BING CROSBY

A Pocketful of Dreams

THE EARLY YEARS
1903–1940

Books by Gary Giddins

Riding on a Blue Note (1981)
Rhythm-a-ning (1985)
Celebrating Bird (1987)
Satchmo (1988)
Faces in the Crowd (1992)
Visions of Jazz (1998)
Bing Crosby: A Pocketful of Dreams —
The Early Years, 1903–1940 (2001)

BING CROSBY

A Pocketful of Dreams

THE EARLY YEARS
1903–1940

Gary Giddins

LITTLE, BROWN AND COMPANY
Boston New York London

Permissions acknowledgments appear on page 694.

First Edition

Library of Congress Cataloging-in-Publication Data

Giddins, Gary.
Bing Crosby: a pocketful of dreams, the early years 1903–1940 /
Gary Giddins. — 1st ed.
p.   cm.
Discography: p.
Filmography: p.
Includes bibliographical references and index.
ISBN 0-316-88188-0
1. Crosby, Bing, 1903–1977.
2. Singers — United States — Biography. I. Title.

ML420.C93 G53 2001
782.42164'092 — dc21
[B]   00-044403

10 9 8 7 6 5 4 3 2

Book design by Bernard Klein

Q-FF

Printed in the United States of America

for Lea and Deborah
and Alice, Helen, and Norman
and Rosemary Clooney

It is a pleasure to think about Bing Crosby.

> — Gilbert Seldes, *The Public Arts*

To be interesting, a man must be complex and elusive. And I rather fancy it must be a great advantage for him to be born outside his proper time and place.

> — Max Beerbohm, *Rossetti and His Circle*

The bearers of the myth of every decade seem to carry in their hands the ax and the spade to execute and inter the myth of the previous one.

> — Murray Kempton, *Part of Our Time*

Whatever might have been bad in the first part of his life, was surely condemned and reformed by his better judgement.

> — Samuel Johnson, *Lives of the Poets*

Let us consider the case of a bodily voice.

> — Saint Augustine, *Confessions*

CONTENTS

Part Two

EVERYBODY'S BING

BING CROSBY

A Pocketful of Dreams

THE EARLY YEARS
1903–1940

INTRODUCTION

There was a time, not so long ago, when it was truthfully said that no hour of the day or night, year after year, passed without the voice of Bing Crosby being heard somewhere on this earth.

— Gilbert Seldes, *The Public Arts* (1956)[1]

His last words were characteristic. Walking off the eighteenth green of the La Moraleja Golf Club, in a suburb of Madrid, Bing Crosby said, "That was a great game of golf, fellas," and then took a few steps and was gone.[2] The three Spanish champions who made up the foursome had ribbed the old crooner about his ratty red sweater and white hat, but Bing and Manuel Pinero won by a single stroke and collected ten dollars. Bing had been in a good mood all afternoon, singing and laughing during the four-and-a-half-hour match, shooting a respectable 85, a lot better than his 92 the day before. He was scheduled to hunt partridge in the countryside the next day; then, on Sunday, fly west to the island resort of Palma de Majorca for more golf before starting home to San Francisco.

But after what was to be his last game, shortly after 6:00 P.M. on October 14, 1977, about twenty yards from the clubhouse, Crosby silently crumpled. The others thought he had slipped. When they realized he had suffered a massive heart attack, they frantically administered oxygen and cardiac tonic injections. An hour later, at Madrid's Hospital de la Cruz Roja, Bing Crosby was pronounced dead on arrival — "cardiac insufficiency due to coronariopathies and valvular sclerosis."[3]

His death was front-page news everywhere. In the United States and Great Britain, his passing was treated as comparable to that of Churchill and de Gaulle. Newspapers then were edited and written by the generation of men and women who came of age during World War II. They remembered Crosby as a shining light during those years, not merely because Der Bingle had made the largest number of V-Discs and army broadcasts, toured in England and France in 1944, and raised $14.5 million in war bonds (a *Yank* magazine poll declared him the individual who had done the most for GI morale) but because perhaps more than anyone else he had come to define — at a time when national identity was important — what it meant to be American.

Yet to the swarming generation born after the war, all the reverence was a mystery. He was known to them as a faded and not especially compelling celebrity, a square old man who made orange-juice commercials and appeared with his much younger family on Christmas telecasts that the baby boomers never watched. He had long since disappeared from movies and the hit parade. If children of the sixties knew his work at all, it was from his perennial hit record of "White Christmas," TV reruns of his *Road* pictures with Bob Hope, and his duet with David Bowie on "Little Drummer Boy." They would have been amazed to learn how advanced, savvy, and forceful a musician he had been in his prime.

That was the cost of having played Everyman too long and too well. Harry Lillis Crosby was the most influential and successful popular performer in the first half of the twentieth century. His was the voice of the nation, the cannily informal personification of hometown decency — friendly, unassuming, melodious, irrefutably American. In his looser and wilder years, when the magnitude of his stardom was without precedent or equal, he had been reckoned the epitome of cool. But universal acceptance demanded of him a willful blandness that obscured the full weight of his achievement. Of the few musicians who had synthesized modernism in popular music and jazz, Crosby received the least serious attention from biographers and critics after 1950. What Edmund Wilson wrote of Charles Dickens's standing in the 1930s describes Bing Crosby's at the time of his death: he had become so much a "familiar joke, a favorite dish, a Christmas ritual" that pundits no longer saw "in him the great artist and social critic that he was."[4]

But more than familiarity laid waste to Crosby's reputation. Popular culture plays by the numbers, and Bing's numbers — and the aesthetic they represented — were shaded by those of rock. His art was now as remote from demotic tastes as classical music or jazz. Four of the last century's most treasured singers died in quick succession in the late summer and fall of 1977: Elvis Presley on August 16, Ethel Waters on September 1, Maria Callas on September 16, and Bing Crosby on October 14. All were American-born and all were celebrated beyond the idioms with which they are primarily associated. Of them, Bing's stature seemed especially secure: his obituaries triggered so many record sales that MCA (Decca) could not handle the orders and farmed them out to other plants, requiring more than a million discs per day. Yet on the twentieth anniversary of their deaths, only Elvis's memory was widely acknowledged in mass media. Two years later *Newsweek* devoted forty-plus pages to "Voices of the Century: America Goes Hollywood," in which Crosby was not mentioned, except to caption a photograph with Frank Sinatra.[5]

In the decade following his death, Crosby's personal stature had been tarnished by a one-two punch.[6] First, there was a savage, ineptly researched biography that ignored his art in its haste to show that yet another departed hero had feet of clay. It was soon followed by a resentful memoir by his alcoholic eldest son, Gary Crosby. Under the law, the dead cannot be libeled, and those books, published in the early 1980s, generated an irresponsible piling-on. Unfounded rumors were passed off as fact.[7] The fading portrait of the imperturbable crooner, the soul of affection, the totem of cool, was replaced by the crude rendering of a pinchfaced, right-wing, child-beating philanderer.

His contemporaries had a more accurate sense of him. Crosby was a phenomenon in the cultural life of the United States long before the war. He had helped lift morale while elucidating the American temperament during the Great Depression, the worst years of privation in the nation's history. Combining musical cultures as no one had ever done (he sang in every idiom short of grand opera), he made the country a more neighborly and unified place. After the war Crosby became an even bigger star, selling more movie tickets and records than ever, serving as a steady barometer of the postwar mood, a bulwark against the reign of paranoia, an outrider of the affluence that followed. Without any dramatic outward change, he had somehow been the right man for successive crises, assertive and optimistic through Prohibition, the Depression, and hot and cold wars. He had the chameleon's ability to reflect his surroundings and the artist's discernment to illuminate them. If Churchill, in his Savile Row pinstripes with his cigars and learned oratory, incarnated the British lion, Bing, in his peculiar motley (shirttails, beat-up hats, torn sweaters, mismatched socks) with his pipe and preternatural calm, embodied the best in American individualism. In 1943 H. Allen Smith observed, "He has been the antithesis of all that the Sunday schools and the Boy Scouts and the 'Y' secretaries taught — and look at him!"[8]

Of the handful of artists who remade American music in the 1920s, Crosby may be said to have had the broadest immediate impact, if only because he reached the largest number of people. He played a decisive role in transforming popular song from a maudlin farrago steeped in minstrelsy and vaudeville into a swinging, racially nuanced, and internationally accepted phenomenon that in one form or another dominated the age. He was by no means alone, yet he attained a matchless orbit of popularity. Most histories of the Depression and the New Deal never mention Crosby, as if the rantings of Huey Long or Father Coughlin exercised greater impact on the public temper than "Brother, Can You Spare a Dime?," "The Last Round-Up," or "The One Rose." Yet as many as 50 million people tuned in every Thursday evening to hear Bing's *Kraft Music Hall* (1935–46). Consider that the hottest TV series of 2000, *Who Wants to Be a Millionaire,* peaked with 36 million viewers.[9]

Popular art listens, absorbs, reflects, harangues, and can, in troubled times, console. Crosby's records were as reassuring as President Roosevelt's "fireside chats." In a national poll conducted in the late 1940s, Crosby was voted the most admired man alive, ahead of Jackie Robinson, Generals Eisenhower and MacArthur, Harry Truman, Bob Hope, and the Pope.[10] Bing was less impressed with himself. He remarked in 1960, "As far as I am concerned, with the exception of a phonograph record or two, I don't think I have done anything that's really outstanding or great or marvelous or anything that deserves any superlatives."[11] Emerson wrote, "Every hero becomes a bore at last."[12] Even to himself.

Except for a confederation of minstrel troupes and chains of vaudeville theaters, the entertainment industry barely existed when Harry Lillis Crosby was born in 1903 to a lower-middle-class Anglo-Irish-American Catholic family. The wax-recorded disc was three years old, and the first nickelodeon was two years down the road. The first regularly scheduled radio broadcasts didn't begin until 1920. Over the next half century, the United States forged the first empire dependent not on strategic colonies but rather on the irresistible sway of its popular arts. Crosby's prestige was crucial in shaping that empire, in spreading a New World style and image. Not the least of his achievements was his role in ensuring the prosperity — in some instances, the very survival — of several major entertainment corporations, including CBS, NBC, ABC, Decca Records, Paramount Pictures, and Ampex tape.

Crosby was the first white vocalist to appreciate and assimilate the genius of Louis Armstrong: his rhythm, his emotion, his comedy, and his spontaneity. Louis and Bing recorded their first important vocals, respectively, in 1926 ("Heebie Jeebies") and 1927 ("Muddy Water") and were the only singers of that era still thriving at the times of their deaths, in the 1970s. When Crosby came of age, most successful male singers were effeminate tenors and recording artists were encouraged to be bland, the better to sell sheet music. The term *pop singer* didn't exist; it was coined in large measure to describe a breed he invented. Bing perfected the use of the microphone, which transfigured concerts, records, radio, movies — even the nature of social intercourse. As vocal styles became more intimate and talking pictures replaced pantomime, private discourse itself grew more casual and provocative. Bing was the first to render the lyrics of a modern ballad with purpose, the first to suggest an erotic undercurrent.

The great cultural critic Constance Rourke identified the three regional stereotypes of nineteenth-century American humor as the Yankee, the backwoodsman, and the minstrel.[13] Bing remains the only entertainer to embody all three, producing in the bargain a twentieth-century composite, often described in his day as the Common Man. Bing's discography, a compilation of 1,668 songs (not including hundreds more he sang on radio), is astonishingly comprehensive. It enfolds the Yankee's Tin Pan Alley, the backwoodsman's western laments, and the minstrel's Old South ballads. It explores every idiom, class, and precinct of American song, from hymns, anthems, spirituals, and novelties to Hawaiian, Irish, light opera, and r&b; he even took a fling at rock 'n' roll. No other performer's catalog is comparable.

During his most prominent years, from 1934 to 1954, Crosby held a nearly unrivaled command over all three key entertainment media, racking up legendary phonograph sales, radio ratings, and motion-picture grosses. At no time was he marketed to one generation or faction of the audience. He may have begun as a Jazz Age emoter for the *College Humor* set, but by the mid-thirties, he was America's troubadour. Bing's influence can be heard in the work of numerous singers in diverse idioms, including Armstrong, whose first foray into popular songs in 1929 was in part a response to Bing's achievement, Jimmy Rushing, Connie Boswell, Perry Como, Billie Holiday, Frank Sinatra, Jimmy Wakely, Roy Rogers, Herb Jeffries, Billy Eckstine, B. B. King, Mel Tormé, Ella Fitzgerald, Rosemary Clooney, Johnny Hartman, Tony Bennett, Ruth Brown, Dean Martin, Ray Charles, and Elvis Presley, who recorded more than a dozen of Crosby's signature hits. Instrumentalists from Jimmy Dorsey to Sonny Rollins have attempted to mimic a semblance of the Crosby cry.

Popular culture, like sports, is beset with statistics, a fixation on chart and box-office rankings, grosses and salaries, and prizes. But whereas sports statistics live forever, pop stats are ultimately transitory and meaningless — no recitation of past sales figures can incline us to listen to Billy Murray records or to read Lloyd C. Douglas novels or to buy Walter Keane paintings. The only pop stats that continue to matter involve artists who continue to matter.

It is impossible to regard Bing Crosby as a historical figure without considering some of his statistics. If nothing else, they reveal his dominance over popular entertainment from Prohibition until the mid-1950s, when his decline as the nation's preeminent muse was signaled by the comeback of a newly charged Sinatra and the arrival of Elvis — the former marketed to adults, the latter to their children. During Crosby's reign, that split did not exist.

- He was the first full-time vocalist ever signed to an orchestra.
- He made more studio recordings than any other singer in history (about 400 more than Sinatra).
- He made the most popular record ever, "White Christmas," the only single to make American pop charts twenty times, every year but one between 1942 and 1962.[14] In 1998, after a long absence, his 1947 version hit the charts in Britain.
- Between 1927 and 1962 he scored 368 charted records under his own name, plus twenty-eight as vocalist with various bandleaders, for a total of 396. No one else has come close; compare Paul Whiteman (220), Sinatra (209), Elvis (149), Glenn Miller (129), Nat "King" Cole (118), Louis Armstrong (85), the Beatles (68).
- He scored the most number one hits ever, thirty-eight, compared with twenty-four by the Beatles and eighteen by Presley.
- In 1960 he received a platinum record as First Citizen of the Record Industry for having sold 200 million discs, a number that doubled by 1980.
- Between 1915 and 1980 he was the only motion-picture star to rank as the number one box-office attraction five times (1944–48).[15] Between 1934 and 1954 he scored in the top ten fifteen times.
- *Going My Way* was the highest-grossing film in the history of Paramount Pictures until 1947; *The Bells of St. Mary's* was the highest-grossing film in the history of RKO Pictures until 1947.
- He was nominated for an Academy Award for best actor three times and won for *Going My Way*.
- He was a major radio star longer than any other performer, from 1931 until 1954 on network, 1954 until 1962 in syndication.
- He appeared on approximately 4,000 radio broadcasts, nearly 3,400 of them his own programs, and single-handedly changed radio from a live-performance to a canned or recorded medium by presenting, in 1946, the first transcribed network show on WABC — thereby making that also-ran network a major force.
- He financed and popularized the development of tape, revolutionizing the recording industry.
- He created the first and longest-running celebrity pro-am golf championship, playing host for thirty-five years, raising millions in charity, and was the central figure in the development of the Del Mar racetrack in California.[16]

*   *   *

Such reckonings count for little and would mean nothing at all if Crosby's art did not merit rediscovery. He was, first and foremost, a masterly, innovative musician — an untrained vocalist of natural charm and robust power with impeccable instincts about phrasing and tempo. He pared away the rococo mannerisms of bygone theatrical styles in favor of the clean melodic line. Lyricists thought him a godsend because he not only articulated words but also underscored their meaning. Crosby, who never learned to read music and could play no instrument except rudimentary drums, had an apparently photographic and audiographic memory. He had only to hear a song to know it.

As an actor, Crosby broke the rules. He was the antithesis of a Hollywood matinee idol — small and average-looking with outsize ears, thin lips, pointed jaw, and a padded midsection that belied his graceful athleticism. He created a new prototype: the unflappable maverick with a pocketful of dreams, a friend to men and catnip to women. The immense success of his 1940s movies has overshadowed his often daring work in the 1930s, when he developed into an accomplished farceur and an exceptional improviser of physical shtick.

A performer of such enormous popularity becomes, inevitably and in spite of himself, a social critic. Crosby, an unreasonably modest man who never took credit for anything musical, let alone social or political, nonetheless played a coercive role in the acceleration of civil rights. He encouraged and pioneered racial integration on stage, radio, and records and in movies; in 1936, after winning the contractual right to produce his own pictures, he hired Louis Armstrong and gave him star billing, a Hollywood first for a black entertainer. A Jesuit by training and temperament, Crosby had enjoyed the benefits of a classical education. He lived in a small parochial world until he was twenty-two. He was a classroom cutup and lover of old show business, not least minstrelsy, but by the time he dropped out of law school, he understood that American popular music was a stew of intermingling ethnicities. He absorbed the influences of performers so diverse that few would have mentioned them in the same sentence, among them, Al Jolson, John McCormack, the Mound City Blue Blowers, Ukelele Ike, Ethel Waters, Mildred Bailey, Van and Schenck, Bix Beiderbecke, and, most decisively, Armstrong.

Perhaps the most telling aspect of Crosby's neglected role in integrating American show business was his calculated decision to attach himself to an ethnic wing. At the time of his death, he was widely remembered as Irish American. Yet not until he reached his mid-thirties did Bing show any inclination to embrace that identity. His mother's forebears had left Ireland for Canada three generations earlier, and his father's Protestant family had been in the United States since 1635. Paramount Pictures had nurtured his persona as the all-American man, without ethnic attachments. The primary semblance of Irishness in his work was his signature vocal technique, the upper mordent, a broken-note adornment imported from Ireland and Scotland that became known as the Crosby cry. Not until 1939, on the eve of the war, did he truly embrace his Irish heritage. Thanks to the antisemitic venom spewed by the radio priest Father Coughlin, Irish American Catholics had come to be associated with intolerance. Bing quietly stepped up to embody a larger truth. As he began to sing Irish songs and play Irishmen and priests, he required no rhetoric to stress the point that nothing was more all-American than its minorities.

Crosby rarely allowed stereotypical Catholic pieties to interfere with the scampish irreverence that informed much of his best work, from the romantic comedies to the *Road* movies. It was even present in his finest screen performances, as the golfing, imbibing, indulgent, yet determined Father Chuck O'Malley in Leo McCarey's great films, *Going My Way* and *The Bells of St. Mary's*. Bing's casual Huckleberry Finn demeanor as a pipe-smoking idler who never dresses up or removes his hat was portended by his odd name, which eclipsed cultural divisions with its unmistakably North American yet faintly Asian (the open-mouthed *aw* surrounded by two grin-making *ee*s) arrangement of consonants and vowels: an Anglo-Danish surname modified by a nickname's New World audacity. In a world of Skips, Whiteys, Blackies, Reds, Pinkys, Shortys, Macs, Butches, and Chips, Bing was a standout moniker, a name that underscored his easygoing modesty. He taught the world what it meant to live the American common man's dream. Aside from his music, that was the best part of his art, perhaps the best part of himself.

Bing was a remarkably autobiographical performer. Yet while the public thought it knew him intimately, his intimates conceded that Crosby was, in many respects, unknowable. They would often remark on his intelligence, humor, and generosity, and then marvel at his contradictions: the melting warmth and chilly reserve, the conservatism and liberality, the piety and recklessness. Bing liked people who made him laugh (he expressed bewilderment that anyone might think him, as many did, a loner) but avoided public displays of affection and introspection. After he lost the soul mate of his early years, guitarist Eddie Lang, he could no more have bared his soul to another man than submit to psychoanalysis. Iron-willed and self-made, insouciant and obstinate, gregarious and remote, he was thoroughly enigmatic, yet hardly unknowable — no man with a legacy as large as Crosby's could be that. Neither saint nor monster, Crosby survives his debunkers along with his hagiographers because the facts are so much more impressive than the prejudices and myths on either side. Bing Crosby was, after all, a poor boy from a Catholic working-class district in turn-of-the-century Spokane who caught the attention of the world and made it better. "Call me lucky," he said. But it was never just luck or even talent. It was also the determination and brains of an alert young man who came along when American entertainment was at a crossroads. He showed it which road to take.

Part One

———

BINGO FROM
BINGVILLE

I will sing with my spirit, but I will also
sing with my mind.
— I Corinthians 14:15

1

THE HARRIGANS

With a mother named Harrigan, you are Irish, I take it?
— Ken Carpenter, *Kraft Music Hall* (1945)[1]

Late in the spring of 1831, Bing Crosby's maternal great-grandfather, Dennis Harrigan, a fifty-one-year-old farmer and carpenter who lived in Schull parish, in the southwestern region of County Cork, Ireland, ushered his family aboard a timber ship bound for New Brunswick, Canada.[2] Leading his wife, Catherine,[3] and nine of their ten children onto the creaking deck, Dennis knew what to expect of the grueling voyage. Still, he counted himself lucky, for few members of his congregation were able to leave at all. Of the 65,000 emigrants who set sail in 1831, only ninety or so from tiny Schull could afford passage, not many of them Catholic.[4] A brave, resolute lot, they gazed westward with tenacious faith as the ship cleared Ireland's southernmost point, the Mizen Head of southwest Cork's Mizen peninsula, once a haven for smugglers and pirates who sought refuge in its impregnable coves.

The Canadian-built vessels were designed not for carrying passengers but for transporting timber, New Brunswick's primary export. To maximize efficiency, the shipbuilders hastily modified the holds and lowered passenger fares by more than two-thirds, allowing greater numbers of Irish families to emigrate and generating the slogan "timber in, passengers out." Dozens of those ships were lost at sea, and many more were decimated by typhus, dysentery, and other diseases. All were cursed with conditions as barbarous as those of slave ships: insufficient food supplies, inadequate sanitation and gender partition, little if any ventilation, berths half as high as those required by law for slavers. The journey averaged six weeks, and the only music heard was the shrill wail of unceasing lamentations.

The wilderness of Canada's eastern provinces promised to be friendlier to the Harrigans. Dennis's siblings had brought over their families the previous year. Now Dennis removed his own family (all but his married daughter, Ellen Sauntry, who arrived in New Brunswick twenty years later as a widow with seven children), fourteen years before the Great Hunger and before the tidal wave of Irish immigration that flooded America's urban centers. His smaller generation of immigrants would explore and prosper in rural America, migrating from the Northeast to the Midwest to the Northwest, building successful farm communities with the logging skills they learned in the Canadian woods. The names of Mizen peninsula's Catholic congregants who left that season and in harder ones to follow took root all across America: Fitzgerald, Driscoll, Reagan, Harrigan, Sullivan, Donovan, Coughlin, O'Brien, Hickey, Mahoney.

They had abandoned a hellish place.

A hundred years had passed since Jonathan Swift offered his "modest proposal" to abate Ireland's poverty, beggary, and congestion by cannibalizing its "Popish" offspring. "A most delicious, nourishing and wholesome food, whether stewed, roasted, baked or broiled," he advised, "a delicacy befitting landlords, who, as they have already devoured most of the parents, seem to have best title to the children."[5] Ireland, cherishing its brood not least as a defense against the privations of old age, tripled its population in the decades after Swift.

But congestion was not the foremost source of Ireland's sorrows. The nefarious Penal Code of 1695 barred Irish Catholics — three-quarters of the population — from owning land and businesses, from voting, and from building schools and churches or attending those that existed.[6] Informants, particularly those who turned in priests, were rewarded. The Act of Union, passed in 1801 amid a blizzard of bribes, threats, and hangings, promised to balance the scales between Ireland and England but in fact gave the dominant country a captive market — fortifying a corrupt system of absentee landlords, toppling what was left of Irish commerce, and dissolving the Dublin-based Parliament. While the Catholic Emancipation Act of 1829 did away with the code, it could not abate the long history of religious enmity.

Ireland became a grim landscape of windowless mud-and-stone cabins, potato-and-milk diets, cholera. The Duke of Wellington observed, "There never was a country in which poverty existed to the extent it exists in Ireland,"[7] and the French traveler Gustave de Beaumont found in the Emerald Isle extremes of misery "worse than the Negro in his chains."[8] In the year the Harrigans set out for New Brunswick, the Mizen peninsula was beset by cholera and famine.

Most likely the Harrigans spoke Gaelic, not English, and could not read at all. They were tough, hardworking, close-knit, intensely religious, and musical. A legend passed down into the twentieth century traces the family's genesis to John of Skibbereen (a town some twelve miles east of Schull), who may have been Dennis Harrigan's father and was known as Organ O'Brien for his fine playing of the church instrument.[9] The importance of music and dance in nineteenth-century Ireland can hardly be overstated, for amusements provided as much solace as the church. After a visit in 1825, Sir Walter Scott described the people's "natural condition" as one of "gaiety and happiness."[10]

When the ship finally docked, the Harrigans made their way through the Miramichi section of New Brunswick to the outlying woods of the Williamstown settlement, six miles inland, where they learned to clear land for tillage and built log cabins that furnished little protection against the winter's freezing temperatures. Dennis's nine children ranged in age from one to twenty. He made capable carpenters of his sons.

Most of Williamstown's Catholic settlers were from Mizen peninsula and were powerfully united by culture and custom. The strongest bond was religious, strengthened by the prejudices of the Irish Methodists who preceded them. A second bond was the tradition of aggregate farming, the sharing of tilled soil between families as in the Irish townlands. A third, consequent to the first two, was the observance of secrecy: the "sinister side"[11] of the Irish character that historian Cecil Woodham-Smith has traced to the days of the Penal Code. A fourth was the heritage of strong, venerated women (Ireland was that rare nation where husbands paid dowries for wives, instead of the reverse) who secured their households. A fifth bond was that of large families — small communes within the larger ones.

Music — the public converse of the secret self — was the sixth bond, taking the form of Irish melodies and rhythms that became increasingly popular and influential in the last half of the nineteenth century, complementing styles developed at the same time by African Americans. It was the custom in Ireland and Africa, but not in Europe, to dance to vocal music; to favor the pentatonic scale, call-and-response phrases, and cyclical song structures; to employ expressive vocal mannerisms, including dramatic shifts in register, nasality, and most especially the upper mordent.[12]

The mordent — a fast wavering from one note to another and back, a fleeting undulation that suggests a mournful cry — was a vestige of the Byzantine influence that dominated European music in the Middle Ages. That influence vanished from most of Europe but endured in the plaintive folk music of Scotland and Ireland, owing to their economic and geographical isolation from the modernizing impact of the Reformation and Renaissance. A 1950s edition of *Chambers's Encyclopaedia* defines the mordent as a "certain oscillation or catch in the voice as it comes to rest momentarily upon a sustained sound"[13] and goes on to qualify it as a basic attribute of "crooning." Among young Celtic singers of the twenty-first century, the mordent-heavy approach is known as *sean nós,*[14] or old style, but it was new to Americans in the 1920s, when Dennis Harrigan's great-grandson pinned the mordent to popular music like a red rose.

Sealing the family's bargain with the New World, Catherine Harrigan, in her early forties, gave birth on September 6, 1832, to her eleventh child, the only one born in North America, Dennis Jr. It would have greatly surprised Bing Crosby to learn that his maternal grandfather was Canadian; he assumed he was Irish born, and wrote as much in his memoir and on his mother's death certificate.[15] (When Bing attempted to trace the family line during a visit to Ireland, he was thwarted by his certainty in the matter.)[16] If Dennis Sr. embodied the trials of transatlantic resettlement, his son — born in

New Brunswick and baptized at St. Patrick's in Miramichi — would personify the westward journey into and across the United States.

By 1835 his family, like so many of Williamstown's interconnected tribes, was earning much of its livelihood from logging and timber. The desirable riverfront land had been taken by previous settlers, but the rigors of clearing tracts acclimated the newcomers and taught them to survive the wilderness. Protestants and Catholics often worked together, united by the hostile environment. Dennis Harrigan's appointment as overseer of highways in 1839 affirmed the increasingly significant Catholic presence. But the old enmities persisted. Catholics were characterized as criminal or rowdy and were severely punished; one man was hanged for stealing twenty-five pennies and a loaf of bread. Catholic children had to travel long distances to escape the schooling of Methodist crusaders. The first Catholic teacher, James Evers, hired in 1846, was falsely accused of sexually molesting a Methodist student and was fired. A petition attesting to his "good moral character" was signed by thirteen parents of Williamstown, including Dennis Harrigan.[17] Evers spent two years futilely defending himself, then cleared out in 1849, at which time the Court of General Sessions at Newcastle concluded that he was a man of "moral and sober habits" and "taught to our satisfaction."

Evers's calamity prefigured that of Williamstown. As Great Britain reduced tariffs on timber from the Baltic countries, New Brunswick's timber industry declined. Town merchants foreclosed on their debts. Opportunities in the western United States lured away the settlers' children. The Williamstown settlement would be little remembered today but for the inordinate number of eminent Americans whose New World roots are in those woods.[18] Dennis Harrigan's descendants alone include, among his grandsons, William and John Harrigan, who built the Scotch Lumber Company in Fulton, Alabama; Emmett Harrigan, head of a major law firm in St. Paul and an unsuccessful candidate for the U.S. Senate; and Ellen Sauntry's brazen Miramichi-raised son, William Sauntry Jr., the millionaire lumber baron of Stillwater, Minnesota, known as "the King of the St. Croix," whose garish mansion, the Alhambra, stands today as a Stillwater tourist attraction. Dennis's great-grandsons include Lyman Sutton, president of Stillwater's Cosmopolitan State Bank; Gordon Neff, whose chain stores introduced supermarkets to Los Angeles; Colonel

Bill Harrigan, who helped rescue the First World War's "Lost Battalion" in the Argonne Forest; bandleader Bob Crosby; and Bing.

Dennis and Catherine passed away within a few years of each other and are presumably buried in a churchyard's unmarked graves in Red Bank, on the Miramichi River. They were almost certainly gone by 1866, the year several of their children, now in their thirties and forties, left for Maine, Wisconsin, and Minnesota. Dennis Jr., however, remained another fifteen years.[19] After attending school in Williamstown and Red Bank, he tried his hand at various jobs. While working as a logger in Newcastle and later as a brewer, he boarded in the home of a friend, Michael Ahearn. In 1867, the year the Dominion of Canada was chartered, he married Ahearn's sister, Katie. Within weeks the couple headed south through Maine and across to Stillwater, Minnesota.

Dennis Jr., one of the most industrious and devout of his father's sons (two or three brothers were thought to be ne'er-do-wells and were probably alcoholic), eventually earned a reputation as a reliable, proficient contractor and builder, specializing in church architecture. Stillwater provided a congenial setting for him to hone his skills; many Miramichi families, including three of his siblings, had been drawn to the prosperous logging and rafting enterprises on the St. Croix River. He also continued with his wife, Katie, the custom of large families. Married in their thirties, the two produced five boys and two girls between 1867 and 1879.[20] They remained in Stillwater until the last was born.

According to the Crosby genealogy written by Larry Crosby (Bing's oldest brother), it was Katie who advanced the family's musical calling. In his account, she "not only baked a wonderful pie, but sang like a bird, and it was common gossip when she was out rowing on the lake, that either Katie Harrigan or an angel is out there singing." Her boys were raised to be practical. In Larry's account, Dennis "wisely brought up four of his sons to be respectively [a] lather, plumber, plasterer and electrician. They could build a house or win a fight, without any outside help." Singing was a pastime, hardly a profession. Two grandchildren of Ellen Sauntry, first cousins to Dennis Jr., "won renown on the stage," to the chagrin of their parents, who considered acting "unmoral."

Katie managed to pass on her love of singing to at least one child, her fourth-born and first daughter, Catherine Helen Harrigan, who was delivered on February 7, 1873, in a boarding room above an old creamery.[21] This Catherine also inherited her father's pious diligence. When her own children — Bing among them — were middle-aged, they reminisced about her "sweet, clear voice"[22] and took care not to smoke, drink, or swear in her presence. A childhood photograph of Catherine reveals a comely round-faced girl who looks nothing like the severe image she presented in later years. In her large, pale eyes, one can see her mother's penetrating stare and her father's hooded lids, both of which she passed on to her most famous son.

A year or two after Catherine was born, the Harrigans moved into a large boardinghouse on Main Street. Many of its thirty or so tenants were from New Brunswick. Dennis probably owned part of the house, but in 1879, when the youngest of his children, George, was born, he was able to secure a home of his own on Second Street, where he took in boarders to bolster his income. In 1881, finding increasingly limited opportunities in Stillwater, he moved the family to St. Paul. Before the year was out, he relocated again, to Knife Falls (now Cloquet), near Duluth, where his fortunes improved. He built that town's first Catholic, Methodist, and Presbyterian churches, as well as a school, and was appointed a church trustee. In 1885, with his reputation as a builder secure, Dennis took his family back to St. Paul for three years. There Catherine, now twelve, and her brother Edward spent their afternoons at the ice palace, he making and she demonstrating ice skates. They were obliged to earn their keep beyond essentials, a Harrigan practice that Catherine, who could skate her name on ice, instilled in her own children.

The West had lured many Miramichi families, including a few of Dennis's uncles and aunts, by the time he succumbed. Most had relocated to Washington and Wisconsin, drawn by the booming economies set in motion by land speculators and lumber barons. Dennis chose Tacoma, a seaport on Puget Sound, about twenty-five miles south of Seattle, where the lumber industry increased the population tenfold in the 1880s. A boom was predicted when the Northern Pacific Railroad named Tacoma its terminus, and in 1884 the city was incorporated from two smaller boroughs of the same name. Signs of progress — electric lights, warehouses, shipways, a hospital — reflected the influx of thousands of blue-collar families drawn by the promise of cheap lumber and land. No city in the nation boasted a higher percentage of families who owned their own homes. Not even the scourge of racial violence halted growth; in fact, it may have helped. Tacoma created international headlines when a mob led by city officials rounded up 200 Chinese residents at gunpoint and forced them to board southbound trains. The United States was forced to pay China an indemnity, but the specter of competitive, minimally paid labor had been subdued.

In 1888 the Northern Pacific Railroad completed its pass through the Cascade Mountains and sold 90,000 acres of timberland to the St. Paul and Tacoma Lumbering Company, which built a sawmill on the tidal flats of Commencement Bay. That year Dennis and his eldest son, William, decided to make their move. Boarding in a Tacoma rooming house, they worked as carpenters until they earned enough to buy a place that could accommodate Katie and the children, who arrived a year later. Dennis was fifty-seven, old for carpentry, but he soon established himself as a contractor and built several notable structures, including Seattle's Hull Building and Tacoma's Aquinas Academy annex, Scandinavian Church, and Dominican Sisters convent.

All but the two youngest children helped keep the Harrigans solvent. William, twenty-three in 1890, worked alongside his father as a lather until he hired on as a streetcar conductor for the Tacoma Rail and Motor Company; Ambrose, twenty-one, was foreman for an electrical-supplies concern; Edward, twenty, worked as a plumber; Catherine, who at seventeen was called Kate, fashioned and sold hats for the G. W. H. Taylor millinery company; her fifteen-year-old sister, Annie, worked at home as a dressmaker; at thirteen and eleven, respectively, Frank and George helped with the chores.

A few years later Kate took a job clerking at Sanford & Stone's popular mercantile store on Tacoma Avenue and was designing hats for a branch of the company that staged amateur theatricals.[23] While appearing in one of those productions, she attracted the attention of an unlikely suitor: a mandolin-playing auditor for the Northern Pacific, Harry Lowe Crosby.

2

THE CROSBYS

*Like unto a saga of old, runs the story of the coming of
the Crosby family into the West.*
— Mrs. George E. Blankenship (1914)[1]

By the time the Harrigans left Canada, the Crosbys had earned distinction in America, initially as seafarers based in New England. They made history sailing around Cape Horn to the Pacific Northwest. Mrs. Blankenship could not contain her enthusiasm in the chapter she devoted to the family's accomplishments in her *Early History of Thurston County, Washington.* "In all the wild experiences related during the compilation of this book," she wrote, "none were more picturesque and interesting than the history of an entire family of stalwart sons and fair daughters with their aged but sturdy father, coming with their own ship, laden with their own goods, their children and themselves, to take their part in conquering the wilderness."[2]

In focusing on Washington State, she traced the Crosbys only as far back as the 1840s, when the illustrious Captain Nathaniel Crosby spurred and pioneered the territory. Larry Crosby's genealogy dove centuries deeper into the paternal line, back to "Vikings and Catholics" who settled in Ireland, Scotland, and northern England.[3] Crosby is a Danish name, meaning "town of the cross" (the suffix *by* is a diminutive of the Danish *burg*). In his account, written with mock lofty diction and printed in faux Old English type, the first recorded Crosbys were of the Irish house of Ardfert, notably the Right Reverend John Crosbie, appointed bishop of Ardfert in 1601. The family spread out over western and middle Ireland to Kerry and Queens, as far north as Tyrone (home to a knight, Sir Pierce Crosby) and as far south as Cork, where the Harrigans also settled.

The family's conversion to Anglicism was coerced during the reign of Henry VIII and was eventually fully embraced. Edmundus Crosby served the king as cantorist at St. John's in Doncaster, and Richard Crosby did likewise as auditor of St. John's in York.[4] The first in the line to reach the New World, in 1635, was Simon, who bought a homestead in Cambridge, Massachusetts. Through marriage, Simon's progeny aligned the family twice over with descendants of the *Mayflower* Pilgrims, who preceded him by fifteen years.

In 1755 Deacon Nathaniel Crosby married into the brood of Elder William Brewster, a *Mayflower* alumnus whose family founded Brewster, Massachusetts, where many Crosbys lived until the early nineteenth century.[5] A generation later his grandson, Captain Nathaniel Crosby, the first in the family's line of sea captains, married Ruby Foster, who traced her ancestry to another noted *Mayflower* passenger, Governor Winslow. Those ties earned Bing membership in the General Society of Mayflower Descendants. But Bing neglected to mention those relations in his 1953 as-told-to autobiography, *Call Me Lucky*, preferring to concentrate on the outstanding men of the sea.

Yet, as Larry discovered, several Crosbys "distinguished themselves in the learned professions and as military leaders in the Revolutionary War." Josiah Crosby, inadvertently overlooked by Larry, signed a declaration of the Continental Congress in Amherst in 1776 as a representative of New Hampshire.[6] The family's most celebrated colonial, however, was Enoch Crosby, who joined the Continental Army at twelve as a spy and claimed to be the model for Harvey Birch, the undercover hero of James Fenimore Cooper's bestselling 1821 novel, *The Spy*. Cooper testily denied Crosby's claim: "I know nothing of such a man as Enoch Crosby, never having heard his name, until I saw it coupled with the character of the Spy, after my return from Europe."[7] But on the evening C. P. Clinch's adaptation of the novel opened at New York's Park Theater (not ten weeks after the book was first published), Enoch appeared in his box to "thunders of applause."[8] Cooper admitted he based his story on an anecdote told to him by Governor John Jay and subsequently conceded he never learned the name of the spy, because "Jay felt himself bound to secrecy."[9] It is known that Jay arranged for Enoch Crosby to enlist as a spy in the British army, and that Enoch refused, Birch-like, his offer of a reward.

Whether Crosby was the prototype for Birch (who exemplifies for Cooper's General Washington "the patriotism that pervades the bosoms of [our] lowest citizens"), the twentieth-century Crosbys were proud to claim a hero of low estate, even as they vouched themselves two coats of arms. Somewhat defensively, Larry explained that heraldry "does *not* denote an aristocratic class, but rather personal merit secured by the humblest as well as the highest." The motto of their Irish arms — depicting two hands, a lion, and three swords — is *Indignante Invidia Florebit Justus* (Despising envy, the just shall flourish). The English arms display three rams and the motto Liberty Under Thy Guidance, the Guidance of the Lamb of God. Bing preferred the Irish emblem, sporting it on the breast pockets of his blazers.

Captain Nathaniel, known as Nathaniel Jr. or Nathaniel II, was the fourth Crosby of that name in a line that produced three or four more.[10] Born in 1810, in East Brewster, Massachusetts, he and his brothers, Clanrick and Alfred, were tutored in the seaman's life by their father, who commanded a vessel out of Cape Cod. In his twenties, Nathaniel moved to Wiscasset, Maine, where he married Mary Lincoln and raised a family. By 1844 his reputation for daring had earned him a commission from a U.S. government agent to command the brig *O. C. Raymond,* charged with taking emergency supplies from Boston to immigrants who poured into the Oregon Territory seeking their fortunes. Reaching the mouth of the Columbia River, he continued to Portland, an outpost of log cabins, and put his crew ashore to build a warehouse for his cargo. That cabin survived as the settlement's post office.

Crosby took to the community, enchanted by the vitality of the frontier and the commercial promise it held, discerning for himself a role amid the burgeoning industries and direct trade routes to Hawaii — still known as the Sandwich Islands — and China. He decided to

transport his family and made one last visit to New England to out-
line his plan. Over the next few years, Captain Crosby traded along
the West Coast and Hawaii, ferrying supplies at government behest
to secure the territory and earning enough money to enable his brothers to purchase the *Grecian,* a 247-ton brig. In September 1849, with
twenty-four people on board, all but five of them relatives, the
Grecian left New York.[11] Clanrick and Alfred served as captain and
second officer. On board were their wives, children, in-laws, housekeeper, and their retired father, Captain Nathaniel Crosby Sr.

Within five months the Crosby brig rounded the Horn and docked
in Portland. The party continued to the small settlement of Tumwater. That town, incorporated three years earlier, consisted of little
more than a blockhouse and a few one-room cabins. It became home
to Clanrick and his family. In partnership with a man named Gray,
Clanrick bought a gristmill and land along the river, eventually building a general store and emerging as a prominent citizen, a leader and
philanthropist. His father also lived there a couple of years but
returned to Cape Cod shortly before his death. Alfred moved his family to Astoria, Oregon.

The man responsible for the emigration, Captain Nathaniel
Crosby Jr., soon tired of sedentary life. Early in 1852 he transported
his family — and the first cargo of spars (poles used in the rigging of
ships) ever sent from the Pacific Coast — to China. After establishing a home in Hong Kong, he returned for a second consignment of
spars, this time from Olympia, the growing settlement at Tumwater's
northern border, soon to be designated capital of Washington Territory. He died in Hong Kong four years later, leaving a widow; two
daughters, Mary and Martha; and a son, Nathaniel. All but Martha
quickly returned to Tumwater.[12]

Clanrick helped young Nat get on his feet, selling him a parcel of
land at Tumwater's north end and employing him at the mill. Nat
took a wife, Cordelia, and prospered for a time, building a spacious,
two-story A-frame house with a small cherry orchard out front. But a
bad investment in steamships annihilated his savings, and he was
forced to relocate to Olympia, where he found employment as postmaster. (Although they lived in the Tumwater house only a few years,
it continued to be known as "the old Crosby home," and in 1949 the
deed was given to the local chapter of Daughters of the Pioneers of

Washington in return for its restoration and preservation.[13] Bing con-tributed $1,800 toward the purchase and gave the Daughters two chairs his grandparents had owned when they lived in the house.) Nat and Cordelia raised two sons. Frank Lawrence, born in Tumwa-ter in 1862, made a name for himself in the Puget Sound area as U.S. deputy marshall residing in Tacoma, thirty miles northeast; his brother, Harry Lowe, born in Olympia on November 28, 1870, devel-oped a less exacting attitude toward life.

Given the eight-and-a-half-year gap between the births of Frank and Harry, each may be said to have been raised virtually as an only child, but it was the younger who became a provincial dandy. Pampered by servants throughout his childhood, Harry was by all accounts a guile-less young man, lighthearted and informal, unburdened by ambition, hail-fellow-well-met — in short, a model for the character Bing Crosby would bring to movies in the 1930s. He was appealing in a ruddy, moonfaced way, favoring broad suspenders and a rakishly tilted straw hat, and he loved music. Accompanying himself on mandolin or a four-string guitar, Harry sang old favorites made popular by roving minstrel troupes, newer novelty songs and ballads, Chinese ditties learned from the Asian servants his mother had brought home from the Orient, and Gilbert and Sullivan. *The Mikado* was the rage of the 1890s, and a cousin of Harry's, Sam Woodruff, famously toured the Northwest as Koko.

Harry sang with an Olympia-based men's choir, the Peep-O'-Day Boys, and played in the city's silver cornet band at about the time Kate Harrigan was singing in a Tacoma church choir. In 1890, after dropping out of college, Harry moved to Tacoma, where Frank lived, and found work as a bookkeeper for the Northern Pacific Railroad's Land Department. For three years he lived in a string of hotels and rooming houses, but his bachelor days were numbered when he encountered the stabilizing glint-eyed gaze of Miss Harrigan appear-ing in a department-store theatrical.

From the first, they seemed oddly matched, a devout Catholic courted by a casual Protestant. Kate was a willful, disciplined young woman who distrusted luck and abhorred sloth. Harry was incapable of raising his voice and trusted less to Providence or God than to goodwill and serendipity. In time, she would come to be characterized as humorless, even autocratic. He never lost the epithet earned as a young man, Happy Harry — though it was amended much later to Hollywood Harry. The women employed in Bing Crosby's offices were more bemused than offended by Dad Crosby's fanny-pinching, in light of Mother Crosby's temperament, which brought everyone, including her sons, to solemn attention.

Music may have sealed their courtship, but Harry's willingness to convert to Catholicism made possible their marriage. He established a standard other non-Catholics would be expected to uphold as a precondition to marrying into the family. The wedding took place in a small wooden church, Holy Rosary, on January 4, 1894, and the couple moved directly into the hotel — St. John House — in which Harry boarded. Within weeks they acquired their first of several houses in the alphabetically configured city. Located in the "backwoods" area of N Street,[14] this house came to Kate's mind fifty years later when a writer solicited her Mother's Day recollections. "One of my warmest Mother's Day memories goes back to before the children were even born," she said, "back to the day when their father and I knew we had established a home for them, a place warm and livable, and I could close my eyes and imagine them there."[15]

3

TACOMA

*There are literally millions of Crosby relatives around
these parts.*

— Burt McMurtrie, columnist (1948)[1]

Kate Crosby wouldn't have to imagine for long. She was expecting
when she and Harry moved into the house at 616 South N Street. On
the third day of the New Year, 1895, Laurence Earl was born at home.
Before the year was out, they moved to a better neighborhood, near
Wright Park, and a bigger house to accommodate Harry's mother,
Cordelia, who lived with them for a few months. In that house, at 110
North Yakima, a second son, Everett Nathaniel, was born on April 5,
1896. The family's fortunes changed when Harry lost his job with the
Northern Pacific and was forced to scuffle for work through the depression years of 1897 and 1898. His plight may account for the four-
year pause before more children arrived. The Crosbys moved twice
more, never beyond the radius of a few blocks in the residential district just north of downtown Tacoma.

Harry's luck changed in 1899, when he was hired as a clerk in the
Pierce County treasurer's office, under Treasurer Stephen Judson,
who had been one of the Washington pioneers of the 1850s.[2] The
family was now able to rent a handsome three-story, many-gabled corner house at 922 North I Street, where their third son, Edward John,

was born on July 30, 1900. Judson was defeated in the Republican sweep of 1902, but his successor, John B. Reed, promoted Harry to bookkeeper. That December Harry celebrated his good fortune by purchasing, for $850, two adjoining lots on J Street, between North Eleventh and North Twelfth, with the intention of building a residence he estimated would cost $2,500.[3] The deed was made out to his wife, who could never feel truly settled in a rental.

Construction at 1112 North J was completed ten months later, in the first weeks of a cold winter. Set on a grassy incline from the street, the wooden two-story frame house had wide eaves and a large front porch with three sets of double columns supporting a roof porch just below the second-story bedroom windows. Harry and Kate permitted themselves the luxury of a piano. Down the street they could see Puget Sound, and only three blocks away stood St. Patrick's, the small wooden church that had served the community for a dozen years and where Edward (Ted) was baptized.

Kate was pregnant again during the construction, with a due date in mid-spring. As the day approached, the stinging April winds suddenly departed and she delivered her fourth son on Sunday, May 3, which the *Daily Ledger* declared AN IDEAL SUMMER DAY.[4]

Kate, who had just turned thirty, and Harry, finally established in the city's middle class, decided that this boy's arrival merited a public announcement. For the first time, they alerted the newspapers of a newborn. When the *Daily Ledger* failed to print the item in "City News in Brief" until May 5, implying with the word *yesterday* that the great event had taken place on May 4,[5] Kate stipulated the correct date for its rival, the *Tacoma Daily News* ("Mr. and Mrs. H. L. Crosby are receiving congratulations on the arrival of a son at their household May 3"),[6] and requested a correction from the *Ledger*, which appeared on May 7.[7]

On May 31, accompanied by Kate's younger brother Frank and his wife (the boy's godparents), Harry and Kate carried the infant to St. Patrick's for his baptism.[8] Harry was disappointed at not having a girl, but Kate placated him by naming the boy after him. For his middle name, however, she chose Lillis, after a neighborhood friend, circumventing a generational ranking of senior and junior (though both Harrys would often use those designations). Happy Harry cradled the infant in his arms, looked into blue eyes that would never darken, and gave forth in song, "Ten Baby Fingers and Ten Baby Toes."[9]

For all the decisiveness with which May 3, 1903, was flagged as Harry Lillis Crosby's birthday, the date proved controversial in and out of family circles.[10] In all official accounts (generated by Paramount, Decca, the Crosby offices, and, most insistently, Bing himself), it was altered by one day and one year, to May 2, 1904. The true date was additionally obscured as two of his older brothers came to believe he was born in 1901. Bing lost the year early in his career at the conniving of Everett, who, acting as his manager, believed he was shaving three.

The first of young Harry's two younger sisters, Catherine Cordelia, named after her mother and her recently deceased grandmother, arrived on October 3, 1904.[11] The second, Mary Rose, with whom Harry developed a particular childhood affinity, followed on May 3, 1906. That Kate delivered four of her six children on the third day of the month is merely an actuarial oddity; that she delivered two on the same day of the same month created birthday havoc, as Mary Rose insisted on having the day to herself.[12] Peace prevailed when Harry's birthday was advanced by twenty-four hours. In later years Mary Rose would triumphantly produce the family Bible in which their father assigned Harry May 2.

By the time Mary Rose arrived, the family fortunes had once again bottomed out. Harry Crosby's benefactor, John B. Reed, was ousted in the 1904 election by his former cashier, Edgar M. Lakin, who advanced Harry to the title of deputy in the county treasurer's office.[13] Of the eight men working in the treasurer's office, Harry had been there the longest. Yet he was fired late in 1905, presumably so that Lakin could reward a political crony. After several more firings, complaints that city employees were being dismissed on trumped-up charges grew widespread. In April 1906 the citizens of Tacoma approved a city charter amendment requiring a public hearing and ratification by a two-thirds majority of the city council before a city employee could be discharged.

The city's indignation came too late to help Harry. In the first years of the century, Tacoma's population had exploded from 38,000 to more than 84,000, but the expected fiscal boom was not forthcoming.[14]

The economy was stymied by the consolidation of the timber industry and railroads. The increase in jobs did not keep up with the number of job hunters. Like many others disappointed with prospects on the coast, Harry began to think about the inland frontier and its burgeoning center, Spokane, 200 miles east, where logging and mining camps were proliferating as fast as they once had in Tacoma. The prospect of a fresh start was made more imperative by Harry's liberal spending.

The very week he was fired, he had come home with tickets for *The Merry Widow*, insisting that they had been given him by a friend. He and Kate "enjoyed every minute of the show," Ted recounted in a fanciful biography of Bing, noting with lingering embarrassment that Harry's "sprees" exacerbated "their financial troubles on the Coast."[15] Just how much embarrassment and debt Harry incurred is no longer possible to ascertain, but given Kate's keen sense of social standing, such difficulties may have sparked her own willingness to leave their home, friends, parents, and siblings, especially her sister, Annie, whose prospering marriage made Kate more envious than she liked to admit. Bing would later praise his father's hunch in recognizing Spokane as "a fine place for a man to raise his family,"[16] but he hinted at a darker motive in lauding it as a place where the people "don't care who you are, what you've been, or what your reputation was before they met you. It's how you handle yourself after you arrive there that counts."[17]

Within a week of his dismissal, Harry was visiting Spokane, soon to become one of the world's great wheat centers. Where wheat is harvested, distilleries and breweries are sure to follow, and Harry landed a job as bookkeeper at the newly developed Inland Brewery. Harry sold the house on J Street to Annie and her husband, Ed Walsh, for a dollar.[18] The nominal figure may indicate the settlement of a debt or the intention to resume ownership at a future date. The Walshes never lived in the house but held on to it for many years before selling.

Harry had to begin work immediately, but Kate was in the last weeks of a difficult pregnancy with Mary Rose and could not withstand the long, jolting rail trip. So he went alone, securing the rental of a roomy four-bedroom house in Spokane's Catholic district and fortifying it with furniture shipped from J Street. Kate and the children moved into a furnished house on South I Street, half a mile from their abandoned home and a couple of blocks from the austere box-frame house in which Annie and Ed Walsh lived and where the children could be distracted. Everett was charged with watching Harry until Mary Rose was safely delivered, though Kate remained ill and in bed for two months.

By early July Kate felt her strength returning, or recognized that the trip could be put off no longer. She said her good-byes and in the grueling midsummer heat transported herself, the baby, the five older children, and several valises to the station. They almost missed the train when the combative Everett disappeared to pursue an altercation with a newsboy. But he was located in time, and the seven Crosbys boarded the Northern Pacific, bound for the Inland Empire.

The times were changing as the Crosbys pulled up roots. The week Spokane's Inland Brewery announced the expansion that made Harry's job possible, a prankster in Chicago yelled "fire" outside a church during the Easter service, inciting a stampede that took the lives of four parishioners, three of them children; and a mob of 5,000 in Springfield, Missouri, destroyed a prison and hanged and burned three black teenagers accused of attacking a white woman, despite the woman's assertion that they were not the culprits. (The mob inadvertently freed nearly forty white bona fide criminals, causing a panic throughout the area.) Three days later, at 5:13 A.M., a fierce rumbling woke San Francisco to the ordeal that demolished the city and stoked fires that raged for three days, taking a thousand lives and leaving 250,000 homeless — the nation's worst disaster since the Johnstown flood of 1889.

It was the era in which Lincoln Steffens damned the shame of the cities and Upton Sinclair revealed that the bodies of Chicago meatpackers who drowned in mixing vats were processed with diseased cows and brought to market. New York tabloids ballyhooed the first of many "crimes of the century" after a deranged wastrel, Harry K. Thaw, defended the honor of his wife, showgirl Evelyn Nesbit, by murdering the architect and libertine Stanford White. His attorneys argued that Thaw suffered from "dementia Americana," and his millions bought him several stays in a mental hospital while Nesbit augured talk-show renown by ventilating her cautionary tale on the vaudeville circuit.

And yet despite unreasoning fears and exploding racial and ethnic hatred, it was an era of heroes — of larger-than-life people who were honored without the slightest taint of cynical apprehension: builders, explorers, educators, thinkers, rebels, scientists, tinkerers, politicians, industrialists, labor leaders. The *Spokesman-Review,* the major Inland paper, published a front-page poll in which regional educators, intellectuals, and writers were asked to name the five greatest contemporary Americans.[19] The same men turned up on ballot after ballot: Teddy Roosevelt topped them all, followed by Thomas A. Edison, Charles W. Eliot, Edward Everett Hale, Andrew Carnegie, William Jennings Bryan, Booker T. Washington, Luther Burbank, Samuel Gompers, J. Pierpont Morgan. These men embodied the American character, enhanced the American profile, avowed an American century. Spokane fit the bill; after driving out the Palouse Indians in 1905, the city sprang forward.

4

SPOKANE

Nicknames are indicative of a change from a given to an achieved identity and they tell us something of the nicknamed individual's interaction with his fellows.
— Ralph Ellison, *Shadow and Act* (1964)[1]

Old Spokane, called Spokane Falls, was little more than a post for trading with the Spokane and Couer d'Alene Indians. When the Northern Pacific Railroad arrived, the settlement boomed overnight, attracting the Wild West's familiar warring elements — "respectable" people, including mining barons, and transient loggers, miners, and other laborers lured by liquor, gambling, and prostitution. The hell-raisers had access to opium, provided by Chinese who had been brought in to lay track and were then forced to live in the town's dark back alleys. The values of the more conservative city fathers began to win out in 1889, the year Washington won statehood, when a fire razed thirty-two blocks of the rowdy downtown district. The towns-men set about rebuilding the city, using red brick and cast iron instead of wood. They imported architects with a taste for terra-cotta. Ordinances were passed to make life harder for those who did not fit in. "Box" theaters, which provided whores and whiskey in balconied boxes, were banned; saloons were shuttered on Sundays.

Spokane (*Falls* was dropped in 1891) flourished as the commercial hub of the Inland Empire, a wintergreen and dun-colored expanse that wrapped its 150 miles around scores of towns, agricultural and mineral riches, forests and streams, seventeen lakes, a rushing river, and falls that were claimed to rival Niagara.[2] The opening of the railway, in 1881, and the Coeur d'Alene gold rush, two years later, transformed the city and its surroundings. But the Northern Pacific's encroaching yards and warehouses spread over Spokane like a blotting shadow, overtaking the riverfront and ultimately sealing the city from its breathtaking views of falls and rapids.[3]

Yet "the Bond which Unites us with the Rest of the World,"[4] as the Northern Pacific characterized itself, brought Spokane undeniable dominance east of the Cascades. The population, which numbered 350 in 1880, had grown to nearly 100,000 by 1906, when Kate Crosby and her children, exhausted and distempered from the blistering heat and rattling journey, stepped from the train into a streaked sunset and saw Harry, smiling in his straw hat beside a rented horse and wagon, eager to show them their new home.

The driver helped load the valises and, turning the wagon north, retraced much of the route Harry took from work every day on the trolley, back through the business district and across the Spokane River to the residential areas. They proceeded east of Division Street, the baseline from which avenues are numbered, to a developing working-class enclave known as the Holy Land, for its Catholic churches, schools, convent, seminary, and orphanage. When they reached the yellow two-story house at 303 East Sinto Avenue, Harry unlocked the door and switched on an electric light, a convenience they had not enjoyed in Tacoma. He pointed out the carefully installed furniture, the groceries, the indoor plumbing.

As the luggage was carried inside, Kate collapsed onto a chair in the living room. The older boys explored the upstairs bedrooms where they would double up — Larry and Everett in one room, Ted and Harry in another, Catherine and the baby in the third. Their parents slept downstairs in a room off the main area. Harry knew the reunion occasioned as much resignation as cheer. In a 1937 account Ted and Larry describe Kate as a woman who renounced self-pity about what she had left behind; she had "acquiesced in her husband's decision to start anew" and considered herself a pioneer now.[5] In later years, however, she complained to Bing that they had arrived with "very short funds" and ran high food and fuel bills, while her husband breezily dismissed her financial worries.[6]

Nothing better symbolized the family's ambivalence about Dad's spending than the acquisition of a "talking machine" during their first Spokane autumn, days after Kate enrolled her three oldest boys in nearby Webster Grade School. (The Holy Land did not yet have a parochial elementary school.) Harry arrived home late one evening with a huge box — a gift, he claimed, from a man who owed him favors. Beaming, he unpacked an Edison Phonograph, a machine that played cylinders with a wind-up lever and amplified them through a bell-like horn. He also brought out recordings of "The Stars and Stripes Forever" and — to soften his wife — "The Merry Widow Waltz." Kate mellowed, and the extravagance was happily accepted. But her concern about Harry's easy way with a buck was not easily allayed; the wariness died hard in her, and she passed it on to her children. Even toward the end of his life, when Bing boasted of his father buying the neighborhood's first phonograph, he allowed that his old man had probably used the grocery money.

The marvelous machine, patented nearly three decades earlier by Thomas Edison, whose hopes for it were no grander than for a Dictaphone, filled the house with trebly, tinny, yet vividly exuberant and often exotic sounds. Radio, as an entertainment medium, was more than twenty years in the future. But for now they had this pipeline to the world and its music. By the time the Edison and its cylinders were replaced by a phonograph that played platters, Dad had a collection ranging from the Peerless Quartet to *The Mikado* to such singers as John McCormack ("Mother Machree," McCormack's theme, was one of his favorites), Harry Lauder, Henry Burr, Denis O'Sullivan, and Al Jolson. Of the Irish tenors, Bing preferred McCormack: "I knew all his songs and I thought he was a wonderful singer with great appeal, great sincerity, and a quality in his voice like a bird."[7] But the sound that mesmerized the boy was the Broadway yawp of the dynamic Jewish minstrel, Al Jolson, whose intensity shattered Spokane's calm surface.

Harry had reason to feel secure about his prospects. A year earlier Spokane's Heiber Brewery, a modern plant with an annual capacity of 110,000 barrels of brew and malt, had switched hands to three partners, John Lang, William Huntley, and Charles Theis.[8] They bought it — and two plots of real estate — for $300,000. Lang, a canny German-born businessman transplanted from San Francisco by way of Tacoma, changed the firm's name to Inland Brewing & Malting Co., bought another six adjacent lots, built a cold-storage plant and bottling works, and opened a wholesale agency in Moscow, Idaho. During this expansion, he hired Harry as bookkeeper. Though modestly paid, Harry was attached to a growing business in a growing community. True, many deplored the shameful product; the company offered home delivery to every part of the city in "plain wagons, plain cases."[9] Even Harry hid his spirits. But the days of temperance fanatics like Carrie Nation were gone, or so most people thought.

The family settled readily into the neighborhood. As Kate recalled, "All around us were young married couples, congenial and all of a sort in tastes, economic position and general outlook. Nobody was wealthy. Everybody was happy."[10] In the fall of 1908, she walked young Harry to the Webster School and registered him in first grade, though he was only five, the proper age for kindergarten. Webster did not offer kindergarten, so perhaps she lied about his age, impatient to get him out from under her feet. Yet Harry had plainly usurped his mother's attentions. Whatever else charmed Kate about her jug-eared, towheaded youngest boy, she cannot have failed to see herself mirrored in his face.

The older boys were different, easier to describe: Larry was bookish, soft-spoken, owlish in glasses not unlike his father's; Everett was pugnacious, a provocateur with little interest in school and defiantly sure of himself; Ted was quiet, a loner, a diligent and imaginative child who wrote stories and studied electronics. The three older boys looked like their father: they had the rounded, fleshy Crosby face and small, dark eyes. Harry, too, had his father's thin nose and thinning scalp. Still, he was decidedly a Harrigan, the only boy to inherit his mother's cool, prominent, hooded blue eyes; her prim lips; and the triangular jaw she got from her mother. Even the way his right cheek folded at the mouth in an irrepressible smirk linked him to Kate. In her later photographs, that smirk is as close as she got to smiling.

The Harrigan moodiness was also familiar, as were his quickness to take offense and his indisputable charm. Everyone who knew young Harry would speak of his constant singing and whistling that heralded his arrival. He was given more leeway than his brothers, his father conceded. "We were both so lenient that it's no wonder our other boys called Bing 'Mother's and Dad's pet.' Not that he was spoiled. He got his tannings. But he — well, he was different in a way. Made it sort of hard to spank him much."[11]

In third grade he was informally and indelibly renamed. It was 1910, the year a local matron, Mrs. John Bruce Dodd, founded a movement to establish a national Father's Day. Harry, six years old, discovered a full-page feature in Sunday's *Spokesman-Review*, "The Bingville Bugle." Written and illustrated by humorist Newton Newkirk, of the *Boston Post*, the "Bugle" was a broad parody of a hillbilly newsletter, with gossipy tidbits, minstrel quips, creative spelling, mock ads, and hayseed caricatures. Harry Lowe told writer Quentin Reynolds that his boy pestered grown-ups to read it to him. He'd point to the page and plead, "Bing! Bing!" until someone gave in.[12]

One older boy he did not have to pester much was fifteen-year-old Valentine Hobart, who lived two doors away. Valentine liked Harry and shared his enthusiasm for the "Bugle," which the *Spokesman-Review* dispersed not in the comics section (its drawings served primarily as teasers for the lengthy text) but in a supplement filled with stories by Jack London, H. Rider Haggard, O. Henry, W. W. Jacobs, and other popular writers. The "Bugle" motto boasted, THE LEADING PAPER OF THE COUNTRY — BRIGHT, BREEZY, BELLICOSE, BUSTLING, and augured with remarkable accuracy the yokel humor that Arkansas-born comedian Bob Burns popularized on Crosby's *Kraft Music Hall* in the 1930s. It incorporated back-fence scuttlebutt ("There was a light in the front parlor of the Perkins' residence last Satterday ev'g until as late as 9:30 P.M. . . . Tom staid a little mite later than usual on this occashion, didn't he Sadie?"); "pomes" by "well knowed pome writer, Miss Sally Hoskins"; recipes for items such as harness grease; drama reviews ("Uncle Tom's Cabin, Played by Real Actor Folks, was Give in the Town Hall to a Large and Intelligent Audience"); and hard news ("Hank Dewberry had a turrible experience with his red bull thet he will remember with loathing as long as he lives").[13]

Harry had an infectious and appreciative laugh, and Hobart took a shine to him, calling him Bingo from Bingville.[14] Shorn of its last vowel, the improbable nickname stuck. Other versions of its origin were later publicized. One had him named for a floppy-eared character in the parody named Bingo, though Newkirk never actually drew such a creature. A Paramount Pictures press release explained that as a boy, Bing played cowboys and Indians, cocking his fingers like a gun and shouting, "Bing bing bing," a tale reprinted for decades to come. Everett, a fount of misinformation, replaced the cowboy story that he helped popularize with a third version, in which Bing's name was earned with a baseball bat, which he used to knock out clean hits called "bingles."[15]

Bing was sensitive about the genesis of his name. Though notoriously free with what Huck Finn called "stretchers" and indifferent to most accounts of his life and career, he corrected Paramount's press release (which perpetuated numerous errors he let stand) in order to ground "The Bingville Bugle" in his history. But he never discussed the more intriguing issue of why a grown man cultivates a childhood nickname. In *The Bank Dick*, W. C. Fields considers a name: "Og Oggleby. Sounds like a bubble in a bath." What then does *Bing* sound like: the direct hit on a spitoon? The NBC chimes? The collision of two martinis? If nothing else, it conveys the affection of its bestowers.

After Hobart named him, only his mother persisted in calling him Harry. In school he signed his work Harry, but even his teachers took to calling him Bing. The name would be used by his wives and lovers, colleagues and partners, family and friends all his life. From the outset of his career, it seemed as natural and fitting and finally as commonplace as Tom, Dick, or Elvis. The name disarms, flatters the wary, demands a certain conviviality of all who approach. Bing. El Bingo. Le Bing. Bing Kuo Shi Bi. Der Bingle. Rarely has a nickname so aptly defined the person it identified. He was Bing at all times, except before the law and the church. He reserved Harry for his alter ego in a running 1940s radio skit (a character of the "Moonlight Bay" era, he explained, his father's generation) and occasions of high seriousness, like meeting the Pope. And he handed it down to his fourth and fifth sons.

Bing was a solid if unremarkable student at Webster, popular and able to hold his own in and out of the classroom, even though he was a year younger than his classmates. To the dismay of his teachers, he did not have to work hard to do well and sometimes appeared to do no work at all. He was considered bright but lazy. A good friend, Francis Corkery (who would become president of Gonzaga University), thought of him as happy-go-lucky, too carefree to be a true leader; he recalled that Bing was always ready to go along when the gang raided fruit trees for apples and cherries. Francis and Bing had jackknives and whittled together. Corkery remembered him as good-natured and always singing. Though shy with girls, Bing was outgoing with boys and good at sports, despite his small stature. In fourth grade Frank and Bing played on the Webster School baseball team. In his dark jersey with striped sleeves and leggings, Bing stands in the front row of a team picture, hands on hips, eager and poised.

Gertrude Kroetch, Bing's fourth-grade teacher, remembered his class practicing ovals in penmanship. She had set a rhythm, counting fours. All the kids did the ovals except Bing, who, finger cocked and one eye closed, shot his classmates one by one with an imaginary gun. Not wanting to interrupt her counting, Miss Kroetch pantomimed her own gun and fired it at Bing, who began to "make those ovals furiously."[16] His mother recalled an afternoon when he was sent home from school with a note. Bing had disrupted the class with his "whispered remarks and pantomime." The next time it happened, he was sent to the principal. "What did [the principal] do?" Kate asked him. "He dealt with me," said Bing. "And?" "That's all. I think I get the idea now."[17] The principal had bent Bing over a chair and whacked him with a yardstick.

Corporal punishment was hardly unknown to him, notwithstanding the parental favoritism. If Dad tended to disappear when a licking was to be administered, Kate was willing; and the children feared her hefty wooden hairbrush and strap. Her implacable authority earned Kate a level of respect denied Harry, but something less than love, perhaps because her approval was so often linked to her ambitions. She was always searching for a star. When Kate thought Ted might become a priest, she relieved him of chores; when she decided Catherine could succeed on Broadway, she insisted on years of piano lessons no matter the cost. The children claimed to venerate her for being steadfast and sensible, yet privately they found her manipulative and severe. One way or another, she was setting up each of them to disappoint her. In later years four of her children — Bing emphatically not among them — conceded that despite their admiration and respect for their mother, they never truly loved her.[18]

In addition to meting out punishment, Kate allocated chores, settled disputes, and governed family traditions. Mary Rose considered her an extraordinary woman but noted that for all the bother over birthdays, they were observed with a cake and never a party. Kate disbursed Harry's wages, and when they weren't sufficient, she emphasized his failure by dramatically resorting to a teapot, her emergency bank. "My father didn't make a great deal of money," Bing said. "My mother raised us on his small salary and we all got through college somehow."[19] Perhaps he hoped to instill in his own children the reverence he felt toward her when he, too, used a strap, with terrible results, as he repeatedly acknowledged. Kate, after all, earned him his success: "My mother was such a wonderful woman and she did so many good things and so much good work and she wanted success and happiness for me. Maybe the Lord, to make her happy, had good things happen to me."[20]

Harry had no illusions about who ruled the roost. Asked to comment on his world-renowned son in 1940, he volunteered:

> My wife really knows much more about him than I do. Not that he's a stranger to me! But Mother — well, you know how boys act toward their mothers. I guess I've always been the easy-going father. Bing takes after me in that respect. Nobody can rush him either. I remember the times I'd come home from work and how often I'd be greeted with the story of some disturbing antic of his during the day. My wife always would say, "Now, Harry, you must speak to Bing. He's been very hard to manage today." I'd look very indignant, promise some sort of punishment, then watch Kate do the disciplining. I just couldn't bring myself to punish Bing — or any of the boys.[21]

Bing considered Harry's serenity his primary legacy. "Whether inherited or not," Bing once said, "his ability to relax has helped me in a life which has had its share of pressure. I don't worry seriously about anything."[22]

A block west of the Crosby home lived Helen and Agnes Finnegan, sisters who taught Bing in fifth and sixth grades, respectively. Helen remembered him as roly-poly and likable, and was proud to claim that he played his first stage role in her class, as a singing jumping bean, one of twelve (Corkery was another) who vaulted across the stage on pogo sticks in a presentation called *Beebee*. In sixth and seventh grades, Bing was introduced to two venerable theatrical conventions, often revisited during his career; he appeared in blackface for a school benefit and in a pink-and-white-checkered dress for a Christmas play adapted from the *Ladies' Home Journal*. His fine voice was much admired. "We think Hollywood has ruined Harry's voice," Helen Finnegan complained to a reporter in 1946. "He sang much better before he became a crooner."[23] Agnes remembered him as clean but sloppy, with his shirttail out, always chewing pencils or gum or both. He had straw-colored hair, a creamy complexion, outsize ears, china-blue eyes, and a tendency toward chubbiness.

Music was always heard at home. As Harry's record collection increased, Bing memorized the latest songs. "I had a constant succession of them in my head. And I had to whistle or sing to get them out."[24] The phonograph was always on, except after supper on Sunday, when the family gathered in the living room to sing. Accompanied by Harry on mandolin or guitar, and by a glowing fire in winter, Kate's contralto fused with Harry's tenor on "When Irish Eyes Are Smiling," "Sweet Adeline," "In the Good Old Summer Time," and "Mother Machree," among others. Harry conducted a male quartet that included himself, Bing, Larry, and Ev. Ted, an inveterate tinkerer, kept his distance from the harmonizing but a few years later made his own valiant contribution by building a crystal radio that picked up new songs from a station in Seattle.

The girls took turns at the piano, recently transported from the house in Tacoma. Harry paid fifteen dollars for cartage, the price of a new suit he was obliged to sacrifice. It was a present for Kate, who wanted the girls to learn how to play and needed cheering up. Her childless sister, Annie, had written to boast how well her husband was doing and rubbed salt in the wound by offering to adopt Kay (Catherine).[25] Only in her children was Kate richer than Annie, yet she made it clear she appreciated the offer and was inclined to consent. This time, Harry put his foot down. They were not so poor that they had to farm out one of their children. By way of saying no, thank you, he reclaimed her piano. Kay quickly revealed musical talent and promised to be a beauty. Kate envisioned stardom for her.

It wasn't Dad, but a member of Kate's family — her youngest brother, George, then a robust man in his early thirties — who became Bing's first idea of an exemplary performer. An enthusiastic amateur, George made frequent visits from the coast. Bing adored him and spent many hours at his side. In later years, when Bing reminisced about George, his voice would rise a couple of tones and the phrases would tumble out with a cantering dispatch:

> My mother had a brother, George Harrigan, a great singer in the Tacoma-Seattle area. He was a court reporter in the local legislature and also in the courts in Seattle and Tacoma, and of course his theme song was "Harrigan," taken from the Cohan song. And he was the biggest favorite singing around that area that ever occurred there. He was a great guy and had a terrific voice — big, high, loud, *powerful* tenor. Anytime he appeared, everybody'd holler, "Harrigan," and he'd go: "H-A-double R-I-G-A-N spells Harrigan / Divil a man can say a word agin me," and I learned a lot just watching him. He could tell stories in any dialect you ever heard of. He should have gone into show business, but he married young, had about five or six children, and never could get away. He'd have been a sensational star with his ability to do dialect stories and sing. He was six foot two, black hair with blue eyes. Handsome man.[26]

During Christmas 1912 Kate, nearing forty, revealed that for the first time in six years she was pregnant. The timing was propitious. Inland Brewery's tank capacity increased by another 25,000 barrels, and Harry received a raise and a new title — cashier. Spokane felt flush. Five years before, Barnum & Bailey's circus elephants refused to step onto the steel Monroe Street Bridge, which collapsed shortly afterward. Now its replacement was completed and was touted as the longest concrete span in the country. Spokane boasted sixty-two miles of paved streets, 600 miles of concrete walks, thirty-five public schools, ten hospitals and asylums, 112 churches. The Spokane–Coeur d'Alene interurban electric railway, leaving every few minutes, transported thousands of swimmers and picnickers to Liberty Lake, the area's most popular resort. The fabulous Davenport Hotel, designed by architect Kirtland Cutter at a cost of $3 million, opened its doors in 1914, attracting celebrities and royalty with its glass pillars and lobby birds, plumbing that siphoned drinking water to every room, and a washing machine to polish silver money.

Even the entertainment world rallied. After city officials banned box and variety theaters, performers were engaged to lure skeptical customers into nickelodeons that were little more than converted storefronts. The first significant theater in Spokane was the Auditorium, built in 1890, with the second-largest stage west of Minneapolis. It presented musicals, operas, concerts, and dramas. The more daring Pantages and Washington theaters offered traveling vaudeville. At the outset of 1915, two movie theaters, the Liberty and the Clemmer, opened their doors. The *Spokesman-Review* crowed, "It is doubtful if any city the size of Spokane can boast of two such moving picture theaters."[27]

In this environment, and with the financial help of Inland Brewery, the ever optimistic Crosbys believed they could finally realize the dream of building their own home in Spokane. Kate got the ball rolling. In June 1911 the Pioneer Educational Society (a Jesuit organization) sold her, "for the sum of one dollar and other considerations," a lot on East Sharp Avenue with a proviso that the buyer erect a "dwelling house worth not less than three thousand dollars."[28] Within weeks Inland Brewery bought the warranty deed for $6,500, enabling Kate and Harry to take out a mortgage. With additional financial help from Kate's sister, Anne, and Harry's nephew Lloyd, a timber executive, construction was completed in eighteen months, at which time Inland Brewery signed a quitclaim for a dollar and agreed to recoup its loan through payroll deductions.

Six months later, in July 1913, the Crosbys left the yellow house they had rented for seven years and moved a few blocks to the two-story clapboard house at 508 East Sharp Avenue, one block north of Gonzaga University and St. Aloysius Church. They could see the church steeple through their rear windows. In the front of the house, a concrete walk led to wooden steps and a porch that ran the full width. The house, painted dark brown and overhung with deep eaves, had four bedrooms plus a sleeping porch on the second floor; the amenities included a coal and wood furnace and two bathrooms. The living-and-dining-room area was appointed with a small fireplace trimmed in brown-stained fir, a bookcase, and a window seat. The modest backyard, ringed with climbable locust trees, abutted an alleylike pathway through which the boys could cut to school. Bing carved his mark on a supporting two-by-four in the basement: H.C. '16.

On August 25 Kate delivered her seventh child, named George Robert (Bob) after her brother George Robert Harrigan.[29] Bing, at ten, was no longer the youngest son. "Mother told me one thing and I really laugh when I think about it," Bob recalled. "Bing was the youngest boy, so he wound up with all the old bicycles, the old clothes, the old roller skates, all of that. And when I was born, in the front room of the house up in Spokane, each one of the kids was allowed to come in and see me. When Bing came in, he said to Mother, lying in bed with me in her arms, 'What is it?' She said, 'It's a boy.' And he said, 'Well, it better be,' and he walked out of the room. And from then on, he took care of me, good care of me. He was a wonderful brother. Outsmarted me all the time."[30]

Gonzaga University is located on East Boone, named for a descendant of Daniel, so the kids Bing ran with called themselves the Boone Avenue gang. Spokane, a mining community at heart, had never completely cleaned away the stain of Wild West excess, and the earliest tales Bing remembered hearing were of local gambling establishments at which his father took an "occasional flutter at the wheels of chance."[31] Miners tramped through regularly, and the downtown alleyways harbored all the secrets that make urban life a trial for the righteous. Bing explored them fully. He knew each alley, theater, swimming hole, rat's nest, playing field, park, and lake. The gang committed petty crimes, landing Bing in the clink more than once; on one occasion Kate, advised of his internment by the arresting officer, told him to keep her son overnight to teach him a lesson. Still, the gang's crimes were piddling ones: swiping candy and ice cream, drinking, smoking anything they could light, putting up their dukes, and sneaking into movie theaters. The urchins in Bing's circle produced a priest, lawyer, doctor, judge, boxer, and football Hall of Famer, as well as an entertainer. Bing stayed in touch with some of them his entire life.

The episode that cemented his stature among his peers — never told the same way twice — involved his challenging one Jim Turner to a fight in defense of his "plump and easygoing" sister Mary Rose.[32] She had been either called "fatty" or caricatured in a picture, which was either distributed to the other kids or drawn on a blackboard. Jimmy Cottrell (later a junior welterweight champ and, with Bing's help, a Paramount Pictures prop man) was a member of the Logan Avenue gang but was present at the 1914 tussle. He remembered a large crowd of kids circling a parking lot (an alley according to Bing, a playground according to Mary Rose), cheering the contestants. Bing bloodied Turner's nose (undisputed), earning his sister's devotion and subdued approval from his parents, especially Kate, who thought him chivalrous.

Bing was closest to Mary Rose of all his siblings, while Kay bonded with Ted. These lifelong pairings were viewed with irony, because Mary Rose — a candid, funny, exceedingly well liked woman who greatly enjoyed Bing's reflected glory — was personally much more like Ted. Kay, who was quiet, private, and fiercely independent, was Bing's double. In later years she never gave an interview, never boasted of her famous brother, never confided in anyone when she was dying of cancer. Of the seven children, only Kay and Bing would never be divorced.

Yet Mary Rose was his favorite. "Whenever I had problems," Mary Rose said, "I always went to Bing and he calmed me down and advised me what I should do."[33] She admired his remarkable memory, apparent from early childhood, and the way he taught himself to do a time step and play drums. His pet name for her was Posie, and he took her ice-skating, sharing his old black skates. "We liked to swim and to skate and none of the others did, particularly," Mary Rose said.[34] Jim Pool, the last of her three husbands, noted that when Everett was managing Bing and found him intransigent, he would ask Mary Rose to intercede. When Bing noticed Mary Rose and Jim driving an old car, he bought them a new one. "In my book," Mary Rose said, "he had it made when he was little. I always knew he'd amount to a lot."[35]

On September 18, 1915, as Bing commenced his final year at Webster, grandfather Dennis Harrigan Jr. passed away at his home in Tacoma, at eighty-three.[36] Bing had been a baby the last time they had seen each other. Six years before, Dennis had been struck by falling timber while inspecting construction of the governor's mansion, and he never entirely recovered. He was survived by a brother, seven children, fourteen grandchildren (half of them Kate's), and a widow, Katie, who would become the subject of the opening anecdote in Bing's 1953 memoir.

In Bing's story, his grandmother Katie, who is dying, asks her "Irishman" husband, Dennis, for his hand. "Katie," he says, "it's a hand that was never raised against ye." Eyes dilating, she answers, "And it's a damn good thing for ye it wasn't!" Upon delivering that insuperable finish, she expires.[37] It's a fine tale, paying homage to a spirited Irish woman, and may have some basis in truth (perhaps regarding Bing's *great*-grandparents). But Dennis died three years before Katie, and neither ever spent a day in Ireland. Bing's confusion on this point is instructive. Bing's family neither visited Dennis when he was ill nor attended his funeral. As an adult, Bing demonstrated a categorical aversion to funerals, memorial services, and hospitals.

Bing's skill as a young athlete was as obvious as his musical talent. Too small to make much of an impression in basketball or football, he was game enough to try hard at both as well as boxing and handball. He excelled in baseball and made the Junior Yard Association and varsity teams year after year, first at third base, then center field. He occasionally fantasized about running off to play professionally, and for a season played semipro on a team sponsored by Spokane Ideal Laundry. In his movies he would often incorporate bits of business to display his agility with a ball, though the closest he came to realizing his pro ambitions was buying a piece of the Pittsburgh Pirates in 1946.

Bing was even better at swimming. He learned the hard way. McGoldrick's lumberyard inhabited a portion of the northern bank of the Spokane River, which was close enough to the Gonzaga complex to disrupt classes with noise and smoke. In the years before the city created a network of public swimming pools, the millpond at the river's bend, bordered by a sandbar and accessed by logs dumped there for storage, was a deadly lure to neighborhood kids. Some drowned trying to brave the swift rapids beyond the sandbar; many more died trying to walk the log booms to and from the pond. Forbidden from going anywhere near McGoldrick's, the Boone gang and others could not resist the challenge.

The boys — Bing and Ted, Frank Corkery and his older brother, Boots, Ralph Foley, Phil Sweeney and his brother, Dan, and half a dozen others — were clustered in the family barn of one of its members when Foley (later a superior court judge and the father of the Speaker of the House Tom Foley) challenged them to join him for a swim in the millpond. They walked south on Standard Street, past

Gonzaga and the vacant lots and the railroad tracks, until they reached the narrow sandbar and saw older boys, including Everett, cavorting in the middle of the river. Despite warnings from passersby and the swimmers, they gingerly crossed a cluster of logs, disrobed, and jumped in. During that first adventure, Bing and Ted were painfully sunburned. They managed to hide their discomfort at lunch, but their vocal suffering alerted Kate that night. She insisted, in vain, that Harry whip them, but she soon took pity and applied a reeking goose grease to their inflamed backs.

As Corkery recalled, Bing was a millpond regular, swimming naked with the others and shocking passengers on the trains that rolled by the log-boom platforms from which they dove. He learned to swim in those currents and revisited them long after the pool at Mission Park opened, six blocks from his home. Jimmy Cottrell swam with Bing at Mission Park but, like him, preferred the excitement of the river: "Bing was a good diver, I admired him. We used to sneak off together to the Spokane River and see who could swim across."[38] Another admirer of Bing's watery talents was Mary Sholderer, one of seven girls in a gregarious and generous German family that fed and looked after the Crosby kids. ("We spent about as much time in the Sholderers' home as we did in our own," Bing said.)[39] She would not venture to McGoldrick's but sometimes walked Bing to the Mission pool, carrying Bob in her arms. She watched him dive and swim, and praised his agility. Mary sang soprano at St. Aloysius and, with three of her sisters, grew old in the family house. The beloved spinsters became known for the birthday parties they threw for neighborhood dogs. Bing never forgot Mary's kindness or failed to visit the Sholderer home when he returned to Spokane.

From Mary and the other kids, Kate learned how well Bing handled himself in the water. In the summer of 1915 he was hired as towel boy for the Mission Park pool locker room. The following summer Kate coddled him into competing in a citywide swimming contest. On the big day, a couple of weeks after graduating Webster, Bing courted the resentment of his brothers as he lazed about, singing Blanche Ring's vaudeville hit "I've Got Rings on My Fingers," resting up for the 2:00 P.M. meet. Kate relieved him of chores and prepared his favorite meal, pork chops. To his initial dismay, Kate also insisted on accompanying him to the pool. She did no harm. He won seven medals, including first place in diving and second place in the 100- and 220-yard speed events. When he resumed work at the pool that week, he was advanced from towel boy to lifeguard.

That same summer Bing added to his finances by caddying. He talked members out of old clubs and played the course on Mondays, becoming obsessed with golf, which replaced swimming as his preferred exercise. During his years in Hollywood, Crosby became an expert golfer, but he had some qualms about keeping a swimming pool and filled in at least one. The presumed reason was his fear that the neighborhood children might have accidents, generating lawsuits. Twenty-three summers after his triumph at the Mission Park pool, Bing attempted to exercise his swimming skills and almost had an accident of his own, at the 1939 New York World's Fair.

Driving back from a golf match with his friend mining heir Harvey Shaeffer, Bing suggested they catch the show at the Billy Rose Aquacade, featuring Eleanor Holm and Bing's friend from Hollywood Johnny Weissmuller, the Olympic swimming champ who became the definitive Tarzan. As Weissmuller introduced the divers, who were climbing up to a fifty-foot board, Bing casually mentioned that he could dive from that height. Shaeffer bet him a hundred dollars he could not. They went backstage. Telling no one but Weissmuller of his plan, Bing borrowed a farcical full-body swimsuit and matching hat and anonymously waited his turn. When it came, he embraced the caper with comic aplomb and was airborne before realizing that his pipe was clamped between his teeth. Fearing it might be driven through his neck, he aborted an intended jackknife in favor of a feet-first plunge. He lost his pipe, incited a furious Billy Rose (who also feared accidents and lawsuits), and collected sixty-five dollars from Shaeffer, who would not accept the plunge as a dive.

Harry mused, "All of our children were musical, but I must admit I had a soft spot in my heart for Bing, because I liked to hear him sing." He brought him down to the Spokane Elks Club and had Bing perform for the members. "The piano player of the Elks Quartet became so interested in Bing's singing that he gave him lessons."[40] Those lessons, if they took place (Bing never spoke of them), would probably have been gratis. Kate took as focused an interest in his singing as in his swimming. "[She] gave me every break," Bing said. "In fact, she took me to a teacher. I had about three lessons and she paid for them and she didn't have the money to spare at the time. I think the lessons cost five dollars a session. He gave me some things to vocalize on, some scales on the piano, and I think I went about three times, but I kept up the vocalizing for a few years — I think it loosened me up. That's the only formal musical training I ever had."[41] In his memoir, Bing claims that the lessons petered out when the professor discouraged pop songs and emphasized tone production and breath control. But shortly after Kate's death, he admitted the trouble was financial: "That fin, you know, every second week, was a little strong for my mother to come up with."[42] Kay's piano lessons, however, continued.

The Crosbys were now facing their worst crunch. On January 1, 1916, Washington went dry. The postboom cleanup, previously directed at gambling and prostitution, claimed one of the city's major legitimate businesses, three years before the rest of the country had to answer to the Volstead Act. Prohibition and the concurrent sale of the big mines brought an end to Spokane's growth years. Inland Brewery failed to accept or prepare for the drought, except with layoffs. Harry survived, at a drastically reduced salary, while the company tried to figure out what to do. The city chemist's confirmation, on January 7, that there was no trace of alcohol in Inland's "carbonated fizz near-beer" did nothing to stimulate sales.[43] As things got worse, so did Harry's wages. During some months he may not have been paid at all: for the years 1915 and 1916, he indicated no employment in his entry in the city directory.

In those dark days, Kate became preoccupied with Bing; just weeks before supervising his triumph at the Mission pool, she dressed her son in finery for his first formal musical performance. At a women's function, he sang typically sentimental numbers such as "Ben Bolt," a poem set to a German melody in 1848,[44] and "A Perfect Day," a 1910 hit by vaudevillian Carrie Jacobs-Bond. For an unsolicited encore, he held a leash in his hand and sang "My Dog Rover," a ditty he loved.[45] With little provocation, he would sing it in later years on well-lubricated hunting and fishing trips, though he never recorded it. Of the songs he sang that day, the one that seemed to bring out the most in him was a recently published secular hymn, "One Fleeting Hour."[46] With a broad range of eight whole notes and a forte-grande top-note finish, it was an imposing showpiece for the twelve-year-old. In the 1970s, when television interviewers asked him about his first experience before an audience, Bing unhesitatingly volunteered a few bars:

> When the twilight of eve dims the sun's last ray
> And the shades of the night gather fast,
> There's one fleeting hour that I've pray'd would stay,
> Full of joy and of pain that's passed.

Yet he never performed it professionally. Bing found his first appearance mortifying. In addition to having to get gussied up, he had to endure a cool reception — nothing like the kind his exuberant uncle George enjoyed.

Bing had never been hesitant about singing for friends, but performing for church groups was another story, inclining him to play harder with the gang. "My mother dressed me up in some fantastic attire, the knickerbockers and the flowing ties," Bing said. "That embarrassed me more than the singing, I believe. And of course the fellas I ran around with all thought singing was for girls or for sissies, certainly not for anyone who was going to be an athlete. Because we were mostly, as a group, concerned with rock fights and going down to the millpond and running logs and hooking rides on railroad trains and robbing the bakery wagon and things of that caliber, which were considered a little more adventurous and colorful than standing up in front of a ladies' sodality and singing 'One Fleeting Hour.'"[47] He was reprieved for a while when his voice changed, after which he was less shy about asserting himself in style and repertoire.

5

GONZAGA

I was eight years with the Jesuits, four high school, four college. Yeah, pretty well indoctrinated.

— Bing Crosby (1976)[1]

As a student at Gonzaga High School, part of the small complex of redbrick buildings on Boone Avenue that made up Gonzaga University, Bing could almost roll out of bed and into class. He was often late. The assembled students listened for his unhurried approach: first the slamming of the back door, then a few bars of whistling, then a popular song as he ambled through his backyard to the end of the block, crossed Boone, and strolled into class. After he began haunting weekend vaudeville shows at the Pantages, he made a point of arriving early on Monday mornings to entertain the class with imitations of the comedians and singers who passed through town. Frank Corkery marveled at his ability to memorize routines down to the corniest gags. Far more unusual was Bing's self-possession — his extraordinary presence of mind.

Once, before physics class, the gang lured Bing into a storage space, then locked him in just as the instructor arrived. Did he bang on the wall of that black hole and holler for someone to let him out? Hardly. He made no sound at all until the instructor, Francis Prange, uttered his first remarks, at which point Bing's voice, crooning "The

Missouri Waltz," floated through the room. The teacher stopped, as did the singing. Prange glanced out the window, looked around the room, then resumed. The mysterious if unmistakable voice sang out a second time. Prange quieted, and so did the song. With the next encore, he trailed the voice to its lair, liberated Bing, and dragged him to the principal's office.[2] It was typical of Bing, a classmate noted, to turn a prank played on him into a more inventive prank of his own.[3]

Gonzaga's history was well known to the community.[4] In the autumn of 1865, Father Joseph M. Cataldo, a Jesuit missionary from Sicily, entered the Inland Empire, traveling on horseback to Couer d'Alene Mission. Within a year he had built a chapel at Peone Prairie, winning the confidence of the Spokane Indians. Under his leadership, a Catholic orphanage and the Sacred Heart Hospital were constructed. In 1881 he began to build a school for Indians on 320 acres of land just north of the Spokane River, purchased for 936 silver dollars from the Northern Pacific Railroad. Coolie labor made bricks from clay on the riverbank where four decades later the McGoldrick Lumber Company appeared. After six years of delays, Gonzaga College — named for the family of Saint Aloysius, patron saint of youth — opened its doors. But by that time Cataldo's intentions were undermined by white settlers, who needed schooling for their own children. They insisted that the two-story building with basement and dormitory attic serve them exclusively. Seven boys, ages eleven to seventeen, arrived the first week, greeted by an eight-man faculty — four priests and four scholastics. By 1900 two more buildings had been added to accommodate increased enrollment and a high-school curriculum. A law school followed in 1912, changing Gonzaga's standing to that of a university.

Jesuit pedagogy in America focused on educating the middle class, extending the liberalism of the Greeks in the cultivation of grammar, literature, rhetoric, and philosophy, in addition to science. "The right word is a sure sign of good thinking," the Athenian Isocrates instructed.[5] Writer Michael Harrington, a self-described "pious apostate," once remarked of his own Jesuit education, "Our knowledge was not free floating; it was always consciously related to ethical and religious values."[6]

Bing's devout mother underscored the moral imperatives encouraged during his eight years at Gonzaga. But the stern principles affirmed by her hairbrush were more unforgiving than the liberal inquiries of the Jesuits. Bing drew on both in creating the character of Father O'Malley (*Going My Way* and *The Bells of St. Mary's*), a paradigm of scholastic progressiveness. Privately, however, he was obliged to bargain his way out of a hellfire that was no more metaphorical to him than a golf club. His inclinations toward wildness could be indulged only in the context of an Augustinian postponement.[7] Bing would have understood Flannery O'Connor's injunction "Good is something under construction."[8] That part of him remained secret and unknowable, rehearsed only in the Sunday masses he attended without fail all his life.

In a 1950s radio interview with Father Caffrey, a genial radio priest, Bing recalled in typically breathless style (substituting conjunctions for punctuation) the "wonderful men at Gonzaga in those days."

> The university was only twenty-five or thirty-five years old then and there was still some of the pioneer staff of the Jesuit order, men around seventy-five or eighty years of age who had come out there in the Indian missions, as Father Cataldo and some of his followers had done, and they were brilliant men, men with great background in the missionary field, and I was much impressed with them, of course, because they had many stories to tell, incidents that happened in the first settlements, working with the Indians, and I was much impressed with their piety. I get a great deal of consolation from my religion, Father, and I think it was firmly embedded in me somehow back there at Gonzaga High and Gonzaga University by the good Fathers.[9]

In his memoir, he credited the priests, whom he invariably describes as powerful and manly, with imparting to him "virility and devoutness, mixed with the habit of facing whatever fate set in my path, squarely, with a cold blue eye."[10] The cold blue eye was in his case genetic, the devotion inculcated, the fortitude willed.

Bing encountered one of the most formidable of those men on his first day, when he and a couple of friends went to register. Father James "Big Jim" Kennelly was a looming but beloved figure, pale-eyed and slope-shouldered, standing six foot three and weighing nearly 300 pounds, garbed in a floor-length black cassock fixed at the waist by a lengthy chain weighted with a ring of keys. As prefect of discipline since 1899, Big Jim was known for flicking his key ring at the bottoms of miscreants with, in Bing's observation, "the accuracy and speed of a professional fly-caster."[11] He was no sadist, Bing quickly added, just a conscientious disciplinarian who was always willing to tuck his cassock into his pants and join the boys on the playing field. Bing may have presumed too much on Kennelly's reputation as a "rah-rah" man and erstwhile star athlete.[12] Asked about his desire to study, Bing allegedly told him, "Yeah, and play some football," escaping the key ring by inches.[13]

With his nearly photographic memory, Bing found that most subjects came reasonably easily. Leo Lynn, Bing's factotum (stand-in, driver) for more than forty years, was a fellow student at Gonzaga and admired his sharpness and style. Bing could "rattle off Latin, was terrible at mathematics, good at Greek and history," he recalled.[14] Despite difficulties in algebra (one semester he wrote an essay called "Why Algebra and Geometry Are Unnecessary in the Modern High School Curriculum"), Bing seemed bound for a conscientious academic career. He received distinctions in history, English, and Christian doctrine and was elected sergeant-at-arms (Frank Corkery was elected vice president) in his first year. With his instantly appreciated sonorous voice, he was chosen to read aloud an original composition to the freshman class. He faced thirty boys in uniform white blouses without a trace of nerves. Come spring, he was one of the fifty students competing in the annual high-school elocution assembly, and one of only fourteen chosen for "public exhibition." He read "Old Watermelon Time."

At Gonzaga's neighboring church, St. Aloysius, Bing put his Latin to use as an altar boy, attending service daily at 6:30 in the morning every third week throughout his four years of high school. *Ad Deum qui laetificat juventutem meum* (To God who gives joy to my youth) was forever imprinted in his memory. "I served mass all over Spokane when I was up there," he said. He served in later years as well, at least twice on transatlantic liners, assisting shipboard priests. "Of course," he observed of those experiences, "I had to use the book. I couldn't remember all the responses, but I guess I got by all right."[15]

Bing Crosby is the only major singer in American popular music to enjoy the virtues of a classical education. It grounded his values and expectations, reinforcing his confidence and buffering him from his own ambition. As faithful as he was to show business, his demeanor was marked by a serenity that suggested an appealing indifference. He had something going for him that could not be touched by Hollywood envy and mendacity. He acted in the early years of his career as if he didn't give a damn, displaying an irresponsibility that would have ensured a less talented man's failure, and he learned to turn that knowing calm into a selling point. Other performers worked on the surface, but Bing kept as much in reserve as he revealed. He was as cool in life as he was in song or onscreen. He was the kind of man who, notified by phone the day after New Year's 1943 that his family was safe but his home had burned to cinders, deadpanned, "Were they able to save my tux?" The Jesuits trained him to weigh the rewards of this world versus those of the next and to keep his own counsel. His brother Bob once said, "As an actor he played Bing Crosby, 'cause he went to Jesuit school all his life. He knew the Jebbies pretty well."[16]

Bing himself was willing to give them much of the credit. Classes in elocution, in which he excelled, taught him not only to enunciate a lyric but to analyze its meaning. At Gonzaga High, education was idealized in the phrase *eloquentia perfecta* (perfect eloquence). Students coached in literature were expected to attain rhetorical mastery as well. However casual a student Bing may have been — however much an underachiever, in the opinion of some teachers — he maintained better than average grades until his last year of pre-law, sustaining a consistent B/B+ average and taking several honors. "We had a lot of experience in public speaking and debating societies, standing on your feet and talking, and doing plays," he emphasized, "and if I have ability as an actor, that's where I got it."[17]

The Crosbys placed great stock in education, less in graduation. Harry Lowe dropped out of school, and so would most of his sons. (Catherine and Mary Rose attended Holy Names Academy, the neighboring convent school, and North Central High, but like most women in working-class families were not expected to attend college.) Yet Kate and Harry labored hard to keep the boys in school as long as possible. When Everett left to take a job, Kate's disappointment was relieved only by the idea that his salary would help the younger boys graduate.

Larry, the oldest, did graduate. He described the family's "common traits" as "natural conservatism, civic and patriotic interests, and devotion to education and learning, even at a time in our early history when such attainments were not common."[18] He proceeded to tally history's most learned Crosbys, without explaining how or if they figured in the direct family line: surgeons, jurists, scholars, writers, reformers, soldiers, and politicians, among them William George Crosby, a legislator in Maine after the Civil War; Howard Crosby, a reformer, clergyman, and writer, and his son Ernest, a prolific if marginal poet; and Cornelia Thurza Crosby, a trout fisherwoman called Fly Rod Crosby, after she outraged an assembly of sportsmen at Madison Square Garden by showing up in a green skirt "seven inches above the floor."[19] Most significant from a musical angle was Frances (Fanny) Jane Crosby, the blind poet and hymn writer, who died in New York City in 1915 at ninety-five, credited with 8,000 hymns, including "Safe in the Arms of Jesus," "There's Music in the Air," and a lyric to "Dixie" with which she attempted to turn that anthem into a Northern rallying cry, called "On! Ye Patriots to the Battle."

On Good Friday 1917 President Wilson read his proclamation of war, and Gonzaga, like most campuses, hummed with patriotic commotion. The exodus of young men began in early June. Larry and Everett, gone from school by then, were instantly caught up in the fever. Larry quit his job as a clerk for New York Life Insurance and applied to officers' training camp at the Presidio, leaving straightaway for San Francisco. Everett, who had left his job as assistant auditor at the Davenport Hotel to pursue greener prospects in Montana, wrote home that he had enlisted in the field artillery. ("I never rode a horse before in my life but I tried not to let the officers know it.")[20] Ted, a year below draft age, went to college, where he spent much of his time writing spy stories set in shady European capitals.

The older boys were away more than two years. Larry served as second lieutenant and commanded the Forty-fourth Company of the depot brigade at Camp Funston, Kansas; after the armistice, he was made camp insurance officer. Ev, a sergeant in the American Expeditionary Forces, was sent from Douglas, Arizona (where he boasted that he won a football game for the Eleventh Division Field Artillery), to St. Aignan. After he was decommissioned, he savored Gay Paree for two years, working part of the time as an American guide, living the high life, mastering French. Kate had hoped the conquering heroes would help pay for the younger boys' schooling and shared her hope that either Ted or Bing would join the priesthood, a future Bing claimed to have contemplated.

An event that occurred when he was a teenager of fourteen made it clear that Bing was probably not destined for the clergy. He had taken a summer job as a property boy at Spokane's prize theater, the Auditorium, and saw some of the finest acts and revues of the day.[21] On the evenings of June 19 and 20, Bing watched backstage as Al Jolson played his standard character, Gus, in *Robinson Crusoe Jr.* It was a role he had created a few years earlier: the canny black servant — in this farce, a chauffeur doubling as Friday — who always saves the day. A whirlwind comedian, Jolson raced around the stage ad-libbing lines and business, even song lyrics. During the show's fifteen-month tour, he was billed for the first time as "the World's Greatest Entertainer."

Bing was spellbound by the electrifying blackface performer. Jolson brought the house down with his spoof of Hawaiian songs "Yaaka Hula Hickey Dula" and the lunatic "Where Did Robinson Crusoe Go with Friday on Saturday Night?" (cowritten by the same team that wrote Bing's early signature song ten years later, "In a Little Spanish Town").[22] Bing and his friends knew and admired Jolson's recordings, but neither records nor all the live vaudeville he soaked up on weekend evenings prepared him for the man's galvanizing energy. "I hung on every word and watched every move he made," he recalled. "To me, he was the greatest entertainer who ever lived."[23] At fourteen, Bing began to imagine himself before the footlights; he kept those dreams to himself.

Harry's fortunes had wavered uncertainly for two years, but at long last Inland Brewery's stockholders "concluded to accept present conditions as to prohibition" and changed the corporate name to Inland Products Company.[24] They authorized the expenditure of $175,000 to erect a modern cold-storage warehouse and convert the brewery into a vinegar factory. Reincorporated in 1917, the firm elected four officers: the three original partners and H. L. Crosby, secretary, whose duties also included selling merchandise from a new retail shop that stocked pickles, sugared cider, ice, candy, ketchup, ice cream, soda water, and near beer.[25] It promoted itself as the "Home of

22 Varieties." Pickles assumed particular prominence after Inland contracted with a distributor that supplied New York's Lower East Side Orthodox Jewish community. A Spokane rabbi regularly visited the plant to certify its pickles as kosher.

Harry would coast reasonably well until 1923, when senior partner Charles Theis appointed his son secretary and laid off Harry, bringing him back as shipping clerk. A man whose father worked as foreman of the plant recalled that as a boy he and his friends visited the shop to buy soda and candy. Mr. Crosby would come out of the back office and wait on them: "A very pleasant fellow, very pleasant. Medium build and, well, he wasn't a handsome guy, but he was a nice-looking fellow. He had a very good personality and everybody liked him."[26]

Harry's own boys were ambivalent; they knew very well who controlled the Crosby house. "She was a matriarch," Bob said of Kate, adding, "we were shanty Irish," to explain the tradition.[27] Kate was strict and hard, though not the terror she became in later years, when Bing's office workers doused their cigarettes and smoothed their skirts because they heard she was in the building. When Bing was young, Kate was the powerful center of his life. Her will ultimately helped drive him from Spokane, but he left with an armor of independence and raw nerve. Kate alone could always threaten his equilibrium. Until she died, her sudden appearance in a room would prompt him to put aside his drink and snuff his cigarette. Peggy Lee recalled a party at the Crosbys' when she and Bing were conversing near the piano. As Mrs. Crosby walked in, Bing maneuvered his glass behind some picture frames.[28]

Asked, as he often was, if he attributed his success to any particular factor, Bing usually answered: "I think my mother's prayers. She's always been a firm believer in the efficacy of prayer and since I was a little boy, she prayed for all of us daily, and had masses said for us and rosaries, and the nuns up in our parish, the Poor Clares, they're a cloistered order — they don't ever get out of the monastery — she would bring them meals and take their laundry out and do all kinds of things, and they always prayed for me and for the family, for our health and our well-being, both spiritual and physical. . . . If I've been lucky, and I certainly have been inordinately lucky, why I think you have to attribute it to the efficacy of prayer."[29] When Bing was not honoring his mother's probity, he would issue credit for his success to producers, managers, and associates, claiming for himself only the good sense to take their advice. If Kate had sent him on his way with a ready supply of confidence, she also instilled in him the old Irish commandment to keep his head down.

Harry's finances intensified the need for his kids to earn money on their own. "Dependability was a necessity in our house with seven youngsters around and a happy life only possible if everyone followed an established pattern of family routine," Kate later explained. "The older ones," she continued, "had to help with the younger ones and they had to try not to be an expense on the family purse. When their clothes and their parties became an item, they had to seek methods of earning their way a little to help out." Bing had no trouble with this. Kate once overheard him tell a friend, "I like a jingle in my pocket that's my very own."[30]

Bing probably worked as many jobs as the rest of the Crosby children combined — in addition to his household chores, which included, at various times, keeping the woodbox full, scrubbing floors, mowing the lawn, and raising chickens in the yard. He was always on the go — early to bed and early to rise, making the most of every waking moment. He was available to milk cows, run errands, and mow lawns. In harvesting season he raced out with other kids to "thin" the apple orchards. Not that he needed authorization to harvest. His friend Benny Ruehl remembered Bing and the other boys stealing cherries from trees in his front yard. "My mother squirted the boys with a garden hose to get them out of the trees."[31] Ruehl also recalled the time one boy successfully dared Bing to bellyflop into a mud puddle, while Harry stood by and laughed. Harry could not help but admire Bing's resourcefulness. His high-school jobs during summer and holidays included — in addition to lifeguard and caddy — postal worker, boxing usher, grocery-truck driver, woodchopper at a resort, and topographer at a lumber camp.

And he still came up short. Delbert Stickney, whose family lived down the street, often went to the movies with Bing. Delbert's mother worked in a department store downtown, and the boys regularly stopped by her counter to bum change for the show. When he visited the Stickney home, Bing would sit in the parlor, singing and pecking a song on the piano with one finger while cradling Delbert's baby niece Shirley on his lap. In 1948 Shirley's daughter suffered an attack of polio and could not afford treatments. Hearing that Bing was stopping in Spokane, Mrs. Stickney went to his hotel and asked for a loan. "No, I won't loan it to you," he told her, "but I'll give it to you. All the quarters Delbert and I borrowed from you including interest must be close to that amount."[32]

For a boy characterized as lackadaisical, Bing had a peculiar affinity for early-morning jobs he could keep throughout the school year. As delivery boy for the *Spokesman-Review,* he rose at four to collect the papers. His whistling and singing carried far in the quiet Spokane mornings as he pedaled his bike from house to house. Occasionally a neighbor raised a window and warned him to keep it down. In 1938 he wrote Charles Devlin of the paper's promotional department, "I hope all my boys may start as carriers. I want them to be workers."[33] All his brothers had routes, he noted, and the girls filled in when the boys were sick. "Of the bunch, I probably developed the least desire for labor . . . but the whistling experience came in mighty handy."[34]

No amount of work could compromise Bing's belief that he was by nature lazy. If indolence was part of the professional Crosby charm, it figured privately as a source of penitence. As Seneca wrote and Bing learned to recite in Latin, "Nothing is so certain as that the evils of idleness can be shaken off by hard work." The habit of rising early came naturally to him. He roused himself on cold winter mornings when it was dark and warmed his hands over an oil drum, waiting for the papers. After delivering them, he had breakfast at home, served mass (if it was the third week of the month), and attended school. One of Kate's friends told Bing about an open position for morning janitor at the Everyman's Club on Front Avenue, a flophouse for transient miners and loggers in the heart of skid row. Bing applied for the job and was hired. For a buck a day that winter, he layered himself in wool clothing and after delivering his papers took a streetcar across the river into downtown Spokane, arriving at five. For the next hour, he tidied the facility, maneuvering around the drunks and layabouts, learning about canned heat (which, liquefied into its alcoholic content, caused blindness and madness) and powdered tobacco and other comforts of the lower depths. He was back home for breakfast by seven, except on days he had 6:30 mass.

Kate proudly described him as "prompt, methodical, sticks to his plans and sticks to his word."[35] She bristled at the notion, promulgated chiefly by Bing himself, that he was idle. "My children were brought up to do for themselves and from the oldest to the youngest they still do. Anyone who works with Bing, for instance, knows he rarely sends or asks for things. He just quietly goes and gets it for himself."[36] Later, in Hollywood, he was known for his entourage of one, Gonzaga classmate Leo Lynn. A butler whom Bing hired in his most baronial years — at the insistence of his second wife — mistakenly assumed Crosby didn't like him, as he wasn't permitted to pack or carry his employer's suitcase or open his car door or fuss over him at all.[37]

"He had a vocabulary like a senator's," Bing's father once said, "and we used to call him Travis McGutney."[38] His way with words, not just his singing and whistling, helped define Bing's personality for his friends. He rolled large words on his tongue, trilled *r*s, fiddled with malapropisms and spoonerisms, and mimicked the lower, upper, and outcast classes, exemplified in minstrel badinage or highfalutin rhetoric. This talent gave him distinction within his gang. Interviewed in the 1940s, childhood friends and neighbors said they thought him more likely to become a comedian than a singer. One pal said he hardly recognized the Bing he knew in the movies until he began making the *Road* pictures with Bob Hope. All that easy banter with Hope, the double takes and primed reactions, the fast wit and easy superiority — that was the way he was in school. His romantic pictures of the 1930s, on the other hand, weren't Bing at all, a friend said; he had never showed that much interest in girls.

The only early crush he spoke of was inspired by one Gladys Lemmon, who survived in the Crosby mythology less for her curly-haired charms than her pun-inspiring name. Upon hearing that Bing carried her books and took her sledding, Larry taunted him at the dinner table as a lemon-squeezer, prompting Bing to hurl a slice of buttered bread that in later accounts metamorphosed into a leg of lamb. The courtship allegedly ended when Bing was forced to wear a starched priestlike collar that made his neck chafe to Gladys's birthday party. It was not his only social faux pas. Margaret Nixon would not invite him to her birthdays because he once stole the party ice cream from her back porch. He was that kind of boy, she said. And Vera Lemley complained that after she broke a date with him, Bing would not talk to her for two years.

If his glib lingo failed to serve Bing as a gallant, it did enhance his standing at Gonzaga High. In his sophomore year he was cited as Next in Merit in elocution (Frank Corkery, who put no less faith in language, won the gold medal) and took first honors in English. Bing's popularity and sportsmanship were affirmed early in the semester: he was elected class consultor and captained the victorious Dreadnoughts in the Junior Yard Association Midget Football League. He also made the JYA baseball team. Posing in his striped red-and-white uniform, he was small, chubby, beaming. Those endeavors proved less meaningful than his admission to the Junior Debating Society, which increased his presence in public-speaking events, though he proved better at elocution than debate. The university magazine, *Gonzaga*, reviewed a recital of Poe's "The Bells" by Bing, Corkery, and two others as "striking and novel," the high point of a contest in public speaking.[39] Bing recited "Romancin'" to a packed house at St. Aloysius Hall and took the adverse position in a debate about limiting the American presidency to a single term of six years.

In 1919, through the efforts of Father Kennelly, football was restored as a major activity at Gonzaga. Its triumphant team produced two players inducted into the Pro Football Hall of Fame. One was Ray Flaherty ("big and powerful — watch out for Flaherty," *Gonzaga* prophesied), with whom Bing remained friendly all his life. Flaherty led the NFL in pass receptions in 1932, helped the New York Giants to the NFL championship in 1934, and retired as coach with the highest winning percentage (.735) in the annals of the Washington Redskins. Ray and Bing were on the Midget team together, and Ray admired his moxie, though he did not think much of him as a footballer.[40] Still, Bing's fortitude was noted after he trimmed down to 135 pounds and learned to handle himself adequately as center. Of a JYA game against Hillyard High (a tie: 19–19), *Gonzaga* reported, "B. Crosby was a tower of strength on defense."[41]

Flaherty conceded that Bing was "pretty good" at baseball. "We played on the Ideal Laundry team in the commercial or business league. We'd play at Mission Park, five blocks up the street from Gonzaga. Oh, we were best of friends, used to chum around all the time, wrestled, played handball, though he didn't play too much handball. Bing was more into entertainment in the evening. He was always a happy kid and was always singing a song. Even though he was a little kid, he was singing. He just was full of music and he was a great whistler. He could really whistle. They used to have these smokers where they'd have kids that liked to box and they'd get a pretty good student body and some outsiders. Bing used to sing at those. He didn't box, I don't think, but he sang and that brought some people in, too. Hell, he could sing like nobody else, sing and whistle. He had a hell of a whistle."[42]

In addition to winning reelection as class consultor in his junior year, Bing was voted Junior Yard Association secretary-treasurer following "a stormy session and a bit of political logrolling."[43] Bing racked up distinctions in English, history, elocution, theology, Latin, and civics and prevailed in reading competitions, scoring coups with "The Dukite Snake" and Macauley's poem of Horatius at the Bridge. "I took those eloquent lines in my teeth and shook them as a terrier shakes a bone," he wrote.[44] Bing, Corkery, and Flaherty enlisted together as charter members of Gonzaga's new glee club. In the club's annual photograph, Bing sports a high pompadour and a roomy jacket. For their first grand concert in St. Aloysius Hall, Bing did not participate in musical numbers but read three selections during intermission.

He fared less well in debate; as part of a two-man team that lost two decisions, he argued against abolishing immigration and forcing Woodrow Wilson's resignation due to illness. Bing, who always took the liberal side, was demoted to an alternate in his senior year. His role in the public debate that year (concerning the League of Nations) was to deliver a recitation at intermission.[45] He had reason to regard his education as Augustine did his own: "Their one aim was that I should learn how to make a good speech and become an orator capable of swaying his audience," the Bishop of Hippo wrote.[46]

Bing looked back with mocking amusement at the rival clubs organized by the most avid speakers and debaters. He founded the Bolsheviks in loyal opposition to the Dirty Six, who commandeered perks such as patrolling varsity sporting events. The "rival tongs," as Bing called them, indulged in free-for-all political debate.[47] Inevitably, a priest — Father O'Brien, a Brit — reproached Bing's clique for embracing a name associated with godlessness. "Apparently his devoutness and his English sense of humor had him confused, for he said we'd be 'cleansed' if we stopped using the name," Bing wrote.[48] Bing also joined the Derby Club, an offshoot of the Bolsheviks, which consisted of six or eight "blades" who sported derbies in class.

Recitation led to other theatrical projects. Gonzaga looked upon theater not merely as a high-school drama-club option but as an undertaking essential to a model Jesuit education. Writing in the university yearbook, instructor William DePuis traced "love of the dramatic" to a pagan worship of Bacchus, which the church adapted to its own ends: "The Mystery and Miracle play taught the sacred story of Christ and the saints. The religious idea yielded gradually to the popular desire for amusement, and the holy day became the holiday."[49] That notion would be employed as a motif in Bing's Father O'Malley films.

Bing enjoyed two genuine theatrical triumphs in his senior year, yet the production that became fixed in Crosby lore was a junior English class presentation of *Julius Caesar* — a prize example of hapless mythmaking. In the February 1919 performance, promoted in the *Spokane Daily Chronicle* with a photo and cast listing, Bing played Second Citizen. His friend Ed "Pinky" Gowanlock played Caesar. According to witnesses interviewed three decades later, the most memorable moment followed Caesar's death, as the rolled-up curtain sprang from its hinges and nearly flattened Pinky. Over time, however, Bing became the center of everyone's memories. According to Ted and Larry, he played Marc Antony and dodged the curtain; according to Everett, he played Caesar and dodged the curtain. According to Bing, in 1946, he played a fallen soldier who dodged the curtain and was rewarded with howls of laughter, for which he took many bows. In 1976 he said that he played a fallen soldier who calmly walked off after the curtain fell. If one accepts Pinky's account, he might well have invoked Plautus's lament *Ut saepe summa ingenia in occulto latent* (How often the greatest talents are shrouded in obscurity). Bing did remark in 1957, when he presented the school with a new library, "In show business, we like to take our bows, even when we can steal them."[50]

Forgotten entirely or at least unmentioned was the Antony Bing played ten months later at the annual Gonzaga Night revelry that preceded the December break. Though it surely stretched Gonzaga's notion of creditable theater, Bing, Corkery, and a few friends offered a minstrel burlesque of Shakespeare, depicting Caesar as a "dark-skinned bone artist."[51] Their performance, a Bolshevik send-up of the Dirty Sixers who appeared in Pinky's version, marked Bing's second venture into burnt cork. Blackface was then too much a show-business convention to elicit accusations of racism. A year earlier the Spokane County Council of Defense put the First Amendment on hold to pass a resolution banning *The Birth of a Nation;* the same community had no qualms concerning traveling minstrel troupes and would have felt cheated had Al Jolson shown up at the Auditorium in paleface.

In the spring the drama and glee clubs presented an Irish playlet, *The Curate of Kilronan,* at St. Aloysius, a production paced with several Irish songs. Once again Bing did not sing, but his acting earned him a notice in the school magazine: he and another student had "used well their experience on the stage and acquitted themselves in fine style as true friends of the unfortunate curate."[52] Bing and his brother Ted were feted afterward at a cast banquet at the Spokane Hotel.

While Bing was charming his way through school, exhibiting less ambition than verve, displaying varied talents that never quite came into focus, Ted nursed his desire to write and worked at it like a professional. Ted was one of *Gonzaga's* most enterprising and prolific contributors, and in his senior year he edited the alumni section. During the summer he interned at the *Spokane Evening Chronicle,* where Larry worked after the war. But everything seemed to fall into Bing's lap, not least the devotion of their mother and a stable of friends. An occasional truant, Bing was all too familiar with the Jug, a room where unruly students atoned by memorizing the Latin of Virgil, Ovid, Caesar — backward, if the offense was serious.[53] Ted, on the other hand, was as steady as they come. Yet even the priests preferred Bing, perhaps because they were gung-ho on sports, and Ted was the only Crosby boy who ducked athletics. Bing sparkled and Ted plodded.

Ted was taller than Bing, his coloring similar — blue eyes, a darker shade of brown hair. A keen reader, he kept to himself, inventing a fantasy life and exploring it in a profusion of short stories, poems, and essays. Bing ended up living much of what Ted imagined. Ted would raise a family in Spokane, where for most of his life he worked at the Washington Water Power Company. In his one book, *The Story of Bing Crosby*, published in 1946, he depicts himself in childhood as a would-be inventor, disowning entirely the years he put into his writing. Yet unlike that frivolous and highly fictionalized account, some of his early stories suggest a darker view of his rivalry with Bing.

Ted's "When Black Is White," for example, published in *Gonzaga* a couple of months before Bing graduated from high school, establishes as its villain Dr. Howard Croye, "a gifted speaker," very popular, and "deeply interested in church work." "Aristocratic in habits and faultless in attire," he charms a millionaire mining magnate into financing his construction of a sanatorium. Howard absconds with the money, eventually returning to the sanatorium to die an agonizing death. In contrast, the dependable center of the story is a journalist, Jim (Ted's middle name was John), who uncovers the deception and brings salvation to the children of Howard and the philanthropist he destroyed.[54]

The month Bing graduated, *Gonzaga* published his sole offering, a poem in celebration of wealth, renown, exotic climes, and dreamy languor. It stood out in stark contrast to Ted's odes to fallen heroes, God, Gonzaga, duty, Crosby seafarers, Lincoln, the Northwest and to those of every other Gonzaga poet, who invariably evoked patriotism, mother, and God.

A King.

> While lying on my couch one night
> I dreamed a dream of wondrous light.
> I thought I was an ancient king
> Of the Mystic East — I heard them sing
> My praises high in accents grand,
> While cymbals echoed loud — and
> As I sat in robes of white
> With vassals kneeling left and right,
> Strong, dusky slaves from Hindustan
> Alighting from the caravan
> Upon their heads and in their arms
> Bore spice and all the Orient's charms,
> While flowed the music soft and sweet
> They piled them high about my feet.

But I was snatched from this away
In rudeness by the dawn of day.
— Harry L. Crosby, H.S. '20[55]

Some believe that only those who admit to themselves that they crave wealth and prestige can obtain them. Only in "A King," a thin, dashed-off indulgence consigned to a volume of juvenilia, did Bing ever come close to acknowledging his ambitions, at least in public. All his life — on radio, in films, press releases, magazines, and interviews — Bing portrayed himself and was portrayed by others as an unambitious man to whom splendid things happened, deservedly, without his ever really chasing fortune. Bing's ambivalence about worldly success was made manifest in the early stages of his career, when he did everything possible to sabotage himself. It was as if success were acceptable only as a gift, unexpected and unsought. Despite his hard work and desperate longing, he never publicly allowed that he merited his special fate.

Fifty-two students received diplomas from Gonzaga on June 9, 1920, the largest graduating class that the high school had ever produced. Students had a choice of pursuing a diploma in a general or classical course, and Bing received his in the latter. Nearly a month before, the class and faculty had celebrated with a picnic and sporting events at Liberty Lake, eighteen miles east, where the graduates rented canoes and swam in the recently opened pool. On June 7 the *Spokane Daily Chronicle* announced the list of those who would speak at graduation, among them two representatives of the student body, Frank Corkery and Bing. In an accompanying photograph, Bing sports a necktie (as do the others) but looks drowsy and exhibits not a trace of the slight smiles the others share.

Graduation exercises took place on a Wednesday afternoon in the gym, and after the Gonzaga orchestra played the overture, "Columbia," Harry L. Crosby was introduced as the first speaker. His speech was "The Purpose of Education," a text that has not survived. Corkery delivered the valedictory. Bing was not awarded class honors, so his prominent role in the ceremony must be construed as an acknowledgment of his elocutionary and speech-making skills. Among other speakers was the Reverend Charles E. Carroll, S.J., prefect of studies, who became dean of the faculty in 1922 and overseer of the Bing Crosby Library in 1957.

Bing had slimmed down in the past year — the chubby, grinning boy of his freshman pictures was now lanky and serious, his face longer and leaner, his voice deeper and more controlled. But he was a year younger than his classmates and looked it. A downtown dance hall refused him admission one evening, sending him away in humiliation. For all his singing, Bing had not yet fixed his star on music, though a friend later recalled his listening to a Jolson record and marveling aloud that by singing a couple of songs Al earned enough money to buy a car.

His taste in music began to lean toward jazz, an almost unavoidable partiality given the raging popularity in 1917 of the Original Dixieland Jazz Band, a second-rate ensemble that had the distinction of making the earliest jazz records. A white band from New Orleans, the ODJB created a sensation in New York with novel, noisy, and irreverent music, including instrumental barnyard imitations on "Livery Stable Blues." Its fans included black songwriter Shelton Brooks, whose "Darktown Strutters' Ball" was the ODJB's first record. (Columbia Records, offended by the loud, poorly engineered performance, shelved it until Victor picked up the ball and produced a series of ODJB hits.)

By 1923 many superior black bands were recording and performing for mixed northern audiences, diminishing the ODJB's status to that of a jazz popularizer. But in the interim, countless bands throughout the country followed the ODJB's lead, blending the rudiments of ragtime, jazz, blues, marches, vaudeville, dance music, and popular songs, and young people devoured their recordings.

Among the performers Bing and his friends recalled listening to — in addition to Jolson, John McCormack, and other singers — were Six Brown Brothers, a saxophone choir (soprano on the high end, bass on the bottom) popular on the vaudeville circuit and through such buoyant recordings as "That Moaning Saxophone Rag" and its own version of "Darktown Strutters' Ball," as well as adaptations of arias, and Art Hickman, the pioneering San Francisco–based bandleader who composed the standard "Rose Room" and codified big band or dance band instrumentation — in effect, setting the stage for Paul Whiteman's orchestra. They listened to Hawaiian bands with steel guitars and comedy records, like Joe Hayman's million-selling "Cohen on the Telephone," and everything else that came through town. Every new record was a mystery until it was played.

In the summer of 1920, with the rigors of Gonzaga University approaching, Bing felt a need to escape Spokane. He was bored with excursions to Newman and Liberty Lakes, where small bands played at dances; he had had enough caddying and swimming for a while. He wanted to see something of the world and break loose even for a short time from the house on East Sharp. After the war Larry returned home, teaching high school while working nights and summers at the newspaper. Everett rushed through Spokane like a storm, traveling on to Portland, where he claimed to be clerking in a hotel.

Bing and his friend Paul Teters resolved to leave town for a couple of months. A want ad in the paper alerted them to a job for two men to work on an alfalfa farm in Cheney, Washington, half an hour away by train, for two bucks a day and board. After securing permission from their parents, they left in the morning and presented themselves for work. The alfalfa farmer was underwhelmed — they were young and inexperienced — and he offered them a dollar each. They grudgingly accepted.

Two decades later Bing bought an 8,700-acre cattle ranch in Elko, Nevada, and insisted that his sons do haying and other exhausting tasks along with the paid cowhands. Gary, the eldest, bridled at the drudgery and years later smiled knowingly upon learning that his father had been no more enamored of farming than Gary had been of ranching. After two weeks of milking cows and putting up alfalfa for forage, Bing and Paul decided to quit. Returning home was out of the question. Luckily, though, Everett Crosby was in Portland, 400 miles west, and he would certainly put them up and maybe find them work. The boys hiked to a water tower where the evening freight train stopped to replenish, and under cover of darkness stole a ride.

They were dusty and rank by the time they pulled into Portland and rushed to the hotel where Everett clerked, only to find out that he did not work there. They were asked to remove their scruffy selves from the lobby. Confused but emboldened, the boys turned their sights on Los Angeles, hopping a southbound Shasta Limited. They got as far as Roseburg, where a railroad bull collared them and put them in a cattle car heading back to Portland. This time they ran into Everett on the street, toting two wicker suitcases full of bootleg hooch. He told them to meet him later at the Shaw Hotel and gave them a dollar for a movie. After the picture show, the hungry boys looked down the street and saw a sign advertising a second-story Chinese restaurant. They split a dish of chop suey and, after Bing diverted the owner by shoving menus off the front counter, raced down the stairs without paying. An alert policeman tracked them to Everett's room and arrested them. Everett paid the lunch bill, and they were released with the magistrate's warning to leave town.

Bing wrote to Kate and told her not to worry, knowing she would worry less about yet another of his minor scrapes than the possibility that he might not want to return to school in September. Kate's brother George met the boys in Portland and took them to the Westdale mills, where they boarded a logging train to a camp Bing's cousin Lloyd operated for Weyerhaeuser Lumber. Jobs were offered: Paul chose to return home while Bing signed on as a topographer scouting trails. Somehow he gashed his knee with an axe — in one retelling, he said he gashed both knees in consecutive accidents. He clearly wanted out of that forest, even in memory. Gonzaga University now promised relief, like mass after a morning at the Everyman's Club.

6

MR. INTERLOCUTOR

*No doubt the appeal of minstrelsy came from these
draughts upon a common reminiscence, stirring some
essential wish or remembrance.*
— Constance Rourke, *American Humor* (1931)[1]

Although Bing quickly decided against becoming a priest, he did
reach a compromise that appeased Kate. Lawyering was reasonably
honorable and solid and would make use of his gifts for elocution and
debate. Kate could also console herself with the fact that law school
would keep him at home for another couple of years. Frank Corkery,
who served mass with Bing, did not think that his friend gave much
thought to the priesthood — not this independent young man who
dreamed of sultanic riches while nosing around in skid-row muck,
who had lately managed to turn what promised to be a brief stint on a
nearby farm into a flight to the coast, an aborted trip south, and a narrow escape from what he liked to quaintly refer to as durance vile.

Gonzaga University was not, however, a mere continuance of high
school. Though the student body numbered no more than 300, many
of them neighborhood boys, the university harbored its own prejudices, directed against day students like Bing, who were not permitted to partake of dormitory activities. Bing and the other townies
were required to leave campus by half past four, except for the one

evening per week when the debating society met. The "boarders," students from outside Spokane, considered Bing's crowd mere provincials and demanded they prove themselves. But Bing never had any trouble making friends. He was "a cheerful and appealing guy," in Ray Flaherty's recollection, "a knowledgeable, very entertaining person to be around."[2] Still, the boarders did not make it easy for him. Though he ultimately disarmed them with his voice, at first he was reluctant to sing formally and switched his musical inclinations to the drums. "I didn't have to learn a feeling for music and for rhythm," Bing observed. "I was born with that."

Had the Crosbys not lived in the vicinity, they could not have afforded Bing's schooling. Boarders paid $265.50 a semester. Day students paid only $80.50 (thirty dollars more than high school), payable on registration day.[3] When he took up drums in the spring of his freshman year, Bing was obliged to pay an additional $7.50 for use of the instrument. When in his junior year he enrolled in the combined college and law course, which conferred bachelor's and law degrees in six years, his tuition per semester increased another seventy-five dollars. Sensitive to his parents' investment in his education, Bing applied himself for the first two years, fulfilling requirements in English, Latin, modern languages (Spanish and French), public speaking, mathematics, and religion. "A man of fair capacity who has conscientiously followed this curriculum," pledged the *Gonzaga Register* of 1920, "will thus be in touch and sympathy with progress in every field of intellectual activity."[4]

Bing was as diligent as one could be about wearing the green beanie required of freshmen. "There is one thing that beats snipe shootin' and that is hunting Freshmen without green caps," the *Register* contended.[5] He matriculated as a member of the largest freshman class so far, at an exciting time in the school's history. That year Gonzaga hired the nationally known coach and former Notre Dame quarterback Gus Dorais.[6] Thanks to Dorais, whose tenure exactly paralleled Bing's (Dorais was long regarded as second only to Bing in bringing recognition to the school), the next four years proved to be the university's golden age of football. Bing was too small to play on the invincible football and basketball teams, but he made his enthusiasm known and was elected to the new advisory board on athletics as one of two assistant yell leaders. In his sophomore year he and thirty-four other students tried out for two baseball teams. Bing made the cut, and Dorais assigned him third base.[7]

All school sports were supervised by the advisory board, controlled by its moderator, Curtis J. Sharp, S.J., a robust personality and erstwhile amateur boxer who had recently arrived at Gonzaga from Anaconda, Montana. He was to Bing an exemplary figure, combining harsh discipline with amiable generosity. Armed with a leather strap that he applied to the backsides of younger students and the hands of older ones, Sharp nonetheless inspired a fervent devotion, perhaps too much so. As a parent, Bing would obtain "a big leather belt — similar to the one I'd backed up to at Gonzaga in the hand of Father Sharp."[8] Bing acquired more than a trust in corporal punishment from Sharp. He admired his poise, his man's-man rectitude, and regular-Joe disposition. Bing often told how in 1937, when he brought his radio show to Gonzaga for a homecoming game and received an honorary degree, he slipped into the locker room to swig the remainder of a pint. In burst Father Sharp. Bing stashed the bottle — "an instinctive return to the habits of my student years."[9] As they small-talked their way out the door, Sharp suddenly stepped back to where Bing had been sitting and retrieved the hidden flask. He emptied it with a gulp and observed, "It wouldn't be right to let a soldier die without a priest."[10] It was Sharp on whom Bing modeled Father O'Malley in *Going My Way*.

Two other instructors Bing had reason to recall with more than usual regard were Father Edward Shipsey and James Gilmore. Shipsey, the chairman of the English department, helped train Bing in elocution, teaching him to roll *r*s, carol vowels, assert consonants, and distinguish the elements, patterns, and meanings of speech. Bing memorized and delivered with gusto recitations by Elijah Kellogg, the nineteenth-century clergyman who wrote "Spartacus to the Gladiators"; Robert W. Service, the popular Canadian poet responsible for "The Shooting of Dan McGrew"; and others. He once said, "If I am not a singer, I am a phraser. *Diseur* is the word. I owe it all to elocution." The enunciation tricks learned from Father Shipsey became habit and mask, a front underscored by his affection for ten-dollar words, faux-British circumlocutions, and spiel worthy of riverboat gamblers. Bing's diction would define his radio persona, frequently bordering on intentional self-parody.

James Gilmore, a young, well-liked chemistry instructor who led field trips throughout Spokane and sang a good bass harmony, was obsessed with inventing a tonic to grow hair. He recruited Bing as a guinea pig, an indication that the diseur's thinning hair was noticeable even in his teens. While his friends were sheared at the on-campus Blue & White Shop ("Tonsorial Art by Tonsorial Artists"), Bing endured private sessions with Mr. Gilmore, who — though unable to save his leery volunteer from a life sentence of "scalp doilies" — eventually brought to market a product called Gilmore Hair-More.[11] Bing grew to care less. Alone among the Hollywood stars of his era and stature, he never concealed his reliance on or distaste for toupees. Unlike John Wayne or Humphrey Bogart, who never appeared without them, Bing wore his only for professional purposes, when he could not get by with a hat. Errol Flynn was so amused by Bing's willingness to attend sporting events, restaurants, and parties without a rug that he once walked over to his table and planted a (photographed) kiss on top of Bing's bare head. Film work was another story. When submitted a script, Bing counted the outdoor scenes where a hat could square the issue, and sometimes demanded more. Writers accommodated him; wardrobe provided every kind of hat, cap, and turban imaginable.

Bing maintained a B average in his freshman year, excelling in English. But playacting and music were becoming increasingly important to him, and he emerged as a school favorite, rivaling his friend and supreme big man on campus Mike Pecarovitch. Mike was the tall, handsome student council president, gifted athlete (a disciple of Dorais, he later coached Gonzaga and Loyola), and leading man in Gonzaga theatricals. He was two years older than Bing, who first supported, then costarred, and finally eclipsed him; Mike could neither sing nor get laughs. Yet most would have bet on Mike to succeed, especially after he appeared in a production of *The Bells* at Santa Clara University and, according to the *Spokane Daily Chronicle*, "drew raves from California critics."[12] If Bing minded in the least playing second fiddle, he must have enjoyed the sublime revenge, a dozen years later, of giving him bit parts in a few pictures. By the 1990s, Gonzaga students could stroll through Pecarovitch Field and study at Crosby Library.

A month into his first semester, Bing performed in a musical program at a smoker with the short-lived Republican Quartette, including his accomplice from the Boone Avenue gang Ralph Foley. Despite the cynical election of Warren G. Harding to the presidency that season, the GOP was not yet synonymous with plutocratic conservatism, certainly not in the state of Washington, where Republicanism was associated with statehood, achieved over long-term Democratic opposition.

A musical event of greater import that year was the release of Paul Whiteman's first record, "Whispering" and "The Japanese Sandman," which sold 2.5 million copies. Whiteman's dance music was far more grounded in Viennese salons than in jazz, yet that record captured the attention of an era, with its novel slide-whistle solo (to which no less than King Oliver paid homage in his 1923 "Sobbin' Blues") and gentle Dixieland ingredients like muted brasses and lively banjo-driven rhythms. Whiteman would dominate the recording industry for the next decade, until Bing supplanted him. His records, released on an average of one a month, enchanted Bing and countless other would-be musicians around the country.

A few weeks later the Gonzaga Dramatic Club presented the comedy *The Dean of Ballarat* in St. Aloysius Hall, to benefit the student band. "Each player seemed especially fitted for his part," the school paper reported, noting that Bing portrayed "a colored aristocrat with the dignity and willingness to receive 'tips' so common to that class."[13] He billed himself as Harry L. Crosby, Jr., A.B. '24, for the first time, suggesting an attempt to try on his father for size, and at least a subliminal acknowledgment that acting was serious stuff but also an improvident activity belonging to the Happy Harry sphere of life. Shortly before the semester ended, he again appeared in blackface, for Gonzaga University Glee Club's minstrel show *A Study in Tone and Color*. Only Bing was featured twice — in a duet with Dirty Sixer Joe Lynch, on "That Shakespearian Rag," and as soloist on "When the Moon Shines." He also played one of four end men who "kept the entire audience in a continuous uproar."[14] Whatever appeal blackface had for the other end men (among them Leo Lynn), for Bing it represented a bond with the mighty Al Jolson, whose talents he broadly emulated.[15]

*　　*　　*

The importance of minstrelsy in the development of America's popular arts can hardly be overstated, and Crosby was steeped in it. The
genesis of American minstrelsy has been credited to an English
music-hall performer, Charles Matthews, who while touring the
South in 1822 became intrigued with Negro music and dialect.
Blackening his face with burnt cork, he offered himself as an interpreter of "Ethiopian" melodies. Contemporaneously, a group of black
performers in New York, frustrated because Negro patrons were not
allowed to attend theaters, staged *Richard III* at the corner of Mercer
and Bleeker Streets. They did not get to tour the country. The minstrels did. Negro minstrelsy, as it was called regardless of the performers' race, was the only acceptable conduit for what was thought
of as native Negro artistry. Though antebellum troupes were white,
the form developed in a forced racial collaboration, illustrating the
axiom that defined — and continues to define — American music as
it developed over the next century and a half: African American innovations metamorphose into American popular culture when white
performers learn to mimic black ones.

In 1830 a little-known black showman, Joel W. Sweeney, invented
or perfected the banjo, minstrelsy's dominant instrument. Yet it was
Thomas "Daddy" Rice, a white entertainer, who became famous for
the discovery he made that same year. When Rice happened to see a
black Louisville stablehand do a whirling dance while singing about a
character named Jim Crow, he made off with the step and the song,
and embarked on a celebrated career. For the sake of authenticity,
Rice also blacked his face with cork, a custom that lasted a
century — until the introduction of Pan-Cake makeup, which facilitated the tradition just as it was drawing to an end. (Cork was arduous to remove, and the pros soon learned to use soap and cold water
only, as warm water or cream pressed it into the pores like gunshot.)

The first successful blackface company, the Virginia Minstrels,
debuted in New York in 1843. (One of its four members, Dan
Emmett, would later adapt a black melody for his most durable song,
"Dixie.") The next year, 1844, William Henry Lane, a black trick
dancer who performed under the name Master Juba, humbled the
popular "Ethiopian imitators" in a dancing competition. It did him no
good: the blacked-up imitators dominated minstrelsy in the decades
before Reconstruction, rallying American songwriting to its first cre-

ative and commercial peak. That summit was symbolized in 1848 by the publication of Stephen Foster's "Oh! Susanna," described by cultural historian Constance Rourke as "a fiddler's tune with a Negro beat and a touch of pathos in the melody."[16]

Minstrelsy was a theatrical mode premised upon the conceit that slave life could be illuminated and prettified by a gallery of grotesques. Its performers had to balance parodic intent with sincere imitation. Caricatures became standardized: the shiftless plantation layabout, Jim Crow; the fatuous urban dandy, Zip Coon; the addled pickaninny, Sambo. Yet many minstrels thought of themselves as actors communicating truths about Negro life, as if the stereotypes were roles as valid as Othello and Aida.[17] In time, the caricatures took on lives of their own, removed from the original intent. "The function of this mythology," Ralph Ellison observed, "was to allow whites a more secure place (if only symbolically) in American society."[18] But for the last generation of white blackface performers, the Negro-ness was all but forgotten. Bob Hope, who did a blackface act in vaudeville, said of the genre's passing, "People thought they were making fun of blacks, but it was just a way of playing characters, you know? Minstrel shows were very large. At one theater where I was playing and getting very little money, I got to the theater late and I didn't have time to put the black on and so I walked out with my regular face. After the show, the theater manager came back and said, 'Don't put that stuff on your face. You got a face that saves jokes.' In those days, you did blackface but you downplayed the minstrel aspect."[19]

In the mid-nineteenth century, as Stephen Foster and other song-writers improved the musical fare, crude dialect songs were replaced by a genteel but equally pernicious type of song, expressing yearnings for the protective hand of dear ol' massa. After the Civil War the minstrel palette became much broader. "If the Negro was set free," Constance Rourke realized, "in a fashion his white impersonators were also liberated."[20] With other minorities streaming into the country, minstrel conventions broadened to include caricaturing Italians, Irish, Jews, Germans, Dutch, Scottish, Indians, Chinese (Asians provided the most durable actors' mask of all)[21] — any group sufficiently different or mysterious enough to warrant parodic deflation. Even women, long imitated by male actors, were invited to participate, although female impersonators never lost their box-office seduction.

"In fantasy, the American types seemed to be joining in a single semblance," Rourke wrote. "But Negro music and Negro nonsense still prevailed."[22]

At its height, minstrelsy was a stylized, codified, and even ritualized variety show. At center stage was the stout announcer, Mr. Interlocutor, who kibitzed with the end-men comics, Mr. Tambo and Mr. Bones. Between them sat the company — as many as seventy men in the larger companies, all corked, bewigged, and attired in loud, mockingly overstated costumes. After an introductory segment of jokes and songs, the olio (variety acts) got under way, presenting dancers, singers, mimics, monologists, sketches, mini-plays, guest performers, and so on. The climax was a walk-around finale, when the entire company let loose on unison banjos or tambourines for a rousing send-off. As an idiom that squelched individuality, minstrelsy inevitably inspired fantasies about disguise. Jolson's film *Mammy* concerns a murderer hiding out in a minstrel troupe. (Well, Officer, he had coal black skin, a huge mouth, kinky hair, and white gloves.) In *The Jolson Story* Al gets his big break by impersonating another performer who can't go on; no one notices the substitution. In dozens of Hollywood comedies, many starring Bugs Bunny, a faceful of soot triggers a total racial makeover. Before Bing can scrub black paint off his face in Mack Sennett's *Dream House,* a black director hires him as a black actor.

Doppelgängers are at the heart of minstrelsy. Over time, they had a baleful influence: people confused racist stereotypes with real people, and those images remained rife in pop culture — especially Hollywood — well into the 1970s. In the short run, though, minstrelsy was considered a boon to the abolitionist movement. It humanized blacks for many whites who didn't know any, undermining the assumptions of barbarism by caricaturing them as sentimental, clever, funny, pompous, stupid, and sexual — human. Minstrelsy embodied a subversive idea, that the distinctions between black and white ran no deeper than a layer of greasepaint. Hidden behind an impenetrably inky disguise, performers were permitted a certain liberality from puritanical constraints, underscored by the nattering horse laugh "yuk, yuk, yuk." After Reconstruction, black troupes were as plentiful as white ones and introduced scores of actors and musicians into show business. They created their own kinds of satire and softened the more abhorrent clichés, greatly influencing succeeding generations of white minstrels. Jolson's alter ego, Gus, is offensive as caricature but is invariably the smartest and gentlest character in the drama; foolish whites are lost without him. In *Bombo* Gus shows Columbus the way to the New World and wins a Moorish princess in the bargain.

The minstrel show was the first unifying form of entertainment America ever knew. Like the circus, the coming of a minstrel troupe was an event, but minstrels — undeterred by the seasons — appeared more frequently than the circus. Not unlike radio or TV, minstrelsy spread the same jokes, songs, dance steps, parodies, puns, and novelties all over the country. Its humor proved deathless: *Why did the chicken cross the road? Who was that lady I saw you with last night?* By the time the form began to morph into burlesque and vaudeville, many individual stars had emerged. To the comically melancholy black entertainer Bert Williams, cork was an indignity he was forced to accept as the cost of integrating the *Ziegfeld Follies.* White performers could afford to be more sanguine. No one who witnessed the graceful Eddie Leonard gliding across the stage singing "Ida, Sweet as Apple Cider" or Eddie Cantor leaping about like a rabbit in a shooting gallery thought of them as impersonators of Negro life. Minstrelsy had become a conduit for the American style.[23] It was buoyant, irreverent, outlandish, and voiced with an oddly alloyed accent that was widely construed as southern.

Bing was enamored of many things southern, personally as well as professionally; he married two southern belles. His longtime buddy Phil Harris used as a theme song "That's What I Like About the South," which comically enumerates the specifics. Bing liked the whole effect, the mystique, the humor, the songs, the speech cadences that chimed well with his bottom notes and vocal affectations. As the character Crosby plays in the movie *Birth of the Blues* tells his disapproving father: "Southern music makes you feel like the circus is coming to town." He found inspiration in the South, in the first recordings by the Original Dixieland Jazz Band and the Mound City Blue Blowers, and more profoundly in the triumphant art of transplanted southern blacks, most particularly Louis Armstrong.

To Bing's generation, *southern* was a synonym for *black:* this was blatantly the case in songs by Hoagy Carmichael, Johnny Mercer, and others — a euphemistic way of saying that the American style of music sweeping the world was rooted in a slave culture. The very cosmopolitan dancer Florence Mills, whom Duke Ellington eulogized in his stride nocturne "Black Beauty," made the case succinctly in the title of her 1926 touring show: *Dixie to Broadway.*

On the occasion of Bing's fiftieth anniversary in show business, an event extolled with a 1975 television special but not by the recording industry he had helped save from extinction, he led a small jazz ensemble into a studio, at his expense, to record the rarely heard LP *A Southern Memoir.* But whose memories were they? For the young Crosby, Dixie was a state of mind and his passport was the faded but inveterately popular minstrel show, which helped bolster his determination to venture beyond his immediate domain. However intuitive and urbane Bing's understanding of jazz, he never lost his adolescent affection for the *dese, dose, yowsuh, yuk-yuk* relics of southernness ritualized in minstrelsy. His recorded performances are rife with words, airs, and slurred inflections that bespeak the show-business customs of his youth. They were especially apparent when he performed with his favorite southern singers, like Connie Boswell. Their 1940 record "Yes Indeed" begins with repartee:

> Bing: Now has you got it, sister Constance? Tell me, has you got it?
> Connie: Whoayeah, I got it, brother Bingstance. Now you knows I got it.
> Bing: Now has you got that rhythm in you, hmmm?

"Yes Indeed," characteristically enough, was a gospel-influenced pop tune written by the highly sophisticated, black northern orchestrator Sy Oliver for the white northern bandleader Tommy Dorsey. It was no more southern than the dozens, if not hundreds, of southern songs turned out by Tin Pan Alley during Jolson's glory years. Gerald Marks, the northerner who wrote "Is It True What They Say About Dixie?," observed, "In those days, New York songwriters wrote about the South because they had a guy who knew how to sing 'em. All those mammies were written by songwriters who never went south of Fourteenth Street. But the minute Jolson got off his knees and left the Wintergarden Theater, the era of southern songs was done for."[24]

The minstrel style was thriving in various offshoots when Bing latched onto the entertainment world. The first broadcast variety show featured Dailey Paskman's Radio Minstrels, in 1924; radio's real triumph was certified five years later with the appearance of *Amos 'n' Andy*. Bing's audience would follow him into the modern world of ballad crooning and jazz while sharing his nostalgia for the old style. Bing appeared in blackface or drag (the minstrelsy of gender bending) in several pictures. Even his loquacious banter, including the lightning exchanges of insults perfected with Bob Hope, was rooted in the verbal contest between minstrelsy's sly end man and the oratorical ringmaster. Bing was equally content to play the lackadaisical Mr. Bones or the inflated Interlocutor.

Gonzaga productions were occasions for fellowship, acceptable impiety, and escape, and Bing often took part. At a second-semester charity bazaar, he and his class erected a tepee and raffled Indian blankets in redface while his mother helped stock and supervise the tearoom. In April, in his own face, Bing and another boy sang solos at the annual Gonzaga Night, held at the Knights of Columbus Hall. Music was provided by the Dizzy Seven, a Gonzaga High School band that had caught Bing's ear. Having already begun to study drums, he was chosen as one of three drummers (Leo Lynn, his future right-hand man, was another) for the Gonzaga band, playing assemblies and sporting events. Soon he began sitting in with the younger kids who made up the Dizzy Seven, though he did not sing with the group.

The pianist with the Dizzy Seven on Gonzaga Night was a high-school senior, Arthur Dussault, who would develop a long-lived, influential relationship with Bing. Dussault had come to Gonzaga in 1920 from Montana. He was the same age as Bing, and so (not having been enrolled in elementary school prematurely) was one grade behind. Dussault first noticed Bing during a football game between the high-school JYA and an unofficial frosh team, which made a lot of noise about teaching them a thing or two but lost. Writing about the game years later, he recalled that Bing played center with startling toughness, considering his small size, winning respect from the other kids. "He had what it took and could give as well as take."[25] In many ways they were opposites. Like Frank Corkery, Dussault was bound for the priesthood, ordained in 1935. He was president of his class, a fabled football hero, and an exemplary student. He had little interest in jazz or dance music, preferring to play organ for the student choir and Gonzaga's orchestra. Bing and Art were never close friends, but their admiration for each other developed in the Dizzy Seven (aka the Juicy Seven) as they lumbered through stock arrangements at school dances. A friend described them as "equals, both strong-willed."[26] Dussault would serve Gonzaga as athletic director, glee club director, dean of men, public-relations director, and vice president; he was called Mr. Gonzaga. A successor remarked, "He was the most honest man I've ever known and an ideal contact for Bing — as was Father Corkery."[27] One of his duties was to enhance ties with the school's most celebrated alumnus, and he succeeded to the point of extracting nearly a million dollars. In so doing, he became something of a Crosby family confessor.

Shortly after publication of Barry Ulanov's 1948 biography *The Incredible Crosby,* Father Art wrote down his remembrances of the first time Bing made his mark singing at Gonzaga. Ulanov had rendered the incident from Kate's point of view, which Dussault dismissed as poetic license, for "Mrs. Catherine Crosby (whom I knew well) was never in our chapel."[28] He remembered the date as December 8, 1922, a holy day of obligation — the Immaculate Conception, a holiday that required Catholic boys to attend mass. For Dussault and about 200 other boarders, that meant the school chapel. Though Bing lived only a block away, he was obliged as a day scholar to attend St. Aloysius.

Art was chosen to ask him to attend the chapel instead, in order to add his voice to a three-part hymn, "Panis Angelicus." The boys thought Bing's baritone would blend with the high tenor (a student) and bass ("Hair-More" Gilmore). Art also hoped he would sing with the choir and take the solo at Communion on "Oh Lord, I Am Not Worthy," a hymn all the boys knew. Bing was reluctant at first, but Art, who was to accompany him on organ, persuaded him: he was going to church anyway, so why not attend a congregation that would consist only of fellow students? Besides, here was a way to please "his many warm friends among the boarders." Bing agreed to give it a try. "Of course, when he soloed, which was really impressive," Dussault wrote, "a goodly number of prayer-goers looked around to see who was soloing."

Bing's immediate reward was an invitation to breakfast with the boarders, the first of many as he made several subsequent appearances at the chapel on feast days, invariably singing a solo. "Bing sang nice," Dussault recalled, "but in a different sort of way."[29] He usually sang the Communion hymn and then joined in with the trio, navigating between tenor and bass with his supple voice. Dussault recalled as particularly beautiful the trio's harmonizing on "Ave Maria Stella No. 2," by A. H. Roseweig (from his collection *Concentus Sacri*). He believed those performances boosted Bing's confidence.

Bing received another shot of inspiration the summer after his freshman year, when he worked as prop boy at the Auditorium and Jolson made his second visit to Spokane. Bing had been fourteen the first time Jolson passed through; he was eighteen when *Sinbad* played two nights in town. "[Jolson] was amazing," Bing said. "He could go way up high and take a soft note, or belt it, and he could go way down. He really had a fabulous set of pipes, this fella."[30] He spoke of unconsciously imitating Al and of the lessons he learned: "I got an awful lot of mannerisms and I guess you could say idiosyncrasies [from Jolson] — singing traits and characteristics and delivery."[31] Bing marveled at how he seemed to personally reach each member of the audience, a feat for which Bing would be credited as a radio crooner. But the difference between working live and electronically was not lost on him. If Bing was inspired by Jolson, he was also humbled. He nursed the lifelong conviction that he could not really hold a stage, not like Jolie. "I'm not an electrifying performer at all," he cautioned one admirer. "I just sing a few little songs. But this man could really galvanize an audience into a frenzy. He could really tear them apart."[32]

Yet they had much in common. Jolson, notorious for his braggadocio (he once followed Caruso with his trademark line, "You ain't heard nothin' yet!"), had once lacked confidence and found it when an older player advised him to try blackface. It worked: "You looked and felt like a performer," he said.[33] A conspicuous bravado, albeit greatly toned down, was no less crucial to Bing's first Hollywood persona, that of the extremely assured if somewhat petulant Romeo who never merely wins a girl but steals her from another. Like Bing, Jolson was of average height, with thinning hair and a weight problem. Al perfected the pseudosouthern slur to the degree that critic John Crosby (no relation to Bing) observed, "He managed to eliminate consonants almost entirely."[34] The formidable Ethel Waters, who shared Bing's admiration for Jolson, could not help but parody his inflections:

"From the day he first stepped on a stage, Jolie always sang as though he expected the next note to be his last 'wah wah' or 'bebee mine' or 'I loav you, honeh, loav, loav you' or 'Californyah, heah I come, Golden Gate.'"[35] Jolson was a baritone who scaled tenor highs and plumbed bass lows, as Bing would, but reigned during an era when most popular singers — Billy Murray, Nick Lucas, Gene Austin — were tenors, often effeminate or sexually ambiguous. The bond between Jolson and Crosby would be strengthened in the years ahead by songwriters, including James Monaco, Buddy DeSylva, and Irving Berlin, who crafted Jolson's signature hits and also played prominent roles in Bing's career. In the end, the tables turned, as Jolson learned from Bing how to handle ballads and exploit recording devices.

Watching *Sinbad* from the sidelines invigorated Bing, and he participated in several theatrical events his sophomore year. At a vaudeville benefit for Gonzaga High School's sports program, he took two turns, playing a satirical sketch with a friend, billed as Ray and Bing, and singing comical songs, as Harry Crosby. In a review of *It Pays to Advertise,* a three-act comedy presented by the Varsity Drama Club, Bing was the only cast member singled out by the student reviewer: "Harry Crosby as the genial press agent 'Ambrose Peale' kept the audience in a constant uproar."[36] A production of the Henry Irving vehicle *The Bells* by the school's Henry Irving Dramatic Society, merited a preview in the *Spokane Daily Chronicle,* which published head shots of the three principals, including Bing, bow-tied and grinning.

Bing displayed few signs of discontent that year, holding his own in class while playing baseball for the varsity and the semipro Ideal Laundry teams. He won a Distinguished citation in English and a Premium (second place) citation in debating. Math and chemistry were problematic, and Father Kennelly made a point of saying that he was worried about Bing's performance in the latter. Bing told him with breezy candor, "Well, Father, there's no use both of us worrying about it." Kennelly may have been too thunderstruck to launch his key ring, but he was a lot angrier when he heard noises one night in front of the Administration Building and marched over for a look. He found Bing supervising a pulley system as his confederates inside attempted to lower to the ground, piece by piece, a set of school drums. Bing, who needed them for a last-minute gig, had previously succeeded in borrowing the drums on several occasions. Getting caught convinced him to save up for a set of his own.

Among his summer jobs was a brief stint at Harry's company, the former Inland Brewery, where he whiled away the time discussing the frustrations of making near beer (they brewed the real article, then "pasteurized it until it was the sissified prohibition stuff") with an old German braumeister. His job was to roll and upend barrels of cucumbers into the briny vats for pickling, and he hated it. He quit after two weeks and never developed a liking for pickles. He did develop an appetite for true beer, not without inadvertent encouragement from his father, who now and then asked him to "rush the can." Local speakeasies sold beer in large tin cans with tops and handles, and Harry would give Bing a quarter to fetch one. When Bing siphoned off some of it himself, he would tell Harry that a bunch of kids had chased him and it spilled. That was known as "dropping the can." One speakeasy Bing knew pretty well was operated by a former fight promoter and con man turned bootlegger. His name was Charles Dale, and he kept the back room of his popular establishment stocked with liquor brought back in suitcases from periodic trips to Butte. Music by bands a lot better than the Dizzy Seven helped Dale lure customers.

Yet notwithstanding an occasional snifter or tin can, Bing hewed to the straight and narrow. Returning for his third year, he enrolled in the School of Law, taking advantage of a program that would confer A.B. and LL.B degrees in six years — two in the College of Arts and Sciences, four in law. His schedule was characteristically full. He attended regular courses in the forenoons and returned to campus five nights a week, between seven and nine, for classes in law. During afternoons, he worked in the office of Charles Albert, an attorney for the Great Northern Railway. Albert's widow, actress Sarah Truax, repeated her husband's favorite story about his former clerk, a likable boy who disappeared from the office to rehearse or nail down engagements for his band. Colonel Albert finally insisted that the stagestruck fellow give his full time to show business. When he saw him next, Bing was pulling down $3,000 a week.

Law may have appealed to Bing's sense of theatricality — it is the one career other than politics that routinely turns out real-life Mr.

Interlocutors. In any case, the decision was not made lightly. When Bing registered for law school, he had not been tested as an entertainer or musician outside school productions. Even by high-school standards, the Dizzy Seven was undistinguished. The workload he embraced indicates his determination to make good on his parents' investment and create his future. Bing buried himself in a curriculum of contracts and quasi-contracts, criminal law, torts, property, logic, procedure (legal bibliography), and debate. Membership in the Debating Society was mandatory for students in the special program, as was attaining thirty credits toward the A.B. He now paid less attention to sports and stagecraft. But working for Colonel Albert brought home the disenchanting truth that lawyering entails more drudgery than drama and was not the instant platform for Ciceronian eloquence suggested by the examples of Clarence Darrow and William Jennings Bryan. Second semester, Bing was back on the boards.

The *Spokane Daily Chronicle* for February 8, 1923, reported rehearsals for an upcoming performance of George M. Cohan's *Seven Keys to Baldpate,* presented by the Gonzaga Dramatic Club with Mike Pecarovitch as the lead. Yet the sole accompanying photo was a head shot of Bing (bow tie, big smile), who played the role of Lou Max, "the crooked mayor's man 'Friday,' the humorous feature of the cast."[37] Bing was described as one of the drama club's "old-timers." The priest who directed the play selected his cast from the entire student body, reported the *Chronicle,* for a version of the play Cohan had specially revised for the East Coast Jesuit school, Fordham. In May the Monogram Club presented a sweater to Father Sharp in recognition of his work in assisting Gonzaga sports. An evening of burlesque and music ensued, during which Bing acted in a three-man comedy sketch and sang in unison with the Gonzaga Harmony Trio.

Enrolling in his fourth year, he continued to work part-time for Charles Albert in the afternoons and took an additional job as night watchman for the Great Northern Railway, studying in a room in its tower on Havermale Island. An acute if fleeting depression hit the country that year, and inevitably the Crosbys felt the impact. Harry, who had been listed in the company books as secretary, was once again let go and then rehired as shipping clerk at a reduced salary. Inland now offered commercial storage in addition to "22 Varieties."

The economic shortfall derailed the ambitions of Bing's eldest sister, Catherine, who upon graduating Holy Names Academy told a reporter that she expected to study music in the East. She remained at home. Everett returned from Seattle and worked as a bookkeeper, but soon left to rejoin the bootlegging trade. Larry worked for the *Chronicle,* as did Ted, who concluded his education with a bang, editing the *Gonzaga Bulletin* and graduating from the School of Philosophy of Letters.

Ted never stopped turning out stories, poems, and essays for the college paper. One tale, "Sunny Skies," tells of an abused wife named Grace Crossland, tormented by a hard-drinking husband and afraid to leave her Westchester mansion. That changes after she visits a dude ranch and meets a cowboy named Hale, who greets people with the phrase "sunny skies." Hale follows Grace home to New York, dispatches her husband, and returns with her to Rancho Los Pinos. The story is chillingly prophetic: Bing's wife Dixie suffered a mild form of agoraphobia, rarely leaving their estate, and though Bing was never the brute of Ted's story, he did drive her away with his drinking early in their marriage. But the truly prescient character is Hale, who emphatically anticipates the public Bing: the cool, capable, optimistic, all-American go-getter who loves horses, operates ranches, and invariably gets the girl.[38]

Bing enjoyed one final theatrical triumph at Gonzaga, when he reprised his role as Ambrose Peale in *It Pays to Advertise,* in November. What turned out to be his last appearance in a school production netted him his first genuine newspaper review. After praising the Gonzaga Dramatic Club for focusing on plays that allow women's roles to be "blue pencilled," to eliminate feminine impersonation (and prove that a drama club can "get along without a woman"), the *Spokane Daily Chronicle*'s critic praised Pecarovitch and Crosby for carrying off "the play's hilarious moments" and continued: "Mr. Crosby bursts over with spontaneity in getting his amusing lines across the footlights."[39]

Neither school, work, nor drama diminished Bing's appetite for music. He listened to everything and without prejudice. He belonged to a generation so dazzled by the sheer availability of diverse music that it did not, unlike subsequent generations, distinguish between hip and square, swing or Mickey Mouse. The only criteria that mattered were whether a performance was interesting and well executed. The father of one of Bing's friends was a record distributor, so many of the latest numbers were available to him. Ted's crystal machine also got a workout. Above all, Bing and his friends spent hours listening to records at Bailey's music shop. They stayed until they were thrown out, rarely buying anything. The mid-1920s signaled an electrifying moment in American music. Jazz and blues were not yet codified as strictly defined genres; there was, instead, a general sense of jazziness and bluesiness. Musical influences from everywhere were fermenting into a whole new brew, and no one could imagine where it would lead; every month brought new sounds to marvel at. Paul Whiteman introduced a nervy Gershwin tune called "I'll Build a Stairway to Paradise." Some listeners were delighted by its bold use of a seventh chord, but most fans were more taken with the trumpet solo, which interpolated two twelve-bar blues choruses right in the middle. A fellow making records under the name Ukelele Ike sang bawdy songs with jazz pizzazz and backed himself on hot ukelele and kazoo. Jolson, who had recorded novelties, now introduced more substantial melodies like "April Showers" and "Toot, Toot, Tootsie (Goo' Bye)." Dance bands paved new ground and gave Whiteman a run for his money — Fred Waring with "Sleep" and Isham Jones with "It Had to Be You."

Many new songs bore the stamp of the South. A group of Whiteman musicians calling themselves the Virginians scored with "I Wish I Could Shimmy Like My Sister Kate." The Peerless Quartet, a perennial on the Crosby gramophone, released "'Way Down Yonder in New Orleans." Arthur Gibbs popularized a new dance with his record of "Charleston." Not everyone understood the racial collusion taking place in the music world, though many who did were outraged and delivered stringent imprecations. *Ladies' Home Journal* located a cause and effect between jazz and rape, and cautioned its readers, "Jazz is the expression of protest against law and order, the bolshevik element of license striving for expression in music."[40] It wasn't entirely wrong: jazz was widely associated with people who broke the law by drinking bootleg hooch in speakeasies. Rape was a stretch, but then most of the jeremiads employed the word to hyperbolize the greater threat of women who freely expressed their sexuality. Liquor,

Ogden Nash wrote, is quicker, and so a syllogism took root: jazz abets drinking, and drinking abets sex; therefore, jazz abets sex, which practiced under the influence of liquor amounts to rape. That *Ladies' Home Journal* failed to hear any musical value in jazz is almost immaterial.

Greater still than the sexual panic was the racial one. To most young people, the hot new music was simply liberating. Few outside the largest cities comprehended how far it went in transgressing the color line. Bing and his friends, for example, probably had no way of knowing that the three songs mentioned above ("I Wish I Could Shimmy Like My Sister Kate," "'Way Down Yonder in New Orleans," "Charleston"), though popularized by white bands, were composed by blacks, two of whom were no more southern than Bing. But Crosby had to realize he was witnessing the vanguard of a music brimming with catchy melodies, exciting rhythms, and weird harmonies, an inclusive multicolored all-American music.

Inspired by Ukelele Ike (Cliff Edwards), Bing carried his father's banjo-uke to outings at Liberty Lake. He never became proficient on it, though he got some mileage from Ike's other instrument, the kazoo. That autumn Bing finally saved up enough to buy a set of drums from a mail-order catalog. The bass drum had a Japanese sunset painted on the skin, which could be illuminated by a bulb inside; a gooseneck cymbal waved from the rim. Those drums were perhaps the most significant purchase Bing would ever make, because news of their arrival circulated as far as North Central High School, where a student piano player named Alton Rinker led a small band that avoided stock arrangements in favor of charts he copied by ear from the latest jazz records. Rinker had a problem. The drummer was no good, and the other boys let him go before he could find a replacement. So when he heard about a law student who lived nearby on East Sharp, with a new set of traps, he figured it was worth a phone call.

7

MUSICALADERS

On the one hand my friends and I would be hunting
after the empty show of popularity — theatrical ap-
plause from the audience, verse competitions, contests
for crowns of straw, the vanity of the stage, immoderate
lusts — and on the other hand we would be trying to get
clean of all this filth by carrying food to those people
who were called the "elect" and the "holy ones."

— Saint Augustine, *Confessions* (c. 400)[1]

The caller introduced himself and asked Bing whether he would be interested in trying out with a band at North Central: would he like to bring his drums over to the Rinker home on West Mansfield for their next rehearsal? Bing unhesitatingly said yes. The Dizzy Seven had faded away. Law was losing its attraction, and no one was bidding for his services as a musician. Spokane had plenty of professional drummers playing in dance bands, and Bing was neither good enough nor experienced enough to join the union and compete with them for work. The fact that he, a fourth-year college student, was asked to audition for a bunch of high-school kids did not affront his ego in the slightest. He was game for anything.

Bing did not know Alton Rinker; and as far as Rinker knew, he did not know Bing. But as soon as he opened the door, Alt recognized him. Alt and his brother Miles, who played alto saxophone in the group, had spent countless summer afternoons at the Mission Park pool. "Every time we went swimming there," Rinker wrote in an unpublished account of his association with Bing, "I would see a young, blond-headed chubby boy, who was older than I. He could swim like a seal and was a good diver off the board. He was well known at the pool and everyone called him Bing."[2] Years had passed and Bing looked older, but he still carried himself with that impressive authority. As Alt introduced him to Miles and the Pritchard brothers, Bob and Clare, he was struck by Bing's composure and sharp sense of humor. After Bing set up the drums and they ran down a few numbers, everyone was happy. "We knew right away that he really had a beat," Rinker recalled.[3] Bing exclaimed, "Oh boy, this is great!"[4]

What was great was the experience of playing music that had some resemblance to the records everyone was listening to. Bob Pritchard played C-melody saxophone, and his brother, Clarence, had a tenor banjo. None of them, including Rinker, could read music, and the only keys they played in were A flat and E flat, which Alt had taught himself on piano: "I don't know why, but these were black keys and looked easier than the white keys."[5] With his acute ear, however, he could adapt arrangements from records and assign appropriate notes to each musician. Among the records they worked on were Paul Whiteman's "Three O'Clock in the Morning," "Whispering," and "I Love You"; Ted Lewis's "When My Baby Smiles at Me"; the Mound City Blue Blowers' "San"; the Cotton Pickers' "Jimtown Blues"; and anything they could find by the incredibly prolific Dixieland outfit the Original Memphis Five and Ukelele Ike.[6] Bing knew the records and had no trouble fitting in. He was so pleased with the group that he stood up from his drum seat and announced he could sing, producing, to prove the point, a tiny blue-spangled megaphone. The boys were impressed. "Now we had a good drummer who could also sing," Rinker wrote, "and it really turned us all on."[7]

In fact, Bing wasn't much of a drummer, and in later years whenever the subject came up, he liked to quote Phil Harris's observation that he had a roll wide enough to throw a dog through. He knew the rudiments and could keep time, but his skills as a percussionist were just about equal to the musical talents of the other guys — which isn't saying much. But they had enthusiasm to spare, especially Alt and Bing, who, unlike the others and unbeknownst to each other, were growing increasingly restless at school.

At first, Alt was concerned about how Bing would feel playing with high-school students. Rinker had just turned sixteen, and Bing was coming up on twenty-one. But the age thing never came up. Perhaps Bing, who had always been a year younger than his friends, liked being the eldest for a change. He established ground rules with Alton early. "I guess I was a little bossy at rehearsals in the way I told the fellows what to play," Rinker recalled. "I didn't talk that way to Bing as he was the drummer and didn't play notes. But after one rehearsal, Bing came over to me and said, 'You'd better not talk that way to me or I'll give you a punch in the nose.' It shook me up and from then on I was careful of how I talked to him at rehearsals."[8]

The influence of the Rinkers — first Alt and later his older sister, Mildred — on Bing's career can scarcely be overstated. His friendship with Alt dominated Bing's life for nearly seven years, ultimately serving as the catalyst for his departure from Spokane and his decision to pursue a life in show business. The association remained the central experience in Rinker's professional life, causing him some bitterness when the friendship died and he realized that despite his success as a radio producer and composer, he would be remembered mainly as an appendage to the Crosby story. But in the beginning, Alton and Bing needed each other. Rinker provided the energy and leadership necessary to spur his pal along. Bing offered Rinker companionship and an entrée to his own clique of college boys, filling a need left by the death of Alt's mother years before and a temporary abandonment by his father. Bing even renamed him, insistently calling him Al, instead of Alt (rhymes with *vault*). Pretty soon Al's friends and family followed suit. Though the relationship ended badly, it is impossible to read the unpublished memoir Al wrote shortly before his death without perceiving an unrequited admiration. On the surface, the young men appeared to be two branches off the same tree.

Al was born on December 20, 1907, the third of four children, on a thousand-acre wheat farm sixty miles from Spokane, across the Idaho state line. His mother, Josephine, was half Cœur d'Alene Indian, and since the farm was on the reservation, the land had been deeded to her tax-free. The eldest of Al's siblings was his sister, Mildred, a skillful bareback rider who rode five miles to school every morning on a buckskin pony with their brother Miles clinging to her waist. In the 1930s she would be celebrated as the "Rockin' Chair Lady," for her record of the Hoagy Carmichael song "Rockin' Chair," and would become almost as well known for her weight as for her swinging bird-like voice. Yet Mildred was a slip of a girl, barely five feet tall; until she was twenty, she weighed less than a hundred pounds. Like the Crosby place, the Rinker home echoed with music. Their father, Charles, played fiddle and called square dances at the community's occasional socials. His wife, Josephine, a devout Catholic who had studied music with the nuns at Tekoa, was a pianist who played by ear — classics, opera songs, and ragtime, including a favorite of Al's she called "Dill Pickles." During the years when the children were young, she sat down at the piano every evening after supper and taught Mildred to play and sing. Al recalled that Mildred favored songs of longing and exotic places, like "Siren of the Southern Seas," "Just a Baby's Prayer at Twilight," "Araby."

When Al was five, Charles hired a tenant to run the farm and moved his family to a house on Spokane's North Side, where he operated an auto-supply shop. Four years later Josephine succumbed to tuberculosis. The distraught widower with four children (including the baby, Charles Jr.) hired and soon married an abusive housekeeper named Mrs. Pierce. "I think he had lost his mind," Al wrote. "Compared to her, the wicked stepmother in Grimms' Fairy Tales was a fairy godmother."[9] Mildred loathed her, and at seventeen she packed a bag, kissed her brothers and bid them and her father good-bye, and left for Seattle, where she stayed with an aunt while working as a sheet-music demonstrator at Woolworth's. She quickly married and divorced Ted Bailey, electing to retain his name because she thought it sounded more American than the Swiss-derived Rinker. As Prohibition went into effect, she began to sing in speakeasies in Seattle and Canada, where she met and married Benny Stafford, a bootlegger.

Meanwhile, Mrs. Pierce issued an ultimatum: Mr. Rinker would have to choose either her and her daughter or his own children. "He must have been under a spell," Al wrote, "because he finally sent us to the Catholic Academy in Tekoa, Washington."[10] The boys were miserable, but whenever their father brought them home, Mrs. Pierce would force him to send them away again. On one occasion when she beat him with a broom, Al hauled off and punched her in the stomach. After that, she agreed to a compromise: Al and Miles were permitted to enroll as boarders at Gonzaga High School. Al began studying piano and found he could pick out tunes by ear and fit appropriate chords to the melody lines — at least if they were in A flat and E flat. Charles Rinker finally shed himself of the wicked step-mother and her daughter, settling a lot of money on them in the process, at which point Alton and Miles returned home and trans-ferred to North Central High.

Even Mildred briefly returned to Spokane, to sing at Charlie Dale's speakeasy. Alton was too young to see her work there, but she enthu-siastically shared with him her collection of records by an exciting new singer, Ethel Waters.[11] Bing apparently did hear Mildred at Dale's, though his recollection of her as "the area's outstanding singing star" was a substantial exaggeration. She appeared locally only once and was little noted; speakeasies were not reviewed. "She spe-cialized in sultry, throaty renditions with a high concentrate of South-ern accent, such as 'Louisville Lou' and 'Hard-Hearted Hannah,'" Bing wrote.[12] She remembered him, too, and in 1941 recalled his early years. "Bing was always a fella to get into trouble," she said. "I expect he spent every Saturday night of his life in jail. But look at him now. For my money, he's the best of them all, male or female."[13]

Bob and Clare Pritchard were living with their aunt and uncle, not far from the Rinkers, when they decided they wanted to play music. For Christmas 1922, they received instruments — a C-melody saxo-phone and tenor banjo — and practiced constantly with Al and Miles, as Al worked up arrangements. After six months they knew six tunes. They drafted Fred Healy on drums, and auditioned him on "Wabash Blues." He sounded okay, but within a few months the Rinkers and Pritchards had improved, while Healy "couldn't keep a good beat on his drums."[14] They broke the news to him and looked elsewhere. Now, with Bing in the group and Miles doubling on clar-inet, they rehearsed at Al's house and played a few high-school dances for money. A student at North Central, Jimmy Heaton, asked if he could play trumpet in the band. Unlike the others, Heaton was an excellent, schooled player; he was the first of the bunch to make a mark in Hollywood, as an ace studio musician. (He played lead trum-pet for Alfred Newman on countless 20th Century-Fox scores.)

Heaton gave the small ensemble a brassy spark, encouraging Al to fashion more intricate arrangements. They called themselves the Musicaladers (as in "musical aiders") and played social gatherings at Odd Fellows Hall, the Elks Club, and the Manito Park Social Club, often with Rinker billed as leader. The Manito job, three dollars a man, was on a Sunday night, and Bing could barely suppress his yawning in law class the next day. His interest in school was fading.

Early in 1924 the band was given a week on the small stage at the Casino Theater and went over well enough to get a repeat engagement. They rented tuxedo jackets and white flannel trousers and thought themselves pros. Bing periodically made his way from the drums to the proscenium to sing such songs as "Alice Blue Gown," "Margie," "St. Louis Blues," and "For Me and My Gal." Al's arrangements, adapted from the latest discs, were invariably up-to-date. "Well, he was very good," Bing said late in life:

> He had a great ear for music, he could play pretty near anything after he heard it a time or two, and play the right harmony, too. He'd pick out a part for each instrument. We had piano, banjo, cornet, clarinet, saxophone, and he'd voice all the harmonies for them, just show them the harmonic line to follow, and we'd be playing the same arrangement as on the record. We were quite a novelty around Spokane 'cause we would have arrangements taken from hit records, which we could play. That really made us unique.[15]

The Musicaladers would take any job, anyplace. "We were non-union," Bing said. "We had no scale, no minimum, no maximum — whatever we could get. It wasn't much, but you didn't need much in those days."[16] One engagement they kept secret was at a second-story Chinese restaurant, the Pekin Cafe, a popular if notorious hangout that trafficked in liquor and prostitution. The Pekin offered the Musicaladers a regular job every Friday and Saturday night for good money. "I was able to allay some of my mother's doubts about the restaurant's respectability by pointing to its most respectable financial rewards," Bing recalled.[17]

The fact that Bing was drinking heavily and not always holding it well became obvious one afternoon when he and his friend Edgie Hogle, who tried to manage the Musicaladers, got into trouble. Bing, who had been at Colonel Albert's office, walked over to Hat Freeman's hat store, where Edgie clerked. Each put up fifty cents, and Bing walked to an alley a block away where a bootlegger sold dollar pints of popskull, a pernicious moonshine whiskey. Later, back at Hat's and properly tanked, Bing and Edgie mulled over a vaudeville act they'd seen the previous evening in which a juggler cast hats over the heads of the audience and made them return like boomerangs. By the time the owner returned, four straw hats had sailed out the door. He fired Edgie and banned Bing from the premises.

Bing's favorite shop, one of his two regular hangouts, was Russ Bailey's House of Music, a record-and-sheet-music store on the corner of Riverside and Post, next door to the Liberty Theater, Spokane's first movie house. Ray Grombacher had built the Liberty in 1915 and now owned Bailey's as well. One of his clerks, Johnnie Bulmer, moonlighted as a drummer and led a band at Liberty Lake. During a late-night waltz, he would focus a light on his bass drum, illuminating a florid sunset that, one observer said, "made Maxfield Parrish's calendars seem somber."[18] According to Bulmer, Bing pressed him for help in mastering the latest licks, and Bulmer gave him pointers "to get rid of him."[19] Bing noted the striped blazer Johnnie wore at the lake and the way he sang "Yes! We Have No Bananas" through a megaphone but did not think much of him as a singer. The feeling was mutual. Bing "always looked like a tramp,"[20] Bulmer groused to a reporter in the 1940s, nursing his envy, for though he chased after the big time, he returned to Spokane an overweight and dyspeptic plumber.

Bing's key interest in Bailey's, however, was not Bulmer. He would pick up Al after school at North Central, and the two would bring their banjo-ukes to the store, lock themselves in a booth, and listen to records until closing time. "We practically lived there," Bing recalled.[21] "We used to wait outside Bailey's music shop for the new records to come in, the Mound City Blue Blowers and the Original Dixieland Band and the Memphis Five and the Cotton Pickers, Jean Goldkette's band."[22] Rinker added, "We couldn't afford to buy [all] the records, so we would buy one, after learning 12 and leave."[23] Bulmer's recollection was not as blithe: "They drove us crazy," he complained. "They'd play some Whiteman stuff over and over, picking up the arrangements by ear. They never spent a dime, so whenever a customer wanted a booth I'd throw them out."[24] Ralph Goodhue, who managed the store, agreed — he couldn't recall them ever buying a record in the hundreds of hours they spent in the glass-enclosed listening room.[25] In 1962 Bing called Bailey's "our jazz classroom."[26] It became his only classroom.

The student of Cicero, Ovid, and Augustine; the declaimer of Horatius at the Bridge; the incipient minstrel; the energetic athlete and yell leader; the devout altar boy; the promising mirror of a rigorous Jesuit education was slipping out of Gonzaga's grasp. The law had not suited him. Had Bing continued in the arts and sciences college, he would most likely have graduated, for he had only two or three months remaining of his fourth year when he dropped out. But in the law school, he faced an additional two years. Kate was on his back, complaining about his slipping grades and lapsed attention, and he bridled, telling her he would rather sing than eat. By spring, Bing was earning more money with the Musicaladers than in Colonel Albert's office and let everyone know it. He saw no contest between following in the footsteps of his uncle George and executing wage-garnishment forms. For weeks he sat in class, whistling under his breath and practicing a paradiddle with pencils on his desktop. He finally told his parents of his decision to withdraw from Gonzaga.

Art Dussault and others tried to change Bing's mind, but the future star — showing the stubbornness that became fabled during his years in Hollywood — was immovable. He left school with little warning, having posed with twenty-seven other law students for the 1924 Gonzaga yearbook. Everyone in the picture wears a necktie or cravat, except Bing, who wears a bow tie; with his hair neatly pomaded and parted on the left, he looks conspicuously younger than the others. Several years later he remarked, "I studied law in college and I can truthfully say that the bar of the state of Washington is the only bar I was ever kept out of."[27] Kate was distraught, Harry encouraging.

Bing was prodded to quit school by Rinker, a reluctant student who did badly in high school and disdained scholastic obligations of any kind, especially those that detracted from the business of music. Al's enthusiasm spurred Bing's, and the successes they enjoyed mitigated their doubts about the ensemble's abilities. Their confidence was not warranted. Jimmy Heaton was the only instrumentalist with real talent. Al's golden ear did not increase his skill on piano, and Bing's musicality was at best unfocused. What kept them running, said an observer, "was their devoted love of jazz and brass balls."[28] They had discovered the great secret of America's new popular music: it let everyone in, even those lacking musical education or conventional technique. All you needed was passion, ambition, a good ear. Rinker and Crosby had all three. Creativity would come later.

The Musicaladers belonged to the first generation of young Americans who bought into the zeitgeist of American popular music through records and a few traveling bands. Among the orchestra leaders passing through Spokane, Vic Meyers, Dwight Johnson, and Abe Lyman spiced their fox-trots and waltzes with jazz. If the captivating new sound was difficult to play well in its toddling stage (only a fraction of the jazz records made during the mid-1920s stand up), it was easy to play badly. The form was methodical, the harmony simple, the rhythm steady — especially as diluted under the Whiteman influence.

With time on their hands in 1924, Bing's gang found another hangout besides Bailey's — Benny Stubeck's Confectionary, which would become a familiar name to Bing's radio audience. Stubeck, a short, stout Bohemian, ran a corner luncheonette that sold newspapers and tobacco. Though Bing retained warm memories of the shop, its owner remembered him and his light-fingered friends with more tolerance than joy. In 1937 the thirty-four-year-old Bing wrote Stubeck a letter admitting that he had stolen Hershey bars from his store and agreeing to pay up if the bill did not exceed three dollars. Stubeck did not send an invoice, as he explained to a reporter: "What the hell, so he now owes me three bucks. He pays me off with publicity. Christ, he's mentioned me fifty or a hundred times on the radio. You heard it, ain't you, saying he's broadcasting from Benny Stubeck's poolroom? Always the clown." Benny recalled Bing as a guy ready with his fists, though not the type to look for a confrontation. "They was all the time getting into fights," either because they were refused entry to a cabaret or because they were "drunker'n skunks on moonshine" or because of girls. "They was always chasing the chickens," getting "clapped up," and coming to Benny, who discreetly arranged for them to see a doctor.[29]

Bing's willingness to fight is much affirmed. On one occasion, a heckler called out, "Hi, pansy," while he was singing "Peggy O'Neil," and Bing leaped off the bandstand and chased him outside, where the police intervened.[30] His fondness for adolescent whoring is less well documented, but it may help explain Bing's widely noted lack of interest in routine dating. The name of only one Crosby girlfriend from the period has come to light, and that because thirty years later her six-year-old nephew sidled up to Bing at Idaho's Hayden Lake Country Club. As the boy stared up at him, Bing engaged him in conversation and was told that the boy's aunt Dorothy had been his girlfriend and that the family scrapbook was filled with pictures of them. As the nephew, Jack Sheehan, remembered many years later, Bing responded, "I've had affection for lots of pretty ladies, Junior. So you've got the goods on me, eh?" A moment later Bing turned to him: "Is your aunt Dorothy Bresnan?" He wrote a note on the back of his scorecard, which was found among Dorothy's possessions when she died in 1973:

> Dear Dorothy,
> Greetings to you and yours. I certainly remember you as a lovely girl. I recall the park dance we attended after you were named May Queen. I'm at the lake for a short spell with the boys. They are becoming excellent golfers. Your nephew is a fine young man, not at all shy. All good wishes to you. Love, Bing.[31]

The scrapbook suggested to Sheehan that the two-year relationship was serious. He surmised that it took place during Bing's final year at Gonzaga and the ensuing one with the Musicaladers. Rinker recalled nothing of the kind, objecting rather primly that Bing "never seemed to get emotionally involved with girls he dated." With Bing, everything was "on a casual fun basis."[32]

For Al, considering his youth, Stubeck's was a pretty heady experience. He and Bob Pritchard were included in Bing's adventures because they were in the band and liked to hang out with him. Al remembered the older boys bringing moonshine and partying with local girls ("not what you would call debutantes") who were considered daring just for taking a swig.[33] Al got sick once, but Bing could usually hold it. Already known for his "sporty hats and fast quips," Bing was much admired for his wit, his singing, and his ability to consume rotgut whiskey at a time when Prohibition made drinking a pastime and a sport. Stubeck was not impressed. "Jeez, that was one wild bunch of clowns, always broke," Benny groused.[34] They kept a jug in his basement, where he allowed the band to rehearse, and at closing time he sometimes found them down there stiff as boards. Benny obviously had a soft spot for Bing and his friends. He was an agent for the *Seattle Post-Intelligencer,* and some nights he piled them into the *PI* truck and drove them home "so they wouldn't get pinched." "Goddamn good customers," Benny later recalled of Crosby and his friends. "Jesus Christ, I can still remember that Bing when he'd walk in and holler, 'Give me a couple of greasy hamburgers and a malted milk.'"[35] Stubeck claimed that Bing later offered him a position with Bing Crosby, Inc.

The Musicaladers' best and steadiest job followed directly from their scandalous appearances at the Pekin Cafe, where George Lareida Jr. heard them. Lareida and his father co-owned the newly established, hugely successful Lareida's Dance Pavilion in Dishman, six miles east of Spokane. George Sr. wasn't overwhelmed by the band at first, but he was duly impressed when an itinerant vaudevillian dropped by for the last show and said of Bing, "That kid's really got something."[36] He asked the boys whether they would be interested in working at his place three nights a week. Lareida Jr. recalled Bing blurting out, "Boy, would we!" The Pavilion was an immense and well-run operation in a hangar of a building (formerly an auto showroom, later a roller-skating rink), where the area's young people went to socialize and dance; it was the first stop on the train out of Spokane. As the band required a car to make its thrice-weekly trips for the summerlong engagement, the six members contributed four or five dollars each to the purchase of a 1916 Model T Ford, without top or windshield.

The bandstand was situated on a platform in the middle of the hall, and everyone danced around it. When Bing sang a ballad, obscuring his face with the megaphone, kids stopped and stared. The repertoire included fox-trots, waltzes, and tangos but was unusually abundant with blues — "St. Louis Blues," "Beale Street Blues," "The Wang Wang Blues," "Stack-o-lee Blues." Lareida's was the one place Spokane's parents generally endorsed. Prohibition was strictly enforced by the teetotaling owners. Anyone who entered the Pavilion intoxicated was asked to leave; bouncers made sure they did. George

Lareida and his father allowed for one exception. They knew Bing often drank before he arrived, but Lareida Sr. tolerated his tippling because he rarely let it show. The son knew better, having found Bing passed out in the men's room near the urinals. "Wake up, you bum, you've got to play tonight," he yelled at him. Bing came to, realized where he was, and grimaced, "Hey, who brung them roses."[37]

On one occasion Bing fell off the bandstand, as he was reminded ten years later, when he wagered a Seattle businessman over the outcome of a fight between a fellow named Handy and a boxer Bing presumably owned an interest in. The businessman wrote Bing that he had met someone from Spokane who offered to "make a little side bet that [Handy] at least doesn't fall off the platform such as in the instance of one of your early crooning experiences at Lareida's Dance Pavilion, Spokane, years ago. Should I cover this bet for you, or should I just let it drop?"[38] Bing's response is not known.

Bing was indulged because he was liked. Lareida thought Al "cold and even a little haughty" but enjoyed Bing and called him the Lip in tribute to his nonstop verbal dexterity.[39] "When you see Bing chewing the fat with [Bob] Hope," he said, "that's the fellow he was."[40] The Musicaladers, excepting Heaton, posed for a photograph used in Lareida's ads. For his first important publicity shot, Bing sat up front beside a tom-tom, holding Miles Rinker's clarinet, wearing the band's latest uniform, a loud, high-buttoned striped blazer and bow tie, smiling boyishly. Seated next to him is Clare Pritchard with his banjo. Bob Pritchard, his alto in hand, stands to Clare's right, his left leg crooked back like a chorine's. Behind them, in darker striped jackets and bow ties, are Miles with his alto and Al, the youngest of the five, looking the most mature. The aggressive glint in Al's eyes contrasts with the smiling cherubs around him. They look pleased, despite their uniformly scuffed shoes. But their appeal to dancers proved unexceptional, and the job led to few others. On the day of Bing's death, George Lareida said, "He was an awful nice fellow": through all the intervening years, Bing had never failed to send him a Christmas card.[41]

The Musicaladers lasted about eighteen weeks at Lareida's, and they never had another job remotely as good. But they kept plugging until the spring of 1925, though exactly how the year after their biggest engagement was spent is lost to memory. Bing and Al ignore it in their accounts, published and unpublished, skipping directly to the dissolution of the band. After Lareida's, Bing wrote, the band skirted by with "whatever we could get" — that is, whatever Edgie Hogle could line up, mostly dances and parties. That the group was losing its steam is clear. It must have been a trying year for Bing, the only member of the band with time to burn. Al was on the verge of flunking out of school, but the others — except Heaton, who had the promise of band work in Los Angeles — were bound for college. Bing hired on as a clerk for the Great Northern Railway, yet continued to spend much of his time hanging around North Central, trying to generate interest in rehearsals and work. Except for Al, the other guys were more concerned with graduating.

Other than Frank Corkery, according to the account by Ted and Larry, Bing now socialized mostly with boys at North Central. Among his drinking partners, Dirk Crabbe best shared his sense of humor and verbal inventiveness. Benny Stubeck's and Russ Bailey's occupied many days, and vaudeville and silent movies occupied many evenings. The first recordings by Bennie Moten out of Kansas City arrived at the shop and became great favorites for a few weeks. Al's home life improved: his father remarried, this time to a "lovely" widow from Stockholm with a conservatory background, who schooled Al in classical music.[42] But Al gravitated to the Crosby home, where he grew fond of Catherine and Mary Rose, whom he had known slightly at school. He recalled that the Crosby house was sparsely furnished, a reflection, he surmised, of the difficulty Mr. Crosby had making ends meet. Al liked Harry ("His dad was anything-goes, a nice guy, Irish guy"),[43] but not Kate ("a real matriarch, ugh, very strict disciplinarian on Catholicism").[44] He and Bing practiced at the piano, and Bing surprised him by comfortably singing E and F, high for a baritone.

By spring 1925 the band was kaput. After graduation, Jimmy Heaton moved to Los Angeles. Miles was heading for the University of Illinois, and the Pritchards were planning to attend Washington State; all had lost interest in being Musicaladers. "Bing and I were left alone," Al ruminated.[45] They became avid golfers, playing with old wood-shafted irons, hickory-shafted woods, and repainted golf balls on a public course at Downriver Park. Al was seventeen and Bing almost twenty-two. For two dollars each, they bought the Model T from the other four boys and stored it in a vacant lot adjacent to the Crosby house. George Lareida was under the impression that they planned to leave Spokane in the spring (he recalled his father giving the boys tires for the trip) but thought they changed their minds when they landed a job at the Clemmer Theater. His memory is not supported by other accounts, however, and the possibility seems unlikely, because Bing and Al had not yet figured out what to do musically in the absence of a band. They learned that at the Clemmer.

Doc Clemmer's theater, at Sprague and Lincoln, had become something of a Spokane institution in the ten years since it was built. The Clemmer was the city's second movie theater, dated only by Ray Grombacher's Liberty, which had opened four weeks earlier. A square four-story building in the neoclassical style of 1915, enviably located across from the luxurious Davenport Hotel, its ornamented off-white brick facade and pillars masked an elaborate interior. Howard S. Clemmer, a dentist turned showman, believed a theater had moral responsibilities and in 1918 persuaded Spokane County to ban *The Birth of a Nation* as "detrimental to the best ends of patriotism."[46] He was much admired for his policy of "juvenile edification" and his Saturday-morning children's hour never failed to attract less than a capacity audience of 900. He wrote and published *The Klemerklink,* a loose-leaf illustrated book that he handed out a page per week to the kids as part of the nickel admission. Doc was a character. He was concerned about redheaded boys, whom he believed bore a "cross of affliction." His Red-Head Club offered free admission and transportation to and from the theater to preteens who suffered that malady; he hired only redheaded boys as ushers. When their ranks were thinned by the war, he announced his willingness to hire redheaded girls, but that drastic step was averted when an official of the YMCA advised him of the surfeit of unemployed boys.[47]

Clemmer had little use for live entertainment, especially jazz. His impact on Bing's life was significant but entirely circumstantial: in March of 1925, just as the Musicaladers were disbanding and Bing and Al were turning to golf, he and his silent partner sold the theater to Universal Pictures. If he had not made the sale, it is almost certain that Bing and Al would have gone separate ways, with what effect on American popular music one can scarcely imagine.

Universal took over on May 1, installing R. R. (Roy) Boomer as manager and approving expenses for a new marquee, carpet, and lighting.[48] Boomer was brought in from San Francisco, where a combination of vaudeville and movies was fashionable. In Spokane he was considered, in Bing's words, "a progressive type, for stage shows were pioneer stuff then."[49] The gala May 9 reopening offered Universal's *The Phantom of the Opera* and a few live acts. Boomer had been scouting for local talent to provide entr'actes between pictures. Bing and Al heard about his inquiries and were determined to audition. But what could they do? They had no band and little confidence in themselves as a duo. Neither one suggested the obvious: a voice-and-piano team. Instead, they drafted three pals, including a boy soprano, and offered themselves as a vocal group, with Al playing piano in the pit. Boomer took them on, assigned them songs, and staged them before a Norwegian tableau.

Boomer proved to have the vision Crosby and Rinker lacked. He tired of their act and fired all the singers save one. "Why, I don't know," Al wrote half a century later. "I guess he saw something in Bing. Perhaps his singing and personality."[50] Boomer also retained Al as accompanist. In what amounted to a shotgun wedding, Bing and Al were finally forced to come up with an act on their own. This time Boomer did not assign them songs; he allowed them to choose. As much as they needed the job, Bing was nervous about accepting it. He had never before sung to paying customers on an otherwise bare stage.

For their first show, with Al in the pit, Bing walked out and delivered a reasonably assured rendition of "Red-Hot Henry Brown," a new tune they had picked up from records by the prolific Irving Kaufman and the Ray Miller Orchestra (including C-melody saxophonist Frank Trumbauer and pianist Tom Satterfield, who two years later would be their bandmates). The audience responded encouragingly, and Bing proceeded with a ballad, "Save Your Sorrow (for Tomorrow)," taken from another Ray Miller record (lyric by Buddy DeSylva, a Jolson songwriter who went on to produce *Going My Way*). The ballad relaxed him, allowing him to purr and trill his high notes, and the reception was warmer still. After two more songs, Bing left the stage, applause ringing in his ears. Boomer was satisfied and told Bing he had the job.

During the next week or so, Bing sang the same songs show after show, but he never got used to having the stage to himself. Everything about his musical drive (the polyphony of jazz) and wit (the banter of vaudeville) demanded a partner he could engage in harmony or horseplay. The situation at hand was more like the sodality meetings at which he sang "One Fleeting Hour." At parties, he and Al had often sung together: Why couldn't they do that now? They would work out a few routines, inject more pizzazz into the show. Bing was so insistent that Boomer agreed to give them a try. But they could not put the piano on the stage, as it would interfere with the projection of movies. Since the pit was shallow, almost level with the orchestra seats, Bing came down from the stage.

Until this point, Bing and Al had worked chiefly from the music of others, copying arrangements and adapting them to the instrumentation of the Musicaladers or offering a conventional recital of familiar songs. Their most fanciful performances had taken place at parties. Invariably, their audiences were dancing, drinking, or otherwise distracted. At the Clemmer, none of the usual formulas would avail. They had to devise an act. Situated with the stage at their backs and an audience out front waiting for the movie to begin, they were expected to fill some fifteen or twenty minutes. What did they perform? Al thought the numbers included "Mary Lou," "Paddlin' Madelin' Home," and "I'm Gonna Charleston Back to Charleston," but he probably confused the 1925 Clemmer engagement with one a year later at the Liberty. (The first two songs were published in the interim.) "I'm Gonna Charleston" may have figured in the Clemmer shows, though not at the beginning; a favorite of bass saxophonist Adrian Rollini, who recorded three versions that summer, the little-remembered song was cowritten by Roy Turk, among whose subsequent hits was Bing's theme, "Where the Blue of the Night Meets the Gold of the Day." Whatever they sang, they went over big. Al said Boomer told them, "You guys are great. Let's keep it this way."[51] He paid each of them thirty dollars a week.

They continued for nearly five months at the Clemmer. One of the most ornately detailed theaters in the Northwest, the place was an acoustical gem ideally suited to Bing's particular vocal projection. A blue, purple, and gray fretwork board — touched with gilt, suspended by wires, and thought to be the first of its kind in any theater — focused the sound while concealing the organ loft and its four-manual, 3,000-pipe Kimball pneumatic organ. The mammoth instrument, which could simulate the range of a forty-four-piece orchestra, was used for intermission solos, recitals, and movie scores.[52] The celebrated Jesse Crawford had played the Clemmer organ from 1915 until 1917, before moving on to Grauman's Chinese Theatre in Hollywood and the Paramount in New York. While Bing and Al were in residence, the instrument was temporarily silenced.

From where the two performers stood, in the pocket of a gently dipping auditorium, they saw a perfect dollhouse enclosure illuminated by no fewer than 1,600 incandescent lamps. Directly above the orchestra was a splendid teal dome ornamented with octagons in gold and beige against a burgundy ceiling. Designer E. W. Houghton had generously dabbed the entire structure with vivid effects and colors. The vestibuled rotunda glimmered with hidden lighting. The floor was a tiled mosaic, the wainscoting marble, the chairs in the eight balconied boxes Austrian oak upholstered in mulberry velour. The "women's retiring room" was furnished with Louis XIV pieces, blue Wilton carpet, cretonne draperies, a telephone desk, and a davenport, lit by beams from alabaster urns trimmed with ivory. Men were relegated to a basement smoking room, situated below the stage, which doubled as a dressing room for performers.

In this setting, Bing and Al gradually honed an act. Al did not have a distinctive voice. He tended to sing high, from the throat rather than from the diaphragm. But he had drive and accurate pitch, and the more the two rehearsed, the more adept they became at harmonizing. They were making it up as they went along, with few examples to follow. Quartet singing had developed out of standard barbershop blends, reaching a popular apex in the recordings of the Peerless Quartet. But the jazzy requirements of an impromptu duet left them to their own devices. The devices they knew best included the hotcha burbling of Ukelele Ike, the florid emoting of Al Jolson, the guttural attack of the blues, and the sentimental wailing of Irish tenors. The minstrel traditions allowed them to try on the masks of black and southern singing, but they were smart enough to distinguish masks from life. In life, they were a couple of young Northwestern Catholics with smooth voices and much energy who had seen very little of the world.

Bing saw no conflict between the blues and Irish tenors, nor was he hampered by a bias in one direction or the other. His key attribute as a troubadour of American song was his capacious appreciation for its diversity, his disposition to follow music wherever it led. He knew instinctively that as long as he kept in mind who he was, he could make any style his own. Al emulated his lead, blending his thin baritone against Bing's poised baritone. Soon they developed a presentation unlike any other. They were buoyant, ingenuous, youthfully appealing.

The adventurous team attempted many variations, encouraged by the generous support of the Clemmer audience, which often included old friends like Art Dussault, who came with a contingent of Gonzagans to cheer them on.[53] Bing brought his drums along once, but that didn't work. Eventually, he eliminated the traps except for a stand-up cymbal. They used kazoos on some pieces and worked up a primitive style of unison scat — a *da-de-ta da-de-ta* — that was rhythmic and novel. Tenors ruled the theater circuit in part because their high, keening voices could easily reach the balcony's last row. Bing had his megaphone but soon realized that the Clemmer's acoustics obviated its need. Besides, people wanted to see his face. The personableness that delighted Bing's friends readily translated to the stage. Bing and Al had plenty of pep, but they also had something most tyro performers lack: charm. They represented Jazz Age bravura in an unthreatening incarnation while offering contemporaries a musical style of their own. When Bing wrapped his gorgeous voice around a ballad, he made familiar lyrics sound fresh and original.

Most of their songs were not familiar. With Bailey's music shop at their disposal, they prided themselves on learning the latest numbers as soon as they arrived in town. Immediately after Gene Austin introduced (on a double-sided smash hit) "Five Foot Two, Eyes of Blue" and "Sleepy Time Gal," Bing and Al adapted and performed them. Wilbur Hindley, drama editor of the *Spokesman-Review* in the 1920s, remembered: "The team of Rinker and Crosby rapidly built up a substantial following. They were often heard at the old Clemmer Theater where they were great favorites — good looking, pleasant appearing chaps with ingratiating smiles and an original method of putting over their songs."[54] Yet for every song they used to showcase their growing skill and enterprise, they were required by management to do another to set the mood for the picture show. Bing described that type of song as a "prologue": a sea chanty for a sea movie, a cowboy song for a western, an exotic aria for a movie depicting Hindustan or Araby.[55] The boys were responsible for finding such tunes, and the exercise proved valuable to Bing, increasing his store of and respect for diverse material. In his 1941 movie *Birth of the Blues,* Bing re-created the Clemmer experience, crooning "By the Light of the Silvery Moon" with an illustrative slide projected on a screen.

The Clemmer had other live entertainment in those months, including singing and jazz piano contests with which Bing and Al had no connection. The most renowned entertainer to perform was the female impersonator Julian Eltinge, whose only appearance in a sound film was facilitated by Bing (along with that of several other faded vaudevillians he admired in his early years) in his 1940 picture, *If I Had My Way.* Still, by October Roy Boomer and Universal Pictures had decided to return to a movies-only policy. The mid-1920s were among the most successful in Hollywood history. The Jazz Age introduced a new style in picture stars; in addition to the abidingly popular Chaplin, Fairbanks, and Pickford, there was sexy Clara Bow and virtuous Colleen Moore, sleek Rudolph Valentino and scary Lon Chaney. Theater managers needed no come-ons to keep their patrons loyal and satisfied.

Once again Bing and Al were unemployed, but this time with a difference. As a Spokane reporter wrote ten months after they left town for California, "all Spokane knew 'Bing' and close behind him followed the ever-faithful 'Al.'" They were established as a team, and they had something to sell. The market in Spokane offered little promise, and they were itching to escape what Bing perceived as the smothering provincialism of the "cornfeds."[56] Bing told Charles Thompson, his authorized biographer, that he was so restless, he applied unsuccessfully for a berth as an entertainer on China-bound ships.[57] If this is true — and it seems unlikely — he must have felt sufficiently confident to part with Al and sufficiently discouraged to follow the maritime path of his ancestors. Actually, Los Angeles was the obvious destination. Al's sister lived there with her bootlegger husband. Everett Crosby was there, too, affiliated with a trucking company that carted hooch. With two siblings already situated, the newcomers were assured of temporary places to stay. Mildred had written Al that she was singing in a speakeasy and doing well. Al figured that she probably knew people who could get them started. He suggested the journey to Bing, who jumped at the idea: "Okay, let's go."[58]

Bing secured his parents' reluctant blessing. Kate had been hard on him for quitting law — her attitude was another reason to skip Spokane. But she and Harry were more equivocal than irate when Bing, who was twenty-two, announced his decision. Years later Harry said, "About the only thing I remember of those times was the day that Bing told us he and Al were going to leave home and go to California in their rickety, painted-up, joke-covered Ford. Mother and I hated to see him leave, but we didn't want to stand in the way of any possible success for him. We thought that such a move might be the beginning for him. We knew he had talent. As it turned out, it *was* the beginning for him."[59]

Al's father and stepmother were concerned because he was so young, but they held their tongues. Al had repeatedly proved himself nothing if not resourceful, and with Bing at his side he could at least count on a memorable adventure, whether or not the move actually led to anything. Al took the Model T to a mechanic for last-minute repairs, after confirming with Bing that he would pick him up the next morning, October 15. The idea of embarking on a road trip of some thousand miles in a machine as ramshackle as theirs did not seem especially perilous. The Tin Lizzy was, in Al's words, "uncomplicated but dependable."[60] It had three floor pedals (stop, low gear, and reverse), an accelerator on the steering wheel, and a crank and pull-out choke out front. The tires were narrow tubes without tread. On the canvas covering the spare a slogan was painted: EIGHT MILLION MILES AND STILL ENTHUSIASTIC.[61] Bing and Al pooled about fifty dollars each, all they had from their Clemmer savings.

Al suffered a nervous, restless night, but he was up with the dawn that wintry Thursday morning. He had decided to postpone his good-byes until he picked up Bing, since they had to pass the Rinker house on the way out of town anyway. He pulled up to Sharp Avenue at nine, only to learn from Kate that the habitual early riser was dead asleep. She told Al to go upstairs and wake him. He did, annoyed by Bing's seeming nonchalance. Bing finally came downstairs with his suitcase, and he and Al carried his drums and golf clubs to the car. As they emerged from the house, a small crowd began to congregate and quickly grew as the two young men packed everything into the backseat.

One neighborhood girl recalled the scene: "It was early in the morning and all of us kids were around. Mrs. Crosby brought out a sack lunch for the boys and when the Ford wouldn't start, Al and Bing borrowed a screwdriver from Mrs. Crosby's sewing kit to fix it."[62] After driving to retrieve Al's suitcase and say good-bye to Mr. Rinker and his wife, they made one last stop at a service station at Boone and Division, where the attendant, an old friend, provided them with a free tank of gasoline. They continued down Division, then turned west toward Seattle, 200 miles away. In a short while, they were up to speed: thirty miles per hour and still enthusiastic.

8

VAUDEVILLE

Crosby and Rinker — Two Boys and a Piano — Singing Songs Their Own Way.
— billing, Paramount-Publix (1926)[1]

It took two days to reach Seattle and another three weeks to make Los Angeles. In later years the often recounted trip was invariably dramatized as the archetypal tale of the Road to Hollywood: a plucky journey of two young men in a rickety outmoded contraption, puttering toward glory. But as they traveled, the recording industry was also taking leaps ahead that would revolutionize communications technology, preparing the way for Bing's ascendancy. Great advancements were ushered in during the very weeks they were on the road. Indeed, the recording industry's dramatic conversion from acoustical to electrical reproduction of music practically coincided with their departure from Spokane. That innovation, which dominated the industry for more than two decades (until the introduction of tape), would help bring Bing's strengths into the spotlight, leading directly to the advancement of his true instrument, the microphone.

More than any other performer, Crosby would ride the tide of technology. He dominated records, radio, and movies throughout a career that would parallel the development of those media in ways ever more suitable to emphasize his talents. Boosted by technology in the beginning, Bing eventually became its advocate and master: In the mid-1940s, he single-handedly transformed radio from a live medium into a canned, or prerecorded, one. Later, the TV industry followed suit. It was through the growth and expansion of electronic media that Bing became so familiar, so prized, so beloved a presence in American life. But the technology never diminished his natural ability to connect with an audience. Near the end of his life, when Bing hit the road for an international tour, many of his older fans were astonished to realize that they had not seen him perform live in four decades.

The year 1925 proved a watershed in the brief and shaky history of the recording business, which, like so much of the communications technocracy, traced its origins to the Wizard of Menlo Park. In 1877 Thomas Edison built a machine that engraved sound on a cylinder wrapped in tinfoil. He called it a phonograph — a neologism from the Greek for "sound writer." But the invention was barely adequate for reproducing a speaking voice, let alone music, and Edison lost interest and turned his attention to the incandescent lamp, thereby missing — as Roland Gelatt, the industry's best historian, points out — an opportunity to record such contemporaries as Jenny Lind and Franz Liszt, not to mention Buddy Bolden, the first widely recognized jazz musician. Edison's apparatus rested for nearly a decade, until Alexander Graham Bell financed and patented what he called the graphaphone, substituting waxed cardboard for tinfoil to achieve far greater clarity. The American Graphaphone Company saw the machine as primarily a Dictaphone, but it renewed the interest of Edison and others, and in 1890 the first commercial recordings were manufactured. They played two minutes, could not be reproduced, and were about as musical as a seance is conversational.

Tremendous improvements were made throughout the 1890s, including the innovation of flat discs and a lateral moving stylus, which its inventor, Emile Berliner, called a gramophone.[2] By 1902 the recently formed Victor Talking Machine Company dazzled consumers with mechanical reproductions of the voices of Caruso and Bert Williams. Yet over the next twenty-three years, the recording process remained essentially unchanged. It was acoustical and manual, and demanded of musicians and singers that they perform into mawlike horns mounted on walls. In 1906, the year Harry Crosby bought his family one of the first phonographs in Spokane, Victor recorded Caruso with an orchestra and manufactured the Victrola, a machine conceived as musical furniture for the home, not unlike a piano. At $200, the Victrola cost more than a used automobile. To be sure, phonographs that did not conceal their workings in mahogany consoles were readily available for less than thirty dollars, but Victor's hot new model for the Park Avenue set reflected a class distinction in the industry's competing systems. The well-to-do bought superior flat discs, while working-class people like the Crosbys continued to buy cylinders until they were no longer manufactured. Cylinders averaged twenty-five to thirty-five cents; discs between one and seven dollars.

John Philip Sousa initially decried "the Menace of Mechanical Music," predicting that "a marked deterioration in American music" would follow as generations of amateurs who had sung and played instruments would now presumably give way to indolent disciples of "canned music."[3] The public disagreed and eagerly purchased everything that was offered, an indiscriminate potpourri of indifferently performed popular music, classics, opera, marches, ragtime, comedy. Records were sold in appliance shops that sold phonographs and in general or grocery stores. In March 1917 Victor announced its imminent release of "the very latest thing in the development of music" — jazz, as played by a spirited, hoked-up white band from New Orleans, the Original Dixieland Jazz Band. "Livery Stable Blues" sold more than a million copies. As Europe reeled from the chaos of the Great War, Americans giddily enjoyed their new role on the world stage. The nation's new confidence resonated in jazz and in a sumptuous dance music played by large orchestras that were at once erotic and genteel. Small independent record companies like Gennett (a subsidiary of Starr Piano) and Paramount (a subsidiary of Wisconsin Chair) put an end to the monopoly enjoyed by Victor and Columbia and generated a musical boom. Between the surging record sales and Prohibition — the government's gift to jazz, guaranteeing work to numberless musicians in speakeasies throughout the land — America was spellbound by the new, raucous, undeniably homegrown music.

With an assist from F. Scott Fitzgerald's stories of swains and flappers, the era was inescapably called the Jazz Age, but it is important to remember that in those years *jazz* — construed as either an exciting or devilish dance music — had a more inclusive meaning than it later acquired. "Livery Stable Blues" was labeled "For Dancing," and even legendary innovators like King Oliver and James P. Johnson played for dancing. Everything with a beat and bluesy tonality was regarded as jazz, from the behemoth orchestras of Paul Whiteman and Vincent Lopez to the rhythm songs and ballads of Irving Berlin and George Gershwin.

Jazz and black music, not for the last time, rescued the record business in the dim deflationary year of 1920. More than 2 million phonographs had been turned out in 1919, a case of overproduction that brought Columbia to the brink of ruin; its stock sank from 65 to 1⅝. The public had grown jaded. The Victrola of 1921 was not much different from that of 1906, nor was popular music, as represented by faceless singers like Billy Murray, the Irish American tenor who recorded hundreds of ditties during the century's first three decades. Blandness in singers who specialized in making records (and had little reputation outside recording studios) was regarded as an asset by songpluggers and publishers who thought of them as little more than shills for sheet music, where the real money was. By contrast, concert performers who made records also helped sell songs, but they were primarily interested in selling themselves.

In 1920 a thirty-six-year-old vaudevillian with a loyal following in Harlem was invited to spell Sophie Tucker at a recording session. Her name was Mamie Smith, and backed by a white orchestra, she was the first African American woman to record the blues and score a major hit. The success of "Crazy Blues" opened doors for black performers, song publishers, and record-company executives. Mamie was not a true blues singer, but she set the table for many, like Bessie Smith (no relation), who were. By 1925 hundreds of blacks had recorded, and the wild, rambling diversity of American voices represented on discs enthralled listeners of Bing's generation, white and black, who found their souls in the simmering footloose rhythms. Aside from the exposure it gave him to a wider range of vocalists and styles, the primitive acoustical technology did not serve Bing, a baritone in a world of tenors, who achieved the clearest articulation when singing into the mounted morning-glory horns that predated more sophisticated microphones.

Electronic recording had been discussed for two decades, but it could not be implemented without a condenser microphone and vacuum-tube amplifier. The need for wireless communication during World War I generated experiments that led to their invention, yet at the end of the war nothing was done to extend their usefulness. Although singers like Bing depended on megaphones to enrich and enlarge their voices, record companies saw no need to change their methods until declining sales signaled the need for improved products. On Armistice Day 1920, the Unknown Warrior burial service in Westminster Abbey was transmitted electronically over telephone lines to a recording machine in another building, an achievement that encouraged further tests. But still the record companies declined to explore the possibilities — until 1924, when prototypes were built for electrical systems that expanded frequency ranges in treble and bass, captured room ambience, and heightened dynamics. Even those improvements, developed by Bell Laboratories, were resisted by the established record companies, which thought the electrical process too much like their hated rival, radio. They capitulated a year later.

The first electrical recordings were released in the spring of 1925. Many critics and musicians complained about distorted sound that lacked the acoustic method's purity. But modifications were made over the course of the year. Endorsements by Toscanini and Stokowski, as well as Sousa, who had long since become an enthusiastic and well-paid endorser of records, helped convert the skeptics. The Victor Talking Machine Company grandly designated November 2, 1925, Victor Day, to crown the blizzard of publicity ballyhoo that preceded the launch of its electric Orthophonic Victrola. Within days Victor was swamped with orders exceeding $20 million.

As noted, another innovation also helped pave Bing's way. One of the most significant corollaries of electric recording was the perfection of the microphone. In 1924 President Coolidge's address to Congress was miked for broadcast, but beyond radio and electrical records, microphones were rarely used in live performances. According to an old theatrical shibboleth, an entertainer who could not project to the balcony's last row was not ready for the big time; Jolson exemplified the leather-lunged belter of songs. With the arrival of the microphone — and instant exit of the preposterous megaphone —

a new and more intimate kind of singing for larger audiences was made possible. Technology changed music. Ironically, mechanics led to a more human and honest transaction between singers and their listeners.

Radio, which now rivaled the phonograph as the preferred mode of home entertainment, was on the verge of the first consolidation of stations. Plans were under way to create a network of local transmitters linked by telephone wires. A year later, in November 1926, the National Broadcasting Company would make its debut, followed the next year by that of the Columbia Broadcasting System. By the time Bing was ready for radio, radio was waiting for the voice made to order to showcase the closeness it could provide. Motion pictures, too, were remade by the new technology. Twenty-four hours before Victor Day, with relatively little publicity, Harry Warner — on behalf of the fledgling motion picture company Warner Bros. — bought control of Vitagraph and its research into sound on film. Talkies would engender not only the movie musical but a subtler and more intimate style of acting. Bing's naturalness would fit in perfectly.

Victor Day found Bing and Al on the last lap of their mud-splattered journey to Hollywood, contending with an increasingly wheezy engine and patched-up, withered tires. In later years they disagreed about many details of their epic three-and-a-half-week road trip, but they differed little on the salient points: they sang nonstop while driving, worked when possible at parties and roadside joints, and saved board money with an old show-business dodge — renting a single room and sneaking the second man in after dark. Their stay in Seattle, early on, was auspicious. They boarded there with a friend of Bing's from Gonzaga, Doug Dykeman, who took them to the Hotel Butler to meet Vic Meyers, one of the best-known orchestra leaders in the state of Washington. (Later he was better known as the state's lieutenant governor, elected to his surprise with help from a facetious campaign conducted by Larry Crosby, in which Meyers donned a white sheet à la Gandhi and promised to install hostesses on streetcars; after his victory, he reneged.)[4]

Jackie Souders led the Hotel Butler's band that weekend, and Meyers asked him to give the boys a chance.[5] Meyers and Souders were each well established in Washington. Bing and Al had heard their records broadcast in Spokane. Souders's recordings from that time were representative of white jazz in the provinces, with a passable rhythm section (de rigueur banjo and slap bass), clumsy instrumental soloists, and nasal tenors with small, fey voices. The fact that the singers are more outmoded than the soloists and arrangements is in large measure a consequence of Crosby's impact. Soon he would put most of those singers out of work. Astute bandleaders in 1925 could not have failed to recognize his lucid individuality. Souders agreed to let them show their stuff.

Al took his place at the piano, and Bing stood by him with a cymbal in hand. They sang in unison on the hot rhythm numbers and featured Bing on a couple of Irving Berlin ballads. The college students, who regularly packed the place on weekends, responded enthusiastically. Next to Bing's full-bodied emoting, the singing of Souders's regular vocalist, Walton McKinney, must have sounded drearily anemic. Both Souders and Meyers made competitive offers to the duo to stick around and work with their bands. Bing and Al discussed the bids that evening, but they were flush with their first triumph outside Spokane and resolved to soldier on to Los Angeles.

By Al's account they bypassed Portland, heading down the inland road through Oregon and the Siskiyou Mountains to California. Bing, however, recalled hitting Portland as well as Medford, Klamath Falls, and San Francisco. On the way, they alternated between fixing punctures and singing. Al wrote, "Bing would sing the melody and I would harmonize. The song 'Dinah' was one of our favorites and we really gave it a good workout."[6] But as they got closer to their goal, Al privately began to worry. He had never written his sister, Mildred, to tell her they were coming and did not know how she would greet them.

Driving 1,200 miles down the coast, they tried to average 200 miles a day. On cold mornings the car would not start, and they took turns with the crank. They went to a movie in Sacramento and were astonished at how much larger (2,000 seats) the theater was than the Clemmer; they marveled at the lavish Fanchon and Marco stage show, with its dancers, singers, chorus line, and emcee. "It was impossible for us to imagine, as we sat in that great big beautiful theater and watched those talented entertainers perform, that in a few months we would be up on that same stage singing our songs," Al remembered.[7] Next morning they reached the San Joaquin Valley, driving past cotton fields and orange groves as the temperature climbed and then heading on to Fresno, Stockton, and Bakersfield, where a gas jockey warned them it was ninety miles to Los Angeles, mostly mountainous, and their jalopy might not make it. But what choice did they have? They switched into low gear and skulked the steep mountain road out of Bakersfield.

At the top of Wheeler Ridge, the flivver either blew and was abandoned (Bing)[8] or held up for the three hours it took to get to the outskirts of Los Angeles (Al: "We made it, but just barely"),[9] where they searched for Sunset Boulevard. They knew Mildred lived a couple of blocks off the thoroughfare, at 1307 North Coronado. It was Saturday afternoon, November 7, when they walked up to her door and nervously knocked. A short, heavyset woman answered and squinted at them for an uncertain moment until Al said, "Don't you know me? I'm your brother Alt." They had not seen each other in nearly three years. "[Mildred] let out a holler and put her arms around me. She was so surprised she couldn't believe it was me."[10] Al introduced Bing while noting silently the weight she had gained. They described their trip and their ambitions, and she offered them a spare bedroom, suggesting that they store Bing's drums in the cellar (where they remained until he sold them a few weeks later). As she prepared lunch, Mildred asked Al about their father and his new wife, Elsa. Al reassured her of their happiness and said that Elsa was taking good care of their brothers. Mildred, in turn, told him about her husband, Benny, who was doing well in the bootleg business. As for herself, she was singing at a speak near Hollywood operated by a friend of hers, Jane Jones. After describing the high-class customers and good tips, she invited them to tag along.

At twilight Mildred, whom Bing instantly took to calling Millie, made cocktails and asked them to sing. In a flash they were at the piano. After a couple of tunes, she walked over and hugged and kissed each of them. "You guys are great," she said. "You should have no trouble getting something going for yourselves."[11] After another drink they asked her to sing. Millie sat at the piano and sang Irving Berlin's "Remember" and Nora Bayes's old hit "Just Like a Gypsy," with, Al recalled, "the same feeling and style which later on would make her a star. I could see that Bing was really impressed, and I was very proud of my sister." Benny Stafford returned in time for dinner

Bing Crosby graduated from Gonzaga High School with a diploma in classical studies in 1920.
Mark Scrimger Collection

Bing practicing his
swing at age four.
*Mark Scrimger
Collection*

Bing's mother, the for-
mer Kate Harrigan,
during the years in
Tacoma.
*Mark Scrimger
Collection*

The infant Bing in Tacoma, with his aunt (Kate's sister, Annie Walsh) on the steps of the Crosbys' J Street home. *Mark Scrimger Collection*

Looking sporty at the new Sinto Avenue house in Spokane, Bing is hugged by his sister Mary Rose. *Mark Scrimger Collection*

Six of the Crosbys on Sinto Avenue: left to right, Catherine, Kate (mother), Bing, Mary Rose, Harry (father), Ted. *Mark Scrimger Collection*

The two-story clapboard house at 508 East Sharp Avenue, one block north of Gonzaga University and St. Aloysius Church.
Mark Scrimger Collection

Gonzaga's main buildings, with the steeples of St. Aloysius to the right.
Bing Crosby Collection, Foley Center, Gonzaga University

Bing, circled, was the youngest in his high school class and looked it.
Bing Crosby Collection, Foley Center, Gonzaga University

With Kate's encouragement, Bing won seven swimming medals, including first place in diving and second place in the speed events. He excelled at baseball, first at third base, then center field, and fantasized about playing professionally.
Mark Scrimger Collection

At a gathering in the Gonzaga University gym in 1919, Bing can be seen near the bottom, over the word *Bazaar*.
Bing Crosby Collection, Foley Center, Gonzaga University

Bing learned to swim the hard way, among discarded logs at McGoldrick's lumber mill on the northern bank of the Spokane River.
Mark Scrimger Collection

Mike Pecarovitch (center) was student council president and frequently shared the stage with Bing (right); by the 1990s Gonzaga students could stroll through Pecarovitch Field and study at Crosby Library.
Bing Crosby Collection, Foley Center, Gonzaga University

Frank Corkery, Bing's boyhood friend and fellow glee club member, later became president of Gonzaga University.
Bing Crosby Collection, Foley Center, Gonzaga University

The Musicaladers posed in a publicity shot for their best and longest engagement, at Lareida's Dance Pavilion (below), originally an auto showroom. Left to right in striped blazers: Bob Pritchard, Clare Pritchard, Bing; in dark suits, Al Rinker, Miles Rinker.
Mark Scrimger Collection

and then drove them to Jane Jones's speakeasy in the Hollywood Hills.[12] The boys liked Benny, thought him "a regular guy."

The speakeasy, which Bing remembered as The Swede's, was a converted private house set back from the road and surrounded by a fence. When the lookout saw Mildred, he let them into a large, crowded room with tables and bar and a small platform for the piano and singer. The place, frequented by movie people, offered working girls as well as booze and song. When the spirit moved her, the proprietress would sing a number or two. Red Norvo, who knew Jane Jones after Prohibition, when he was married to Mildred and living in New York, described her as a large woman with a brassy style. Customers preferred what he called "cooing types," like Mildred or Tommy Lyman, a peripatetic singer-pianist who played chic clubs in New York and Europe and liked to stop by Jane's when he passed through town.[13] But it was Millie who grabbed the audience with her repertoire of melodramatic warhorses such as "Ships That Never Came In." Large tips — her only salary — always flowed like wine.

In the years to come, Millie would recall Bing's really gauging the spirit of the room that night and many that followed, shouting, "Sing it again!" or "Give the lady a twenty!"[14] When customers requested favorites, she dragged a bar stool over to where they sat. Bing was amazed when actor Eugene Pallette put a "Benjy" on her for two choruses of "Oh Daddy."[15] He liked to tell the story of the evening when he and Al listened to Millie until closing. When the three arrived home, they slumped in the living room and talked until she announced that she was going to bed. Then, rising to her feet, she reached under her dress and pulled down her bloomers. A shower of twenty-dollar bills, dozens, hit the floor, covering her small feet.

On his first evening in Hollywood, however, Bing may have been too smashed to notice anything. Benny Stafford kept buying rounds, and Bing downed them all. By the time the foursome left, at two, Bing had rubber legs. During the next few years, he would develop a reputation as a lush, but when genuine stardom beckoned, his talent for nursing one drink or forgoing a cocktail at all convinced many that he was never a true alcoholic. "There has been a lot of talk about Bing being a heavy drinker when he was young," Al observed. "Every once in a while when I worked with him he would go on a little binge, but he was not a steady drinker."[16]

The next evening Bing and Al drove to the Cocoanut Grove at the Ambassador Hotel to see their former colleague from the Musicaladers, Jimmy Heaton, who was playing trumpet in Ray West's orchestra. Jimmy was delighted to see them, and as the next day, Monday, was musicians' night off, he suggested an outing. Jimmy drove his friends down to San Diego, where they stopped to visit his cousins (the Carr brothers, who had a band), then continued across the border to Tijuana, where Al and Bing were shocked by the aggressive whores who tried unsuccessfully to lure them into their shacks. On the way back they stopped at Ryan Airfield near San Diego, where Lindbergh's *Spirit of St. Louis* was assembled a year later. For three dollars, Bing and Al took a ride in the rear open cockpit of a plane, circling over the ocean. With the wind blowing in their faces, they were scared to death and held on with white-knuckled grips. Al recalled, "When we landed we couldn't get out of that old Jenny fast enough."[17] For Bing, the flight had long-lasting repercussions. He would avoid planes whenever possible for most of his life, preferring train travel or ocean liners. He was uneasy about heights, and in hotels reserved rooms on the lower floors.

Bing and Al continued to live with Millie for a week or so, and she took them under her wing, making calls on their behalf and introducing them to her show-business friends. Mildred Bailey would one day be recognized as one of the first of the great women jazz singers, the key transitional figure between Ethel Waters and Bessie Smith and band singers like Billie Holiday and Ella Fitzgerald. Her small, light voice inclined to a whirring vibrato when she sang high notes, and her time and enunciation were exemplary. She was bedeviled, however, by a fierce temper, enormous pride, and a lonely soul that she attempted to soothe with food and compulsive cooking. She did not smoke or drink. Al thought she used the great dishes she prepared and her pets — a fleet of dachshunds — as a substitute for children. As sentimental as she was high-strung, she was an easy touch and a formidable enemy. Like many musicians, trombonist Milt Bernhart assumed that she was black when he heard her on the classic records she made with Teddy Wilson.[18] When he mentioned that to Red Norvo long after her death, Red chuckled and told him a story that he thought summed her up.

In the 1930s, after Mildred became a star on radio and a headliner with Paul Whiteman's orchestra, a rival singer began spreading rumors that she was black, and a Hearst columnist picked up the story. Whiteman didn't care in the least — he'd have hired black musicians if his management hadn't talked him out of it. But Mildred was incensed. By this time, she and Red were married and traveling together as members of Whiteman's band. One day she asked Paul if he was still friendly with William Randolph Hearst, whom the band-leader had known during his salad days in San Francisco. Paul said he was. Hearing this, she demanded that Whiteman phone Hearst and have the columnist fired. Whiteman complied, as did Hearst. A couple of years later, as Millie and Red emerged from a theater, a man in a threadbare overcoat walked over and asked, "Miss Bailey?" The former columnist apologized for what he had written, conceding that he deserved to lose his job, and turned to go. Mildred, convulsed with tears, asked his name and how she could reach him, then went to Whiteman and got him rehired.

She had always been fond of Bing, and despite a misunderstanding or two, they would remain loyal to each other, the one invariably nam-ing the other as his or her favorite singer. Bing credited Millie with the start of his career and reciprocated in full, engineering the White-man job that took her to the big time. In 1951 he assumed all her medical costs when she became fatally ill. Indeed, Millie got along better with the easygoing Bing, who liked a good time and shared her advanced and expansive musical tastes, than with her brother, who thought her "a little too barrelhouse."[19] Al, who forgot that Bing had heard Mildred in Spokane, was at once proud and a little miffed about the bond between the two. "I guess he hadn't expected to find that I had a sister with so much humor and who was so hip," he wrote. To Bing, she was *"mucho mujer,* a genuine artist, with a heart as big as the Yankee Stadium, and a gal who really loved to laugh it up."[20] He admired her jazzy slang (a dull town was "tiredsville"), which was new to him. Clearly, the role she played in launching their careers was not limited to providing introductions and arranging auditions.

Bing understood Millie's rare abilities as a singer, her unaffected-ness, understatement, and versatility. And she saw in him the real thing, an antidote to the prissy aesthetes who had no swing or feeling for the blues. Bing, having won prizes in elocution, admired her impeccable diction; she encouraged his innate affinity for focusing on the language of a song, its meaning, the special story it told. She played records for him and Al, including Ethel Waters, Bessie Smith, and her pal Tommy Lyman, whose "Montmartre Rose" — the maudlin account of a Parisian courtesan with "a true heart of gold" — she played constantly.[21] She listened to it so often that more than half a century later, Al could recite the lyric:

> *And each tear is a token*
> *Of some heart that's broken*
> *In your garden, my Montmartre Rose.*[22]

More significantly, it appears to have been Millie who first told Bing of a young man in Chicago whom he had to hear if he was going to be a serious singer: Louis Armstrong. What makes this advice particularly fascinating is that as of November 1925, Armstrong had yet to record as a vocalist (beyond a scat break at the end of a Fletcher Henderson side) and Mildred had yet to travel to Chicago or New York to hear him. She was familiar with Louis's trumpet playing from his records with Henderson and Bessie Smith and may have advised Bing to study his instrumental work, which had musicians nationwide buzzing. Millie told Norvo that she advised Bing of Armstrong's genius for inventing melody; possibly she was referring to his powers as a trumpeter. But Norvo thought she was speaking of his singing. Armstrong often sang at jam sessions, so the advance word in the jazz grapevine may have been enough to inspire Mildred's praise. Barry Ulanov said of his old friend, "Mildred was two things: very hip and very much a gossip. . . . She'd pick up on anything and if anyone would have known about Louis she would have known."[23] Whatever the circumstances, Bing soon put Louis on a pedestal; their association would prove momentous musically, professionally, and — in advancing integration in show business — societally.

During Bing and Al's first few days in California, nothing came of Mildred's efforts on behalf of her lodgers. Bing hooked up with his brother Everett, who was selling trucks as a front for moving liquor. Ev also wanted to help the boys. What happened next is unclear.

According to Bing, Mildred arranged an audition with Mike Lyman, the brother of bandleader Abe Lyman and the proprietor of the Tent Cafe.[24] Bing rented a tux and borrowed the accessories from Everett. Early accounts suggest that they did not get the job, although Bing would later claim that they worked the Tent Cafe as long as three weeks. Al would deny that he and Bing ever played the Tent Cafe; but he also disputed another audition of which there is no doubt. This one was arranged by Ev at the Cafe Lafayette. Harry Owens, who would play an important role in Bing's career (as the composer of "Sweet Leilani"), led the band at the Lafayette, and Ev was a frequent customer. Having fared poorly with a "big, brassy and rhythmic" orchestra, Owens fired his expensive star soloists and switched to "the sweet 'corn' of ballads and violins."[25] Success followed, and Everett pressed Owens to audition the boys. Owens tried to dissuade Ev from encouraging his kid brother in a career as unstable as show business, but Ev insisted that the kid had his mind set.

Owens agreed to the tryout, and Bing and Al showed up in time to sit through an hourlong rehearsal. Then they took the stand, Al at the piano, Bing with a small cymbal in his hand. Before they completed their first number, the orchestra musicians, who had been filing out for their break, stopped and came back to applaud the finish. "Bing had a terrific beat," Owens recalled, "but the voice was the thing."[26] He scheduled them for the show on the following Tuesday; their opening went over well, but afterward Owens told them that he lacked the budget to offer a regular job. By his own subsequent reckoning, Owens "missed the boat" and allowed the duo to sail away into Paul Whiteman's orchestra. Yet he recalled the young Bing with affection: "What a sweet guy he was and so sincerely grateful."[27] In the last days of 1925, Bing told a reporter that he and Al got their start in Los Angeles at the Lafayette.

Their real start, however, came when Mildred heard about open auditions for Fanchon and Marco, a sister-and-brother team famous in vaudeville as dancers, now producing traveling vaudeville units for Loew's California circuit. Mildred drove the boys to the audition at the Boulevard Theater and ordered them to relax: "You're good and I know they'll like you."[28] Fanchon, Marco, and their brother, Rube Wolf, sat quietly in the orchestra seats, watching the young performers. When their turn came, Bing and Al did a few rhythm songs

("China Boy," "San," and "Copenhagen"), to which Bing added some business on kazoo, and two comical numbers ("Paddlin' Madelin' Home" and "Five Foot Two, Eyes of Blue"). They were hired at seventy-five dollars each per week for a thirteen-week tour in the new revue, *The Syncopation Idea.* Rehearsals began immediately at the Boulevard. They found themselves on a bill with jugglers, a dog act, a dance team, and a sixteen-girl high-kicking chorus line. The show opened on December 7, a month to the day since their arrival in Los Angeles.

Like most new acts that clicked from the first, Bing and Al evoked proven vaudeville traditions while pushing the boundaries. Not the least of their assets was the same sort of youthful jazz-inflected exuberance and worry-free winsomeness that characterized their loose harmonizations. They were a handsome team, Al with his wavy black hair and dark eyes and Bing with his lighter color and piercing baby blues. Their easy manner and horseplay disarmed audiences dazzled by the charge of their rhythm numbers and the beauty of Bing's sonorous baritone on ballads. They presented themselves as cutups no less than singers and enjoyed themselves tremendously onstage. Vaudeville was hard, but fun. Bing saved the shirt he wore during the run of the revue. It had a false front and buttoned in the back for speedier changing.

Bing may have been a jazz hound, but he had learned the value of sentiment, not only from the great tenors of his youth but from a famous vaudeville team whose popularity was as fleeting as theatrical memory. In 1976 Bing remarked, "The ballads I sang a lot like Joe Schenck of Van and Schenck. I imitated him. I imitated McCormack, Jolson. I took a lot from Jolson. . . . We sang a lot of scat. What Ella Fitzgerald does now, only she does it about three hundred times better, and I think Cleo Laine does a lot of it, Mel Tormé. That's what we were doing. We would sing a chorus straight and sing scat the next chorus and then go back to the lyric for the climax or something. And we'd sing a lot of comedy songs too. We lifted a lot of comedy from Van and Schenck and all the other acts that played Spokane at the Pantages Theater."[29] The report in *Variety* on Whiteman's 1926 signing of Bing and Al describes them as "youths who have been doing a Van and Schenck type of act in picture houses."[30]

Gus Van and Joe Schenck were the best-known tenor-baritone team in vaudeville, having starred for several seasons in the *Ziegfeld*

Follies. They achieved particular success in a minstrel sequence singing Berlin's "Mandy" (revived by Crosby in the 1954 *White Christmas*). Van was a dark, rumpled man who (Brooklyn-born, like his partner) favored southern speech affectations but used his deep baritone to master other dialects as well; *Variety* reported that he could do "Hebe, Irish, Cockney, Wop, Dutch, and Coon."[31] He also harmonized with and anchored Schenck's tenor. With his pale eyes, round face, and sweet voice, Schenck brought an Irish lilt to the day's sentimental songs. Like Rinker, he worked from the piano. Like Crosby and Rinker, Van and Schenck imparted the contagious rapport of old pals from the same neighborhood.

In their filmed appearances, performing songs like "Nobody But Me" and "He's That Kind of Pal," Van and Schenck exhibit surprisingly similar harmonies to those of Rinker and Crosby. And yet Bing's fascination with solo tenors like Schenck or Skin Young (Whiteman's high-pitched singer-violinist) can hardly be detected in even his earliest recordings. One thing Bing and Al did not learn from Van and Schenck was scat. Nor is it likely they did much of it before the spring 1926 release of Louis Armstrong's startling "Heebie Jeebies" — the first widely noted instance on records of an old New Orleans vocal style, which substitutes nonsense syllables for words.

By that time, Crosby and Rinker had made the papers. On New Year's Day 1926 the *Spokane Daily Chronicle* headlined the first in a series of bulletins, LOS ANGELES CAPTURED BY SPOKANE PAIR; RINKER, CROSBY MAKE THEATRICAL HIT.[32] The story told of the bumpy trip two months earlier, the discarding of the "delapidated flivver," the audition for Fanchon and Marco, the success of their singing and "humorous comedy sketch," and a purported contract (never realized) that promised to launch them on the big-time Orpheum circuit. The article closed with references to the Crosby and Rinker families and to Roy R. Boomer of the Clemmer Theater, who had brought the pair to "the attention of the theater-going public." After a month in Los Angeles at the Boulevard and Loew's State, the Fanchon and Marco unit went on tour, opening in the nearby suburb of Glendale and then making brief stops on a western route that took in Pasadena, Pomona, and Riverside. This was followed by full weeks at theaters along a triangular route that went south to San Diego, north to Long Beach, and west to Santa Ana and finally San Bernardino, where they played three days before returning to Los Angeles for another week at the Boulevard.

They were no longer alone, on- or offstage. A week after Bing and Al auditioned, Fanchon and Marco held another audition at Loew's State, where they paired two attractive female dancers, Bobby Thompson and Doreen Wilde, who arrived separately but knew each other from previous shows. Doreen was a few years younger than Bing but was far better traveled. As a young girl in El Monte, a small town east of Los Angeles, she studied ballet with Ernest Belcher (father of dancers Lina Basquette and Marge Champion) and Spanish dancing with Eduardo Cansino (father of Rita Hayworth), among others. She was appearing in specialty acts in high-priced nightclubs by the age of seventeen. She toured with the Duncan Sisters, Ken Murray, and Jimmy Durante ("quite young, very ugly, played a wicked piano"), worked from Hawaii to New York, and received a hundred-dollar tip from Al Capone and free tap lessons from Bill Robinson. ("He taught me everything I ever knew about tap," Doreen recalled.) She was dismayed to find that her mentor could not enter a restaurant in her company. Yet thanks to Robinson and another black dance legend, Peg Leg Johnson, with whom she toured, Doreen developed a style that combined tap, ballet, and contortionist body twisting featured in her eye-opening publicity photos. Doreen had almond eyes, a wide mouth, and black hair bobbed in the manner of Louise Brooks.[33]

Fanchon recognized in her a spry youthfulness comparable to that of Crosby and Rinker, and he sought a partner for her. By happy coincidence, he chose Bobby Thompson, whom Doreen had met touring in the first mainland production to play Hawaii. Bobby was a few years older; she could sing as well as dance; and she was blond and beautiful — the perfect complement to Doreen. Fanchon asked them to work up a number with a couple of boys who were just getting started but were "really good."[34]

"She brought two boys out," Doreen recalled. "Al Rinker was tall and thin with curly black hair and played a piano like you've never heard before. Bing was a character. He was sort of short and stubby and he had a special way of singing. They were very cute. We liked them right away and they liked us."[35] During rehearsals they devised a routine in which Doreen danced as Bing sang "Mary Lou," a brand-new song by an unlikely coalition of bandleader Abe Lyman, pianist J. Russel Robinson (formerly of the Original Dixieland Jazz Band), and filmmaker George Waggner (best remembered as director of *The Wolf Man*). Bing's performance of the song went over so well, however, that they cut the dance. "Mary Lou" was a constant in the boys' act that year. It was arguably the first of Bing's signature songs, though he did not record it until 1976, when he celebrated his demicentennial at London's Palladium. On that occasion, he said, "Fifty years ago I stepped on the stage of a little neighborhood theater in West Los Angeles [always pronounced by Bing with a hard *g*]. And my big ballad that afternoon was a plaintive little plea. . . ."[36]

In the course of doing a grueling four shows a day, five on weekends, Bing, Al, Doreen, and Bobby grew close. At first the relationships were platonic, "just like brothers and sisters." They boarded in the same hotels and on one occasion got bounced during a Shriners' convention when the foursome was caught sleeping in the same bed ("the only place we could get," Doreen would recall). Soon they came up with a quartet number — one that stayed in the show: "Before the ensemble came out for the finale, why Bing and Al and I came out and Bobby and I did the Charleston and they banged up the piano and Bing hum-drummed. He loved to do that — just snap his fingers and tap his feet. He was a doll." One incident that gave them something to laugh about concerned Doreen's specialty dress, which had long sleeves with underarm slits, "so you could do your walkovers and lift up your arms."[37] While visiting her dressing room during a show, Doreen's mother noticed the slits and helpfully sewed them up. After making a costume change and walking onstage, Doreen realized that she could not do her number and backed off.

By now Bing was beginning to enjoy the showbiz life a little too eagerly: the high-kickers in the chorus line, the contraband booze, the gambling joints on both sides of the border. He could hardly believe his luck, singing for good money without a worry in the world. Away from the Jesuits and his mother for the first time in his life, he inhaled as much life as his lungs could handle. "For in that youth of mine," confessed Augustine, apparently in a similar mood, "I was on fire to take my fill of hell."[38] Bing was a long way from home, and he wanted to keep it that way. On their evening off, when the troupe arrived at the Hotel Santa Ana, Bing wrote a chatty letter to a friend in Spokane, Dirk Crabbe, using Mildred's home as the return address.

Sunday

Dear Dirk—;

How's everything and have you watered any showcases* of late? Received a letter from Walter the other day and he tells me that you and the little Anderson girl are quite thick. I expect you will be pulling off that marrying business before long. Good groceries at their hut anyhow so you're not so dumb at that.

We came in here from Long Beach yesterday and this is a pretty little town of about 75,000 souls. Long Beach is the niftiest town I was ever in. Swell golf courses, good bathing and beauteous gals. I was indeed sorry to leave. We play San Bernardino and then go into L.A. for a week before going to Frisco, Oakland etc which territory will consume about 10 weeks.

Received a copy of the Chronicle containing a clipping relating to our work. I expect a number of the cornfeds up there thought it was applesauce, but it is all quite true. We have been very fortunate and are situated now in an envious position which should make us some real dough. At any rate I am sufficiently satisfied with this locality to stay here as long as I'm getting groceries and a flop and if I ever return to Spokane it will be merely for a visit. People up there have no conception of the opportunities presented down here, both commercial and recreational. Long Beach has only 100,000 people but it makes Spokane look like Tekoa. Of course the larger towns are even more wonderful.

I have seen Hazlett Smith several times at the Ambassador. The next time I am in L.A. we're going to get together and do things. He certainly plays classy looking twists.

While in San Diego I ran into Pete and Ed Smith (Kappa Sig from U.SC.) and of course we must go to Tia Juana and get stiff. Am enclosing a portrait taken in the Holy City. We had just come from the Foreign Club where I won some dough. Hence the happy grin. While

---

*"Watered any showcases" refers to the ritual of peeing in the flowers after a night out drinking; the *Chronicle* clipping is the January 1, 1926, article previously cited; *envious* was used synonymously for *enviable* in those days; the Ambassador Hotel housed the Cocoanut Grove; "classy looking twists" refers to women; the Foreign Club was the largest gambling house in Tia Juana (now Tijuana); Jay is Jay Eslick, a San Diego–based drummer and booking agent from Spokane and longtime drinking buddy of Bing's; Ray Johnson led a band.

down there in San Diego we stayed with Jay at the Beach and we didn't miss a thing.

Was quite surprised to learn that Wink and Alice are still clubby and that Betty and Ray Johnson are likewise afflicted. Understand that the Band might go to Frisco in which visit I shall probably see them there. I hope so.

There are certainly plenty of filthy bands around L.A. Tone don't mean a thing. Rythm [sic] and heat are the only requisites together with novel arrangements. There are so dam [sic] many hot sax-men down here that it isn't even peculiar. All the good men make plenty dough. Anywhere from 85 to 150 per week and the cafe jobs are a snap.

Well Dirk I fear this letter is getting a bit lengthy and tiresome so will cease. Drop me a line soon and give me all the dirt on the boys & girls. Say hello to the gang.

Your friend
Bing.[39]

The fledgling entertainer did not entirely leave the Jesuits behind with the cornfeds. "He was always drunk," Doreen said. "After every show at night he just got himself plastered, yet he would never miss mass. I don't know how he even made the shows, but he was up to go to church every Sunday morning. It was a riot." As ever, he was loquacious: "When Bing talked he used words that made you feel like an idiot. Even an intelligent person would feel like an idiot because he used words that were not in the dictionary, but they sounded good." Most of all he was funny — "funny to talk to, funny when he ate."[40]

For a brief spell, Bing and Doreen were romantically involved, but Bobby was the one he fell for, the first in a line of sweet-faced, sharp, showbiz troupers with whom he was smitten. To Al, who took up with a brunette in the chorus line ("16 Lightning Flashes — Fanchon's Own Steppers"), Bing's romances were casual and all too typical of show-business relationships. But according to Doreen, who met her own true love on the vaudeville circuit, Bing and Bobby ("the most fantastic couple") were quite serious. "Very much in love. They really were," she said. "They were going to get married in Tia Juana, but her mother said she wasn't going to let her get tied up with a poor singer, so they separated."[41]

On returning to Los Angeles in early February, Bing and Al bought a secondhand Dodge to continue the tour and squire their girls. The second lap of *The Syncopation Idea* brought them to San Francisco with stopovers in Oakland and Sacramento. The stay in the Bay Area precipitated Bing's long friendship with the Hearst family. A young stage-door Johnny named Bill called on Doreen at Loew's Warfield, where they played a highly successful week in a show that also featured the new Garbo film *(The Torrent)*, comedy shorts, and selections from *Carmen*. Doreen demurred, complaining that she was too tired to go out after five shows a day, and suggested he call on her during the revue's next tour of San Francisco. She was unaware that Bill, a Berkeley student, was William Randolph Hearst's son and a Crosby-Rinker fan.

Of his first encounter with Bing, William Hearst Jr. said, "He was very gentle and unprepossessing — not pushy at all. You'd never know he was a show person — always smiling and grinning and very easy to get along with."[42] Bill invited Bing and Al to a party at his father's San Simeon estate. The boys asked Doreen, Bobby, and another dancer to go with them. They were put up in cottages for three days, visiting the main house only at dinner (some twenty-five guests were catered to). They saw Marion Davies once, during an early-morning swim. She waved.

All this a mere thirteen weeks after they pulled out of Spokane.

Upon finishing in Sacramento and returning to Los Angeles, Bing and Al learned they would not be required for the next Fanchon and Marco tour, unlike Bobby and Doreen, who went directly into rehearsal. They found themselves, to use the show-business euphemism, at liberty. Having saved some money, they took an apartment in the San Fernando Valley and scoured the trade papers for work. They were now experienced vaudevillians and didn't need Mildred or anyone else to tell them how to find gigs. A few weeks later they learned that *Will Morrissey's Music Hall Revue* was casting at the Majestic Theater; they auditioned and were hired at the same price as before, seventy-five dollars each. Morrissey's shows were coproduced by Arthur Freed, an erstwhile vaudeville performer who, as a producer in the 1940s and 1950s, would redefine the movie musical at MGM. In 1926 he was already a successful songwriter with access to financial backing.

According to Bing, the producers rechristened the Majestic the Orange Grove Theater for the duration of the show, "thinking that tag would give it more verve."[43] The company rehearsed for weeks, but the ill-fated presentation was forced to open a day late, on April 30; the costumes had not arrived on time.[44]

Bing and Al were not initially featured. Freed remembered, "We loved Bing, but didn't know what to do with him because the show was already running. So we put him in the pit to sing between acts and he went over so big that we had trouble raising the curtain for the second act!"[45] In truth, Bing and Al worked on an elevated stand in the pit for four months until the revue hit San Diego. The show's chief attractions were Midge Miller, Morrissey's wife; Eddie Borden, a sketch comedian who parodied Aimee Semple McPherson and others; singer Lee Kent; comedian Eddie Lambert; an adagio team; and a chorus line. Those were the acts expected to entice customers. Bing and Al were gravy. Yet night after night, the audiences — rich with important Hollywood movers and shakers — responded mostly to Two Boys and a Piano, demanding encores that stopped the show.

Bing began to meet some of the brightest talents of the day. During the first month of Morrissey's revue, the English musical *Charlot's Revue* opened at Hollywood's El Capitan Theater, fresh from a triumphant run in New York. It introduced America to three established stars of the British stage: Beatrice Lillie, Gertrude Lawrence, and Jack Buchanan. Morrissey, who was friendly with producer André Charlot, arranged for Bing and Al to see a Wednesday matinee; they were bowled over by the show's sophistication, fast pace, and love of language revealed in extended comic skits. One night after the curtain fell, Morrissey invited them to accompany him to a party Charlot was giving for his headliners. They drove to a house in the Hollywood Hills and, in Al's words, "tried to play it cool," sipping Mumm Extra Dry champagne and meeting the stars.[46] Late that evening Charlot's pianist sat down at the Steinway, and Lillie cracked everyone up with her double entendres and mock scowls in material such as "Susannah's Squeaking Shoes," followed by Lawrence with a signature number ("I Don't Know") and a Noël Coward ballad. Buchanan did a medley from the show. Morrissey, by this time feeling no pain, rose and asked if everyone would like to hear a few songs by the young men in *his* show. "We were full of champagne and ready," Al recalled.[47] He went to the piano as Bing pulled out his pocket cymbal, and they dashed through "When the Red, Red Robin Comes

Bob, Bob, Bobbin' Along." Asked for a second number, Al suggested the Tommy Lyman number Mildred always played, "Montmartre Rose." Bing agreed and ladled his best syrup on the plight of that sorrowful *fille de joie,* his high notes receiving full attention and much applause, notably from the three English stars, who rushed to him with compliments. It was a heady moment: the beginning of his ascendancy as Hollywood's own crooner. Lillie and Buchanan later worked with him, but Bing never recorded "Montmartre Rose."

At another party, Bing met a young musician who, after fitful encounters over a period of more than twenty years, became one of his closest friends, Phil Harris. "I was working a place called Edgewater Beach Club, one of the first of the beach clubs, with Henry Halstead, who had a pretty big band on the coast," Harris recalled. "Bing came in for just one night with a private party and we kind of hit it off because I was playing drums then and he played that cymbal. He was doing comedy songs, something like — I used to kid him about it later — 'Aphrodite, where'd you leave your nightie last night' or something. We hit it off pretty good."[48] He went to see Crosby and Rinker in Morrissey's show, which he characterized as an "Olsen and Johnson kind of thing," referring to the vaudeville team known for shameless hokum and lunatic jokes.[49] Phil was most impressed by Bing's timing: "He was singing those rhythm tunes pretty good — I don't remember him doing any ballads. Those things were rolling."[50]

But Morrissey was having trouble making ends meet. At one performance he informed the audience that the show could not continue because Freed had reneged on payments. In the audience was the agent and future producer Edward Small, who offered to underwrite the cost of completing the performance. Morrissey had other troubles, however, including drinking heavily and bouncing the cast's checks. Everyone was relieved when the show went on tour. But before the company pulled out of Los Angeles, Morrissey arranged for himself and several members of his cast to appear at an extravagant benefit for the American Legion at the Olympic Auditorium. Bing and Al found themselves on a once-in-a-lifetime bill of some thirty acts, among them Eddie Cantor, Tom Mix, Fanny Brice, Pola Negri, Jackie Coogan, and one of Bing's perennial idols, Charlie Chaplin.

One admirer who phoned their apartment was Jack Partington, a producer of stage shows for two key theaters in the Paramount-Publix chain: the new Metropolitan in Los Angeles and the Granada in San Francisco. Bing was out on the golf course, so Al went alone to see Partington, an amicable man who got right down to business. He liked the act and wanted to sign them for his two theaters. Al initially tried to act casual, but when Partington offered them $300 a week, twice what they were earning with Morrissey, he quickly accepted. Bing could hardly believe it when he heard the news that evening. The next morning they drove to Partington's office and signed a two-month contract that was to take effect after they fulfilled their commitment to Morrissey.

When the Morrissey revue opened in San Diego, the duo was finally raised from the pit to a platform that extended beyond the stage. The local paper raved about their up-to-date selection of "red-hot mama songs" and credited them with "stealing the show from those billed as stars." It described Bing and Al as "two young men whom the audience . . . wanted to take home and use for permanent amusement."[51] Some women who could not take them home made themselves available backstage, but these admirers were not numerous enough to keep the show in the black, and after the company made the jump from four days in San Diego to a full month in San Francisco, empty seats indicated greater trouble ahead.

The situation got worse after Bing took the opportunity to resume his friendship with Bill Hearst, who insisted on taking the entire cast, not least the chorus girls, to the campus at Berkeley. Hearst's frat brothers provided a washtub filled with pure gin, an ice block, and a decorative orange that was supposed to camouflage the liquid as punch. Plastered along with the rest of the performers, Bing pulled a Bea Lillie, singing his repertoire of risqué songs, including "Where'd Ya Stay Last Night," the Aphrodite/nightie number that had so amused Phil Harris. "Our show bordered on the — shall we say outré?" Bing later admitted,[52] but he denied that the Hearst party was the orgy implied by campus officials, who suspended a few students and prohibited the rest from attending Morrissey's midnight shows, thus hastening its demise. Bing felt guilty about the blow to Morrissey, perhaps more than he would have had he not signed the impending deal with Partington. But Berkeley's entire student body could not have saved the show. In September the company traveled to Santa Barbara and folded within a week.[53]

*   *   *

Partington revised the team's contract to encompass a two-month obligation, between September 18 and November 19, beginning and ending in San Francisco. Bing and Al had a week to kill before the commitment began, and when they read in the paper that Paul Whiteman and His Orchestra, on whose records they had teethed, were arriving by rail to play a month at Grauman's Million Dollar Theater, they decided to join the welcoming throng. The band, recently returned from Europe, was at the peak of its popularity. Al recalled that as they approached the station early in the morning, he and Bing "were more than excited."[54] They watched in awe as such celebrated musicians as trumpeter Henry Busse and tiny banjoist Mike Pingitore stepped onto the platform, followed by the great man himself — oversize in everything but his razor-thin mustache. "We stood watching until they all got off," Al wrote, "then drove away knowing that we had seen the most famous band in the world, in the flesh."

Whiteman opened the next day, September 16, and Bing and Al were there when the curtain rose, revealing some thirty musicians in blue-and-gray uniforms. The maestro bowed and lifted the baton, and, in Al's words, "the sound was like nothing we ever heard," big, full, and beautiful, with a complement of violins to soften the brasses and saxophones.[55] Busse played his puckish trademark, "Hot Lips," Pingitore his bracingly strummed "Linger Awhile," and Wilbur Hall his fleet "Nola" on trombone and "The Stars and Stripes Forever" on bicycle pump. A vocal trio drawn from the band, made up of trombonist Jack Fulton, guitarist Austin (Skin) Young, and violinist Charles Gaylord, rendered sweet, high-pitched harmonies. Fulton, in his effeminate, almost flaccid style, sang a new song, "In a Little Spanish Town," through a megaphone. Bing liked the number and quickly added it to his repertoire, but the singer who caught his attention was Skin Young, whose "sensational" style and "tremendous range" was, he recalled, reason enough to attend the show a second time. Bing claimed, "He could not only sing things like 'The Road to Mandalay,' he could sing blues songs and fast rhythm songs and he could make sounds as uninhibited as a pre-Cab Calloway."[56] Bing's high praise is not supported by Young's pallid recordings, but his description uncannily portends the Crosby emerging that year.

Two days later Bing and Al were back in San Francisco, featured players in Partington's *Purple and Gold Revue,* which within a week was revised and renamed *Bits of Broadway.* Paramount-Publix billed them as "Crosby and Rinker — Two Boys and a Piano — Singing Songs Their Own Way." They delighted audiences and reviewers, one of whom singled out Bing's customary "Mary Lou." Shortly before the company was set to return to the Metropolitan in Los Angeles, *Variety* ran a review by its San Francisco–based reporter, Robert J. Landry (later the trade's managing editor). The boys' first major notice appeared under the heading NEW ACTS and ignored the rest of the revue.

> Crosby and Rinker
> Songs
> Granada, San Francisco
>
> Two boys from Spokane and not new to show business, but new to picture house work. They appeared with Will Morrissey's Music Hall Revue, and were a success in a show that was a flop. Bringing their methods to the Granada, they registered solidly and on the crowded Sunday performances practically stopped the show.
>
> The duo works with a piano and minus orchestral accompaniment. Blues of the feverish variety are their specialty. They are well equipped with material, presumably their own. Young and clean cut, the boys found a quick welcome. When they have completed their weeks locally, they will unquestionably find a market for their wares in other presentation houses.
>
> Wherever the public goes for "hot" numbers served hot, Crosby and Rinker ought to have an easy time.[57]

In Los Angeles, a tougher town, *Bits of Broadway* expanded to include a fourteen-piece pit orchestra, additional acts, and the banjo-playing emcee, Eddie Peabody, who was entrusted with much of the responsibility for keeping the show running on time (a necessity as the four and five daily performances were programmed around an unwavering movie schedule). For their spot, Crosby and Rinker commenced with the surefire "Five Foot Two" and then debuted their version of the new song appropriated from Whiteman, "In a Little Spanish Town." The stage was dimmed except for small blue spots trained on each of them. Microphones were not yet in use, but as Al recounted, the team had the complete attention of a capacity audience of 2,500 when they did the tune. It instantly became one of their biggest successes, a signature song like "Mary Lou," and the first in the long string of modern standards associated with Bing — if only during his season in vaudeville.

Composed by young Mabel Wayne, "In a Little Spanish Town" is a Latin-tinged waltz built on alternating dotted-eighth and sixteenth notes with two-measure lulls at the end of each phrase. It gave play to Bing's rhythmic pluck and provided Al with plenty of room for piano fills. The lyrics came from the team of Sam M. Lewis and Joe Young, whose hits included "Rock-a-Bye Your Baby with a Dixie Melody" and other Jolson benchmarks as well as the duo's standby, "Five Foot Two, Eyes of Blue." For some reason (perhaps in deference to Whiteman or because he wearied of it), Bing did not record "In a Little Spanish Town" until 1955, when he cut a jazzy piano-trio version for a radio broadcast and released it on an album.

To dress up their rhythm songs, Bing and Al began to interpolate unison scat breaks in imitation of two trumpets. King Oliver and Louis Armstrong had made this kind of thing famous in jazz circles, but it was certainly novel and possibly unprecedented in vaudeville. Suddenly, Bing and Al found themselves routinely stopping the show. This is not showbiz hyperbole; they stopped the proceedings flat as the audience howled for more. The emcee, Eddie Peabody, whom Al thought was jealous but who may simply have been trying to keep the show on schedule, did everything he could think of to throttle the audience, but to no avail. Time had to be allotted for two or more encores. For Bing and Al's second week at the Metropolitan, the show was revised as *Russian Revels*. Most of the revelers who bought tickets were drawn by the coolly irreverent cutups from Spokane. Those two offered something fresh and modern, and they put over their art with energy and humor and without airs.

Red Norvo, a vaudevillian of eighteen, was laid up with typhoid fever in a small hotel not far from the Metropolitan when Bing and Al did the Partington shows. "When I got strong enough," he recalled, "I walked across the park over to a theater and I just felt like going in 'cause I'd been sick so long. The thing that knocked me out was Rinker and Crosby. Just crazy. They pushed a piano out on stage, a little upright that Al played. Bing had a little cymbal hooked on the edge of the piano, you know, with the lid back? And they'd sing and they were scat singing even then. Their time was good and they did cute tunes. I would say it was jazz in those days, yeah. It was a sharp act."[58] They did scat exchanges on kazoos ("terrible sounding things," Bing said);[59] incorporating a trick picked up from Mound City Blue Blowers records, they played them into coffee tins. "It gave out a wah-wahing sound I thought jazzy," Bing explained.[60] During the third week at the Metropolitan, the show was reworked as *Joy Week,* and Crosby and Rinker were billed second to Peabody.

They were the Jazz Age personified, two clean-cut white boys bringing a variation on black music to the vaudeville stage with panache and charm. They represented something borderline radical: a trace of danger, a current from a generation that threatened to bust out of old and settled traditions. At no time between the Civil War and Prohibition had the nation's young people clamored for a music of their own or rebelled against the songs of their parents. Partly because the jazziness of Two Boys and a Piano stopped a few stations north of the genuine article, the young men — Bing was twenty-three and Al two months short of nineteen — suggested youth and daring in a way that did not send the "cornfeds" running for cover. They charmed everyone yet were harbingers of a break with conventions, a fissure gradually developing in the American family. Bing, especially, signaled the change with his easy wit; cool, distant manner; and unmistakably virile baritone. When he sang a song, he created drama.

Al, who had idolized Bing for so long, knew his partner communicated more powerfully as a soloist than through his hotcha settings for two voices and encouraged his partner to do more ballads, more solos. Al's arrangements were loosely harmonized, drawn from jumping instrumental numbers. The blend of his voice with Bing's was edgy, not self-consciously adroit in the manner of the old barbershop quartets nor as rigorous and inventive as the Mills Brothers or Boswell Sisters, who followed on their heels. But their loose open-collared style worked in their favor. They improvised until a routine was nailed, then stuck with it, as every vaudeville team did. Yet Bing and Al were able to contrive the illusion of spontaneity; each audience felt that it was seeing something different from what others saw. When Bing sang alone, the attitude of the audience changed from jokey camaraderie to rapt empathy. Drawing on the soulfulness of Irish laments, Jewish theater, and African American blues, Bing could take a ballad to the cliff's edge of sentimentality without going over.

He was too honest, too respectful to be manipulative. The audience could trust him with its emotions.

Before their first week at the Metropolitan was up, Bing was handed a note backstage: Paul Whiteman wanted to see them. "We thought someone on the bill was kidding us," Bing told columnist Ed Sullivan in 1939. The next morning Bing answered the phone at the apartment and was about to hang up when Jimmy Gillespie convinced him that he really was the manager of Whiteman's band and that the invitation was definitely on the level. The great man was completing his run at the Million Dollar Theater in a couple of days and wanted to see Bing and Al in his dressing room tomorrow. "After the phone call, Bing and I just looked at each other," Al remembered. "We still couldn't believe it wasn't a joke. When we talked it over with Mildred, she said, 'It doesn't sound like a joke to me. This may be the chance you've been waiting for.' We hardly slept that night."[61]

9

WHITEMAN

Home is Never Home
Without PAUL
A White Man
A Good Man
A Great Man
— *Variety,* signed by thirteen
(white) members of the New York
musical community (1927)[1]

In late 1926 no American entertainer outside the movies was more famous, more acclaimed, or more caricatured than Paul Whiteman. Within a year Charles Lindbergh would fly across the Atlantic and forever raise the stakes on fame. But for the moment, the tall, egg-shaped Whiteman was the darling of the media — he could make news by announcing his latest plan for a diet. Fastidious in his bearing, he was the first genuine popular-music superstar, an idol mobbed coast to coast at railway stations in every city he played. When he returned from his first tour of Europe, in 1923, he was welcomed at the dock by New York's mayor and police commissioner as well as by the heads of the musicians' union, executives from the Victor Talking Machine Company, and seven bands, one playing from an airplane circling the arriving ship. To the delight of the hundreds of fans waiting at the dock, a skywriter lettered the air with HELLO PAUL. To many,

Whiteman personified the Jazz Age. You could scarcely avoid his mug, an illustrator's delight, the original happy face: a swatch of slicked-back black hair, symmetrical brows and eyes, razor-thin waxed mustache, two chins.

He was born in Denver, in 1890, the son of music educator Wilberforce J. Whiteman, who abominated jazz and broke with his son because of it. They were testily reconciled after Paul became celebrated as a national resource. (Two of the elder Whiteman's other students, bandleaders Jimmie Lunceford and Andy Kirk, would become leading figures of the Swing Era; he must have considered himself a total failure.) Whiteman first attracted some attention in California, where he led a Barbary Coast ragtime outfit while holding down a viola chair in the San Francisco Symphony. After a stint in the navy, he organized a popular ballroom band in Los Angeles. In 1920 he opened in Atlantic City and signed with Victor. An instant favorite with the haut monde, he soon moved to New York's Palais Royal as sales of his first record, "Whispering," soared into the millions. Whiteman became internationally recognized after he presented *An Experiment in Modern Music* at New York's Aeolian Hall in 1924. That concert introduced George Gershwin's "Rhapsody in Blue," with the composer at the piano. Whiteman himself was not a composer, but he was a powerful arbiter of taste and considered himself a dedicated advocate of jazz. Although "Rhapsody in Blue" later became world-famous as a symphonic work, the original version arranged by Ferde Grofé was a jolting — even rickety — montage of orchestral bumps and moans, beginning with a yawning clarinet cadenza, punctuated by pounding piano, and finishing with a lovely concerto-like melody. Though by no means a blues, it shivered with blues shadings.

The Aeolian Hall concert was more than a premiere; it was a distillation of Whiteman's argument with the music establishment. A passionate believer in American music, he had insisted that a native classicism was in blossom, inspired by lowborn jazz, far beyond the realm of academic composers and European tradition. This concert was intended to make his case; as far as the critics were concerned, it did. From that point on, Whiteman was promoted as the King of Jazz. Yet no jazz was played at Aeolian Hall, except for an introductory performance of the creaky "Livery Stable Blues," which Whiteman offered as an indication of jazz in its "true naked form."[2] It was something to laugh at, a prelude to the scrupulously arranged and executed music Whiteman offered in its place — a concert ballroom music with damp rhythms and minimal improvisation.

Whiteman was on the wrong boat. By 1926, when his star had risen still higher after another successful European tour and he and Mary Margaret McBride had published their book, *Jazz,* he knew it. His mistake had been in thinking of jazz strictly as inspiration for serious music, a resource rather than an art in itself. The same year he overwhelmed critics at Aeolian Hall, another landmark musical event had taken place, one that went unnoticed by the major dailies. Louis Armstrong had arrived in New York to play with the orchestra of Fletcher Henderson, Whiteman's relatively low-profile African American counterpart. Armstrong's impact was instantaneous, immeasurable, and absolute. He had transformed the music of Henderson and his chief arranger, Don Redman, and countless others, not least Whiteman. He infused the basic building blocks of true jazz — blues, swing, and improvisation — with depth and exhilaration. Whiteman was not about to give up his expansive instrumentation, semiclassical repertoire, or vaudeville variety, but now he was hungry for honest-to-God jazz musicians.

After extensive listening and long chats with Henderson, Duke Ellington, and others, Whiteman concluded that the best jazz musicians were black, and he proposed to sign some, including his friend ragtime pianist and songwriter Eubie Blake. His management came down hard: in addition to all the lost bookings in the South and some in the North, he would risk humiliating his black musicians, who would be relegated to separate entrances, dining and boarding facilities, and even toilets. Whiteman acquiesced but countered with his determination to hire black arrangers. He wasn't the first to do so: his chief rival, Vincent Lopez, had challenged the Aeolian Hall triumph with a competing concert of his own, commissioning new pieces by Henderson and W. C. Handy. Whiteman moved more slowly: a few years later he would trade arrangements with Henderson while a young black composer, William Grant Still, would emerge as his most prolific staff writer. In the interim, he went looking for white musicians who could play authentic jazz, the real thing. So he was intrigued when his manager and financial adviser, Jimmy Gillespie, raved about an act at the Metropolitan, two young men, one a terrific baritone. Whiteman said, "If you think they're the bees' knees, bring 'em to me."[3]

The day after they got the call, Bing and Al walked backstage at the Million Dollar Theater and knocked on Whiteman's dressing-room door. Gillespie admitted them. Bing remembered the huge Whiteman sitting on a bed "looking like a giant Buddha, and he had a pound of caviar in his lap and a bottle of champagne on his breakfast table . . . the ultimate in attainment."[4] In later years the more homespun Rinker remembered Whiteman sitting in his dressing gown drinking beer, but when Bing and Whiteman were alive, neither Rinker nor anyone in the room contradicted Bing's often repeated recollection. If Bing did inflate his depiction of Whiteman's "habiliments of success,"[5] it would not be surprising. His vision of the orchestra leader is remarkably consistent with the aspirations of Bing's boyhood poem "A King," the dream now conferred upon a real monarch (of sorts), "in robes of white / With vassals kneeling left and right."

In his memoir, Bing said they performed a few numbers in the dressing room, perhaps to disguise the fact that Whiteman had offered them a job without having heard them. Instead, he had dispatched two trusted musicians to the theater to see whether Crosby and Rinker were as good as Gillespie claimed. Pianist Ray Turner dismissed them as "cute,"[6] but violinist and arranger Matty Malneck was impressed. Malneck said of their act, it was "like hearing a great jazz player for the first time."[7] Malneck (yet another former student of Wilberforce Whiteman) was one of the band's few advocates for recruiting genuine jazz players, so his word was good enough for Paul.

According to Al, Whiteman made a point of saying that he had seen the act before making his offer. "You guys are good," he told them. "How would you like to join my band?" He offered them a featured spot at $150 a week each. They would begin by touring the Balaban and Katz circuit and wind up in New York, where Paul was scheduled to open his own nightclub and perform in a Charles Dillingham show on Broadway. They would be paid extra for their work in his club, for Broadway, and for each Victor record they made with the band. With options, the contract could bind them for five years. "Well, how does that sound?" he asked. "Go ahead, boys, talk it over."[8]

The two young men exchanged grins. Bing spoke up. "Al and I don't have to talk it over, Mr. Whiteman," he said. "We accept your offer. How soon would you want us to start?" "As soon as possible," Whiteman told them, at which point Al said to Bing, "Say, what about our contract with Jack Partington?" (They were signed to Partington through November.) Whiteman thought for a moment and advised them to complete the contract and join the band for its three-week stay in Chicago. "That will give you a couple of weeks to relax," he said. The next day they returned to Whiteman's dressing room with Al's dad to sign the papers. Before taking off on his tour, Whiteman shook hands with them and said, "So long, I'll see you sprouts in Chicago."[9]

Mildred was delighted, as was Partington, relieved perhaps that they intended to honor their contract. Eleven months and one week before, Bing and Al had left Spokane in a Tin Lizzie, "just to see my sister and hoping we could get something going," Al marveled.[10] Now they were about to work with their idol, scaling what Bing described as the Mount Everest of show business.[11] Al thought he was living a Horatio Alger fable. Bing credited luck. Yet it would be a mistake to discount the appeal and originality of their act. Audiences loved them, and Whiteman wasn't risking much. He wanted something fresh and jazzy, something for young people, and who better than these two clean-cut kids? He had no way of knowing that in signing them, he had put into motion the career of the first in a long line of white musicians who popularized real black music (jazz, not mammy singing) for a white public. This was ten years before Benny Goodman launched the Swing Era, thirty before Elvis Presley rocked.

Bing and Al marked time at the Metropolitan, reprising *Russian Revels*. But a couple of days later, the pair chalked up another first: a chance to make a record. Don Clark, a saxophonist who had worked with Whiteman before starting his own band, led the Biltmore Hotel Orchestra and had a Columbia Records session booked for October 18; he invited Bing and Al to sing the vocal choruses on two numbers. On ethical grounds, they should have passed; legally they were pushing their luck. They had just signed with Whiteman, a Victor artist who expected them to make their wax debut under his auspices. They accepted instantly. "We were kind of excited to hear how we would sound," Al explained.[12] Clark gave them lead sheets for two tunes, asking them to work up a harmonized chorus on each. The material was undistinguished: "I've Got the Girl!," a weak tune by Walter Donaldson, who later wrote some of their most important Whiteman records, and "Don't Somebody Need Somebody," a throwaway by Abe Lyman, the cowriter of "Mary Lou." No major recording career got off to a more dismal start than Bing's.

The session took place in a hastily converted warehouse at Sixth and Bixel, and was engineered acoustically. Bing and Al had to sing into a megaphone-like horn built into the planks of the recording booth. The Lyman tune was abandoned when Bing and Al could make nothing of it, and Peggy Bernier, a vaudeville trouper with pretty eyes and long bangs, fared no better. For all the good it did the boys or Clark, "I've Got the Girl!" ought to have been junked, too. Singing into a horn for the first time, Bing and Al could not sustain the blend of their voices. As a result, their recorded chorus is dominated by Al's higher voice, though it is moored by Bing's weighty, more controlled timbre. They sing Rinker's treatment of the nattering tune energetically, inserting a measure of scat at the first turnback and attempting a unison portamento that got away from them. The performance did not do justice to their act — but then again, it wasn't meant to. Their names did not appear on the label, and their complicity was further disguised by an accident: the record — backed with another Clark performance, "Idolizing," vocal by one Betty Patrick — was inadvertently released at a fast speed.[13] Bing and Al sound like chipmunks.

The day after the session, *Variety* ran an item on the boys' extraordinary new contract with Whiteman, to begin "in Chicago in the Publix houses."[14] Weeks later the *Spokane Chronicle* reported that "they made a number of Columbia phonograph records,"[15] along with other ballyhoo that suggested a boneheaded attempt at public relations, probably by Everett. Not surprisingly, "I've Got the Girl!" promptly disappeared. Bing never spoke of it, and it lay unknown to avid Crosby collectors until 1951, when Ed Mello and Tom McBride published the first Crosby discography and failed to include it. After showing it to Bing, Larry Crosby wrote Mello, "Bing is well pleased."

But he pointed out that Bing told him his first record was with Don Clark's orchestra "in 1926 or 1927 for Columbia — he thinks with Al Rinker. Do you have any record on this?"[16] A year later a collector in San Francisco found a copy. Larry's doubt about Rinker was not shared by Bing, who recalled their duet well enough to sing a few measures for interviewers as late as 1976.

They finished at the Metropolitan with *Joy Week* on October 28, and two days later hit San Francisco to fulfill their debt to Partington. Before leaving, they sold their Dodge, and Mildred gave them a farewell party. Partington's revues rotated weekly — *Dancing Around, Jazz à la Carte, Way Down South*. In the cast of the first two was Peggy Bernier, on whom Bing developed a crush that would later blossom into a woozy affair. But Bing and Al spent most of their time in San Francisco playing golf on the public links and — eager to impress Whiteman — working up new songs. During their final days with the company, they were preoccupied with the problem of filling a two-week interval before heading for Chicago. They may not have noticed the quiet revolution taking place in American entertainment: NBC had just launched the first radio network. The boys decided that after ending their run in *Way Down South*, they would visit Spokane. They made calls to line up a job. Within days the *Spokane Chronicle* trumpeted their return and a "big production" scheduled for the Liberty Theater.[17]

Their reception at the Northern Pacific depot was a modest rendition of *Hail the Conquering Hero*, with a clamoring retinue of family and friends. Al's family had relocated to Los Angeles, so they stayed at Bing's home. Kate pointed out that her son had gained weight. Surrounded by neighbors on the Crosby porch, Bing sat a four-year-old named Mary Lou Higgins on his lap and sang "Mary Lou." She began sobbing uncontrollably.[18] The prodigal sons palled around with the gang, squired women, played golf at Downriver Park, and did four shows daily. Ray Grombacher, who operated the Liberty — and the adjoining music shop that had been Al and Bing's graduate school — hired them for five days at the fancy price of $350. They opened at 11:00 P.M. on the evening before Thanksgiving, opposite a popular Paramount comedy, *We're in the Navy Now*, starring Wallace Beery and Raymond Hatton. That night their old stomping ground, the

Clemmer Theater, made do with *Stella Dallas* and no live acts. The Liberty's newspaper ads emphasized the movie but added: "And then just to make it the best show in town Ray A. Grombacher presents Bing Crosby & Al Rinker in their own original novelty."[19] The ad included pictures of the pair in matching jackets and bow ties, along with their billing, "Two Boys with a Piano and a Voice."

"We were both a little nervous," Al remembered. "It was a lot different playing to all of our hometown friends."[20] But after the first show, the nervousness disappeared. They headlined in a "six-act pot-pourri"[21] at the "midnight matinee"[22] and went over big. The *Spokesman-Review* reported "songs and songalogues last night, with Rinker at the 'ivories'; Crosby lent the jazz touch to the act by playing a solo on cymbals. The big crowd went wild over their mixture of harmony and comedy."[23] The *Chronicle* further mythologized their flivver (comparing it to Elijah's "flaming chariot") and their ascendancy "to affluence in the song world," and noted their impending departure for "Gotham's high-priced whirl."[24] No mention was made of the coming tour of Chicago and the Midwest. The big news was that they would appear on Broadway in a Charles Dillingham production.

"It isn't what the boys do, but the way they do it," one reporter concluded, citing Bing's "timely crashes on a diminutive cymbal."[25] For five days they performed at three, six, seven, and nine. Grombacher boasted that on the first day alone, 9,000 people saw the show and another 1,500 were turned away. At last he was compensated for the records Bing and Al did not buy at Bailey's. Yet for Bing the memory of their visit was compromised: "Somebody sneaked into our dressing room and stole our money while we were on stage, a heinous thing to do to a fellow in his home town," he recalled.[26] They were able to earn some of it back with a show in the Italian Gardens of the Davenport Hotel, but they were not sorry to leave town. Bing's family and friends cheered and wished them luck as the boys boarded the Great Northern to join Paul Whiteman's band, the most famous in the world. Spokane did not lay eyes on Bing again for eleven years.

The train was three days getting to Chicago. Relying on a friend's recommendation, they taxied to the Eastgate Hotel on Michigan Avenue. ("This time we checked in double," Al recalled, referring to their old dodge of going two for one.)[27] Whiteman was booked for three weeks in Chicago, a different theater each week. He closed at the Chicago Theater on the Saturday the boys arrived, and would hit the Tivoli — with Bing and Al — on Monday. On their last day to themselves, Bing and Al toured the city, learning the ways of the elevated train, which they would be using to get to the theater on the South Side. Bing attended a football game. His old friend Ray Flaherty was in town, playing with the New York Yankees, and Bing sat on the bench. They went out afterward for drinks and dinner, and Bing told Ray that there would be a pass in his name at the Tivoli.

Monday morning — December 6, 1926 — they packed blazers and got to the theater as the bandstand was set up. Whiteman arrived at noon, delighted to find them waiting: "Well, I see you made it, and right on time."[28] He introduced them to the musicians ("They seemed very pleased to have us with them," Al recalled) but asked Bing and Al to sit out the two afternoon shows, to get a feel for the production from backstage. The show dazzled them as much as it had in Los Angeles. By evening they were nervous but raring to go. Whiteman gave them a pep talk and went to work. Al described their initiation:

> The first evening show was about to start and we were all made-up and ready. There was a full house out front. Whiteman told us that we would go on about the middle of the show and that he would introduce us as Crosby and Rinker, who were making their first appearance with his band. Well, our turn finally came and Paul walked out and started our introduction. What he said was far different than what we had expected. He told the audience that he had heard two young boys singing in an ice cream parlor in a little town out west, called Walla Walla. "They sang some songs and I wondered what they were doing in Walla Walla. These kids were good, too good for Walla Walla, so I asked them to join my band. This is their first appearance with the band and here they are. I want you to meet Crosby and Rinker. Come on out boys." The little piano was moved on stage and Bing and I came out from the wings. All I know is that we got a big hand after our first song and even more applause on our second number. To top it all, we were called back for an encore. That was our first appearance on the big time. You can bet we were two happy guys. Whiteman came over

to us after the show and said, "Well, how do you feel? I knew they'd like you. Welcome to the band!"[29]

Whiteman's introduction established a receptive mood in the audience but failed to impress the names of his recruits on a *Chicago Daily News* reporter, who referred to them as Bing Rinker and Bill Crosby.[30] A small incident after the show presaged Crosby's immense impact on popular music. One of the three songs he and Al performed was "In a Little Spanish Town," a nervy choice considering they had originally nabbed it from Whiteman and his trombonist-singer Jack Fulton, who sang it at the Million Dollar Theater. Before they left for the hotel, Whiteman notified Fulton that the song would now be done by the new boys. Fulton was irate and let everyone know it. Al felt guilty and half a century later took pains to justify himself. He told a Crosby biographer that he and Bing did not realize it was Fulton's number; he wrote in his memoir that Whiteman forced it on them. (In fact, Whiteman allowed them to choose their own songs.) Perhaps Bing also felt pangs — he did not record it for nearly thirty years.

Jack Fulton, however, had recorded it with Whiteman three months earlier, and his version was just then reaching the stores. By Christmas it was the biggest record in the country. Whiteman had no choice but to return it to the man who made it nationally famous. Yet Paul's switcheroo served as a warning to those present: the effeminate, semifalsetto style typified by Fulton and the other musician-singers was not long for this world.[31]

Bing's stay in Chicago was eventful for other reasons, too. After Whiteman completed his week at the Uptown Theater, he reserved the cavernous Orchestra Hall for two days of recording, on December 21 and 22. The first produced three acceptable instrumentals. The second was less productive. "Bunch of Happiness," a feature for the band's high-voiced trio — Fulton, Young, and Gaylord — was deemed unsatisfactory and shelved. The same fate befell "Pretty Lips," a Walter Donaldson tune designed to introduce Crosby and Rinker. Though four takes failed to jell, the arrangement showed enough promise to warrant another try at a later date. The session's only acceptable number was a rendition of Ruth Etting's "Wistful and Blue." Coupled with an instrumental from the day before, it was the first of nearly one hundred titles Bing and Al recorded under White-man's aegis. Dated as it is today, their record debut was novel in 1926.

Max Farley, a Whiteman saxophonist, arranged "Wistful and Blue"'s odd eighteen-bar theme for the orchestra, but the vocal cho-rus was treated separately; the singers were backed by viola, guitar, and bass. Matty Malneck, waiting for this kind of opportunity, arranged the vocal passage, using his viola as a third voice in unison with Bing and Al. With Wilbur Hall strumming guitar and John Sperzel keeping a yeoman beat on bass, they sing a straight chorus with a two-bar break, followed by a stop-time scat chorus that evolves into a chase between voices and viola. Rinker's voice dominates the duet, but it was the general jazziness of the vocal interlude — not the individual talents of the singers — that made the record a turning point for Whiteman; this zesty brand of singing was unknown to most of his public. Bing credited Malneck's arrangement with helping him and Al forge "a new style . . . a vocal without words."[32]

To hip musicians in Chicago, however, scat had been the rage for months. Bing and some of the other adventurous musicians in Whiteman's band heard it that very week from the master himself, Louis Armstrong. If mobster Al Capone ruled the city, Armstrong ruled its music. Whatever he played was instantly picked up by other musicians. The previous spring OKeh issued his Hot Five recording of "Heebie Jeebies," and it caused a sensation, selling some 40,000 copies thanks to his inspired vocal chorus — a torrent of bristling grunts and groans in no known language. Pianist Earl Hines later claimed he knew musicians who tried to catch cold so they could growl like Louis; and Mezz Mezzrow, the marijuana-pushing clar-inetist, recalled, "You would hear cats greeting each other with Louis's riffs when they met around town . . . scatting in each other's face."[33] Before Louis, scat singing could be heard on records by Cliff Edwards (Ukelele Ike) and Red McKenzie (Mound City Blue Blow-ers); Bing and Al had admired and imitated them in Spokane. But the ad libs on those records were often disguised by kazoo or comb. They had little of Armstrong's rhythmic thrust and none of his melodic ingenuity.

At the time Whiteman pulled into town, Louis was fronting the Sunset Cafe band, with Hines as his musical director. The place was run by Joe Glaser, a Capone acolyte who several years later would become Armstrong's manager, building the powerful Associated Booking Agency in the process. In Chicago he billed his star in lights as "The World's Greatest Trumpet Player." The Sunset was located on the main stem of black Chicago but served an integrated audience. Because its band played a good two hours after most others retired, the club became a second home to many of the best white musicians in town, among them Bix Beiderbecke, Hoagy Carmichael, Tommy Dorsey, and Frank Trumbauer.

Whiteman introduced Bing and Al to the Sunset and other hot spots in Chicago. One can only imagine Bing's initial response to Louis's irrepressible genius, especially if Mildred Bailey had primed him for an experience bordering on the Second Coming. All his life Bing surrounded himself with people who made him laugh. In Armstrong, music and humor were inseparable. Bing was bowled over one evening when Louis revived a routine he had developed in New York in 1924, putting on a frock coat and dark glasses and preaching as the Reverend Satchelmouth. The Gonzagan found Armstrong's irreverence almost as revelatory as his music. He had a front-row pew and knew exactly what he was hearing. When asked in 1950 who had influenced him most, Bing replied, "I'm proud to acknowledge my debt to the Reverend Satchelmouth. He is the beginning and the end of music in America. And long may he reign."[34]

The band headed east, and at every Paramount-Publix theater it played — in Cleveland, Detroit, St. Louis, Indianapolis, Youngstown, Cincinnati — Bing and Al went over well. As the old year turned new, Whiteman broke the house record at St. Louis's Missouri Theatre and was held over for a second week. Throughout January 1927 the band traveled through one triumph after another, until it boarded a train out of Cincinnati bound for New York's Grand Central. Whiteman's return generated the usual hoopla: a motorcycle escort to Times Square for festivities at the Paramount Theater, then downtown to City Hall, for Mayor Jimmy Walker's greeting; finally, the motorcade headed uptown for lunch at the Hotel Astor.

Whiteman had five days before opening at the Paramount on February 12, and little time to rest. When he was not supervising and ballyhooing Club Whiteman, which was set to open February 18, the last night of the Paramount engagement, he was recording. On February 10 he used his Walla Walla boys in tandem with Fulton, Young, and Gaylord on an ersatz Asian novelty, "Shanghai Dream Man," complete with gong and woodblocks. The five-man choir (Bing and Al disappear in the soup) carols "shing-a-ling-a-hi-lo." Grofé's gloomy arrangement seemed to foretell the events of two days later, when Crosby and Rinker became the punch line in one of show business's fabled Waterloos.

On screen: Dolores Costello in *The Third Degree*. On organ: Jesse Crawford. Main attraction: "The Jazz King (in person)."[35] The Paramount, flagship of the Publix chain, was a jaw-droppingly opulent theater and the quintessence of big-time entertainment. Whiteman's musicians liked to pretend it was just another gig — even if it paid them $9,500 for the week. *Variety* loved their show, complaining only that it was short. "Whiteman could do an hour easily without really getting started," yet he crammed "the smartest, quickest, snappiest routine of his career" into forty-two minutes, beginning with Jack Fulton piping "In a Little Spanish Town."[36] Toward the end of the set, Whiteman introduced his dynamic find "from the coast." *Variety* was pleased: "Rinker and Crosby, a smart two-man piano act who sing ditties differently and are of the Van and Schenck class. After Whiteman gets through grooming the boys, they will be plenty in the money." The critic went on to note that they "vocalised two numbers and accepted as many encores."[37]

No one else remembered it that way. Not only were there no encores, but the audience sat on its hands, quiet as the grave, a freeze-frame. For the next two days, Bing and Al repeated the act that had always wowed them in the Midwest — to more silence. The theater manager wanted them out, and Whiteman complied. "They laid dinosaur eggs," he recalled.[38] No one could explain it. "Wistful and Blue" was a successful record and pleased every audience, except in Whiteman's citadel. On the road to New York, he attempted to integrate Bing and Al into the orchestra rather than bring them on as a specialty act. The idea of carrying singers who did nothing else was unheard of, so Whiteman had them sit with the band, pretending to play prop instruments — violin for Bing, guitar for Al, each with rubber strings. Audiences throughout the heartland had been pleasantly surprised when a small piano was rolled onstage and the two young men stood up to do their numbers.

Yet in New York, Whiteman could not give them away, and he tried, situating his boys in the lobby, where fans who could not get in to one show milled around waiting for the next. Bing and Al wheeled a spinet into the vestibule to entertain, but the crowds there were no more appreciative than those inside. Whiteman used them as backup singers: "We sat in the band and we hummed background for Johnny Fulton, who sang solos, and for Skin Young and things," Bing recalled.[39] He says in his autobiography, "I couldn't explain it then. I can't now."[40]

After years of thought, Al concluded: "New York taste very much leaned toward the Jewish type of thing,"[41] meaning Jolson, Sophie Tucker, Eddie Cantor, George Jessel, and others "who put over songs with much more emotion and broad showmanship." He and Bing "were more intimate and sang our songs in a more modern way."[42] That fails to explain why the warblings of Fulton, Gaylord, and Young were so well received. Some said the Paramount itself defeated them, particularly since they sang without microphones or megaphones. But that fails to explain the hostility they faced in the lobby. Al noted, "We had been influenced by the new jazz feeling popular with young people and understood and appreciated by audiences *outside* of New York."[43] Yet in 1926 New York was running over with jazz bands. The reason for the boys' failure may lie in a combination of all these factors, plus an undefinable negative vibe, nothing more concrete than that they were perceived as young and impudent. One observer referred to their "collegiate and cocky air."[44] Whiteman, trying to fix the blame twenty years later, told columnist Ben Gross that a Paramount executive sent a telegram forbidding him from allowing Crosby a solo.

The second-story blocklong Club Whiteman opened on Broadway and Forty-eighth Street to a packed, star-studded, bring-your-own-hooch crowd in which Prohibition agents mingled with Governor Al Smith and Mayor Jimmy Walker; two rival club owners, Jimmy Durante and Texas Guinan; Charlie Chaplin, Jeanne Eagels, Gloria Swanson, and Harry Warren. Evangelist Aimee Semple McPherson dropped by a few days later, bringing greetings from Whiteman's father, who was conducting her choir. Entered by a carpeted staircase, the ornate black-and-gold room could accommodate between

900 and 1,000 customers. As a result, what passed for a full house in other places (a hundred filled tables) was a disaster at Club White-man. The bandleader introduced a singer he discovered in Chicago, but in her first New York visit, Ruth Etting did not fare much better than Crosby and Rinker.

In three months Paul would unload his 50 percent interest and retract his name. Meantime, he used the club to give Bing and Al another shot at New York. But he scheduled them during intermissions between the floor shows. They worked by the side of the stage under a spotlight, Al at a white piano adorned with Paul's caricature. Without microphones, they were unable to claim the attention of the audience. After two nights the perplexed Whiteman dropped their act. He allowed them to earn their keep, however, opening and closing the bandstand curtains.

Bing and Al served as stagehands for nearly three weeks, a humiliation they accepted with aplomb, not that they had much choice. On at least one occasion, Bing was assigned a mallet to pound the chimes, offstage, during the climax of the 1812 Overture. Describing his "heartbreak" in his 1954 memoir, Bing insisted, "We were prepared to go back to Los Angeles or even to Spokane,"[45] but he was more candid to his biographer Charles Thompson in 1976: "I couldn't care less, really. I knew that Whiteman had to pay us — we were contracted and I just felt something'd show up."[46] Besides, Bing had the chance to disport himself in the speakeasy and musical life of New York. He basked in a world he could scarcely imagine back in the listening booths of Bailey's House of Music. He was bedazzled by glittery Harlem: the Cotton Club, where the late-night audiences sparkled as much as the elaborate revues; Connie's Inn, where Allie Ross's band invited top jazz soloists to sit in; Smalls' Paradise, an enormous basement that accommodated 1,500 people and offered Charlie Johnson's band and sometimes Willie "the Lion" Smith; the Lafayette Theatre, where you could catch Duke Ellington when he wasn't midtown at the Kentucky Club or the Plantation Café. Another midtown mecca was the Roseland Ballroom, where you could hear the best black jazz musicians, in Fletcher Henderson's band, or the best white ones, in Jean Goldkette's. Bing was in the right place at a transitional time. Come December, Ellington would debut at the Cotton Club, an engagement that would bring

New York jazz to the attention of the world. If Bing was inclined to soak up too much bootleg whiskey, he was soaking up just as much music.

The results were soon evident. A week after Club Whiteman opened its doors, Paul boarded the band in Atlantic City for a week of recording at Victor's Camden studio. At the first session, he asked Bing and Al to blend with his three tenor voices on a selection only slightly less risible than "Shanghai Dream Man." "That Saxophone Waltz," on which the five men hum "do-do doodle-doodle do" in indistinct unison, is of interest only because Bing's tones are vaguely discernible and the eight-bar setup for the vocal was pilfered after three decades by Richard Rodgers for "Edelweiss." Three days later Paul gave them another shot at "Pretty Lips," something of a companion piece to "Wistful and Blue," yet a distinct improvement. After a natty theme statement by saxophone virtuoso Chester Hazlett, a transition ignited by thumping bass sets up the vocal episode, again with Matty Malneck's viola echoing the singers. The distinction between Bing's round lower tones and Al's flavorless higher ones is unambiguous, yet they blend well, especially in the chase section with Malneck.

Whiteman knew he had something special in Bing, and if New York put any doubts in his head, Malneck was there to allay them. Three days later Whiteman recorded Matty's intricate arrangement of a wonderful recent song by Will Marion Cook and Donald Heywood, "I'm Coming, Virginia," with Bing taking his first solo and Al harmonizing only on the final scat chorus. Yet four tries failed to produce a satisfactory take, and they left the studio in a state of bitter frustration. Three days after that, on March 7, at New York's Liederkranz Hall, Whiteman's faith was rewarded as the band essayed another Malneck arrangement, "Muddy Water," a song recently introduced by Harry Richman, the egocentric headliner who graduated from burnt cork to top-hat-and-cane elegance. It was the work of white composer Peter De Rose, at the outset of a career that produced "Deep Purple" and "Wagon Wheels," and black lyricist Jo Trent, whose "Georgia Bo-Bo" Louis Armstrong had recorded the previous year. This time Al was left out altogether.

"Muddy Water" did not electrify the music world. It was no "Heebie Jeebies" or "Heartbreak Hotel," though sales were respectable. Yet

Crosby's first recorded chorus — thirty-two measures — was every bit as radical. Nothing remotely like it had been heard before. The song, with its bucolic theme of an idyllic life "down Dixie way," was cannily appropriate for a Dixiephile like Bing. Yet his delivery is never patronizing or sentimental. He bets everything on his rhythmic phrasing and gives each word its due. The introductory trombone, answered by strings, and a bold unison ensemble chorus promise a jazz record; but only the vocal, backed by viola and rhythm, make good on the promise. Though stilted and even formal, Bing's time and articulation are assured, especially on the bridge, where he emphasizes *there* and *care* with trilling vibrato that displays his growing affinity for swing.

No singer had ever come close to swinging on a Whiteman record or with any other white ballroom band. For that matter, in early 1927 hot vocals were practically unheard of on records by black orchestras. Except for a single brief scat break by Armstrong that he strongly disfavored, Fletcher Henderson confined vocals to Don Redman's singspiel. The earthier territory bands of the Midwest tended to limit vocal choruses to novelties. Crosby's very presence was singular. He was the first ever full-time band singer, not an instrumentalist who doubled on vocals.

As an indication of just how standout a performance "Muddy Water" is, one need only listen to it in tandem with other vocal records issued the same year. The bestselling singer of 1927, by far, was Gene Austin, with three number one hits. An innocuous tenor who two years earlier was little more than a Cliff Edwards imitator, Austin hit paydirt with "My Blue Heaven," considered the all-time top seller for years, some say until Bing's "White Christmas" in 1942. The four other most successful vocal records of the year were Whiteman's "In a Little Spanish Town" (vocal by Fulton), Sophie Tucker's "Some of These Days," Ben Bernie's "Ain't She Sweet" (with singers Scrappy Lambert and Billy Hillpot), and Whispering Jack Smith's "Me and My Shadow."[47] Sophie, a rowdy alto with a vibrato that could hold its own with a tailgate trombone, was the lustiest and most masculine of the lot. Smith, true to his name, whispered his songs into lullabies. The others piped in an effete manner that suited the gender-bending tastes of an era when transvestites were among the top attractions in vaudeville.

Variety reckoned 1923 as the peak year for cross-dressing acts, most famously the phenomenally successful Julian Eltinge, who a decade earlier had a Times Square theater named for him. Indeed, transvestism had become another school of minstrelsy, about which one critic opined, "Just as a white man makes the best stage Negro, so a man gives a more photographic interpretation of femininity than the average woman is able to give."[48] Bing had played black and female in grade school and would again, but as a singer the primary quality he projected was one of virility. The women fans who would ensure his success on radio were less smitten with his soft microphone crooning than with the fact that he was unmistakably of the opposite sex, which could not be said of Gene Austin and company. In the collective memory of popular music, the nasal Rudy Vallée is thought of as Bing's predecessor; he did, in fact, precede Bing as a star. But his breakthrough came in 1929, two years after "Muddy Water," and was less the youthful step forward it was claimed to be (especially by Vallée) than a brief throwback to the effete style Bing ultimately put to rest. Vallée does not speak to us; but Bing in 1927, though far from the finesse of his maturity, does. He makes one telling misstep in "Muddy Water," inflecting "down on the delta" with a Jolsonesque tremor that suggests the old Broadway aesthetic. Otherwise, he is ours — a modernist.

Two days after "Muddy Water," Whiteman reinstalled Bing and Al as performers at his nightclub. Two weeks after that, the band opened on Broadway in the musical comedy *Lucky*, with Mary Eaton, Walter Catlett, Skeets Gallagher, and Ruby Keeler. The show, a tale of a Ceylonese pearl diver and her conniving father, boasted lavish sets and a score by two great songwriting teams, Kern and Harbach and Kalmar and Ruby. But nothing could induce people to buy tickets. Whiteman appeared for nearly thirty minutes in a cabaret scene that began at 11:00 P.M., allowing the band time to perform nightly at his club as well. The song assigned Bing and Al, "Sam, the Old Accordion Man," was ignored by the critics; theatergoers were apparently no more hostile to it than to the rest of the evening, which closed after seventy-one performances. Whiteman rewarded Bing with a solo number at the club, but by then the room was draining more money than it brought in. (Whiteman shuttered it on May 24, three days after *Lucky* folded.) Knowing the show and the club were fading, he could think of nothing to do with his protégés beyond dispatching them on vaudeville tours.

Once again, Matty Malneck came to the rescue. He arranged for Bing and Al to meet a friend of his from Denver who was having a rough time in New York — a wildly kinetic singer, pianist, and tune-smith named Harry Barris.

10

RHYTHM BOYS

They were trying to get him to make a solo record, but he laughed — said it was silly, no one wanted to hear him alone.

— Cork O'Keefe (1946)[1]

As frenetic as Bing was calm, Harry Barris, at twenty-one, was the quintessence of Jazz Age show business, or at least thought he was. He played piano, sang, joked, and wrote songs (though he had yet to sell any) and was brazen with confidence. Small, wiry, and moon-faced with glittery eyes, and dark hair slicked back and parted in the middle, Harry had already logged more miles than Bing and Al combined. He was born in New York, on November 24, 1905, to a Jewish family that relocated to Denver when he was in his teens. He studied music in high school with Wilberforce Whiteman, who took a liking to him, and at fifteen played local dances with a small band that included Glenn Miller, Ted Mack, and Matty Malneck. He enrolled at the University of Denver in 1923 but did not last long. Harry liked to claim he was expelled for playing piano after hours. (Told he could play until 10:00 P.M., he cracked, "That's when I get up.")[2] His predicament was exacerbated by incipient signs of the alcoholism that tormented him all his life.

He toured briefly with Gus Edwards's revue *School Days* and played for a short while in Paul Ash's orchestra in Chicago, but mostly he toured as a single for Paramount-Publix with his Blu Blowing Baby Grand. Along the way, he married and a daughter was born. *Variety* caught up with his twelve-minute act in St. Louis and acclaimed his showstopping "nut songs," which had the audience "tied in knots." The reviewer concluded, "Young, peppy, and goofy is this young man Barris. And he can help any show."[3] Harry tried to convince Whiteman of that when he arrived in New York, but the bandleader was full up with pianists and singers. He soon found a job at bandleader George Olsen's club, where his hotcha style of banging the piano lid on the beat and mix of ragtime and nonsense songs won him a modest following, though not enough income to support a family. Bing would later remember his act as "sort of a metropolitan type Fuzzy Knight" — a reference to the western actor who started out as a hillbilly pianist and bandleader.[4]

One of the first people Barris looked up in New York was an old friend, Jimmy Cavanaugh, who toured in vaudeville performing original material, none of which caught on. After the two downed a few beers, Cavanaugh showed Harry a lyric he was working on and asked whether he could do anything with it. Harry walked to the piano and fashioned a melody; they called their song "Mississippi Mud." Malneck, determined to help three fish out of water, told Harry about Bing and Al, suggesting they might team up. Harry was initially skeptical: if one of them played piano, what would he do? But Matty arranged a meeting at which Harry banged out his new tune, and the rapport was instant. "The next day we went over to Barris's apartment," Al recalled, to work out a routine:

We fooled around with some ideas and we tried out some three-part harmony. We were all baritones but I had the highest voice so I sang the top part. Barris sang the middle part while Bing sang the low part. . . . One of Harry's tricks in his solo act was to slam the top of the piano for an effect and make the sound of a cymbal with his mouth. This sounded great and all three of us were getting our kicks at the way we sounded. We all came up with ideas. Bing took most of the solo parts and Barris and I would fill in with answers or a rhythmic scat background. Although we weren't conscious of it, we were creating an entirely new style of singing pop songs. We were far more jazz oriented than any other singing group of that time. . . . We were greatly influenced by the great jazz musicians we had heard and were working with. We were very free and uninhibited. We had a solid beat in our rhythm numbers, but we could also give a pretty ballad an individual and personal feeling. In two more days we had put together two complete songs, "Mississippi Mud" and "Ain't She Sweet." We sang the songs for Matty Malneck and he was bowled over. He said, "If Whiteman doesn't flip over you three guys, he's gotta be nuts."[5]

Whiteman flipped. He installed them in his dying club the next Saturday night, bringing in a second white spinet to match the first. The house was nearly full. Paul introduced them as the pianos were wheeled out. Bing stood between them with his cymbal. According to Rinker, they "slammed the piano lids and carried on. You can bet the audience at the Whiteman club could hear us now."[6] The crowd not only listened but stopped dining, drinking, and talking, and applauded enthusiastically for both numbers. Barris had the least distinctive voice of the three, but his sizzle and high-strung energy inspired Bing and Al, whose curtain-pulling days were now over.

Whiteman could not wait to get them into the studio — and not just them. Whiteman had never given up on his desire to hire bona fide jazz soloists, and Bing and Malneck made him more determined than ever. The best white players were in Jean Goldkette's band, but Paul was reluctant to raid another orchestra; in any case, several of Goldkette's stars were none too eager to wade into a sea of Whiteman strings. Instead, he co-opted four of the five musicians who worked in Red Nichols's famous recording unit, the Five Pennies.

Nichols was a competent but rarely inspired cornetist who had created a fascinating small band with timpani and a clever ratio of written to improvised music. Though Whiteman made a fuss over him, Nichols ultimately chafed at playing what he considered compromised jazz. He came on board in February and was gone by summer. Still, Whiteman managed to capture a couple of his best cornet solos on the same session that introduced Barris, on April 29. Max Farley orchestrated a new song by Harry Woods, "Side by Side," with a vocal chorus worked out by Barris that incorporated a stutter — "Oh, we ain't got plenty of muh-muh-money / Maybe we're ragged and fuh-fuh-funny." Bing sings the bridge solo, backed by the harmonizing of Al and Harry, and reasserts a touch of Jolson schmaltz in his quivering cadences.

Bing was more himself on Malneck's adaptation of "I'm Coming, Virginia," the song he and Rinker had flubbed at a previous session, with Barris adding only a hot-cha-cha coda. Here Bing captures the originality of "Muddy Water," combining his deft time with a full, relaxed articulation of the words. Contrary to Al's suggestion of a diligent jazz influence, two surviving takes show that their scat routines were worked out to the last detail. Yet Bing's imperturbable vocal, Matty's writing, Nichols's solo, and the band's skill combined to make "I'm Coming, Virginia" the best and most authentic jazz record Whiteman had ever made.

Harry did not participate in the May recording of "I'm in Love Again," and Bing and Al were relegated to the choir, backing Charles Gaylord, except for a brief and undistinguished solo passage in which Bing reveals a hoarseness that would plague him for years, ultimately altering his sound and style. Two weeks later Whiteman presented his new vocal trio on an innocuous if cheerful Buddy DeSylva, Lew Brown, and Ray Henderson tune called "Magnolia," a record that introduces their patter style, each spurring the others with spoken or sung interjections punctuated by Barris's cymbal-like *hahh!* The song, replete with topical references to "sex appeal" and movie queens Clara Bow, Lillian Gish, and Gloria Swanson, was an excuse to focus attention on the band's recent jazz recruits, now including Jimmy Dorsey, who solos on alto saxophone, and the innovative jazz and symphonic drummer Vic Berton, a Nichols associate, who bounces the ensemble with pedaled timpani and choked cymbals.

By now they had decided to call themselves the Rhythm Boys, a play on the Happiness Boys, one of the first successful radio acts. The boss, presenting them as Paul Whiteman's Rhythm Boys, arranged an independent recording contract for them at Victor and brought them back to the Paramount when the orchestra was hired for an unprecedented six-week engagement, at $10,500 a week. Not much attention was paid to the other acts or the film (Lois Moran in *The Whirlwind of Youth*). Whiteman's first week was so successful that Sam Katz, the president of Publix, wanted to double the length of the band's stay. Paul's touring commitments prevented it, but to make each week special, Katz brought in Crosby and Rinker's prior boss, Jack Partington of San Francisco's Granada Theater, to design the thematic productions. As the movie changed to W. C. Fields in *Running Wild*, so the band suddenly found itself wearing sailor suits aboard the USS *Syncopation*, while Whiteman conducted from a gun turret. The production changed weekly — among the titles were *Rushia, Jazz à la Carte*, and *Fireworks* — and the audiences were as receptive to the new singers as the *Variety* reporter, who lauded their spot as "a stellar opportunity in itself."[7] In a succeeding notice, the reviewer pointed out that the show lacked comedy except for "the natural laughs in the delivery of the jazz vocal trio." In the patriotic *Fireworks*, the band — including the two "blues yodeling plebes from Spokane" — performed a "cute" number with pop guns.[8]

Midway through the Paramount run, the Rhythm Boys formally debuted on records, singing the first two numbers they had rehearsed, now tricked up as medleys and accompanied only by Harry's piano and Bing's cymbal whacks. "Mississippi Mud" is oddly structured: a twenty-two-bar chorus with a sixteen-bar middle section. The lyric is catchy (though marred by the term *darkies*, which was eventually changed to *people*), and the melody is propelled by accents on the first beat of almost every measure. Bing recorded it three times over the next seven months. Though the Rhythm Boys' version is not as effective as those that followed, it confirmed the trio's style as part music and part wisecracking comedy. A scat passage introduces them one at a time: Bing, then Al, then Harry, who finishes with a *hahh*. After a unison chorus in which Bing takes the lead in the middle section, the patter leads to an interpolation of "I Left My Sugar Standing in the Rain," where Bing displays for the first time on record his sustained balladic tones as well as his humor and wordplay — in the spin he puts on the spoken phrase "I don't know" and the spoonerism "irregardless and respective." The second number employs "Ain't She Sweet" as a rapid windup to Barris's "Sweet Li'l." Bing instructs the others at the outset, "If it's gonna be good it must be fast," and when they close with an exchange of scat breaks, he mimics a tuba (*bub-bub-bub bub-a-bub-bub-bub*), the modest beginning of a trait for future mimics.

Those recordings are not especially good, and *darkies* aside, have not aged well. Barris is too jumpy, though Rinker proves fairly adept at scat, and the humor is intrusive. Still, "Mississippi Mud" became hugely popular, and they performed it nightly at the Paramount and at the Whiteman club, establishing it as their signature song. Everyone who saw them remembered the number as a Jazz Age anthem. It secured Barris's role as the new brains of the outfit, supplanting Al, who was both grateful and annoyed. Bing was no less ambivalent. "Barris was and is remarkably talented," Bing wrote. "He writes songs as easily as other folk write a letter. In addition he can sing and he's a good comedian. But while he could do all of these things, he knew he could do them. And because he gave the impression of knowing all there was to know, Al and I called him Little Joe Show Business."[9]

Their hard work on the arrangements is evident from the alternate takes, which are virtually indistinguishable from the masters. The Rhythm Boys never achieved anything approaching the buttery harmonies and unison drive of the Mills Brothers or the Boswell Sisters, but their inventiveness and pep influenced both of those groups and countless other vocal teams, some of them rank imitators. Donald Mills and his brothers heard Bing with the Rhythm Boys: "He had a great voice *then* and, actually, some of our music came from listening to what they were doing."[10] Despite their burgeoning popularity, the Rhythm Boys were humbled when Jack Fulton's falsetto la-di-da vocal in an otherwise upbeat arrangement of "My Blue Heaven" generated the biggest Whiteman hit of the year. Spokane's *Daily Chronicle* stayed loyal to its hometown boys, however, commending "Mississippi Mud" and their new partner (mangled as Jack Barriss): "The variety of jazz put into these pieces is distinctive and unique and includes rapid fire patter, bits of solo work, minor chords and close harmonies with deft business on the piano and with the cymbals."[11]

Yet Bing's recorded work over the next three months provided him with few chances to shine. His hoarseness had worsened, and Whiteman felt it best to bury him in the choir. He is so off-mike and whispery in his solo on "The Calinda" — faux Africana tarted up with a weird haunted-house arrangement — that one is surprised Whiteman agreed to release it. On "It Won't Be Long Now," notable for Tommy Dorsey's solos on trombone and trumpet, the Rhythm Boys add little to Malneck's jazzy arrangement. In November the band toured the Midwest. When it arrived in Chicago, the trio was assigned a recording session of its own. Victor declined to release "That's Grandma" (until 1942), a comical, swinging number with a unison scat chorus backed by Harry's piano and Bing's cymbal; the prattling lyric by Bing and Cavanaugh concerns a chipper grandma and relies on allusions to popular entertainers like Eddie Cantor and Moran and Mack. Far more intriguing is "Miss Annabelle Lee," in which Bing huskily parodies sentimental balladeers of the day and improvises a six-bar passage — his first scat solo on records.

It was a warm-up. The next week's sessions represented a turning point, a crucial shift in the Whiteman band that led to the most durable music — along with "Rhapsody in Blue" — of Paul's long career. Two selections recorded at the November 1927 dates, "Changes" and "Mary," established Bing as the choice singer among Whiteman's musicians, some of whom would now regard him as one of the band's top soloists, period.

Whiteman's determination to hire first-rate jazz players paid off that fall. In August Whiteman, Jimmy Dorsey, the Rhythm Boys, Jimmy Gillespie, and Henry Busse had traveled to the Million Dollar Pier in Atlantic City to hear the Jean Goldkette orchestra. They were especially interested in its brilliant young arranger, Bill Challis, whom Dorsey had been pressing Whiteman to hire. The Goldkette organization, based at the Graystone Ballroom in Detroit, included more than twenty bands. Goldkette himself was a French-born failed concert pianist who did not much care for jazz and rarely appeared with the bands touring under his name. By mid-1927 he was devoting most of his time to his booking agency, and his most important band, the one with the great jazz musicians, was rumored to be on its last legs. In Atlantic City Challis invited Whiteman to guest-conduct a number. Afterward, Paul told several of the musicians that he did not want to be responsible for breaking up the band but that when the time was right, he hoped to hear from them.

Challis was the first to join, when Whiteman opened at the Paramount on September 10, a couple of weeks before the Goldkette band collapsed. Goldkette's main jazz stars, including cornetist Bix Beiderbecke and saxophonist Frank Trumbauer, elected to go to New York and work in a big band organized by saxophonist Adrian Rollini. "I was offered a job with Rollini, too, but I liked the idea of the fiddles, all those reeds, all that brass," Challis recalled. "I thought, well, that's for me, that's what I've been looking for, a lot of instruments, a lot of things to do. Plenty of records."[12]

An admirer of Whiteman's key arranger, Ferde Grofé, Challis spent his first weeks "watching and learning, finding out who did what and listening to all the shows."[13] He was put to the test when Whiteman reached Indianapolis. That week other major Goldkette refugees drifted into Whiteman's band, first bassist Steve Brown, then Beiderbecke and Trumbauer. While they rehearsed their opening at the Indiana Theatre, a very green piano player, singer, and songwriter named Hoagy Carmichael stopped by to visit his old friend Bix, who introduced him to Whiteman. Hoagy's first piece, "Washboard Blues," had recently been recorded by a local group, Hitch's Happy Harmonists, with the composer on piano. Whiteman liked it. He told Hoagy that if the tune had lyrics, he would use him to sing them at the band's next recording session in Chicago.

Late that night Whiteman knocked on Challis's hotel room, with Gillespie, Carmichael, and a pedal organ in tow. The organ passed from arranger to arranger, depending on who was working on deadline. Challis recalled, "Paul asked Hoagy to play 'Washboard Blues' and asked me to arrange it for when we got to Chicago."[14] By the time the band opened at Chicago's Uptown Theater, however, Paul had second thoughts about Hoagy's singing and asked Bing to cover for him. Carmichael remembered Bing's coming around while he rehearsed and casually asking to see the lyric, explaining that he simply liked the song and wanted to learn it. "Paul wanted some insurance," Hoagy realized. "If I couldn't do it, he wanted someone who could. Bing was being kind. He didn't want me to know I might flop."[15] Hoagy made the record, and though it failed to get him a job with Whiteman, it marked the beginning of his long and fruitful association with Bing. For his next assignment, Challis determined to use Whiteman's regular singers, all of them — the hot trio and the sweet trio.

Walter Donaldson's "Changes" could not have been more aptly named. As Challis adapted it, the song embodied the changes in the Whiteman band: the old guard giving way to the new, the old dance-band aesthetic succumbing to the improvisational vitality of jazz. Of course, the title also suggested the bullish transformations in a nervous pre-Depression America that, during the previous six months alone, had witnessed Lindbergh's flight, Sacco and Vanzetti's execution, Babe Ruth's sixty home runs, and *The Jazz Singer*, the first feature-length talking picture. A song-plugger representing Donaldson's publisher gave "Changes" to Whiteman, who handed it to Challis, who reversed the usual roles of the two vocal trios. The sweet trio sings the first theme in strong midrange unison; the Rhythm Boys follow with a high-voiced harmony, singing four bars and scatting four more. The third theme is all Bing, followed instantly by a glorious cornet improvisation from the astonishing Bix. Though Donaldson's lyric concerns the changing of musical keys (with a gratuitous reference to "many babies that he can squeeze"), the melody employs few notes; Bing's episode consists almost entirely of repeated Gs, which he caps with a trombonelike melisma. "What I liked about Bing," Challis marveled, "was there were fast words in there and they came out beautifully — excellent enunciation." Challis underscores the energy of the soloists with exchanges between the winds and strings and a deep bottom bolstered by three baritone saxophones. "Paul said use whatever I wanted and I did."[16]

One man who was not happy with the changes was Henry Busse, Whiteman's long-serving trumpet star whose rickety muted approach had once been considered "hot." When Challis omitted him from his arrangement of "Washboard Blues," Busse protested, pointing out that his contract guaranteed him a role in every Whiteman record. His jealousy would snowball as Beiderbecke increasingly usurped his position. He could not fail to notice that Whiteman treated the young and troubled newcomer like a son. (Paul and Bix had in common fathers almost Kafkaesque in their disapproving rage.) Bix was a heroic magnet for Chicago's young white jazz musicians, who never gave a thought to the likes of Busse, and Bing was immediately accepted into that golden circle. They would hang out at a storefront speakeasy on State Street known as the Three Deuces, after the notorious brothel called the Four Deuces. Mezz Mezzrow recalled a midnight jam at the Deuces in November: "[Bing] beat time all night with his hands, like he was at a Holy Rollers meeting. Under Bix's spell, everybody was a genius that night."[17]

Two days after "Changes," another Donaldson tune defined the band's stylistic divisions. In Malneck's mischievous arrangement, "Mary" entangles Busse and Bix much as "Changes" connected the sweet and hot singers. After an ensemble introduction, Busse's muted trumpet states the theme in damp staccato over a starchy *bum-cha bum-cha* rhythm. Then Bix takes over the brasses for the verse, delivering them and the entire ensemble into the sunshine of swing.

Toward the end of the performance, Bix begins his flaming eight-bar improvisation with an impatient rip and, leading the brasses in contrapuntal figures, all but drowns out Busse's reprise of the theme.

Yet Bix isn't the key soloist. Bing is. Voice restored, he sings his chorus with exemplary finesse, articulating details at a cantering tempo and balancing rhythmic heat with vocal cool. He reshapes the melody, improving Donaldson's cadences, displaying a jazz license all his own. The kind of liberties he took, however subtle, were not often appreciated by songwriters and publishers, who were known to threaten legal action over an altered note or word. Bing shows no trace of the Jolson influence, but he avails himself of an influence that had lain dormant: the upper mordent, also known as a pralltriller, that wavering catch in the voice preserved in the folk singing of Ireland, Scotland, and northern Africa. In his final phrases ("You wouldn't let my castles come tum-tum-tumbling down. . . . What are you waiting for, Mary?"), Bing employs mordents on *down* and *Mary*.

Unlike "Changes," "Mary" was not a hit with the public but was a triumph with the new guard in Whiteman's band. Challis and other members lobbied for more Crosby features. To insiders, Bing was becoming something of a Bixian hero. Just as Bix proved that a white musician could be an expressively nonconformist jazz player, Bing showed that a white male vocalist did not have to sound like a Floradora girl. Bing thought like a musician; he had his own sound; he improvised; he had time.

Throughout the year, carbon microphones were increasingly replaced by new condenser microphones, which favored singers with an intimate approach. In Bing's case, the mikes registered his fetching throatiness and nuanced phrasing. By the end of 1927, they were used with greater frequency in theaters, too, thanks in part to two show-business milestones that fall. On September 18 CBS Radio began broadcasting, giving NBC some badly needed competition and emphasizing improvements in the electrical reproduction of sound; on October 6 Jolson's picture *The Jazz Singer* opened on Broadway, justifying the Warner brothers' faith in Vitaphone and hastening further advances in audio technology.

Two days after Christmas *Show Boat* opened at the Ziegfeld, a turning point for the American musical theater and, as it happened, a milestone for Bing. Whiteman assigned Challis "Ol' Man River" from the magnificent score by Jerome Kern and Oscar Hammerstein II. Challis went to work, preparing the chart for Bing. That week White-man debuted on NBC with his own show. Scheduled to sing, Bing alerted his family. But those in Spokane who huddled around their radios were disappointed when he sang and was not identified — an indication of how inside his reputation was. "Ol' Man River" would help change that. Challis and Malneck worked at a hotel piano, trying different voicings for the song. Malneck tuned the strings "à la Venuti,"[18] a nod to Joe Venuti's method of playing with the bow under the violin's soundboard and the horsehairs tied over the strings, enabling him to play four-note chords. The inevitable dissonances were incorporated in ensemble passages backing Bing. Whiteman himself chose the buoyant tempo; he emphasized to Challis that he was making a dance record, not a semiclassical piece. On Broadway, Paul Robeson sang it an octave lower than Bing, who delighted the rehearsing musicians when he took it up. Challis recalled, "He could do that and make it sound good. He had good intonation. Took the whole tune and went right on up. You didn't have to tell him what to do, he just did it and did it nicely."[19]

The record was a sensation; months later Whiteman sought to extend its success by recording another version with Robeson and a choir. But Bing's triumph was singular. Coming on the heels of such sentimental Whiteman bestsellers as "Together" (vocal, Jack Fulton) and "Ramona" (vocal, Skin Young), it created a stir among musicians and fans, expanding Whiteman's following among younger listeners. Cultural historian James T. Maher, in high school at the time, believed Bing's version spoke specifically to his generation. Johnny Mercer was transfixed by it: "It seemed to me he employed a completely new and different style which sounded more natural and effortless than any I'd ever heard."[20] Britain's young were mesmerized as well. As Alistair Cooke recalled, "Word ran through the English underground that a genuine jazz singer — and a white man! — had appeared in the unlikeliest place: breezing along on the ocean of Paul Whiteman's lush 'symphonic' sound."[21] Even an older Bing, notoriously parsimonious with praise for any of his records, begrudgingly mentioned "Ol' Man River" as one of two favorites (along with his 1939 "My Isle of Golden Dreams"): "I made a good record of 'Ol' Man River' when I was with Whiteman. It was a good arrangement anyhow and I thought what I had to do on it was adequate."[22] He surely recognized the source of the climactic line in Hammerstein's lyric: "I was at the same time," confessed Saint Augustine, "thoroughly tired of living and extremely frightened of dying."[23]

Bing was elated to be surrounded, finally, by some of the country's most admired white jazz players. He roomed with Bix at New York's Belvedere Hotel, where many of Whiteman's musicians were quartered. The two friends listened to and discussed music constantly, whether they were sober or spinning. Bix held his liquor better than Bing, who frequently fell into a stupor. Of the men he most often named as musical influences — Jolson, Armstrong, and Beiderbecke — Bing was personally closest to Bix. He memorized his cornet solos, scatted his phrases, and was particularly taken with Bix's devotion to modern classics, from Eastwood Lane and Cyril Scott to Claude Debussy and Igor Stravinsky. As critic Larry Kart would observe, Bix's blend of American jazz and European classicism was "a romantic sound — gentle, intimate, and tinged with nostalgia. And those were the qualities that soon would mark Crosby's style."[24]

Bing and Bix spent a lot of time at a speakeasy down the street from the Whiteman club's old spot. The place had a piano on the balcony, where, despite the speak's loud goings-on, Bix and other musicians exchanged ideas. "I didn't contribute anything but I listened and learned," Bing recalled. "I felt my style then was a cross between Al Jolson and a musical instrument. I was now being influenced by these musicians. . . . Bix, Bill Challis, even Frank Trumbauer would make suggestions to me for my vocalizing and I'd give it a try."[25] When Trumbauer organized a session for OKeh Records early in 1928, he hired Bing along with Bix, Malneck, Chester Hazlett, Jimmy Dorsey, Min Leibrook, and pianist Lennie Hayton, among others (paying Bix fifty dollars, Hazlett thirty dollars, and the rest twenty-five). He even selected two numbers created by the Rhythm Boys. Trumbauer's recording of "From Monday On" was never issued, but "Mississippi Mud" is a jazz classic, albeit one often found distasteful because of the patter between Tram (as Trumbauer was known) and Bing. Though they avoid heavy dialect, their routine is decidedly in the idiom of blackface vaudeville acts like Moran and Mack, with Tram stuttering his lines. The only soloists are Bix (a resplendent chorus) and a strikingly relaxed Bing, upholding his end of the patter without missing a beat of the song.

With his jazz players pressuring him to feature Bing as a soloist, Whiteman made him a regular at recording sessions, though he buried him in the choir almost as often as he brought him into the limelight. Yet Whiteman was canny enough to give Bing numbers that suited him — especially after "Ol' Man River" topped sales charts in March. Remarkably, Bing participated in more sessions in 1928 — about three dozen — than he would again until 1940. Those record dates track the artist in development, as he jettisons the Jolson flutter and the stiffness that marred "Muddy Water." Bing developed a uniquely spirited sangfroid. No matter how jazzed-up the setting, he negotiated the words, rhythm, and melody with a polished timbre and flawless enunciation. Even on off days Crosby's instrument radiated confidence. Most of his predecessors who were not belters belonged to the genteel school and sang with effete head tones. Bing conveyed a chest-tone approach, making full use of his diaphragm. His vocal mask was complete and mature. But his most extraordinary gift was to communicate naturally. While other pop singers employed ponderous or flaccid tones, Bing sang the same way he spoke. His style avoided the mannerisms of style; his art seemed artless, even effortless.

One example is his stunning chorus on Grofé's breakneck version of *Show Boat*'s "Make Believe." The instrumental chorus is ornate, but Bing's vocal, backed by Steve Brown's stomping bass, marries rhythmic panache to pitch-perfect articulation and underscores the lyric's meaning despite the charged tempo. Tom Satterfield reflected Challis's influence in his finest arrangement, "There Ain't No Sweet Man That's Worth the Salt of My Tears," a jazz classic with Bix driving the ensemble and Bing rattling his first word — a rhythmically italicized *I'm* — for a sensational entrance. The song's unchanged gender reflects the obstinacy of song publishers, who would not allow singers to alter pronouns; Bing was not permitted to sing "there ain't no sweet gal." Since the great majority of songs were conceived as male entreaties to women, the sanctity of pronouns discouraged the employment of female singers, a convention Whiteman eventually breached when he hired Mildred Bailey.

At a February session Bing sang the obscure "Sunshine," notable only as his first recording of an Irving Berlin song — a handsomely executed but commonplace beginning for what would turn out to be

a mighty collaboration. Within weeks he was also featured on Malneck's strongest arrangement since "I'm Coming, Virginia" (perhaps
his finest ever), the definitive version of "From Monday On," for
orchestra and all six singers. A Barris original, with input from Bing
on the lyric, the song was first recorded by the Rhythm Boys in January. That performance marked Bing's debut as a whistler and includes
an awkward Al Rinker chorus that publicly revealed what everyone in
Whiteman's fold knew: a huge musical gap existed between the former Musicaladers. Malneck's version, made six weeks later, was
something else, an arranger's fantasia.

Matty devised an elaborate setting for "From Monday On," beginning with Fulton and company mooing the introduction in tenor
range. The Rhythm Boys scat an interlude, and Bix charges in with a
high note and full chorus as the saxes carry the theme. Matty confined Al to the choir and let Bing carry the main vocal chorus. In the
best-known of three surviving takes, Bing tags a couple of words
(*skies, on*) with Jolsonesque vibrato, though he lightened up on the
later takes. He is otherwise loose and robust, and the record has a
joyousness that has lost nothing over the years. To a musician like
Challis, "He sang a song right, in the register you wanted to hear it. If
it was up to me who the singer would be, it was usually Crosby. He
enunciated and he had presence. He could hit a low A flat, maybe a
little lower, and his top note was F, but he didn't have a preferred key.
I always used my own judgment."[26]

"High Water," Whiteman's pretentious attempt at a hymn, typifies
what jazz players loathed about his music but is perversely amusing
for Bing's spoken interlude — a parody of Jolson — and for his evident relief when swinging the chorus. "What Price Lyrics?" by Barris,
Bing, and Malneck, is a chatty send-up of *moon/June* rhymes (Bing
offers *Sammy/mammy*) and finishes with a round of scat. "Lovable" is
a negligible Richard Whiting melody, brightly arranged by Challis.
Bing's stellar chorus makes the most of Seymour Simons's lyric ("others just imitate / kisses that you create") and is characterized by canny
breath control and minor embellishments, prefiguring his mature
style. (For some reason, "Lovable" was released only in England.)
Challis's "My Pet" intrigues because three takes exist in which Bing
improvises very different eight-bar segments, combining scat and
words on the first, borrowing Armstrong licks for the second, and
finding himself on the third.

*   *   *

Most of the songs of the period were not appreciably better than "My Pet," and many that Bing tackled were worse, for example, "I'm Afraid of You" or "It Was the Dawn of Love." But every so often a gem came along, suggesting another reason that Bing was the ideal man for the time. Songwriting was entering a new phase of sophistication and subtlety. Only parodies could accommodate the *June/moon* rhymes, mother worship, patriotic gibberish, and coon song outrages that had dominated Tin Pan Alley for nearly a quarter of a century. The 1920s brought talented songwriters able to embrace the Jazz Age blend of Prohibition, flaming youth, exotica, and sex. Among the most enduring were Walter Donaldson ("Makin' Whoopee," "Yes Sir! That's My Baby"); Spencer Williams ("I Ain't Got Nobody," "Everybody Loves My Baby"); Jimmy McHugh and Dorothy Fields ("I Can't Give You Anything but Love," "Doin' the New Low-Down"); Bert Kalmar and Harry Ruby ("Nevertheless," "Three Little Words"); and Buddy DeSylva, Ray Henderson, and Lew Brown ("Button Up Your Overcoat," "The Best Things in Life Are Free").

Yet by 1928, after *Show Boat,* even the songs of those progressive talents seemed transitional. Something new was going on. You heard it in the swinging ingenuity of Lorenz Hart and Richard Rodgers ("Manhattan," "Thou Swell"), the sexy wit and minor keys of Cole Porter ("Let's Do It," "You Do Something to Me"), the invigorated melodies of the prophetic Irving Berlin ("Blue Skies," "How About Me?"). With the arrival of book musicals on stage and later in film, American songwriting entered a golden age, an explosion of melody and harmony to rival the recently faded glory days of Italian opera. Crosby was the era's first great voice and interpreter. He made lyrics understandable, worthy of attention.

Good songs liberated Bing. On "Louisiana," written by J. C. Johnson and Andy Razaf, Challis introduces him with a brassy fanfare and a "waaaah" from the vocal choir, launching a marvelous supple chorus in which Bing fulfills the promise of those elocution distinctions he earned at Gonzaga. Unfortunately, the exuberance of that performance was torpedoed the next afternoon by the mutiny of Whiteman's old guard.

Furious at the attention lavished on Beiderbecke, Henry Busse was at the boiling point. No one could recall exactly what set him off, but in the last hour of a recording session, he loudly berated Paul. The bandleader snapped back at him. Another old-timer, drummer Hal McDonald, sided with Busse. The dispute ended with the two stomping out of Liederkranz Hall and the Whiteman organization. With one scheduled tune left, a dejected Paul canceled work till the next day and put out a call for replacements. Despite the calamity, the postponed tune emerged as a Whiteman benchmark. Satterfield adapted Rodgers and Hart's "You Took Advantage of Me," a hit song introduced by Joyce Barbour and Busby Berkeley in the revue *Present Arms*. The record is celebrated for the riotous chase chorus (a conversational but formally precise exchange) by Bix and Tram and the vocal that follows. Bing had the unenviable task of upholding a high level of invention, but as Bix's biographer, Richard Sudhalter, has observed, "Bing Crosby, entering immediately afterwards, catches the mood exactly, voice brimming with obvious pleasure at what has just gone on."[27]

That number represented not only the end of the old Whiteman band but the end of the orchestra's historic eight-year association with Victor. Chiefly because of a perceived rivalry with another Victor bandleader (Nat Shilkret), Whiteman signed with the accommodating Columbia Records. He was so miffed at Victor that on May 12 he allowed a Fox Movietone newsreel crew to film him tearing up his contract at the stroke of midnight (when his association with Victor officially ended). Worried by the large number of records Whiteman had stockpiled at Victor, Columbia wanted him in the studio immediately. To underscore its commitment to the band, the company paid Whiteman the singular tribute of designing him his own disc label: a pale blue potato-shaped caricature of Paul set against an orange-and-green background. Yet a thorn lurked behind the pastels. Columbia's engineers were not as good as their Victor counterparts at capturing the band's plush sound. Worse, the sessions were run by Eddie King, a jazz-hating producer who encouraged Whiteman to revive his old sound; the winged phrasing of a Bing or Bix gave him no pleasure.

Meanwhile, Bing was enjoying the good life, whether on tour or at home base. The money was good and the booze was plentiful. Every city the band played — Chicago, Minneapolis, Detroit, Erie — provided him with a golf course by day and speakeasies by night. In New York the Rhythm Boys were in demand for private parties thrown by or for such celebrities as Mayor Walker, Buddy DeSylva, and Beatrice Lillie. Other nights the guys headed for Harlem, for mixed-race jam sessions in Fletcher Henderson's basement or shows at the Cotton Club and other venues starring such titans as Duke Ellington and Ethel Waters. On Broadway the boys soaked up songs in such shows as *Oh, Kay!*, with Gertrude Lawrence and a Gershwin score; *Oh, Please!*, with Bea Lillie and music by Vincent Youmans; *Funny Face*, with Fred Astaire and another Gershwin score; as well as *Hit the Deck!* (Youmans) and *A Connecticut Yankee* (Rodgers and Hart) and more — entertainment without end. Bing, Al, and Harry were present at *Midnight Frolic*, an exclusive show atop the New Amsterdam, when Maurice Chevalier made his American debut. They met Maurice Ravel at a Whiteman session and attended his concert at Mecca Auditorium. They spent numerous evenings doubled-up with laughter at the Parody Club, home to the vaudeville anarchy of Clayton, Jackson, and Durante. The great Durante never failed to convulse Bing. But maybe the Rhythm Boys spent too much time together; they were beginning to get on one another's nerves.

"We couldn't decide which of us was boss," Bing recalled. "Every three or four weeks we decided to break up, then the next day we'd get back together again."[28] Bing could be cantankerous and was becoming unreliable. Some nights he was so green from drink that he had to be held up at the mike; on other nights he did not show at all. Barris was never without his flask, constantly nipping. Al tried to keep up, no easy task when he double-dated with Bix, but remained the most responsible — "I was too young to keep up with them"[29] — and was sometimes perceived by the others as a scold. The women they saw were chorus girls, of which there was a limitless supply.

When Whiteman played Philadelphia in December 1927, Bing met two roommates, Ginger Meehan and Dolores Reade, who were appearing in the road cast of Eddie Dowling's *Honeymoon Lane*. The women would remain in his life, but as the wives of men with whom he had lifelong associations: in 1930 Ginger married Johnny Mercer, and three years later Dolores married Bob Hope. Dolores recalled, "Back in the Philadelphia days, if they couldn't find Bing, they'd say, well, where was he last night, and they'd go and look for him under one of the tables."[30]

Francis Cork O'Keefe, the dapper manager who later advised Bing, also saw him at the Philadelphia engagement, having taken the train from New York because "people had been raving about a guy with Whiteman." He found Bing "nervous and shy."[31] O'Keefe may have been the first to suggest that he go out as a single, but Bing dismissed the idea; he did not even want to make a record under his own name. "I sat in the first row," O'Keefe told an interviewer in 1946. "Harry Barris was the piano player, the clown of the crowd. Bing had the worst sore throat, but I heard him and liked him. I went backstage to say hello to the guys and met him. He had something, but then he was just another one of the fellows. They were trying to get him to make a solo record, but he laughed — said it was silly, no one wanted to hear him alone."[32] O'Keefe worked on him for better than a year, to no avail. He was not ready.

Bing was more focused on Ginger Meehan, a quietly pretty, Brooklyn-born brunette with delicate features — just the type he preferred. One night in New York, at nearly 1:00 A.M., Bing wired Ginger at Philadelphia's Emerson Hotel: ACCORDING TO US STATISTICS THERE ARE 7 MILLION PEOPLE HERE BUT WITHAL IM A STRANGER AND MISERABLY ALONE BECAUSE YOURE NOT ALONG LOVE UNDYING BEST REGARDS TO DOLORES AND STUFF. BING.[33] The affair continued on and off through the summer. When Whiteman pulled into Chicago in July, Ginger was already there, in the road company of *Good News*. Bing wired her at the Selwyn Theater: WOULD LIKE TO SAY HELLO THIS EVE AFTER YOUR PERFORMANCE SAY AT ELEVEN FIFTEEN. BING.[34] Six days later he wired her a few minutes before she went onstage: WOULD LIKE TO CALL YOU TONIGHT IF BUSY SUE ME BING.[35] Ginger didn't sue, but the romance fizzled, possibly because Bing became enamored of another *Good News* cast member, the star, Peggy Bernier, whom he had met twice before — at Don Clark's recording session and in Jack Partington's San Francisco revues. Bing's infatuation with Peggy, who could keep up with his late-night carousing, lasted several months, unlike most of his romances, which were as fleeting as stops on a vaudeville circuit.

The good life took its toll on the Rhythm Boys. Whiteman complained that they no longer seemed as dedicated to their work. They stayed out late and looked beat at the early matinees. When the movie went on, they would repair to a nearby speakeasy and sometimes could hardly tear themselves away in time to make the next show. Merwyn Bogue, a worshipful young Whiteman fan who became popular in the 1930s as Kay Kyser's trumpet player and comic foil, Ish Kabibble, got a close look at them on and off the bandstand. He first saw the Rhythm Boys when Whiteman opened at the Perry Theater in Erie, Pennsylvania. "The audience went wild"[36] as the trio, backed by Rinker on a tiny organ, belted out "Mississippi Mud." Bogue attended all four shows every day of the engagement, and designated himself the boys' guardian after he tailed them to a speakeasy one afternoon:

> The boys muttered a password through the little peephole. A door opened, and we all went inside. The owner must have considered me part of the group. But nobody knew me from Bephus, and I sat off in a corner by myself. The three of them got something to drink, scooped handfuls of peanuts from a glass penny machine, and sat telling stories. I was so afraid they would be late for their next show that I appointed myself their timekeeper. . . . When I finally said ["Hey, fellows, you better start walking back or you'll miss your next show"], they looked at me as if to say, "Who are you?" But they got up and left. After this had happened a few more times, one of them said, "Thanks kid." They were never late for a show that whole week.[37]

In 1949, when Ish Kabibble had a spot in the Crosby movie *Riding High,* he asked Bing "if he remembered a kid in an Erie speakeasy who always got him to the theater on time. He did a double take, swung his golf club at another wad of Kleenex, and said, 'Was that you? Hey, those were the greatest peanuts I ever ate!'"

The boys' most grievous sin was their failure to "grow the act." Whiteman assigned them roles on recordings, but he expected them to develop new material for concerts and their own record dates (which, like the band's, were made at Columbia). In Bing's estimation, "I don't think we were too serious about our work, it was just something we liked to do, we enjoyed it and never really made a conscious effort to improve ourselves. Although we looked for new material all the time, it was difficult to get all three of us together at one time for a rehearsal. About the only time we did is when Whiteman had something for us to do with the big band and then we had to be there or we'd get the old sack."[38]

Whiteman had no intention of firing them, but he was losing patience and noticed that some theater audiences continued to resist the trio's charms. As *Variety* observed, "There seem to be a lot of people in a picture house audience who don't know what they're trying to do or what it's all about, but it's funny, hot, and good."[39] In July Whiteman summoned the boys to his office and, as Barris recalled, told them, "I'm taking the band on tour and if it's okay with you, I'd like to place you on a vaudeville circuit."[40] They had little choice. In a sense, Paul was exiling them from the band. He hoped that independence would straighten them out and spur their creativity. If they could cultivate audiences on their own, they would be a more attractive component in the orchestra's presentations when he brought them home. Meantime, he would be increasing his income, taking a percentage of their tour in addition to receipts generated by the band. Paul promised that they would rejoin the orchestra when it returned to New York and that in the interim he would continue to use them on records.

On August 1 he gave the news to the press: the Rhythm Boys would be playing the Keith-Albee, Orpheum, and Proctor vaudeville circuit. Whiteman did, as he promised, bring them in for several studio sessions, but otherwise the boys were on their own for six months, through February 1929. While the band toured in the East, the Rhythm Boys traveled to their first stop: the Proctor Theater in Yonkers. They played most major Midwestern cities and a few eastern ones, dipping as far south as Nashville, usually to great acclaim. At each venue they were introduced by a life-size plywood cutout of Paul and a transcription of his voice. "Ladies and gentlemen," it proclaimed, "I take great pleasure in presenting to you my Rhythm Boys."[41]

They began the tour in high spirits. The double challenge of big-time vaudeville and autonomy invigorated them, though not musically. For a while they worked out a comedy dance routine to "Baby Face," taking turns as they parodied what Al described as "dime-a-dozen dance routines by second rate hoofers."[42] Despite the jokey intent, those "corny" steps proved a useful part of Bing's apprenticeship; he used them throughout his career, not only in routines with Bob Hope and Fred Astaire but in comic time steps and hand gestures that defined his persona in numerous films and TV shows. The boys also worked out a comic mind-reading routine, with Harry and Al engaging the audience as Bing did the swami bit onstage in a turban (prefiguring a routine in the 1946 *Road to Utopia*). Bing acknowledged, "We had indifferent success. We went up and down. It depended. See, we'd been in vaudeville a lot and we'd been watching a lot of comics and we wanted to do comedy. And as a result, we weren't singing hardly anything. And the managers of the different hotels and theaters objected to this strenuously. They thought they were booking a record seller, you know."[43]

Playing only two shows a day, beginning at 2:00 P.M., Bing and Al spent mornings on the golf course, renewing their friendship and perfecting their games; they played about equally well and always for a small amount of money. To their surprise, most of the best private courses in each city granted them admission. Harry didn't play, but he kept busy writing songs and nursing his flask. In Columbus, Ohio, they shared a bill with Jack Benny, who, learning of their mania for golf, asked whether he could join Bing and Al in a game. They had already made arrangements at the Scioto Country Club (where Jack Nicklaus learned to play) and so changed their reservation to a threesome, arriving early the next morning in their plus fours. After three or four holes, Bing hit his ball over a fence into a cow pasture. "That's a new ball," Bing complained, and climbed over the fence to get it.[44] As he searched the pasture, Al and Jack heard a frightful bellowing and turned to see a mammoth black bull galloping toward Bing. As they yelled warnings, Bing took off like buckshot, barely making it over the fence in time. Shaken, they laughed it off, as they tended to do with most things.

The Rhythm Boys usually managed to look good onstage in their blue blazers and white flannels. Harry stood five foot six but usually sat at the piano; Bing was five nine and Al five ten. *Variety* recognized them as a potential hit "with the younger generation, particularly the flaps [girls]"[45] but was less pleased with the material. Robert Landry, who had written the first review of Bing and Al in San Francisco and was now reporting from New York, saw "ample room for improvement" in the fifteen-minute act: "Little too much of sameness about the horseplay. More rhythm and melody and less slamming of the music rack suggested." With "elimination and improvements," he thought, they would be "a consistent zowie."[46] They ignored the advice, preferring to rack up hilarity on- and offstage.

Bing's favorite city on tour was Chicago, where the trio played one week in September and another in November. As he grew friendly with Louis Armstrong, they began to inspire each other. Bing had learned much from Louis about style, spontaneity, time, and feeling. Armstrong was the fount from which Bing's swinging and irreverent but emotional approach to song developed. Louis returned the admiration, picking up on Bing's timbre and his way with ballads, which he soon added to his repertoire. Occasionally Louis even paid Bing homage by covering his songs or inserting a telling mordent. Writing in the 1960s to a friend, he discussed Bing at length: "Shortly after I witnessed my first hearing of Bing's singing, he started making records with his Trio and different bands. Then, later, by himself. And *that did* settle it. There were just as many colored people 'buying air,' raving over Bing's recordings, as much as anybody else. The chicks (gals) were justa swooning and screaming when Bing would sing. . . . The man was a Natural Genius the day he was born. Ever since Bing first opened his mouth, he was the *Boss of All Singers* and Still is."[47]

One night Armstrong took Charlie Carpenter, his valet and subsequently a lyricist ("You Can Depend on Me") and Earl Hines's manager, to the Grand Terrace Ballroom, which stayed open until 4:30 A.M. The Rhythm Boys stopped by at 2:00, after finishing their own gig. Charlie was too young to drink but marveled at Bing's thirst. When he ran into Bing thirty years later on a television soundstage, he told him, "I haven't seen you since 1928, Bing, but I still remember you were tore up." Bing laughed and said, "I probably was because in those days I was really putting it away."[48] He was consuming more than liquor.

Louis's influence on Bing extended to his love of marijuana, which he alternately called mezz (after Mezz Mezzrow), gage, pot, or muggles. Bing didn't develop the lifelong appetite for it that Louis did, but he enjoyed it in the early days — it was legal — and, like Louis, surprised interviewers in the 1960s and 1970s by suggesting it be decriminalized, to set it apart from more harmful and addictive drugs. Bing's eldest son, Gary, argued that pot had a lasting effect on his father's style: "If you look at the way he sang and the way he walked and talked, you could make a pretty good case for somebody who was loaded. He said to me one time when he was really mad, ranting and raving about my heavy drinking, he said, 'Oh, that fucking booze. It killed your mother. Why don't you just smoke shit?' That was all he said but there were other times when marijuana was mentioned and he'd get a smile on his face. He'd kind of think about it and there'd be that little smile."[49]

Gary's theory is hardly the strangest explanation of Bing's preternatural cool, which in the early years of his career suggested indifference rather than the composure for which he became famous. It was as if he had not fully committed himself to the idea of making himself a success. He made no attempt to hide his stumbling inconsistency, except in letters home, which were often accompanied by mementos and gifts. His younger brother, Bob, finishing high school, received regular updates on Bing's fortunes: "He'd write me quite often, tell me about the cities he played and what was happening in the orchestra. He sent me records of the original Dorsey brothers band and a lot of jazz things with Frankie Trumbauer and Bix Beiderbecke and some of the great musicians; a lot of Louie Armstrong, that was one of his favorites. Told me at one time, 'I'm sending you a tennis racket and a whole tennis outfit. I want you to learn how to play tennis because that's a great way to meet people.' And he sent me from Saks Fifth Avenue a very expensive racket and beautiful sweater and the shoes and the whole thing and a book of instructions by Bill Tilden."[50]

About that time, Bing posed — uncharacteristically natty — for an eight-by-ten sepia portrait, his hands tucked into the pockets of a double-breasted jacket, with a handkerchief peaking from the breast pocket, and his tie carefully arranged with a dimple below the knot. His eyes are luminous and his hair thinning; a rakish, ready smile is crowned by an exactingly trimmed mustache. In his caption on a copy he sent his brother Ted, Bing wrote, "brush by Fuller." His inscription also included a question without a question mark: "Am I too suave or sveldt."[51]

He was neither when he finished the November 1928 week in Chicago. During that visit Bing's romance with Peggy Bernier blossomed, though they were not especially committed to each other. A series of beaux awaited Peggy at the stage door. To Bing, the *Good News* cast was a chicken coop and he was the fox. He dated one of Peggy's two roommates and tried to get the other on the phone. But Dixie Carroll, who turned seventeen the day before the Rhythm Boys opened at the State-Lake Theater, had heard plenty about Bing's reputation and refused his call. (A year later in Hollywood, she would take the name Dixie Lee and meet Bing face-to-face for the first time.) Still, Bing could not bear to part with Peggy, a playmate who could hold her liquor better than he, and when Harry and Al took the train for the next gig, in Rockford, Illinois, he promised to leave the next day and get there on time. After a serious night of saloon-hopping, Peggy poured him onto a train. Bing passed out and slept the distance, but it did him no good; he was in such bad shape when the train pulled in, the police hauled him to jail and kept him overnight, refusing to let him use the phone.

Harry and Al panicked. They went onstage as a duo for two shows, kibitzing their way through comedy numbers and haphazardly filling in Bing's part. "We were sure something awful happened to Bing," Al said, "maybe an accident."[52] After the second show they called the hotel, and Bing answered, groggy and chagrined as he admitted why he had not been able to call them. They took revenge by asking an Irish actor to impersonate the theater manager. The actor marched up to Bing's room and accused him of betraying his partners and breaching his contract. Bing abjectly apologized, asking the manager not to punish the other two for his transgressions, until Al and Harry could take no more and stopped the charade. He accepted the prank, smiling in relief.

While his Rhythm Boys cavorted through the Midwest, Whiteman enjoyed a series of triumphs in the East, including a Carnegie Hall celebration of his tenth year in New York. On the same September day that Whiteman recorded a garish medley of Christmas carols, among them "Silent Night" (a song that would one day become a Crosby annuity), an apoplectic theater manager in Toledo brought down the curtain on the Rhythm Boys in retaliation for what he con- sidered a vulgar joke: "Say, Harry, do you know how to cure a horse from frothing at the mouth?" "Why no, Bing, how do you cure a horse from frothing at the mouth?" "Well, Harry, you teaches him to spit."[53] The boys were happier when they were in New York, and the band made better records when they were around.

One of them is Challis's arrangement of Willard Robison's faux-rural hymn, "'Taint So, Honey, 'Taint So," the first record ever to begin with the singer entering before the band, which comes in a millisecond later. It was a startling thing to do, and a rumor grew that Bing was unable to pitch the correct note until the tenth take, when Challis had to prompt him with a pitch pipe. Challis denied the whole story: "I wanted to start off with a vocal, just a prank sort of, so

I gave him the note he starts on. I think Paul beat off, or I did, well, anyway, he came right in and sang it. No problems or anything. And no problems with changes of key. He had a wonderful ear."[54] "'Taint So" is also notable for a balky bassoon solo by Trumbauer and dark Venuti-influenced strings behind Bing's vocal.

Another standout, Walter Donaldson's "Because My Baby Don't Mean 'Maybe' Now," opens with a chorus in which Bix Beiderbecke improvises figures that are closely shadowed by the band's written phrases (a passage that shows why Ellington admired Challis). But the record is best known for Bing's jaunty vocal; he completes several phrases with spirited *bu-bu-bu-boo*s. Young fans began to note Bing's spoken interjections, like "why say there" on "Wa Da Da" or "tell it" on "My Suppressed Desire" — which *The New Yorker* helpfully classified as not a "profound study in psychoanalysis, but [a] record full of surprises."[55] In truth, the record's only revelation is Bing's blithe eight-bar scat episode.

The Rhythm Boys were back in New York to play Christmas week at the Palace (*Variety* praised Bing's ballad and the threesome's "modulation of the vo-do-de-o stuff")[56] and Newark's Proctor on New Year's Eve. The day before closing at the Palace, Bing made two records with the Ipana Troubadours, a radio orchestra led by Sam Lanin that included several of Bing's jazz buddies (the Dorseys, Vic Berton, Manny Klein), though you would not know it from the staid arrangements. Bing's hiring indicated his growing stature among top musicians. He got to sing a very good song, "I'll Get By," with a somewhat husky voice and tinge of Jolson, and a very bad one, "Rose of Mandalay," which he nonetheless enhanced with his intrepid zip.

On February 5 Whiteman inaugurated *The Old Gold Hour,* a successful series on WABC (the New York flagship of the Columbia Broadcasting System), airing Tuesdays at nine. Whiteman liked to tell how he originally offered the show to the president of NBC, who turned him down because his network already had a cigarette sponsor. Despite jealous sponsors, radio was about to enjoy a crushing if provisional triumph over its hated rival, the recording industry, aided by the stock market crash later in the year. Records were expensive, and radio offered free entertainment subsidized by advertising accounts. Even before the crash, the new medium flaunted its power. When the Radio Corporation of America took control of the Victor Talking Machine Company in 1928, it established RCA Victor, a division intended to manufacture nothing but radios (it produced 4 million that year alone). RCA would have been happy to wipe out the phonograph altogether. Instead, Victor officials held the fort, and RCA became the leading record label of the 1930s. Still, as late as 1939, when records rebounded with sensational sales, the networks tried to keep them off the air.

Old Gold initially paid Whiteman $5,000 per broadcast hour for sixteen weeks. William S. Paley, who had just been elected president of CBS, knew the bandleader's popularity would draw stations nationwide to his network, especially when the band went on the road, broadcasting from a different city each week. Old Gold had other concerns. Its deal required Whiteman to present his Rhythm Boys — the trio evidently had an influential fan in the tobacco business. Perhaps the executive was fond of "Mississippi Mud" or thought a young trio would lure young smokers or recognized a musical turnaround taking place, favoring baritones over tenors. Maybe all three motives figured in his rationale. For a turnaround was indeed in the air. Sponsors wanted people to keep their radios on as much as possible, as a soothing background for millions of potential consumers. Higher voices are better for reaching theater balconies, but lower ones are more appealing in living rooms. Radio's superior sound captured the subtle nuances of deeper voices.

Whiteman cheerfully reinstated the Rhythm Boys at double their salaries ($300 each). He had another use for them beyond radio. A few months earlier, in the fall of 1928, when Herbert Hoover was elected president, Paul had agreed to star — for two-fifths of the net — in Universal's "super-special 100 per cent talker," *King of Jazz.* Carl Laemmle, Universal's president, and Jimmy Gillespie signed the contracts at New York's Harmony Club, agreeing to go into production in March with director Wesley Ruggles. Nothing about this production would go as planned.

11

OF CABBAGES
AND KINGS

Get yourself set for the biggest news you've ever heard
since the advent of the audible screen. . . .
— advertisement, *Variety* (1929)[1]

The first screenwriter assigned to the project had little sympathy with
Whiteman's ideas.[2] When their discussions collapsed, the film was
rescheduled for the fall and the band planned to head for the Coast
in May. Now there were four months to fill, but Whiteman's plate
never remained empty for long. A couple of unexpected opportunities
had come his way shortly before the New Year. Florenz Ziegfeld celebrated the first anniversary of his production of *Show Boat* by launching two new shows in December: an Eddie Cantor musical, *Whoopee,*
on December 4, at the New Amsterdam Theatre, and a completely
revised version of his after-hours nightclub revue, *Midnight Frolic,*
three weeks later on the New Amsterdam Roof. *Whoopee* was a
smash, but George Olsen, its featured bandleader and the conductor slated for *Midnight Frolic,* battled with Ziegfeld, who accused him
of reserving his best arrangements for leading lady Ethel Shutta,
Olsen's wife. After Olsen quit or was fired, Ziegfeld hired Whiteman
for both shows at a salary rumored to be the highest ever offered a
bandleader.[3]

On December 29 Whiteman moved his operation into *Whoopee*
with much fanfare and not a little calamity. When Paul gave the

downbeat for a dance sketch, the band segued into one piece while lead trumpeter Charlie Margulis started another. Certain that everyone else was wrong, the crocked Margulis figured he could fix things by playing extra loud. Musicians recounted Whiteman sputtering, "Get me a pistol. Somebody kill the son of a bitch. I'll tear him apart with my hands!"[4] For the finale, the stage rolled over the pit, scaring the hell out of Whiteman, who had not been warned of this innovation in stagecraft. He ran out and, realizing his mistake, could not get back in. Cantor went on a tear, parodying Paul with a drumstick for a baton. The delighted audience assumed it was all planned.

After the curtain, the band and numerous luminaries took the elevator to the *Midnight Frolic* on the lavish roof, fashioned by Austrian theatrical designer Joseph Urban with pastel colors and lights, glass balconies, and a "pearl" curtain that was actually made of transparent medical capsules painted silver. The roof boasted a chic kitchen with matching prices. Ziegfeld stars, including Fanny Brice and Helen Morgan, stopped by to sing one or two numbers, but the *Frolic* was Whiteman's show. He was more at home in a nightclub than in a pit trying to tailor his music to actors.

During this time, the Rhythm Boys were playing their week at the Palace. They finished the engagement the same night Whiteman entered the cast of *Whoopee*, and two days later they were back on tour, in New Jersey and Pennsylvania. They were not scheduled for *Whoopee*, although Bing was whisked into the studio to record a fast, impeccably articulated version of the Eddie Cantor showstopper "Makin' Whoopee." By mid-January Whiteman was also on the road, playing weeks in Cincinnati and Detroit, where he hired Andy Secrest, an able if uninspired trumpet player who could handle the jazz solos when Bix was ailing. Returning to Manhattan for the February 5 commencement of his Old Gold show, Paul resumed double duties at the New Amsterdam for nearly three months. When in town the Rhythm Boys occasionally appeared in the roof shows and even in *Whoopee*, performing an interpolated song. More often they were sent on area tours, returning Tuesdays to take their places on the Old Gold broadcasts.

Meanwhile, in Hollywood, to mark his son's twenty-first birthday, Carl Laemmle Sr. appointed Carl Laemmle Jr. general manager of Universal and dropped the much publicized and hugely expensive Whiteman film in his lap. Junior immediately replaced Wesley

Ruggles with Hungarian director Paul Fejos (whose succès d'estime of 1928, *The Last Moment,* details the last days of a suicide) and assigned the script to Edward T. Lowe (whose thin vita later included Poverty Row Charlie Chans and Bulldog Drummonds). Both men were dispatched to New York, and one can scarcely imagine what Paul made of them. Fejos proposed a history of the orchestra with actors playing the musicians. Under no circumstance was Whiteman going to make a movie about his band without his band; he could not believe anyone would suggest such a thing. Universal obliviously informed the trades that an eight-week shooting schedule would begin June 1 so that Paul could return home for the August racing season at Saratoga. But the start-up was delayed again when Fejos and Lowe limped back to Hollywood. They were accompanied by Ferde Grofé, whom Whiteman asked to orchestrate the score; at least *he* could get started.

Concurrently, something entirely unexpected happened to popular music: it got younger. The new sound was favored almost exclusively by women, and the object of their passion was not Bing but rather Hubert Prior Vallée, a singer, saxophonist, and bandleader who renamed himself Rudy in honor of his idol, saxophone virtuoso Rudy Wiedoeft. As a Yale undergraduate who spent six years earning a philosophy degree, Vallée led a sticky-sweet band called the Yale Collegians. He believed he possessed rare insight regarding his generation's musical tastes, which he construed as a desire for rah-rah Ivy League songs, adapted European ballads, and mildly risqué novelties about stupid or easy girls. Briefly the public validated his judgment. In 1928 he brought his band, renamed the Connecticut Yankees, into New York's Heigh-Ho Club, achieving widespread recognition as WABC aired his sets. When he opened at Keith's 81st Street in February 1929, success became spectacle as mounted police cordoned off an area to accommodate hundreds of fans, many of them teenagers.

Vallée's trademark appurtenance was a small megaphone, his greeting a jaunty "Heigh-ho, everybody," his sound a dry, nasal baritone that detractors (they were legion) derisively characterized as "crooning." By March Vallée had three simultaneous hit records. By June he was starring in a hit film, *The Vagabond Lover,* which was advertised, "Men hate him — women love him." By 1930 he had published the first of three unintentionally hilarious autobiographies, fabled for their pettiness and vaunted modesty. ("I apparently have always been like the great surgeon who is too busy performing his superb and skillful operations to take any bows for what he does so easily and naturally.")[5] By 1931, after watching Crosby perform, Vallée, whose theme song was "My Time Is Your Time," proved sufficiently astute to observe to friends, "My time is short." Yet Vallée's startling popularity helps explain Bing's strangely uneven recordings in the months before he left for California. They suggest a bout of indecision, as if Bing had lost his compass and was no longer certain what kind of singer he wanted to be.

Bing was now twenty-five and prized by the musicians he admired as well as numerous fans. With Whiteman granting him the freedom to freelance for Columbia sessions, he was in demand to provide "vocal refrains" for studio orchestras. Before the Vallée hysteria set in, Bing was on a roll. He demonstrated confidence at a date by a Sam Lanin outfit, inflecting Spencer Williams's "Susianna" with a felt ebullience, cannily shading the lyrics with his measured breathing. On the British evergreen "If I Had You," he embellishes the melody and stresses the vowels, often with a slight turn or mordent. The next day he was on hand for the Dorsey Brothers Orchestra, a recording unit copiloted by Jimmy and Tommy, the battling brothers from Shenandoah, Pennsylvania, two of the most sought-after freelancers in New York. Glenn Miller arranged the material, and for the first time Bing's chorus was backed by the ingenious guitarist Eddie Lang. On "The Spell of the Blues," Bing bends notes for bluesy effect and, despite one Jolsonesque ringer, is clearly his own man. He is no less assured on Cole Porter's "Let's Do It," encouragingly supported by Lang. Best of all is "My Kinda Love," a flimsy song that he projects stirringly without a trace of the frangible crooning style.

Several days after Vallée's theatrical breakthrough, however, Bing recorded with Whiteman and for the first time appeared discombobulated. He sang two waltzes — including his second Berlin tune, "Coquette" — in a key too high for him and in a style that might be described as a poised croon, deft but diffident. The second tune, "My Angeline," was deemed unreleasable; a week later Bing gave Whiteman an acceptable version, but even then his top notes were soft.

Bing was clearly in a state, and we can only speculate about what threw him. Perhaps he would have been more himself if Challis, not William Grant Still, had arranged "Coquette." Perhaps he withered under the glare of the despotic anti-jazz producer Eddie King. Perhaps he simply had a bad day. Most likely, Vallée had gotten to him in a way drink never did, as witness the far more significant follow-up session.

On March 14, encouraged by the Vallée phenomenon, Columbia offered Bing his first date under his own name. He was backed by three Whiteman musicians (violinist Matty Malneck, pianist Roy Bargy, guitarist Snoozer Quinn). All his experience during the four years since the Musicaladers should have been consolidated in this hour, yet the records are unaccountably lifeless. Spurred by the vitality he achieved on "My Kinda Love" with the Dorseys, Bing chose to rerecord it, but this time he overloaded the song with self-conscious vocal techniques; for the first time, he was thrown off-kilter by a doubled-up tempo change. On the wholly undistinguished song "Till We Meet," he sounds not unlike singers he was in the process of demolishing.

By contrast, he was in splendid form a few weeks later, in April, for arguably the best of the Rhythm Boys sessions. "So the Bluebirds and the Blackbirds Got Together," by Harry Barris and Billy Moll ("I Want a Little Girl"), recounts an ornithological covenant while advancing the merrily subversive subtext of miscegenation, a theme previously explored in 1924, when Eva Taylor, accompanied by Louis Armstrong, recorded "I'm a Little Blackbird Looking for a Bluebird." Bing begins the number with his hand cymbal and sings his solo parts with aplomb, using mordents and a midrange croon, but without the corn of "My Kinda Love." Later passages suggest a rapping modernism, and the unison harmonization shows the trio at its best. In case anyone doubted the soloist's identity, "Louise" begins with a phone call for Bing ("I wonder who could be calling when I'm recording," he grouses. "Louise? That's different.") The phone found its way into their live act. On some nights the routine had Hollywood on the line, calling for Bing to make pictures. And why not? After all, Hollywood had called Rudy Vallée.

Returning to the studio with Whiteman, Bing appeared perplexed once again, casting about for style. He did as well as could be expected on the ineffable Jolson tearjearker "Little Pal," tossing in a tearful mordent and somehow managing to sound rational. The potentially vital "Reaching for Someone," a Challis arrangement recorded on Bing's twenty-sixth birthday, is marred by his misguided attempt to vocally mimic Tram's saxophone glissandi at the turnbacks, a tasteless conceit in an otherwise fine performance and one he never repeated. Bing, Tram, and Bix all enliven "Oh, Miss Hannah," a southern song ("the moon am shining bright"). Bing stresses the word *roses* with a mordent employed not for sentiment but to underscore rhythmic pulse, and swells the final cadence. Yet at the same session he is indifferently orotund on Gus Edwards's "Orange Blossom Time."

Unlike Armstrong, who was born practically fully formed, Bing flirted with styles before settling into one unremittingly his own, one that would prove applicable to every kind of song. His natural reserve led him toward an economy of expression, but the times encouraged his inclination toward grandiloquence. To a certain degree his dilemma was created by his obligation to fulfill Whiteman's requirements. When he was afforded good material, Bing could make the whole band shine. But Paul's more bombastic pieces demanded a stolid projection. The miracle of Bing's tenure with the band is how consistently he held himself apart from its pomposity. Like Bix, Bing seems to open a window and let in fresh air almost every time he stands up to solo. Only in the spring and summer of 1929, Vallée's brief time in the sun, did Bing blink. He was the one, after all, who should have been moving into the limelight, not that mewling throwback to the kind of dullards he and Louis Armstrong were consigning to oblivion.

Bing's musical confusion did not detract from his appetite for good times, leading to one professional and personal lapse that almost ended in disaster. Whiteman's orchestra played a two-week engagement at the Pavillon Royal on Long Island's Merrick Road. On Sunday, May 12, Bing, Al, Harry, and Mischa Russell, a violinist in the band, entertained some *Ziegfeld Follies* girls at the apartment of a wealthy friend. Late in the afternoon their host proposed a sailboat cruise on Long Island Sound. As they launched onto the water, Bing leaned against the rail, hoisted a glass of champagne, and began a song just as the boat hit a wave. He was tossed overboard. Wind drove the boat 300 yards before the skipper could come about. Bing's expertise as a swimmer saved him. He was treading water and laughing when they fished him out — reason enough to return to New York and resume the festivities.

At 2:00 A.M. the Whiteman foursome and the Ziegfeld girls repaired to the apartment of one of the chorines. They slept late and missed the bus Whiteman had chartered to take his musicians to Long Island. When they realized that there was no way they could make the gig in time, they knew they were in serious trouble and had no recourse but to apologize profusely. Whiteman threatened to fire them. The boys had never seen him angrier. Yet he calmed down when they promised to reform. Asked years later whether Bing had been hard to handle, Paul replied, "No, he was never hard to handle. But sometimes he was hard to find."[6]

On May 24, a week before the Whiteman caravan headed west, Bing made his second date as a leader. Backed by three musicians, this time including Lang on guitar, he covered Vallée's adaptation of a German song, "I Kiss Your Hand, Madame," humming, whistling, and finishing with jazzy adornments. But then he lost his moorings on "Baby, Oh Where Can You Be?," missing a note and veering out of tune on a scat break. Even his usually flawless time failed him. Bing needed a break from New York.

The *Whiteman–Old Gold Special* chugged out of Pennsylvania Station on May 24, a privately chartered train of eight coaches, two for baggage alone, another for Paul's Duesenberg. The party of fifty included thirty-five musicians, managers, a crew of audio experts, staff arranger William Grant Still, the vice president of P. Lorrillard (Old Gold footed the bills), and reporters, most notably *Variety's* Abel Green, who filed regular dispatches along the way as, over the course of twelve days, the band performed — in addition to weekly broadcasts — free concerts in sixteen cities, from Philadelphia to Salt Lake City. It was a public-relations bonanza, the showbiz story of the year. When they did not have a hall, the band performed on the train's extended observation platform, and no one complained when local radio stations set up microphones. Indeed, the sponsor was overjoyed to have the whole country tracking the bandleader's journey to California. "This is a nite club, all stag, on wheels," Green reported, "except that the club is going all hours, day and night."[7] In Nebraska the band entertained 4,500 at Omaha's City Auditorium in the afternoon and 1,500 at the Lincoln train station at night. In Denver Whiteman participated in a much photographed reunion with his parents. Throughout the trip black porters ("Ethiops" in the parlance of *Variety*) greeted him as king and treated him accordingly.

Shortly before the band left New York, the premier violin-guitar team of Joe Venuti and Eddie Lang signed on as members of the troupe (previously they had been contracted for individual recordings), and they provided much of the journey's intramural entertainment, not all of it musical. Along with banjoist Mike Pingitore and violinist Wilbur Hall, they formed a string quartet to serenade the king at dinner. Venuti was a dedicated practical joker. Heading through Utah and finding Bix in a dead sleep, he gathered sand buckets (used to extinguish fires) from passenger cars and heaped the sand on Bix's lap, the adjoining seat, and the floor. When Bix came to and blanched, Venuti reassured him that they had safely emerged from the worst sandstorm in years. Bix protested, "Why didn't someone wake me up? I could have suffocated."[8]

Lang and Venuti were two prodigiously talented Italians from Philadelphia. After Bix, they were arguably the most influential white jazz musicians of the 1920s, serving as a sort of template for the famed European jazz ensemble of the 1930s, the Quintette du Hot Club de France, which featured guitarist Django Reinhardt and violinist Stephane Grappelly. They blended their instruments in virtuoso ten-string exercises that combined classicism and swing in astonishing breakneck exhibitions, but they were also capable of poignant lyricism. Inseparable in their school years, they remained personally and musically close and had no need for arrangements; once they agreed on a key, they could improvise all evening. Yet as individuals they could not have been more different. Venuti, a physically imposing man with a growly voice and temperament, was a resolute gambler and joker, said to be the only man to nettle the placid King of the Cowboys, Roy Rogers. (When they shared a stage bill in the 1940s, Joe struck up a conversation with Roy as he awaited a cue astride his palomino, Trigger; while they conversed, Venuti triggered the horse with his violin bow, producing an immoderate erection that convulsed the audience.) Joe was a loner who worked when he felt like it, an eccentric and natural comedian — just the type of personality Bing relished.

Lang was his polar opposite: quiet, thoughtful, responsible, a ruminative Catholic. Bing came to regard him as a counterpart. Eddie was one of the few people in Bing's life to get beyond the role of a jester or playmate and become a genuine confidant. He was Bing's most intimate friend, almost certainly the closest he would ever have. Until Lang's tragic death in 1933, they traveled together, making wonderful music on records and in films. Eddie's wife, Kitty, whom he met in 1920, when she was touring in a *Ziegfeld Follies* road company and he was playing banjo with a band in Philadelphia, described him as a "shy boy with black, curly hair and grey-green eyes. He could barely say hello, but he had the sweetest smile I ever saw."[9] They eloped in 1926, enduring rough times until the good jobs began coming Eddie's way. He introduced Kitty to Bing in a nightclub: "Eddie and I were with Jimmy Dorsey and his wife Janey. Bing came over to our table and sat down for a few minutes. He was a happy-go-lucky sort of fellow, a perfect gentleman at all times, though he had had a few drinks. Eddie told me afterwards that he believed this guy Bing would go places as he had everything going for him once he settled down to business."[10]

"Well we are wending our way westward and having a truly marvelous time of it," Bing wrote home to his mother. After detailing the itinerary, he penitently reassured Kate: "If nothing else our return to Whiteman has been fruitful because of this trip. Not only are we having a great time but my name is being prominently featured in the newspapers and in the broadcasts and considerable invaluable publicity thus redounds to me. What awaits us on the Coast is as yet problematical and whether we get much of a break in the picture or not I can't tell now. However, I intend to bear down heavily and really try to accomplish something worth while."[11] He told her that they figured to be in Los Angeles on June 20 and that she could write him in care of Everett, who had recently married the former Naomi Tillinghast and settled in what Bing later described to Kate as a "cute home."[12]

The band pulled into Los Angeles early on June 7 for a covert huddle with Universal officials, then continued to San Francisco to play a week of vaudeville at the Pantages Theater. The official arrival in Los Angeles, preceding yet another week of vaudeville, was accompanied by the usual ballyhoo at Central Station: speech by the mayor, key to the city, all the contract players Universal could muster as a welcoming committee, plus a crowd of 500 fans. This was Whiteman's first visit to California in three years — he had been away since the time he recruited Bing and Al. Carl Laemmle brought the musicians to the lot to show off a clubhouse he had built for them, called Whiteman Lodge, complete with rehearsal room, fireplace, billiard tables, library, lockers, and showers. Transportation problems were solved when a Ford dealer offered each of Whiteman's men a Model A roadster, almost at cost, the payments to be deducted from their salaries over the course of their stay. Whiteman ordered thirty-five. Bing chose a convertible. As a promotional gimmick, each roadster sported a prominent spare tire with the potato-head caricature, which became a carrot for highway patrolmen who learned that if they followed one long enough, they would get to issue a summons or two.

During an impromptu interview, Whiteman made the ominous remark "I haven't seen the script yet, but I can tell you one thing. Jazz is losing out to the slower rhythms. You might print that and quote me!"[13] If his statement was intended as grievance, he himself was partly to blame, having decided to hire a team of conventional writers like Mabel Wayne (who wrote Whiteman's hit "In a Little Spanish Town") and L. Wolfe Gilbert (who wrote the Jolson classic "Waiting for the Robert E. Lee"), when he might have had his pick of the sophisticated songwriting talents lighting up Broadway. He also chose to leave Challis at home in favor of Grofé and Still. Whiteman's concert violinist, Kurt Dieterle, thought he made that decision because Challis was too painstaking and slow for the Hollywood mill. Challis, however, was not nearly as slow as scriptwriter Ed Lowe. When Whiteman checked in with the front office on June 24, he was flabbergasted to learn that there was no script. Furthermore, Grofé complained that time and again he was asked to score a tune and after finishing the job was told the tune had been scrapped.

Aside from radio broadcasts, the band had nothing to do except golf, party, drink, and drive around, all on the Universal dole. Mischa Russell was arrested for drunk driving and held by a peculiarly liberal turnkey; when some of his friends visited the lockup, they were informed that Russell and his jailer had gone to the movies but that they were welcome to wait if they liked. Comedy turned to tragedy six weeks into their stay when several musicians took off in a fleet of cars for a gig in Santa Barbara. Venuti broke from his lane to pass a slow-poke and crashed into an oncoming vehicle. His wrist was badly mangled; for a while it was feared he would never play again. His passenger, Mario Perry, an accordionist and one of Whiteman's earliest associates, died en route to the hospital. The two women in the other car, though unharmed, filed suit against Venuti and Whiteman. Hollywood had become a nightmare.

Bing stayed out of trouble. "Universal gave the boys two hundred dollars a week, each boy," Kurt Dieterle recalled, "and we also had the Old Gold broadcasts — that was another fifty dollars. The first three months they were rewriting the story, five of us who were golfers — Chet Hazlett, Roy Bargy, Bing and Al Rinker, and myself — went and joined Lakeside. Hazlett bought a regular membership and the rest of us bought associate memberships for five hundred dollars. We didn't do a lick of work as far as the orchestra. The five of us went to Lakeside in the morning, played a round of golf, each with our own caddy. After lunch we would play another eighteen holes."[14] Bing, Dieterle, and Mischa Russell rented a house for the summer on Fairfax Avenue and hired a cook. They visited Universal only on payday. Bing recalled Whiteman's saying, "Well, thanks a lot for managing to get over here for your checks — thanks a lot."[15]

In those days, the membership of Lakeside Golf Club was dominated by the film industry, and Bing became friendly with several actors, including Richard Arlen, Buddy Rogers, Oliver Hardy, and Johnny Weissmuller. But his entrée into Hollywood really began to take wing after the Rhythm Boys, alone among the Whiteman musicians, sought a steady job. "We are trying to line up some extra work while here but the rehearsals and radio just about make it impossible," Bing wrote Kate, overstating their labors:

However, we plan an opening at the Montmartre cafe in Hollywood for a short time to see how it works out. This will help to tide us over during our enforced idleness. Picture work is, of course, possible for the trio, but we are prevented from doing any of this until the Universal picture is completed, and even in that it is quite probable that we'll be left on the cutting room floor. In the meantime I am going to make some screen tests for MGM, as has been suggested to me quite often since my arrival here, and, who knows, something may come of them?[16]

The Rhythm Boys were a hit at the Montmartre Cafe, but nothing came of Bing's MGM tests or of subsequent tests at Fox, where casting director Jim Ryan complimented Bing's singing and asked him to read lines for chief of production Winfield Sheehan. Bing recalled Sheehan's saying, "Very good, but the ears are wingy." Bing told the tale on TV in 1971: "I thought he said, 'The years are winging,' and I said, no, I'm twenty-whatever-I-was-then. He said, 'No, the ears are winging, there's no way we can photograph you, it would be a lot of big problems.' He said, 'I'm afraid that there just isn't a place for you in pictures.' I went on my way and the years went by and I finally belonged to the same church he did, Blessed Sacrament out in Beverly Hills. He used to sit in the third row, so when I went to communion, I'd come back and as I passed him I'd go [he mimed flapping his ears]."[17] Bing never forgot the slights of those days and polished the particulars like old silver. To Jim Ryan he attributed the crack "A camera pointed straight at you would make you look like a taxi with both doors open."[18]

Though he continued to make the studio rounds, Bing did not seem especially ambitious to those who worked with him. A member of Whiteman's radio cast, Dorothea Ponce of the Ponce Sisters, who occasionally sang with Bing, remembered: "He didn't seem star material at the time. He was simply a part of the weekly program with the Rhythm Boys. I never thought of him going out on his own and leaving them."[19] Bing rarely showed his hand. Sometimes he appeared not to know what cards he was holding. Rudy Vallée told of Bing's diffidence one evening in Baltimore, when he shared a bill with the trio:

Above the chatter of the diners the Rhythm Boys might just as well have stayed in bed; no one was paying the slightest attention to them. But suddenly a hush fell upon this crowd of Baltimore's elite. One of the Rhythm Boys was singing a song called "Montmartre Rose," and even though he lacked any amplification or means of channeling his sound waves to us, his voice commanded instant silence [and] when he finished the crowd applauded wildly and cried for more. As though he were oblivious to their shouts and applause, almost as though he were hard of hearing, he threaded his way back through the tables and passed by our sax section, not more than a foot and a half from me. I was struck by the lack of expression on his face, which was a mask of complete indifference. Bing Crosby was a hit and didn't even know it![20]

Bing undoubtedly did know it, but he was not inclined to let on, then or ever. Although he sang solo on Whiteman's broadcasts as often as he sang with the trio, neither he nor his partners acknowledged the inevitable split that had to come. Whiteman attempted to stifle his ambitions, threatening to fire him if he continued to seek screen tests. Yet pressure from Everett and established agents was building for him to go out on his own. They all wanted a piece of him.

The young Hollywood crowd was captivated by Bing's casually handsome composure. After the Second World War, an observer suggested that if a celestial visitor arrived at a cocktail party seeking an earthling leader and was directed to a group in which Bing was chatting with Winston Churchill and Douglas MacArthur, it would probably assume Crosby was the guy in charge. Even in 1929, when he was scrambling after a new career and shying from responsibility, peering at his future through the mist of rotgut whiskey and generally preferring a life on the fairway, Bing imparted a near regal nonchalance. His innate propriety deflected the kind of vanity that curdles into narcissism. The distinct warmth that defined his singing and later his acting made him seem cool yet approachable. A young contract player named Sylvia Picker observed, "Truthfully, there wasn't a girl in town who wasn't nuts about Bing Crosby."[21] His working-class man's-man insouciance was found no less fascinating by men. He had none of the brilliantined conceit and manicured irony rife in Hollywood. He came across as an extraordinary ordinary guy.

The Rhythm Boys worked the entire month of July at Eddie Brandstatter's Montmartre Cafe on Hollywood Boulevard. They were billed as Paul Whiteman's Rhythm Boys and touted as the "Musical Sensation of Los Angeles," "America's Foremost Entertainers,"[22] and, in a stretch even by Tinseltown's standards, "Direct from Ziegfeld's Roof in Their First Appearance Outside of New York."[23] The second-story café was a blocklong room with banquet tables (packed for fashionable luncheons), a small dance floor ringed with tables, and a band-stand. It was the hot spot of the moment, and fans routinely crowded under the ornate marquee to see who entered: a mix of celebrities and coddled would-be stars of the new all-talking picture business. The *Los Angeles Evening Express* trumpeted Brandstatter's coup in luring the trio away from New York ("at great expense"),[24] and the club boasted increasing receipts as young Hollywood turned out every night to be in on something new and adventurous.

Bill Hearst and his college friends from San Francisco were regu-lars, as was another acquaintance from vaudeville days, Phil Harris, who had just returned from a long tour of Australia and was playing drums and coleading a band. "The Montmartre was *the* place, that and the Cocoanut Grove," said Harris. "And that's the first time I heard him do a ballad, 'I Kiss Your Hand, Madame,' and he knocked the roof in with it. When Bing finished, I mean, I never heard any-thing like it, you could hear a pin drop."[25] The crowd demanded an encore, and the boys reprised their flagwaver, "Mississippi Mud." The trio was invited to countless parties, including one in Catalina at which Bing and Al ended up squiring Lita Grey Chaplin, recently divorced from Charlie Chaplin, and her friend, starlet Catherine Dale Owen. One thing led to another, and the Rhythm Boys were soon engaged for a week in a vaudeville package at the Orpheum, billed second ("syncopated song, melody, comedy you will talk about for months") to Lita, "California's own crooning beauty."[26] They played two shows daily at the Orpheum, then rushed to make their evening sets at the Montmartre.

Among the starlets and hopefuls who crowded the Montmartre was a young couple, each recently signed to Fox. He was Frank Albertson, the busy character actor who would be remembered as Sam Wainright in *It's a Wonderful Life* and the lecherous millionaire robbed by Janet Leigh in *Psycho*. At that time, he was a fleshy-faced second lead and a friend of Bing's, eager to introduce him to his beau-tiful seventeen-year-old date. She was Dixie Lee, an introverted but temperamental southern-born actress and singer who dyed her dark hair platinum blond and was fully expected to make the transition from starlet to star. Frank and Dixie had worked together in two films, in the star-studded chorus of *Happy Days* and as the second leads in *The Big Party* (both released in 1930). Before she arrived in

Hollywood, Dixie had won a singing contest in Chicago that eventually led to a job understudying Peggy Bernier in *Good News*. Known as Dixie Carroll in those days, she had heard about Bing from her roommates, Bernier and Holly Hall, both of whom complained about his habit of last-minute cancellations. "I just wanted to meet this character once and tell him off," Dixie said in 1946. When Bing did call her in Chicago, wanting to meet her, Dixie asked one of her roommates to handle him: "You tell that guy I'm not in the habit of going places to meet anybody — especially him."[27] Yet at the Montmartre, seeing and hearing him for the first time, she coyly asked Frank to introduce her to him by her real name, Billie Wyatt. Dixie and Bing struck no sparks that night, but Bing was flattered when she returned to hear him sing, especially when he found out she was the well-known Fox starlet Dixie Lee.

In late August, nearly three months after his arrival in Hollywood, Universal presented Whiteman with a script. He read it with disbelief. To his utter bewilderment, the studio intended to make him a leading man in a conventional love story. Hollywood's incomprehensible, always unsuccessful attempts to make romantic figures of rotund or oddball music personalities would eventually sink the cinematic aspirations of performers ranging from Kate Smith to Liberace to Pavarotti; it is to Whiteman's credit that he was appalled rather than tempted by Universal's blandishments. Paul prepared to leave California as soon as possible. He would return when the studio could assure him that it had a reasonable story idea. If Whiteman was mad, the Laemmles were livid: they had already spent $350,000 and had nothing to show for it. After broadcasting on August 27, Whiteman's troupe boarded the train for New York and an emergency job Jimmy Gillespie had lined up at the Pavillon Royal. They had a stowaway in Hoagy Carmichael, who had come west on his own without the prospect of work and without finding any; he shared a berth with Bing.

In fact, Whiteman made off with much more than Hoagy. At a party in New York a year earlier, he had met Margaret Livingston, who played the vamp in the bulrushes in F. W. Murnau's masterwork, *Sunrise*, a movie Whiteman adored and screened repeatedly. Though married to his second wife, Paul devoted much of his California sojourn — when not in attendance at the dozens of parties thrown in his honor by such film luminaries as Marion Davies, Richard Barthelmess, and Ronald Colman — to his courtship of Livingston, who was filming on the Universal lot. In 1931, after he complied with her ultimatum to diet, they married; they remained a devoted couple until his death in 1967.

He did no less well on the musical front, as Bing and Al finally found a way to favor their benefactress, Mildred Bailey. Paul made it clear he wasn't hiring anybody, including Hoagy, but Bing and Al knew that if they could get Whiteman to hear Mildred, he'd fall under her spell. Millie became friendly with several guys in the band that summer. She took them horseback riding in the Hollywood Hills, cooked up a storm, and served her home brew, which created quite a sensation, as decent beer was hard to find. Bing and Al encouraged her to throw a party for the band and its leader. Whiteman, a prodigious beer drinker, happily accepted the invitation. As Bing recalled, "Paul didn't know it at the time, but he was a goner when he walked into the house."[28]

Hoagy, Roy Bargy, and pianist-arranger Lennie Hayton took turns at Millie's Steinway. Rinker describes what happened next: "Finally, Bing turned to Mildred and said, 'Hey, Millie, why don't you sing a song?' No one had ever heard her sing but they all joined in, 'Yeah, c'mon, Millie, let's have a song.' At first, Mildred acted reluctant, but I knew it wouldn't last long."[29] She asked Al to accompany her on "(What Can I Say, Dear) After I Say I'm Sorry," and "she sang the hell out of the song." After a brief silence everyone started to cheer, and Whiteman, who had been in the kitchen, asked who was singing. Bing barked, "That was Millie, Al's sister." Whiteman joked, "Don't tell me that there's one in the family who can sing!" He then walked over, kissed her, and asked for an encore. "All her past experience singing in speakeasies and night spots came out as she sang. Her small, pure voice gave the songs feeling and meaning, and you knew you were hearing a singer who was very special," Al wrote.[30] That night Paul hired her to sing the popular lament "Moanin' Low" on Tuesday's Old Gold show. Weeks later she was on the train to New York, a contract in her purse — the first "girl singer" to tour with an orchestra. A year later she was the highest-salaried performer on Whiteman's payroll.

*　　*　　*

On the previous occasion when Whiteman played the Pavillon Royal, Bing had fallen into the Long Island Sound and almost lost his job, if not his life. This time he had a dire experience of another sort. Bing and his brothers told the story so often that it became family lore, the details mutating in the telling. Apparently the evening began when Kitty Lang rounded up some Ziegfeld girls for a party and Bing found his companion less than stimulating. In their 1937 fictionalized biography, Ted and Larry Crosby say he left the table and walked to the bandstand to hear a new song, "Singin' in the Rain," and returned to find his date "pouting." The gerund has the ring of discernment, because Bing could not abide pouting and found emotional neediness as unpleasant as emotional dishonesty.

He left for another speakeasy, where a Valentino wannabe — padded shoulders, greased hair parted in the middle — recognized him and bought him a drink. Bing joined the stranger's party, embarking on a forty-eight-hour brandy binge. He came to in a strange hotel room and stumbled into the bathroom seconds before the front door was blasted open by machine-gun fire and his companions were sprayed by bullets, all wounded but none killed. Bing stayed in the bathroom "for what seemed hours,"[31] until a cop opened the door and asked him who he was, eliciting an innocent-bystander routine that Bing claimed surpassed anything he did in the movies. The next day he learned he had spent two days in the hideout of Machine Gun Jack McGurn, the dapper Capone killer who had taken part months earlier in the St. Valentine's Day Massacre and had slit the throat of singer (later, thanks to McGurn, comedian) Joe E. Lewis.

However mortified Bing may have been by his behavior — and if the McGurn story was embellished, his predilection for a binge was not — he continued to make professional strides. During the band's weeks in New York, before Universal summoned them back to resume (or begin) work on *King of Jazz*, Whiteman and Columbia refused to record the Rhythm Boys because they had failed to develop any new material. Barris was not included in any sessions at all. But Bing was still in demand for studio work.

He had finally exorcised the demon Vallée and was now intent on insulating himself from the word *crooner*, a term that due chiefly to Vallée was almost always used disparagingly, often implying deviance. Boston's Cardinal O'Connell denounced crooning as a force for evil and invited parishioners to share his "sensation of revolting disgust at a man whining a degenerate song, which is unworthy of any American man."[32] Pundits followed suit. The *Springfield Union,* enraged to the point of grammatical chaos, reviled crooning as a "gratuitous insult to that intelligent person which rightfully expects a better return for its expensive investment in radio equipment."[33]

What, we may ask, were such laughable denunciations really about? Is the subtext nothing more than fear of homosexuality, and if so, why all the indignation over Vallée and not the Nick Lucases, Gene Austins, and Jack Fultons who preceded him? We may agree, from a musical point of view, that Vallée and company were "whining," but the diatribes, with their emphases on manliness and words like *degenerate* augur Hitler's excuses for banning Weimar artists. In truth, Vallée was a big, convenient target. The real prey was the entire sexual undercurrent manifest in the Jazz Age, particularly its music, which along with Prohibition lured women into saloons and crossed racial boundaries. A youth music almost by definition implies rebellion, family tension, the potential for anarchy.

Bing's singing was nothing if not virile. He would cause a far greater furor than Vallée, but the Cardinal O'Connells of the world could never tag him with imputations of effeteness. After Bing achieved his breakthrough, the word *crooner* would usually be used descriptively or with admiration. In September Bing recorded for the first time in four months, since the high-strung "Baby, Oh Where Can You Be?," and gave free reign to his natural tones. His heartiness uplifts Grofé's arrangement of "Waiting at the End of the Road," an Irving Berlin song memorably introduced in King Vidor's black musical film, *Hallelujah.* This was the pre-Vallée Bing, restored and confident. His effortless swing was the flash point for the session, which proved to be Bix's last with Whiteman.

Bix, drinking excessively, was coming apart at the seams and ruined several takes. A few days later Paul put him on a train for his family home in Davenport, Iowa, hoping he would cure himself. Paul kept him on salary for months, until it became clear he would not be coming back to the band. Bix returned to New York, though, and freelanced on several sessions — playing a memorably affecting solo on his last as a leader, "I'll Be a Friend (With Pleasure)." He died in August 1931 at twenty-eight. "Every once in a while he'd wake me up in the middle of the night, and make me change beds with him," recalled Bing,[34] who refused to concede that Bix was an alcoholic, maybe because, like himself, he could go without liquor for days at a time. But Bing was kidding himself, more than twenty years after the fact, when he wrote of a man who often started his day with four ounces of gin, "In the end, it was his lack of sleep and his physical exhaustion which broke his health and killed him."[35]

Bing's third session under his own name, in late September, was little better than the first two and suffered from pompous, non-jazz accompaniment. Columbia probably wanted to disabuse him of his inclination to scat or embellish. On the movie tango "Gay Love" (written by Oscar Levant and Sidney Clare for *The Delightful Rogue*), he emotes with a purple bravado that prefigures his hit recording of "Temptation," the movie tango composed for him a few years later, sobbing the high notes and employing a robust attack no one could misconstrue as crooning.[36] No less operatic is his work with Whiteman on two Vincent Youmans songs, "Great Day" and "Without a Song." On the former he staunchly sings the verse before disappearing into a trebly choir. "Without a Song," however, taken at a peppy tempo that displeased its composer, is a Crosby coup of the sort that encourages one to speculate on how inspiring it must have been to, say, Frank Sinatra, who was fourteen when the Youmans numbers were released on a hugely popular platter. Bing's phrasing, breathing, vibrato, and projection are superbly coordinated, and he pins the high note free and clear, demonstrating hardly a trace of his or anyone else's mannerisms. His vocal is the more remarkable for crowning an otherwise dreary arrangement.

Bing is more in his element and again in marvelous voice with Whiteman on Lennie Hayton's pert arrangement of "If I Had a Talking Picture of You," backed by Lang and Venuti. The chemistry between Bing and Eddie is fully realized on "After You've Gone," a delightfully cool William Grant Still arrangement with voicings that blend rather than separate the strings and the winds, as well as a climax that includes an Andy Secrest solo in the style of Bix and a Joe Venuti solo in a style all his own, complete with sparkling break. Directly after the session Whiteman returned to Hollywood, with the band following a day or so later. This time there was no hoopla, no dispatches from the front, no broadcasts, just a quick jaunt to get the damn movie made.

*　　*　　*

On October 22, 1929, a few days before the Whiteman band regrouped in Hollywood, Charles Mitchell, chairman of National City Bank, responded to the sense of dread enveloping Wall Street with consoling words: "I know of nothing fundamentally wrong with the stock market or with the underlying credit structure."[37] On October 23 Paramount and Warners called off their negotiations for a merger that might have completely altered Hollywood history — not a moment too soon. Twenty-four hours later, Black Thursday, the market imploded as nearly 13 million shares were traded at a loss of $6 billion. The band arrived in Los Angeles a day later; like most Americans, the musicians were undistracted by the crash. Few of them were in the market, and no one believed that the panic on Wall Street would be anything more than a brief inconvenience. In days that followed, experts reassured the country that the market had stabilized. But on Tuesday, as Paul resumed broadcasting, the bottom fell out; nearly 16.5 million shares were traded at a loss of three times the money circulating in the entire nation. Hollywood digested Black Tuesday with *Variety*'s famous headline: WALL ST. LAYS AN EGG.

Few Americans were worried even at that stage, certainly not members of the Whiteman band, several of whom had secured raises just before the trip. No one saw the big bad wolf of the Depression slavering at the door. Nor could anyone have imagined that, by a Hollywood-style contradiction, the nation's financial ruin would have an even more salubrious impact on the fortunes of show business than Prohibition. True, the movie business would never again enjoy the figures of 1929, when 23,000 theaters were visited by an average of 95 million people a week. By 1936 the number of screens would be shaved by a third and would not rise beyond 20,000 until the 1980s. The number of weekly filmgoers would also decline permanently, slashed by radio and television and the Internet to a late-nineties average of 22 million. Still, never was escapist entertainment needed more than during the Depression. Hollywood rose to the occasion.

As the wolf settled in for a lengthy stay, entertainment provided solace and balm. But reduced prices and varied giveaways were not enough to lure people into trading hard-earned pennies for filmed vaudeville. They wanted magic and romance and novelty; stories with happy endings and a chastened wolf. Whiteman's *King of Jazz* would turn out to be a mammoth casualty of that demand — a sad irony, because Universal's was the most magical revue of an era in which every studio felt obliged to release an oversize, vaudeville-style parade of talent. Had *King of Jazz* been finished on time, it almost certainly would have been a smash hit. Instead, because of the delays that plagued the production, the first film revue announced was the last to be released; it would appear just as the excitement surrounding "audible variety" ended.

When Universal signed Whiteman, it had no major stars, an inconvenience the studio hoped to disguise with Whiteman's status and a supercolossal production. Junior Laemmle decided that the solution to his script problems was a variety show. His writer, Edward Lowe, could stay on to provide continuity between the numbers, but Laemmle sought a top theatrical showman to replace his director, Paul Fejos. Whiteman lobbied for John Murray Anderson, a former dancer with whom he had worked at the Paramount Theater in 1928 and whose lush and innovative direction of *The Greenwich Village Follies* (1919–24) thrilled Broadway. He was hired at $50,000, half Whiteman's salary, but an extraordinary sum considering his total lack of movie experience. Anderson, the nucleus of a formidable crew, brought in set and costume designer Herman Rosse, who won *King of Jazz*'s only Academy Award (he later worked on set decor for *Frankenstein*), and choreographer Russell Markert, who went on to create the Rockettes at Radio City Music Hall. Junior asked Anderson to meet with Fejos and cameraman Hal Mohr to discuss the use of a twenty-eight-ton crane and boom camera built for the just released musical *Broadway*. He then fired Fejos but retained Mohr — an innovator in color photography — and two other cameramen, color expert Ray Rennahan and special-effects wizard Jerry Ash. Anderson insisted that Universal shoot the entire picture in the two-strip process (red-orange and blue-green) developed by Technicolor.

Never before had a Hollywood studio bestowed upon a first-time director as much money and control as Universal yielded to John Murray Anderson; nor would any studio follow suit until RKO imported Orson Welles from New York a decade later. Whatever he desired, he received — dozens of extras in flamboyant and costly foreign costumes, a 500-foot bridal veil, the first-ever Technicolor cartoon, film rights (estimated at $50,000) to "Rhapsody in Blue." He did accept a few constraints. The nightclub act of Clayton, Jackson, and Durante held out for too much money, and negotiations with Rodgers and Hart fell through. But he was able to reassign the score to the team that had written his recent Broadway flop, *John Murray Anderson's Almanac:* Jack Yellen and Milt Ager, old-school songsmiths whose many hits included "Ain't She Sweet," "Hard-Hearted Hannah," and "Happy Days Are Here Again." He kept only two of Mabel Wayne's tunes, including the waltz "It Happened in Monterey."

Anderson also recruited sixteen chorus girls and two sister acts: the Sisters G, a Yiddish vocal and dance team from Europe, and the Brox (originally Brock) Sisters, a close-harmony trio who got their start by auditioning for Irving Berlin on the telephone from their home in Edmonton, Canada. They became regulars in Berlin's *Music Box Revues,* including one in 1924 staged by Anderson. The Brox Sisters were already in Hollywood; along with Cliff Edwards, they introduced "Singin' in the Rain" in MGM's *The Hollywood Revue of 1929.* Bing became smitten with the pretty married one, Bobbe.

Junior, preoccupied with his production of *All Quiet on the Western Front,* not only allowed Anderson three months to rehearse and shoot the picture but permitted him to improvise sequences as he advanced, shooting acres of film. A script was transcribed after the fact. Rehearsals began November 6, but as of December 11 Universal had yet to nail down a final cast. An ad in *Variety* boasted "the biggest news you've ever heard since the advent of the audible screen . . . a luxury of song, dance, music, and joy."[38] The promised lineup of performers included Joseph Schildkraut, Mary Nolan, Ken Maynard, and Hoot Gibson, none of whom appeared in the finished film. The shooting was fraught with problems. The Technicolor lighting was so severe that it peeled the varnish off the violins (a Warners technician measured the heat on a closed Technicolor soundstage at 140 degrees). It was impossible to move the crane, erect sets, or film dancers while recording music, a problem Whiteman solved with a prophetic fiat: "Let's prerecord it."[39]

Most early recording engineers in the movies were moonlighting radio technicians, who considered prerecording an affront to their craft. They played out the old debate between live (radio) and canned (records) entertainment, a debate that peaked in 1946, when Bing produced the first transcribed network radio show. The soundmen argued that the public had accepted direct recording in earlier films and pointed to disastrous attempts at dubbing in Fejos's *Broadway*. Although a few musicals had been prerecorded in part — most notably, "The Wedding of the Painted Doll" in MGM's *The Broadway Melody* a year earlier — live recording remained the standard procedure until 1932, when Paramount prerecorded *Love Me Tonight* and Warners followed suit with *42nd Street*. Whiteman, though, was adamant and he prevailed. That decision not only expedited the filming but produced clean musical tracks. The cast mimed to records as carpenters hammered the sets, just like in the recently departed days of silent movies.

No incident in this period is more emblematic of Bing's ambivalence about stardom and success than his arrest that November for drunk driving. As maddening as the seemingly endless production of *King of Jazz* was, the picture held tremendous promise for Bing. His screen tests and auditions had led nowhere, but Whiteman offered him a prominent role in what everyone expected to be one of the most important pictures of the coming season. In addition to numbers with the Rhythm Boys, he would be featured as soloist in a lavish episode built around the key song in the Yellen-Ager score, "Song of the Dawn." He scuttled his chance.

The trouble began with a tiff during the rehearsal of "A Bench in the Park," a Brox Sisters number for which the Rhythm Boys provided harmony. As recalled by Bobbe Van Heusen, née Brox, Bing arrived on the soundstage cheerful and slightly flush with drink. Bobbe had argued with him about his drinking before. This time she got mad. "I was told to sit on his lap during the number and I refused. I wouldn't do it," she said. "It was really silly, like kid stuff, you know. But I wouldn't do it. So he went out and got drunk and he practically drove through the lobby of the Roosevelt Hotel in Hollywood. And of course he was arrested, and came to rehearsals with two detectives for the rest of the picture."[40]

Despite several versions of the tale and the disappearance of Bing's arrest record, no one disputes the basic facts. After the rehearsal and argument with Bobbe, Bing walked to Whiteman Lodge, where an elaborate studio-catered party was in progress, celebrating the end of the first week's filming. The musicians played, Bing sang, and shortly after midnight, a woman asked him to drive her to her hotel. As they approached the Roosevelt, Bing made a left turn into an oncoming car with such force that he and his passenger were knocked over the windshield and onto the pavement. He was fine, but the woman was bloody and unconscious. Bing carried her into the Roosevelt lobby, where the house doctor assured him that she was all right. Just then a policeman collared him and the other driver — who in Bing's account was more inebriated than he was — and took them to Lincoln Heights jail.

Kurt Dieterle, the violinist Bing roomed with, observed, "Well, Bing is a boy that does what he wants when he wants to do it. This night I went out for a date after I had my dinner, and the woman cooking for us said, 'How about Mr. Crosby?' I said, 'Just leave it on the stove, he'll be back later, I'm sure.' I went out and came home. He wasn't home yet, must have been after twelve, one o'clock. I was in bed when the phone rings, and who was it? Bing. I said, 'Where in the hell are you?' He said, 'I'm in jail.' Said he got into a confrontation. 'It's cold here, bring me a couple blankets.' That was the end of our apartment with Bing. I gave it up and moved in with Roy Bargy and his family."[41]

The next morning Jimmy Gillespie arranged bail and a trial was set for the following week. Bing agreed to plead guilty and pay the fine, but at the hearing he could not resist riling the judge. He arrived in court directly from the golf course, wearing green plus fours, an orange sweater, and check socks. The judge, noting the H.B.D. (had been drinking) complaint, asked if he was familiar with the Eighteenth Amendment. Bing's reply ran along the lines of "Only remotely" (according to his brothers' account)[42] or "Yes, but nobody pays much attention to it" (according to his own).[43] He was sentenced to sixty days.

Unable to contact his friends, Bing stewed in his cell for a day, until his brother Everett discovered he had not come home. Bing was stung by the severity of the sentence, and Whiteman was irate. The combined pleas of Ev, Whiteman, and Laemmle succeeded in getting him transferred to a Hollywood jail with a liberal visitation policy. After a great deal more pleading, Bing's new jailers agreed to a scheme that allowed him to work at the studio under police escort and return to his cell after the day's shooting. But it took two weeks to make that deal, and Whiteman could not or would not postpone "Song of the Dawn." He gave the number to John Boles, a thirty-five-year-old former World War I spy and stage actor who had made the transition from silent to talking films with his chesty operatic voice and conventional Hollywood good looks: dark hair, trim mustache, square jaw, gleaming eyes. As the closest thing to a movie star in the cast, billed second to Whiteman, Boles was an obvious choice for the number, an ersatz aria with the martial optimism expected of at least one song in every Hollywood revue.

Bing steamed, complaining repeatedly to Everett that Paul should have waited for him. Whiteman, sick of waiting, argued that he could not afford to postpone a major production number, though at this stage he undoubtedly felt little compunction in lowering the boom on Bing. Whiteman barely acknowledged him when he returned to the set. Bing's continuing obsession with the accident and its aftermath is evident in his repeated assertion — until the day he died, decades after there was any reason to airbrush the story — of his innocence and relative sobriety. He may indeed have been the victim of a bad driver and a zealous cop. But it was his brazen court performance that ruined his chance and required him to explain to Kate why he would not be featured as promised.

In one of his memoir's oddest passages, Bing considers what might have happened had he performed "Song of the Dawn" in *King of Jazz*. Observing with a trace of resentment that it "certainly helped" Boles, he concludes that it all worked out for the best, because the number might have short-circuited his career. "He had a bigger voice and a better delivery for that kind of song than I had," Bing wrote. "My crooning style wouldn't have been very good for such a number, which was supposed to be delivered à la breve like the 'Vagabond Song.' I might have flopped with the song. I might have been cut out of the picture. I might never have been given another crack at a song in any picture."[44]

Bing had a gift for mocking his own powers: note the humble reference to his "crooning style." But any doubts he or anyone else may have entertained about his ability to sell "Song of the Dawn" had been put to rest right after the film wrapped, when he recorded it with Whiteman. Bing never sounded more determined to prove how stentorian he could be; yet even belting that operatic rubbish, he lightens an overwrought arrangement with a touch of impudent swing. Still, he had self-inflicted a professional wound, and his indignation and guilt would not let it heal. Bing suffered several disappointments during the next year. Sometimes he feared he would never get another shot at Hollywood, while Boles, who had made many films, continued to make many more. However facetious Bing meant to be in his 1953 memoir, his desperation back in 1930 was real, and it survived in his fixation on a song and a movie that are no better remembered than John Boles.

On New Year's Eve the picture's production was threatened again by a car accident, in which violinist Mischa Russell suffered four broken vertebrae and trombonist Boyce Cullen a broken arm, though this time the other driver accepted full blame. A week later, in an attempt to quell rumors of catastrophe, Paul, Grofé, Anderson, Rosse, Markert, and featured vocalist Jeanette Loff took a seasonal-greetings ad in *Variety,* announcing their joy in completing *King of Jazz.* When that failed to squelch the gossip, Junior Laemmle arranged for reporters to visit the set to watch him shake hands with Whiteman.

Bing's jail sentence was ultimately reduced by a third, and he was released before the New Year. Bobbe Brox never did allow Bing to sit on her lap for "A Bench in the Park," which was consequently staged with the Rhythm Boys chirping behind the bench. "He had to come to the rehearsal with those detectives and he looked so terrible. He didn't like it very well," Bobbe recalled, laughing. "But he was so charming, so very charming. I loved Bing and we were good friends for a long, long time. He was lots of fun — great sense of humor, fun to be with. But he did something a lot of boys do at that age. They do not know how to hold their liquor. That was the only thing about Bing that I didn't like. Of course, he grew up, thank goodness, and never did that anymore and we remained friends."[45]

In her last years Bobbe claimed that she and Bing might have married but for his drinking. Apparently she had forgotten that a year earlier she had married William Perlberg, who booked the sisters and had helped secure the Montmartre engagement for the Rhythm Boys. Perlberg later became a film producer and worked closely with Bing. After she ended their long marriage (some thirty-five years), Bobbe married another Crosby associate, songwriter Jimmy Van

Heusen. Bing sent them a telegram in 1969 that, in Bobbe's recollection, read: "I can't tell you how much pleasure it gives me to see my two oldest friends married — to each other."[46]

The film finally wrapped on March 11, 1930, and by then the Whiteman band had resumed its theatrical jobs in Los Angeles and San Francisco, reaping tremendous gates. (*Variety* reported that when the band went into "Rhapsody in Blue," a woman advised her girlfriend, "That's the Old Gold theme song.")[47] During the weeks leading up to the film's April 20 premiere in Hollywood and May 2 premiere in New York, Whiteman ceaselessly plugged the cast and songs on radio and recorded the main tunes for Columbia. Universal announced that Anderson would be retained to direct a second film with Whiteman. Everyone was hopeful.

They were whistling in the dark. At $1.5 million, *King of Jazz* cost more than four times the average musical. Translated into today's dollars, the budget was as high as a modern special-effects action extravaganza (about $75 million) — this in a year when movie tickets averaged thirty-five cents. The industry began to realize that the vogue for filmed vaudeville was over shortly before *King of Jazz* debuted, when Paramount Pictures released *Paramount on Parade* (a revue packed with real stars) and saw business fall sharply in the first weeks. Universal's hopes sank precipitously. *King of Jazz* opened well at the Los Angeles Criterion. *Variety* projected first-week receipts of $18,000. But business tapered off so badly by the third day that the theater took in only $13,000. *Variety* ran an unusually vicious review, attacking Anderson ("who knew nothing about picture direction and didn't seem to know any more either at the finish of the film")[48] and accurately predicting a two-week life span. Most critics, however, were dazzled and supportive.

As Bing feared, Boles was singled out (typically: "John Boles throttles all competition in the singing cinema")[49] while the Rhythm Boys were mentioned only in passing. The picture did well in Philadelphia, fair in San Francisco, and died in Indianapolis. Yet Universal believed the public could be swayed, and pulled out all the stops for the New York debut at the Roxy, presenting the film in tandem with a stage show that starred Whiteman and George Gershwin.[50] Mordaunt Hall in the *New York Times* wrote, "There is no sequence that isn't worth witnessing and no performance that is not capable in this fast paced picture."[51] But for once, there was too much Whiteman. The public, surprisingly, favored *All Quiet on the Western Front,* Lewis Milestone's scalding World War I film, which saved Universal's hash and won Junior Laemmle an Academy Award for best picture. Junior would not be picking up options on Whiteman or Anderson (indeed, he threatened to sue Paul over food and telegram expenses). Nor would he make any more musicals for a while, though he approved nine foreign versions of *King of Jazz,* including a German edition emceed by Joseph Schildkraut, with two additional numbers by the Sisters G, and a Hungarian one with Bela Lugosi.[52] Junior would find his forte in monsters and vampires, initiating the great Universal horror cycle of the 1930s. But the Depression defeated him, and when his splendid 1936 film of *Show Boat* stumbled at the box office, he left pictures for good at age twenty-eight.

Universal took a million-dollar bath and did not begin to recoup until the picture was reissued in 1933, on the coattails of *42nd Street.* (Bing, by then a major star, was embarrassed to find himself top-billed.) Yet as the *New York Times* and other papers noted, *King of Jazz* was a singular film, and it endures as Anderson's triumph. Its ingenious visual effects bely his novice status and proved highly influential. It remains a Rosetta stone of early American pop, incarnating a multicultural display intended for a white middlebrow audience. The picture begins with Bing's voice, singing through the credits ("Music hath charms, though it's classy or jazz"), and ends with "The Melting Pot of Music," an extravaganza featuring leggy Spanish dancers, men in jodphurs, and concertina, bagpipe, and balalaika players (but no Africans), all ultimately dissolving into the image of Maestro Whiteman taking a bow. We are told at the outset that "jazz was born in the African jungle to the beat of the voodoo drums," but the only black person in the film is a smiling six-year-old girl cradled in Whiteman's lap for a laugh.

King of Jazz exists in a bubble of racial and mercantile timidity. All references to blacks are aged in minstrel conventions, among them a snippet of "Old Black Joe" and dancer Jacques Cartier decked out as an African chieftain, dancing in silhouette on a gigantic drum. Yet the Cartier number underscores the film's tremendous impact: the silhouette trick was used by Fred Astaire in his tribute to Bill Robinson in *Swing Time*; the drum dance was developed by Robinson himself in *Stormy Weather*. Many of Anderson's ideas were imitated in later pictures, from the miniature musicians climbing out of a valise (*Bride of Frankenstein*) to cardboard skyscrapers (*42nd Street*) to concentric tuba and trombone orbits (the two-reeler *Jammin' the Blues*). Visual abstractions for "Rhapsody in Blue" are abundant with tropes later elaborated by Busby Berkeley: pianist Roy Bargy morphing into five pianists, aerial shots, giant dislocated heads, kaleidoscopes.

Musically, the film is dreary except for "Rhapsody" and the few examples of jazz, which consist of Lang and Venuti playing "The Wild Dog" and the numbers involving Bing. Despite the hullabaloo over "Song of the Dawn" (Boles, in a bolero outfit, looks and sounds as dated as the rouged and lipsticked tenors in other scenes), Bing is handsomely represented and in excellent form. He swings the song behind the opening titles as well as a spiritual lip-synched by a Walter Lantz cartoon character, interpolates a *bu-bu-bu-boo* in top hat behind the Brox Sisters; and jives two numbers with the Rhythm Boys. Whether he is on- or offscreen, his voice is buoyant and bright, agelessly rhythmic. The Rhythm Boys sequence is the best evidence we have of how enchanting they were at their peak and how natural Bing was in front of a camera from the start. Al Rinker is tall and handsome, standing with his hand in his pocket. Harry Barris is so chipper, he can't sit still. Yet on "So the Bluebirds and the Blackbirds Got Together," only Bing adds deft physical touches, waving his hand, inclining his head. For "Happy Feet," Al and Harry play two pianos and Bing stands in the middle. As Harry pretends to execute a dance step, Bing gives the camera a wide-eyed look that momentarily breaches the fourth wall. Bing's light marcelled hair is receding and his rouge is a bit thick, but he is utterly relaxed. With his double takes and mock solemnity, he is our contemporary, winking across time.

The Rhythm Boys continued with the band when Whiteman left California to play Canada. Incredibly, Paul was barred from entering the country at Vancouver: orchestra leaders, he learned, were "entertainers" and "as such could play from theater stages, but not at dances."[53] After days of wrangling, the tour detoured for a week to Seattle and Portland before finally heading home to New York. But a contretemps that week permanently poisoned the waters between Paul and Bing.

In his memoir Bing explains that a bootlegger dunned him for money he claimed was due for a quart of "day-old pop-skull";[54] when Bing contested the debt, the bootlegger demanded money from White-man, who complied over Bing's objection and then deducted the amount from Bing's salary. That led to an argument, Bing wrote, that ended when Whiteman told him, "When we get to Seattle, we'll part friends and that'll be the end of it."[55] Years later, however, Bing related a different version of events to his second wife, Kathryn: Whiteman had confronted him in front of the band and accused him of stealing his liquor. "I was outraged by that and quit," he told her.[56]

In any case, neither Bing nor his partners quit in Seattle. They traveled with the band back to New York and made the break shortly after arriving. They had several reasons beyond Bing's pique, chiefly a desire to return to California. A couple of days after his jail sentence was commuted, Bing had encountered Dixie Lee again at a party, and they had continued to see each other almost every night. Now, in New York, he was inconsolable without her. One evening he tele-phoned her from his room at the Belvedere and fell asleep without breaking the connection. His roommate, Frank Trumbauer, found him in the morning cradling the phone. The cost was $130.75, paid by Tram, who saved the bill as a souvenir. Barris, too, had become infatuated with a singer, Loyce Whiteman (no relation to Paul), who demonstrated sheet music in a Glendale shop. Al didn't have a steady girl, but he was no less determined than the others to stay off the road. After three years and four months, the trio decided to break with Whiteman and return to Los Angeles.

On April 30, the morning after an Old Gold broadcast, Bing told Whiteman of their intentions. Paul agreed to abrogate their contract but asked them to keep it quiet so as not to interfere with his immi-nent premiere at the Roxy. "It was time to go out on our own and also the right time for Paul to let us go," recalled Al. "His band payroll was very high and his contract with Columbia was soon to end. On our part, the Rhythm Boys had not followed through on our own record-ings and we didn't seem to have the incentive to pursue our record-ing career. It was a friendly parting and we wished each other good luck."[57]

For Bing, the "pop-skull" incident may have added to a grudge he was already carrying. In February — a month before *King of Jazz* wrapped, but after Bing's work on it was done — Paramount rushed into production a Nancy Carroll musical called *Honey* but could not settle on a leading man. They needed an appealing young actor who could sing. Studio chief B. P. Schulberg asked songwriter Sam Coslow for a recommendation. Coslow had known Bing in New York and now heard rumors that he was ready to leave the band. He drove to Loew's State, where Whiteman was working, and found Bing heartbroken about losing "Song of the Dawn" and eager for a real movie part. "He was confident he could get by with it," Coslow recalled in his autobiography. All Bing wanted was the same $200 Whiteman paid him, a standing contract ("After all, I have a steady job with this outfit"), and guaranteed parts for Al and Harry. Coslow relayed the good news, and Schulberg sent two talent scouts to Loew's State to audition Bing. "For about 24 hours, he was under consideration," Coslow wrote. "But the following day they auditioned a young actor named Stanley Smith. He couldn't sing very well, but somehow he got the part — don't ask me why."[58] Stanley Smith was one of the ineffectual tenors in *King of Jazz.*

Bing thought Whiteman had nixed the deal. That seems unlikely. Weeks earlier Whiteman had allowed him to participate in MGM's *The March of Time,* a blockbuster that threatened to dwarf all the other movie revues. Bing was retained for two scenes and billed as "Bing Crosby, Paul Whiteman Soloist." *The March of Time* was a strange mixture of stage veterans (Weber and Fields, Fay Templeton), newcomers (Skin Young, Benny Rubin), and extravagant production numbers. Bing sang "Poor Little G String," backed by an all-girl orchestra and the Albertina Rasch Ballet, but was little more than a prop in his second scene, made up as an old man with wig and mustache listening to a boy violinist. Just as the picture neared completion, the *King of Jazz* fiasco sobered MGM's accountants. Rather than pour more cash into a sure loser, MGM not only shut down its "giant screen carnival" but destroyed most of the film stock. The more expensive numbers were recycled into later pictures,[59] but all that remains of Bing's labors is an eight-by-ten glossy.

In later years Bing's tributes to Whiteman were reserved, if sincere: "I'm impressed by how kind he was. When I was younger and more hot-headed, I used to think he should line my pockets with more gold. But I confess he owes me nothing. It's the other way around."[60]

They had little more to do with each other beyond a few radio appearances. Whiteman had his own troubles. Old Gold dropped his show, and his record sales evaporated. After he opened at the Roxy, he fired ten musicians and shaved the salaries of the survivors by 15 percent. Bing's timing had not failed him. The musicians Whiteman let go were his jazzmen — among them Lang, Venuti, Hayton, and Challis. For three years, beginning when he hired his Walla Walla boys, Paul had intelligently felt his way into jazz. Now he returned to his old formula (though he later recruited such jazzmen as Jack Teagarden and Red Norvo).

Challis thought the band began to slide downhill in 1929 and blamed radio, which consumed arrangements as fast as jokes. The luxury of taking one's time to perfect a piece was sacrificed to the demand for quantity. Worse, radio counted blandness as an asset, desirable to sponsors and song-pluggers. Challis briefly freelanced for Henderson and Ellington, until he could no longer ignore the hated medium and signed on for three years with Kate Smith.[61] By the early days of the Swing Era, he was considered old hat and was soon forgotten; not until the mid-1970s was he rediscovered by jazz fans. As for Whiteman, his celebrity and energy kept him afloat for years, but he never recovered his reign. He abandoned jazz just as it was about to enjoy a sweeping triumph in America's mainstream. An embittered, cynical public demanded a new and honest music that spoke directly to its dreams and fears. Few in 1930 could have imagined that the scepter would fall to a twenty-seven-year-old Rhythm Boy.

12

DIXIE

They say I left a trail of broken hearts behind me when I left California for New York. Now I wouldn't do a thing like that. The fact is I left a trail of broken bottles and unpaid bills.

— Bing Crosby (1931)[1]

For years a story circulated on the Fox lot about an eye-level chink in the exterior of one building's wall. The culprit was peppery Dixie Lee. Whenever she passed, a swain or two could be depended upon to whistle, "I wish I were in Dixie."[2] On one occasion she picked up a stone and hurled it in the direction of her tormentor with such force as to cause the damage, which naturally came to be known as Dixie's Hole. Dixie was no pushover, but she was a relatively typical product of the era: a shapely, shy, talented, if not especially ambitious teenager for whom show business was as much a lark as a living. In an age of infinite chorus lines (employed on the stage, in movies, at nightclubs), not even a depression could quell the demand for attractive young women with educated legs or lilting voices or inviting smiles. Dixie was lovelier than most and more capable; on film she radiated sauciness in a smart, sad-eyed way. She had a strong unaccented shopgirl's voice and, like her contemporary Jean Harlow, was fashionably plebeian. Harlow, however, was the tough-broad type, whereas Dixie was vulnerable, acerbic but wounded.

From the time her father enrolled her in an amateur contest, she handled each show-business opportunity with aplomb. By the time she was eighteen, Dixie possessed a glamorously quizzical expression, as if she saw irony lurking everywhere. She was a knockout, with large brown eyes, a full lower lip, round cheeks to cushion a firm nose, and blond (or red or natural brown, depending on the year) hair falling in waves down the right side of her face. Men found her captivating, but like Bing's, her appeal was genderproof; women were disarmed by her straight-arrow modesty. At five foot three and 115 pounds (as she informed the editor of her hometown newspaper), she somehow conveyed stature. Rory Burke, daughter of Bing's lyricist Johnny Burke, thought she gave the illusion of height: "She had this tall look to her, lean and slim. I always think of her in a beautiful white gown with that beautiful blond hair."[3]

She was born Wilma Winifred Wyatt on November 4, 1911, in a handsome plank house with pitched roofs and a small covered porch in the Walnut Hill section of Harriman, Tennessee, to Evan Wyatt and the former Nora Scarbrough.[4] Her family had lived in Tennessee for generations; her grandfather, Jim Wyatt, was known throughout local counties as a singer and vocal coach. Billie, as Wilma was known from early childhood, was four when the family relocated to Memphis. The move may have been the result of her father's career as an insurance salesman or may have stemmed from the desire to escape the scene of tragedy: Billie's two older sisters had died of rheumatic fever within a year of each other. After seven years in Memphis, the Wyatts moved to New Orleans, where Billie grew friendly with the slightly older Boswell sisters (they later sang offscreen in one of her movies), and then — when Billie was fourteen — to Chicago.[5] Three years later, she wryly recalled, "my theatrical career began."[6]

"I loved her dearly," her lifelong friend Pauline Weislow recalled; they had met in high school. "Oh, she was very sweet, most generous, but shy. Her parents were nice people, no money at all, really. I used to go over to her house and we would borrow clothes from each other. Her dad would cut my hair when he cut hers. He was gentle, but he knew his own mind."[7] Indeed, Mr. Wyatt was a voluble socialist given to tirades against organized religion. Billie was having a difficult time in high school and spoke to Pauline of quitting, when — in May 1928 — her father entered her in an amateur "blues singing" contest.[8]

She made up a pseudonym "so all the kids wouldn't know it was me if I lost."[9] Performing as Dixie Carroll, she triumphed.

One of the judges was popular singer Ruth Etting, who must have noticed how much Dixie's style owed to her own. Etting, apparently flattered, took an interest in her. The contest prize was a job at a roadhouse, College Inn, and Etting and music publisher Rocco Vocco arranged for Dixie to borrow a piano, pianist, and arrangements.[10] In October a talent scout passed through and offered her a part in the traveling company of *Good News,* which was then playing in Philadelphia. With her mother as chaperone, Dixie reluctantly agreed, realizing she would have to learn to dance at rehearsals. That turned out not to be a problem. Dixie was so proficient that after six weeks she was transferred to the Broadway company. When the star who created the role of Connie Lane, Mary Lawlor, became ill, Dixie subbed for her for nearly two months. A Fox agent spotted her and signed her to a contract to take effect when she completed her commitment to the show, which included a return to Chicago as lead understudy. When Dixie and her mother finally arrived in Hollywood, Fox's chief of production, Winfield Sheehan, informed them that there were already two young Carrolls in town, Nancy Carroll and Sue Carol, and that her professional name would be Dixie Lee.

Dixie was quickly put to work and extensively promoted. "I was a big shot because I was a Broadway star," she said, "yeah, I'd been on Broadway seven weeks!"[11] She was featured in two 1929 pictures, *Fox Movietone Follies* and *Why Leave Home?,* and rushed into five more for release in 1930.[12] In *Happy Days* she was given a flamboyant number, "Crazy Feet," backed by thirty-two tap dancers.[13] So when Dixie reencountered Bing at a party in January 1930, she was several rungs up the ladder while he was a recently paroled singer who had just been rejected for picture work by the very man who was investing heavily in Dixie.

Several people later claimed credit for their second meeting. Holly Hall, Dixie's roommate back in Chicago, told her husband, Bobby O'Brien (later a writer for Bing), that she made the match. But where? David Butler, who directed Dixie ten years before he directed Bing (in *Road to Morocco* and others), said the party was at his place. Sol Wurtzel, who produced Dixie's films at Fox, claimed the party was at his place. Richard Keene, an actor who appeared in *Happy Days,* said he was the party's host — but in July, by which time Bing and Dixie had been steadies for six months. The first to speak up, however, was Marjorie White, an actress who appeared with Dixie in *Fox Movietone Follies* and *Happy Days* and said in the *Los Angeles Times* the week Bing and Dixie were wed that the party was at her place.[14] Wurtzel attained distinction of another kind, advising Dixie, "If you marry him, you'll be supporting him for the rest of your life."[15] Others agreed, including Dixie's father, who considered him "a useless, good-for-nothing type."[16] Dixie never forgave those who disparaged her husband. "Everybody's saying they made Bing," she said years later. "The same ones who told me, Don't marry him — he'll never amount to anything. Bing's sweet to them, but I can't be."[17]

That they deeply loved each other no one doubted. But though the marriage blossomed for the better part of a decade, publicly extolled as a fairy-tale romance, the story of Bing and Dixie is not a happy one. In the shorthand of Hollywood mythology, Dixie began drinking to keep up with Bing, then put her foot down and forced him to quit. As a result, his career took off while hers disappeared. As insecure as Bing was confident, Dixie was not ungrateful to escape the limelight, but by then her own drinking had gotten out of hand. Warning signs were apparent long before they tied the knot.

At first, Bing's drinking was uncontained while Dixie's was a less noticeable compulsion. Her high-school friend Pauline, who later danced in *George White's Scandals* and became a member of Dixie's Hollywood support group, observed, "I think what happened was she tried to compete and she was a shy person. She was afraid she couldn't come up to the expectations of other people who she thought were so talented, and she couldn't really talk to people unless she'd had a drink. Bing was private and Dixie was not only private, but unable to share anything that was wrong."[18] Flo Haley, the widow of Jack Haley (the Tin Man in *The Wizard of Oz*) and for many years a Crosby neighbor, recalled Dixie as "a darling little girl. And she didn't drink before she met Bing. It was the waiting for him at night, after the show, before they went home, that she'd have a drink. He'd say, 'One for the road.' But she didn't have the tolerance he had. If she took more than two, it would bother her and then she'd have another one."[19] In her final years Dixie confided in her doctor and friend,

Dr. George J. Hummer, about her insecurities. "She was an introvert," Hummer observed. "She said that she died every time before she went onscreen or onstage. You'd never know it by looking at her work. But when she used to sit down and talk to me about her stage fright, it was real, you know, very real."[20]

Bing, though he denied it, was also familiar with stage fright, which he attempted — not always successfully — to curb with drink. Before he courted Dixie, he was infatuated with an older, much-married beauty of the era, Adeline Lamont, who hunted and drove racing cars and was known to friends as Buster. According to Buster's daughter-in-law, actress Marsha Hunt, Bing was needed at the studio (presumably for the unfinished *The March of Time*) and panic ensued when he could not be located. He was traced back to Buster's home in Coldwater Canyon, where he had attended a party the previous evening, and was found under her bed, terrified of having to report for work. "He was so shy, so nervous, that he was hiding out, or so the story went," Marsha Hunt recalled. "But that elaborate, casual, laid-back style that he was so famous for must have been a carefully drawn cover for great self-consciousness. Boy, what an act of grace and understatement and charm."[21]

He was somewhat less than graceful in his marriage proposal, which Dixie recalled as a kind of self-improvement decision, as though he'd taken to heart Saint Paul's dictum to put away childish things and saw her as a means to a long-postponed maturity. His brothers write in their biography that Bing told the other Rhythm Boys, "What I need is some responsibility, somebody for me to look out for, and somebody to look out for me, and in spite of my depleted financial condition, I think I'll take the bull by the horns and get married."[22] Reminded of that passage by a reporter in 1946, Dixie said it was not far from the truth.

During the first weeks of their courtship, Dixie lived in the beach home of Mabel Cooper, a rehearsal pianist at Fox and a few years her senior and very protective. Mabel's son, child actor Jackie Cooper (his first film was *Fox Movietone Follies*), wrote of Bing's constant hanging around, especially on weekends: "When I went outside those Sunday mornings, there would be Bing Crosby, asleep on the front porch swing, in his tuxedo and shoes with a flower in his buttonhole. I would get him a pillow and a blanket."[23] Bing was so infatuated with Dixie that he ventured to forewarn his mother. In early April, when

Bing had been seeing his future wife for three months and was set to leave on his last tour with Whiteman,[24] he closed a letter to Kate: "Incidentally I met a girl the other night whom I think you'd like. Her name is Dixie Lee and she works for Fox. Been taking her out quite a bit lately, and she's kind of got me winging. Don't get alarmed though, nothing serious yet. Or maybe there is. Love. Harry."[25]

The letter undoubtedly masked apprehension about bringing up women, or romance, with his mother. But there was another issue, too. In considering marriage to Dixie, Bing was contemplating a step that, though taken by Kate herself, could only appall her. The son she fancied as a priest was considering a marriage out of faith, into the religion to which his father had been born. This cannot have been a casual decision, yet he did not insist that Dixie convert.

In the nine months between the beginning of their courtship and the day of their secretive wedding, Bing became increasingly determined to support Dixie and avoid the burden of being known as Mr. Lee. Dixie was skeptical at first (she found him "spoiled even then. He wore plus fours and yellow socks and hoped for a break in pictures"), but she soon succumbed.[26] Although only eighteen, she displayed a nearly maternal dedication to his future. The cost was ruinous. In effect, she adopted Kate's role, taking Bing in hand, pushing him forward, mothering him — hardly an auspicious tack for conjugal bliss. Her belief in Bing reassured and flattered him. But at twenty-seven, he continued to hold discipline at bay.

Bing's final solo with Whiteman, recorded shortly before the last tour, was a song written for a Maurice Chevalier film that Bing might have adapted as his slogan, "Livin' in the Sunlight, Lovin' in the Moonlight":

> *Things that bother you, they never bother me, I think everything's*
> *   fine,*
> *Living in the sunlight, loving in the moonlight, having a wonderful*
> *   time.*
> *Just take it from me, I'm just as free as any dove.*
> *I do what I like, just when I like, and how I love it.*
> *I don't give a hoot, give my cares the boot, all the world is in rhyme,*
> *Living in the sunlight, loving in the moonlight, having a wonderful*
> *   time.*

With the Whiteman association over, the Rhythm Boys could hardly wait to return to California's sunshine, though as Al conceded, "The opportunities for performing and finding work were not as available as in New York."[27] Dixie, anxious to keep Bing in town, encouraged him as the group made the rounds. They found a brief stint on radio, and then cooled their heels for a few weeks until a young agent, Leonard Goldstein, landed them a week's work at $250 each on a two-reeler, a last-ditch try by Pathe Exchange to skirt insolvency. The movie, a halfhearted burlesque of the hoariest of melodramas, concerns a greedy landlord who threatens to evict an old man and his daughter into the cold. It was first conceived as a showcase for Yiddish character actor Nat Carr. As the tailor in jeopardy, Carr is admired by the boys at Tait College (a nod to *Good News*), who call him Ripstitch and spend their time playing ukeleles and shooting craps. The Rhythm Boys were to be included among the college boys. On May 23, the day they made their last Columbia record (an amiable version of "A Bench in the Park"), a script was submitted to producer Fred Guiol and director Ray McCarey for *Plus Eights,* a title they changed to *Two Plus Fours.*

The most amusing aspect of *Two Plus Fours* is that the Rhythm Boy singled out for stardom by Ray McCarey (brother of Leo McCarey, who went on to create Bing's Father O'Malley pictures) was Harry Barris, on whom he ladled key lines, close-ups, and even the girl. Harry has pizzazz to spare, but his collegiate wiseguy stuff was old hat even then. Al gets lost in the crowd while Bing seems inattentive and bored, even at the end when he sings a solo verse of "The Stein Song" (a current Rudy Vallée hit), affects a dancer's bearing from the waist up, and then bops the landlord on the head while doing a comical entrechat with fluttery hands — mock-balletic poses that would recur throughout his career. Shot in five days at a cost of more than $19,000, it previewed mid-June, shipped early July, and disappeared, taking Pathe with it.

Yet Bing persisted in the belief that he could make it as an actor, despite his lack of experience (beyond plays at Gonzaga), his ready acknowledgment of his thespian limitations, and his looks, which did not jibe with the vogue in leading men. He was appealing, to be sure, with azure eyes and handsome features, but he had those wingy ears, a rapidly receding hairline, and an expanding waist. In just about every interview he ever gave, Bing was consistently and unreasonably modest about his abilities as an actor. He even, perhaps disingenuously, remarked that he won his 1944 Oscar because the good actors were away doing war work. (His rival nominees included Cary Grant and Charles Boyer.) He insisted that all he ever did was play himself.

The wonder is that he was so certain playing himself would do the trick. Bing quietly, pragmatically weighed his strengths and limitations, confident that the former would carry the day. In the long view, he probably shortchanged his dramatic talents by clinging too closely to the Bing Crosby persona. Yet in 1930 that persona existed only in his mind. His belief that he could beat the odds by being himself followed from his conviction that he could remake himself as a "type," a new movie genus, *Bingus crosbyanis*. In learning to play himself, he had to invent himself. And he invented himself as a man whose decency others might want to emulate.

Rumors circulated that he took bit parts whenever he could; Bing or the Rhythm Boys were said to have been involved in such obscurities as *The Lottery Bride* and *Many a Slip*, either blending into crowds or landing on the cutting-room floor. One newspaper reported that Bing and Dixie were slated for MGM's film of *Good News;* if in fact they were considered for that adaptation, Bing must have been especially galled to learn that the juvenile lead went to Stanley Smith (who had recently beat him out for a part in *Honey*), while the femme lead went to the oddly disconsolate stage star Mary Lawlor, who lacked Dixie's spirit.

While the Rhythm Boys were spinning their wheels, agents were more than willing to take a chance on them. Bing all too casually encouraged more than a few, including Everett, who did not quite understand the business yet; William Perlberg, who had arranged the Montmartre job; and Edward Small, who sued when Bing hit the big time. But the guy who came through in their hour of need was Leonard Goldstein. Years later, when Goldstein was reaping a fortune with quickie westerns and lowbrow franchises (Ma and Pa Kettle, Francis the Talking Mule), he regaled journalists with his claims of discovering Bing: "I found him in the gutter. He chucked a cigar butt, and there I was right after it."[28] *Two Plus Fours* had not helped either of them. Now he had a better idea.

Goldstein had first heard Bing and Al when they were with the Morrissey revue. His twin brother, Bob, later a power at Fox, was then manager of Abe Lyman, renowned for leading the orchestra at the Ambassador Hotel's Cocoanut Grove. Leonard tried in vain to get Lyman to hire the Rhythm Boys. When Lyman left the Grove in 1926, his pianist, Gus Arnheim, took charge for three years. Arnheim, in turn, left for a lengthy tour; during the years the Rhythm Boys were making their name with Whiteman, he traveled to Europe and enhanced his reputation before returning to the Grove in early 1930. Goldstein knew Arnheim would appreciate what Lyman had declined. The Grove's manager, Abe Frank, agreed to hire the boys at $450 a week, $50 less per man than they had received from Whiteman. Goldstein was not happy and neither were the boys, but they accepted the offer. Gus Arnheim and arranger Jimmy Grier, a friend and fan of Bing's, were ecstatic.

The Ambassador Hotel, with its private bungalows, intrigued the film crowd from the time it opened on Wilshire Boulevard in 1920. Abe Frank knew that a nightclub on the premises could not miss. Within a year the main ballroom was transformed into the 1,000-seat Cocoanut Grove, complete with prop palm trees and fake monkeys grabbing fake coconuts. By 1930 the style was Hollywood Moroccan; the palms and monkeys were set against white stucco arches, and a red carpet extended from the top of a wide stairway in the hotel lobby all the way to the Grove. The Depression could not lay a glove on the place. Limousines crowded the entrance at night. On July 14 at 10:00 P.M., Arnheim featured the Rhythm Boys in his two-hour broadcast over KNX, a powerful station that covered the Pacific Coast and reached as far inland as Colorado. The next night he officially introduced them to the audience at the Grove, and they were a sensation.

Much of young Hollywood had heard the trio at the Montmartre a year before, but the Grove was more established and posh, well known for its star nights and college nights, and as the venue (through 1936) for the Academy Awards ceremony. The Grove merged society (royalty, mobsters) and moviedom, a flush following that adored the Rhythm Boys, who appeared nightly and at Saturday teas. "We would show off our latest outfits generally on Tuesday nights, which is when the Hollywood crowd of that time gathered regularly at the Cocoanut Grove," director Mervyn LeRoy recalled. "We would all have the same table, week after week. We went to see, and to be seen."[29]

If you couldn't get in, you could hear them on the two-hour radio broadcasts. Anthony Quinn, a kid who would later appear in three of Bing's movies, never missed a broadcast. He was the only one in his Mexican American neighborhood with a radio: "All the kids from all over would gather out my window and I would turn the sound up so that they could hear [Bing]. So he was quite a hero to us."[30]

Arnheim's was strictly a sweet band, but he admired good musicians — he apprenticed such jazz stars as Woody Herman, Budd Johnson, and Stan Kenton. He recruited Loyce Whiteman, who was courted by the recently divorced Barris, and Irish tenor Donald Novis at the same time as the Rhythm Boys but counted on the trio to add zest to a fourteen-piece outfit that, by Paul Whiteman's standards, was stiff and impassive. One band member whose life was transfigured by Bing was Russ Columbo, a capable violinist who knew just enough Joe Venuti licks to handle a two-bar break. Russ doubled as singer with two other musicians in a high-voiced trio, but what made him stand out were his dark good looks. A Valentino type with slicked-back hair, he was personable and alert, smiling as he played. After observing Bing for a few months, he began to appreciate what could be done with a microphone (he could barely be heard without one) and realized he was a light baritone, not a tenor, and could put over a ballad in a manner not unlike Bing's. Some listeners claimed they could not tell the difference on evenings when Bing failed to show and Columbo went on in his place. Neither Goldstein nor Bing was amused by the similarity; Columbo soon left Arnheim to embark on a successful if tragically short-lived career.

At first the Grove engagement seemed charmed. Bing spent his days at the golf course and encountered little pressure on the job. He behaved. Movie stars said hello and became friends. For a change, Al did some drinking while Harry continued to nip at his flask, but Bing generally abstained. In those first few months, Bing established himself as a ballad soloist with no little help from Barris, whose songwriting efforts finally paid off in tunes discerningly tailored to the Crosby cry. They worked out a schedule with Arnheim. Once a night, between dances, they performed one of their numbers alone on the bandstand. For the rest of the evening, they sang choruses with the band. Al noticed something he had not seen before: "When the Rhythm Boys or Bing were singing from the bandstand all the dancers . . .

would practically stand still and watch us and when the band took over they would dance again."[31]

The more observant gawkers may have realized they were witnessing something historic: Bing's innovative perfection of a new instrument, the microphone. It was his ultimate ally, perfectly suited to his way with dynamics and nuance and timbre. As he explored gradations in projection, Bing collaborated with the electric current as if he were romancing a woman. He played the mike with a virtuosity that influenced every singer to follow, grounding it as a vehicle of modernism. Overnight, megaphones became a joke, as the tradition of vocal shouting receded into an instant prehistory. Two years earlier Al Jolson had been at the peak of his popularity; now he would be recast as the beloved reminder of old-fashioned show business. With the microphone elaborating the subtleties of his delivery, Bing was reinventing popular music as a personal and consequently erotic medium.

The modern style of American popular singing, as distinct from the theatrical emoting of the minstrel and vaudeville eras, dominated the interpretation, understanding, and even the composition of contemporary songs throughout the Western world for most of the twentieth century. That style was originated by four performers, each to some degree rooted in jazz and blues: Bessie Smith, Ethel Waters, Louis Armstrong, and Bing Crosby. The first to make their influence felt were Smith, born in 1894 in Chattanooga, Tennessee, and Waters, born two years later in Chester, Pennsylvania. Both women were formed in the crucible of tent shows and black vaudeville; their talents were tried and tested by audiences that dared them not to be great. Inevitably, they became rivals, and Ethel's popular triumph over Bessie, whom she described as "all champ"[32] and whom her contemporaries acknowledged as Empress of the Blues, represents a moment when the black blues tradition was assimilated by mainstream American pop.

In their day Smith was the least widely known of the four, but as the finest heavy-voiced blues singing (some said shouting) contralto of the era, she influenced Waters and Louis Armstrong. She established vocal techniques intrinsic to the American style, notably an undulating attack in which notes are stretched, bent, curved, moaned, and hollered. Smith perfected and popularized an old style of melisma that Jeannette Robinson Murphy captured with lively accuracy in an 1899 issue of *Popular Science Monthly*. Attempting to instruct white singers in the art of "genuine Negro melodies," Murphy asked:

> What is there to show him that he must make his voice exceedingly nasal and undulating; that around every prominent note he must place a variety of small notes, called "trimmings," and he must sing tones not found in our scale; that he must on no account leave one note until he has the next one well under control? . . . He must often drop from a high note to a very low one; he must be very careful to divide many of his monosyllabic words in two syllables. . . . He must also intersperse his singing with peculiar humming sounds — "hum-m-m-m."[33]

Murphy titled her article "The Survival of African Music in America," but as musicologist Peter Van Der Merwe has shown, the stylistic elements she enumerated could also be found in Celtic music, particularly the Irish *caoin,* or lament. That may help to explain why the impact of Bessie Smith and other blues singers was felt most profoundly not only among Sephardic Jews, who shared with African Americans the tradition of the pentatonic scale, and Italians, who reveled in operatic projection, but by the Irish in precincts like the one in Spokane. Smith brought to modern American popular music the freedom to ad-lib melody and rhythm. Given her range of little more than an octave, she proved that emotional power does not depend on conventional vocal abilities.

Ethel Waters was another story. Though initially characterized as a blues singer, she came to embody the aspirations of black performers determined to make it on "white time." With her lighter voice and higher range, she may have lacked the weighty sonority of Bessie Smith, but her superb enunciation and gift for mimickry established her as a virtuoso capable of irrepressible eroticism (she was the queen of the double entendre) and high-toned gentility. Sophie Tucker, one of the giants of white vaudeville, was so taken with young Ethel that she offered to pay her for singing lessons. Young white jazz acolytes of the 1920s were mesmerized by Waters and Smith, but it was Ethel's smooth, articulate attack that had the greater appeal for Bing when Mildred introduced him to her records. If Bessie belonged to the blues, Ethel stood astride the whole swirling tapestry of American song.

Like a world-shaking conqueror — Alexander the Great razing Thebes yet creating Alexandria — Louis Armstrong was the most extreme force American music had ever known. A man of exceptional generosity, Armstrong would have been incapable of consciously destroying anything. Yet having assimilated almost every valuable tradition in nineteenth-century vernacular music, sacred or secular, he offered a comprehensive revision that supplanted them all. Born in the direst and most violent district of New Orleans, in 1901, he liberated American music instrumentally and vocally, uniting high and low culture. The mandarins wanted an American voice, and here it was — improvised yet durable, serious yet ribald, resolute yet startling. Musicians were permanently transformed by him and his music; they went away feeling freer, more optimistic, ambitious, and willing to take risks. Louis anchored — as Bessie Smith could not — blues as the foundation of America's new music. He proved — as Ethel Waters could not — that swing, a seductive canter as natural and personal as your heartbeat, was its irreducible rhythmic framework.

Bing Crosby was the first and, for a while, the only white singer who fully assimilated the shock of Armstrong's impact, and his loyalty never wavered. A year before he died, while playing the London Palladium, Crosby learned of the death of his friend, lyricist Johnny Mercer. The BBC requested an interview and sent a camera crew to the theater. Joe Bushkin, the pianist and leader of Bing's quartet, recalled that Bing was very upset and spoke at length to the reporter of his friendship with Mercer; toward the end of the interview, Bing added, "I loved his singing." Afterward, Bushkin told him how glad he was that Bing had mentioned Johnny's often neglected singing. They reminisced about Mercer, when out of the blue, Bing said, "I gotta tell you, Joe, do you realize that the greatest pop singer in the world that ever was and ever will be forever and ever is Louis Armstrong?" Bushkin said, "Of course, I love Louis's singing." Bing said, "It's so simple. When he sings a sad song you feel like crying, when he sings a happy song you feel like laughing. What the hell else is there with pop singing?"[34]

One of the most significant things Bing learned from Louis was that the contagious pulse later called swing did not have to be exclusive to jazz. It was a universally expressive technique that could deepen the interpretation of any song in any setting. However subtle or modest, that pulse created a steady grid while focusing the song's momentum. Bing's uncanny ability to hear "the one" — the downbeat of each measure — was unheard of among white singers in the 1920s. It never left him. Jake Hanna, the drummer in Bushkin's quartet, insisted, "Bing had the best, the absolute best time. And I played with Count Basie and that's great time. You just followed him and he carried you right along, and so unassuming."[35] Most of the singers who imitated Bing in the twenties and thirties — Russ Columbo, Perry Como, Dick Todd — took the superficial aspects of his style without the jazz foundation, which is why so much of their work is antiquated. Bing, on the other hand, did not imitate Armstrong; he understood that Louis's message was to be yourself. That meant not simulating a black aesthetic but applying it to who he was and what he knew as a Northwestern third-generation Anglo-Irish Catholic, reared on John McCormack and Al Jolson, Dixieland and dance music, elocution and minstrelsy, comedy and vaudeville.

In addition to exemplary time and articulation, Bing was blessed with sterling pitch. "He was always on target," said Milt Hinton, who played bass with the Bushkin quartet. "He was very theoretical about his singing, about diction and dynamics and things like that. I said, 'How in the hell do you do that?' He said, 'Well, I get in my car and go to the golf course and I'm singing in my car, and when I'm playing I'm singing.' His selection of words and what the meaning of a particular word was — he would really think about it, you know. You usually just hear a guy sing, but Bing knew the meaning of words and how he wanted the band to accent those certain things."[36]

To the mix as developed by Smith, Waters, and Armstrong, Bing added three elements that proved crucial to the fulfillment of popular singing: his expansive repertoire, expressive intimacy, and spotless timbre. Those facets grounded him as the first great ballad singer in jazz. Ethel Waters recorded a few ballads before Bing, but in a bold, plangent style more appropriate to vaudeville than romance. Bing prompted singers — and instrumentalists — to go beyond the familiar repertoire, even as he inspired songsmiths to handcraft ballads suitable to his singular talent. His sound had little precedent: rich, strong, masculine, and clean. Listeners who were put off by vernacular growls and moans could understand his relatively immaculate approach. Having absorbed his early influences, he rarely borrowed the expressive colorations of the blues. His one accommodation to the pervasive use of melisma was the Irish mordent. His phrasing was his own, aggressive yet gentle, heartfelt yet humorous.

Few patrons at the Cocoanut Grove could have foreseen how far Bing's renown would advance. But thousands of fans, even at that early stage, knew they were hearing something new and personal — a performer who sang to you, not at you, who told a story, who made you cry and laugh. The movie colony adopted and championed him. Veteran actor Walter Huston remembered him in those days as "one of the most likable, friendly fellows that I have ever met."[37] Most of those cheering were of the younger generation. Lupe Velez introduced Bing to Gary Cooper, who became a good pal; they sailed together, often with Richard Arlen. When Bing finally won the attention of the studios, he turned down generous offers from Fox and Warners to follow Cooper to Paramount; a year later he named his first son after him.

Songwriters and publishers often dropped by the Grove, as did directors and producers. So did childhood friends, including Bing's Gonzaga rival, Mike Pecarovitch, who now coached at Loyola and occasionally brought his students to hear Bing. Bud Brubaker, a Pecarovitch ballplayer who later became operations manager at Del Mar racetrack, recalled, "It was always jam-packed. They had a small dance floor and everybody was dancing. The Rhythm Boys would come out and sing six or eight songs during the evening's program and Bing was already the leader. His style was completely different than anybody else. We'd dress semiformal and everybody had a date. It was Prohibition so they couldn't serve booze. You brought your own. What you'd do is order fruit punch or something like that and they would bring you a setup and then you'd pour your own under the table. No one bothered you."[38]

One of Bing's most eminent fans was Duke Ellington, visiting Hollywood to make his feature debut in the Amos 'n' Andy vehicle *Check and Double Check*. Duke's spot required him to introduce the Kalmar and Ruby song "Three Little Words," but at rehearsal it was evident that the three members of his brass section assigned the vocal could not handle it. When another trio fared no better, Ellington told the producer to hire the Rhythm Boys. Given the decree against exhibiting white singers with a black band (never mind that the stars of the movie were white actors in blackface), the boys were set up behind the backdrop with a separate microphone. The number was filmed and recorded live. As they sang, the three Ellington musicians lip-synched — it was the kind of charade parodied in *Singin' in the Rain.* Ellington asked the Rhythm Boys to sing on the record, too, and by December "Three Little Words" topped every sales chart in the country. During the next decade Ellington refused to hire a male vocalist until he could find one (Herb Jeffries) who sang à la Bing.

Another movie deal was sealed at the Grove, but this time the request was for Bing alone. Edmund Goulding, who was writing and directing a Douglas Fairbanks musical, *Reaching for the Moon,* was so entranced by Bing that he asked executive Joe Schenck to hire Crosby to sing "When the Folks High Up Do the Mean Low Down," the jazziest number in the Irving Berlin score. Bing's screen time is little more than a minute: he bursts into an ocean-liner lounge with a greeting, "Hi, gang!" and sings one rocking chorus, arms waving in rhythm, then listens as the song is reprised by leading lady Bebe Daniels and June MacCloy, a Paramount starlet on loan. When the footage was edited, United Artists cut out all but one of the songs and released the film as a romantic comedy — enraging Berlin, who never allowed UA to use his work after that.

Bing's was the only number that survived. He shot it late at night (again, without prerecording), after finishing a set at the Grove. "We went in cold as cucumbers," recalled June MacCloy. "We heard the song and they just told us where to come in. It seems to me Bing may have had a chance to sing the whole song and that it was cut down. I think he liked having the job, because we were well paid, but he was disgusted because we were supposed to do another song that was never shot. Edward Everett Horton was also in the film and he talked with Bing quite a bit. They laughed and talked a lot. Everyone liked Bing, he was very likable. He didn't change keys on things. Everybody was pleased about that. Once in a while, when they were getting ready to take another shot, he'd be by the piano, but they never had to change the key for him."[39]

Fairbanks insisted that the crew break every day at four for tea, and though Bing did no filming during the afternoons, he liked to drop by and the cast liked having him. Songwriters and musicians who visited to carouse with Fairbanks also wanted to meet Bing. As far as MacCloy could see, all Bing drank was tea. "We started laughing, like 'What kind of sissy stuff is this?' But we liked it. We were quite tickled that Fairbanks insisted that the grips have some too. There was caviar and everything on the table, and I'm talking about the real good stuff. They must have spent a bloody fortune on that. Bing used to come to those and everybody wanted him to sing, because we had been down to the Ambassador, always dressed to the nines, to hear him with Al Rinker and Harry Barris, who were flying. After that he still sang at the Ambassador, and every time I had a date and went down there, Bing gave me recognition from the stand. I was very pleased about that and my date would say, 'Oh, you know him, you know Bing?'"[40]

Bing's friendship with Louis Armstrong, presaged by Mildred Bailey, begun in Chicago, and advanced in Harlem, now deepened in Los Angeles. Louis reminisced:

In 1930 I went out to California to join the band which was playing at Frank Sebastian's Cotton Club. Bing and his Trio were really romping with Gus Arnheim's Orchestra at the Cocoanut Grove Hotel in Hollywood. The Cotton Club was out in Culver City. Every night between their outfit and our outfit, we used to *Burn up* the air, *every* night. . . . Yea — Bing & Gus Arnheim & Co would broadcast first every night and leave the ether wave sizzling hot. Just right for us when we would burst on in there from the Cotton Club. Oh, it was lots of fun. The same listeners would catch both programs before going to bed. After Bing — the band — Mr. Arnheim and boys would finish work at the Grove they would haul ashes over to the Cotton Club where we were playing and swing with us, until Home Sweet Home was played. Sometimes he would come over wearing his sharp uniform, the one I admired so much. It was a *hard* hitting blue with white buttons, which made him look (to me) like a young Captain on some high powered yacht. That's when he and Dixie Lee were CANOEING.[41]

On September 29, with Bing reaping what by Hollywood standards was at least a nascent success and apparently controlling his drinking, he and Dixie quit canoeing, discarded the advice of those who thought she was sacrificing a hot career to a ne'er-do-well, and tied the knot. Dixie applied for the license under her birth name, thereby keeping the wedding — at the Church of the Blessed Sacrament in Hollywood — a secret until the morning of the day it took place; the license made out to Wilma Wyatt and Harry Crosby raised no flags. Not even her mother knew until the day of the ceremony, when she and a dozen others received phone invitations from the couple. Dixie's bridesmaid was a friend from high school, Betty Zimmerman. Everett served as best man and provided his home for the reception.

The question of religious differences was kept quiet. Most people in and out of Hollywood assumed Dixie had taken her vows, but she remained outside the Catholic Church until a conversion on her deathbed. If Bing asked her to convert early on, he willingly accepted her refusal to do so. Kate Crosby, on the other hand, harbored a resentment that came roaring to the surface when the marriage almost collapsed in the 1940s. Dixie agreed to raise the children Catholic, though she did not attend church — a father-and-sons ritual — and was not pleased when the eldest boy, Gary, suggested he might like to become a priest. "Mom never bad-mouthed the church," Gary remembered. "On the contrary. Even though she wasn't a Catholic, she was the one who stayed on our case about showing up for mass on Sunday and meeting our other religious obligations. 'If you're going to be in a religion,' she would lecture us, 'if you're doing something you believe in, then you do it all the way.' Whenever Grandpa Wyatt started in on one of his tirades against the pope and big-time religion, she shushed him on the spot."[42] Even in 1930 Bing never missed mass, no matter how late or wild the previous evening.

One Spokane paper loyally reported, BING CROSBY WEDS ACTRESS,[43] but another accurately reflected the typical coverage: SPOKANE BOY WEDS FILM STAR.[44] Bing was thought to be coming up in the world. How far he had to go was implied by the account in the *New York Times,* headlined, DIXIE LEE IS MARRIED: "Dixie Lee, film actress, was married today to Murray Crosey, 26 years old, orchestra leader, at a simple church ceremony."[45] Most of Dixie's fans got Bing's name right but were not particularly wowed by her choice of husband. Basil Grillo, who was "very enamored of Dixie Lee in those days," remembered, "I was in college and absolutely heartbroken. I couldn't figure out why she would marry a lousy crooner." Grillo would eventually direct Bing Crosby Enterprises, earn the crooner his fortune, and learn that "Dixie was a very bright, smart woman, with the sharpest tongue anybody could ever imagine. She cut him down to size fast. Man!"[46]

The *Los Angeles Times* concluded its report, "There isn't to be any honeymoon trip as both young people are too busy in their professions at this time to be able to spare time to go away."[47] Dixie later acknowledged that they did not honeymoon because they were strapped for money. They had yet to find a home and for two weeks lived in Sue Carol's house while Sue visited New York. Carol had become one of Dixie's closest and most protective friends, along with Pauline Weislow and Alice Ross, who later worked as Dixie's secretary.

Dixie was a magnet for mother hens. Flo Haley recalled, "She was damned sweet. She never hurt anybody. But she was sensitive, way down, and she didn't have a sister. She needed people around her, like someone to console you, to say, 'Come on, we'll go after this and do that.'"[48] Sue assuaged Dixie's fears and sheltered her on and off the Fox lot. Eight years older than Dixie, she had social status and knew the ropes. The two women became inseparable; when Sue's marriage to actor Nick Stuart came apart, she stayed with the Crosbys. They had both been relieved to marry and leave the business, though Sue demonstrated more than a touch of sentiment when she named her daughter Carol Lee, fusing the names Hollywood bestowed upon her (Sue was born Evelyn Lederer) and upon Dixie.

Those two weeks at Sue's were all the time Bing and Dixie had to cement their marriage. On October 14 Dixie, on loan to Paramount from Fox, was sent to New York (Astoria Studios) for a Clara Bow picture, *No Limit,* intended as the "It" girl's comeback. Bing resented putting her on the train but was in no position to suggest she stop working. By the time she returned, more than two months later, things appeared to be turning his way. In preparation for Dixie's homecoming in late December, he planned a reception at the train station and asked Louis Armstrong to preside: "Oh — Daddy Bing — Harry Barris and Al Rinker — they gave me all sorts of inducements, etc. to just go down to the station and sorta toot a few hot ones as she hit the ground from the train," Louis recalled.[49] But Armstrong had romantic plans of his own that night. As the Rhythm Boys serenaded Dixie, Bing had more to commemorate than her arrival. In her absence, his confidence as a singer had turned a corner.

*   *   *

Bing made only eleven records with Arnheim, between October 1930 and May 1931, and they pack a wallop. They mark the end of Bing's career as a dance-band vocalist and a redefinition of his style, from Jazz Age emoter to poised soloist. Moreover, they served as calling cards, bringing him to the attention of three men — Mack Sennett, Jack Kapp, and William Paley — who helped ignite the Bing Crosby Era, a quarter century stretch during which no other performer rivaled his dominance in popular entertainment.

Significantly, only one of the Arnheim sides features the Rhythm Boys, yet the three best-remembered Bing vehicles are the work of Barris. Small wonder that Rinker was feeling "more dissatisfied" with his role in the Rhythm Boys.[50] The trio's last appearance on records was a capable version of "Them There Eyes," a song memorably claimed by Billie Holiday in 1939. The harmonizing is sure, but compared with Bing's solo discs, the net effect is pallid; the sound of the trio could no longer compare with the sound of Bing alone. A scat episode dominated by the zealous Harry and a breezily swinging final chorus feel frozen and of a fading era. Still, the record was a hit, a last hurrah boosted by their frequent radio renditions. It was quickly swamped by the revelation of Bing's new ballad style.

If his microphone experience at the Grove cured him of the need to belt out a song, his jazz experience indemnified him from the temptations of anemic crooning. Bing soared beyond the restraints of the Arnheim band, which though adept at a jumpy rhythm was too hidebound to really swing. He pitched his vocals as much from the throat as from the diaphragm in an attempt to minutely control shading and breathing. This was a calmer, steadier Bing, even on inferior songs. He subtly winks at the lyric of "Fool Me Some More" and provides the record's only rhythmic jolt by syncopating the first beat of his last eight bars. He imbues Berlin's negligible "The Little Things in Life" (cut from *Reaching for the Moon*) with the authority of a man willing to sell a song on its own terms.

On good songs his heightened authority is unmistakable. A major tune that year and a Grove favorite was James P. Johnson's "If I Could Be with You (One Hour Tonight)," which became a jazz classic with the release of three highly inventive hit records by Louis Armstrong, McKinney's Cotton Pickers (with Benny Carter), and the Mound City Blue Blowers (with Coleman Hawkins and Pee Wee Russell).

The melody inspired jazz musicians, and Bing's rendition inspired Barris to concoct a secondary theme, which Jimmy Grier arranged as accompaniment to Bing's vocal. Bing liked the second strain so well that, at his suggestion, Harry asked Gordon Clifford to write a lyric, transforming a countermelody into a song, "It Must Be True." Arranged by Grier over a lazy two-beat with a chorus of Bing's most impetuous whistling to date, the recorded version was released as the flip side of "Them There Eyes" and exceeded it in popularity. The second Crosby-Barris-Grier record, early in the New Year of 1931, proved to be a milestone.

"I Surrender, Dear" renovated Bing's professional stature on several counts. Barris configured the melody after hearing Bing sing a variation on "Lover, Come Back to Me," and Gordon Clifford wrote the lyric. From the time Bing introduced it, the song was hugely popular at the Grove and on radio; he was often asked to sing it several times in an evening. The recording is startling, calling attention to itself with an unconventional arrangement that defied dancers with its frequent change-ups in tempo and manner. Grier had written a concert-style orchestration of a popular song, and though the effect superficially resembled Whiteman's more inflated numbers, the result was cogently novel. It begins with an introduction by trombones and strings, essays the verse with sixteen bars of fox-trotting strings followed by jazz trumpet and solo clarinet, and then sets the stage for Bing's entrance with a splendid two-bar ensemble transition. Even his chorus, elaborately supported by the band, has a change-up: he sings the bridge over modified stop-time rhythm. The ensuing instrumental chorus starts with trombone and strings intimating an Eastern strain, and leads to muted trumpets and responsive violins, a stop-time clarinet, a bridge that suggests a Polish wedding dance, and a finish that combines rigidly marching trombones and a crescendo from which Bing's voice glides for a brief reprise.

With Bing wrapping the word *dear* around a shapely mordent, sculpting dynamics, and impeccably articulating every word and pitch in a climbing melody that parallels the rising ardor in his voice (or vice versa), the performance is if not his finest to date, then certainly his most paradigmatic. Bing's huskiness is wonderfully captured by the Victor technicians (a perquisite of recording with Arnheim), and his projection is at once forceful and restrained. The success of the record amplified his national reputation and all but buried the Rhythm Boys; for as popular as they were, radio audiences wanted to hear that astonishing singer with the throb in his voice, not a trio of hepcats. Perhaps the prime indication of Bing's elevated stature was Louis Armstrong's cover of "I Surrender, Dear," which Rudy Vallée — in recounting Armstrong's influence on Bing, Russ Columbo, Mildred Bailey, and others — proclaimed a masterpiece.[51] Before the year was out, Louis covered two more Crosby signature tunes, "Wrap Your Troubles in Dreams" and "Star Dust," and often paid homage ("I'm Confessin'") to his friend with crooning asides and telling mordents.

Louis was not alone. Bing was now imitable, not only in the positive sense but also as an object of parody. When Bing leaned too heavily on mannerisms, he courted the kind of mockery that, on the heels of his movie breakthrough, unleashed a generation of *bu-bu-bu-boo* impressionists. Only Dixie had the temerity to emphasize the danger, and did so with devastating precision late in 1931, in Rudy Wiedoeft's Vitaphone short *Darn Tootin'*, singing Bing's hit of the moment, "I Apologize." She reveals no overt indication of parody, but her droll mordent-heavy performance is spot-on. Bing got the message, after a period of testing, indulging, and rejecting diverse affectations. At his next Arnheim session, Bing turned in a rigorous performance of "Thanks to You," investing trite material with a glowing conviction as fresh and innovative as anything heard in American song. That same day he recorded the romping "One More Time" and the finest of Barris's songs (lyric by Ted Koehler and Billy Moll), "Wrap Your Troubles in Dreams," in which Bing combines whistling and singspiel and finesses a bel canto second chorus variation. He continued to explore emotional range, from the vibrant "I Found a Million Dollar Baby (in a Five and Ten Cent Store)," with its jaunty release and soaring finish, to the amorous "At Your Command," backed only by its composer, Harry Barris, and complete with an interlude of faux-Rachmaninoff pounding.

With records like "Thanks to You," Bing heralded the end of song-pluggers and the tyranny of sheet music — although he appeared on more sheet-music covers than anyone else. Neutral or detached renditions designed to boost the song gave way to individualized interpretations. In blending and mainstreaming all he had learned from

Jolson, Armstrong, Waters, and others, Bing personalized and deepened pop. Jazz adapts material with a brashness expounded in Trummy Young's song "Tain't What You Do (It's the Way That You Do It)." Bing showed that a popular singer could be just as much in command. Yet he created an illusion of commonality. Bing, like Jolson, was unique, but unlike Jolson, he was at the same time Everyman. Jolson threw himself at his listeners; Crosby made his listeners come to him. Jolson inspired them to cheer him; Crosby seduced them into contemplation. Most radio fans did not know what he looked like, yet they responded to him with the sighs and blushes usually reserved for movie idols.

Dixie was thrilled at Bing's progress but distraught at the state of their marriage. In the two months since she returned from New York, Dixie exhausted herself trying to keep up with his nightlife while doing justice to her own career. On March 4, two days after the "Thanks to You" session, she announced her intention to file for divorce. "We have been married only about six months," she told an Associated Press reporter, "but we have already found out that we are not suited to each other. Our separation is an amicable one, and the only reason for it is that we just can't get along."[52] Amicable it was, for the simple reason that she neglected to inform Bing, who learned she was charging mental cruelty when Everett phoned to read him the newspaper account. Dixie vanished and Bing didn't know her whereabouts for ten days, until a friend persuaded her to call him from her hideout in Agua Caliente.

Bing had been drinking and carousing again, but that was not the primary issue for Dixie. The intolerable thing was that she never saw him. At first she traipsed about with him every night, staying late at the Grove and then moving on to the Cotton Club and other places, overimbibing and not much enjoying it. Dixie was nineteen and wanted her husband, not the party swirling around him. Sue Carol and others at Fox noticed how exhausted she looked. Dixie, realizing she could not live both of their lives, made an agreement with Bing: he would not go to her job, and she would not go to his. They would meet on weekends. But Bing often preferred to spend that time playing golf or baseball. There were nights he stayed out till the small hours while she waited up, a nervous wreck, taking one drink and then another in the vain hope of getting to sleep. Another source of contention was his gambling, an unlikely habit for a man later known for his financial prudence, but one that in those years consumed his income.

Putting aside his fear of flying, Bing chartered a single-engine plane and headed for the Mexican playground where they had spent weekends at the track and casino.[53] Dixie was amazed that he was willing to board such a contraption and was moved by his entreaties. But she was now in the catbird seat and made a fateful bargain, demanding that he quit drinking and take control of his life. The Agua Caliente pact became part of Crosby family lore. According to Bob Crosby, Dixie made Bing's career possible when she weaned him off alcohol. Yet the weaning was a two-year process, and at the end of that time Dixie would be fighting her own battle with booze. Bob conceded the devastating impact her drinking had on her health and her relationship with Bing, but steadfastly maintained, "It was to me one of the finest marriages that I have ever seen. . . . You couldn't escape feeling the love between the two of them."[54]

It is difficult to contemplate their disenchanted marriage, which caused much misery even as it was universally acclaimed as idyllic, without disquiet. Yet it is no less difficult to imagine their not marrying, considering how forceful Dixie was in turning Bing around and how large a role their mythic romance played in the public imagination. As Bing's star rose and Dixie's dimmed, rumors spread of her sacrifice. By the 1940s the hearsay gained traction when reports of their troubled marriage made the gossip columns and Walter Wanger produced a picture allegedly based on Dixie's plight (*Smash-Up, the Story of a Woman*, 1947). Bing considered bringing suit, but his attorney correctly pointed out that the public would never connect the film to him and Dixie unless he publicized his outrage. For even then, the Crosbys were popularly known as a model couple.

The public was not entirely deceived. Dixie was crazy about Bing, whom she privately called Angel. Her dramatic getaway had apparently been an attempt to save the marriage; she never filed suit and the place she ran to — a resort Bing loved, where they had shared happy times — suggested her hope for a honeymoon furlough. Dixie later said she asked Bing if he wanted her back because he could not countenance divorce. He assured her that as they were married only six months, it would not have been "much of a megillah to get it annulled."[55] Agua Caliente was their chance for a clean break, and they didn't take it. The papers announced their reconciliation on March 15.

Bing promised to reform and, despite several slips during the next couple of years, so successfully took control of his drinking problem that it all but disappeared. Until this point, his story threatened to turn into a prototype for the plight of music's slow suicides: from Bix Beiderbecke and Charlie Parker to Hank Williams and Elvis Presley. But Bing's tale took a radical turn. He would achieve a complete personal reversal, exercising jurisdiction over every minute of his day. If Prohibition found him exploring the lower depths, as he had as a child, working before dawn at the Everyman's Club, the Depression would help him to reassert the rectitude he had exhibited on those same mornings at mass. Instead of joining the ranks of defiant young artists who crash prosperity's gate only to be undone by its rewards, he would learn to savor — with disarming modesty — the public's adoration and the privileges of power. As the Depression deepened, he would become a standard-bearer for community and survival.

As a result, most of Bing's friends endorsed his belief that — unlike Dixie and his sons — he was never truly alcoholic, because true alcoholics do not remain casual drinkers, as Bing did, nursing a scotch for hours or enjoying an occasional blowout with no disruptive effects. They chalked up his hell-raising days to the culture of Prohibition and paraphrased Saint Augustine's reflection "Our real pleasure was simply in doing something that was not allowed."[56] Yet Bing had displayed undeniable symptoms of clinical alcoholism — blackouts and binges and self-destructive conduct. In time, the years 1927–31 would represent to him the abandoned period of his wildness, an alcoholic maze that devoured one Bing Crosby and delivered another. Dixie's decree inaugurated his transformation. Yet like many who possess a genius for self-control, Bing was impatient with those who did not.

13

PROSPERITY IS JUST AROUND THE CROONER

Boys, I admit I never heard of a crooner in slapstick comedy, but until we flung 'em, nobody ever heard of a custard pie in slapstick comedy. All I know is, this boy entertains. . . . I'm going to sign Crosby.
— Mack Sennett, *King of Comedy* (1954)[1]

If Bing had good reason to believe in luck, having fallen upward every step of his career, he now had reason to marvel at rehabilitation. For suddenly grand doors were opening.

The first of three powerful gatekeepers was the smart and daring record producer Jack Kapp, a genial businessman with an unerring memory for names and faces, who knew every facet of the record business. Kapp began working at thirteen in his family's store, the Imperial Talking Machine Shop, and it was said he understood records the way Irving Thalberg understood movies. His lifelong dictum was an accusatory question: Where's the melody? His ability to assess popular taste was considered all but infallible. If the negative face of Kapp's demotic appetite was an implacable aversion to music he did not like, there was plenty that he genuinely loved; he was a pioneer in signing jazz, blues, and country artists and was the first to record cast albums of Broadway shows. In 1934 he would create Decca Records and transform the industry, but in 1931 he was general manager for the Brunswick label, building an imposing roster —

the Mills Brothers, the Boswell Sisters, Victor Young, Cab Calloway, Glen Gray, Duke Ellington, and his personal favorite, Guy Lombardo.

In March Bing engaged an established entertainment lawyer, Roger Marchetti, who along with Everett prevailed upon Kapp to listen to a few of Bing's Arnheim recordings. Kapp already knew Bing's singing from the Whiteman days and did not need persuading. He signed him to a six-month contract with a renewal option favoring the company, which was then controlled by Warners. A couple of weeks later, Kapp traveled to California to supervise his first Crosby session, recording "Out of Nowhere" and "If You Should Ever Need Me." The latter, a negligible song, is memorable only for a singular reprise with an intimate barrel-down Crosby low note that fluttered the hearts of his fans.

But "Out of Nowhere" was a benchmark, an outstanding song by Hollywood composer John Green, who a year earlier had written the melody of "Body and Soul" (one of the most recorded songs of all time, though Bing, oddly enough, never sang it). Expertly backed by Bennie Krueger's orchestra and recorded with vivid immediacy, Bing emphasizes the song's balladic drama with parallel caesuras, or pauses, that also underscore rhythmic momentum. Marred only by a touch of Jolsonesque whinnying on the verse, his performance is rife with details, especially in his opening chorus: the mordent on *free,* the full two-bar sustain on *me,* the bravura selling of *nowhere.* He attacks the last chorus with a huskier mask and reveals Armstrong's influence by syncopating the phrase *with my memories.* By April "Out of Nowhere" was a top-selling record, the first released under Bing's name.

An unexpected dividend of his first Brunswick recording was an invitation to appear with the Rhythm Boys in a potboiler, *Confessions of a Co-ed,* singing "Out of Nowhere." The picture, his first job at Paramount, was the sort of thing Hays Office censors were supposed to stamp out (coed gets pregnant by one man, marries another, leaves him for the first). Bing appears mercifully early, at the school dance, wearing a terrible slicked-down hairpiece. His solo number is sung in his reveling jazz mode; he does justice to the song but projects little in the way of movie-star charisma. In distinct contrast, the trio number that follows is restrained and dry — his partners clearly hold him back. A dancing couple interrupts Bing mid-song for no other reason than to shout his name: a salute to the growing fame of his suave moniker.

Bing owed one more session to Arnheim, who provided him with two bouncy numbers. Bing is irrepressible on "I'm Gonna Get You," inserting the comment "'cause I'll never stand for that" in the space of two beats, transfiguring a nothing song into a frolic. "Ho Hum!," with Loyce Whiteman, is notable as the first of Bing's numerous recorded duets with women singers. His ease and wit are unmistakable, but the trite number scarcely indicates his particular genius for the format. Bing would establish the duet as a pop-music staple, raising it to a level many emulated in vain. He inspired other singers with his spontaneity, humor, and professional empathy, all of which Loyce experienced on the night she opened at the Grove. Arnheim had called her to the stage for her first solo, and Bing could see that she was trembling with fright. He escorted her to the mike and sang the opening phrases with her; when she was able to continue alone, Bing smoothly backed off the bandstand. The "Ho Hum!" session was significant for another reason: it marked the end of his sideman career. He now placed himself squarely in the hands of Jack Kapp and would nestle there until Kapp's death in 1949.

According to Sam Coslow, the song "Just One More Chance" originated when his partner, Arthur Johnston, came up with the title and four suitable notes: "The next phrase ["to prove it's you alone I care for"] popped into my brain like a flash."[2] They discussed the futility of writing a song without an assignment, and Johnston suggested they fashion it for a singer, not a production: how about Bing? They tailored the melody to his "croony ballad style." Bing, who loved it, rehearsed with Johnston and then introduced the song on a midday radio show, *Musical Cocktail*.[3] He sang it again that night on the Grove broadcast. The impact was incredible. Clubgoers demanded encores, and radio fans besieged stores for a record that didn't exist. Kapp returned to Hollywood and put his operation on red alert. He set up a session and asked Bennie Krueger, a Brunswick artist and friend, to contract a band. Krueger assembled a small group with piano, bass, clarinet, and three or four violins and voiced the instruments to make the band sound larger, an inventive (and economical) trick that would become a trademark of Kapp recordings. Within two weeks the disc was in stores, and Kapp promoted the hell out of it.

"Just One More Chance" easily outsold "Out of Nowhere," dominating sales in June, until it was supplanted by two more Crosby hits in July, followed by another in August, two more in September, and four more in October. And so it went: Bing would continue to average sixteen charted singles per year through 1950, peaking in 1939 with twenty-seven (a feat broken only by the Beatles in 1964, with thirty), never falling below double digits until 1951, when he placed nine singles in the top twenty-five. This unparalleled twenty-year accomplishment is not likely ever to be equaled.

Coslow observed of "Just One More Chance": "Never before, and never since, has a song of mine been established as a smash hit so quickly."[4] Yet it does not rank among Bing's finest performances; indeed, many of his records that year are stylized to the point that they seem far more dated than his jazz choruses with Whiteman, not to mention his incandescent recordings of the mid- and late thirties. Yet these were the sides that established the Crosby style and fashion. "Just One More Chance" was considered prototypical Bing, an obvious choice for lampooning by animators (he was a favorite target of Looney Tunes) and comics. He sings, whistles, and hums; exhibits an unusual degree of nasality; goes over the top fusing mordents to *bu-bu-bu-boo*s. If "I Surrender, Dear" was a hit, "Just One More Chance" was a phenomenon.

Bing was about to become the defining voice of his era, and for many people, this was the salvo that announced his arrival. It did for him, in 1931, what "All or Nothing at All" would do for Frank Sinatra in 1943, what "Heartbreak Hotel" would do for Elvis Presley in 1956, what "I Want to Hold Your Hand" would do for the Beatles in 1964. The sales for "Just One More Time" were relatively modest, a fraction of those Bing achieved a few years later, but large enough to alter his standing. He could no longer be claimed exclusively by jazz fans who knew him way back when or by insiders at the Cocoanut Grove. The buzz was heaviest in colleges and among women. Most of his enraptured fans had never seen him and didn't really know anything about him. But as far as they were concerned, Bing, at twenty-eight, was young and he was theirs.

The second gatekeeper was, by Hollywood's turnstile standard, a legendary has-been: the original king of comedy, Mack Sennett. He visited the Grove in early May and was, according to his often fanciful memoir, taken with Bing and with his fans. He was amazed by the number of "sophisticated and show-wise people [who] were repeat customers."[5] Mack invited Bing to his table for a drink and asked him to visit the studio and make some tests. As Sennett tells it, his crew thought him crazy to think he could combine crooning and slapstick, to which Sennett responded, "All I know is, this boy entertains."[6] In truth, he extended a similar invitation to Arnheim's popular tenor Donald Novis.

One of Sennett's writers, former actor and director Earle Rodney (who would cowrite all six of Sennett's Crosby pictures), was surprised by the auditions and explained why to his son, Jack Hupp, one of the more ardent Crosby fans at Hollywood High. Hupp recalled: "He told me Bing and Novis had been out to the studio. And Donald Novis had one of the most beautiful tenor voices you ever heard. I thought it was interesting, because my father said that when Novis got through singing, the guys out there had tears in their eyes. But the thing he noticed about Crosby was he had a great sense of comedy, which I got a kick out of, because Bing hadn't acted and he didn't do any comedy at the Grove. My father said, 'You know, Crosby is not only a wonderful singer, but he's got a real fine sense of comedy.' He was impressed."[7] Sennett, who discovered or directed most of the great silent-screen comedians (Charlie Chaplin, Buster Keaton, Harry Langdon, Fatty Arbuckle, Mabel Normand, Harold Lloyd, Ben Turpin, among many others), had recently made a distribution deal with Paramount's Adolph Zukor. Like every other producer, he was looking for actors with good voices. A singer with comic timing was a godsend.

If Bing wanted to cut loose from the Rhythm Boys, he was not admitting as much to himself or them. Just as he had insisted that Sam Coslow find roles for Al and Harry in *Honey,* he attempted to involve them in the Sennett films. The letter he received from Sennett's assistant general manager on May 18, 1931, confirmed an agreement for an option on the services of all three in a picture to go into production on or before June 15; it stipulated that Sennett had fifteen days to exercise the option and that the three men would be paid $1,000 a week while engaged in the production. Bing signed ("Rhythm Boys by Bing Crosby")[8] and Al and Harry initialed the letter on May 20, a Wednesday. They must have felt emboldened by the deal, because on Saturday the Rhythm Boys failed to show up at the

Cocoanut Grove. They had long complained about Abe Frank's refusal to raise their salaries, and now, as the job approached its first anniversary, they declared grievances, insisted that their contract was up, and — presumably advised by Bing's lawyer, Roger Marchetti — walked off the job.

It has been argued since Bing's death that he betrayed Al and Harry, as if he could have remained tied to them any more than Armstrong could have remained tied to King Oliver's Creole Jazz Band or Sinatra to the Tommy Dorsey Orchestra. Certainly, Bing played at best a passive role in the breakup, ignoring its inevitability until his less assured partners forced the issue. That he attempted to involve them in the Sennett venture suggests his ambivalence about striking out as a single, despite his solo success. But the Rhythm Boys no longer created anything new — why bother when the customers wanted to hear Bing? They rarely saw one another except on the job. Bing represented something daring and refreshing in music, while the trio, with its conventional harmonies, usually voiced in thirds, was now significantly outclassed by two vocal groups that had once been inspired by them: the Boswell Sisters and Mills Brothers each enjoyed their first hit records that year.[9]

Al was the first to speak of leaving; he had been champing at the bit as early as March: "I had become more and more dissatisfied with my role as part of the Rhythm Boys. Harry Barris was writing songs, Bing was becoming recognized as a soloist, and I was somewhere in between. The Rhythm Boys no longer always performed as a set group, as we did with Whiteman, and I saw no future for me in the present situation. I didn't have the voice or the ambition to be a solo singer, but more important, I wanted to get into something that I thought was more legitimate."[10] The trio was simply going through the motions and sometimes didn't even do that. When Bing or Harry arrived late or missed a show, Arnheim would cover for them by casually rescheduling their numbers, increasing Abe Frank's ire.

A blowup was inevitable. In his memoir, Bing concedes the failings of the trio, but not without resentment at Frank's intransigence. "Toward the end of our engagement at the Grove," he recalled, "we didn't take our responsibilities seriously enough to suit Abe Frank."[11] Bing justifiably insisted that the trio was grossly underpaid, and Frank justifiably pointed to the shows he missed, usually on Tuesdays, when Bing was reluctant to conclude his long weekends with Dixie. But the squabble turned rancorous. Bing and his advisers probably felt that the Grove was holding him back, but they never came right out and said so. Instead, Bing looked for an affront that would justify his leaving. He found it: "When I failed to get back for the Tuesday-night show once too often, he docked my wages." Bing packed up. "Of course Abe was within his rights legalistically speaking," he acknowledged, "but I thought he was pretty small about it, so I quit."[12] The Rhythm Boys were nothing without Bing, so Al and Harry also quit, presenting a unified front. They claimed to be on strike, demanding a raise and the repeal of Bing's fine.

On May 28 the *Los Angeles Illustrated Daily News* asked the "question being mouthed feverishly among radio fans":[13] What happened to the Rhythm Boys? A week later the paper reported that despite "an army of listeners' frets and complaints," they would not return "unless contractual difficulties between them and the proprietors of the Cocoanut Grove, not to mention the musicians' union, are ironed out."[14] The union got involved after Frank filed a complaint, in which he admitted that the original contract had lapsed but insisted that he was entitled to a nine-month option or financial remuneration. Implausibly, the union sided with management and imposed a blacklist that remained in effect for four months, during which time the trio could perform neither on radio nor on records. "My run-in with Abe Frank was the end of the Rhythm Boys," Bing concluded.[15]

He could afford to feel sanguine, however, with the sealing of the Sennett deal. Why Harry and Al did not participate in the two-reelers is not known. Perhaps they were tiring of the backseat and did not want supporting roles in vehicles created around Bing. Rinker never commented on the decision, except to describe Bing's acceptance of Sennett's proposal as "a wise decision" and admit that the group's demise "was a relief to me."[16] In any case, Sennett and Bing renegotiated the contract to their mutual benefit, amending the price from $1,000 for the trio to $600 for Bing.

The Rhythm Boys never officially announced their breakup, and fans continued to hope for their reappearance, even as Frank advertised a contest for replacements. The three contest winners —

including Jack Smith, who continued to work on radio and as host of TV shows like *You Asked for It* — called themselves the Ambassadors.[17] Radio reviewer Kenneth Frogley dismissed them as "an imitation. Has lots of pep, but not enough genuine melodic music." Barris served as the group's music director. Arnheim and his announcer, Nelson Case, had asked Loyce Whiteman to convince Harry to return. She found him drunk and helped get him into shape. He needed money and accepted the offer. If anyone still had illusions of the Rhythm Boys' getting together, Harry's work with the Ambassadors scotched them.

"Barris, Bing, and I parted on the best of terms," Rinker recalled in the unpublished memoir he wrote shortly before his death in 1982. "Bing went to his Mack Sennett job, Barris stayed on at the Grove for a while, and I went my own way."[18] Al's way was, according to a *Variety* account in July 1931, initially paved by Bing Crosby Ltd., a short-lived alliance between Bing, Barris, and Marchetti, which paid him a salary and may have facilitated his first job, touring in vaudeville on the same Fanchon and Marco circuit that had provided him and Bing with their start nearly six years earlier.[19] In that period Al began to compose and completed his first successful piece, "Peter, Peter, Pumpkin Eater" (debuted by Whiteman at the Metropolitan Opera House and recorded by him). For a while he was part of the vocal group backing Kay Thompson on radio. Then, in 1936, he became producer and director of CBS music programs (his first show was a substantial hit, *The Saturday Night Swing Club*) and prospered.

Harry did not fare as well. While continuing to direct the Ambassadors, he married Loyce and created an act with her. Having completed Frank's disputed option, Harry and Loyce were in good standing with the union and free to move on. They worked at New York's Park Central Hotel and toured the country, settling for a while in Las Vegas. He played with several big bands through the 1940s, briefly leading one of his own, and backed comedian Joe E. Brown on his tours of army camps. But Harry's drinking was out of control; it cost him his songwriting talent — he never had another hit after 1935 — and, eventually, his marriage. Until his death in 1962, he survived on royalties and the ministrations of the Bing Crosby office.

In addition to recording "I Surrender, Dear" and "Wrap Your Troubles in Dreams" three times each during Harry's life (and once after his death), featuring them in Sennett and early Paramount films, and performing them often on radio and television (thereby ensuring their value as annuities), Bing saw to it that Harry received regular movie work, including credited bits in at least eighteen Paramount pictures, seven of them with Bing. In all, Harry appeared in more than fifty movies between 1930 and 1950, usually as a band member, pianist, or emcee. His finest screen moment is as the jivey, gum-chewing accompanist who encourages Irene Dunne to rag "Can't Help Lovin' Dat Man" in Universal's 1936 *Show Boat*. The movie roles were Bing's way of helping him without appearing to hand out charity. (He did as much for many old friends.) Harry told his daughter, Marti, that a guest shot with Bing on radio paid the hospital costs of her birth.[20]

Marguerite Toth, the receptionist in the Crosby office at 9028 Sunset between 1945 and 1962, said, "I know he supported Harry Barris when Barris was so sick. I believe he paid the house payment to keep it from foreclosure."[21] Basil Grillo, who managed Crosby's finances, spoke of a confidential list of old friends of Bing's: if anyone on the list was in need of financial help, he was to provide it, no questions asked. "I was given carte blanche to see that Harry was taken care of," Grillo recalled, "just as I was given carte blanche to take care of Mildred Bailey's hospital bills. It was a losing battle with Harry, but we did the best we could."[22] Harry titled his last song "Never Been So Lost."[23]

And Al? "I specifically don't remember doing anything for Al," Grillo said. "Mostly because as far as I know, he didn't need anything. At least it was never brought to our attention."[24] Al's daughter, Julia, concurred: "Dad didn't need any help from Bing. Dad made a very good living. He produced radio shows and that's how he met my mother, on the Kay Thompson show — she was a singer, Elizabeth Rinker. He had a good job and we lived very well, I'd say upper middle class. He called himself a runaway Catholic and said he left the church because his knees hurt. There was no rift between him and Bing, no betrayal. What was Bing supposed to do? Slow his life down — put it on hold? That's crazy."[25] Yet in Al's memoir, written in part to counter a scurrilous attack on Crosby that claimed Al as its primary source,[26] he expresses a nearly morose anxiety regarding the distance between them, at one point consigning himself to the KOBBC club, an acronym among insiders for "kissed off by Bing Crosby."

In spite of his frustration, Al acknowledged Bing's decency toward him. But no matter what Bing did, it never felt right to him. In 1943

Whiteman invited Al to participate in a broadcast reunion of the Rhythm Boys. "It had been over 12 years since the Rhythm Boys had split up," Al wrote, "and I was rather surprised that Bing, who was now an established star, would agree to appear." When they met at the studio, the band applauded, and the show was a great success. "After rehearsal," Al continued, "Bing invited me out for a game of golf at the Bel-Air Country Club. We had a good match and were just as competitive as when we last played together over 13 years ago." Yet he was offended because when he asked Bing why he did the show, Bing told him he figured "he owed Whiteman a favor," when by Al's lights he should have done it "out of sentiment." Later he learned that Bing was offered and refused his usual fee, insisting that it be divided between Al and Harry, an act that merely fueled his suspicions: "This was a nice gesture, but I'm inclined to feel that it was his way of squaring things up with us."[27] When four years later Al sent him a song he had written, "Suspense," Bing recorded it, though it was neither good nor successful. What Al wanted was no longer possible: an intimate channel to Bing, founded on sentiment.

They met for the last time in 1973, when Al was attempting to produce an original musical program for television, *The French Quarter.* He showed it to Phil Harris, who suggested it would be perfect for Bing and phoned him. Bing instantly agreed to do the show, before seeing the script. A conference was arranged. "When he arrived at the meeting, he was very friendly and seemed glad to see me," Al wrote. "He and I reminisced at lunch about the old times." They went up to Phil's hotel to play the score and show Bing the dialogue and story. "He was very attentive, and after we had gone over the show, he seemed very pleased and said he would be glad to do it." Al wanted something more. "Although he seemed to have friendly feelings toward me, I no longer cared whether his friendliness was genuine or not. Too many years had gone by, and who he was and what he did no longer mattered to me."[28]

Skitch Henderson, a pianist who made his reputation as a regular on one of Bing's 1940s radio shows, said, "When Bing closed the door on you, it never opened. And I think Rinker, who I didn't know well, but I knew him as a performer and respected what he had been, had his heart broken. Something happened between them. Nobody knows what it was."[29] Rinker knew, or thought he did. Shortly before he died, he offered an explanation to his old friend Kurt Dieterle, the violinist who had roomed with Bing during the *King of Jazz,* and to Don Eagle, a musician turned writer, who interviewed him for a magazine piece. "Al wasn't too assertive," Eagle noted. "I asked him, 'When did the turning point come?' He says, 'One night I drove Bing home in my car when he was living with Kurt on Fairfax in West Los Angeles. I dropped him off and Bing wanted to borrow some money from me, which I didn't have or was not going to loan or something like that. So he slammed the door of the car and walked away.' He said from then on a strain was there."[30] Dieterle added, "Instead of loaning him the money, Al lectured Bing on his behavior. Bing wasn't someone you lectured."[31]

Now on his own, working with Mack Sennett's Educational Pictures in the Hollywood Hills, in 1931, Bing turned out four two-reelers in three months — two in June, a third in July, a fourth in August. On average, each involved no more than two days' shooting. Sennett later said he had briefly doubted Bing's ability to carry the pictures and hired comedian Arthur Stone to share the load. Yet Bing completely dominates the shorts, which are fascinating for the way they establish in embryonic form the Crosby persona — exuberant and mischievous, dreamy and stubborn, often callow, sometimes petulant — that would emerge in Bing's feature films of the 1930s.

The first short, *I Surrender Dear,* received a limited release on the West Coast but was broadly redistributed in September, after Bing triumphed on national radio. Educational could then advertise him as "California's famous discovery who has become the country's favorite overnight." Moviegoers were pleased, and so were the trade papers. *Photoplay* reported, "The [Sennett] shorts . . . not only get over the Crosby voice, but the Crosby personality, which seems to be quite sumpin'."[32] *Motion Picture Herald* thought "the baron of baritones" (as he was billed) "personable," adding that he "can act sufficiently to put over his songs and has a really beautiful voice."[33] *Variety* agreed: "Crosby displays capital comedy sense, plays with assurance and certainty."[34]

Today it is difficult to grasp the degree to which radio threatened Hollywood. Many theaters suspended projection of films at 7:00 P.M. and piped in *Amos 'n' Andy,* which might otherwise have kept patrons at home. Sennett realized that just as talking pictures offered audiences a chance to hear the voices belonging to beloved faces, they provided a chance to see the faces belonging to beloved broadcast voices. In the world of Bing's two-reelers, everyone knows how Bing sounds, but no one knows what he looks like. And since Bing never carries ID, the only way he can prove himself to women or police officers is to sing. His resonant low notes and seductive phrasing invariably win the day and the girl.

The motif of Bing's voice as universally recognizable was a bit presumptuous, since the first four Sennetts (two more followed in 1932) were shot *before* Bing succeeded on network radio, when his fame on the airwaves was based almost exclusively on Arnheim's West Coast broadcasts and his guest appearances on other local programs. Yet even then, Bing and other invisible singers were accused of seducing wives and daughters with their laryngeal wiles. Radio's role in the battle of the sexes had greatly changed. Back in 1923, when mostly men donned earphones to surf the air on crystal sets, a Mrs. Cora May White of Minneapolis divorced her husband because "radio mania"[35] had alienated his affections. Now men complained of perverse crooners beguiling their women. Their scorn provided another theme for the Sennett shorts. Bing, embodying a rare balance of humility and audacity, never merely wins the girl: he steals her, usually from one of her parents (never both) and her fiancé, who loathe radio crooners and conspire in vain to foil his unstoppable charms. A class distinction is explicit in these battles. While Bing is a regular Joe, the foiled suitors are rich and prissy (effeminate Franklin Pangborn plays the unlikely lover twice) or European and prissy. They usually end up falling into a pool of water or getting whacked on the backside as Bing drives off with the lady.

I Surrender Dear is unusual among the Sennetts in allowing Bing to indulge in vaudeville verbosity and banter, a result of the teaming with Arthur Stone. He mimes his own recording of "Out of Nowhere," using postures he picked up in his barnstorming days with Al and Harry. The second short, *One More Chance* (for which his salary was raised to $750), is more overtly personal and departs from the formula to present him as a married salesman, Bing Bangs. He parodies "I Surrender, Dear" with lyrics about a laundry detergent (leading to a routine later recycled and much improved in *Road to Singapore*), before leaving with his wife, Ethel Bangs, for California. They endure many disasters on the way: an Indian threatens to scalp Bing, who, wearing a wretched hairpiece, says, "Maybe you're right, so far it's only a bald spot." When Ethel announces her intention to leave him for her lover, Percy, Bing confronts her in a nightclub scene that recalls his public rewooing of Dixie, and sings "Just One More Chance." It's an extraordinary moment, because the real Bing shines through in all his swinging, funny, improvisational glee.[36] His spontaneity clearly startled actress Patsy O'Leary, who looks genuinely surprised when he kisses her and cannot keep a straight face as he rocks the tune. He concludes by finger-popping his cheek.

A lingering instinct for minstrelsy is pursued in *Dream House*. Bing plays singing plumber Bing Fawcett, who accidentally gets black house paint on his face, leading a black casting director to hire him as a black actor. When he kisses the leading lady (before spiriting her away from his rival and her mother), he inadvertently gives her a blackface mustache and goatee that suits her mannish hairdo, as he dons a womanly turban.[37] Transvestism is more salient in *Billboard Girl,* in which the swishy brother of Bing's paramour pretends to be her (he wears his sister's undergarments for authenticity) and Bing can't tell the difference. Bing ultimately whisks the real sister away from her fiancé and irate father, whose objections echo those expressed in life by Dixie's dad. While making this film, Bing realized he could avoid hairpieces by wearing hats, and wore one in every scene.

Before Sennett's cameras rolled, Marchetti and Everett had invited offers from radio and vaudeville. Having picked up a few pointers from Leonard Goldstein, Everett mailed two records — "I Surrender, Dear" and "Just One More Chance" — to William S. Paley, president of the Columbia Broadcasting System. What Kapp and Sennett had done for Bing on records and in movies, Paley could accomplish on network radio. The prize was a nightly fifteen-minute show that would be relayed by the network all over the country. A CBS representative offered Bing an audition with the proviso that he come to New York, but Bing had qualms about making the trip. He was beginning to realize his Hollywood dreams and did not want to be apart from Dixie. Yet when word got back that Russ Columbo was pursuing the same course, Bing agreed to give it a shot. For his resourcefulness, Everett was officially signed on as Bing's manager.

Yet Paley had never received Everett's package. While Bing was ruminating about the audition, the CBS chief was on board the SS *Europa,* en route to the Continent. On his third day at sea, or so it was related in a CBS press release, Paley heard "I Surrender, Dear" wafting from the stateroom of a fellow passenger. He ascertained the name of the singer and radioed his New York office for information. Upon arriving in Europe, Paley was advised of Bing's fame in California, shown a Sennett short, and warned that "radio and theatrical impresarios were vying in submission of contracts to the young baritone."[38]

This was not entirely true. Roger Marchetti was asking $2,500 per week for Bing, an astronomical fee that, as *Variety* reported, "drew a batch of yawns."[39] The best offers the lawyer received were an RKO vaudeville tour at $1,500 and a featured spot in *Earl Carroll's Vanities* at $1,000. NBC expressed interest, but not beyond a three-figure salary. Nonetheless, Paley instructed Columbia to sign Crosby for a sustaining show at $1,500, a remarkable sum for a show subsidized by the network in the hope of luring a sponsor. (Kate Smith received a third of that for her sustainer.) In later years Paley would embellish the story, making it a near perfect match for Mack Sennett's: the CBS underlings tell him he's crazy (Bing is a drinker and unreliable), but he overrules them and mandates a contract.

Bing was signed to a fifteen-minute show, Monday through Saturday: the routine would be three vocals, one instrumental by the band, and no talk except by the network's announcer. In Bing's recollection, Paley wanted him on the air right away but had to wait while Marchetti settled the American Federation of Musicians ban instigated by Abe Frank. CBS was taking no chances. It postponed its announcement of Bing's signing until the AFM ruled that his unfavorable status applied only to Los Angeles.[40] The stall allowed Marchetti to settle with Frank before he learned of Bing's improved finances; Frank demanded a payoff of $7,500, which was nearly two-thirds of what he had paid Bing for a year's work at his club. Still, the delay was no more than a week or two, and Bing arrived in New York on August 11. CBS scheduled his debut for August 31, a Monday evening at 11:00 P.M. Bing did not make it.

Part Two

EVERYBODY'S BING

Bing's voice has a mellow quality
that only Bing's got. It's like gold
being poured out of a cup.
— Louis Armstrong, *Time* (1955)[1]

14

BIG BROADCAST

The thing you have to understand about Bing Crosby is that he was the first hip white person born in the United States.

— Artie Shaw (1992)[2]

The two weeks preceding the broadcast were busy ones for Bing, who had not been back to New York in fifteen months. A few days after his arrival, he was booked by Jack Kapp for a three-hour session that proved momentous on two counts. Bing worked for the first time with Victor Young, the conductor and composer soon to emerge as one of Hollywood's finest musical directors and someone with whom he developed a particularly close and lasting rapport.[3] And he was paired with three important songs that he forged into all-time standards: "Star Dust" (Bing was the first to record Mitchell Parish's lyric to Hoagy Carmichael's magical, Bixlike melody, verse and chorus), "Dancing in the Dark" (from *The Band Wagon*), and the less sturdy but much revived "I Apologize." They represent Bing in his ardent, pleading mode, technically assured but studied, as though he were mining to the fullest a commercially viable approach.

He spent several days auditioning theme songs for his radio show. The title of the leading candidate, fashioned for him by composer Fred Ahlert and lyricist Roy Turk, underwent two revisions: first, it was transposed from "When the Gold of the Day Meets the Blue of the Night" to "When the Blue of the Night (Meets the Gold of the Day)"; then the word *when* was replaced with the more intriguing *where*. The other leading candidate was "Love Came Into My Heart," written by nineteen-year-old Burton Lane and Harold Adamson for *Earl Carroll's Vanities of 1931*. Bing learned about it from music publisher Jack Robbins, who asked Burton to play it for the singer. "Bing came up to [Robbins's] offices," Burton recalled, "and I played the song and he liked the way I played it and he asked me to accompany him when he auditioned the song for the studio. He was not auditioning himself — he was auditioning two songs, mine and 'Where the Blue of the Night,' which was a much better song. So we were ushered into a room at CBS, the two of us, and apparently we could be heard by people in another office who would make the decision. The other song was chosen and it was perfect, a lovely song."[4]

Harry Barris's daughter, Marti, said "it broke his heart"[5] that Bing did not choose "I Surrender, Dear" as his theme, but strong financial and musical reasons justified his preference. A successful theme song, mandatory in the 1930s (every top band and radio star had one), might identify an entertainer for decades, accruing mechanical royalties with each performance. Ahlert and Turk cut Bing in on the copyright, allegedly because he worked with Turk on the song's verse, ensuring him a significant income over the years. Although Bing was accused of making a deal with Ahlert and Turk, which the team denied, his consideration of the Burton Lane tune and his reputation among songwriters indicates that this was not the usual case of quid pro quo authorship.[6]

Bing was in a position to demand cut-ins on dozens of songs (as Jolson did before him and Presley after), but he appears to have been scrupulous about taking credit only on those to which he made a contribution; he shares the copyright on twenty-three (including seven he never recorded), almost all collaborations with friends, chiefly Barris, Young, and Johnny Burke, and only two of any commercial significance — his theme song and Victor Young's enduring melody "I Don't Stand a Ghost of a Chance with You."[7] Bing went on to write several parodies that he recorded privately and pressed on a handful of discs for friends, but he had no illusions about his songwriting talent. Late in his life he wrote, "I really think I'd trade anything I've ever done if I could have written just one hit song."[8]

Financial considerations aside, Bing's choice was eminently musical. "Where the Blue of the Night" is an ideal signature tune because
the main eight-bar phrase can be played in just about any tempo,
lending itself to compression and dramatization. The lyric is relatively
neutral (unlike, for example, the dejected avowal "I Surrender, Dear"),
and although the melody resembles Gilbert and Sullivan's quintessentially British "Tit-Willow," it has the unmistakable appeal of an
Irish lullaby. Wistful and nostalgic, the song boasts a rousing release
suited to Bing's range and attack, and works equally well in either
three-four (it was conceived as a waltz) or four-four time. Bing recorded it in November, backed by Bennie Krueger's band and Eddie
Lang's splendid guitar, an exceptional, well-tempered performance,
devoid of vanity and honeyed with understated emotion. The song
became so closely associated with him that few recorded it except in
homage. Yet Bing remained undecided about his theme when the
show premiered, a week after the tryout with Lane. By then, some
thought he was beginning to look undecided about singing at all.

August 31, 1931, was a cool, dry Monday in the twilight of Prohibi-
tion, just before the bleakest years of the Depression. The two front-
page stories could not have been more reflective of the times: a
Brooklyn gunfight (residue of a gang war between Dutch Schultz and
Mad Dog Coll) had taken the life of a teenage girl, and President
Hoover was pledging to fight the payment of bonus reparations to
World War I veterans. (When some 15,000 veterans encamped in
Washington the following summer, he allowed federal troops to burn
them out.) Prosperity was nowhere near the corner, but the New
Deal was, and Bing, though a moderate Republican by disposition,
was about to emerge as its crooning oracle. The ascendancy of Every-
man Bing began on network radio with a strange and fitful birth.

Bing's Monday evening 11:00 P.M. debut was much publicized.
The Sunday New York Times "Listening-In" column featured a large
photograph of Bing and a capsule rendition of Paley's shipboard discovery.[9] Yet when listeners tuned it at the appointed time, they heard
CBS staff announcer Louis Dean tell the radio audience that the
scheduled program would not be heard. Instead, Fred Rich and the
Columbians — a compact edition of the CBS Studio Orchestra —
would perform. Listeners expecting to hear Bing on Tuesday night

heard another announcer declaim a second postponement; Fletcher Henderson's band filled in.

Finally, on Wednesday evening, September 2, an ebullient third announcer, Harry Von Zell, ended the mystery: "Here is the moment you have been waiting for, the delayed appearance of that sensational baritone, Bing Crosby, whose singing has made him the favorite of California through the mediums of the motion picture, the vaudeville stage, and the radio." Von Zell explained that the singer had recovered from a severe case of laryngitis and could now "bring you his inimitable song interpretations."[10]

Insiders drew the obvious conclusion: drunk again, another opportunity almost blown. Bing noted in his memoir that he was variously thought to have suffered a hangover, laryngitis, stage fright, nodes on his vocal cords, and blacklist troubles. His own explanation was that he had exhausted his voice singing at four or five clubs and parties a night while making the rounds: "The pipes just gave out, and I couldn't produce hardly a sound. Just hoarse. Tired."[11] A Paley biographer claims that the CBS head was at home during Bing's delayed premiere and was so angered by Bing's unstable performance that he phoned the studio and ordered Crosby pulled off the air; feeling "giddy" with power,[12] he then assigned a twenty-four-hour guard to keep Bing sober. According to a biographer of Bing, the singer was on a three-day binge.[13] Both stories are demonstrably untrue. Paley was in the studio for Bing's debut, which was transcribed (the first and last songs Bing sang that night have been released on records), and Crosby showed up for daily rehearsals. There is no reason to doubt his own account. Bing was a public drinker who never attempted to hide or disavow his conduct; no one saw him drunk on those evenings, while many saw him at work or at rest during the afternoons, among them agent Cork O'Keefe, who told a background reporter in 1946 that Bing had lost his voice and "mooned about the hotel for three days, heartbroken."[14]

Moreover, his condition was diagnosed by Simon Ruskin, an ear, nose, and throat specialist whose patients included members of the Metropolitan Opera, Gertrude Lawrence, Mary Martin, and other entertainers. On Wednesday Everett Crosby summoned Ruskin to the station twenty minutes before Bing went on the air. In 1949 the doctor told a field reporter for *Time* that that evening Bing had a head cold and postnasal drip, which infected his vocal cords. He said that Bing griped, "It's no use, let me go back to California," to which Ruskin, referring to his pricey ministrations, retorted, "Don't be silly, Bing, you're working for me now."[15] Ruskin thought the infection caused Bing's voice to drop, making it huskier and more attractive to the radio audience.

Bing wasn't incensed at the drinking stories (here is a man who, in the blush of his success in 1931, told journalist Joseph Mitchell of his "trail of broken bottles"),[16] but he was offended by rumors that he had had an attack of nerves, rumors that undermined his reputation for imperturbable confidence. "I don't think I have ever had stage fright or what we in the trade call 'flop sweat' in my life."[17] On that score, witnesses take issue. Agnes Law, the CBS librarian, brought material to the studio and found him "pacing the floor too petrified to open his mouth to sing."[18] The show's recording engineer, Edgar Sisson, said that during the rehearsals Bing appeared nervous and grumbled about the microphone, which lay flat on the stand rather than hanging from a boom as was customary at recording sessions. Bing spent much of his rehearsal time trying to get comfortable with the setup. The engineers respected his concern and admired his understanding of the technology — especially when a few weeks into the program, he arrived with a copy of his new record, "Sweet and Lovely," and declared, "This is what I want to sound like."[19]

Gary Stevens, a precocious fifteen-year-old gofer in the publicity department, idolized Bing and made certain to be present on the Monday he was originally scheduled to air. The show emanated from the twenty-second floor of Paley's newly acquired building at 485 Madison Avenue. "When I finally got a glimpse of him, he was shorter than I envisioned and he had sparse hair, brownish blond, and was fairly thin. He wore an outlandish outfit, kind of a pink coat and blue-green slacks and an ill-colored shirt. And he was very, very nervous. Late that afternoon, after a three-hour rehearsal where they did the eight or nine songs to be used for the week, he left, and sometime after five there was a big huddle and when they came out, the word was he wasn't going on."[20] Among those in the huddle were Ralph Wonders, the head of CBS's artists bureau; bandleader Fred Rich; and Paley himself, who left after the decision was announced.

Bing's apprehensiveness was made evident by his request that Victor Young conduct his first show. He had already made certain that Eddie Lang and Joe Venuti were on hand. Bing had no complaints about Rich, who resumed his duties the next week and for the rest of the series. But on that first night he wanted a conductor who understood him, and Young was available as of Wednesday to supervise rehearsal and broadcast. Premiering on Tuesday was never a consideration. Artie Shaw, a member of the CBS Studio Orchestra, recalled Bing affecting an attitude of indifference at rehearsal, but believed otherwise: "He wanted it badly. You don't get that by accident. Bing was never a matinee idol. He developed a screen personality that worked because it was based on who he wanted to be — casual, relaxed. But it was a tense sort of relaxing because you knew he was working at it. Bing wasn't Bing any more than Bogart was Bogart."[21]

Yet on the third day the tension apparently disappeared. "No nerves," Gary Stevens insisted. "Very relaxed. He was in the same outfit I saw him in Monday afternoon, pink jacket and open shirt, greenish or aquamarine slacks, and he was very casual. He loved being around musicians. When I got there, about ten minutes before he went on, he was in animated conversation with a few musicians before they took their places and were ready to go on the air."[22] Paley was in and out of the control room all evening, and Stevens was instructed to alert radio editors at the dailies and prepare any information they needed.

At eleven Harry Von Zell intoned, "Fifteen minutes with Bing Crosby" while the orchestra — with Tommy Dorsey soloing — played Victor Young's "Too Late" in the background. Bing sang "Just One More Chance," "I Found a Million Dollar Baby," and "I'm Through with Love," resting his voice during an instrumental. He was not at his best. He sounded almost too tense to whistle, though CBS reportedly asked him not to on behalf of Morton Downey, its resident whistling singer.[23] Instead, he exchanged halting la-di-das with Joe Venuti's violin and first came alive near the finish of "Just One More Chance," ringing forth on the phrase "all the while." His wobbly mordents were overstated (almost as baldly as in Dixie's "I Apologize" parody), but by the closing "I'm Through with Love," he was warmed up, beaming on the release. Inspired by Venuti's obbligato, he attacked the final eight bars with brio.

Stevens thought he was "sensational. It knocked me out — I knew something new had happened. We had a crooning, nasal, tenor society — Downey, Vallée — and this had a refreshing macho quality. Bing moved with the band. He was the first ballad singer who had rhythm with him."[24] Artie Shaw concurred: "There are virtuoso performers who have not found an identity. That thumbprint is missing. With Bing you knew right away who he was. And you knew that he knew. He really is the first American jazz singer in the white world. Bing was an enormous influence. You couldn't avoid him. He had a good beat. He was a jazz singer, he knew what jazz was, and could sing a lyric, say the words, and make you hear the notes. Bing could swing. When he sang, the tune swung, whatever it was."[25] After the show wrapped, Stevens found himself in an elevator with Paley and Ralph Wonders. As they descended to the lobby, Wonders broke the silence and asked Paley what he thought. Looking at his shoes, Paley quietly replied, "I hope he's got it."[26]

By the end of the week, affiliates were calling to inquire about Bing and to report on the excitement in their communities. Fans phoned or sent letters and wires. Requests for interviews poured in from the press. Several out-of-town editors asked to meet Bing and watch the show (there was no studio audience). The country was suddenly mad for singers: Paley immediately added the Boswell Sisters to his team, which already included the immensely popular Downey and Kate Smith. NBC could not believe it. With two networks (the Red and the Blue), NBC thought of itself as the invincible ruler of the air. Suddenly Paley was crooning his baby into position as a real competitor. NBC had fired Russ Columbo on August 21; but after Bing signed with CBS, NBC's vice president John Royal rehired him for a nightly show that directly followed Crosby's. He advised the press, "Both artists are the same style singers," instigating a "battle of the baritones" that prefigured the Crosby and Sinatra duels of the 1940s.[27]

Despite the superficial resemblance, Columbo was the obverse of Crosby. He was a crooner merely, a ballad singer who initially favored a tenor range and could barely handle an up-tempo number, let alone swing. If Bing represented a synthesis of jazz and pop, Columbo was a limited stylist who held his notes a tad too long. Yet Russ echoes throughout Bing's developing years like a night wind, pursuing him in every medium — the first of many celebrated singers to consciously imitate Bing, affirming and codifying his influence.[28]

Staff announcer Ken Roberts was an avid admirer of Bing. Only twenty-one, he had listened to him in the Whiteman years and was thrilled to be assigned to Bing's show. He began with the second broadcast and remained until a sponsor took charge and demanded a more inflated voice. He recalled that Victor Young was brought in "strictly for Bing" because he was a friend and "knew his style," which included placing Eddie Lang right behind Bing, "giving him the rhythm," and Joe Venuti at Bing's side, providing obbligato.[29] Sixty years later Roberts, one of radio's ubiquitous announcers for decades, reminisced about Crosby's first weeks on network radio:

> It was a wonderful time, but I must say that as much as I loved him, I didn't know him. He was a very private person, at least in the studio. He would come in and do his job. He was not temperamental at all, easy to work with, but as soon as he was finished it was good-bye. At first the only conversation we had was "Good evening, Bing, how are you?" "Hello, Kenneth, how are you?" That changed after a few weeks on the air. I was walking up Madison Avenue, a few blocks from CBS, and I saw Bing standing in front of a bookshop, looking in the window. I stopped alongside and said, "Hi, Bing, how are you?" He said, "Oh, hello, Kenneth, how are you? You read that book yet?" He pointed to some esoteric book — it could have been Schopenhauer. And I said, "No, I haven't," and he said, "Well, you should." And from then on it was very warm between us, until he got a sponsor.
>
> He used to wear porkpie hats in some crazy shade of green. He was cute — a nice fella. His style was so marvelous, so effortless and beautiful and knowledgeable. The show would begin with the theme, "Where the Blue of the Night Meets the Gold of the Day," and then I would say, "Welcome to another fifteen minutes with Bing Crosby and tonight Bing starts his show with . . . ," and he'd sing his song. The show was an immediate success. Tremendous. He was a real star. The song-pluggers were around all the time — radio was their bread and butter. But with Bing it was no longer the song that sold the records, it was the artist. [30]

Roberts's observation underscores the great paradox about Crosby: he was a man whom the audience thought it knew almost as well as a member of the family but who was, in fact, known to very few. Cool and efficient in his private manner, he was, in Roberts's words, "exceptionally intimate when he sang. He never bellowed. He never sang out as he did when he was with Whiteman, as on 'High Water.' Once he got his show he learned what a microphone was. We liked his easiness, the intelligence behind his interpretation of the lyrics. Everything he did depended upon intelligence and he certainly had that."[31]

Bing was now shaking up the entertainment world. In March 1931 CBS had seventy-seven affiliates. Three months after Bing's debut, it had ninety. The November issue of *Radio Log and Lore* categorized the new radio voices (Columbo was "King of Crooners"), describing Bing as "recording artist and entertainer extraordinary." At the close of his first week on the air, two of the top five sheet-music hits — "Just One More Chance" and "I Found a Million Dollar Baby" — were songs he had sung on his first broadcast. His success was contagious. Four days after he premiered, Kate Smith found a sponsor, raising her salary sixfold. A few weeks later Jesse Crawford interpolated Bing's record of "Just One More Chance" in his performances at the Paramount; that raised eyebrows because Crawford was contracted to NBC. Seven weeks into Bing's broadcast, *Variety* noted that Rudy Vallée impersonators had given way to something new: "Radio circles and song pluggers who have just returned from road tours report that they heard at least one or more Crosby-Columbo imitators locally in every city they visited."[32] *Variety*'s tabulation of October record sales showed Bing with three of the five top sellers in New York (no. one, "I Apologize"; no. two, "Sweet and Lovely"; and no. five, "Goodnight Sweetheart") and Los Angeles (no. one, "Dancing in the Dark"; no. two, "I Apologize"; and no. four, "Sweet and Lovely").[33] The Groaner from Tacoma, as Tommy Dorsey tagged him at a rehearsal,[34] was now, in Duke Ellington's words, "the biggest thing, ever."[35]

Bing's sustaining program lasted as long as it did — two months — because Ralph Wonders, encouraged by Everett, told prospective sponsors they would have to pony up $3,000 a week, which was considered exorbitant for an artist who had yet to prove himself more than a fad. (Actually, as noted, Kate Smith received that amount, a far greater raise for her than it would have been for Bing, who was already paid half that by Paley.) Before long, however, a contract was negotiated with Certified Cremo, a cigar-making subsidiary of American Tobacco, ruled by the notoriously despotic George Washington Hill. For four months Bing was infelicitously known as the Cremo Singer. Carl Fenton conducted the orchestra, which included few (if any) regular jazz players except Lang and Venuti, and David Ross announced — the ideal choice for a ludicrously pretentious company, known for its bizarre obsession with clean tobacco. Ross rolled his rs and contrived fancy pronunciations in reading copy that might have reduced a lesser man to giggling:

> Good evening, ladies and gentlemen! The manufacturers of Certified Cremo present for your listening pleasure Bing Crosby, the Cremo Singer. While you are listening, light up a Cremo and discover real smoking enjoyment. Your eyes can't tell you whether a cigar is clean or whether it is made by unsanitary methods. Smoke Certified Cremo and *know* that your cigar is clean. Cremo, made in the famous perfecto shape that is the mark of fine cigar quality, is the only cigar in the world finished under glass. Fifty-six health officials endorse Cremo's crusade for cleanliness. And now, Bing Crosby, singing . . .[36]

Ross, who pronounced *singer* "sing-ah" and might have served as inspiration for Groucho Marx's "thank yow" sketch in *A Night at the Opera,* was the typical radio announcer of the era and, in fact, had just received the annual gold medal in the field, which titillated Cremo's sense of status. Younger announcers like Ken Roberts and Harry Von Zell were trying to humanize the medium but faced an uphill battle. Ross had the sort of delivery that Bing — who ultimately did more than anyone to popularize a chummy radio style — routinely parodied, once he was allowed to speak. His early sponsors would not permit Bing to utter a word on air. Ironically, this constraint worked to his advantage, as the contrast between the naturalness of his singing and the announcers' pomposity intensified the sense of intimacy he cultivated.

The most important result of the Cremo series was that it established Bing as a prime-time performer from coast to coast. The sustainer had originally been aired at 11:00, in part so that it was heard at 7:00 out West (California had not yet accepted daylight saving, so there was a four-hour difference in 1931), where CBS hoped Bing might put a dent in *Amos 'n' Andy*. That hopeless cause was teased in *Sing, Bing, Sing*, the Sennett short that Crosby made the following year. Bing's character, a radio singer, signals his plans to elope over the air; then that night, the girl's father intercepts and taunts Bing with the line "Thought I'd be listening to *Amos 'n' Andy*, didn't you?" CBS attempted to increase Bing's New York following by adding an early show to his schedule on Tuesdays at 8:45. His success in that time slot motivated the network to broadcast him exclusively at 7:00 P.M., causing much consternation among West Coast fans who were working or did not otherwise have access to radios at three in the afternoon. With Cremo writing the checks, however, the issue was solved: Bing made two nightly broadcasts Monday through Saturday, at 7:00 for the East and 11:00 for the West.

For all his notoriety and success, Bing was not breaking any ratings records. But three days after he debuted for Cremo, he began setting the first of many career records that would never be broken. On November 6 he embarked on a ten-week stint at the Paramount Theater (the stage where he and Al Rinker had bombed) for what turned out to be the longest streak by any entertainer in the theater's history. Midway through the initial engagement, Paramount renewed his contract for another ten weeks — four more at its Broadway theater and six at the Paramount Theater in Brooklyn. When he closed in Brooklyn, Bing returned to the Broadway theater as the vocal star in a George Jessel revue for an additional three weeks. In total, he commanded Paramount's two New York stages for five months without a break. During most of that time, Bing's daily grind consisted of four stage shows — at $2,500 a week — and two fifteen-minute daily broadcasts, plus various charity shows, guest appearances, recording dates, and concerts.

Inevitably, Bing's vocal problem — the huskiness — returned. Paramount, concerned about its contracts, sent him to the same specialist who had treated him before the CBS debut. This time, Dr. Ruskin found him "happy-go-lucky"[37] and assured Bing that his only problem was a minor node, a hard blister, on one of his vocal cords; because of it, a slight cold might generate congestion and swelling. Ruskin told him he could have it surgically removed but advised against it. An operation could have an unforeseen effect on his voice, while the harmless node contributed to an appealing timbre. Over the next few years, an echoey and pleasing throatiness served as Bing's signature sound. (It could also render him downright hoarse, as on the record "Snuggled on Your Shoulder.") He suggested that Bing rest his voice, allowing it to heal on its own. Bing compromised; he curtailed its use when he was not working. For years fans debated whether Bing secretly had surgery, so completely did the huskiness disappear in the mid-1930s, but he evidently did not. In 1933, when Paramount Pictures signed Bing to a contract, his voice was insured for $100,000 by Lloyd's of London, which insisted on a proviso: Dr. Ruskin had to stipulate that he would not operate, as the node was an essential component of Bing's "vocal charm."

On opening night of the Paramount engagement, Lillian Roth, Gus Edwards, and the dancer Armida made stage appearances to wish him well. As was customary, Paramount stage shows changed weekly, along with the movie — he opened opposite Ruth Chatterton in *Once a Lady* — and supporting stars. Bing's duties required him to emcee as well as sing and act in sketches, all good preparation for the movies and the kind of radio shows he would pioneer in a couple of years. He began to draw on his inveterate fascination with the-sauruses. Though prohibited from speaking on the air, onstage he could be quite "gabby," as he put it.[38] Blending verbal gimmicks ("alliteration and other fancy devices")[39] with jaunty phrases and current slang, he produced a distinctive speech pattern all his own. "I can only go so far with big words," Bing explained, "then I have to return to the vernacular to finish what I have to say."[40]

Because Bing was a radio persona, Paramount management decided to actually introduce him as a disembodied voice — or something close to it. During his first number he was displayed as a dark blue silhouette. *Billboard* complained that all one could see of him as he sang "Just One More Chance" were his white flannels. Where was the logic in that, the reviewer wondered, especially as Bing "registered heavily" in his second number, "As Time Goes By," bathed in white light and seated on an ascending pipe organ played by Helen Crawford (Jesse's wife).[41] In a more bizarre setup, Bing had to swing over the first few rows in a seat welded to a crane. The theater was dark except for a spotlight on his face. Once, the controlling mechanism got stuck during a performance, and Bing was forced to crawl along the crane's shaft — amid gales of laughter — until he could safely drop to the stage.

Microphones were stationed everywhere, two in the open and the rest hidden, so that Bing could perform freely in just about any position. Diversity was key. In one show he sang "Wrap Your Troubles in Dreams" as a lead-in to a dance by the scantily clad Vanessi, who rumbaed; then he serenaded ballerina Harriet Hoctor with "I Surrender, Dear" as she danced on her toes and leaped over hurdles in a simulated steeplechase. A mike was hidden in each of the hurdles, and Bing walked from post to post, singing one phrase at each, until finishing the song.

Variety praised his professionalism: unlike most singers, "he saw an audience before he saw the inside of a radio studio."[42] But business was not much better than average the first week. The theater manager, Jack McInerny, remembered Bing occasionally having an attack of nerves and bracing himself with a drink — though nothing like in the Rhythm Boys days, he added. McInerny recalled him as "very pleasant, talked to the stagehands, joked with everybody, easygoing, but a little nervous before a show."[43] He relaxed when the Mills Brothers, one of the most ingenious and melodious of close-harmony groups, appeared for three delightful weeks. Bing never felt more at home than when surrounded by good musicians, and though he performed only one number onstage with the brothers, between shows they repaired to the steps out back and jammed.

In October Bing and the Mills Brothers participated in a two-sided record, *Gems from George White's Scandals,* sharing the platter with Victor Young's orchestra, the Boswell Sisters, soloist Tommy Dorsey, and radio tenor Frank Munn, whose contribution includes the unspeakable "That's Why Darkies Were Born." The highlight of the session was "Life Is Just a Bowl of Cherries," for which Young asked Bing, the Boswells, and the Mills Brothers to devise different interpretations that he could juxtapose into a single arrangement. Engineer Edgar Sisson recalled that "Bing rehearsed one-tenth the time the others did" and amused everyone present by spontaneously altering the line "You can't take your dough when you go-go-go" to "You can't take that good dough when you go" because, Bing explained, *go-go-go* "seemed awkward."[44]

Yet the arrangement permitted no interaction between Bing and the Mills Brothers; after sharing three weeks with them at the theater, Bing was determined to rectify that. On December 16 he arranged — accidentally on purpose — to record with them. Taking a busman's holiday, Bing wandered into the studio to watch the brothers rehearse with one of Bennie Krueger's units. After a while he asked to get in on a number. They ran down a routine on "Dinah," a jump tune chiefly associated with Ethel Waters. Bing began fooling around, scatting. He asked the engineers to record a take simply as a test. Everyone liked it so much, a second take was made. Kapp was probably not present, for no actual recording was scheduled, but when he heard it he knew he had a jewel. He released the second take of "Dinah" on a disc with Bing's earnest version of Victor Young's "Can't We Talk It Over," recorded days later at the Paramount Theater, sedately accompanied by Helen Crawford's Wurlitzer. In the first days of 1932, "Dinah" was the hottest record in the country, the second top-ranking hit for the Mills Brothers and the fourth (under his own name) for Bing. It endures as an irresistible pop classic.

"Dinah" is emphatically a record of the early thirties; Bing slightly overdoes the parallel mordents and scats with a two-beat stiffness. Yet his phrasing is sure and inventive, and he swings buoyantly, especially when riffing with the brothers. The entire performance is dazzling fun, flowing with energy and good cheer. Bing was most expressive in his lower midrange, as here, sculpting every note while breezing over the rhythm. After the Millses sing a unison double-time chorus, Donald Mills scats a two-bar platform from which Bing leaps into a sixteen-bar improvisation. The Armstrong influence is evident in his ensuing riffs (especially on the long-unissued and more larkish "test" version), yet he is utterly himself. Donald, not yet seventeen at the time, recalled, "Crosby and us were great friends. We enjoyed one another. He was a wonderful person. When we made 'Dinah' or 'Shine' [two months later], we didn't rehearse. We just said, 'Well, we'll do this, you do that,' and we recorded. No arrangement."[45]

Over time, business at the Paramount improved. Reviewers noted Bing's equanimity — he did not appear to mind having to sing while obscured by a bevy of dancing girls — as well as his "quiet line of clowning" and his innovative decision to plant his main microphone in the orchestra pit, several feet in front of him, so that he stood bare before the audience, like Al Jolson. The front office (Paramount-

Publix) booked Russ Columbo into the Brooklyn theater during part of Bing's Broadway run to exploit the battle of the baritones. But it tilted its booking powers toward Bing, whose shows were more elaborate and included several of the most talented and popular performers of the era, notably Kate Smith, Eleanor Powell, Lillian Roth, Cab Calloway, the Boswell Sisters, and Burns and Allen. Paramount increased his salary to $4,000 when it extended his contract (it did not renew Columbo's), a tribute as much to his personal stability as to his drawing power.

Which is not to say he didn't slip up a few times. Frieda Kapp, Jack's widow, recalled the Paramount run as the period when Jack began pressuring Bing to dispense with the trademarks that had given him cachet ever since the Whiteman years. Jack summed them up as the "bu-bu-bu-boos," by which he also meant scat singing and jazz. Kapp was determined to establish Bing as the first entertainer who was all things to all people, and as his instincts usually proved sound, Bing grew to depend on them. But it was not always easy, and one of their discussions apparently sent Bing on a bender. "That was the beginning of Bing's success, taking away the *bu-bu-bu-boos* at the Paramount Theater," as Frieda remembered it. "I remember very well that [Jack] took the *bu-bu-bu-boo* away from him and he did not appear that night at the Paramount. They found him drunk somewhere. After that, of course, he went back and became a great success."[46]

His sporadic unsteadiness was also apparent on the air. "A couple of times during the early weeks, I remember him fumbling on the radio," said Burton Lane. "I never saw him drinking, but if he blew a lyric, there would be talk on the street, you know, around the music publishers."[47] Artie Shaw remembered a broadcast when Bing "was so drunk he was staggering. He wouldn't stay near the mike, somebody had to hold him there."[48] In Shaw's opinion, the problem was Dixie. The scuttlebutt had it that she had come to New York to keep him off the sauce but was drinking too much herself.

Shortly before Bing took off for New York, Dixie Lee embarked on a nightclub engagement in Los Angeles at the Embassy club. She arrived in New York after completing the gig, and friends said they seemed happy together. "Bing and Dixie were living at the Essex

House, which was very new, and Mildred and I were married and staying with Joe and Sally Venuti, nearby on Fifty-fifth Street," Red Norvo recalled. "And so we gave parties at Joe's apartment, the six of us, and they were wonderful."[49] Bing and Dixie bought a white terrier and named it Cremo. "Dixie came to the studio once or twice," Ken Roberts remembered, "and she was like a little waif. I heard after that she drank a lot. I don't know. Bing had a reputation for drinking, but I never saw him drunk. When he was working he was very serious."[50] Yet a turnabout was taking place. At Dixie's urging, Bing had straightened out, but in trying to keep up with him and in warding off loneliness when he worked late, she now turned increasingly to alcohol.

Meanwhile, Everett ran rampant, pulling strings, making deals. "Everett was running Bing's life at that time," or so it seemed to Gary Stevens. "He was all business, looking out for Bing's welfare on a very strict, cold basis."[51] He was not greatly liked or respected. Ken Roberts thought that "he just kind of latched on to this brilliant young brother."[52] Everett was known as a tippler and a chaser. Members of the Paramount stage crew[53] described an incident that occurred when Everett followed Bing onstage as he was about to climb onto the seat of the crane that suspended him over the audience. During their hurried conversation, before the curtain rose, Everett noticed they were standing near a trapdoor that opened on the girls' dressing area. Somehow he managed to fall through the trap as the crane took Bing on his ride. The orchestra had to play extra loud to cover the shrieking from down below.

In the all-time classic Everett story, however, he plays a bit part. "There was a shoeshine boy near CBS at Sunset and Vine in Hollywood," Artie Shaw recalled, "and he was working on one man, when the man he just finished gave him a dime tip, which was a normal tip back then, and walked away. So the shoeshine boy says, 'Thanks, Mr. Crosby,' and the new customer says, 'Was that Bing Crosby?' And the kid says, 'No, that's the wrong Crosby.' Everett was known as the wrong Crosby for the rest of his life."[54]

Yet for all his rough edges, Everett proved an effective deal-maker as the Crosby phenomenon billowed. Young Gary Stevens helped the process along by convincing CBS's three vocal stars — Kate Smith, Morton Downey, and Bing — to pose for a picture he placed in the

New York World-Telegram; it was quickly picked up by the Associated Press. Bing refused to wear his hairpiece for the picture, the last time that would happen in a publicity shot.

In January Mack Sennett asked Bing to complete a biographical card for his public-relations office. Everett filled it out, creating bits of the Crosby myth that persisted from one press release to another, from one screen-idol magazine to the next. He got little right beyond eyes (blue), hair (light), pastimes (golf and swordfishing), and current address (the Essex House). But he did create Bing's official birth date of May 2, 1904. Though he shaved only a year from Bing's real age, Everett thought he was being canny; he figured Bing had to be thirty-one or thirty-two and that he was doing him a favor keeping him in his twenties in what promised to be his breakthrough year in movies. He declined to fill in height and weight, identified his first Sennett film as *One More Chance* (it was *I Surrender Dear*), and traced his nickname to his childhood affection for popguns. Unable to resist adding a little more color, he appended a few Whiteman tales and the comment: "claims his watch has been in every pawnshop across country."[55]

Everett could afford to make the pawnshop crack, because those days were behind Bing. With Dixie on furlough from Fox, she made the rounds with him. They enjoyed their relative prosperity, his increased renown, New York, and each other. Bing focused intently on singing and rarely turned down an opportunity to work. He sang so often, it's a wonder his node didn't cause greater affliction. On a Saturday evening in February, toward the end of the Paramount engagement, Bing moonlighted at New Jersey's Newark Armory at a Radio Artists Ball, where a dollar ticket rewarded fans with Crosby, the Mills Brothers, the Boswell Sisters, Nick Lucas ("Tip Toe Through the Tulips with Me"), and Bennie Krueger's orchestra. Five evenings later he hightailed it from his last show at the Paramount to the Columbia studio where Duke Ellington was setting up. Between midnight and one, they recorded two Ellington arrangements of W. C. Handy's "St. Louis Blues." Although they admired and liked each other (Duke created his concerto version of "Frankie and Johnny" for Bing's radio show in 1941; the last recording Bing made in the United States was for a memorial tribute to Duke in 1977), this was the only time Bing formally recorded as a soloist with Ellington and one of the few times he recorded the blues.[56] A pity on both counts, for the result is a gem — or, more precisely, two gems.

The second (B) take was initially released and remains the best known of the two, beginning with a slap-tongue introduction by baritone saxophonist Harry Carney and proceeding with glowing choruses by trumpeter Cootie Williams and trombonist Joe Nanton. After a short piano transition, Bing sings two twelve-bar choruses, backed by a covey of clarinetist Barney Bigard, Carney, and guitarist Fred Guy, whose dynamic strumming suggests a banjo. Bing continues with the two sixteen-bar refrains (Ellington dispenses with the tango rhythm of the original), backed at first by Nanton and then by the previously noted trio. He coolly improvises phrases with such authority that when he forgets the lyric, he is able to unhesitatingly fake — in true blues tradition — a closing refrain. At which point the tempo is doubled as the great alto saxophonist Johnny Hodges wails a chorus, setting up a stirring passage by Bing, one of the finest examples of scat singing in that era. He concludes at half tempo with the beautifully modulated line "And I love my baby [critic J. T. H. Mize astutely singled out the "slow and deliberate tilt on *baby*"][57] till the day I die."

That closing phrase probably clinched the choice of take B, but the verdict was actually settled on a question of gender; in Bing's first try, the St. Louis woman pulled "that gal around," instead of the man she was supposed to be pulling. The A take has rewards of its own, beginning with an orchestral introduction and a ferocious Cootie Williams solo that establishes a far earthier mood, peaking with one of Bing's headiest jazz moments on record. Before Hodges completes his double-time chorus, Bing — Louislike — leaps in and commands the saxophonist's last four bars as a scat runway for his own elated chorus. In neither version does Bing make an effort to mimic expressive blues techniques. He enjoyed, as did Ellington, the contrast between his level tones and the band's idiosyncratic timbres. The record was reviewed later that year in Britain's *Gramophone*: "After the ballad performances to which Bing has been devoting most of his time lately the brilliance of his rhythmic style will be surprising, even to those who remember the days when, with Harry Barris and Al Rinker [he] created quite a sensation as a hot singer."[58]

Bing played it both ways, hot and cool, all season. If the material was uninspired, as it often was, he managed to wring something personal from it anyway, for example, "Starlight," a poised though raspy-voiced reading of an undistinguished ballad that shows how comfortable he had become as a stylist, no longer trying so hard to turn or sigh a note. Jack Kapp's persistence in getting him to simplify his attack paid off without diminishing Bing's gift for drama. He gives full measure to the bygone lament "My Woman," transforming an awkward song into a charmer with mild echoes of jazz and tango.[59] Eddie Lang was invariably at his side, a kind of jazz conscience. In arranging "Paradise," Victor Young allowed Bing and Lang to waltz the last sixteen bars largely on their own, and on "You're Still in My Heart," he had Lang double-time the second chorus.

The most popular Crosby recording that month was a stunning reunion with the Mills Brothers on "Shine." A minstrel song fashioned for a revue in 1909 by two black songwriters (Ford Dabney and the influential lyricist-publisher Cecil Mack), "Shine" did not achieve success until the 1920s, by which time its self-pity and ethnic clichés ("Just because my hair is curly / Just because my teeth are pearly") were more likely to invite parody than outrage. In 1931 Louis Armstrong had made the song an exuberant virtuoso showcase, practically transforming the epithet "Shine" into a badge of honor. In their 1932 version, the Mills Brothers politely phrase the outmoded lyric. Then Bing jumps in, imbuing every word with swing, rhythmically and sonorously overwhelming the trite caricature. When the Millses reprise the chorus, Bing interpolates spoken responses that suggest a benign carny barker ("man's got curly hair!" "also got pearly teeth!") and adds an Armstrongian "ohhh, keep on smiling." Bing's scat solo on "Shine" was his most inventive to date, surpassing "Dinah" in its rhythmic variety and assurance.

He fared less successfully on Victor Young's "Lawd, You Made the Night Too Long," an incongruously heavy-handed record with Don Redman's elegant orchestra and the Boswell Sisters, with whom he does not interact. Sadly, that was the last time he appeared on record with the Boswells, though they worked together on radio numerous times. It was also the last time he recorded in New York before embarking — that very afternoon (April 13) — on the tour that brought him back to Hollywood.

Bing's departure from New York had been hastened in part by Cremo's surprise decision, in February, not to renew his radio contract. George

Washington Hill saw no need to explain why. According to one observer, the clean-cigar company was shocked to discover, after four months, that women who faithfully listened to Bing did not smoke cigars. Another traced the rupture to one of Hill's advertising boasts, "There is no spit in Cremo." Bing's show had become notorious for its distasteful commercials, shudderingly recited by announcer David Ross ("Spit," he would begin, "is a horrid word"), concerning the dreadful effects of saliva.[60] The story went that one of Hill's lieutenants manufactured a private run of hand-rolled (and tongue-sealed) cigars and distributed them with the Cremo label. Hill was allegedly mortified to realize that those Cremos did undoubtedly contain spit and withdrew all sponsorship for the product.

Bing and Everett were not overly worried at first. CBS had every intention of keeping Bing on the air until a new sponsor could be found. Yet the network forbade him from including Dixie in the show, perhaps fearing that a wifely presence would undermine his potency as a heartthrob balladeer. Bing was sufficiently concerned about his future in radio to accept the injunction, which hammered home the career reversals that had taken place in the seventeen months since they were married. Cremo's retreat was not untimely. Bing had failed to give his voice the prescribed rest, so Dr. Ruskin sent him to another specialist, Chevalier Jackson, who apparently frightened him into a brief repose. As Bing related to biographer Charles Thompson, Jackson warned him that surgery might turn him into "a boy soprano" and advised, "If you rest and don't even answer the phone — don't talk, don't do anything — [the nodes will] recede."[61] Bing took ten days off before resuming broadcasts, again with Fred Rich's band, but only three times a week. Cremo's layoff also made it easier for him to return to California to shoot the two remaining shorts on his Sennett contract. While Bing continued working the Paramount, Everett was less preoccupied with finding him a new sponsor than with lining up a feature film to make the trip worthwhile.

Meanwhile, Bing's standing in show business reached a new plateau. During the week of his last Cremo appearance (February 27), Bing was honored with a midnight dinner at the Friars Club — "a particularly funny night," according to the club's chronicler, Joey Adams, and the first time the industry paid him tribute.[62] The speakers included Jack Benny, George Burns, Irving Berlin, Rudy Vallée,

William Paley, George Jessel, Walter Donaldson, and Damon Runyon. At the end of the evening, George M. Cohan presented Bing with a lifetime membership card made of gold. In March the public joined in a roast of the whole crooning triad, stimulated by a song, "Crosby, Columbo and Vallée" ("Who do husbands hate their wives to listen to? / Crosby, Columbo and Vallée!"). Vallée sued to have his picture removed from the sheet music but could do nothing when Merrie Melodies lampooned him and Bing in a cartoon of the same name.

(Over the next decade Bing would be caricatured visually, vocally, or both in numerous animations, not always kindly. In depicting him as a cad, the parodies echoed the plots of the Sennett shorts in which he abducts women from their suitors. In a May 1936 cartoon, *Let It Be Me,* Mr. Bingo is a spats-wearing cock of the walk, who croons for PBC [the Poultry Broadcasting Company] and seduces and abandons an innocent hen in favor of a curvaceous French capon. The hen's dumb-cluck boyfriend avenges her by smashing a radio and punching Mr. Bingo before marrying the hen. They have five chicks, one of whom chirps *bu-bu-bu-boo.* Merrie Melodies quickly followed it with *Bingo Crosbyana,* this time prompting a suit in which Bing's attorney, John O'Melveny, argued that the title character was depicted as a "vainglorious coward." The complaint had no motive beyond harassment. Warners cartoonists gave Bing a wide berth for a couple of years, during which his representatives developed a better sense of humor. Bing was back on the drawing board by 1938, albeit less derisively.)

A blanket skewering of radio itself provided Bing with his opportunity to return to Hollywood in style. The talk of Broadway in early 1932 was William Ford Manley's play *Wild Waves,* which satirically traced the rise of a broadcast star. One of its producers, D. A. Doran, was affiliated with the story department at Paramount Pictures and persuaded the studio to purchase the film rights. By February Paramount let it be known it was considering Bing for the lead role. A New York *Daily News* columnist cheered, "Should be Bing's meat!"[63] Paramount negotiated with Sennett and Everett to obtain Bing's participation and signed him to a one-picture deal — a deal that would have Bing working his way west in just about every Paramount-Publix theater en route.

*   *   *

As his star rose during the first six months of 1932, Bing began to extricate himself from a surfeit of agents. Early in the year, Ev was taking 10 percent of his income while Marchetti was taking another 20 percent. Bing was obliged to the lawyer for getting him out of the mess at the Grove and vetting his CBS contract, but he now rankled at paying him a fifth of his earnings when they were on opposite coasts and Marchetti no longer did much, if anything, for him. Having organized Bing Crosby, Ltd., with himself, Bing, and Barris as equal partners, Marchetti demanded $100,000 for his third. Bing wired another Los Angeles attorney, John O'Melveny, to handle the situation. O'Melveny represented Sue Carol and once helped Dixie with her Fox contract; he had seen Bing at the Grove and was later introduced to him by Sue at a party she gave for Bing and Dixie when they were married. His negotiations with Marchetti resulted in the astonishingly low settlement of $15,000 and established O'Melveny as a permanent member of the Crosby organization, representing Bing in all legal matters for the rest of their lives.

Edward Small presented more of a problem. Bing had stopped paying him his 10 percent, claiming that Small verbally released him from their 1930 contract on the condition that Bing settle with him upon his return to Los Angeles. Small denied ever relieving Bing of his obligations. When the Paramount deal was rumored, he sued for $20,000, based on his estimate of Bing's two-year earnings as $200,000 ("I wish that were true," Bing told a reporter);[64] when the movie deal was confirmed, he enlarged his demand by an additional $85,000. Newspaper accounts feigned surprise that such sums could be earned from crooning, and Bing bristled at having his finances publicized. After one of his Paramount salary checks was attached by the sheriff, Bing settled out of court.

Bing needed a publicist. His brother Ted (third-oldest of the siblings, after Larry and Everett) had made a game try in December 1931 from his home in Spokane, pitching Bing's story to *Time*. Ted received a smug response from a member of the editorial department with the improbable name Eleanor Hard: "I am afraid the Bing Crosby suggestion won't be suitable for FORTUNE. Thanks for your suggestion, however."[65] *Fortune*? He wrote back that he had meant *Time,* which recently ran a story on Alice Joy, "The Dream Singer," a vaudevillian who did a daily fifteen-minute show. "The incidents in

Doreen Wilde (above) appeared with dancer Bobby Thompson in the same vaudeville show (*Syncopation Ideas*) that introduced Crosby and Rinker to California audiences, 1925.
Alison McMahan Collection

STAGE AND FILM EVENTS

LOCAL BOYS ARRANGING VARIETY TOUR

These two Spokane boys, Alton Rinker (left) and Harry (Bing) Crosb have recently completed a successful engagement with Fanchon and Marc dancing artists, in Los Angeles, and are now making arrangements for a Orpheum booking. It has been learned from the California city. The appeared at the Clemmer theater this summer. Rinker is a pianist an Crosby is a humorist and talented vocalist.

On January 1, 1926, the *Spokane Chronicle* reported on Al and Bing's first variety tour. *Bing Crosby Collection, Foley Center, Gonzaga University*

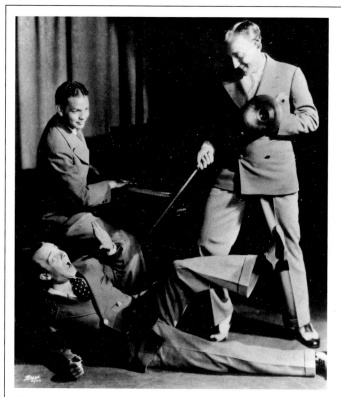

The Rhythm Boys at play: Al Rinker at the piano, Harry Barris on the ground, Bing with cymbal and baton.
Mickey Kapp Collection

Paul Whiteman's photograph helped sell the sheet music for the Rhythm Boys' biggest hit, "Mississippi Mud," 1927.
Gary Giddins Collection

"Am I too suave or sveldt . . . Brush by Fuller." Bing, mustachioed and natty, had this picture taken in New York and inscribed it to his brother Ted. *Howard Crosby Collection*

Gus Arnheim led the famous orchestra at the Cocoanut Grove. *Elsie Perry Collection*

A publicity photo of Bing and Eddie Lang, the highest-paid sideman in the country before his untimely death. *Gary Giddins Collection*

Six scenes from the short subjects Bing made for Mack Sennett. In *Dream House*, he gets black housepaint on his face, leading a black casting director to hire him as a black actor; in *Billboard Girl*, the swishy brother of Bing's paramour pretends to be her and Bing can't tell the difference. Note that he almost always wore a hat to avoid the dreaded "scalp doily."
Jon Protas

Larry Crosby was brought on board to handle Bing's publicity and collaborated with brother Ted on a fictionalized biography.
Bing Crosby Collection, Foley Center, Gonzaga University

Jack Kapp revolutionized the recording industry and chose many of Bing's songs between 1931 and 1949.
Elsie Perry Collection

Three Crosby brothers, top to bottom: bandleader Bob, Bing, and manager Everett ("the wrong Crosby").
Ron Bosley Collection

The October 1934 issue of *Radio Stars* celebrated the crooner who helped place radios in millions of homes.
Gary Giddins Collection

Bing's ambivalence about tobacco sponsorship was evident in a 1944 print campaign in which he allowed himself to be quoted only on the matter of friendship.
Eric Anderson Collection

In the weeks before his 1931 network radio debut, Bing auditioned a couple of songs as his theme before settling on "Where the Blue of the Night (Meets the Gold of the Day)"– a perfect choice. *Gary Giddins Collection*

When Rudy Vallée first heard Bing, he observed, "My time is short." Bing thumbs through *Radio Mirror* with Rudy on the cover, 1933. *Courtesy of the Academy of Motion Picture Arts and Sciences* her rise to fame are not nearly so startling as those to be found in a history of Bing's," he argued: "[Bing] heads the list of radio singers — he is in his third month at the New York Paramount — his motion picture 'shorts' are breaking records — his records are best sellers — and his latest success is in song writing."[66] Though Ted harbored aspirations as a manager and writer, he was disinclined to leave Washington. Brother Larry, on the other hand, was raring to go, and Bing gave him the job of redefining his reputation as one of professionalism and sobriety. The FDR era was about to commence. Within a year Prohibition would be repealed. There was no reason to drink anymore — except maybe the Depression.

15

THE CROSBY
CLAUSE

*Listen in on the hilarious secrets and romances your
radios never reveal!*
— Paramount advertisement, *The Big Broadcast* (1932)[1]

Paramount and Bing closed the deal on *Wild Waves,* which was retitled *The Crooner* and *Broadcasting* before the studio settled on *The
Big Broadcast.* On April 13 Bing, Dixie, and the terrier, Cremo,
embarked on a five-month tour of the Paramount-Publix circuit in an
elaborate publicity drive for the picture, which was scheduled to
shoot midway through the tour, beginning June 11. During the seven-
week westward leg of the journey, Bing broadcast fifteen-minute
shows Mondays and Wednesdays at stops where the theater chain
had him booked; upon arriving in California, he would play local
venues for a month and make the film, then resume a schedule of
broadcasts and theaters as he worked his way back to New York. Bing
had hoped to bring along a small combo with Joe Venuti and Jimmy
Dorsey but was obliged to settle for just Lennie Hayton, who served
as musical director and conducted theater-pit orchestras, and Lang,
who worked at Bing's side, seated on a high stool that allowed them to
share a mike. Bing called Eddie his "good luck charm."[2]

A couple of weeks into the tour, *Variety* ran an ad cosigned by
Everett Crosby and William Paley, in which Bing says "THANKS

EVERYBODY See You in the Fall."[3] Bing's brother identified himself as the singer's personal manager, and Paley was credited with "personal direction," which reflected nothing more than his desire to keep Bing on his network.

Dixie and Kitty Lang grew close during the trip. Kitty remembered, "Every town we went to, we were alone most of the time due to rehearsals and shows the boys were doing. We only saw them at dinner or after the last show of the evening." Bing and Eddie spent off-hours shooting pool, playing cards, and talking music. Bing "always listened to Eddie's advice as to how to sing certain phrases in a tune," Kitty said.[4] In booking their accommodations, Everett invariably arranged connecting rooms. While the boys rehearsed, the girls went horseback riding or shopping in the morning, occasionally taking in a movie in the afternoon.

The tour zigzagged — Detroit, Chicago, Buffalo, Boston, New Haven, Chicago (again), Minneapolis, St. Louis — before touching down in Los Angeles. In Boston Bing joined Jack Benny and George M. Cohan in a minstrel show and, using a pseudonym, entered an amateur-talent contest at the behest of two vaudeville chums, Les Reis and Artie Dunn. He lost. In Chicago Bing recorded five tunes with Isham Jones's orchestra during the first stopover, and four with a Frankie Trumbauer unit during the second. Those sides produced Crosby's classic versions of two of the most indelible and rhythmically energized songs in the American canon, both created by black songwriters.

Maceo Pinkard's hugely popular "Sweet Georgia Brown" was written in 1925 and was introduced by bandleader Ben Bernie. The song is disarmingly fluent given its distinct qualities. Structurally, it avoids the prevalent *aaba* format in favor of *abac;* harmonically, it employs a cycle of fifths but averts the tonic chord until midway; melodically, it is uncannily buoyant, making a slow treatment virtually impossible. Bing's performance with Isham Jones, whose dance band was studded with jazz players (including Woody Herman), is jubilant. Lang strums a two-bar transition to introduce Bing, who is loose, unhurried, letter-perfect. Bing rarely begins phrases on the one, preferring to coolly syncopate them against the ensemble rhythm. No singer of that era understood as well as Bing Louis Armstrong's proclivity for superimposing implied rhythms over stated ones. But where

Armstrong flows, Bing inclines toward a two-beat lockstep, underscored by his practice of adding words to heighten swing; for example, in the space of the phrase, "I'll tell you why and you know I don't lie, not much," he sings, "And I'll tell you just why, you know that I do not lie, not much."[5] A Bixlike solo by trumpeter Chelsea Quealey and Jack Jenny's graceful trombone precede his scat solo and handsomely embellished reprise.

Bing's sparked rendition of Shelton Brooks's "Some of These Days," a milestone song of 1910 that became Sophie Tucker's theme a year later, is even more successful. By any measure, it is one of his greatest performances. Reunited with Trumbauer, who led an ensemble of his regulars plus Lang and Hayton (who dictated the arrangements at the session), Bing is in peak voice and eager to please. Lang begins with vigorous strumming, almost as if the record had faded up on a number in progress, and four bars later Bing rides in — swinging and bending notes, indulging a fetching cry (no mordents today), even clipping a few high notes, while perfectly enunciating the virtually rhymeless lyric. In his superb scat solo, Bing emulates Bix and the result is rhythmically more varied than his usual ad-lib choruses; he inventively uses riffs, rests, and a diminished scale — harmonizing with Lang's turnback chords at bar sixteen. Solos by Lang, trumpeter Nat Connant, and Tram may be smoother, but Bing's solo is the one that stays in the mind, not least his closing, "tweet, tweet, tweet, twee twee."

Bing was in exceptional form in Chicago, giving indifferent songs like "Lazy Day" and "Cabin in the Cotton" more than their due. He rises to a dramatic righteousness on the latter, as if, having been mockingly entwined with Columbo and Vallée, he were determined to sever himself from the depiction of crooners as small-voiced wimps. A couple of weeks later, Bing explained to a reporter, "A crooner is someone who always sings softly, never raising his voice to full strength. I raise mine to full volume whenever the song calls for it."[6] Yet before he left the Windy City, he confided to Tram that he felt his future lay not in music but in the movies.[7]

On June 12, the day after shooting was originally scheduled to begin, the Crosby party arrived at L.A.'s Union Station and was greeted by the Biltmore Hotel Orchestra (chief rival to the Cocoanut Grove band) for speeches courtesy of Paramount's public-relations department. Bing and Dixie rented Sue Carol's house, where they had lived in lieu of a honeymoon, and Eddie and Kitty took an apartment. "But we always stayed close together," Kitty recalled.[8] The start-up for *The Big Broadcast* was delayed until July 5. That gave Bing time to fulfill his obligations to Sennett and film a promotional reel for Paramount's series *Hollywood on Parade.*

The final two Sennett shorts employed the same basic formula as before, but the scripts now reflected Bing's renown as a national radio personality and the general disparagement of crooning. In *Sing, Bing, Sing,*[9] Franklin Pangborn fires a gun at Bing and crows, "It's always open season for crooners." That film also includes the first allusion in the series to the Depression. When the girl's father vows that his daughter will never marry a radio singer, Bing replies, "That's where you're wrong. Prosperity is just around the crooner." Bing's final film for Sennett, the appealing *Blue of the Night,* indulges in a few inside jokes (Bing pretends to be a reporter named Jack Smith, the name of his successor at the Grove) but is more notable as the screen debut of his theme song and for his lovely rendering of "Auf Wiedersehen," a song well suited to the lush timbre of his midrange.

For some reason, Bing never recorded "Auf Wiedersehen," but he sang it again in the first of the four *Hollywood on Parade* publicity shorts he made in 1932 and 1933. None of the stars were paid for their appearances in these one-reelers, which pretend to depict them candidly, though every shot was carefully staged. In the one made to promote *The Big Broadcast,* actor Stu Erwin, his costar, has the distinction of delivering the first documented joke about Bing's fabled fortune, when he announces that Bing appears "by permission of his broker." Bing does a routine with two other stars of the picture, George Burns and Gracie Allen, who greets him as Morton Downey. "No," Bing tells her, "I'm Rudy Vallée."

In the 1950s, when television ravaged movie box office receipts, movie studios fought back with everything from biblical spectacles to 3-D projection to double-D bottle blondes, not to mention the trinity spelled out by Cole Porter: "If you want to get the crowd to come around / You've got to have glorious Technicolor / Breathtaking Cinemascope and / Stereophonic sound."[10] In the early 1930s radio was just as threatening; it bedeviled the record and motion picture industries and every other area of entertainment that required people to leave their homes. The movie studios were stymied in trying to subvert its growing power. *Amos 'n' Andy* did not work as a movie, and musical revues were dead on arrival.

Radio's monstrous intrusion may be inferred by the first important picture to reflect radio culture, the 1931 horror epic *Frankenstein*. Updated to the twentieth century, James Whale's film is dizzy with radio talk and apparatuses as the scientist bridles electricity to replicate life, wearing earphones and muttering about correct frequencies. His creation has two bolts resembling vacuum tubes in its neck to attract electric current that will transform it into virtual humanity. *Frankenstein* captured the unstated fear of electricity — its invisible inroads into everyday life.

The statistics were ominous. In 1930 fewer than a third of American homes had radios; by 1935 fewer than a third did not. The average listener spent upward of four hours a day beside an entertainment device that cost nothing beyond the purchase price yet supplied constant diverse programming. Between 1930 and 1932 weekly movie attendance and receipts fell by a third. Theaters offered double features (generating the need for more product and the assembly of B-picture units and studios) and two-for-ones or half-price tickets. When those gambits failed, movie houses resorted to outright giveaways: hams, dishes, and, ultimately, money — a Fox exhibitor copyrighted Bank Night, a lottery to which more than 4,000 theaters subscribed. As if the challenges of radio and the Depression weren't bad enough, the church intervened. The Motion Picture Production Code, created in 1930 by Catholic publisher Martin Quigley and a Jesuit priest, Daniel Lord, had exerted influence among the faithful. But as of mid-1934 it would be taken up and strictly enforced by the studios — good news for Shirley Temple; bad news for Nick and Nora Charles, who were sentenced to separate beds.

The Code loomed as particularly baleful for Paramount, Hollywood's most sophisticated studio, home to the movies' randiest performers, Mae West and Maurice Chevalier; the unfettered anarchy of the Marx Brothers; outlandish director Josef von Sternberg and his Trilby, Marlene Dietrich; and resplendent director Ernst Lubitsch, who was appointed head of production when he could no longer explore boudoir sallies, ménage à trois, and the joys of theft. Those talents raked in a fortune, and soon they would all be gone. Yet in 1932, when Bing and eight other radio acts were recruited for *The Big Broadcast,* Paramount did not anticipate the coming chill. Nor could it foresee the impact Bing would have on its fortunes or that of the industry. It simply hoped to capitalize on Mack Sennett's notion: if the country was crazy over radio singers, maybe it would pay to see what some of them looked like.

After signing Crosby, Paramount made two shrewd decisions. The first was to jettison every aspect of William Manley's *Wild Waves* except the radio-station setting, turning a satire into a variety show. Manley had started out as a radio writer (*Snow Village Sketches*) and achieved his success on Broadway by crunching the hand that fed him. Hollywood, however, sought a rapprochement with radio and its listeners. Bing was to be the most prominently featured of the several CBS radio stars Paramount hired for the picture, and it seemed reasonable to have him play some version of himself. Still, in presenting Bing Crosby as a character named Bing Crosby, the film took the cult of personality a step beyond established custom.[11]

True, Laurel and Hardy used the same names on- and offscreen, and a few stars routinely appeared in roles that combined their real first names (Al Jolson usually played a guy named Al, Eddie Cantor almost always played a guy named Eddie) with made-up surnames, as Bing did in the Sennett shorts. In 1932 Jack Benny and Burns and Allen were extending their vaudeville personae into radio characters of the same names, a practice that would confuse a generation of listeners. (Asked if Jack Benny was really cheap, the professionally ditzy Gracie Allen replied, "Am I stupid?") Bing never appeared as Bing in any of his subsequent pictures, but his movie character, established in his first feature, would remain fairly constant from one film to the next. Audiences would presume the man onscreen was no different at home: exceptionally likable if, as revealed in *The Big Broadcast,* not entirely admirable.

Paramount's second smart move was to assign the picture to Frank Tuttle, who in 1932 was one of the studio's most highly regarded contract directors. A Yale graduate who had served as assistant editor at *Vanity Fair* and as publicist for the New York Philharmonic and

Diaghilev's Ballets Russes (he married dancer Tatiana Smirnova), Tuttle came to Hollywood as a writer and was encouraged to direct by veteran filmmaker Allan Dwan. He was tall, lean, bespectacled, donnish, and famously efficient; he helped found the Screen Directors Guild. Tuttle had made stars of Clara Bow and Eddie Cantor in silent pictures and would do as much for Bing, Alan Ladd, and Veronica Lake in the 1930s and 1940s. Indeed, no one played a more prominent role than Tuttle in Bing's first decade in Hollywood. They worked together on six pictures between 1932 and 1939, and when Bing formed his production company in 1945, he hired Tuttle to direct its first feature. Bing once named him and Leo McCarey as his two favorite directors — a remarkable statement, as McCarey was widely ranked with John Ford and Frank Capra as one of America's greatest filmmakers in the years between the advent of sound and the end of the Second World War.

Yet Tuttle was soon forgotten, his reputation demolished by his craven performance before the House Un-American Activities Committee in 1951.[12] Tuttle had been a Communist Party member for eleven years, breaking off in early 1949. After a witness named him and his career was put on the line, he signed a loyalty oath and appeared as a friendly witness, confirming thirty-six names the committee already had and inadvertently adding three more (wives of the accused). Tuttle's liberal politics were well known in the years before he joined the party and dismayed no one, certainly not Bing. During the filming of *The Big Broadcast,* Tuttle introduced Bing to John Bright, a screenwriter *(The Public Enemy)* who was raising money for the defense of the Scottsboro Boys. Bright asked Bing for a contribution. "He asked me one simple question," Bright remembered, and quoted Bing as follows: "Nine colored boys in the South accused of rape. They didn't do it. How much do you want?"[13] Bing wrote him a check for $1,000.

Looking back on that incident, Bright attempted to explain Bing's generosity. "He had worked with black people in the music industry all his life and had never shown any prejudice. That was the early thirties. Later on, he became very, very reactionary."[14] In truth, he was far from reactionary and rarely discussed politics at all. Despite his resentment of confiscatory wartime taxes and a traditional Catholic's distrust of change, his conservative inclinations tended to be undercut by his live-and-let-live disposition. Nancy Briggs learned as much in 1960, when she worked as Basil Grillo's secretary in the largely Republican offices of Bing Crosby Enterprises, Inc. "I was at the water cooler getting a drink," she recalled. "I was so proud, I had just gotten a JFK button. Larry [Crosby] came back and said, 'You don't wear that in this office.' And all of a sudden there was Bing — he just appeared out of nowhere. He said, 'Larry, you don't tell anybody what to do in this office.' He said, 'You don't tell anybody not to wear a JFK button or a Republican button or a Communist button if they want to.' Larry kind of folded and Bing said, 'Good luck, Nancy,' and walked off."[15]

Bing was tagged a conservative for criticizing FDR during the 1940 election, for appearing in a Chesterfield-sponsored propaganda short during the Korean War, and for supporting religious causes, like The Christophers (a progressive organization also supported by Jack Benny and Eddie "Rochester" Anderson), yet he let it be known that he opposed the Vietnam War, advocated the legalization of marijuana, and despised Richard Nixon. In politics, he publicly declared himself only once, for Wendell Willkie, the most liberal Republican presidential candidate of the century, after Theodore Roosevelt. He instantly regretted it, and though he later appeared on radio with Democrat Alben Barkley (Truman's vice president) and played golf with President Kennedy, he never again professed sides, never allowed himself to be exploited by or photographed with a politician. Basil Grillo said, "He didn't believe actors should be influencing people on serious matters. It didn't make any difference what it was . . . he thought actors should not use their prominence that way."[16]

Like several men important in Bing's career (Buddy DeSylva, David Butler, Stuart Erwin), Frank Tuttle had worked with Dixie before he encountered Bing, directing her in Clara Bow's futile comeback, *No Limit,* which Dixie had filmed shortly after her wedding. But he bonded quickly with Bing, who, like many actors, enjoyed working with Tuttle. "He was very much a gentleman," Tuttle's daughter Helen Votachenko observed of her father, "not at all abrasive."[17] Bing especially admired his comedic talent. With few exceptions, most of his work was bland, but given the right story and performers, Tuttle could summon forth a visual flair worthy of his masters, Ernst

Lubitsch and René Clair. He made his name with the startlingly inventive 1926 Eddie Cantor silent comedy, *Kid Boots,* and in 1933 he directed Cantor's finest talkie, *Roman Scandals,* the giddiest anti-fascist pro-socialist picture of Hollywood's golden age. Today Tuttle is best remembered for the 1942 Graham Greene thriller, *This Gun for Hire,* the scathing portrait of capitalist venality that paired and made stars of Alan Ladd and Veronica Lake. But *The Big Broadcast,* his thirty-ninth picture, is perhaps his most charming film. It not only launched Bing but initiated a successful series at Paramount and helped revive the benighted musical, which got an even bigger boost a few months later with the release of Warner Bros.' *42nd Street.*

An homage to René Clair,[18] who pioneered the blending of musical and visual effects in such influential films as *Sous les Toits de Paris* and *Le Million, The Big Broadcast* is a brisk confection that marries song, sex, comedy, and trickery and might almost be considered an American *Le Million,* with radio replacing opera as its setting. Tuttle adapted several of Clair's trademarks, among them long traveling shots, miniature sets, accelerated motion, recitatives, sound effects, and silent sequences, adding his own touches, including animation, visual puns, and clever editing that integrates into a Hollywood setting footage of entertainers (Cab Calloway, Kate Smith, Arthur Tracy, Vincent Lopez, the Mills Brothers, the Boswell Sisters) who were shot at Astoria Studios in New York.

Writer-producer Benjamin Glazer concocted a story, and George Marion Jr. dressed the bare-bones situation with details drawn from Bing's own life. But if Paramount had no qualms about presenting Bing in the role of a reckless, alcoholic libertine, it drew the line at allowing his ears to wave and his pate to shine. Bing was required to spend the better part of a day at the House of Westmore, while Wally Westmore's protégé, Harry Ray, fitted him for a hairpiece and glued back his ears. Wally, who later named Bing his all-time favorite client, flatly refused to work on the singer when he first arrived at Paramount, and tried to discourage the studio from signing him. His animus stemmed from an evening two years earlier when he had taken his wife to hear the Rhythm Boys at the Cocoanut Grove and Bing retched onstage. So it fell to Harry Ray to overcome Bing's aversion to a procedure described by the makeup clan's chronicler, Frank Westmore: Ray had to "stick back the ears and then wrap Crosby's head with a turban until he was sure they'd stay pinned back."[19] Ray tried to convince Bing to have surgery to flatten his ears (recently under-taken by George Raft), but Bing refused, much as he loathed the daily ritual. "It was terrible," Bing remembered. "They put this glue back there and it hurt, it would sting, and after a few days, the skin would get raw. Oh, I hated it. They kept popping out — the lights would be hot and all of a sudden one of these things would pop out, and the director would holler, 'Cut! Fix that guy's ears.'"[20]

Tuttle was more concerned with Bing's acting. After screening the Sennett shorts with Glazer, he expressed his delight with Bing's voice and personality, and concern about his awkwardness: "Bing didn't seem to know what to do with his hands." Tuttle's fears were allayed as soon as they began shooting. "Bing was extremely cooperative and his sense of comedy was first-rate from the opening shot," he wrote. "His approach was casual and he liked to move around. We worked out interesting pieces of business so that he wouldn't have to just stand there and deliver a number." The physical business minimized Bing's tendency to gesticulate, and his acting improved markedly. Tuttle admired Bing's predilection for working with top performers and learning from them, and he got a kick out of Bing's verbal gifts: "Between shots he spoke a language of his own, a slang-enriched Americanese that is almost impossible to describe, but was amusing as it was unique."[21]

Bing did win one argument against Hollywood conventions. He refused to accept top billing, reasoning that if the film tanked, it would sink his career. Although he played the lead role, Bing was second-billed to Stu Erwin, who had a track record in movies. (By contrast, Guy Lombardo refused to appear in *The Big Broadcast* after learning he would be billed below Crosby.)[22] Bing considered his judgment vindicated the following year, when Kate Smith's much ballyhooed *Hello, Everybody!* turned out to be her movie hail and farewell. He believed that if she had been billed as one of many per-formers rather than as the sole reason for making or seeing the pic-ture, she might have survived the debacle. Billing aside, few radio stars were able to make the transition to movies; after Bing, the most successful was Bob Hope, who debuted at Paramount six years later in *The Big Broadcast of 1938*.

Bing never took his stardom for granted. Even when he topped the Quigley box-office poll five years running (an unprecedented achieve-ment), his movie contracts always contained "the Crosby clause," as it became known in the industry, enjoining producers from billing him alone above the title. His insistence on sharing credit — or blame — prompted David O. Selznick to cite him as the smartest man in movies. (Selznick had another reason to value his acuity. In 1937 Bing sent him a note to suggest Hattie McDaniel for the role of Mammy in *Gone With the Wind,* to which Selznick replied, "Dear Bing, Thanks for the suggestion. And also for not wanting to play Scarlett.")[23]

Almost two decades later, when *The Country Girl* was released in 1954, much was made of Bing's courage in playing an alcoholic, because of his own past. Yet from the beginning, his movies were filled with autobiographical references that track every stage in his life, from his drinking days to his love of horses and sports to his problems dealing with his sons. Those allusions range from inside jokes to blatant reenactments and contribute to a portrait of a highly unorthodox film idol, one who always got the girl yet was most admired for playing a celibate. Audiences and critics often failed to notice the darker aspects of his persona and the way it linked Crosby's life and art. Consider *The Big Broadcast.*

The picture opens with a shot of an electric speaker, from which a voice announces, "Clear all stations for the big broadcast!" As the camera pans over a board of publicity photos of radio stars, the performers come alive one by one and sing a few bars of their theme songs, beginning with Bing's peppy strain of "Where the Blue of the Night." During the ensuing credits, an orchestra plays "Please," one of only two songs ("Here Lies Love" is the other) written for the film, and the first of many hits tailored for Bing by the resourceful team of lyricist Leo Robin and composer Ralph Rainger.

The only sound heard in the first episode is the beating of a clock, a ticktocking rhythm to which the action is precisely measured, partly through the use of reverse action, still frames, and other camera tricks. When the sponsor, Mr. Clapsaddle, tromps down the corridor, a terrified cat liquefies and slides under a door. The first words are not spoken but displayed in a wire that fills the screen one word at a time, like the typed opera review in *Citizen Kane:* BING ISN'T HERE YET. Panic ensues. When a station manager motions for Cab Calloway to fill in for Bing, music supplants the ticking and a clarinetist mimes on a rubbery instrument (literally a licorice stick, slang for clarinet). Clapsaddle, who is the president of Griptight Girdles, orders the station to fire Bing — the Griptight Troubadour — for chronic lateness. The scene cuts to accelerated footage of Bing driving a cab through traffic while the cabdriver lounges in the backseat. Bing screeches to the curb and is mobbed by hundreds of women, including an elderly lady who leaps from a wheelchair, all in silence except for the musical score. Disheveled, covered in lipstick, Bing races to the studio in time to sing the last line of "I Surrender, Dear."

Bing is absentminded, we are told, because he is in love with Mona Lowe (Sharon Lynne, whose every appearance is augured by a few bars of Ralph Rainger's "Moanin' Low"), whom he plans to marry. This disturbs Anita, secretary to station manager George Burns, who tells her Bing isn't her type. She sighs, "Yes he is. He's everybody's type. That's the trouble." Anita is played by sloe-eyed Leila Hyams, an alluring former model and vaudevillian whose brief Hollywood career included a couple of shock movies (*Freaks, The Island of Dr. Moreau*) and an enchanting and largely improvised two-minute scene teaching Roland Young to play drums in Leo McCarey's *Ruggles of Red Gap*. The purehearted Anita will surely win Bing from the haughty vamp, or so we think, especially after Mona suddenly elopes with a millionaire.

A trio of telephone operators harmonize over Mona's perfidy, which Bing doesn't know about: "He blew out of here so bright and breezy / And he's probably in some speakeasy." Cut to Stu Erwin as jilted millionaire Leslie McWhinney, getting drunk in the same speak where Bing, unaware that he too has been jilted, is buying rounds. Bing attempts to cheer him up, but is crestfallen to find that Leslie has never heard of Bing Crosby. After learning from a newspaper headline how low Mona is (much as the real Bing learned from a newspaper that Dixie had taken a powder), he gets loaded with Leslie, as Arthur Tracy and his accordion maul "Here Lies Love." A sensational traveling shot through a model of the city shifts the scene to Bing's art deco apartment, where he convinces Leslie that they have no choice but suicide. As soon as he raises the subject, the cinematography changes: Crosby looms in a doorway, Leslie is beset by shadows (a parody of James Whale's horror style at Universal). The radio blares "I'll Be Glad When You're Dead, You Rascal You." They turn on the gas and collapse in a stupor, hallucinating a skull and ghosts and . . . no, not Frankenstein's monster, but Arthur Tracy and his accordion.

Anita drops by with the joyful news that Bing was not fired after all. Finding the men unconscious, she carries them to the bedroom, where the waking Leslie nervously asks Bing, "Are we married?" During a nicely handled mistaken-identity scene about who is in the shower (it's Anita), Bing inadvertently mangles his theme song, substituting *when* for *where* and transposing the lyric ("and the blue of her eyes crowns the gold of her hair"); either no one noticed or no one thought it worth retaking. Anita emerges from the shower and reveals herself as Leslie's beloved and Bing's adoring angel. Encouraged by her to rethink his life and career, Bing deadpans one of his best lines: "You sing into a little hole, year after year. And then you die."

Bing falls for Anita but regrets taking her from the magnanimous Leslie, who buys the troubled radio station and arranges an all-star broadcast to save it. Happily, the plot takes a backseat to a couple of privileged musical interludes: Bing's brief but lively chorus of "Dinah," accompanied by a rhythmic and uncredited bootblack (anticipating Fred Astaire's "A Shine on Your Shoes" number in *The Band Wagon*), and a beautiful "Please" by Bing and Eddie Lang, who was cast at Bing's insistence. Then Mona returns — to a crashing orchestration of her theme — and Bing is once again besotted. She has had her marriage annulled, she declares, and has made off with a fat settlement. Bing, reenacting the Peggy Bernier debacle in Chicago, goes off with her, assuring Leslie he'll be back in plenty of time for the big broadcast. But when the forlorn Leslie tracks him down, Bing gets rid of him by pretending to be soused.

Leslie has a brainstorm: he'll pass off a Crosby recording as the real thing. The rest of the film veers between an extended silent sequence in which Leslie attempts to find a record late at night and interpolations of the radio stars, introduced by their respective announcers (". . . the songbird of the South with her Swanee music, your own Kate Smith"). Unable to locate a playable disc, Leslie commences a caterwauling impersonation of the reckless crooner, backed by Lang. Just then, Bing coolly arrives and croons to his lover, Mona, who sports a black eye (that'll teach her), thereby saving his job while following his worst impulses. Bing goes off with the shameless vamp. Anita settles for Leslie.

Critics complained that the film and Bing's character were unbelievable. *Variety* was unusually captious, grousing that *The Big Broadcast* was neither exposé nor documentary, predicting that it would fail everywhere but "the hinterland." The critic nonetheless considered the picture a "credit to Crosby as a screen juve possibility" despite a "dizzy and uncertain role which makes him misbehave as no human being does." (The piety of that last comment was ingested with more than a grain of hilarity by Bing's friends.) The reviewer was especially troubled by scenes depicting Bing's tardiness, which, he insisted, could have "no foundation in fact, for the biggest of ether names know better." He was also affronted by Sharon Lynne's false bosom ("so artificial it's bound to be noticed by the femmes") and bangs.[24]

Some reviewers revised the script in their heads, refusing to accept what they had seen, for example, the *Spokesman-Review:* "Bing is unable to decide whether he prefers Miss Lynne, the siren, or Leila Hyams, the sweet girl from Texas, and in the end Miss Hyams turns out to be Erwin's old sweetheart from the great open spaces."[25] Others ignored the plot to announce the arrival of a new star. The *New York Daily Mirror:* "No radio star ever has photographed better, or faced the cameras with greater poise and assurance than the pleasing Bing."[26] The *New York American:* "Bing Crosby is the star, make no mistake about it. The 'Blue of the Night' boy is a picture personality, as he demonstrated in his two-reelers. He has a camera face and a camera presence. Always at ease, he troupes like a veteran."[27] In its newspaper advertisements, Paramount cut to the chase: "Stars of Stage, Screen and Radio in a lightning-fast, romantic drama of Radioland! Listen in on the hilarious secrets and romances your radios never reveal!"

The picture did only fair business in New York, where the radio stars could be seen in person, but made a fortune around the country, far surpassing expectations. The studios turned out eleven musicals in 1932 (down from seventy-eight in 1930), and five made money, four of them for Paramount: two Maurice Chevalier classics (Ernst Lubitsch and George Cukor's *One Hour With You,* Rouben Mamoulian's *Love Me Tonight*); the Marx Brothers' *Horse Feathers;* and *The Big Broadcast.* The fifth was Leo McCarey's Eddie Cantor entry, *The Kid from Spain,* for Samuel Goldwyn. But Chevalier bedroom farces were on the censors' death list — even *The Big Broadcast* put them on their guard (Leila Hyams's shower scene, revealing her ankles, was excised in Ohio and Pennsylvania) — and Cantor and the Marxes represented a fading stage tradition transferred to movies.[28]

Bing embodied something native and new. Paramount, reeling from the Depression, banked its future on him. Despite several popular films, the studio lost nearly $16 million in 1932, and in the first days of 1933, Paramount-Publix went into receivership. After a bloodbath that consumed its production heads and pushed even foxy Adolph Zukor "upstairs," the company was reorganized as Paramount Pictures. In the time between the premiere of *The Big Broadcast* at New York's Paramount (October 14) and the bankruptcy hearing (January 26), the studio offered Bing a $300,000 contract for five pictures to be made over three years and announced that he would star in *College Humor* come spring. Other studios had also bid for Crosby's services, but Paramount had two advantages: it was the first major studio to come calling, and it was home base to Gary Cooper, whose friendship and advice meant a lot to Bing. In many respects, the two men were alike. Privately, what Frank Tuttle said of Cooper applied equally well to Bing: "Despite his friendly warmth, he never let you get really close."[29] They were the sort of friends who could spend days together on a fishing boat without feeling the slightest inclination to unburden themselves. As film actors, they were perceived as strong, solitary, men's men, taken to heart by a public that gleaned a comforting familiarity in their reticence.

In December *Variety* reported, FILM MUSICALS ARE BLOOMING.[30] Hollywood was beginning to understand the kind of entertainment a bowed and bleeding nation demanded — not the Lubitsch touch but a hearty American slap on the back.

16

BROTHER, CAN YOU SPARE A DIME?

He would sing at the drop of a hat. He would sing all the time. He'd sing when he was riding a bicycle, he'd sing when he was walking down the street, he'd sing on a train — he had a singing habit.
— Rosemary Clooney (1991)[1]

Launched by *The Big Broadcast,* Bing Crosby's career soared in a steady arc, a trajectory ascending with greater velocity every year until, at its late-1940s pinnacle, he would be transformed from an actor-singer-star into an incontestable national icon, a match for motherhood, apple pie, and baseball. Pundits would resort to epic encomiums, saluting him, not untypically, as "the first of the Universal Common Men."[2] Even before then, the adulation was such that, in the recollection of his eldest son, it blurred the boundaries between "God and dad, because everybody revered both of them." Looking back at his early childhood, Gary Crosby recalled, "People crossing streets, running up to the side of the car, or, if I was in some place, coming over and kneeling in front of me to tell me what a wonderful man he was and what a thrill it must be to be his son, and how they loved him so much, and he had done so much for them, and his singing was so great, and it went on and on and on, the way people spoke about God."[3]

Before a society invests its dreams in an individual, particularly one without military power, it must detect in him the exemplary tribal disposition. Bing was quintessentially American, cool and upbeat, never pompous, belligerent, or saccharine, never smug or superior. He looked down on no one and up to no one. In an age when other nations invested everything in despots, America could feel proud not only of Bing but of its pride in Bing.

The transformation was gradual and largely unforeseeable, ultimately tethering Bing and the country in a pact neither could afford to break. Having left his wildness behind him and having attained prosperity far beyond that of Whiteman or the "ancient king" of his high-school reverie, Bing was able to mine a magical perquisite of old Hollywood, the power to remake oneself. He was free to choose and reject aspects of his past, or images from his imagination, to concoct the better man he resolved to be. In Hollywood, shopgirls became queens, cowards warriors, gay men Don Juans, scoundrels gentlemen, and gentlemen mugs. Bing created the most astute role of the era, and he played it exceedingly well for forty-five years — never more engagingly than during the 1930s, when his metamorphosis was fresh and providential. During Prohibition he had been a drunk. During the Depression he became, FDR-like, an aristocrat of the people: a North Star of stability, decency, and optimism.

Yet while he allowed the Paramount publicity department and brother Larry to reinvent him in a blizzard of press handouts, he found the conversion from entertainer to secular priest disturbing. It violated his sense of irony and modesty. "That modesty is real, realer than anybody understood," Barry Ulanov, his first biographer, would later reflect. "Quite apart from faith, in the sense of something you believe in and follow, he had in his education an introduction to some of the greatest thinkers the world has ever known — tough, philosophical minds." In short, Ulanov argued, he was too well educated *not* to be modest. "Audiences felt that about him," he continued, "and didn't feel envious — they didn't feel this guy should not have so much talent, success, and money. I never heard that, not once. Audiences were knocked out by him because they recognized in him a person who did not exaggerate his skills, who even had doubts about those skills."[4] The taller he stood, the more Crosby ducked flattery. "He is a very odd individual," wrote Adolph Zukor of the man who rescued his movie empire from insolvency. "He doesn't like to listen to praise. He likes to listen to criticism."

Modesty sobered his ambition without weakening it. Though Bing insisted he was a mildly talented, profoundly lucky entertainer (never an artist), he did not turn to Providence to guide his career; he relied on hard work and astute, obstinate bargaining. Bing had reason to credit his success to the help and advice of others, yet he was the one who pulled the strings in forging an entertainment corporation without precedent. If Bing was disinclined to make claims for his gifts, he wagered aggressively on his market value. His reputation for knowing his own mind grew in the early 1930s as he played simultaneous career chess with the bosses of movies, records, and radio, casually moving his pieces until one opponent after another conceded defeat.

He knew that however much he might enrich himself, he could only enrich his masters more. As they accepted the unassailable logic of his position, they lined up for a piece of the action. The emerging house of Crosby served as a template for subsequent entertainers who gambled on the same trifecta: first recordings, then radio or television, finally Hollywood. Only Frank Sinatra in the forties, Elvis Presley in the fifties, and Barbra Streisand in the sixties, each working the Crosby strategy, came within hailing distance of his success — though a great many others tried — and only Bing and, to a far lesser degree, Sinatra enjoyed a consistently successful broadcasting career, as opposed to specials and guest appearances. But career statistics tell only a part of the story. No other pop icon has ever been so thoroughly, lovingly *liked* — liked and trusted. Bing's naturalness made him credible to all, regardless of region, religion, race, or gender. He was our most authentic chameleon, mirroring successive eras — through Prohibition, depression, war, anxiety, and affluence — without ever being dramatic about it. He was discreet and steady. He was family.

His later success on all fronts was so profound, it is difficult to believe that in 1932, while Paramount was preparing to launch him as a major film star, Bing thought he might be washed up on the air. His association with CBS had soured — perhaps, he feared, for good. After Cremo canceled him and he returned to Los Angeles, Bing continued to appear for CBS on a sustaining show that paid him no salary except for a default guarantee of $400, should he not have a theatrical job in any given week. CBS was motivated to make certain he did, not only to save the fee but because the network booked his vaudeville appearances for a 10 percent commission. As if those terms weren't invidious enough, CBS asked Bing (and other artists) to accept a 15 percent cut in June, promising a raise when his contract was renewed. He agreed, only to learn on July 15, when the old contract expired, that CBS demanded an additional cut of 20 percent, reducing his default payments to $250. Again he consented, waiving the promised raise and taking the 20 percent cut. But when the new contract arrived on July 18, two weeks into the production of *The Big Broadcast,* he discovered that CBS's artists bureau had increased its commission for his concert performances. CBS was treating him like a mark. That evening, an hour before his broadcast, Crosby informed the network's New York office that he would not appear. A week later he casually announced that when the picture wrapped, he would take off for the Mexican coast on a fishing trip.[5]

But Bing was less confident than he sounded. He postponed the fishing excursion two weeks and appeared free of charge on *California Melodies,* an evening series on the CBS affiliate, KHJ. In *Variety's* interpretation, Bing was "giving his services gratis once a week . . . to show that CBS can't do without him."[6] Ev flew to New York, assuring him that the free broadcasts were having a softening effect. Bing left for his vacation in mid-August and spent two weeks cruising Mexico's waters, deep-sea fishing with Eddie Lang, Lennie Hayton, and actors Lew Ayres and Nick Stuart, returning with an ill-suited if symbolically carefree mustache. When he learned that CBS would not budge, he refused to broadcast until a sponsor was contracted. Not an easy task. The public may have been clamoring for Bing, but the Depression had advertisers anxious and uncertain.

Meanwhile, his theatrical appearances drew capacity crowds in Oakland, Los Angeles, Glendale, Pasadena, Riverside, Pomona, and San Bernardino. He broke Jolson's house record at San Francisco's Fox Theater, taking in $40,000 for the week. On September 16, the day after he closed at the Fox, Bing recorded for the first time since May. "Please" was timed for the premiere of *The Big Broadcast,* and its punning lyric shaped a melody that ideally suited Bing's style. Whole notes at the beginning and end of the leading phrase ("Please lend your little ear to my pleas") showcase Bing's beseeching timbre, the first generating a hiccupy mordent and dramatic entrance. Bing's record, with Anson Weeks's band and Lang's guitar, was an enormous success, topping sales charts in November and December — an early example of marketing synergy between movies, records, and radio. Paramount adopted "Please" as the title for a Crosby two-reeler and required him to reprise it in his second feature film, *College Humor*. The song remained a staple of his career: He re-recorded it in 1940, scoring a second hit, and parodied it nearly twenty years after that for a TV skit in which his sons instruct him in rock 'n' roll, turning the mordent into a Presleyan split vowel ("pli-ease"). One young listener who discovered the song in those years was John Lennon, who credited it as the inspiration for the Beatles' "Please Please Me."

Those successes worked in Everett's favor as he labored to put Bing back on radio. Working against him, in addition to his brother's increasing reputation for willfulness after the CBS walkout, was corporate suspicion (perhaps mixed with desire) that the rage for Crosby, though heating up, might fizzle out. Under the circumstances, no one knew for sure if Everett's formidable asking price was high or reasonable or, just possibly, low.

The most powerful of advertisers was the tobacco industry, which shamelessly marketed cigarettes with the flapdoodle once lavished on snake oil. The carnage wrought by tobacco was first noticed in the early 1930s, with the increase in lung cancer; in 1932 the *American Journal of Cancer* traced the disease directly to cigarette tar. Cigarettes had been tagged coffin nails long before the turn of the century, but those imprecations were often dismissed as puritanical caution against anything pleasurable. Big tobacco, with a pleasurably addictive product and infinite funds, blithely promised better digestion, weight control, and improved speaking and singing abilities. Camel urged a regimen of five cigarettes at Thanksgiving dinner, one after each course; Lucky Strike claimed support from "20,679 Physicians."[7] Everett opened negotiations with Chesterfield.

Bing and Dixie left for New York on October 5, arriving as "Please" began topping sales lists everywhere. They lived in New York for the next five and a half months, until filming began on *College Humor*. While Everett worked to nail down a sponsor, Bing secured himself a new agent at Mills-Rockwell, the powerful musical concern whose client list included Duke Ellington, Cab Calloway, the Mills Brothers, Glen Gray, Don Redman, and Victor Young. An offshoot of the Rockwell-O'Keefe Theatrical Agency, it was run by Irving Mills, Tommy Rockwell, and Cork O'Keefe, who lined up November concert bookings as Everett hammered away at Chesterfield and Bing enjoyed weeks of suspenseful leisure.

October 14 was a memorable day. It began with Bing recording three songs: "Here Lies Love" from the picture, as well as two songs he established as standards, Irving Berlin's "How Deep Is the Ocean?," and his collaboration with Victor Young and lyricist Ned Washington, "I Don't Stand a Ghost of a Chance with You."[8] Within hours *The Big Broadcast* began its run at the Paramount, establishing him at last as a Hollywood player. In the evening, while shmoozing on the street near the Friars Club, Bing was introduced to Bob Hope, a fast-talking comic and vaudevillian then appearing on Rudy Vallée's radio show and on Broadway in *Ballyhoo of 1932*. Bing's friendliness surprised and gratified Hope. They were the same age; Bing was twenty-six days older, though his purported 1904 birthdate convinced Bob that he was himself the older man.[9] But Bing's career had advanced well beyond that of Hope's. Six weeks later they shared a bill at the Capitol Theater, with Bing headlining and Bob (*Ballyhoo of 1932* had flopped) as emcee.

The Capitol engagement lasted only a week, December 2–8, but that was long enough for Bing and Hope to dream up routines that emerged as unexpected highlights on a workaday bill with comic acrobats, radio impressionists, and the Abe Lyman band. "I did an act, you know, impressions," Hope recalled, "and so I talked Bing into doing it at the Capitol and it just played like gangbusters. We'd play two politicians meeting in the street and we'd say hi, hi, and then we'd go into each others' pockets, or two conductors who end up dueling with their batons, and it went over so big — stuff they really laughed at."[10] Their chemistry blossomed between shows at a nearby saloon, O'Reilly's, where the two traded show-business tales and quips and made each other laugh. Bing, a model audience for anyone he thought funny, flourished in the presence of gifted performers, and Hope admired his confidence, speed, and ease — his willingness to try new things. "Bing's career was doing pretty good, coming along," Bob said, "but he was just the same then as he always was, a good straight-ahead guy."[11]

Reviewers who caught only the first day's shows missed out. *Variety* praised "Bu-bu-bu-Bing" for his "baritoning" and lauded Lang as "a guitarist whose swell strumming detracts at first but eventually helps out the Crosby singing," ignoring the rest of the bill.[12] The *New York Herald Tribune* cheered Bing for a "merry return, combining songs and comedy in a pleasing act" and added that Hope's material was old but effective.[13] No one wrote of the Crosby-Hope interplay, but Bob's brother returned with a (silent) movie camera and captured their infectious energy. Hope broke big the next year, playing a lead in Jerome Kern's *Roberta,* six years before making his first movie with Bing.

After months of dickering, Chesterfield signed Bing to a thirteen-week contract, two CBS broadcasts per week at $2,000, beginning January 4, 1933, with Lennie Hayton conducting. Chesterfield initially offered the show to NBC, which Bing tried to interest in creating a broadcasting outlet in San Francisco, permitting him more time to make movies. NBC seemed sympathetic, but those talks ended when Lucky Strike, an NBC sponsor, objected to a rival cigarette company's being represented on the network. Chesterfield knew the feeling: it had stalled sealing Bing's contract on the grounds that his Cremo connection was too fresh in the public mind.[14] Chesterfield decided seven months was an appropriate buffer to rid Bing of the Cremo taint.

For Bing, who smoked cigarettes when he did not have a pipe, the Chesterfield deal marked the beginning of an on-and-mostly-off relationship that lasted twenty years, producing two radio shows, *The Music That Satisfies* (January–April 1933) and *The Bing Crosby Show* (1949–52) and several print campaigns. The association troubled him and his mother, who badgered him not to shill for tobacco. But Chesterfield had given him what he considered a badly needed break, and he maintained the affiliation partly out of loyalty. Even so, he refused to be shown in print ads with a cigarette in his mouth, especially after a magazine ran an ad in which the art director had penciled one in. In a 1944 ad he neatly avoids the product altogether. Pictured at a desk, its open drawer overflowing with cigarette cartons, an improbably well-dressed Bing reflects, "There's no friend like an old friend and that's how I've felt about Chesterfield ever since I first sang for them several years ago."[15]

As soon as the radio deal was signed, Paramount — its executives flaunting the success of *The Big Broadcast* while fighting off creditors — announced that *College Humor* would go before the cameras in April, after the Chesterfield show ended. The studio was treading water, chaotically. Until 1931, when ticket sales sharply declined, Paramount had ignored the Depression, acquiring new theaters, a music division, and massive debt. Now the studio filed for bankruptcy, and in the course of a bitter restructuring, two of Hollywood's pioneers, Jesse Lasky and B. P. Schulberg, were forced out. Adolph Zukor, whose extravagant policies helped put the company in jeopardy, was appointed chairman of the board, a face-saving charade to camouflage his removal from the seat of power. A lot was riding on Bing.

Crosby, too, had avoided facing the Depression in his work. But in the months before he launched *The Music That Satisfies* and during the weeks it aired, he resumed a prolific recording schedule. At an early-morning session on October 25, he addressed the Depression musically for the first time. Two of the three planned songs were negligible items by Harry Woods (whose "Side by Side" had done well for the Rhythm Boys). With Hayton conducting an ensemble of five winds, four strings, and rhythm, Bing began with a firm reading of "Linger a Little Longer in the Twilight," extending to his mate a promise to "dream our cares away," then whistling like a chirpy bird. "We're a Couple of Soldiers" is a maudlin muddle about combating hardship with patriotic diligence: "Trouble and hard luck we face with a grin / Like regular soldiers we never give in." Hayton's arrangement begins with marching brasses, and as Bing sings the second chorus, a slight flutter suggests he might crack up, which is precisely what happened on the second take, the first of the semilegendary Crosby breakdowns, known for his quick-witted and off-color ad-libs. Bing sings with authority for more than two minutes, until Eddie Lang waffles an arpeggio that Tommy Dorsey critiques in an extended raspberry, convulsing the singer. What makes the ensuing minute hilarious is Bing's and the band's insistence on completing the take as he steadies himself for a measure or two and then cracks up again. At the coda, he ad-libs: "We're a couple of nances, Uncle Salvi and me. Station house!" *Nance* is period slang for a homosexual; Uncle Salvi is Eddie Lang (born Salvatore Massaro); the station house is showbiz overstatement for the fate of performing truants.

The session grew suddenly serious for the next selection, a song from a new Broadway revue, *Americana,* with a melody by Jay Gorney and an emphatic lyric by E. Y. ("Yip") Harburg.[16] Instead of trite metaphors, "Brother, Can You Spare a Dime?" paints vivid images of veterans ("half a million boots went slogging through hell"), laborers, and farmers who believed they were "building a dream," only to find themselves destitute and forgotten. Bing recorded his version three weeks after *Americana* opened. Brunswick rushed the platter to stores, and within two weeks it was the best-selling record in the nation — the one Tin Pan Alley hit that addressed the darkness in American life. Columbia quickly issued a version by Rudy Vallée that begins with a spoken introduction (he describes the song as "poignant and different"),[17] and Jolson sang it on his radio show. But other versions pale beside Bing's, a perfectly pitched statement of protest and empathy, dignified but not somber, rueful but not bitter, heroic but not overwrought. As Studs Terkel would later note, he "understates [the song] beautifully," all the better to allow the words to "explode."[18] Bing's record emerged as an emblem of the era.[19]

After Bing recorded his single perfect take of "Brother, Can You Spare a Dime?," emotions ran high in the studio, and Bing's way of diffusing them was to swing some jazz. Lennie Hayton was supposed to conclude the session with a couple of piano solos, but he never got around to them. Instead, Bing instigated a duet with him on Victor Young's first hit, recently revived by the Mills Brothers, "Sweet Sue — Just You." The rollicking result is in some respects as stunning as the number that preceded it, though it remained a secret for thirty-five years. Bing and Lennie claimed the tune in a loose treatment that begins with stride piano in the style of Fats Waller. Bing enters cocksure, coolly exchanging phrases with Lennie and deftly interpolating — in his scat chorus — a passage from the solo Bix Beiderbecke played on an otherwise bombastic 1928 recording by Paul Whiteman.[20] He is bright and moving, as if tempered by the Depression song. Yet Kapp rejected "Sweet Sue," which did not see the light of day until 1967.

Days before Bing's "Brother, Can You Spare a Dime?" achieved instant prominence, Franklin D. Roosevelt was elected president. Though neither man was especially happy about it, Roosevelt and Crosby became associated in the public's mind as twin forces against the unknown. Just as he had haplessly incarnated the excesses of Prohibition, Bing would emerge as a source of strength and community in that precarious era when parents dreaded the approach of Christmas, and bank robber John Dillinger commanded grudging admiration. There were those who longed for take-charge guys like they had in Europe — Mussolini, who made the trains run on time, and Hitler, soon to be appointed chancellor of Germany. From 1929 Studebaker marketed an automobile called The Dictator. But most sought the reassurance FDR inspired as a man of the people, no matter how highborn, and the reassurance they found in Crosby, an entertainer of the people, a straight shooter and good guy, with a voice as resonant and natural as every Joe imagined he produced in the shower and as chivalrous as every Jane imagined of her heart's desire. Bing, approaching thirty, had no real competition for the job. In the sound of his voice, people knew who they were and where they stood.[21]

After vacationing with Dixie in Miami Beach and playing a week at a theater in Baltimore, Bing debuted his Chesterfield series on January 4, 1933; he was on twice a week, Wednesdays and Saturdays, from 9:00 to 9:15. Arguing that listeners might be tired of "Where the Blue of the Night" and wanting to purge memories of his previous affiliation, Bing's sponsor urged him to change his theme, so for a short while he used "Just an Echo in the Valley," one of his sappier records, which consequently became a major hit. Once again Bing was prohibited from speaking on air; Norman Brokenshire did the announcing. On the first broadcast he sang "Please," "Love Me Tonight," "How Deep Is the Ocean?," and, because of time constraints, half of "Echo in the Valley." Hayton conducted an instrumental number. *Variety* found it "highly palatable stuff if not particularly distinguished. Crosby and Hayton are both adept but the presentation is quite formula."[22] The announcer was criticized for his "rather saccharine overly benign wordage." Radio fans had no such reservations. In February the show ranked ninth in *Variety*'s nationwide survey, and in a poll limited to singers, Bing ranked first, trailed by Vallée, Downey, and Columbo.[23]

He continued to pack them in at theaters as well. Irving Mills negotiated an impressive $3,000 for a week at the Albee in Brooklyn (he shared the bill with vaudeville legends Weber and Fields). In March Bing returned to the Capitol Theater to share a bill with Eddy Duchin's band and Milton Berle, who relished the marquee — BERLE DUCHIN CROSBY — though, in fact, Bing hijacked the audience, performing numerous encores and clowning with the comedian for the finale.[24]

It is tempting to imagine that every time Bing stepped out on a stage in 1933, his last year as a concert performer until 1975, aspiring singers experienced jolts of recognition. Within ten years the pop-music terrain would be crowded with his musical offspring — among them Perry Como, Dick Todd, Herb Jeffries, Bob Eberle, Buddy Clark, Andy Russell, Bob Carroll, Dick Haymes, Bob Stewart, and Tony Martin, who remembered, "We all loved to sing like Bing — to listen to Bing was taking lessons."[25] In the same period, Bing's influence reached country singers like Jimmy Wakely, Roy Rogers, and Eddie Arnold, and European singers like Paris's Jean Sablon or London's Jack Cooper, Denny Dennis, and Sam Costa, who noted, "All the singers tried to be Crosbys. You were either a high Crosby or a low Crosby."[26] Even Count Basie's majestic blues shouter Jimmy Rushing revised his style after hearing Bing. Rushing, who named Bing, Louis Armstrong, and Ethel Waters as his favorites, was "a high Crosby," according to Costa's formulation.[27] The finest "low Crosby" was Billy Eckstine, who covered numerous Crosby hits and bred a generation of bass-baritones known among musicians as the Black Bings.[28]

Yet none of those singers, however popular or distinctive, provided Crosby with any real competition. Only one singer challenged him. Right before Bing played the Capitol, he and Eddie Lang worked a week at Jersey City's Journal Square Theater. In attendance, with his girlfriend and future wife, Nancy Barbato, was seventeen-year-old Frank Sinatra, who credited Bing's performance that day with his own decision to embark on a musical career. Sinatra set out to fulfill his ambition immediately; by 1934 he was singing with the Hoboken Four, with whom he auditioned for Major Bowes and his *Original Amateur Hour*. One of the quartet's numbers was an imitation of the Crosby–Mills Brothers record, "Shine."

Despite his tremendous impact, Crosby was going through a transitional period, as he attempted to jettison mannerisms in favor of a more level, straightforward, speechlike approach. At the same time, he was helping define the American songbook by introducing a batch of important new tunes. For Sinatra, Bing's 1933 recordings provided a trove of durable material as well as a guide to vocal devices he could use, reject, or revise. Consider Bing's hit record of "Street of Dreams," with its ominous lyric by Sam Lewis and dramatically ascending melody by Victor Young.[29] Bing begins with a dark rendition of the verse, establishing the theme of opium-induced dreams; stresses the first chorus with mordents; and, inspired by Tommy Dorsey's breathless chorus (thirty-two bars without a rest), demonstrates his skillful phrasing in the finale as he glides without a pause into and out of the release. Sinatra, nine years later, discarded the sinister verse as well as Bing's fluttery mordents but retained the breathless phrasing, meticulous enunciation, and feeling for the song's drama.

If Sinatra thought Bing's 1933 records dated, Bing himself seems to have chafed at the pedestrian arrangements. In "Try a Little Tenderness," a love song peculiarly germane to the Depression ("women do get weary / wearing the same shabby dress"), he spurs the sluggish tempo with adornments like the unexpected high note on *happi-NESS*. In a recording with Guy Lombardo of "You're Getting to Be a Habit with Me," he counters the band's hopelessly rigid inflections with his own infallible rhythmic pulse and caps his first chorus with a blues locution. Surprisingly, Lombardo's clipped brasses, buttered reeds, and staccato rhythms propel Bing (much as Lombardo-style arrangements had roused Louis Armstrong to fanciful flights a couple of years earlier). Bing's embellishments are relatively mild, but his time is vigorous, particularly on "You're Beautiful Tonight, My Dear," a second-rate song made unaccountably affecting in his sure interpretation. His buoyant scat solo and reprise on "Young and Healthy" are insurgent statements of self in the face of Lombardo's stuffy rectitude. "Young and Healthy" and "You're Getting to Be a Habit with Me," both from *42nd Street,* were combined on a platter that topped sales charts twice within a month — first one side, then the flip.

For Bing's next sessions, Kapp returned him to the arms of old friends, but despite Bing's evident enthusiasm, the results are uneven. Lennie Hayton backed him with a crew that included Artie Shaw, Tommy Dorsey, trumpeter Sterling Bose, and forgotten drummer Stan King, who knew how to drive home an out-chorus, as on "I've Got the World on a String." Yet the session's highlight turned out to be the last record by Bing and the Mills Brothers, "My Honey's Lovin' Arms." Bing vigorously romps the first chorus, the brothers imitate instruments in the second, and Bing ad-libs against the scrim of their harmonies in the third. This savory performance boasts a rapid-fire in-joke that Crosby expert Fred Reynolds has noticed: in the third chorus (of take A), Bing does an easily overlooked but unmistakable Jolson imitation on the line "I know that I belong." Bing's teaming with the Mills Brothers had been initiated by the singers, not Kapp, and from now on it would continue only on the radio.

A couple of weeks later, with four violins added to the mix, Bing covered Ruth Etting's hit "You've Got Me Crying Again" and gave his all to the Depression tearjerker "What Do I Care, It's Home," almost overcoming Roy Turk's quatrain: "It's a weathered shanty / On a barren mountainside / You may think it's rough / But mom and I are satisfied." The material was marginally better at a session with the Dorsey Brothers, for which Bing played a supporting role, singing single choruses as he had in his Whiteman days. Two faux-preacher numbers, "Stay on the Right Side of the Road" and "Someone Stole Gabriel's Horn," elicit his asides in southern dialect. Yet Bing and the band — including the masterly trumpet player Bunny Berigan — grill the smart, energetic arrangements to a turn.

On nearly all his recordings, at his radio broadcasts, and in theaters, Bing was backed by Eddie Lang, sitting at his right elbow, sharing a microphone, steadying him with strummed chords, leading him with calculated arpeggios, pacing him with a lissome yet resolute accompaniment. He "just made you feel like you wanted to ride and go," Bing said.[30] They looked out for each other on- and offstage. "Eddie had everything to do with the radio show," said Barry Ulanov, "but he also took a great deal of responsibility for Bing as a person, Bing as a singer, Bing as someone who could be a front man for the music that Lang loved."[31] In return, Bing stipulated that Paramount include Eddie in all his projects, specifically guaranteeing him a speaking role in *College Humor*. Lang's Paramount contract, netting him $15,000 per Crosby picture plus a salary of $1,000 a week while touring, made him the highest-paid sideman in the country.

Eddie was apprehensive about his part in *College Humor*. He was suffering from chronic and painful laryngitis and worried that he might not be up to it. Bing encouraged him to have his tonsils removed, and the doctor assured Eddie that a tonsillectomy was a safe and simple procedure. The operation was scheduled for Sunday morning, March 26, at ten, so that Eddie would be able to leave for the Coast with Bing on Wednesday. A few days earlier Dixie had asked Kitty Lang to join her and Sue Carol on a steamship voyage that would take them to California via stops in Bermuda and Cuba. Kitty wanted to go but told Dixie that she could not leave Eddie during the operation and would travel by train with the boys. As he was wheeled into the elevator, Eddie asked her to buy a racing form so he could pick her a winner on Monday.

When Eddie came out of surgery, the doctor told Kitty he was fine but heavily sedated and suggested she go home. She refused, and remained by his bed for hours with a racing form in her lap, comforted by a nurse who told her that patients often slept that long. At 5:00 P.M., the nurse took his pulse and raced from the room. An oxygen machine was wheeled in, but he had hemorrhaged and it was too late. "I must have screamed, for I remember hearing a child start screaming, too, and realized that it was someone down the hall and that I must not frighten this child," Kitty recalled. A doctor gave her an injection, and she felt her throat constrict until she could not speak. "Someone must have called Bing on the phone, he was at the Friars Club. Needless to say, he came right over and into the waiting room. He fell on his knees with his head in my lap and started to sob, 'Kitty, he was my best friend.'"[32]

When the news was announced, the radio networks observed a minute of silence for the luminous twenty-nine-year-old musician who more than anyone else invented jazz guitar in the era before Django Reinhardt and Charlie Christian. Kitty waived the autopsy, and Eddie's brother Tom made arrangements to send the body home to Philadelphia, where friends and relatives filled the family home. Eddie's father, who had built him his first instrument out of a cigar box and thread, paced the floor for days while Kitty sat in a trance. She lost thirty pounds. "I remember someone touching my shoulder and telling me that Bing had arrived to take me to the funeral. Poor dear Bing, my heart went out to this great man who was sitting on top of the world as the greatest singer the world had ever known, and yet he lost the one companion who had been instrumental in putting him there."[33]

The service was hell for Bing, his first taste of the madness of celebrity. He was accustomed to autograph seekers in person and through letters; these he efficiently answered, usually plugging his current projects. But until now he had been mobbed only in *The Big Broadcast,* and that was for laughs. At Eddie's service, people closed in on him and turned the ceremony into a circus. In their haste "just to touch him," in Kitty's words, they overturned pews and the appalled priest was forced to implore mourners to take their seats. Bing was already phobic about hospitals and funerals, but this was unendurable, an intrusion on his and the family's grief, and he resolved never to let it happen again. A welterweight named Marty Collins volunteered to protect Bing, who was impressed with his manner and effectiveness. Afterward, when Bing and Kitty had a moment alone, he asked her to Los Angeles to stay with him and Dixie, promising her a home as long as she wanted. Dixie had become pregnant during filming of *The Big Broadcast* and was expecting in June. They needed her, he said. Kitty joined them in April, and Bing looked out for her all his life. But a part of Bing died with Eddie, and he never allowed anyone else to get as close.

Bing's public statements were typically reserved, mostly mourning the loss of Eddie's talent. He elaborated a little in 1939, writing that Eddie "had good sense and saved me from many a jam. And I don't mean music session. Naturally, when I got into a musical solo spot, it was a great comfort to have such an artist with me. Eddie made me do my best when the break came, and I give him full credit."[34] Mutual friends were astonished by Bing's seeming lack of emotion. Only a few intimates were allowed to see how tortured he was by Eddie's passing, having advised him to undergo the operation. "Joe Venuti confirmed he was absolutely wrecked," Barry Ulanov said, "and I don't think he was capable of that kind of attachment again."[35] In his 1948 biography, Ulanov suggests that Lang's death hastened Bing's retreat from jazz. But surely the influence of Jack Kapp and the obligations of stardom would have channeled him into the mainstream with or without Eddie. Bing's recordings had long reflected his inclination to move in and out of jazz, and as Ulanov wrote, his jazz style "might have proved too strong for complete public acceptance."[36] Yet in Eddie Lang, he had a partner on- and offstage, a trusted friend with the same musical moorings, the same attitudes, the same rhythmic pulse.

Bing tracked down Dixie in the Caribbean and phoned her to ease the shock of Eddie's death. When Dixie, Sue, and Everett's wife, Naomi (who took Kitty's place on the voyage), arrived in Hollywood, Dixie moved in with Sue. Bing followed on the Santa Fe *Chief,* traveling with Mary Pickford, the eternal waif of silent pictures and a loyal Crosby fan; her companion, Countess DiFrasso (American heiress Dorothy Taylor, subsequently an escort of mobster Bugsy Siegel); and Sue's husband, Nick Stuart. Dixie greeted them at the Pasadena station. Bing and Dixie moved in with Sue and Nick and then rented the Stuarts' home while they traveled. With Paramount paying the musician and line charges, Bing was able to complete his Chesterfield contract on the West Coast. Paramount wanted as much of Bing as it could get. A couple of weeks into *College Humor,* the studio prepared him with a new script *(Too Much Harmony),* to go into production almost immediately. It also announced plans to feature Bing in a musical version of a stage play *Cloudy with Showers* (never made) and a series of two-reel shorts, all of which reinforced his decision to go Hollywood for good.

In anticipation of their first child, the Crosbys began to build their first real home, at 4326 Forman Avenue in the Toluca Lake area. Dixie's dad, Evan Wyatt, supervised the construction, which included a miniature balcony off the front hallway. At a party, actor Jack Oakie asked Wyatt its purpose and was told, "That's so Bing can sing to his guests as they arrive."[37]

Paramount requested Bing to fill out a publicity questionnaire. This time Bing and not Everett provided the answers. Eleven years later Ed Sullivan discovered the form in his files and published it in his syndicated column.[38] It is an illuminating portrait of Bing and the period. Bing gave his New York address (160 West Fifty-ninth Street) as home, his name as Harry Lillis Crosby Jr., and his childhood ambition "to be an actor." His favorite fictional heroes: Robin Hood,

Robinson Crusoe, François Villon.* Real-life hero: Theodore Roosevelt. First radio job: with Al Rinker on KFI, Los Angeles, 1927. First childhood job: selling the *Saturday Evening Post*. Married: Dixie Lee. No children. Five outstanding figures in history: Jesus, Richard the Lion-Hearted, Napoleon, Disraeli, Lincoln. Outstanding figures of 1933: in sports, Babe Ruth; in theater, John Barrymore; in literature, Shaw; in music, Ravel; in politics, Mussolini. Favorite stage actors: Alfred Lunt, Katharine Cornell. Film actors: Helen Hayes, Lee Tracy. Radio artists: Burns and Allen. Comedian: Jimmy Durante. Dish: Lobster diavolo. Flower: gardenia. Jewel: diamond. Axiom: Take it easy. Least favorite color: lavender.

Of which compliments was he most proud?: "Ring Lardner wrote me, saying he was glad I was returning to the air. My wife generally comments favorably on my efforts and my dad maintains I sing better than Jolson. Coming from this unbiased source, I treasure this highly." Favorite fan: "My mother, because she is very sincere and never hesitates to criticize when she figures criticism is due." Did he ever fail to make a broadcast?: "On various occasions, while broadcasting in California, I found the thoroughbred delights of Caliente superior to the prospect of facing a mike." How would he retire: "I would go nicely to California — buy a home, a boat, a car. I'd take up some light business (i.e., buy a piece of a prosperous business); travel abroad a bit; fish and golf in the interim, and visit the various racetracks. And raise a small family." Good memory? "Quick memory, but retentive power bad." Prompt for appointments?: "Yes, that is, lately." Favorite expressions: " 'Yeah, man,' is one of them." What broadcast of his own did he recall with the most pleasure? "Opening night on the Chesterfield program. After all hope had been abandoned, it was infinitely pleasurable after many months to get a break again." Favorite song: "Sweet Sue." Favorite classical number: "Prélude à l'apres-midi d'un faune." Least favorite: "No dislike for anything musical, but Beethoven and Wagner leave me unresponsive." Favorite books: *Of Human Bondage, Point Counter Point, A Farewell to Arms, Round Up* (Ring Lardner). Favorite poets: Keats, Browning, Shelley,

---

*François Villon is today remembered as a very real fifteenth-century French poet. But early in the last century he was transfigured into a popular fictional character in such works as Robert Louis Stevenson's story "Lodging for the Night," Justin H. McCarthy's novel *If I Were King*, and Rudolf Friml's operetta *The Vagabond King*.

Longfellow. Quotation: "'Full many a flower is born to blush unseen and waste its sweetness on the desert air.'" Eccentric? "In dress, tend slightly to the bizarre." Hunches? "Sometimes I bet a hunch on a horse. A horse named Bingo won at Latonia and paid 40 to 1. Professionally, I don't go by hunches."

A year before Sullivan published those answers, humorist H. Allen Smith included a chapter on his attempt to research Bing's life in his book *Life in a Putty Knife Factory* (1943). Allen excerpted a twenty-four-page "bio-book" that Bing filled out at CBS in 1933, which restates and amplifies comments in the Paramount press book, for example, his response to "What would you do if you had a million dollars?" After observing that he would go to California and buy a prosperous business, fish, golf, visit the track, raise a small family, he continues:

> If a million bucks ever came my way, I could doubtless distribute a considerable amount to relatives, etc., in loans, and still have enough to carry out the program described. I'm pretty socialistic in this connection and really don't think anyone is entitled to or should have more than they need to live comfortably. My wants are comparatively simple and with half a million I could possibly scrape along somehow. In point of fact, if I ever connect with the aforesaid amount, I'll wash up.[39]

Small wonder the CBS bio-book was suppressed! In addition to the familiar Crosby wit and verbiage, and the predictive limning of a character he would play in movies throughout the 1930s, Bing suggests he just might be the sort of wild-eyed usurer capable of pulling the lever for Norman Thomas.

College Humor took its title from the popular magazine that H. N. Swanson founded in 1920. Initially intended as a potpourri of jokes, cartoons, and verses collected from undergraduate newspapers, it earned a reputation in the 1930s for launching talent; its contributors included S. J. Perelman and Philip Wylie. The jokes are now as antediluvian as those in *Joe Miller's Jests* and not as funny, but they underscored a view of college as an interval consecrated to sex, puns, and football, much the same view propounded by Paramount in its rash of college movies, beginning with the Marx Brothers burlesque, *Horse*

Feathers, and going downhill from there. As a genre, movies set in college peaked in the silent era, a time when Knute Rockne made higher education synonymous with football and *Good News* translated his Barnumesque hoopla to Broadway, inspiring enduring film parodies by Harold Lloyd (*The Freshman*) and Buster Keaton (*College*). Campus musicals (not dramas, as Paramount discovered with *Confessions of a Co-ed*) drew audiences throughout the 1930s and 1940s, disappeared in the 1950s, rallied in the 1960s as social protest movies, and resumed their more lunatic pedigrees in the frat house and slasher epics that followed.

The movie *College Humor* is maddeningly inane and dull, and would be no better remembered than *College Rhythm, College Swing,* or *College Holiday* if not for Crosby's involvement. But it was a hit that validated the genre, produced three popular songs, and substantiated Bing's box-office appeal. In the long run, the film proved of greater significance to Bing for professional associations that took root. Director Wesley Ruggles was sitting pretty with an Academy Award nomination for *Cimarron* when he was given the assignment, boosting its A-picture cachet. A former Keystone Kop and the director originally announced for *King of Jazz,* Ruggles was the first husband of actress Arline Judge, a friend and drinking companion of Dixie's, later renowned for her front-page marital escapades. Ruggles's association with Bing outlasted the marriage and led, in 1938, to Bing's breakthrough performance in *Sing You Sinners.* Screenwriters Claude Binyon and Frank Butler separately went on to write more than a dozen of Bing's most important films, including *Sing You Sinners, Going My Way, Holiday Inn,* and most of the *Road* pictures. Sam Coslow and Arthur Johnston, who wrote the score, had already given Bing "Just One More Chance" and would turn out several more of his signature hits. According to Coslow, *College Humor* was the "prize that every songsmith in the land coveted."[40]

Most of the cast were pretty long in the tooth to play college students, but the atmosphere was convivial, especially for Bing and his pals Richard Arlen and Jack Oakie. Like Bing, Arlen was an expert swimmer and spirited carouser, but he grew intense and stiff in front of a camera — never more so than as the hulking, unshaven, hard-drinking football star who, after expulsion from school, turns painfully maudlin. As his roommate, Oakie, a gifted comic ham, endures a disturbingly violent initiation into the fraternity before replacing Arlen to win the big game. Oakie described a ritual required to make Bing starlike: the glued ears ("many's the time Dick Arlen and I flipped those ears loose to get off early")[41] and the donning of corset, padded shoulders, shoe lifts, and hairpiece. Oakie razzed him as "the robot of romance."[42]

Bing, oddly enough, does not play a student (that would come a year later), but rather Professor Danvers of the drama department, a representative of the adult world, albeit one who teaches by singing and is swooned over by coeds, including Barbara Shirrel, Arlen's girl and Oakie's sister, played by the appealing Mary Carlisle. After defending Arlen against expulsion, Danvers loses his job and runs off with Barbara, becoming a successful crooner. "You can hear him but you can't see him," marvels Oakie, spooning with his girl to the car radio. Bing's role was pumped into the script as an afterthought — it's Oakie's movie — and he doesn't show up for reels at a time. He's a one-man chorus in the first half, singing a few strains while the plot is tugged forward by the students. In the second half, he continues as a musical commentator while displaying world-class obtuseness about women, especially Barbara, whose infatuation ("He's a swell egg," she confides) provides him with the picture's one memorable line. He has just been dismissed and is furiously packing his belongings when she walks in and asks him, "Do you mind if I take off my shoes?" He retorts, "I wouldn't care if you took off your, ahh, shoes."

Bing doesn't exactly underact; he doesn't do much acting at all. When he plays anger, his breathing seems rehearsed, and he's little more than an extra during the big game. Still, while Oakie mugs like the devil to keep the film alive, Crosby and his husky easygoing voice steal it. The picture is a creaking antique, but Bing's performance is attractive in a way that Oakie's entertaining shtick and Arlen's histrionic glowering are not. The best of his songs, "Learn to Croon," is introduced as a classroom sing, with a Kate Smith lookalike delivering the line "just bu bu bu bu." "Down the Old Ox Road," which concerns a lovers' lane and is expanded by a long recitative, caused controversy. As directed by Ruggles, it becomes, in Coslow's opinion, "a sneaky bit of lyrical quasi-pornography."[43] Everyone can find the Ox Road, the production demonstrates, except three long-nosed virgins who wear glasses and oversize collars and are definitely out of place on a campus that thrives on sex and touchdowns. Burns and Allen are wasted as Scottish caterers.

The picture represented a break for Mary Carlisle, a twenty-year-old blonde with a provocative glint in her eye who was under contract to MGM but on perennial loan-out to Paramount for college movies. This was her biggest part to date, and Bing liked her well enough to cast her in two subsequent films, by which time he had the clout to approve his leading ladies. They became friends on the second film (*Double or Nothing*, 1937), but on the first he kept to himself, retiring to his dressing room as soon as he completed a scene and to the track or golf course at the end of the day. She admired his professionalism: "I worked with Lionel Barrymore and a lot of good actors, but Bing had something about him that was so natural, like Spencer Tracy. They were thinkers, very intelligent, and Bing was well read and terribly funny — he had a really marvelous vocabulary. He always knew his lines. It was always something else that went wrong in a scene, never Bing."[44]

One morning, however, he appeared to revert to his old ways. "We had a big set with an orchestra," Carlisle recalled, "and Bing wasn't there. So they did a lot of rehearsing and then about ten-thirty, I was going back to my dressing room because he hadn't arrived, when the big doors opened and up drives Bing. He stops and says, 'You know, I don't think I'm gonna make it today.' I guess he'd been out on the town, but he was absolutely charming and you couldn't be mad. I said, 'You're a very bad boy.' But that was the only time. He was wonderful. He didn't get mad, didn't argue, wasn't temperamental. He was just nonchalant about everything."[45]

Well, almost everything. Carlisle noticed that he was self-conscious about his weight and height; he wore his watch on his inside wrist because, he told her, it made his hands seem less pudgy. And he wore lifts. He once told the diminutive Alan Ladd, who followed him at Paramount Pictures, how pleased he was that Ladd was shorter than he was. Bing maintained that he was five nine, but an office secretary, Nancy Briggs, recalled a visit to his home when he wore slippers and she realized he was just about her height — five seven.[46]

The shooting of *College Humor*, in the spring of 1933, coincided with a siege of paranoia on the Paramount lot. Dwarfish Emanuel Cohen was appointed chief of production that year, and no one knew from one day to the next whether the studio would survive or for how long. It might have gone under if not for Mae West's two 1933 megahits, *I'm No Angel* and *She Done Him Wrong,* which grossed more than $2 million each and earned West a place on the annual Quigley box-office poll, the first Paramount player ever to make the list. The uncertainty encouraged the manipulative Cohen to sign West, Gary Cooper, and Bing to personal contracts, much to the horror of his bosses, the bankers in New York, who controlled Paramount's purse strings and canned him in retaliation, in 1934. The pervasive fear worked its way through the ranks and, if nothing else, sparked a carefree social whirl.

The center for partying on Paramount's lot was Gary Cooper's dressing room, prominently located on the stars' row of bungalows and adjoining that of Carole Lombard. Bing once remarked that the reason they all gravitated there was that Gary was so well liked and Carole told the raunchiest stories. Coop's happy hour became a ritual for drinking, singing, and trade talk. Marlene Dietrich liked to stop beside Bing's dressing room to hear him sing and play records, especially those of Richard Tauber. "The crooner confided to me that Tauber had taught him to breathe properly and how to modulate his phrasing," she wrote. "This common passion brought us together."[47]

Contract players at Paramount were inclined to huddle in defense. Everyone knew the studio was in dire trouble, so its stars were sometimes needled as also-rans. MGM was said to have the glamour queens and Warners the stalwart men. Yet Paramount was beginning to forge a new, postcontinental style with Bing, Coop, Lombard, Fredric March, Cary Grant, Miriam Hopkins, George Raft, Charles Laughton, and Claudette Colbert. West and Dietrich were huge, but the approaching hooves of censorship threatened their commercial value. A symbolic changing of the guard occurred when Josef von Sternberg, Dietrich's cunning director and a specialist in erotic decadence, walked into the Paramount commissary and found Bing at his table. "The air was electric," wrote columnist Harrison Carroll in 1934. "Bing looked up and said politely: 'I came in here and I was hungry, so I just sat down at a table.' . . . Sternberg turned on his heel and went to another table."[48] Within two years Sternberg was gone from Paramount, and soon after from Hollywood.

Workers before and behind the cameras survived the months of uncertainty by playing as hard as they worked. A secretary remembered, "At five, the cameras stopped and out came the bottles and everyone screwed on the desks."[49] Her image conveys the whistling-in-the-dark gaiety of a studio that produced hit after hit yet remained on the brink of collapse — a studio that, unlike all the others, had a revolving door where the head of production sat. To make things worse that summer, the technicians went on strike. Bing, who forever maintained his common touch with crews, earned their respect by asking about the dispute in the studio canteen and leaving money with instructions to "keep the boys in beer for the rest of the afternoon."[50]

College Humor was rushed into theaters in June, barely a month after principal photography ended. Reviewers were remarkably forbearing. The *New York Times* considered it "an unsteady entertainment" but detected "heartily amusing patches" and especially liked Bing for his "sense of humor and his subterranean blue notes."[51] The *Los Angeles Times* approved Bing's "most important role in this peppy film music comedy."[52] *Variety* reported, "Crosby makes his best showing to date with a chance to handle both light comedy and romance. His pale face make-up is the only flaw so it looks like all he needs is a new paint job and another good role."[53] The reliably condescending *Time*, however, thought it a "frantic little absurdity," fit for "rural cinemaddicts whose tastes in diversion have been shaped by wireless" and observed of Bing his "inappropriate calm which is his chief distinction."[54]

The critics were kinder than the censors. James Wingate of the Hays Office warned against the use of *hell, pansies,* and *punk,* and anything that could be construed as satirizing college life: "In this connection," he wrote a Paramount executive, "[we] suggest that the college president be played straight and not as a heavy paunchy man, or in any other derogatory manner. Also, we would recommend that you do whatever you can to minimize the bitterness of the theme of the picture, which is that a college education does not necessarily spell success in later life."[55] Bing and other cast members promoted the film onstage and on the air, and the public — not just *Time*'s rubes — lined up for tickets, filling the studio's coffers at theaters around the country.

*　　*　　*

Two long-term intimates joined the Crosby circle during the making of *College Humor*. Paramount's publicity campaign included a beauty competition to crown Miss College Humor. The winner was an exquisite young woman from Tucumcari, New Mexico, with golden hair and porcelain skin, named Bessie Patterson. Her prize was a bit part in a Crosby film, but because she was underage, she did not collect for a few years. When the time came, Bing introduced her to Johnny Burke, who became his most accomplished lyricist and Bessie's husband. The often tumultuous marriage of the Burkes would parallel that of Bing and Dixie.

Leo Lynn reentered Bing's life while Bing was driving down Sunset Boulevard and noticed his Gonzaga classmate crossing the road. Leo was a few years older than Bing, but they had appeared together in school concerts and plays. Bing pulled over and asked what he was doing in Hollywood. Leo explained that he was working as driver and assistant to English actor Clive Brook. Bing said he needed someone, too. Leo gave Brook his notice that afternoon. He remained Bing's aide-de-camp until Bing's death, a quiet, omnipresent, loyal keeper of the keys for forty-four years.

"Leo was almost the shape of Mr. Crosby," said Alan Fisher, the Crosby butler in the 1960s and 1970s. "A peculiar-looking guy. Leo's eyes were slightly odd, but they were blue and he was stocky, as Mr. Crosby was in those days before he became thinner. So Leo became his stand-in and driver and would do anything personal for Mr. Crosby."[56] Leo was always around, a shadow, easy to be with, diffident but friendly. "Bing never had an entourage, never," Rosemary Clooney said. "The entourage was Leo. That was it." Bing was comfortable with Leo. They had no need to keep up a conversation, and Leo could read his mind when he got in a mood, like the time in the 1950s when he recorded with Clooney and the producer's friends packed the control room. "Bing would do things I could never figure out," Clooney recalled. "He sat in a chair facing the wall and I said, 'You want to go through with this?' and he said, 'I'll be with you in a moment.' He wanted the people out of the control room, but he didn't say it. You were supposed to divine these things sometimes with him. But Leo came back with his sandwich and saw right away what was going on."[57]

Still, despite the Gonzaga connection, Leo was an employee before he became a friend, a fact that helped define his role as Bing's right-hand man, a member of the inner circle who knew his place, a place somewhat belied by his working-class manner and reserve. Phil Harris turned the spotlight on Leo whenever he came to see his Las Vegas nightclub act: "There's a friend of mine in the audience I want you to meet. His name is Leo Lynn. You can't get through to see Bing Crosby without going through him."[58] After Eddie Lang's death, Bing unburdened himself to no one. Leo, who played life as close to the vest as Bing, mirrored the change in him. He was a different kind of confidant — one who didn't unload his confidences or expect others to unload theirs.

17

UNDER
WESTERN SKIES

*I'd like to be able to sing like the crooners. The reason is
a crooner gets his quota of sentimentality with half his
natural voice. That's a great saving. I don't like to work.*
— Bing Crosby, *Time* (1934)[1]

Paramount was determined to keep Bing in harness. Two months
after wrapping *College Humor,* he began shooting *Too Much Harmony,* enjoying little rest in the interim beyond a week in May spent
with Dixie at Palm Springs. On returning to Hollywood, he agreed to
shoot six shorts and, within days, accompanied director Arvid E. Gillstrom to Yosemite Park to make two, *Please* and *Just an Echo.*[2] In the
first, Bing once again plays Bing. Driving his car, he comes upon a fair
maiden with a flat tire and an overbearing clownish suitor. As it hap-
pens, she teaches singing and Bing — looking younger and more
attractive than in *College Humor* — asks for lessons. After dispatching her beau, Elmer Smoot (Vernon Dent doing a malevolent Oliver
Hardy), in a vocal contest, Bing drives into the sunset with her, pecking her on the lips and nodding his head to seal his accomplishment.

In *Just an Echo* Bing proves he can stay on a horse, as a forest
ranger who orders campers to douse their cigarettes. One miscreant
is his captain's daughter, with whom he, once again, rides into the
sunset. Bing disliked *Just an Echo* — he thought it poorly edited —

and it disappeared, apparently for good. When *College Humor* exceeded box-office expectations, the studio realized Bing was too important for two-reelers and abruptly canceled the four remaining shorts.

Instead, he participated in another *Hollywood on Parade* promotional short, exchanging compliments with Mary Pickford, Paramount's first major star and the queen of Hollywood royalty. She retired that year, at forty, but returned in 1935 to introduce Bing in the MGM Technicolor two-reeler *Star Night at the Cocoanut Grove*, a film terminally dated except for Bing's complacent, almost alien intelligence and his measured rendering of "With Every Breath I Take." That same unassuming flair is evident in the Paramount reel, as he, every inch the film star, genially accepts Pickford's praise. Eight years earlier he had grudgingly roused himself from sleep to accompany Al Rinker to California. Now he felt flush, confident of his success — and he wanted his parents at hand. Kate and Harry, in their early sixties, were ready to enjoy easier times. After twenty years in the small brown house near Gonzaga, they left Spokane for a new life. For a while they lived with Bing, who wrote his brother Ted about selling the house: "I don't imagine the folks will ever return there, except for a visit. This climate is less rigorous and accordingly better for them."[3] Months later he bought them a place of their own in Toluca Lake, at nearby 4366 Ponca Avenue. Harry Crosby readily took to Hollywood: "He'd sit down on a bus and introduce himself," Bing marveled. "'Harry Crosby Sr., I've got a few clippings,' and he'd show my clippings."[4] Mother Crosby discovered the ponies.

In June Bing reunited with bandleader Jimmy Grier, Gus Arnheim's former arranger at the Grove, for three recording sessions, followed by a fourth in August. Bing's pleasure in working with Grier cannot in itself explain the magnetic extravagance of his singing on those dates. Perhaps he was expressing his delight in his success or his happiness with Dixie or anticipation of their first child or solid roots indicated by their new home or all of the above or something else entirely. But never before had Bing performed with so much nervy adrenaline; his voice seemed to burst with vitality. Neither Brunswick nor Columbia, the label that eventually acquired ownership of the records, ever thought to collect the Grier sessions for an album, yet they are all of a piece: exuberant readings of mostly second-rate songs, exemplifying the jazz creed, Tain't what you do, it's the way that you do it.

The first order of business was to record the tunes from his films. Much of the material was grim, expressing the mood if not the substance of the Depression in narratives of lost, doomed, or betrayed love. Bing's stout delivery, cradled in richly detailed arrangements, is at once heroic and haunted. He told an interviewer that same year, "I won't sing sappy songs. A crooner gets enough criticism. There's no reason to invite more barbs by singing mush."[5] None of the fourteen titles recorded that summer is mushy. "Learn to Croon" may be replete with la-di-das, but the attack is bolder than any singing of the day short of opera. Yet so unaffected is Bing, he creates the illusion that anyone could sing as well. Even his flawless intonation and splendid timbre have an unschooled, artless quality — the sound of a passionate American rearing back and singing full bore. "Moonstruck," also from the film, begins with a *moon/June* cliché and never gets much better, but it is emboldened by the assertiveness of Bing's delivery. "Down the Old Ox Road," inverting the usual order of tempo adjustments, begins swinging and then slows down.

Better was to come. "I've Got to Pass Your House to Get to My House," an odd Yiddische minor-key melody by Lew Brown, has had no life beyond Bing's original recording, yet he embraces the sad plight of the narrative with such sympathetic brilliance — aided by Ellingtonian muted brasses to underscore the rhythm — that he enhances it with an intensity due an art song. Victor Young's undistinguished "My Love" begins with a surprising allusion to John McCormack; Bing enters unexpectedly high before settling into a more comfortable midrange. With his forceful conception and execution, he turns a minor song into a satisfying experience, soaring into the clouds at the end of the release. "Blue Prelude," trumpeter Joe Bishop's mesmerizing melody (it was briefly Woody Herman's theme in 1940), was outfitted with a Gordon Jenkins lyric and an Ellingtonian arrangement, plus strong rhythm-section work and a fitting clarinet solo by James Briggs. Bing's dynamics are most impressive in his rattling last eight bars, but his overall attention to detail confers a structural design virtually unheard-of on a pop record.

The most successful of the Grier records and a huge national hit for Bing was "Shadow Waltz," from *Gold Diggers of 1933*. Most of Al Dubin's lines end in the maladroit phrase "to you":

In the shadows, let me come and sing to you.
Let me dream a song that I can bring to you.
Take me in your arms and let me cling to you.

Bing takes the vowels in stride, building an overall arc for the performance that complements Harry Warren's loping melody. In some of his inflections (*song/bring*), one can hear the nascent style of Dean Martin, another young singer — fifteen at the time — who learned his trade by imitating Crosby. After the first chorus, Bing attacks the verse a beat early, for dramatic emphasis. "There's a Cabin in the Pines" was one of several cabin songs (in the cotton, on the hilltop, in the sky), but Bing puts aside its rustic innocence in favor of jazzy cadences and subtle backbeat phrasing. His mastery of time is no less marked in his rubato treatment of the verse of "I've Got to Sing a Torch Song."

Bing's immaculate bell-like projection deepens "The Day You Came Along," from *Too Much Harmony,* as does his canny breath control, as he punctuates the turnback after the first eight bars with a wordless exclamation; he turns an unimportant, repetitive song into a rousing anthem, building to a climactically rhythmic finish. His alchemy is perhaps most luminous on the cryptically dark "Black Moonlight," from the same film. The arrangement begins with pizzicato strings answered by growly brasses and descending saxophones and advances with rhythmic change-ups and vivid voicings. Emotional yet stoic, Bing displays all he knows about breathing and enunciation and dynamics to articulate its mood and import. These performances refuted the critics who disparaged his allegedly anemic crooning, and demolished singers who could do no more than croon.

Shortly after the June sessions, Gary Evan Crosby was born at Cedars of Lebanon on June 27, 1933, weighing seven pounds six ounces and named after Gary Cooper and Dixie's dad. Richard Arlen had bet Bing $100 that the baby would be a girl and that his newborn son, Richard Jr., would marry her. Instead, the infants were christened together and feted at a baby-dunking party at the Crosby home. Weeks before, Kitty Lang had arrived to live with the Crosbys; they never spoke of Eddie's death and funeral, three months earlier. She helped Dixie shop for layettes and other items she would need in the hospital and stayed with her through the delivery. She then ran into the waiting room to tell Bing. "He was so happy. It was good to see him smile again. He said, 'This calls for a celebration.' Did we go to Chasen's? Not exactly. We went to Sid's Ice Cream Parlor for a banana split."[6] Gary Cooper, delighted by his namesake, brought over a crib with *Gary* carved on it. Bing tried to match him with Kitty, who admired him on the screen, but she shyly demurred. Bing told her, "Now that I have a son, I want him to be proud of me. I'm really going to settle down."[7]

For the next few years, he doted on Gary, taking him everywhere, not least the racetrack and swimming. Gary was said to be exceptionally bright; Bing claimed that he could sing in tune when he was a year old. Gary would watch his father sing, and cause much hilarity by moving his lips and mimicking his movements. But he was a difficult, colicky infant, and Dixie was intimidated by the hospital nurse. Kitty thought the nurse, who insisted that Gary was having temper tantrums, less than sympathetic. When she convinced Dixie to hire an "old-fashioned nurse," the colic disappeared. Kitty showed Dixie how to bathe and feed her baby; "although she was scared to death, she managed quite well."[8] At one point Dixie fell and broke her elbow, fueling rumors that she was drinking. Bing rushed home from Catalina Island to take her to the hospital. When Gary was four months old, the Paramount publicity department issued a four-page press release, quoting Bing as hoping his son would be an actor and singer "a million times better than I am" — though he was not going to push him into the profession. "Whatever he wants to do, we'll smooth the road as far as it is possible to do so."[9]

All he demanded, Bing purportedly said, was that Gary, unlike himself, finish college. He also stipulated that his son be a regular kid, no different from any other. He would be raised like a "typical American boy."[10] But not entirely typical. In July, responding to threats in the wake of the Lindbergh kidnapping, Bing sought a bodyguard to protect his wife and child. He offered the job to Marty Collins, the fighter who had come to his aid at Eddie's funeral. Collins remained on the payroll for three years, after which Bing helped him open his own bar.

The energy of the Grier recordings and the joy of fatherhood did not hold for *Too Much Harmony* — a rote backstage musical with a lackluster performance by Bing. The picture was directed by former vaudevillian and Chaplin protégé Edward Sutherland and was written by Joseph L. Mankiewicz, who idolized Bing and mimicked him at parties. Again, Bing's role was an afterthought, this time in a project originally intended for the other two stars. In 1929 Jack Oakie and Skeets Gallagher had enjoyed popular triumphs with two films, *Close Harmony* and *Fast Company;* the latter is an adaptation, by Mankiewicz, of Ring Lardner's *Elmer the Great* and remained Oakie's perennial favorite among his own pictures. *Too Much Harmony* was devised as a reunion for Oakie and Gallagher but was shelved until producer William LeBaron got the idea to move them into the background of a romance built around Bing.

Mankiewicz's story, for which he received a larger screen credit than Sutherland, concerns Broadway headliner Eddie Bronson (Bing), who is torn between the nice girl who adores him (Judith Allen) and the faithless, gold-digging bitch who uses him (Lilyan Tashman). The outcome, unlike that of *The Big Broadcast,* holds no surprises. The film begins with Bing singing the final measures of "Learn to Croon" at a Chicago theater, establishing continuity with *College Humor* not only for Bing but for Coslow and Johnston, who wrote the score. (They learned they had the job from Everett at Gary's christening party.) They wrote worthy songs, notably a hit sequel to "Please" called "Thanks." Yet two superior numbers, "Black Moonlight" and "The Day You Came Along," were maddeningly assigned to Judith Allen and Kitty Kelly, who could neither sing nor synchronize their lips. Allen's song was dubbed by a singer whose streetwise head inflections, a cross between Dixie Lee and Ethel Merman, are a far remove from her highborn speaking voice. Kelly appears as the salty paramour of a producer, Max Merlin, played by a language-mangling Jewish comedian, Harry Green; in an instance of kitsch imitating life, her number was created for her because she was the paramour of producer William LeBaron.

Another cast member with connections was Mrs. Evelyn Offield Oakie, Jack's mother on- and offscreen, a feisty lady who left a trail of anecdotes. She once convinced a Bank of Hollywood teller to give her all of Jack's money the day before the bank folded. On the set she regaled the actors with tales as they sat around her on canvas chairs emblazoned with their names. When her chair tipped over, Bing helped her up, asking, "Are you all right, Mrs. Offield?" "Bing," she said, "I noticed that my name wasn't on the chair and it kind of upset me."[11] Bing admired Oakie, a master of double takes and sheepish grins, and insisted that he did not mind his rampant scene stealing, his "twisting you around so that his face was in the camera while you talked to the backdrop." He reasoned: "Sooner or later there would be a spot in the picture in which I'd sing a song and Jack would be in the trunk."[12]

One of Bing's best scenes is in the baggage car of a train, when he sings, all too briefly, "Boo Boo Boo," another attempt to cash in on his trademark; the tune rouses him more than the cast or script. Yet the most elaborate number belongs to Kitty Kelly. "Black Moonlight" is an outlandish indulgence in which, through a trick of lighting, street-walkers and dancers decked out in Harlem drag change from black to white and back, while Kitty's lips move in blissful disregard of the words she is supposed to be miming. The jokes were older than the actors telling them. At one point Oakie and Gallagher exchange a breakneck string of vaudeville jokes, including the one — "How can I keep my horse from frothing at the mouth?" — that got the Rhythm Boys banned in Toledo.

Bing was not happy about his billing, especially on the pre-release posters. Paramount was giving him star treatment despite his opposition. The company argued that his name was the movie's biggest asset and ought to be played to the hilt; in any case, the press materials were printed and it was too expensive to redo them. But Bing was intractable. He insisted they place his name on the same title card as Oakie, Gallagher, and other principals, and the studio complied, creating new credits, ads, lobby cards, and press packets.

Completed after five weeks, in mid-August, the film was distributed in September. Reviews were mixed. The *New York Times* found many "quite lively" scenes but cautioned admirers of "Mr. Crosby's peculiar ballads" that they might be "disappointed by his attempts to register admiration and affection."[13] *Variety* approved his ability in "the trouping department."[14] The ludicrous Hearst columnist Louella Parsons was delighted with Kitty Kelly and her voice and thought the whole picture "swell," except for Judith Allen.[15] She counted herself, along with her son, as converted Bing fans — small wonder, as Mr. Hearst was set to produce Bing's next picture.

The majority of local reviewers held their collective nose, but adverse reviews notwithstanding, the public flocked to the box office. *Too Much Harmony* was a smash in every region. Several theaters extended their bookings, a rare occurrence in 1933. In Pittsburgh it was the first major draw in months; in Cincinnati it successfully competed with the road-show megahit *Dinner at Eight*; in Indianapolis, despite major competition and a dearth of ads, it beat everything else on the street; in New York it broke the Paramount Theater's house average and raked in $60,000 in one week — "like the old pre-depresh days," *Variety* crooned.[16] Receipts from Europe were just as dazzling. In two weeks *Too Much Harmony* did more business at London's Plaza Theatre than any movie since the advent of sound.[17]

The picture that clinched Bing's place in the coveted circle of top-ten box-office attractions, as calculated in an annual poll of exhibitors conducted by Quigley Publications, was not made at Paramount. It came from MGM, at the behest of Marion Davies and her powerful lover, William Randolph Hearst. The irony was much appreciated on the Paramount lot: in attempting to boost Davies's flagging popularity, Hearst borrowed two of Paramount's leading men (first Bing in *Going Hollywood*, then Gary Cooper in *Operator 13*). In Hollywood's pecking order, this was akin to Rolls-Royce renting upholstery from General Motors. The decision to borrow Bing was initiated by MGM lyricist and former coproducer of the Morrissey revues, Arthur Freed. With his partner, Nacio Herb Brown, Freed had written a fervent new song, "Temptation," that he believed only Bing could put over. Davies was charmed by Bing. But the jealous Hearst fretted about his reputation as a womanizing hell-raiser (he surely recalled the Berkeley frat party that got his son Bill and Bing into trouble) and had to be persuaded. *College Humor*'s box-office receipts helped. He was undoubtedly comforted by the success of *Too Much Harmony*, which broke during the filming of *Going Hollywood*.

Paramount agreed to the loan-out, reasoning that a little MGM stardust could not hurt the value of its property; besides, Hearst always paid his way. Everett, who closed Bing's deal, put to good use the rumors about Davies's leisurely way of working. He negotiated a payment of $2,000 a week above and beyond a lump sum. This produced a windfall as the picture, slated to shoot between August 30 and October 13, wrapped several weeks late, netting Bing $75,000 and leading *Time* to describe him as "probably the world's best paid male singer."[18] Bing relished *Going Hollywood* for the partying and the clique of top-notch talent.

It had all begun when Cosmopolitan, the production company Hearst created for Marion Davies, bought a treatment called *Paid to Laugh,* by Frances Marion, a prolific scenarist of the silent era who also directed a few Davies films. A synopsis was given to playwright and novelist Donald Ogden Stewart, then at the beginning of a stellar career as a screenwriter — *Holiday, Love Affair, The Philadelphia Story* — that was curtailed twenty years later by the blacklist. He completed his final draft in August, by which time six songs were written by Brown and Freed, the team that put the MGM musical on the map in 1929 with *The Hollywood Revue of 1929* and *The Broadway Melody.* Supervising the musical score and fashioning some of the most refined movie arrangements of the era was Lennie Hayton, who became a mainstay of the Freed unit in 1942. Davies, at thirty-six, was six years older than Bing and looked it; she required a premier cinematographer and found one in George Folsey, who shot *The Big Broadcast* among numerous other black-and-white films and would also become a Freed unit regular, setting Technicolor standards in pictures like *Meet Me in St. Louis* and *Ziegfeld Follies.* Walter Wanger, soon to be a major force in Hollywood, was chosen to produce.

Last on board was director Raoul Walsh, a legend at forty-six, though his best work lay ahead of him (*The Roaring Twenties, High Sierra, The Strawberry Blonde, White Heat*). He accepted the picture because he was eager to work with its two stars. Walsh had known and admired Bing as far back as the Cocoanut Grove ("he had come a long way with talent and a big future sticking out all over him"),[19] and he wanted to meet Marion, by then a reluctant actress, often maligned as Hearst's Galatea by those who had never seen the superb comedienne's work. Born to an Irish Catholic family that prospered in the Garment Center, Raoul grew up in a posh Manhattan town house bustling with servants and visited by the celebrities of a fading era, among them Edwin Booth, Diamond Jim Brady, Buffalo Bill, and John L. Sullivan. Yet, like Bing, he had a yen for the wild side, which he exercised swimming in the East River and frequenting Bowery saloons and bordellos.

Walsh was fifteen when his mother died and an uncle took him to Cuba. He made his way to Mexico, where a job driving cattle led to parts in western movies and an apprenticeship with D. W. Griffith, who cast him as John Wilkes Booth in *The Birth of a Nation*. He developed into an instinctive and stylish filmmaker, renowned for dynamic action scenes; an early triumph was *The Thief of Bagdad*, with Douglas Fairbanks. Though Walsh directed few musicals during his long career, he loved the sentimental ditties of old New York, and several of his most hard-bitten pictures are cued to those songs. Wearing an imposing eye patch, the result of an automobile mishap, he was not averse to drinking and brawling. He was popular with actors, though he could be acerbic on the set, grumbling his pet phrase "otra vez" — Spanish for "another time" or "not now" or "let's get the hell out of here," depending on his inflection.

Stu Erwin was again recruited as a rich, nebbish producer. Walsh filled out the cast with Fifi D'Orsay as the bad girl competing for Bing's attention, comic Patsy Kelly as Marion's pal, and sour Ned Sparks as a film director. Hearst summoned them all to San Simeon, his 350,000-acre estate, commanding thirty miles of shoreline. Bing reluctantly boarded a plane with the director and the songwriters. They were ensconced at the castle for the week, rehearsing and socializing with, among others, Winston Churchill, who puffed on a cigar and generally ignored them. One night at dinner, Marion, who was born and bred in Brooklyn, asked Walsh if as a boy he had ever visited Rockaway Beach. When he assured her he had, she named him Rockaway Raoul, which Bing amended to Rollicking Rockaway Raoul.

Except for exteriors filmed at Walsh's Encino ranch, the film was made on the MGM lot, where Marion had a bungalow fit for the mistress of the world's wealthiest press lord: fourteen rooms. The powers at MGM were tiring of Hearst, especially his tirades about Norma Shearer, executive Irving Thalberg's wife, and the roles he thought Marion and not Shearer should have been given, like Marie Antoinette and Elizabeth Barrett. For her part, Marion was tired of the whole routine. Hearst pushed her into unsuitable parts and rammed her down the throats of his tabloid readers, and she went along to please him. Yet she had long ago proved herself a sparkling comic actress with a trenchant gift for mimicry, especially in such movies produced by Thalberg and directed by King Vidor as *Show People,* remembered for her hilarious spoofs of Mae Murray and Gloria Swanson. Neither she nor Hearst thought filmmaking should crimp a good party, however, and they let Wanger worry about the hopeless task of keeping the train on track. The costs eventually exceeded $900,000, making *Going Hollywood* Marion's most expensive movie, and consequently a money-losing hit.

The aspect of talking pictures that most bothered Marion was having to learn dialogue. Taking literally the idea that one could memorize something one slept on, she kept her script under her pillow. "But that didn't work," she admitted. "When I got on the set, I didn't know one line of it." Nor was she inclined to walk the block and a half from her bungalow to the set before eleven. She refused the assistant director's pleas, with the excuse that she was studying her lines. "Bing got mad at me every once in a while, but W.R. never did. He used to coax us not to work."[20] Bing would arrive at nine, make up, and wait two hours for Marion, who was accompanied by a five-piece band that serenaded her between shots. They would listen to pop tunes for half an hour, at which time Walsh would tear himself away from such pursuits as driving golf balls into a canvas net or playing cards or conducting the band, to discuss the first scene. Then they repaired to lunch, a two-hour production in Marion's bungalow, described by Bing as Lucullan: Rhine wines, foie gras, chicken in aspic, Bombay duck. Now they needed to make up again, after which they paused for another musical interlude, and finally prepared to shoot around five. "Flushed with the success of our first scene," Bing noted,[21] they were ready to tackle another, but either the crew punched out or Hearst stepped in to avoid overtime. Alone, Marion did her close-ups. "That was kind of smart of me, anyway," she said.[22]

Soon a competition in pranks evolved, as Raoul encouraged Bing to trick Marion into acting scenes when the cameras were not rolling and the mikes were off. Once, Marion, who was terrified of horses, looked out from her bungalow and saw Bing and Raoul on white steeds, determined to ride into her living room; she locked the door in the nick of time. The day they shot "We'll Make Hay While the Sun Shines," Bing and Marion had imbibed an excess of Rhine wine. The scene required them to stroll through a field of eight-foot cellophane daisies that waved from side to side like pendulums. Bing and Marion, waving a bit themselves, found the swaying reeds so nauseating that they could barely stand. Marion cried out for Bing to hang on to her, and they made a pact not to look at the daisies. In the completed film, they walk through the scene with Bing singing to the sky and Marion gazing raptly at the side of his face.

They became good friends. "He was very cute and very sweet, and he was crazy about his wife Dixie," Marion said. He talked about Dixie constantly, phoning between shots, until Marion suggested he pretend that she was Dixie to rev up their love scenes. "Oh, no," he told her, "you're not nearly as pretty." "I understand that," she said, "but just close your eyes." Marion named Bing and Cooper as her favorite leading men, for the same reason: "Gary would give the star the benefit of the scene. Only a real man does that, and Bing did that, too. Other actors don't."[23] Bing described Marion as generous, charming, funny, with a "heart as big as Santa Monica."[24] Both of them enjoyed the irascible Walsh. At a wrap party at San Simeon, Bing announced that he and Arthur Freed had written a song about Walsh, set to the melody of "The Bowery." He performed it, complete with spoken interlude in which he mimicked Walsh's voice and manner:

> *Rollicking Rockaway Raoul*
> *When clad on the beach in a towel,*
> *He's terrific, colossal, stupendous, and grand.*
> *He's the lay of the land, of the land.*
> *Oh, the Bowery, the Bowery,*
> *He never goes there anymore.*
> *A good pal and true,*
> *That old Kerry blue,*
> *Rollicking Rockaway Raoul.*

[Spoken] Hello, Greenwood! Greenwood! Get me a bottle of that Royal George. What? No Royal George? Oh, Newman, is it too late to replace Greenwood? And where's my Bull Durham, goddamnit, where's my Bull Durham? No Bull Durham? Nuts! I tell you what we'll do, Bing, we'll go over to Davies' bungalow. Maybe she'll pop out with a drink. Okay, let's go. Wait a minute, wait a minute, wait a minute. There's Waange-er, Wanger. Turn 'em over quick! Wanger's here. Bing, otra vez.

Rollicking Rockaway Raoul,
He thinks highbrow operas are foul,
But bimbos and sailors and chippies and such,
He gives them that old Rao-oul Walsh touch.
"Otra vez," "otra vez,"
We'll never hear that anymore.
And now that we're through,
MGM can go screw,
Says Rollicking Rockaway Raoul.[25]

As Bing's best attempt at lyric writing to date, it reveals a more penetrating talent for satiric observation than for love songs, and he wrote several more in later years. This one was recorded on the spot (after giggling through the opening lines, he sings it with characteristic esprit) and found its way to the underground circuit of Crosby collectors. According to Walsh, MGM moguls were so incensed by the song's last line and the implication that Walsh and associates fiddled while studio chief Louis B. Mayer burned (even if Hearst, and not MGM, footed the bill), they barred Bing and Walsh from the lot for life and would have fired Freed but for an ironclad contract.[26] Except for a B-film by Walsh — who enjoyed a dazzling twenty years at Warners — and Bing's appearance in the Cocoanut Grove two-reeler, both in 1935, neither man worked at MGM until after Mayer was deposed, in 1951.

Going Hollywood was forgotten for decades, until excerpts appeared in the 1974 compilation *That's Entertainment!*, reviving interest in a fascinating film. By then the Bing persona had become so upright, at least in memory, that one chronicler of film musicals described "Temptation" as "a drunken paean to lust and self-loathing [and] the last thing one associates with Crosby."[27] That may be true today, but it wasn't in 1933. In two of his first four movies, Bing played a man with a drinking problem; in one he attempts suicide, and in all four he lusts and is lusted after, usually by two women. *Going Hollywood* was the formula as before, but with intriguing twists.

Marion's Sylvia is a French teacher at an impossibly stuffy girls' school where the rest of the faculty is spinsterish, butch, or old. Transported by the voice of Bill Williams (Bing) on her contraband radio, she quits her job and pursues him — despite his consistent rejections — to his hotel bedroom, train stateroom, and movie set, calmly disparaging his hot-tempered fiancée and leading lady, Lili (D'Orsay). Sylvia is a female version of the Sennett Bing, who invariably runs off with the affianced. Here, he is passive and vulnerable, while Sylvia dogs his tracks, refusing to be thwarted. The comical sparring for power between Erwin's producer and Sparks's director parallels the catfights between Sylvia and Lili. Sparks riotously mimics Walsh, grousing and grumbling, contemptuously walking off whenever the producer arrives on the set. At one point he snarls at his stars: "Off to Rockaway Beach for the both of ya, if you don't get this right."

Davies is fun to watch, in part because she is so clearly uninvolved with the proceedings, sleepwalking through scenes and almost falling over during a dance routine that unflatteringly reveals her pudgy legs — she looks at her feet like Ruby Keeler and waves her arms to keep upright. One remarkable shot is an almost gratuitous example of what George Folsey's glamour photography could achieve for an aging ingenue. Sylvia lies in bed at school, listening to Bill on the radio, and the camera gazes at her face for an astonishing ninety-plus seconds, with only two brief cutaways. In a soundstage scene, she appears in blackface as an extra — Bill doesn't recognize her — yet charmingly reveals herself with a beautifully unadorned smile. Bill reaches past her to a black boy and rubs his cheek; "I's real, Massa Williams," the kid says. Erwin, who also fails to recognize her, tells her she's changed quite a bit. "It's the climate," Sylvia deadpans. But it is more than climate; it's going Hollywood, which means she walks onto a set with no thespian experience and is chosen — after Lili conveniently throws a fit — to play the lead in the picture. Ever the mimic, Marion/Sylvia does a mean Fifi/Lili.

Though it was Marion's production, with Bing taking second billing for the first and last time until he accepted character parts in the 1960s, Bing dominates the film, greatly assisted by a terrific score. Inexplicably, he never recorded the title song, but when he sings it in a production number set in Grand Central, reenacting his own recent decision to leave New York, he is at his indomitable, swinging best. "Beautiful Girl" allows him to reveal his increasing ability to handle varied bits of business, singing as he walks around his hotel room, followed by Sterling Holloway and a microphone. He glides through a six-minute production number and romances Marion with "After Sundown," pouting like a teenager when she declines to sleep with him that evening. She changes her mind, however, only to find him in Lili's room. The Hays Office found that acceptable but vainly lobbied MGM to change the title: "no Hollywood title should be used which would tend to undo the efforts made to disabuse the public mind of the unfavorable impression of Hollywood which formerly obtained."[28]

Sylvia does not find it acceptable, and when she gives him the cold shoulder, Bill does what Bing might have done in years past. He goes on a bender in Mexican bordellos, precipitating the best scene in the picture. An unshaven derelict, Bill stares into a shot glass, reeling between hallucinations of the dark and evil temptress Lili and the good and golden Sylvia. "It was all very Russian Art Theater," Bing later explained.[29] He sings "Temptation" at his purple best, imbuing a melodramatic yet weirdly seductive style of pop with stentorian, heartbursting, operatic gusto — part Jolson on his knees, part McCormack in his cups, and all youthful bravado. Keep your head down, his mother might have said, but go for broke in song.

The initial response to *Going Hollywood* was positive. Needless to say, Hearst papers could not contain themselves. Louella had an attack of literary vapors trying to do justice to its immortal glory: the picture "stands supreme as a perfect example of good entertainment with a heroine beautiful enough to make every other girl wish she could be a Marion Davies." Lest anyone think she was prejudiced, she added, "She is so lovely that a murmur of admiration went through the theater, both in the scenes where she wears regulation street dress and again in the beautiful costumes in the motion picture scenes."[30] The *New York Times* critic thought it "sprightly and jocular."[31] *Time* grudgingly conceded that it surpassed previous attempts at movies featuring radio singers, but could not resist disparaging Bing as a reformed Vallée imitator.[32] *Time* ran a letter weeks later from Jackson Leichter, one of Paul Whiteman's radio writers, who corrected several errors, including the Vallée crack, and closed with a prediction: "Crosby's popularity will grow. He has brains, a growing wisdom, a recently acquired balance. He's good for America."[33]

*   *   *

Variety gauged *Going Hollywood* as "an emphatic moneymaker," but despite strong openings, it failed to become the runaway hit that would have earned back its investment. MGM soon buried it. The trade paper was on firmer ground when it declared Bing "the present day disc best seller."[34] Other record companies attempted to lure him away from Brunswick and Jack Kapp, who paid him $400 a disc plus royalties. Victor offered him five times that. Kapp parried with a history lesson, comparing Brunswick's steadfast buildup with the wobbly loyalties of Victor and Columbia, which Bing had learned about firsthand during his time with Whiteman.

Bing did not need the lecture. He liked and trusted Kapp, who had an ace in the hole. Jack himself was fed up with Brunswick, which rejected his bid to head the company, and determined to start a label of his own, with Bing's contract as collateral. If anyone could defy the majors in the middle of the Depression, Kapp was the man, and Bing would be in on the ground floor; indeed, he would *be* the ground floor. While Jack considered his options, he continued to advance Bing's transformation from crooner to all-American troubadour.

A week after the Victor offer was rejected, Jack recorded Bing with a plush Lennie Hayton studio ensemble. He devoted half the session to slightly accelerated versions of songs from *Going Hollywood,* "Beautiful Girl" and "After Sundown." With two additional songs, he routed Bing on a new trail. "The Last Round-Up" was the year's most improbable hit, introduced at the New York Paramount by Irish tenor Joe Morrison, who was heard with George Olsen's band. Written by an erstwhile cowboy, Billy Hill (whose "There's a Cabin in the Pines" had fizzled for Bing), it was a sensation in spite of the incongruity of song, singer, and band; Olsen's Columbia record, with Morrison singing the refrain, dominated sales charts for two months. Victor and Brunswick raced in with bestselling versions by bandleaders Don Bestor and Victor Young. But Kapp, convinced there was far more to round up, simultaneously released another two versions, by Guy Lombardo (Brunswick 6662) and Bing (Brunswick 6663). Lombardo's sold almost as well as Olsen's (they accounted for two of the year's ten bestselling discs). But Bing's version, nestling directly under Lombardo's, had the more lasting impact. His melancholy moonlit cry sold the tune with the authenticity of a true western balladeer. When he sang it at the Los Angeles Paramount, the audience leaped to its feet and cheered, as if for a patriotic song. Afterward, Gene Autrey took up the song, and Paramount slapped the title on a Randolph Scott western.

"Crosby was one of the main fellas in those days and if he sang a song and it was a halfway decent song, it became a hit," Roy Rogers recalled. "And what we would do, we'd take those big top hit songs and build a story around them and use them to name our pictures."[35] Rogers himself would not become known as King of the Cowboys for nearly a decade, but he realized even then that Bing's way with western songs made them more appealing than did the gruff country singers of the early 1930s. Many other cowboy and country singers agreed, and over the next few years Bing's influence turned up unmistakably in the work of several western balladeers who admired his timbre, enunciation, and feeling.

Bing, in turn, recorded dozens of western songs. Three years after "The Last Round-Up," Paramount devised a horse opera for him, *Rhythm on the Range,* introducing the Sons of the Pioneers, the group that brought Roy Rogers to Hollywood. In years to come, when Roy went out on his own, Bing covered several of his hits, notably "Tumbling Tumbleweeds" and "Cool Water." An ironic intersection in their careers took place in 1944, when Roy premiered "Don't Fence Me In," by the least likely of cowboys, Cole Porter, in *Hollywood Canteen,* and Bing (with the Andrews Sisters) scored the hit, selling millions. "The Last Round-Up" echoed in western circles as late as 1947, when Autry made a movie with that title, underscoring his homage by including a rendition of an intervening Crosby hit, "An Apple for the Teacher."

Yet the most resonant of Bing's cowboy records, by far, was made at the same session as "The Last Round-Up," although it did not initially sell as well. Bing's version of "Home on the Range" turned a little-known saddle song into the most renowned western anthem of all time. In November 1933, when his record was issued, the origin of "Home on the Range" was obscure and widely debated. Folklorist John Lomax, who said he learned it from a black saloonkeeper in Texas, published it in 1910, in *Cowboy Songs and Other Frontier Ballads.* In 1925 a sheet-music arrangement found modest popularity; two years later Vernon Dalhart, the operatic tenor turned hillbilly singer, recorded it for Brunswick. California's radio cowboys picked it up from him, and in 1930 the movies' first crooning western star, Ken Maynard, recorded a version. Not until Bing sang it, however, was the song embraced as a national hymn, so popular as to generate a farcical plagiarism suit that had the unintended benefit of spurring an inquiry into the song's history. It was traced to a poem, "Western Home," written in the 1870s (without the chorus or the phrase "home on the range") by Dr. Brewster Higley, whose neighbor, Dan Kelley, set it to music.

Bing's stirring performance transforms a nostalgic lament into an ode to pioneering, a dream of shared history, a vaguely religious affirmation of fortitude in the face of peril. He made it a Depression song that ignores the Depression, expressing longing, awe, and grace. Bing's subtle embellishments enhance the melody, and his projection and control are unfailingly dramatic, particularly during the soaring eight-bar release. His record offered a transcendent secularity, a well from which all Americans could drink. More prosaically, it anticipated the golden age of gentle-voiced singing cowboys and the Irish sentiment of the John Ford westerns that followed on their heels. FDR acknowledged "Home on the Range" as his favorite song. John Dillinger escaped jail with a wooden gun and drove off singing "The Last Round-Up."

Bing recorded "Home on the Range" twice in the late 1930s, neither version as compelling as the one from 1933, but the performance about which he was most likely to regale friends occurred on August 16, 1935, when Bing and Dixie visited Saratoga for the races. They attended a dinner for the turf riders. "I didn't, uh, skip any drinks that were passed around," he recalled.[36] Afterward, they went to the Arrowhead nightclub, where Guy Lombardo's band was broadcasting:

> And it came over the NBC network that Will Rogers had just been killed up in Alaska with Wiley Post, and they were putting together a memorial program — picking people from all over who could do things in tribute to Will Rogers, and they wanted me to sing "Home on the Range." I was going to have to do it in about ten minutes, and I was a little shaky, from the sauce and from the realization that it was a solemn occasion, and it was a song he dearly loved, and they thought it should be used, and I couldn't remember the words. The time was drawing closer and closer and I kept asking if anybody knew the words. I knew the first line, of course, "Give me a home," and all of a

sudden I'm on the radio. And that was the first time that I really had flop sweat, my palms were wet, my brow was damp, and they were playing the introduction, and there I was. Obviously, I had sobered up a little by that time, and I sang the first line, thinking, "What the hell is the second line." And it came, and then, "What's the third line," and it came. And it kept coming, kept coming, until I was finished. And I was really finished then. I went home and lay down.[37]

18

MORE THAN A CROONER

Bing Crosby — he's a different kind of ladies' man, because he appeals to men! That's the truth! Have you ever heard of the Malden, Massachusetts Bing Crosby Club? There's not a sixteen-year-old microphone-struck girl in it; no sir! That Bing Crosby Club up in the New England state is composed of men all over twenty years of age and every one an athlete.

— Robert Trout, *Wilkins Coffee Time* (1933)[1]

Shortly after going cowboy, Bing inaugurated a CBS radio series for Woodbury ("for the skin you love to touch"), a manufacturer of women's soap based in Cincinnati. The show represented a significant leap in his transition from radio crooner to radio star. Instead of two fifteen-minute recitals a week, the Chesterfield schedule, Woodbury gave him a thirty-minute program once a week, with an announcer, supporting players, and guests. Above all, radio could now boast: Crosby speaks! This came as no surprise to the millions who had seen him do that very thing live and onscreen. Nor was it a revelation to fans who had heard him plug his films in radio promotions. But on his own shows he had never been permitted to talk directly to his radio following.

At first, his new freedom counted for little. The funny, relaxed, quick-thinking, verbally dexterous Bing was nowhere to be found. He stiffly intoned pro forma introductions like "I have the pleasure of singing tonight the feature song from Ben Bernie's new picture, *Shoot the Works.*" Bing had conjured up a personality in pictures. Now he had to find a complementary one for the air.

Easier said than done. Radio comedians invented personality trademarks that were consistently harped on, whether or not they were true to life — Jack Benny's cheapness, Eddie Cantor's pep, Ed Wynn's zaniness, Gracie Allen's dizziness, Will Rogers's horse sense, Joe Penner's idiocy. But Woodbury had hired Crosby as a romantic figure who would appeal to its female customers. Turning him into a jokester was never an option, and Bing didn't give his producer and writer, Burt McMurtrie, much to work with: singer, film star, nice guy. What's more, he was uneasy without a script. The stubborn confidence Bing displayed in devising his film persona was less in evidence when it came to radio, though he knew what he would not do. He refused to accommodate a studio audience or replace his theme song with a Woodbury jingle; when an advertising agent from New York indelicately criticized his work, he threatened to walk. His contract called for thirteen shows at $1,750 per broadcast. By the second season he commanded $6,000, keeping nearly half and paying for the orchestra and arrangements with the rest, thereby securing control over the show's contents.

McMurtrie had produced Paul Whiteman's Old Gold shows and hailed from Spokane. He understood Bing's style and potential as well as anyone but could do little more than suggest the rudiments of a radio identity for him. On the first show, Bing sang "Thanks," "Tomorrow," and "The Last Round-Up"; bantered with announcer Ken Niles about cosmetics; and introduced Lennie Hayton's instrumentals and a vocal by a teenage singer, Mary Lou Raymond. *Billboard* liked the show, relieved that "he neither whistled nor dabbled in his famous impromptu obbligatos."[2]

A livelier atmosphere started taking hold in December, after Bing prevailed upon Woodbury to sign the Mills Brothers as weekly regulars, singing their own numbers and — significantly — backing his. Though little noted or remembered, their hiring represented a landmark for racial integration in radio and music, preceding by two years Benny Goodman's road tour with Teddy Wilson and by three Jack Benny's signing of Eddie "Rochester" Anderson. When the Mills

Brothers were unavailable, Bing sustained the broadcast's high spirits with the Boswell Sisters, whom he famously introduced as "three girls with but a single thought: harmony. And what harmony."

Hayton, basking in the attention of the movie studios, did not renew his Woodbury contract after the first season. His replacements included Gus Arnheim, Jimmy Grier, and ultimately Georgie Stoll, who conducted the orchestra on more than half of Bing's seventy-two Woodbury shows, from mid-1934 through the end of 1935.[3] Like Bing, Stoll was an Armstrong fanatic, but little of that emerged in his arrangements, which, judging from the three surviving episodes, were rather stuffy and unswinging. Other regulars on the show included the singers Kay Thompson, Irene Taylor, the Three Rhythm Kings, and the Williams Sisters — Laura, Alice, and Ethelyn. Alice went on to work with the Music Maids, a popular addition to *Kraft Music Hall* during Bing's tenure.

The show was an instant ratings success. The *New York World-Telegram* observed that of the radio singers who had won so much acclaim only two years earlier, Bing alone maintained "the same level of popularity," adding that he might easily have sustained the Woodbury ratings through the summer had he not "put his foot down" and insisted upon a vacation.[4] The same paper conducted a national radio poll, publishing the results in February 1934. Bing won Best Popular Male Singer and the Boswells, Best Harmony Team. With the Boswells or the Mills Brothers at his side, Bing didn't need much in the way of guests, and he had few good ones — mostly dull comics and stillborn starlets. Radio had yet to become acceptable to Hollywood's supernovas, many of whom would later snub television for the same reason: it was free and common. But in plugging his concurrent movies, Bing scored appearances by his leading ladies, notably Carole Lombard, Kitty Carlisle, Miriam Hopkins, and Joan Bennett, prefiguring the movie colony's delayed appreciation of radio as a publicity bonanza.

Bing's years of undergraduate oratory had taught him that great speakers don't pontificate to the great unwashed. They make contact with their fellows. That was Bing's natural way, enabling him to speak as intimately via the microphone as he sang. Orotund announcers were on their way out — they were silly at best, snobbish at worst. Bing occasionally reached for their affectations (his Woodbury performance of "Just a-Wearyin' for You" is painfully genteel), but he got over the temptation quickly, poking fun at the highfalutin by italicizing a rolled *r* or inserting a ten-dollar word in his plainspoken repartee.

Bing was not the only radio personality who tailored his style to speak to individuals at home rather than to a massive congregation. Nor was he the only one to understand that the public responded to a well-spoken man as long as he refrained from talking down to them. Bing may have learned a trick or two from President Roosevelt, that master of aristocratic candor, whose "fireside chats" debuted seven months before the Woodbury show.[5] With 60 million people tuned in to his first Sunday-evening broadcast, March 12, 1932, FDR spoke warmly and directly, without patronizing folksiness or condescension: "My friends, I want to tell you what has been done in the last few days, why it was done, and what the next steps are going to be."[6] He said it was safe to put money in the bank, and people did. His secretary of labor (and the nation's first female cabinet member), Frances Perkins, recalled, "His face would smile and light up as though he were actually sitting on the front porch or in the parlor with them."[7] Roosevelt's inauguration won Outstanding Broadcast in the *New York World-Telegram* poll.

Roosevelt had begun using radio when he was governor of New York. He was more practiced than Bing in projecting personality through speech. Yet he applied basically the same techniques of directness and enunciation that Bing had mastered in selling his musical style. On one occasion FDR seemed to acknowledge Bing's influence. According to Eddie Cantor, during a March of Dimes broadcast from Warm Springs, Georgia, the president tested the microphone by "crooning in a cracked baritone, 'When [sic] the blue of the night . . . bub-bub-bub-boo!'"[8] The wonder of it is that so few, beyond Bing and Roosevelt, recognized radio's unique power to convey rapport and empathy.

Still, compared with what he later achieved on radio, Bing sounded hesitant on the Woodbury show, though his artless, neighborly way struck a chord. Listeners who once tuned in to hear the crooner now discovered a friend. Bing, logically, began to infuse the show with elements of his personal life. After he attended the Rose Bowl game between Stanford and Columbia in 1934, he talked about it over the air. After Dixie gave birth to twins during his summer break, he employed them in a song cue: "Speaking as the father of twins, I might say, in fact I will say, that it is a double pleasure to be back on this program again. As a result thereof 'I'm humming, I'm whistling, I'm singing.'" The dialogue was often fairly stilted, but it was appealingly modest, even adorable, and usually revealed his singular personality:

> Niles: Say, have you learned much about [the twins]?
>
> Bing: No. It's a new racket for me. But what would you like to know?
>
> Niles: Well, tell me something about them, anything.
>
> Bing: Well, twins usually look alike, having been born more or less under the same conditions and having no preference in the matter.
>
> Niles: There you go, Bing!
>
> Bing: Sure, and if they resemble their mother, they have what might be called a flying start in life.
>
> Niles: What if they resemble their father?
>
> Bing: Well, in that case, they should be held right side up and patted lightly on their respective backs.

Niles was invariably upbeat, nudging the audience about Bing's linguistic playfulness. Bing was more earnest, taking his time, peppering convoluted phrases with slang, and averting banality with little more than a slightly reticent, vernacular charm.

It was too vernacular for Woodbury. On the surface, the company seemed content with its spokesman. Before Bing took his summer break, the sponsor celebrated his success with a giveaway:

> Niles: We think you'll agree the Woodburys have done two very important things this year. They've brought Bing Crosby back to this radio audience, with whom he is such a favorite. And they've created a ten-cent size of Woodbury's facial soap in order that new millions may enjoy the blessings of this scientific beauty aid at a price never heard of before. Tonight Woodbury's makes you an extraordinary offer. In exchange for ten cents, one dime, Woodbury's will send you an attractive gift, the Woodbury loveliness kit [and] an autographed photograph of Bing Crosby. . . . Please send a dime, not stamps.[9]

Yet despite solid ratings, the marriage between sponsor and spokesman was rocky. Woodbury argued that Bing's cool delivery did not confer enough dignity on its products. That impression solidified after *Variety* conducted a street-corner poll on sponsor recognition: fewer than one-fourth of those queried knew who paid Bing's bills. For his part, Bing had a hard time with Woodbury's idea of dignity, as expressed in commercials that managed to insult the very women it hoped to reach. One sketch began with Ken Niles confiding to Bing that he was in love with a woman he had never seen. When Bing tells him he is "full of that boulevard gin," Niles explains that she wears a mask. Two songs later Niles reveals that she removed the mask and was so homely that he pretended not to know her. "Sure glad you didn't get stuck with her," Bing commiserates, to which Niles responds: "The poor thing, Bing, and you know, there are hundreds just like her, who if they only knew about Woodbury's facial soap might easily capture such a prize as Bing or, ah, me."

What really rankled Woodbury was Bing's effectual control of the series. By May 1935 the company made clear its intention to challenge him. The first showdown took place after Bing announced on the air that his friend, actor Andy Devine, would be a guest the following week. The sponsor told Bing that Devine could not appear because his voice, a comically strained gargle caused by a childhood accident, was unsuitable for the air. Next week Bing arrived at the station with Devine and calmly refused to go on unless Andy accompanied him. Minutes before airtime Woodbury backed off and inadvertently launched Devine's long career as a radio entertainer.

Bing refused to relinquish authority in choosing songs or guests, and the company refused to renew his contract, which was up June 11, 1935. Yet even with the end in sight, the clashes continued; at one point Bing would have walked (John Boles, of all people, was hired as an emergency substitute) had not CBS convinced him to complete his obligation. After Woodbury, Bing would not be at liberty for long. NBC became interested in him late that summer when Bing appeared alongside the Dorsey Brothers as guests of *Kraft Music Hall*'s ratings-challenged host, Paul Whiteman. By December Bing would be Kraft's new host, commencing an eleven-year run that not only redefined the variety show — it reinvented the image of Bing Crosby.

One reason professional strife never got the better of Bing is that he always had so many fish to fry. Pursuing work and play with equal dili-

gence, he consigned virtually every minute of his day to a schedule —
to the dismay of his family, which was not always accorded prime
time. While Woodbury was pulling its hair, Bing shot one picture
after another: four features and one short subject between January 29, 1934, and January 19, 1935. After he completed *Too Much
Harmony,* Bing owed Paramount one picture on his original contract.
Chagrined by the difference in quality between MGM's *Going Hollywood* and its own Crosby vehicles, the studio resolved to make it a
first-rate production. Paramount could ill afford to lose him and had
recently endured a reminder of his finicky independence.

Paramount's stars had been assigned small parts in a film of *Alice
in Wonderland,* in which they were disguised by makeup intended to
approximate John Tenniel's illustrations. While the other contract
players signed on, Bing (through Everett) opened negotiations.
Although he could not see the point of appearing under a mound of
makeup, he agreed to participate on two conditions: a week's salary
and permission to do another picture for an outside studio. Paramount agreed to the first and balked at the second. Furious at Bing's
intransigence, the studio offered his part to Russ Columbo before
settling on Cary Grant. It also signed Lanny Ross, a tenor who
became popular on the *Show Boat* radio hour, promising a big buildup
and casting him in *College Rhythm* (opposite Jack Oakie as a football
star). As insurance against Crosby, Ross was marginally more viable
than, say, John Boles, and the executives knew it.

They also knew that Bing had been damn shrewd to avoid *Alice in
Wonderland,* a miserable flop, and that although Everett served as his
cover, Bing made the decisions. As Bob Crosby once noted, "A lot of
people thought Everett was a financial wizard, but he wasn't. He
would maybe get a call from someone that would want Bing to make a
picture, and he'd go to Bing and say, Do you want to do it or don't you
want to do it? And Bing would say yes or no or I want more money or
I'd like to read the script, whatever."[10] While Lewis Carroll took Paramount to the cleaners, Bing prepared for the adaptation of another
British classic, by Carroll's young Scottish contemporary, James M.
Barrie.

The Admirable Crichton, a comedy about class divisions and the
perfect butler, had been Hollywoodized as a silent film, *Male and Female,* and was now decked out as a musical, ominously titled *Cruise*

to Nowhere. Enigmatically renamed *We're Not Dressing,* the result was frothy and absurd but vastly entertaining, the class war having been reduced to a more dependable formula of boy meets girl, annoys girl, wins girl, rejects girl, and walks into sunset with girl. In this instance, the girl is a rich and haughty brat, played by Carole Lombard, and the boy a lowly sailor (who wants to be an architect, so it's all right) employed on her yacht. The yacht sinks and, mirabile dictu, all the stars drift to the same spot on an apparently deserted island, where the sailor's skills create a turnabout, placing him in charge. An elaborate joke involving Lombard's panties (an example of pre-Code raffishness) uncovers the presence elsewhere on the island of a pair of natural scientists. Before the castaways learn they are not alone, however, the sailor (Bing) has brought Lombard down a peg, and they are chastely reconciled.

The making of *We're Not Dressing,* including three weeks of shooting on Catalina Island, was a happy experience for everyone, especially Bing and Lombard, who became fast friends (although she was then engaged to his rival Russ Columbo).[11] It was an important picture for her, the first to suggest the screwball flair for comedy she unleashed in *Twentieth Century, My Man Godfrey, Nothing Sacred,* and other films before her much lamented death in a plane crash. She had not been the studio's first choice. Miriam Hopkins demurred because she thought the script trivialized Barrie, and Paramount unsuccessfully asked MGM for the loan of Karen Morley or Mae Clarke (Charles Butterworth and W. C. Fields were also sought, presumably for the role played by Leon Errol). Two years earlier Lombard had turned down the Leila Hyams part in *The Big Broadcast,* which might well have salvaged Carole's faltering career. She leaped at the offer of a second shot in a Crosby picture.

Carole, bemused by Bing's cool tact, played off it between takes in a series of practical jokes. Bing enjoyed her dedicated swearing — "colorful epithets" he described as "good, clean, and lusty. Her swearwords weren't obscene. They were gusty and eloquent. They resounded, they bounced. They had honest zing!"[12] With amazement, he described her dash to the ocean after inadvertently dousing herself with wintergreen: "She appeared practically unclothed," he wrote, the adverb added as a gentlemanly euphemism.[13] She occasionally enlivened the set by flashing him. While breakfasting at Catalina's St.

Catherine Hotel, where elderly regulars stared disapprovingly at the movie clan, she "came slinking in" and loudly cried, "Bing! Did I leave my nightie in your room last night?"[14] For two days she sent Bing a one-word telegram every fifteen minutes or so: the word was NOW. "The fact that she could make us think of her as being a good guy rather than a sexy mamma is one of those unbelievable manifestations impossible to explain," Bing wrote. "She was the least prudish person I've ever known."

Carole had one weak point, however; she could not stand to have her face touched, and one scene called for Bing to slap her. At her request, he refrained during rehearsal, but when the scene was filmed, she responded violently. Howard Hawks liked to take credit for creating Lombard as a comic actress by encouraging her to kick John Barrymore in the balls in *Twentieth Century*. According to Bing, she required no coaching; she kicked, punched, bit, screamed, tore off his toupee, and finally "wept hysterically."[15] Bing recalled that he refused to do a second take and that some of the tantrum was actually used, but it wasn't. In the film, she returns his slap with a kiss.

Bing also had trouble with Bruno, the ship's pet bear, whom the sailor is obliged to soothe with a lullaby, "Good Night Lovely Little Lady." One scene in which he narrowly averted disaster did get into the film. While brushing the bear's fur, Bing sings "She Reminds Me of You." Bruno suddenly tries to get away. Bing grins but continues lip-synching while manfully holding on.

Norman Taurog directed *We're Not Dressing* with brisk confidence, sprinkling story points amid musical numbers, not allowing a dull moment to intrude in its seventy-four minutes, thanks to a splendid cast — Burns and Allen (never better), Ethel Merman, Leon Errol, Ray Milland — and no less than six songs expertly rendered by Bing as the radiant, funny Lombard gazes at him, alternately happy and dismissive, but mostly happy, especially during his swing chorus on "May I?" The film's luminous look was created by photographer Charles Lang. Like many great stars, Bing developed a keen interest in cinematography, realizing that its masters influenced not only a film's veneer but the actors' glamour. More than half of his fifty-four features (excluding those in which he makes cameo or one-song appearances) were shot by just four of Hollywood's most accomplished cameramen: Lang, Karl Struss, Lionel Lindon, and George

Barnes. Lang worked on six Crosby pictures, and his contribution here is evident in the sharp black-and-white contrasts, plush shots of Catalina, and unmistakable aura surrounding the principals.

Though cheeky and adult, *We're Not Dressing* lacks the sophistication of the year's best comedies, *It Happened One Night* and *The Thin Man,* but remains a standout among the musicals of 1934. *Dames* and *The Merry Widow,* though more assured, restate the tried-and-true formulas of Busby Berkeley and Ernst Lubitsch. By contrast, *We're Not Dressing* and *The Gay Divorcee* (the first film in which Fred Astaire and Ginger Rogers assume lead roles) augur the musicals to come, for they are built around virtuoso American performers, not the stock juveniles, backstage wannabes, and Continental rascals of the past. Ballyhooed by Paramount for featuring more Crosby songs than any of its predecessors, *We're Not Dressing* proved that Bing could enchant audiences through three-minute vocal close-ups and offered his most informal and amusing performance to date.

He was immeasurably aided by Mack Gordon and Harry Revel's energetic score, which exploits his gifts for jazz and lullabies. Bing had known the team in New York — they entertained at his Friars Club send-off — and loved the way Gordon, an ebullient man and lively singer, demonstrated his new songs. For their first Paramount picture they wrote "Did You Ever See a Dream Walking?," which became an outstanding Crosby recording at the close of 1933 — boldly expressive and stoked with understated rhythm. *We're Not Dressing* was their second film, and no less than five of its songs became Crosby hits: "May I?," "Once in a Blue Moon," "She Reminds Me of You," "Good Night Lovely Little Lady," and "Love Thy Neighbor." Inevitably, Gordon and Revel were hired for his next film, which went into production in April, the same month *We're Not Dressing* opened at Grauman's Chinese Theatre to the usual lively crowds.

Most critics found it breezy fun and generously lauded Bing (the *New York World-Telegram* called him "an excellent comedian"), while *Time* reliably snorted: "Interspersed liberally with shots of Crooner Crosby's blank, adenoidal face, *We're Not Dressing* is fair entertainment, easy-going, incredible and sanitary." If the movie was all those things, it was clearly because of and not in spite of Bing — not least the sanitary part. Bing looks desolate during his big love scene, which lacks the anticipated kiss. Lombard supplies heat in her revealing gowns, as does an exasperated Bing, when he drags her off and chains her to a tree. "I suppose a fate worse than death awaits me," she says. "How do you know it's worse than death?" he replies. "You've never been dead, have you?"[16] Bing's acting had improved, though he was still given to moonfaced pouts. A breakthrough would occur late in the year with *Here Is My Heart*. But first came the gender-reversal comedy, *She Loves Me Not*.

Miriam Hopkins did not know Bing would be her costar when she accepted the role of Curley Flagg, a nightclub hoofer who witnesses a murder and hides out in a Princeton dorm, disguised as a boy. The role of college student Paul Lawton was first offered to Gary Cooper, who refused it because he feared Hopkins would steal the picture, her forte. A busier, twitchier actress never lived, though she could be highly effective in dramatic roles. *She Loves Me Not,* however, was farce with a pedigree, first as a novel (by Edward Hope), then as a Howard Lindsay stage hit, which was packing the Forty-sixth Street Theater as the film went into production and did not close until four months after the movie's release. All the play's political satire was deleted, but Paramount retained a few barbs about salacious movie producers and arrogant press flacks. Gordon and Revel wrote three songs, but Ralph Rainger and Leo Robin contributed the picture's immensely popular ballad, "Love in Bloom." One Paramount executive demanded that their song be pulled, citing it as too sophisticated for the general public.

Hopkins's scene-stealing shenanigans were legendary,[17] but her confidence was shaken when she saw that the picture would now be perceived as a Bing Crosby vehicle. The imperturbable Bing, fast becoming renowned for his letter-perfect first takes, knew how to handle her, as she explained to interviewer John Kobal:

> And do you know another *doll* was Bing Crosby. Oh my God! We did *She Loves Me Not*. Now I thought I was a dramatic actress, you see, and I want to rehearse everything first. I was on his radio show all the time, and I said, "Bing can't we rehearse this show?" He ran through it once and we went out and sat in his car and had a cigarette. And I said, "Can't we do it again?" And he said: "Sweetie, no! We'd get stale. Let's just do it, you know, we've got the line. I'll say something and [you] ad-lib back and forth with me." Well, there was one scene in *She Loves*. I

said: "Bing, I'd *like* to rehearse this with you." He says . . . , "Now, you know very well, you've been in the theater and New York, and I'm just a guy who dropped a load of pumpkins." I said, "What do you mean, 'dropped a load of pumpkins?'" And that was the famous line, "I'm just a guy who dropped a load of pumpkins," you know. Oh, but so darling![18]

Kitty Carlisle, who played the university president's daughter and Paul's true love, considered Hopkins surprisingly nice, "the most generous of colleagues, offering to rehearse before each scene."[19] Carlisle had appeared in only one other film, *Murder at the Vanities*, but — trained in opera and theater — she tended to look upon Hollywood from an aristocratic perch, condescending and ambitious. Yet she was startled by Bing's singing. "I was a serious singer, I had studied seriously, and I was impressed by his technique, his effortlessness, the fact that his voice was so much bigger and more available for, really, operatic roles than you saw in the movies. To me there was Bing Crosby and then everybody else." She also marveled at his unaffectedness: "He certainly didn't pamper himself. He'd come in chewing gum and eating chocolate and then just begin to sing and it was melting." They had little in common and nothing to talk about, she with her "European social training" and he "a man's man who got along very well with the crew." She could recall only one personal moment off the set, when Bing showed her "a very pretty, rather modest diamond necklace. He said, Did I like it, did I think [Dixie] would like it? I said I think she'd adore it."[20]

Bing was enthusiastic about the film, but the overall pressure was beginning to tell. Bing confided to Ted his need for a break:

I am three weeks along into *She Loves Me Not* a collegiate comedy with a couple songs, from the play now current in New York. It has a terrific script, great dialogue, and grand situation. I don't see how it can fail to be a great laugh picture, and fine for me.

Dad had some teeth out the other day and was a little out of line for a bit, but is okay now. I have been so busy I haven't seen much of mother or anyone else for that matter, but at last reports she was in good health and spirits. Everett is, of course, living the life of Riley, and his family are well.

I finish the picture in another week, the radio May 26th, and following this plan on resting for possibly a couple months. Feeling a

little tired, and further income in May & June will put me in a very dis-
agreeable income tax bracket. So I might as well rest as give it back to
Uncle Sam. I am trying to pick up a ranch near San Diego, not too
elaborate, and if successful, you can come down and start me off rite
on some intensive gentleman farming.[21]

Elliott Nugent, a successful stage actor, director, and playwright,
directed *She Loves Me Not* with little flair, from a script by producer
Benjamin Glazer. The film has dated badly, in part because Hopkins,
in her determination to be funny, goes so far over the top that no one
can reign her in, certainly not Bing or Eddie Nugent, who plays Paul's
housemate, Buzz (the role that made Burgess Meredith a Broadway
star). The most persuasive bits poke fun at Hollywood: Buzz's father
(George Barbier) is a producer who intends to capitalize on Curley's
notoriety by putting her in a picture (replacing one Yvonne Lamour, a
name that was considered satirical until Dorothy Lamour came to
town). He promises his backers that her clothes will be ripped off in
every scene, while she remains a virginal victim of circumstance.[22]

She Loves Me Not is of interest for the way it cuts against the grain
of the era's other transvestite movies, in which women invariably play
men as serious and sexually repressed. Hopkins's Curley Flagg is initially hesitant about entering the dorm. But as soon as she loses her
hair to Paul's scissors and trades in her clothes for Buzz's pajamas, she
becomes sexually ravenous, while the boys act like affronted fops.
Paul stammers and turns schoolmarmish: "Now you listen to me,
Curley Flagg, I got no more interest in you than I have in the United
States Senate." But the joke is muffled, because Curley is very girly —
mascara will do that. Only a murderous goon is, briefly, confused by
her wiles; he figures she's gay.

Bing, who turned thirty-one during filming, is an absurdly seasoned undergraduate. He offers a few comical double takes (notably
a Stan Laurel turn at the end), but his vest buttons do not close. "He
was very good in movies except that he didn't look right," Kitty
Carlisle remembered. "He had a behind the size of a barn. There's a
shot in *She Loves Me Not* where he turns and walks — I mean, it was
like a ship leaving shore. But Bing could make fun of anything about
himself. He was not at all pompous."[23] A mystery to several leading
ladies who felt neglected by him off the set, Bing — as he once said

of his association with Bob Hope — preferred to save it all for the camera, a practice that clearly pays off in his duets with Kitty. However aloof he may have acted between takes, he genuinely lights up as he sings to her "Straight from the Shoulder" and "Love in Bloom," at the thirty-minute mark. Kitty, too, registers delight when they sing together. One reason the duets are so convincing is that Nugent shot them live, an unusual and risky decision. "Why we did it live I'll never know," Kitty said. "I never asked questions. I got onto the set at nine and there was a little orchestra and we recorded. I was so nervous I thought I'd jump out of my skin. We did it two or three times and that was the end of it."[24] Watching footage of Carlisle and Bing, Paramount's pint-size studio chief Emanuel Cohen must have imagined he was brewing his own version of Nelson Eddy and Jeanette MacDonald. He signed Kitty to Bing's next film.

"Love in Bloom" handed Bing another megahit, topping sales charts for nearly four months — six weeks in the number one slot. That year the Academy Awards initiated a best song category, and "Love in Bloom" was nominated. It lost to "The Continental" (from *The Gay Divorcee*) but paved the way for a Crosby statistic that is not likely to be broken. Between 1934 and 1960 he introduced more songs that were nominated for Academy Awards (fourteen) and more that won (four) than any other performer; Astaire and Sinatra tie for second place with eight nominations each. Bing thought "Love in Bloom" "a good melody, easy to remember, a lovely song."[25] Kitty expected it to become her theme. Neither was pleased by what happened to it. As Jack Benny told the story, he and his wife, Mary, went to a supper club one night, and the bandleader asked him to sit in. When Benny stepped up and borrowed a violin, he noticed an arrangement of "Love in Bloom" on a music stand and played it with predictably amusing results. A columnist wrote about his impromptu performance, and the next time the Bennys went to a club, the band serenaded them with "Love in Bloom" as a joke. "So I decided to adopt it as my theme song," Benny explained.[26] Overnight the melody became a Pavlovian laugh-getter; no matter who played or sang it, audiences howled. "I always took umbrage at that," Bing said.[27] Kitty felt she had been robbed.[28]

Few moviegoers noticed at the time, but Bing's looks changed after *She Loves Me Not*: his ears were finally liberated. During one scene, midway through filming, the hot lighting repeatedly loosened the spirit gum. According to Frank Westmore, "this happened no less than ten times," whereupon "Bing furiously refused to allow the errant ear to be stuck back."[29] Bing recalled, "They said you've got to put them back, we've got half the picture with your ears in — you put 'em out, you'll look like a taxi with both doors open and you'll never match the other scenes. So I said, all right, I'll put 'em back for the rest of this picture. We had a couple weeks to go, and then the next picture, that was the end of it."[30] Wally Westmore involved himself in the battle, convincing Manny Cohen that Bing's ears did not affect his voice.

Audiences paid little attention to his ears, but thanks to Lang's astute camera work, they did begin to notice a unique and endearing physical aspect of his speech: the fluttering cheeks and popping lips when he pronounced *w* or *b* words. A phrase like "Well, what is it?" suggested a goldfish recycling oxygen, a tic that kept mimics busy for years.

She Loves Me Not outgrossed all of Bing's previous pictures. This time most critics were disarmed, and not just the Louellas. Otis Ferguson of *The New Republic* noted a plug in the film for Chase National (which had Paramount by the throat) but praised it for its honest professionalism. "Bing Crosby sings pleasantly and even acts a bit," he wrote.[31] *Time* considered it "creditable," reserving praise for Hopkins ("squeaks and wriggles pleasantly") and the new songs while remaining mum on the singers.[32] An especially perceptive analysis of the Crosby phenomenon appeared in the *New York Herald Tribune*. After noting Bing's obvious appeal to women, the writer continued:

> Perhaps it is his uncompromising masculinity and obvious inability to overplay anything that make him so innocuous to his own sex. Unlike most of the other radio names, he never seems to be trying to be charming. The toothy smile, the Sunday School superintendent's unction [play] no part in the Crosby technique. He borrows something from the old deadpan school of slapstick comedy and something from the insouciant ogle of the professional masher to produce an effect of being congenitally at home and sure of himself anywhere — not working hard in the least, just taking it as it comes.[33]

The better the public came to know Bing, the better it liked him; the more it learned, the more it wanted to learn. Paramount, having signed him to another three-picture deal, put its publicity department into overdrive to maximize the attraction of his personality. Of the several full-page ads it purchased in *Variety*, one took a conspicuously novel tack: a caricature of a man pushing a stroller and the boldfaced headline SHE LOVES ME NOT IS BING CROSBY'S GREATEST TRIUMPH SINCE THE TWINS!

While Bing was shooting films, flogging soap for Woodbury, and recording, Dixie was on every bit as tight a schedule. She learned about her second pregnancy a few months after she gave birth to Gary. Kitty Lang, who helped nurse her as well as the infant, had briefly left for New York to settle Eddie's affairs, promising she'd be back before Dixie delivered. She returned to find Dixie suffering from chronic back pain. An X ray revealed twins. Despite her distress, Dixie was pleased when tiny Monogram Pictures called and asked her to star opposite Robert Armstrong in a quickie production they promised to complete in less than two weeks. She asked Kitty to be her stand-in so they could continue to spend afternoons together. Kitty's own life had just taken an upward turn. Dixie's friend, Alice Ross, now working as her secretary, located a small home for Kitty in Toluca. With help from friends (Richard Arlen's brother-in-law was the contractor), Kitty rebuilt it to suit herself, a niece, and two dogs. When one of the dogs took ill, she took it to the local veterinarian, Dr. William Sexton. She became Kitty Sexton.

Knowing that Dixie was pregnant, the film crew showed her every consideration. Kitty was paid handsomely — $200, nearly three times the going rate for two weeks of extra work — and the shoot presented no problems. But the songs unnerved Dixie, who feared everyone would compare her with Bing; she steeled herself with a few drinks before making the prerecordings. The film, *Manhattan Love Song*, was of no consequence, and Dixie looks pallid. Shortly after it was completed, in her fourth month, she experienced contractions and her cautious doctor ordered her to bed, forbade parties and alcohol, and limited her time with Gary to visits in her bedroom, where she remained for the next four months. Bing made up for it by being "a doting father," Kitty remembered. "As a result, Gary did become a little spoiled."[34]

The twins were born six weeks premature, weighing less than four pounds each, on July 13, 1934. Their arrival was treated as a major news story. When Bing allowed them to be photographed with Gary for the press the following September, the *Los Angeles Times* ran the picture on its front page, right-hand column above the fold. As the babies lay in the incubator, Kitty visited the ward with Bing and asked him about their names. He said, "Well, I'll name the largest one Dennis Michael, after my family, as he looks more Irish, and Dixie can name the other."[35] Dixie chose Phillip Lang, Phillip from the Greek "lover of horses," and Lang after Eddie. When Ted's wife, Hazel, had delivered twin girls a few months before, Ted wrote Bing, "You have to have three of a kind to beat a pair of queens." Bing now wired his brother, "A pair of kings arrived today."[36]

With only thirteen months separating Gary and the twins, two nurses were added to the household. Gary, resenting the interlopers, began acting out to claim the attention of his parents. The fraternal rivalry would remain a constant in the boys' lives, generating countless fistfights and feuds and ultimately resulting in a break between Gary and Phillip. As her strength returned, Dixie grew bored. The nurses took over her chores with the babies while she took up tennis, revealing a genuine talent for the game until a kidney infection forced her to give it up. That, Kitty thought, "started Dixie drinking more than usual, particularly as it meant she was sitting home again."[37]

In the weeks between the completion of *She Loves Me Not* and the birth of the twins, Bing bought a sixty-five-acre property in Rancho Santa Fe, twenty-five miles north of San Diego, five miles from Del Mar. The large adobe ranch house, with exterior walls two feet thick and a white wraparound porch supported by beams and posts, was built a hundred years before, and Bing hired architect Lillian J. Rice to restore the cultivated simplicity of the nineteenth-century Spanish style. At the same time, he modernized it, adding a new wing, a tennis court, and a swimming pool. Dixie decorated with sturdy wooden furniture, brass adornments, gingham and chintz, keeping it spare to protect valuables from the three infants, whose maple cribs were aligned in one room, with a rocking chair separating Gary's from those of the twins.

Except for one historic recording session (Decca's first) on August 8, Bing was free until late in the month, when filming on *Here Is My Heart* began. He and Dixie spent much of that time at the ranch, where her health improved as they entertained friends. Publicity photographs of Bing and Dixie, looking trim, youthful, even enchanted, on the tennis court or by the pool glisten with romance. Bing invested in his first racehorses and kept riding mounts at the ranch. He even labored with the work crew on the construction site for days, returning to Hollywood with callused hands. That did not fit the image of the self-made prince and his devoted princess, so publicity photographs focused on Bing in his yachting cap and Dixie — incandescently blond — in a bathing suit, the loving pair incarnating a fantasy as appealing as any movie.

Back at Toluca, the old routine ensued. Bing returned to work while Dixie sat disconsolately at home. Her own career was little more than a memory, despite the just-released *Manhattan Love Song,* of which *Variety* reported: "Film shows the potential value of Dixie Lee and Helen Flint, both of whom can go places if properly handled, especially Miss Flint."[38] Dixie enjoyed Bing's triumphs but envied them a little, too. She wilted when obliged to meet the press, always as an appendage to Bing, never as an accomplished entertainer in her own right. A few drinks helped her face his clamorous public. Kitty suggested to Bing that Dixie needed a mink coat and other accessories suitable to her station as a star's wife. "You're right," he told her. "I never thought of it."[39] The next day the two women went on a spree and bought everything Dixie wanted. At other times Dixie was loath to spend money at all.

With Larry Crosby acting as her agent, Dixie was signed to star in a Paramount film, *Love in Bloom.* She of course had no say concerning the title, which exploited Bing's song (though it was not performed in the picture) and underscored her connection to the singer. But she was adamant that Paramount not promote her as Mrs. Bing Crosby. Paramount hardly promoted her at all. Dixie had the central role but was billed fourth, after Burns and Allen and Joe Morrison, the tenor who introduced "The Last Round-Up" — a strange choice for a leading man at Bing's studio until one remembers that the Crosby-style baritones who overwhelmed the business a few years later were not yet on the scene. Morrison proved no more tempting to moviegoers than Lanny Ross and left the business within a year. So did Dixie. And yet *Love in Bloom,* though negligible, contains her best work. She brought pathos to the shamelessly clichéd role of a street-smart trouper from the dregs of show business, and her sole musical number — Morrison did most of the singing — is the picture's undoubted highlight.

Most of the figures involved in the production had worked with Bing, including producer Benjamin Glazer, director Elliott Nugent, and songwriter Mack Gordon, who composed the unmemorable songs without his partner, Harry Revel, though Revel received screen credit anyway. But Dixie, never one to visit her husband's sets, did not know the crew, and the crew did not know her. They were all embarrassed by their first meeting.

Dixie had dyed her hair a golden red, and on the first day of shooting, Kitty was sent to wardrobe to find a matching wig and a dress so that she could serve as her friend's stand-in during lighting tests. The wardrobe mistress fitted her with a wig that might have suited Harpo Marx and a tight sheath dress. As Wally Westmore worked on Dixie in her dressing room, Kitty, feeling like a stuffed sausage, waited on the set. When the assistant stage manager called for cast and crew, she draped a full-length mink over her shoulders, put on dark glasses, picked up a script and Dixie's purse (which Dixie had asked her to safekeep), and joined the others. Cameraman Leo Tover (*College Humor*), mistaking Kitty for the star, panicked. He had been told Dixie was pretty, he mumbled to his assistants. While Kitty baked under the lights, Tover circled his team for a pep talk, imploring them, for Bing's sake, to make Dixie look good. Minutes later Larry brought in Dixie, groomed to gleaming perfection in a pleated dress. Tover ordered Kitty to work in street clothes.

Love in Bloom effectively marked the end of Dixie's career. She was twenty-three, though she looked older and warier. *Variety* said she played her part "excellently,"[40] but only Larry thought it would boost her standing. Convinced that the experience "built up her confidence,"[41] he convinced Jesse Lasky to give her the lead in his doomed 1935 Fox production *Redheads on Parade,* in which the twins — not yet nine months old — make their debut and Dixie plays opposite the recurring John Boles. Larry wrote Ted it was "sure fire to make her a star — the only gal in it. She made some great records for Decca, & is singing and acting swell as I told her she does better without liquid stimulant — more natural."[42] But the picture bombed. Aside from a few radio spots (notably a star turn on Al Jolson's *Shell Chateau*) and two records with Bing, Dixie enjoyed no more professional hurrahs. The stage jitters that had always plagued her increased to the point where she declined to appear in public. Yet, as the wife of one of the most adored men in America, her name was known to everyone.

Another career ended, tragically, on September 2, 1934, when Russ Columbo died in a bizarre shooting accident, at twenty-six. Though no longer a major rival, he had continued to shadow Bing, aiming for a career in movies. Appearing in the tawdry *Broadway Through a Keyhole* (based on Ruby Keeler's affair with a mobster when she was young), he did well enough to land a contract with Universal. But Latin lovers were out of season, and his *Wake Up and Dream* was a disaster; that it provided him with his first hit in two years, "When You're in Love," could be largely attributed to the controversy surrounding his death.

Russ had been killed while visiting a friend, Hollywood photographer Lansing Brown, who showed him a set of antique dueling pistols, not realizing that one pistol held a live charge. When it went off accidentally, the bullet ricocheted off a mahogany desk and through Columbo's eye. A new Columbo legend sprang to life as Carole Lombard, who called Russ "the great love of my life,"[43] and other friends conspired to keep Russ's ailing mother from learning of his death; they regularly sent her checks and letters purportedly mailed by her son from various European cities where he claimed to be in great demand. The charade continued until Mrs. Columbo's passing, two years after Lombard lost her own life. At the funeral, Carole had sobbed uncontrollably, comforted by Bing, who served as a pallbearer. Five years later she married Clark Gable. In January 1942, while returning from a midwestern tour to promote U.S. bonds, Carole Lombard died in a plane crash, at thirty-three.

Larry's disappointment with Dixie's retreat from show business was matched by his general frustration with the entertainment world and his brothers. He wrote to Ted: "Bing too heavy — testy & hard to handle. May quit anytime. Ev a big shot, etc. The future — *very* indefinite. All depends. This is a *tough* racket! Nothing done in a business way! Merit is the last thing that counts."[44] Yet at that very moment, Bing's film acting was rising to a new level. While Dixie vainly went through the paces of her comeback, Bing completed the picture that would at last convert his detractors and secure his position as a captivating comic actor — *Here Is My Heart*. Improbably, the plot hinges on antique dueling pistols.

Adapted from Alfred Savoir's play *The Grand Duchess and the Waiter* (filmed in 1926), the picture reunited Bing with director Frank Tuttle and inaugurated his long collaboration with his favorite cameraman in the prewar period, Karl Struss. Having served up "Love in Bloom," Leo Robin and Ralph Rainger helped Bing to three more brass rings with their new score: the perennial jazz standard "Love Is Just Around the Corner" (written by Robin with Lewis Gensler), the bygone "With Every Breath I Take," and the classic ballad "June in January," which dominated sales charts for nearly two months.

As casting began, Paramount sounded out the idea of promoting Bing and Kitty Carlisle as a new romantic team by asking exhibitors for their opinions. The results convinced Manny Cohen he was on the right track. The pair's costars included some of the finest character actors in the business: Roland Young, Alison Skipworth, Akim Tamiroff, and William Frawley (a longtime Crosby pal), as well as the mysterious Marian Mansfield, a fetching and enthusiastic young woman whose only other appearance in pictures was a minor role in Dixie's *Love in Bloom*.

Once again Carlisle was touched by Bing's professionalism and modesty. "He was always right, Johnny-on-the-spot. We had Alison Skipworth and Roland Young and Reginald Owen, three first-class stage stars, much older than we were, and we were doing a scene with them, and he turned to me and he said, 'What the hell are we doing starring in this movie with those folks?' He could not get over the fact that they were the supporting cast."[45] According to Tuttle, the script was written by Harlan Thompson (who shares screen credit with Edwin Justus Mayer) with an assist from playwright Vincent Lawrence, who was hired to write an extended love scene between a waiter (Bing) and an impossibly lofty White Russian princess (Kitty). "They played it to the hilt," Tuttle wrote. He believed that Bing had "developed into a first-rate comedian" and was especially tickled by an episode in which Bing serves the Russians while wearing a fake mustache that falls into their soup: "He played this broad scene with the telling seriousness of an accomplished farceur."[46]

The story concerns a radio singer named J. Paul Jones, who, having made his first million, sets out to do all the things he dreamed of doing as a boy, including fishing dead center in the Atlantic Ocean, singing "Yankee Doodle" to the Sphinx, presenting dueling pistols owned by John Paul Jones (no relation) to the Naval Academy, and marrying a princess. He already has one of the pistols and learns that the second is owned by Princess Alexandra, in Monte Carlo. Money and class drive the plot. To get access to the princess, he pretends to be a waiter, secretly purchasing the hotel to further his ruse. When he discovers that the high-living Russians are penniless, he surreptitiously stuffs their purses with cash. As in *We're Not Dressing*, he brings the highborn down to his own exemplary plane. "You can't offend royalty," his hotel manager cautions. "No, you probably can't," Bing says, "but let's make an effort anyhow." He ultimately lands his princess and converts her family to capitalism, offering one relative an honest day's work as a hotel doorman.

The Ruritanian romance between commoner and royalty was old hat long before 1934, but Bing gives it a new twist, playing the commoner as an Everyman American of such good and honest disposition that Old World values crumble before him. His performance is utterly relaxed and infectious. He more than holds his own with those eminent stage actors, taking quiet command of every scene, confidently inserting Bingisms: a pet phrase ("keep it shady") or a cowboy inflection or an Oliver Hardy chin waggle. Bing's love of the old comedians is particularly apparent in a scene in which he adopts the mustache and squint made famous by Jimmy Finlayson, a ubiquitous actor in the classic shorts of Mack Sennett and Hal Roach.

Tuttle, who propels the film at a clip, is no less sure of the material. A sequence in which several servants squeeze Bing into his waiter uniform is worthy of Lubitsch, and a strangely disconnected passage in which Bing stalks a man down a corridor is his homage to silent comedy. No little credit must go to Karl Struss, who won the first Academy Award for cinematography, for *Sunrise*. Bing finally looks handsome, every vestige of callowness gone. Struss shadows Bing's features to make them appear chiseled and strong, while his eyes are limpidly romantic. In one diverting scene, the camera is all but stationary as Bing governs and sustains the action on his own: he is in his room, listening to his own record of "June in January," whistling a duet, reading a paper, changing from a robe to a dinner jacket, singing along. When his recorded self finishes with a head tone, he kibitzes, "Well, you made it."

Paramount knew it had something special and issued several publicity shots, most featuring Tuttle, including one with Kitty and Bing hanging on to the director's tall shoulders. As usual, Bing did not allow himself to be billed alone or above the title; in the ads Carlisle's name is the same size as his. But billing, publicity, and good reviews did not help her case at Paramount, which deemed her neither beautiful nor charming enough to go the distance. "There was something in *Photoplay* that I was sort of the young star of the year. And I got notices," she recalled. "I really thought I was on my way. That's why I was so surprised when they paid me off and sent me home."[47]

The reviews focused on the leading man. "Bing Crosby is something more than a crooner; he is a comedian with a perfect sense of timing," declared the New York *Daily News*.[48] The venture was praised by *Variety* as "an excellent example of musical comedy picture making," especially Bing's duet with his own recording.[49] Even *Time*, which months earlier had found the Crosby face blank and adenoidal, capitulated: "To cinemaddicts who share the Princess' feeling about crooners, *Here Is My Heart* will reveal that Bing Crosby is not only an accomplished singer but a talented comedian."[50] Marquis Busby expressed the consensus in the *Los Angeles Examiner*: "As I see it, Clark Gable, Fredric March, and Gary Cooper had better take a good look at the writing on the wall. They'd better hurry and take some singing lessons. Now all the studios are looking for another Bing Crosby."[51]

Yet *Here Is My Heart* was for many years a forgotten film, out of circulation since the 1930s. Paramount's copies rusted, and the picture was presumed lost, though Bing's version of the commoner had a lingering afterlife. Billy Wilder reworked it in his script for Lubitsch's *Ninotchka,* in which a Soviet snob succumbs to the American way, and in his self-directed *The Emperor Waltz* (1948), starring Bing as a phonograph salesman who brings to heel an Austrian countess. Then in July 1977, three months before his death, Bing invited film preservationist and Crosby collector Bob DeFlores to his home to screen for him some rare short films Bing had not seen since they were made. At the end of the day, he offered DeFlores anything he wanted from his nearly complete vault collection, including a pristine duplicate of the original print of *Here Is My Heart*. The picture's long neglect is puzzling because it is central to Bing's canon, both for the quality of his performance and for launching his new image as an all-American character: a plucky, eternally boyish, self-made millionaire with a common touch and uncommon voice.

Midway through shooting *Here Is My Heart*, Tuttle threw a party for Bing and Dixie to celebrate their fifth wedding anniversary, a lavish Beverly Hills affair climaxing with a midnight swim. It had been a blessed year — the twins, the ranch, a career of limitless horizon. On Christmas Day, shortly after the film debuted in New York, Bing celebrated the reopening of the Santa Anita racetrack in Arcadia, a bedroom community northeast of Los Angeles. It was a momentous occasion. The original Santa Anita was built in 1907 and failed quickly; but the new one, constructed at a site several miles from the first, brought racing back to the San Gabriel Valley for the first time in twenty-five years. Bing invested $10,000 to secure box seats. Hardly a day passed that he did not visit his investment.

On Christmas night he sang "Silent Night" on the radio, initiating a tradition that continued for forty-three years and associated him as closely with Christmas as anyone since Charles Dickens, if not Santa Claus. When the 1934 Quigley poll was tabulated, Bing was seventh among the top-ten box-office attractions, the first and — until 1936, when Gary Cooper scored — only Paramount male to make the list. One other Paramount player, Mae West, also ranked, for the last time, in a field dominated by stars at Fox (Will Rogers, Janet Gaynor, Shirley Temple) and MGM (Clark Gable, Wallace Beery, Joan Crawford, Marie Dressler, Norma Shearer). For Bing, who became a fixture in the poll, placing in fourteen of the next twenty years, the victory signaled a new beginning. He was about to take charge of *Kraft Music Hall* and, with Jack Kapp, revolutionize the record business.

19

DECCA

I know how to keep my pulse on the multitude.
— Jack Kapp (1947)[1]

The cornerstone years of the Bing Crosby legend stretch from 1934 to 1954, peaking in the middle and late 1940s. During those two decades his popularity attained an unexampled luster at home and abroad. What changed in 1934, to accelerate the public's acceptance of him? After all, he had been a successful entertainer for nine years — he had recorded much of his finest music while triumphing on the stage, on the air, and in motion pictures. The answer has less to do with the nature of his work than with Bing's willingness to redefine his public role. He was now on the verge of reinventing common-denominator aesthetics, creating a national popular music that pleased everyone. The cost, in the opinion of many observers, was encroaching blandness.

Like the once knavish, now suburbanized Mickey Mouse or the once succulent, now prim Betty Boop, Bing had to be housebroken. America's puritan strain always kicks in when disaster strikes, especially after a long night of partying, as though depressions and plagues and floods and earthquakes were retribution for staying out till dawn. Time to sober up and knuckle down. But whereas Mickey and Betty became so innocuous as to be of no use except as corporate symbols and souvenir adornments, Bing blossomed in the process. His own moralistic streak emboldened him as an actor and personality. What his singing forfeited in muscularity, it gained in poignancy. When he periodically reasserted his jazz chops, he revealed a maturity and eloquence that often trumped his Jazz Age triumphs. In this regard, Bing's metamorphosis suggests Chaplin, who reduced his Tramp's original sadistic streak in favor of a pathos that afforded him far greater nuance. Like Charlie, Bing never totally abandoned his scampish irreverence, as became clear in the 1940s *Road* movies. Nor was his stubborn streak diminished, as corporate chiefs who crossed him or underestimated his resolve learned to their dismay.

The new Bing, projected in the mid- and late 1930s, was propelled on four fronts: movies, records, radio, and public relations. In each arena he was guided by knowing and determined pilots, true believers.

Six months before his death, Bing was asked by a radio interviewer whom he would most like to thank for his success. He gave what had become his standard answer: "I think it would be the A and R man at Brunswick and then Decca Records, Jack Kapp. I was just going on the air for the first time when I signed with him and he had me on a recording program that embraced every type of music — sextets, choral music, light opera, liederspiel, jazz, ballads, comic songs, plays, recitations. . . . And that kind of diversified record program, I believe, was the most important thing in the advancement of my career. I thought he was crazy, but I did what he told me." The interviewer observed that Bing simply took hold of every opportunity, to which Bing rejoined: "I wasn't doing it. He was doing it. He'd say, 'You ought to do this,' and I'd say, 'Oh, Jack, this is silly.' And he'd say, 'You come on down and do it,' and I'd do it because I thought he was a nice guy and he had good taste. I know I didn't have any. I just did it because he wanted me to."[2]

Jack Kapp and Bing Crosby had at least four things in common: outsize ears, a love of Al Jolson, remarkably retentive memories, and the belief that in matters of taste, the public is usually right. The last did not come naturally to Bing, but Jack patiently converted him, one record at a time, overcoming Bing's misgivings and downright disdain. Jack did not live long enough to witness the inevitable split between mass taste and his own, though it is entirely possible he might have rolled with the punches for another generation. Bing, who lived long enough to feel abandoned, attempted to roll and even rock, following the dictum of the man he increasingly prized as the principal architect of his career. Kapp's law was simple: melody. His brother, Dave, during a vacation in Virginia, photographed a statue of Pocahontas with her arms raised in prayer and added Jack's mantra as a caption, "Where's the melody?" Dave mailed the picture to Jack, who enlarged it, printed several copies, and posted them in Studio A and other strategic places in the Decca offices.

In Bing, Kapp recognized the ultimate melodist, a true bard for the times. It was Kapp who stubbornly clung to the idea that Bing could become America's voice, the first Everyman singer. He had to combat cynics who characterized Bing as a mewling crooner, which was easy enough, but he also had to mollify and restrict Bing while convincing him of his potential. Jack, who could not play or sing a note, was Bing's most formidable collaborator. "I regard his association with me as something of a sacred trust," Kapp would write in 1949. "Moreover, I believe there has been a mutuality of faith, and from that mutual faith came the renascence of an industry which was once decadent and which is now a source of world-wide entertainment and cultural education."[3]

Bing trusted him unequivocally. "All the song-pluggers that used to annoy the artists asked him to record their songs or sing them on the radio," recalled Frieda Kapp, Jack's widow. "But he wouldn't. He would say, 'If Jack says I should do it, I'll do it.' That's how loyal he was."[4] Asked to name the important people in his career, Bing offered a fairly consistent list over the years, including his mother and father, Everett, Leo McCarey, William Paley, John O'Melveny, Buddy DeSylva, and one or two more. But he always began with Jack and always for the same reason: his policy of musical diversification. Bing rarely included anyone in that litany with whom he had a personal or formative association, except his parents and Everett. Unless specifically asked, he did not short-list Al Rinker, Paul Whiteman, Harry Barris, Eddie Lang, Louis Armstrong, Bix Beiderbecke, or even Dixie. He kept a separate mental file for the power brokers and advisers who had helped him mold his career, publicly honoring them yet keeping them at bay. As much as he and Jack liked each other, they rarely socialized. As far as Frieda could recall, they never dined alone.

Frieda could not figure it out: "Bing was very, very fond of my husband, but he was a cold person to know. We bought a house on East Sixty-fourth Street during the war, when the prices were down to nothing, a beautiful five-story house. And Bing came to New York one year, and Jack would have loved to have him come to our house. But he wouldn't. The next day in the studio, Jack says, 'What did you do over the weekend?' He said, 'Oh, I went to a Jewish show.' So Jack says, 'What did you do in a Jewish show? You don't understand Yiddish.' Bing says, 'I didn't have to. The woman sitting next to me told me what was going on.' Jack would have been proud to show him that house, but Bing would never let anyone get that close. But Jack was crazy about him."[5]

Bing was crazy about Jack, too; he forbade his business manager from auditing Decca royalty statements (until after Jack's death), for fear of embarrassing him. "If he was your friend, he was a good friend," Frieda said. Yet he could be oddly unfeeling. In the late thirties, the Kapps stayed at the Beverly Hills Hotel during the summer months, while Jack recorded. One night they threw an elaborate party in Bing's honor at the hotel swimming pool, with Jimmy Durante leading the orchestra. "There must have been about two, three hundred people there that night," Frieda recalled. "Hours go by and no Bing. Never showed up. Never showed up. Forgot."[6]

Nothing underscored the bond between them more than Bing's steady refusal of incredibly lucrative offers from rival labels — at one point nearly $6,000 a disc. "The idea of working for anyone else was preposterous to me," Bing wrote, "and I never gave those offers serious consideration. With Jack I felt that I was in the hands of a friend and that whatever he told me to do was right."[7]

Bing's allegiance made Decca possible. The record industry hit rock bottom in 1932 and 1933, and yet — as Kapp complained to anyone he could buttonhole — the companies stubbornly refused to lower the price of discs, which sold for seventy-five cents or a dollar. In 1921, 110 million discs were sold; Paul Whiteman's "Whispering" alone accounted for 2 million sales. In 1933 the total figure was down to 10 million. Many people were certain that the business was bound for obsolescence. Desperate to recoup a fraction of their losses, record labels merged or dissolved. By 1934 only two were standing: Victor, which was shielded by RCA's radio network, and the American

Record Company (ARC), a branch of Consolidated Film Industries, which monopolized the market for bargain discs (stock arrangements, unknown singers) in chain stores like Woolworth's. As a holding company, ARC acquired Columbia and several smaller labels. Artist royalties counted for little in that climate, when the average disc moved a thousand copies and hits were tabulated in the realm of 40,000 sales, sometimes as few as 20,000. "Love in Bloom" was considered a smash at 36,000. Yet Bing refused the big advances, wagering that Kapp could restore the industry.

Jack Kapp was born in Chicago on July 15, 1901, the eldest of four children.[8] His Russian immigrant father, Meyer, became a distributor for Columbia Records in 1905 and opened the Imperial Talking Machine Shop, selling phonographs, discs, cylinders, and sheet music. Jack went into the business immediately after high school and displayed a singular flair for sales; he was said to have memorized the catalog numbers of every record in the store's inventory as well as the addresses and phone numbers of faithful customers. He married Frieda Lutz, his childhood sweetheart, in 1922 and with his younger brother, Dave, opened the Kapp Record Store. Four years later he joined Brunswick-Balke-Collender, a company that made bowling balls and billiard tables and operated Brunswick Records and its race affiliate (distributed largely in black neighborhoods), Vocalion. Put in charge of Vocalion, Jack hired a black recording director, J. Mayo Williams, and scouted, signed, or produced such legendary musicians as King Oliver, Jimmie Noone, Jelly Roll Morton, Earl Hines, Andy Kirk, and Louis Armstrong (whose OKeh contract he dodged by releasing the discs as Lil's Hot Shots), as well as hillbilly, blues, and jug bands. He also worked with established Brunswick stars such as Al Jolson, Fletcher Henderson, and Ted Lewis, developing personal relationships with them all.

In 1930, largely as a result of Jolson's hugely successful hit "Sonny Boy," which Kapp recorded over the protests of his employers, Warner Bros. bought Brunswick for $5 million and relocated Jack to New York, where he worked with comptroller Milton Rackmil. As general manager of recording, he hired Victor Young as his house conductor and signed Bing, Mildred Bailey, the Mills Brothers, the Boswell Sisters, Glen Gray, Cab Calloway, and more, an exceedingly smart roster. But Warners had not figured on the Depression and soon wanted out of the record business. While maintaining ownership (the sales value was meager), Warners practically gave the company to ARC on a ten-year lease, hoping for royalties down the road. With Brunswick now established as ARC's flagship, Kapp recorded more than ever. The company dispatched him to England in 1932, to sell Brunswick's British franchise to the audacious stockbroker, Edward R. Lewis.

Three years earlier Lewis had taken control of the foundering English Decca Company and turned it around. The mysterious name, Decca, coined in 1916 by a company that produced the first portable gramophone, has no meaning. According to Decca producer and historian Geoff Milne, it was devised, like Kodak, as a word that can be pronounced only one way anywhere in the world. Lewis needed a source for American artists, and Brunswick was ideal. By 1934 Bing sold more discs in England than in the United States; "Please" exceeded 60,000 sales and "The Last Round-Up" 80,000, double the numbers in America. Despite discrete backgrounds, Kapp (the Chicago Jew) and Lewis (the future knight of the realm) spoke a similar lingo concerning records. Lewis endorsed Jack's conviction that the industry's salvation lay in marketing premium performers on premium labels at bargain prices. They hatched a plan.

When Brunswick's president, Edward Wallerstein, disclosed that he was going to Victor, Jack was certain the company would appoint him president. In April 1934 Kapp, Rackmil, and Columbia sales manager E. F. Stevens induced Lewis to finance a 50 percent option on the still independent Columbia for what Lewis described as "the astonishingly low price of $75,000," plus an option to buy Brunswick from Consolidated Film.[9] The idea was to fold Columbia into Brunswick, creating a new combine that would in turn be purchased by English Decca. Arriving in the United States for the first time, Lewis was greeted at the dock by his lawyer, Milton Diamond, and an underwriter. (Curiously, he sought the participation of William Paley, who declined; four years later, after the industry rebounded, thanks largely to Decca, Paley's CBS bought ARC for nearly ten times as much — a bargain even at that price.) Kapp assured Lewis that in the unlikely event he was blocked from Brunswick's presidency, he would resign and take Bing, whose contract had an escape clause allowing him to leave with Jack. Lewis went home thinking the deal was set. But as soon as he arrived in Southampton, Diamond summoned him back. They had been betrayed.

Consolidated Film's ARC had bought Columbia (for $70,500) and reneged on the Brunswick option. "We decided there and then," Lewis recalled, "to form a new record company."[10] Kapp prepared to resign, as promised, and so did Rackmil and Stevens. On the surface, the venture seemed nuts. All but Lewis would be leaving lucrative positions without even having an office to go to; indeed, for several weeks they operated out of Milton Diamond's suite. But Kapp convinced Lewis they had everything but financing: the most popular singer in the United States as well as the goodwill of numerous top artists, producers, and distributors who liked and believed in Jack. Furthermore, he was certain they could cut a deal with Warners Bros. to buy a pressing plant and office space that had fallen into disuse when ARC took Brunswick off the movie studio's hands. Above all, they had a radical idea: premium records at discount prices.

Lewis believed, contrary to common wisdom, that "the end of an unparalleled slump" was the ideal time to start a company. He was convinced of a "terrific latent demand for records," if they were affordable.[11] The men made their plans, and on July 14 Lewis sailed home once again. Two days later Kapp resigned his post at Brunswick. He wired Bing, who agreed to stick with him in the absence of a written contract, for a $10,000 guarantee. Jack immediately announced the formation of a new record company, Decca, with himself president (Lewis grudgingly allowed him the title, believing he held the balance of power as chairman and chief stockholder), Stevens vice president, Rackmil treasurer, and Diamond secretary. English Decca issued 25,000 common shares, holding 18,000, which it used to procure subscriptions to raise a $250,000 operational base. Remaining shares were divided among Jack (1,250), Stevens (750), and Warners (5,000). When Jack declared that a Decca disc would sell at fifty cents, the industry rolled its eyes and groaned. "If Decca can't get 75 cents for Crosby, Casa Loma, etc., just as Brunswick, then what's the use?" a nonplussed *Variety* asked.[12]

The loyalties Kapp had cultivated paid off instantly. Brunswick thought its roster impregnable, but every artist represented by Rockwell-O'Keefe followed Bing to Decca — Glen Gray's Casa Loma band, the Mills Brothers, the Boswell Sisters, Jimmy and Tommy Dorsey. Victor Young hired on as Decca's music director and house conductor. Guy Lombardo, Isham Jones, Ted Lewis, and Earl Hines also made the leap, as did such new additions to the Kapp family as Chick Webb, Ethel Waters, Art Tatum, Noble Sissle, Johnny Mercer, Jimmie Lunceford, and Bob Crosby, a middling singer who, at twenty-one, was appointed front man for a cooperative orchestra that made its name combining swing and Dixieland. Within a year Jack enjoyed the particularly sweet coup of signing Louis Armstrong, the beginning of a twenty-year association with Decca. Kapp gutted Brunswick's production team, too, recruiting engineers and producers, among them J. Mayo Williams and Joe Perry, who he asked to set up Decca's Los Angeles studio and supervise recording sessions by Bing and others.

"We lived in Oakland," Joe's widow, Elsie Perry, recalled, "and Jack Kapp called us about six o'clock in the morning, and he said to Joe, 'I want you to go to the office today and quit your job.' He says, 'I'm forming Decca and I want you with me.' And so Joe — 'cause he loved Jack Kapp, they were like brothers almost, you know — went to the office and he put in his resignation. The next year Jack asked us to move to Los Angeles."[13] Joe went on to produce such classics as Bing's "White Christmas," Jolson's "Anniversary Song," Armstrong's "When It's Sleepy Time Down South," Nat Cole's "Sweet Lorraine," Ella Fitzgerald's "Stairway to the Stars," and Judy Garland's "You Made Me Love You."[14] Bing named a racehorse after him, Decca Joe.

Jack also engaged, no less brusquely, his brother, Dave, who was working as a talent representative in Chicago, averaging ninety dollars a week. Jack told him to make a field trip to record a singer in the Midwest. When Dave complained, Jack said, "Don't you understand? We got a new record company and you're with us" — at fifty dollars a week.[15] Dave was so effective developing the hillbilly catalog that Decca cornered the country-music market for years. While Jack was recruiting staff and performers, Warners — as he predicted — solved the problem of office and studio space. In exchange for its 5,000 shares of Decca stock, it turned over a New York office building at 799 Seventh Avenue, a factory that made radio transcriptions, pressing equipment, and a $60,000 promissory note.[16]

Decca's key asset, however, was Bing. The entire operation was launched at his feet, literally: the Los Angeles studio was built at 5505 Melrose Avenue, across the street from Paramount's south gate. Contrary to widespread assumptions, he received none of the precious stock. "Everybody thought Bing had gotten a lot of money, a lot of stock," Frieda said, "but he never got one penny. In later years he bought [Decca shares] and Jack said to him, 'Why are you buying stock now?' Bing laughed, 'Well, now I know the company is good. Now I have faith.'"[17]

Decca barely survived its first year. Brunswick, fearful of Kapp's pricing, moved some of its own catalog recordings to its twenty-five-cent subsidiary, Melotone. (Budget labels trafficked in cheap pressings of pop tunes by studio hacks or catalog items by established artists.) Kapp responded quickly. Decca Records, he told the trades, would sell not for fifty cents, but for thirty-five cents, three for a dollar. Furthermore, he emphasized, Decca was not a budget label; it did not stint on production costs in ways that affected the product or consumer. Instead, song-publishing royalties were reduced (1.25 cents instead of two), as were advances to artists. Kapp argued that increased sales would more than compensate for those reductions and encourage the artists' concern with commercial viability.

To ensure higher volume, he pursued the burgeoning jukebox trade, a by-product of Prohibition's repeal, which — with 25,000 units around the country — had became the largest single market for records. A juke, in southern argot, was initially a roadhouse or brothel, but by the mid-thirties the term encompassed any place with inexpensive entertainment. The boxes replaced live music in bars and branched out to ice-cream parlors and restaurants; they were impervious to the usual seasonal slumps in record sales. The jukes had already proved friendly to Bing's Brunswicks, particularly in the South and East. Mezz Mezzrow wrote that even Harlem hipsters, who would not play anyone on their jukes but Louis Armstrong, made an exception for "Where the Blue of the Night," and not only because Bing was considered one of them: "That was a concession to the sentimental chicks, too, because they were starved for sweet romance and they sure didn't get much of it from Louis's recordings."[18]

Kapp also invested in large-scale advertising. He hurled his first print ad straight at Brunswick's head:

DECCA SCOOPS MUSIC WORLD

Here they are — your favorite stars of radio, screen and stage — in their greatest performances of instrument and voice! *Not* obsolete records, cut in price to meet a market, but the latest, newest smash hits — exclusively DECCA. Hear them *when* you want — as *often* as you want — right in your own home.[19]

But for all his apparent confidence, Kapp had plenty of worries. Decca was using old and inferior equipment. Most of the first 200,000 records were intended for jukes but were pressed at ten inches in diameter, one-sixteenth of an inch too large for the standard machines. The distributors returned them. The corrected copies wiped out Decca's capital, requiring a crucial cash infusion from English Decca. Worse, Kapp's rivals underhandedly warned dealers not to do business with Decca, insisting that the company was unsound and cheated its creditors. Kapp hit back with a million-dollar defamation suit, specifically accusing Victor, Brunswick, ARC, Consolidated Film, and Columbia of predatory business tactics. The suit never went to court, but the rumoring ceased. Kapp was a man possessed. He scheduled four or five sessions a week, supervising more than 200 records in a few months, almost all by prominent artists. Yet the record that guaranteed the company's survival was a novelty by two unknowns.

Mike Riley and Eddie Farley led a Dixieland band at the Onyx Club on Fifty-second Street, near Kapp's office, and wrote a song, "The Music Goes 'Round and Around," that pleased their audiences. Kapp encouraged them to work up a lyric and recorded six versions before he deemed one good enough to release, in the autumn of 1935. By December it was the hottest tune in the country, a phenomenon, selling more than 100,000 copies and endlessly covered. (Columbia Pictures produced a dreary musical of the same name.) "At least everyone can sing Whoa-ho-ho-ho," Kapp wrote, "and that is what made the song a hit." He recorded a version for children by Mae Questel, one for "swing addicts" by the Boswells, one for "the old time tune trade" by Haloran's Hooligans, and one for "the evergrowing Armstrong cult."[20] *Variety* called "The Music Goes 'Round and Around" "a freak tune,"[21] but it put Decca in the black in its second year.

By 1938 the number of jukeboxes would increase tenfold, accounting for 13 million records, mostly at thirty-five cents, a price Brunswick and others had to meet to stay in business. That year Kapp would introduce one of his most telling innovations: record sleeves with cover art. Other Kapp breakthroughs included Broadway cast albums and dramatic recitations, songs and playlets commissioned specifically for records, and liner notes. In 1939 the industry would sell 50 million records; 18 million of them — 36 percent of the entire market — were blue-label Deccas. By then Jack's enterprise would represent more than a corporation. It was the people's record company. Consumers went to stores and asked for Deccas, ignoring the competition. Parents handed their children a dollar bill and told them to bring back three new Deccas. Brand loyalty inevitably advanced Bing's status as the people's singer.

On August 8, 1934, four days after Decca was incorporated, Kapp conducted the session that would produce the label's first two catalog numbers, Decca 100 and Decca 101. The performer, of course, was Bing, but the material was unusual, to say the least.

Music sales have always been stoked by new material. In the 1930s songwriters, song-pluggers, publishers, radio, and movies thrived on novelty. For his final Brunswick sessions, Bing featured mostly fresh material, not all from his own movies. "Little Dutch Mill," a lightweight ditty and one of two he recorded as a favor to its composer, Harry Barris, strutted its way to the top of the sales lists, as did his radiant performance of "Did You Ever See a Dream Walking?" But Bing also enjoyed hits with more venerable numbers, like "Dinah" and "Home on the Range." Mindful of that, Kapp decided Decca would offer something so old that it was new: not the latest tunes you heard on radio for free, but quality songs of a sort that charmed generations. For Decca 100 he selected sentimental evergreens by Carrie Jacobs Bond, "Just a-Wearyin' for You" (1901) and "I Love You Truly" (1906).

Subsequent, uncharmed generations have speculated that he chose such weary songs because they were in the public domain and cost-effective, which was far from true. Bond, who died in 1946 at eighty-four, operated her own publishing house and was a bear for royalties. They were not Kapp's first choices; he resorted to them only when Bing flatly refused to attempt the sham operetta of Oley Speaks's "Sylvia" (1908) and Victor Herbert's "Ah! Sweet Mystery of Life" (1910), arguing "That's not for me, that's for the high-class singers."[22] Kapp was determined to reposition Bing as the foremost interpreter of American classics. It was not enough just to take away his *bu-bu-bu-boo*. Hoping that the Bond songs had raised his sights and confidence, he wrote Bing on August 30:

> After listening to "Just a-Wearyin' for You," there can be no doubt of your ability to do songs of a semi-classical nature as well, if not better, than any singer in the country today. I feel our judgment in this regard is wholly justifiable. There is one thing I'd like to call to your attention. The public today wants an unadulterated Bing Crosby, without any frills. They think that the combination of his voice tinged with a natural feeling which he possesses, is unsurpassed. I agree with them and I think that the frills should be avoided, as well as "hot" songs. You have in your grasp the opportunity to be the John McCormack of this generation. You can achieve that much more easily than you think. By doing what we are discussing and by following thru both on records and on radio, you will reach a popularity, which, in my opinion, will be as great as ever enjoyed by any singer in this country. Think it over Bing. I do not mean to be presumptuous, but the masses want melody combined with soul, which is yours. Nobody can touch you there.[23]

Small wonder that by the 1940s, Jack was denigrated by many insiders as Killer Kapp, for killing Bing's early greatness in a relentless exploitation to sell more and more records. Bing grew up admiring McCormack and other Irish tenors his father played on Edison cylinders, but he had long since become a far more important artist, a first-rank innovator, one of the most influential singers of all time — with the exception of Louis Armstrong, the most forceful that America had ever produced. Through Bing, American popular music came of age and found a beat, learned to strut on the stage of modernity, relaxed the prejudices that isolated pop, jazz, country, and every other idiom he addressed. By 1941 the deeply satisfied Kapp could boast, "If he hadn't diversified his talent, he would remain just a popular singer of popular songs."[24]

Bing's unique position, his ability to sing so many different kinds of music, reflected the myriad styles he assimilated. Kapp appreciated that, but in singling out McCormack as a career template and encouraging Bing to deflect hot songs, he hoped to remake him as a smoother, less mannered, ultimately less expressive singer, a kind of musical comfort food. To the degree that he succeeded, he made possible the singular career that allowed Bing to repeatedly remake himself. The erstwhile symbol of Prohibition and now the Depression would be reborn yet a third time as an unchallenged icon of World War II and a fourth time as the gladdening troubadour in an age of postwar paranoia (his peak years) and a fifth time as the avuncular skipper of the affluent 1950s. Had Bing not leveled his style, the mainstream would likely have left him behind, a Dixieland dinosaur bewildered by changing times and not the show-business titan who enjoyed an additional twenty years at the epicenter of American tastes and attitudes. Bing's renovation was never so complete, however, as to undermine the rhythmic ease that set him apart. A score of Jack Kapps could not have scuttled the self-possession, adroitness, and Armstrongian musical wisdom that permitted him to glide over changing times with discriminating aplomb.

That much was indicated at the first Decca session, when in addition to the Carrie Jacobs Bond songs, which sold modestly, he sang two others for a second disc that sold even more modestly but produced two Crosby classics. These songs were also timeworn, but the mood Bing created supersedes nostalgia. "Let Me Call You Sweetheart" (1910), one of two vaudeville standards (along with "Meet Me To-night in Dreamland") by Beth Slater Whitson and Leo Friedman, is a paragon of melodic simplicity, with few notes and many of them dotted halves. Bing cuts the sentimentality with his dauntless clarity, extracting real emotion from the enchantingly artless melody. The flip side, "Someday Sweetheart" (1919), was a jazz standard said to derive from a Jelly Roll Morton melody and encouraged Bing to rock a little.

On the early Decca sessions, Bing was backed by the journeyman Georgie Stoll orchestra, from the Woodbury show. Happily, it kept a low profile on "Someday Sweetheart," making its first entrance at the release and providing room for the soloists. Bing saunters in on the fourth bar of pianist Joe Sullivan's introduction and sounds transported, as though back in Chicago in the days of Bix and Eddie. He sings with riveting lucidity and command, alternately nudging the beat and reclining on it. For the instrumental passages, Stoll outdid himself, writing handsome interplay between reeds and brasses and wittily shadowing Bing at the outset of his deftly embellished second chorus, which closes with Bing's original and much imitated eight-bar vocal coda.[25] It is a masterpiece, though not the sort Jack Kapp was looking for.

For Bing's second Decca session, Kapp reverted to the usual formula of covering new hit songs, to which the public responded with greater sympathy. Jack chose "The Moon Was Yellow," a tango in the "Temptation" mold, as the A-side for one disc, but the B-side, Ray Noble's "The Very Thought of You," stimulated sales and became an all-time standard. Bing was a bit hoarse at that date, which also produced the satisfactory "Two Cigarettes in the Dark" and the lamentable "Sweetheart Waltz." He exhibited a new and short-lived mannerism that reflected Kapp's injunction to sing in a style suitable to light classics — a high, sighing head tone to cap phrase endings. For his third Decca session, Bing was back on the terra firma of songs written for his pictures. He scored his first megahit for Decca with "June in January" and delivered a far more expansive interpretation of "Love Is Just Around the Corner" than the one heard in *Here Is My Heart;* spurred by a lively rhythm section, he swings, embellishes, and whistles. With the release of three new movies during the spring and summer of 1935 (*Mississippi, Two for Tonight,* and *The Big Broadcast of 1936,* in which Bing made only a cameo appearance), Bing feared an overload and restricted his recording activities to four sessions for the entire year, focusing mostly on his movie songs, with two crucial exceptions.

An enduring irony of America's secular religious life is the influence of Jews in promoting Christmas songs, most obviously Irving Berlin's "White Christmas." Kapp's role in this regard was considerable: he overcame Bing's adamant refusal to venture into the field. In keeping with his determination to offer classical pop from an earlier period, Kapp asked him to record the nineteenth-century hymn "Adeste Fidelis" (a John McCormack hit in 1915) and "Silent Night," which Whiteman had recorded when the Rhythm Boys were out of town. Bing had sung the latter on his Christmas Woodbury show, but it was one thing to go caroling, even on the air, and another to mix religion with the rank commercialism of records — "like cashing in on the church or the Bible," he argued.[26] Bing repeatedly spurned Kapp's requests, insisting that he lacked "sufficient stature as a singer to sing a song with religious implications."[27]

The situation was resolved when Father Richard Ranaghan of the St. Columban Foreign Missionary Society, recently returned from China, was referred to Bing as someone who might help him raise money for his mission in Hanyang. Ranaghan hoped to generate funds at American churches by showing an old film of China depicting famine and orphans. He wanted Bing to underwrite a new negative and arrange for the loan of sound equipment to record a narration. According to Bing, his brother Larry suggested that he also sing a few songs on the soundtrack, which could be released on a special white-label Decca, selling at five dollars, with all royalties going to the mission. Accompanied by celesta and the Crinoline Choir, Bing sang an abridged medley of "Adeste Fidelis," "Lift Up Your Hearts," and "Stabat Mater." But to release a disc, Kapp had to have a B-side. Knowing the money would go to a worthy cause, Bing agreed to record "Silent Night."

Bing's readings are surprisingly stiff, with halting rests and strained top notes, but "Adeste Fidelis" — despite his rusty Latin, resulting in a couple of mispronounced vowels — is flavored with a choirboy candor and a lovely mordent on the first syllable of *Bethlehem*. Having broken the ice, Kapp convinced him to record full-blown versions of "Adeste Fidelis" and "Silent Night" nine months later, accompanied by Victor Young's orchestra and the Guardsmen Quartet. Oddly, Bing and the choir sing *dominum* when they mean *dominus* in the former (not until his definitive version of 1942 did Bing conquer classic Latin), an otherwise cautious but subtly individualized performance. Gilbert Seldes wrote, in 1956, of "Bing's special endearing quality [that] makes everyone want to appropriate him," and asked, "how can one take possession better than by seeing the essential more clearly or catching the miraculous trifle that others have missed?" He cited as an example: "A long time ago, when I first heard his recording of 'Adeste Fidelis,' I imagined that I caught in the last bar of the song a tiny, delicate syncopation." He thought it "right and reverential."[28]

Bing was downright cowed by "Silent Night," with its more profound religious history; it was introduced at a midnight mass on

Christmas Eve 1818. An awkward key does not help him, though Bing's final chorus is poignant. One imperious reviewer conceded, "His style is reverent and the effect is not as incredible as you might have thought."[29] According to Bing, the recording generated $250,000 in royalties, but little of it went to Ranaghan's cause. The missionary was killed in a traffic accident shortly after the soundtrack was made, and Japan's invasion of China ended contact with the St. Columbans. As a result, royalties were dispersed to sundry charities in the United States and abroad, from convents in India to leper colonies in Africa.

Kapp's devotion to evergreens received an unexpected boost when Bing inherited the lead in *Mississippi,* a role created for Lanny Ross, the tenor Paramount hoped to establish as his rival. The film, co-starring W. C. Fields and Joan Bennett and boasting a score by Lorenz Hart and Richard Rodgers, was just getting under way when Paramount-Publix mutated into Paramount Pictures. Adolph Zukor was kicked upstairs to preside as outlying chairman Barney Balaban became president, and Ernst Lubitsch — a sublime director who thought he could improve the work of every other director — was disastrously miscast as chief of production, replacing Manny Cohen after not quite three years at the helm. Lubitsch survived barely a year, at which point Balaban appointed Y. Frank Freeman head of West Coast operations. But Freeman, a onetime Coca-Cola executive and a southerner with antediluvian racial notions, knew and cared nothing about making movies, so he delegated the job of running the studio to his assistant, William LeBaron.

Balaban himself looked at a rough cut and was so disenchanted by the colorless Ross that he halted production and offered the part to Bing. Director Eddie Sutherland, who remained friendly with Bing after *Too Much Harmony,* was delighted and so were Rodgers and Hart — but not for long. Lubitsch declared that Bing "was going to be a great artist,"[30] yet he had reservations about *Mississippi*'s score and expressed them to its producer, Arthur Hornblow Jr. Bing was also displeased. Backed by Balaban, he requested new songs. When Hornblow insisted on retaining the Rodgers and Hart music, Bing came up with a compromise. The songwriting team would provide him with a new ballad, and he would interpolate the minstrel aria "Old Folks at Home," a Stephen Foster song with an ancient pedigree in the record business. Len Spencer, the first nationally recognized recording star, scored one of the medium's earliest coups with his rendition in 1892. Until Bing revived it, the song had not been successfully recorded since 1919.

At it turned out, the agreement benefited everyone. The best of the original songs were employed, Foster's melody did little damage, and "It's Easy to Remember," the new ballad Rodgers and Hart were obliged to write, turned out to be a major hit and one of the most beloved songs in their matchless oeuvre. Still, Hart was incensed by Bing's intransigence concerning "Old Folks at Home." He declared they would never again write for Bing, who, in turn, declined to record their songs until the patriotic "Bombardier Song" of 1942. A shame all around, though Hart's antipathy toward the interpolated Foster is easy to understand.

Interpolations were commonplace on the stage and in films. Most of the studios had songwriters under contract who, in exchange for salaries, gave up their publishing royalties. When a studio purchased film rights to a Broadway score, the royalties went to the songwriters, so in order to generate royalties for itself, the studio would replace some of the Broadway songs with those by its own writers, who in many instances were hacks. Needless to say, this galled the Broadway writers. Rodgers and Hart would not hear of it; their contract specifically mandated that they provide all the songs for *Mississippi*. The Foster song violated their contract and particularly offended them because of its theme of a former slave who longs for the old plantation.

Bing did not see Foster's song in that light, and he sings the lamentation with tremendous vitality. In his interpretation, it becomes a universal venting of desire for the lost places none of us can ever regain. Yet for all the emotion he wrings from the lyric and despite its undeniable historical appropriateness, his performance is enfeebled by Foster's minstrel grammar and the allusion to *darkies* (in later years Bing sang *people*). In the picture, Fields opines that the song won't last two weeks because "people can't remember the tune," then walks away whistling it. Jack Kapp must have been whistling, too; with that song, Bing led the way to a trove of nineteenth-century public-domain standards, and within a year he, Armstrong, the Mills Brothers, and other Decca artists were reviving them in bunches.

Rodgers and Hart were more insulted than injured when the movie credited Foster's song, retitled "Swanee River," to them.[31] But their chagrin should have been tempered by Bing's renderings of their genuine songs, two of which became number one hits. He uses a touch of parlando on "Soon," emphasizing his range with high sighs and chesty curves, and delivers the definitive interpretation of the marvelous "It's Easy to Remember." Its deceptive simplicity — a string of B flats that arcs to a D natural — and the sloping release suit him as well as the wistful lyric and lulling tempo. A third song, "Down by the River," elicited an indifferent recording but is sung with great relish in the film, building to a rousing finish.

One fourteen-year-old in North Dakota who never forgot that finish was Norma Egstrom, who saved her pennies to see Crosby movies as an escape from her abusive stepmother. Years later, after she had changed her name to Peggy Lee and become a regular performer on Bing's radio show, she told him about seeing *Mississippi*: "He had lost the girl and sang 'Down by the River' and I was crying so, because I wanted everything to turn out right for him. And when I told Bing how heartbroken I was, he took me all over San Francisco, one place after another, searching for a pianist who knew that song, and sang it to me. Imagine your idol singing that song to you."[32]

On paper, the film promised a concoction worthy of Ziegfeld: Bing's songs and W. C. Fields's comedy. Sutherland, close to both men, seemed the ideal director. He knew that no one could ad-lib or steal a scene like Fields, who, though drinking heavily, was inspired throughout the shoot. In one of his funniest routines, he recounts his battle with Indians ("I unsheathed my Bowie knife and cut a path through a wall of human flesh, dragging my canoe behind me"). Bing, who often broke up during their scenes together, did not mind the upstaging. A longtime fan, he memorized Fields's best lines. Sutherland grew concerned, however, as the story — a moldy Booth Tarkington play that had been filmed twice before[33] — shifted in Fields's favor. He felt obliged to warn Bing: "I'm worried now that he's going to be so funny, he's going to steal the picture from you." Bing shrugged it off. "Is it good for the picture?" Sutherland said it was great. Bing told him, "Forget it, it's got my name on it, what do I care what Fields steals? I'm not a fundamentalist. This is business. If it's funny, okay. I think he's great, don't you?"[34]

Still, rumors of rivalry between them were rife. Crosby was reported to have demanded recuts after a preview (the changes he mandated actually occurred when he came onboard), and Fields was said to have disdained his singing. They were, in fact, friends and Toluca Lake neighbors, occasionally playing golf and drinking together. "Fields had real affection for Bing Crosby," Robert Lewis Taylor wrote. "In turn, Crosby had an idolatrous, filial attitude toward Fields, whom he always called 'Uncle Bill.'"[35] When Fields went to visit him at Del Mar racetrack a year later, Bing bought him an expensive pair of binoculars. Film preservationist Bob DeFlores recalled that upon visiting Bing's baronial home in Hillsborough in 1977, he drawled, "Nice little lean-to you have here." Without missing a beat, Bing provided the citation: "Bill Fields, *Poppy,* 1936."[36]

The only downside of the production for Bing was that his weight had increased to 190 pounds and he was obliged to wear a girdle, a nuisance he accepted with more equanimity than he did the requisite toupee. By this time, however, he made a point of avoiding the scalp doily by wearing hats in as many scenes as possible. Charles Lang devised several fancy shots — reflections in mirrors, Bing singing through harp strings — and managed to make him appealing even with a mustache and muttonchops, about which he remarked to Quentin Reynolds, who profiled him for *Collier's,* "Looks like hell, don't it?"[37] The story wasn't much, with Bing as a sensible Philadelphian who refuses to engage in a duel, thereby losing the love of Gail Patrick while earning the adoration of her kid sister, Joan Bennett. (Frank Capra had used the same device of rival sisters and family honor the previous year in *Broadway Bill,* which he remade in 1950 as a vehicle for Bing.) Reviews were mixed, but despite strong competition in a spring rendered heavily Gallic by *Les Misérables* and *Cardinal Richelieu,* it made pots of money.

Paramount was so pleased that it renewed Bing's contract in a three-year, nine-picture deal, at $125,000 a film, plus a salary of $15,600 for each week past the eighth one devoted to any film, plus a new clause that had become singularly important to Bing.[38] Crosby's negotiators initially suggested twelve pictures at $200,000 each; they did not expect to get it, but in maneuvering toward common ground, they finally wrangled from Paramount permission for Bing to make one film annually for another studio. That set off fierce competition for his services, with offers coming in from such past associates as Fanchon and Marco, Hearst's Cosmopolitan Productions, Manny Cohen, and film pioneer Jesse Lasky, who had been ousted by Cohen and now vainly sought to launch a production company with Mary Pickford. Bing signed with Cohen, who already owned an interest in his services, to coproduce an independent feature for Columbia Pictures in 1936.

The new Paramount covenant began poorly. One remarkable indication of the studio's confidence in Bing was its perverse reasoning in deciding to release a turkey called *Two for Tonight*. Initially, it promised to be a sure-fire production: reuniting Bing with Joan Bennett, Frank Tuttle would direct a farce adapted by George Marion Jr., shot by Karl Struss, and supported by such expert hams as Mary Boland, Thelma Todd, and Ernest Cossart. Resting at Rancho Santa Fe, Bing lost twelve pounds in preparation, while Mack Gordon and Harry Revel wrote the songs. What they produced was a calamity. Tired of the usual froth, Tuttle was preoccupied with adapting Dashiell Hammett's *The Glass Key*, one of his best pictures, and allowed *Two for Tonight* to lurch between screwball comedy and romance with timeouts for music. The romance amounted to little: Bing and Bennett "meet cute" when he rolls downhill in a runaway wheelchair and she is scooped onto his lap. "Going my way?" he asks. "Apparently," she says. For comedy, Tuttle turned to the silent era for a long, elaborate bout of seltzer-squirting, his homage to a Laurel and Hardy pie-throwing epic.[39]

The inchoate script required retouching by several hands, leaching whatever strength it might have had as a satire of the New York stage. The songs were weak, though Bing mined three hits for Decca. He fared less well with his character, a cipher surrounded by lunatics. Once again he is insensible to the good girl's true love, preferring bad girl Thelma Todd. His singing, however, is electric, despite self-deprecating crooning jokes, whether swinging "From the Top of Your Head to the Tip of Your Toes" or emoting "Without a Word of Warning."

During post-production, the film was sheared to barely an hour's running time. If they had cut another forty minutes, they might have had a very good two-reeler. There was talk of shelving it entirely rather than dilute Bing's box-office clout. Instead, it was slated for late-summer release as a test. Bing was already known to be critic-proof; if audiences would pay to see him in this, a picture guaranteed to elicit bad reviews and negative word of mouth, Bing's box-office power would be affirmed rather spectacularly. As it happened, *Two for Tonight* turned a handsome profit and was held over at several theaters. Nor were reviewers uniformly censorious. Graham Greene, writing in the London *Spectator,* considered it "very amusing and well written entertainment" and described Bing as "attractively common-place."[40] On the other hand, Greene disdained the Irving Berlin songs in RKO's *Top Hat,* the year's one indisputably great hit musical, which deservedly trounced *Two for Tonight* when they played rival theaters in New York.

The year was turning out to be a personal triumph for Bing finan-cially; between records, radio, and movies, he grossed more than $500,000. In other respects, he was treading water. His pictures made money but did little to enhance his stature. Mae West, enjoying her last year as a box-office queen, was Paramount's top draw, fol-lowed by Claudette Colbert, Gary Cooper, and Bing. Other studios, however, were dominated by their musical stars — Astaire and Rogers at RKO, Shirley Temple at Fox, Eddie Cantor at Goldwyn, Jeannette MacDonald and Nelson Eddy at MGM. Weeks before *Two for Tonight* opened, Paramount sought to make amends by announc-ing what it considered a classy project. Bing's next film would be *Tony's High Hat,* costarring Metropolitan Opera contralto Gladys Swarthout. Apparently, the studio neglected to consult Bing, who publicly declined. The plot, counterposing jazz and the classics, was a familiar gambit in the 1930s. Bing did not like the story idea and con-tended that he could not hold his own with an opera star. But Para-mount, intent on finding a more credible answer than Kitty Carlisle to MGM's MacDonald or Columbia's Met star Grace Moore, con-vinced Bing to make a test with Swarthout and reannounced the project with a more didactic title, *Opera Versus Jazz.* After Bing and Gladys sang "Home on the Range" and "Thunder Over Paradise" for the ears of the bosses, the project was nixed. Swarthout was teamed, instead, with John Boles in *Rose of the Rancho.* Two years later she left Hollywood for good.

The Swarthout episode may have indirectly stung Jack Kapp, ironically enough, considering how closely Paramount's misguided ambition jibed with his own desire to establish Bing as a singer of light classics. The day *Variety* printed Paramount's announcement of *Tony's High Hat,* August 14, Bing took out his frustration on Jack in an argument that was recorded and covertly circulated.[41] It was Bing's first time in the studio since "Silent Night," six months earlier, and his first session with the Dorsey Brothers in more than two years. The session was brought about by Rockwell-O'Keefe, the agency that had arranged for Bing to take over the *Kraft Music Hall.* Cork O'Keefe hoped to find a berth on the show for the Dorseys, too. Their band was an obvious candidate, its very sound a reflection of Bing's musical influence; as drummer Ray McKinley once explained, "The emphasis on the trombones was to give the band a Bing Crosby quality."[42] Bing had not heard the new Dorsey band, which was playing the Glen Island Casino in New Rochelle, and as he and Dixie planned to spend much of August at the Saratoga races, Cork hoped to lure him out to listen. When Bing complained that he did not want to brave the crowds or don the hairpiece, Cork suggested a record date.

Tommy and Jimmy Dorsey were two of the most temperamental men in the music business. Known as the battling Dorseys, they battled chiefly each other and were not exactly enjoying their much touted, celebrity-studded engagement at Glen Island — not with Tommy, the mandarin loner, taking all the bows as conductor and Jimmy, the acerbic tippler, giving him the fish eye from the reed section. One evening, weeks before Bing traveled to New York, Jimmy griped about a tempo and Tommy tromped off the stage, never to return. Thus ended the Dorsey Brothers and commenced two of the most successful bands of the Swing Era. For the immediate future, however, O'Keefe wanted them both on *Kraft.* He pleaded with Tommy to do the record date, and Tommy relented. He would do it for Cork and Bing, he said, but would not speak to his brother. August 14 was a sizzler, but tempers were cool when Bing arrived. The brothers were happy to be reunited with him, if not with each other, and were primed — both were perfectionists — with solid arrangements (probably by the band's pianist, Bobby Van Eps) of the five songs from *Two for Tonight.*

The first few hours were highly productive. Though slightly hoarse, Bing completed the five tunes without incident. Much joy is evident in "From the Top of Your Head to the Tip of Your Toes," which glistens with Bing's jauntiness. "Takes Two to Make a Bargain" is a thin number, but Bing and the musicians (Jimmy takes a clarinet solo) are off and running, with Bing rhythmically interpolating the phrase "I'd like to know" and upping the ante in an embellished second chorus. By "Two for Tonight" Bing sounds a bit worn and raspy, but notwithstanding a couple of spent high notes, he phrases with pleasing élan. Then they took a break.

In addition to the *Two for Tonight* score, he was scheduled to record his number from *The Big Broadcast of 1936*, Robin and Rainger's "I Wished on the Moon." It was his sole contribution to a picture carried by Jack Oakie, Lyda Roberti, and the wonderful Nicholas Brothers. Bing sang two choruses under a full moon in a rustic setting and received top billing. Kapp knew the appealing song could be a hit.

Precisely what ensued in the studio is unclear, though alcohol was evidently poured on fresh wounds. Jimmy was a serious drinker and easier to get along with than Tommy, so it is not unlikely that he and Bing took the break together, consoling each other with their beefs. Bing had two gripes: the Swarthout story, announced that morning, and a fight he was waging at Paramount in an attempt to share in royalties on songs written for his movies. In fact, he was scheduled to meet with Manny Cohen in Saratoga to discuss their imminent production, for which all the songs would be written by independent songwriters and published by Rockwell-O'Keefe's music wing, Select, guaranteeing Bing's participation. At Paramount Bing's demand was blocked by Lou Diamond, the hard-working, generally well liked supervisor of Paramount film shorts and the head of Famous Music, one of the studio's two music-publishing subsidiaries. Though owned by Paramount, Famous operated independently; Diamond, unmoved by Bing's pull, refused to cut him in on songs — a perquisite that later became standard in Hollywood contracts, including Bing's. It didn't help that Bing and Diamond could not stand each other. According to Sid Herman, Diamond's successor at the firm, they were incapable of discussing the matter. Famous Music controlled publishing rights for "I Wished on the Moon."

After the break, while Kapp was absent, Bing informed the band that he would sing only a single chorus, like in the old days when he was the male vocalist who appeared in the middle of an instrumental performance with a vocal refrain. During the rehearsal Kapp walked into the control booth and couldn't believe what he was hearing. Bing groused that he was unable to sing more than a chorus because he was hoarse, a fact amply demonstrated by his work that day. Jack tried to convince him that he could no longer get away with a solo refrain, but Bing, who never raised his voice in an argument, remained childishly rigid as the band sat around, waiting for the final decision. The altercation was recorded — at Kapp's instigation, perhaps with the intention of later showing Bing how badly he had behaved. But it also shows how funny Bing could be even when sloshed and threatening.

Jack: Come on will ya, Bing? Sing.

Bing: You wanna make this thing . . .

Jack: I want you to sing.

Bing: . . . the way we rehearsed it or not?

Jack: Sing the first chorus. I don't care what you do after that, but sing the first chorus.

Bing: No.

Jack: Well now, you're a little bit arbitrary. . . .

Bing: No, I don't think so. I think you're being arbitrary.

Jack: I leave it to the jury.

Bing: Man gets a record free [crowd laughter] with a beautiful arrangement, he don't want, you don't want my vocal chorus.

Jack: [shouts over him] Hey, Rockwell-O'Keefe, come on out of there, let's get with the game. Come on.

Bing: [shouts back] Let's go over to Victor! Let's go to Victor! They'll take it! Come on.

Jimmy Dorsey: Brunswick will take it, grab it up in a minute.

Jack: Yeah, Brunswick *will*, too.

Bing: You want it that way?

Jack: For Christ's sake, come on.

Bing: Jack, you've got fifteen minutes.

Jack: All right, you can make it in six.

Bing: You want it that way?

Jack: Come on, sing the first chorus.

Bing: The boys don't want to sit around here . . .

Kapp: They do.

Bing: . . . and listen to this endless bickering. They want to either get it made or go home.

Jack: I know! They want to go home!

Bing: And I'm sure I'm similarly minded. And I won't even make any excuses.

Jimmy: Let's make "Dippermouth."

Bing: All right. [crowd laughter]

Jack: Come on, Bing. Sing the first chorus.

Bing: No.

Jack: You might as well do it right.

Bing: Let's not do it at all.

Jack: But why do that? Seems like it'll be a terrific hit.

Jimmy: Who is this guy anyway, what happened?

Bing: Who?

Jimmy: That guy.

Bing: You know the son of a bitch.

Jack: Oh, what's the difference? You're in the picture, aren't you? Son of a bitch or no son of a bitch, you're still in *The Big Broadcast*.

Bing: I might get myself taken out. What do you think of that?

Jack: Yeah, well, I'll tell you what you do. If you get yourself taken out, we'll make it two ways. One my way and one your way. If you get yourself taken out, I'll release your way. If it stays, you gotta make it my way.

Bing: Is that a bargain for you? [crowd laughter] How do you like that? Would you like a dance record of "Wished on the Moon" with a vocal chorus, me singing it, or not? No? G'bye.

Jack: If you turn back the clock four years, it'd be entirely different. We can't do it now. I'm telling you we can't do it. C'mon, c'mon.

Bing: I'm on my way, Jack.

Jack: C'mon, c'mon, Bing.

Bing: Nooo, what have I got to do? Swear out an affidavit? You want that, Jack?

Jack: Listen, do whatever you want, Bing. I'm not going to argue with you. This means more to you than it does to me.

Bing: Jack, it don't mean a fuck to me.

Jack: Well, you sing it in *The Big Broadcast*. The picture will . . .

Bing: I think it would be a nice record with just a swell arrangement and a vocal chorus.

Jack: In all my experience, I've never seen you in such an arbitrary mood.

Bing: Well . . .

Jack: And I want to tell you, you just — just because you happen to have it in for a fellow by the name of Diamond.

Bing: No, that's not it — that's partly it, yes.

Jack: I say this, though, it has nothing to do with the song. He can be a son of a bitch, but if the tune is great, you should do it right.

Bing: It's got nothing to do with it.

Jack: Yes, it has.

Bing: My reasons for doing it this way are threefold.

Jack: All right, give me the first one.

Bing: First I'm very hoarse . . .

Jack: [shouts to control booth] Are we getting this down?

Bing: . . . this afternoon and I don't think I can sing any more than one chorus and do it well. Secondly, the guy who controls the tune is a pirate.

Jack: Well, supposing he is?

Bing: Thirdly, I think the record as discussed and arranged would be an interesting salable piece of property which you can well afford to have on your shelves. [crowd laughter]

Jack: That's where it would probably stay!

Bing: Now, if you want it that way, say yes and if you don't, say no and let's stop fucking around.

Jack: Up to you, Bing.

Bing: I'm telling you what I want to do.

Jack: I can't argue with you if your mind is made up.

Bing: Been made up for days.

Jack: It has?

Bing: . . . talked it over the phone, we discussed this at great length.

Jack: Who did you discuss it with?

Bing: Uhhh, T. J. Rockwell. Might as well put him in the middle. [much crowd laughter]

Jack: Do it any way you want. I don't care. What can I do?

Bing: Maybe I can't even do it, Jack. I don't know.[43]

He did it, barely, his tones taut and breaking. Years later Kapp, who preserved the recorded contretemps in Decca's archives, liked to complain that Bing won the argument but that the record did not sell. In fact, "I Wished on the Moon" was a substantial hit, outselling the *Two for Tonight* songs and crowning Decca's sales list before the movie was released — a telling example of a song's appeal overriding a singer's failings and possibly gaining a touch of mystique from the surprising brevity of the vocal. Subsequent disputes between Bing and Jack are neither documented nor rumored. Perhaps Bing was genuinely chagrined by the episode. In any case, he doubled his recording agenda for the next year, resuming Kapp's program in November with two long, back-to-back sessions, scoring a number one hit with "Red Sails in the Sunset" and doing nearly as well with "On Treasure Island" (a bewitching performance marred by an uncharacteristically corny Victor Young arrangement) and the songs from the movie on which Bing was currently working.

Bing's sessions, almost all with Jack present if not presiding, became known as the easiest in the business. He would arrive early, chew gum and smoke his pipe, read the racing form or newspaper, run down the material if it was new to him, and stick a pencil behind his ear. When he and the band were ready, he stepped over to the microphone, on which he habitually parked his gum, and, on average, completed five songs in two hours. He coined a couple of descriptive phrases: a Kappastrophe was an arrangement Jack disliked; those Jack approved were Kapphappy.

Bing and Dixie returned to California in early September so that Bing could begin preparing for *Anything Goes,* the hottest ticket on Broadway and the most expensive Crosby project to date. The movie rights alone cost $100,000; the negative cost topped $1.1 million. If Larry Hart had a snit over "Swanee River," imagine how Cole Porter must have felt about Hollywood's treatment of his worldly musicals. In New York he was toast of the town. In Hollywood he was just another ink-stained wretch whose songs were not controlled by Famous Music. When RKO turned his *The Gay Divorce* into *The Gay Divorcee,* it canned his entire score except "Night and Day." *Anything Goes* was another story. It was Porter's masterpiece. Howard Lindsay and Russel Crouse had written an outstandingly droll book, set entirely on an ocean liner, but it was Porter's urbane words and music that made it a theatrical event. Paramount retained only four of the show's twelve songs, discarding "All Through the Night" and commissioning a ching-chong Chinese minstrel number called "Shanghai-De-Ho."

Censorship was at issue. The Motion Picture Production Code, introduced by Will Hays in 1930, had proved largely ineffectual (even Hays's perverse resolve, agitated by the Hearst papers, to squelch Mae West had came to little) until the summer of 1934, when he hired Catholic journalist Joseph Breen as an enforcer. No sooner did Paramount purchase the rights to *Anything Goes* than Breen was told that the plot involved a gangster who impersonates a priest while toting a violin case with a machine gun. "As you know," he cautioned the studio, "recently official censor boards have been deleting scenes of machine guns in the hands of anybody but police and other properly organized bodies."[44]

Breen ultimately acceded to the machine gun, but not the "definitely suggestive"[45] "All Through the Night" ("you and your love bring me ecstasy"), and warned that the showstopper "Blow, Gabriel, Blow" might be interpreted as a burlesque of religion. After Breen went to work on the title song, Paramount hired the unrenowned Brian Hooker (a lyricist for Rudolf Friml!) to revise Porter's lyric. Yet despite three rewrites and submissions, "Anything Goes" was relegated to background music for the credits. "I Get a Kick Out of You" and "You're the Top" were cleansed of allusions to cocaine, Minsky dancers, and Holy Moses, for what Breen termed "obvious reasons."[46] The Leo Robin–Frederick Hollander interpolation (one of three), "Shanghai-De-Ho," offended him, too, not because it burlesqued Chinese people, but for the "plainly vulgar meaning"[47] of the line "Soon the chows and Pekinese will stay away from cherry trees."

The script was trimmed of dozens of words and phrases ("hot pants," "we'll rub him out," "snatch") and situations, including one in which it could be construed, the censors grumbled, that a woman passenger was asking directions to the ladies' room. Not all was lost. With Lindsay and Crouse adapting their own book, they salvaged much of the original story, and the cast was outstanding: Ethel Merman re-creating her role of chanteuse Reno Sweeney; Charlie Ruggles, deftly handling the comedy (though the New York critics lamented the absence of Victor Moore, who created Public Enemy No. Thirteen on the stage); Ida Lupino, underemployed but enticing; and Bing, a costume-changing stowaway pursuing Lupino and pursued by Merman.

Because Bing's role had to be revised from that of a juvenile, the new songs were intended to play to his strengths. Two succeed: "Sailor Beware" is an energizing though pointless diversion, and "Moonburn" represents Hoagy Carmichael's first movie sale. (Bing helped another old friend by arranging a bit part for Eddie Borden, who toured with

Crosby and Rinker in the Will Morrissey revue.) Hoagy's song employs period slang — "Get away from that window before you get moonburned," Roscoe Karns told George Raft in *Night After Night* — and offers a balmy interlude, though the version heard in the picture does not compare with the jamlike record Bing made for Decca with pianist Joe Sullivan, guitarist Bobby Sherwood, and an unknown bassist. "Truck on down," Bing tells Sullivan, and they do, for a "hot" classic.

The movie is no classic. Despite its ups, it suffers from a discursive, flattened feeling that restrains the zaniness. Director Lewis Milestone, justly celebrated for the 1930 *All Quiet on the Western Front,* was an odd choice for a musical; he promptly returned to dramas. He employs fancy shots and wipes, abetted by Karl Struss's exquisite photography, but the tempo is uneven and the remaining Porter songs are stiffed, either because Merman is too brazen or Bing too controlled. They excel musically and comedically on "You're the Top" yet fail to indicate a dalliance; nor do they make much of the (bowdlerized) lyric's polished wit. The critics were generally pleased. *Variety* wondered whether Bing's jazzy singing was added "for the special benefit of the boys at the Famous Door," a New York jazz club.[48] *Time* loved it, including the new songs, describing it as "rapid, hilarious and competently directed by Lewis Milestone."[49] The Legion of Decency also thought it "hilarious" and "a good picture" but refused to recommend it because of "suggestive dialogue and double-meaning lines."[50]

Audiences flocked to see *Anything Goes,* extending its run in New York, Chicago, Hartford, Kansas City, Birmingham, Denver, and elsewhere. The picture received an enormous boost from Bing's new sponsor, Kraft, which plastered the title on delivery trucks and ordered salespeople to spread the word. Paramount arranged tie-ins with magazines and special promotions in menswear and music shops. Though radio continued to hurt theater receipts, the ether did wonders for Bing, and not just in marketing synergy. *Anything Goes* was the last picture he made before taking over *Kraft Music Hall.* His subsequent movies reflected an augmented stature. Kapp proved that Bing could be America's voice. *KMH* repositioned him as every American's neighbor.

20

KRAFT
MUSIC HALL

*Two unpredictable bad spots — (1) Bing muffled a top
note. (2) Elissa Landi lost a page. Bob Burns had one
very long story that took too long for the laughs. There
was so much fun and frolicking by cast it probably was
not so enjoyable over the air.*

— H. C. Kuhl, *KMH* program report (1936)[1]

Jack Oakie, a popular guest in the early days of Bing's tenure on *Kraft
Music Hall,* liked to recount a cherished story about an appearance
by Detroit Symphony Orchestra conductor Ossip Gabrilowitsch, who
was also a concert pianist. Shortly before airtime, as Oakie told it,
while humorist Victor Borge was warming up the studio audience,
director Cal Kuhl realized that the show was running long and anx-
iously asked Bing to instruct spectators not to applaud. "You're kidding," Bing said.[2] Kuhl was adamant. There must be no applause,
especially for Gabrilowitsch: "Now listen, we know he's going to murder 'em, and if they get started applauding for him, he'll louse up our
time."[3] Bing made the announcement.

The program was in progress when the pianist arrived, an entrance
recalled in loving detail by Oakie, who was fascinated because
Gabrilowitsch was married to Clara Clemens, the daughter of his
idol, Mark Twain. Oakie watched him doff his large-brimmed fedora

and cape and pace silently, awaiting his turn. When Bing introduced him, Gabrilowitsch marched to the piano and, in Oakie's telling, "gave one of the greatest performances of his career! He played the last notes, lifted his hands, and held them above the ivories in a dramatic pause." The audience was quiet as a tomb. He just sat there, dazed. "Those silent moments, which must have seemed an eternity to him, must have been one of the greatest shocks of his life," Oakie observed. Finally, he bestirred himself and, as if in a trance, walked off the stage and out of the building. Afterward, Bing wanted to know what was troubling the maestro. "Bing," Oakie asked, "did you tell him about the no-applause business tonight? 'Oh, my God!' was all Bing could say. 'Oh, my God!'"[4]

This is classic show-business apocrypha: the setup, the details, the specific names, the vivid movielike finish. It even has a second punch line. So thunderstruck was the musician, he left the building without his cheese basket, the sponsor's much coveted gift to each guest. Though something like that may have — or certainly should have — happened during radio's golden age, Oakie's story is as much a fabrication as his idol's "Celebrated Jumping Frog of Calaveras County." Ossip Gabrilowitsch never appeared on Bing's show. Oakie himself appeared only once before Gabrilowitsch's death. The pianist on that occasion was Alexander Brailowsky; Oakie was rebuked by the director for "discourteous" mugging during his spot.[5]

But Oakie's nuanced telling gives the game away, underscoring the absurdity of the tale: Victor Borge didn't relocate from Denmark to the United States until years later, and he joined the Crosby show as a regular cast member, not as an audience warmer; Bing's musical guests were invariably involved in patter with the star; *Kraft Music Hall*, like all network programs, was a minutely timed operation, and radio did not permit the luxury of "silent moments" (Bing would be on the mike in an instant), especially when time was short. Above all, Oakie ignored a unique component of the show: applause was *always* forbidden, by directive of Crosby himself, who found it disruptive and contrived. Bing particularly disliked what he called "organized applause" at the start of the show, before he had done anything — or so he argued — to merit it. Had he been able to persuade his sponsor, he would have had no audience at all. Listening to disc transcriptions of Bing's early Kraft shows, one is startled by the rapid intros and outros surrounding musical numbers, the absence of any kind of mitigating response, the consequent fast pace and easy, nothing-special ambience. One wouldn't know an audience was present, but for its frequent laughter.

During Bing's reign, *Kraft* became a lightning rod for comic yarns, some of which were actually true, for example, the often told tale of David Niven and the bounteous cheese basket. Every guest received a large wicker hamper containing pounds of the sponsor's products, individually wrapped in cellophane, festooned with ribbons, and tied to a teakwood tray. Shortly before he was scheduled to appear, Niven was warned by Samuel Goldwyn, to whom he was under personal contract, that the producer was entitled to whatever he was paid for his radio work but would magnanimously allow the actor half. "When I got home," Niven wrote in a memoir, "we meticulously removed half the spread from the jars, cut every cheese in half, every sardine in half, then with an envelope containing a check for half my salary from the show, I sent the lot to Goldwyn inside half the basket."[6]

Bing's *Kraft Music Hall* generated droll postmortems in part because it represented something different for radio. It had become a way station for entertainers high and low and was a must for Hollywood notables plugging their wares. A pleasure for listeners and performers alike, thanks chiefly to Bing's even keel on air and behind the scenes, *KMH* erased Hollywood's last resistance to radio as a low-life competitor. Here was fresh ground, on which hillbilly comedian Bob Burns and longhair icon Leopold Stokowski could mix it up under the benevolent gaze of ringmaster Bing. The show was so effortlessly amusing, the humor so unforced, that the audience assumed it was largely if not entirely ad-libbed. This assumption was shared even by people supposedly in the know, like the press. They believed *KMH* to be, no less than the numberless talk shows spawned in its wake, a playful hour in which Bing and friends shot the breeze, joked, performed, and periodically took time out so the announcer could sell cheese.

That a program as complicated as *KMH,* with its repartee, musical numbers, commercials, and skits, could be produced off the cuff was about as likely, in 1936, as Ossip Gabrilowitsch wandering off the set in silence. But the assumption was an unbeatable tribute to Bing's finest and longest-running characterization, as the relaxed, neigh-borly, decent, straight-shooting, genial host who was too much him-self, too much a creation of his own lazy tempo to read a script or mind cues. Whenever Bing cracked up or misread or stumbled over a lovingly intoned ten-dollar word or scooped a punch line with his plucky baritone, he contributed to the illusion of spontaneity. The genuinely impromptu moments, for Bing was no slouch at quips, were isolated. Never mind the thousands who (quietly) attended his weekly broadcasts and saw the artists standing around a mike with scripts in hand; the radio-listening audience had its own mind, and in that realm Crosby was simply not the rehearsal type. As his radio per-sona grew in stature, it subsumed the personae he created on records and film.

The Kraft-Phenix Cheese Company had introduced the *Kraft Music Revue* in 1933, for the express purpose of promoting a faux-mayonnaise concoction called Miracle Whip. Doubling as sandwich spread and salad dressing, the new product appealed to Depression purses and deficient palates and received a dynamic send-off with a program that starred Al Jolson, music commentator Deems Taylor, and Paul Whiteman, whose Rhythm Boys then included Johnny Mercer. An immediate success, that show, like all network shows, was created by the sponsor's advertising agency — in this instance, the powerful J. Walter Thompson, specifically Thompson's visionary chief of broad-cast production, John Reber. Writer Carroll Carroll, who played a decisive role in unleashing Bing's radio id, wrote of the man who put him on the agency's payroll: "The fact that I met the unbelievable Reber, one of the most inspired and inspiring showmen of the Golden Age of Radio, while he was clad in Chinese red pajamas is the only thing that kept me from being scared to death of him."[7] Reber, a tall, gaunt man, had launched hit programs for Rudy Vallée, Burns and Allen, Eddie Cantor, and Edgar Bergen, among others. Carroll con-tributed to most of those shows but came into his own as sole writer of the New York–based *Kraft Music Revue*.

When Jolson took sabbaticals to work in California, as he often did, Reber — knowing that radio waves were especially responsive to deeper voices — sought personable baritones to fill in. He employed a few unknowns who remained unknown, compensating for their mediocrity with an impressive rotation of celebrated guests from Broadway, jazz, and opera. When Jolson left for good, Reber renamed the hour *Kraft Music Hall* and promoted Whiteman to host. Whiteman, typically, presided over a showcase for his musicians and band, contrary to Reber's desire for a more diverse variety program. To Reber's relief, Whiteman refused to change his modus operandi, freeing J. Walter Thompson to pursue — now that Woodbury proved Bing had the makings of a radio personality — the hottest baritone of all. Whiteman, in turn, was picked up by Woodbury.

During his fruitful August trip to Saratoga, the day after the recording session with the Dorsey Brothers, Bing appeared as Paul's radio guest for what the cheese company regarded as a de facto audition. He also sang that evening at Whiteman's opening night at the Riviera Club. Four months later, in December, the *KMH* baton officially passed from the bandleader to his erstwhile crooner — a formality spread over four Thursday-night shows, for which Whiteman served as host in New York while Bing was wired in from Hollywood, taking his cues on the telephone. The audio engineer responsible for this sleight of hand was a young wizard named Murdo MacKenzie, who went on to record and eventually transcribe and produce Bing's radio ventures for three decades.

Bing was paid $3,000 for each of those four performances, a series that began shakily despite long rehearsals. Following the "Miracle Fanfare," announcer Ford Bond introduced Whiteman, who explained that the featured guest was not in the Music Hall, but in Hollywood with Jimmy Dorsey's "swell" orchestra. This was to be a big night, Whiteman continued, because "Bing is not only a swell singer and a swell guy, but he happens to be one of the best friends I've got in all the world. So naturally, I'm mighty happy to have him with us."[8] As a token of his esteem, Whiteman offered a medley of Crosby hits, from "Mississippi Mud" to "I Wish I Were Aladdin." Then the microphone passed to Bing.

The verdict at Thompson was divided, but the enthusiasm of director Cal Kuhl carried the day; he was placed in charge of the show. Kuhl wrote in his program report, "[Dorsey] still nervous at playing for Bing. It'll wear off shortly."[9] He also noted the more pressing problem of Bing's tendency to stand too close to the mike. For the third show, a lectern was placed in front of Bing to force him to keep his distance. On the last of the four dual broadcasts with Whiteman, a comic named Bob Burns came into his own. A vaudevillian from Van Buren, Arkansas, billed as the Arkansas Traveler, Burns had appeared occasionally with Whiteman and Rudy Vallée, to little response. He personified the kind of rube humor that amused Bing back in his "Bingville Bugle" days and would now thrive as Bing's sidekick on *KMH* and in two films. *KMH* even signed him as Bing's summer replacement, and Paramount starred him in his own low-budget films.

On January 2, 1936, broadcasting over station KFI at 7:00 P.M. Pacific time from NBC's Studio B, a temporary setup on the back lot at RKO, Bing finally presided as sole host of the *Kraft Music Hall,* his radio home for the next decade. From the beginning, *KMH* juggled classics and pop, the concert stage and Hollywood. On the first show, teenage violinist Ruggiero Ricci played a classical number and director Cecil B. De Mille participated in a scripted interview. Don Wilson announced, Jimmy Dorsey's band underscored Bing's rhythmic zing, and Burns demonstrated a musical instrument of his own invention: a brass contraption made of sliding pipes with a funnel at one end, resembling a kitchen-sink trombone but sounding more like a jug. He called it a bazooka, after the sound it made, and his featured numbers became so popular that the name was later appropriated by the army for short-range rocket launchers.

Burns's job included welcoming the audience (the studio accommodated 400) and asking it to withhold what other stars craved. He appeared just before airtime, introduced himself and the host ("that fella back there in the corner is Bing Crosby"),[10] and said:

> The Kraft people welcome you all here and ask you not to applaud, but if you find something funny, feel free to laugh. Now, when the green light turns to red, we will be on the air. And then, when the red light goes off and the green light comes on again, if you feel like applauding, please do.[11]

In his program report for the first show, Kuhl complained about Bing's stubborn hugging of the mike and worried, "Show may need a bit of working over to find correct formula to the Crosby style and personality."[12] Improvement was immediate. Following the second installment, Kuhl exulted, "Crosby in fine fettle. Show changed from opening program and now is more in the Crosby style, which is distinctive and different."[13] He found it well engineered and fast moving, especially praising contributions by classical pianist Mischa Levitski and commentator Rupert Hughes. Bing even held back on the mike. The jazz and humor quotient were raised by old friend Joe Venuti, whose impertinent, monosyllabic wit invariably made Bing laugh and who, in the argot of musicians, could swing you into bad health.[14] On the next few shows, guests included John Barrymore (who arrived in his cups yet, steadied by Bing, flawlessly rendered Hamlet's soliloquy), Percy Grainger, Joe E. Brown, Leopold Stokowski, and Marina Schubert, a minor actress whose singing made her an early *KMH* favorite.

The February 6 show was memorable. Walter Huston's dramatic reading fell flat, but he enchanted listeners by reminiscing about his years in vaudeville and movingly croaking a song — in effect, a prelude to his triumph in the 1938 musical *Knickerbocker Holiday* and his renowned recording of the score's only hit, "September Song." Elusive Russian pianist Josef Lhevinne, however, showed a slackening in his fabled technique; "the mike is cruel," Kuhl wrote.[15] Most important, that night marked the *KMH* debut of Bing's new announcer, Ken Carpenter.

Don Wilson was well known as Jack Benny's corpulent foil, and *KMH* wanted a fresh personality to serve as Bing's man. Ken Carpenter was made to order. Mildly stentorian and quick on his feet, he was a sincere, gentle, and never unctuous pitchman. Like Benny's Wilson, Carpenter became an essential part of the show, an agile straight man who relished every opportunity for clowning. Bing called him "a genuine professional radioman. He made me look good every time. He could do a lot of things with that big voice of his. He'd kinda surprise you. He could break you up putting on some kind of character — a rube or something like that."[16]

Carpenter was born in Illinois in 1900 and, after relocating to Los Angeles, was hired to emcee the Cocoanut Grove broadcasts featuring the Rhythm Boys. At the time Bing took over *KMH,* he was reminded of Ken's abilities listening to him announce the Rose Bowl. The chemistry between the two men was evident: they both loathed pomposity. Carpenter was even willing to accept the task of manually ringing the NBC chimes — the network's famous three-note trademark — before it became a push-button job. Their association was all business but engendered mutual loyalty. Ken announced other programs (including *The Edgar Bergen/Charlie McCarthy Show, One Man's Family,* and *The Lux Radio Theater*) but was known chiefly for his long association with Crosby. Like Murdo MacKenzie, he left *KMH* with Bing in 1946 and remained with him through his last radio series, in 1962. In 1976 Ken presented Bing with the Armstrong Award in recognition of his pioneering work in the medium.

KMH, an instant success, would ultimately reach a weekly audience of some 50 million, a Thursday-night ritual across the country. Riotous laughter and roof-raising musical numbers were not the goal; the idea was to engage the listener's smile and sense of involvement, as if *KMH* were a family circle that just happened to comprise superb musical entertainers. An open-house feeling was underscored by the diversity of Bing's guest list, which has never been equaled. Suddenly radio was an eminent address — not just an obligatory promotional stop. For a while the movie studios held out, restricting their biggest stars and imposing arbitrary conditions on those they let appear; players contracted to 20th Century-Fox, for example, were required to mention studio chief Darryl Zanuck. B-list players appreciated the exposure as well as the work; concert artists relished the chance to be heard by millions. No other program in broadcast history did as much to introduce Americans to classical music and its stars, whom Bing chaperoned with casual respect, presenting their talents as a non-medicinal contrast to the pop tunes handled by himself and Jimmy Dorsey's twelve-piece band.

In his first year alone, Bing's *KMH* visitors included Spencer Tracy, Alice Faye, Andrés Segovia, Charlie Ruggles, Leonard Pennario, Dorothy Wade, Lotte Lehmann, Ann Sothern, Bronislaw Hubermann (who insisted the piano be retuned to European pitch while the show was on the air), Patsy Kelly, Emanuel Feuermann, Lyda Roberti, Virginia Bruce, Grete Stuckgold, Edward Everett Horton, Albert Spalding, Binnie Barnes, Rudolph Ganz, Joan Crawford, Ernestine Schumann-Heink, Efrem Zimbalist, ZaSu Pitts, Fritz Leiber, the California Society of Ancient Instruments, Louis Prima, Rose Bampton, the Avalon Boys, Frank Morgan, Bette Davis, Fyodor Chaliapin (who slowed the show by ad-libbing but utterly enchanted

Bing), George Jessel, Norma Talmadge, Edith Fellows, Pat O'Brien, Toscha Seidel, Martha Raye, Frances Farmer, Norman Taurog, Jean Arthur, Bert Wheeler, Robert Taylor, Robert Young, Dolores Costello, Louis Armstrong, Alison Skipworth, Elizabeth Rethberg, Dorothy Lamour, Joan Bennett, Ruth Chatterton, Slip Madigan (the football coach), Josephine Hutchinson, Warren William, Iona's Hawaiians, Cary Grant, Elissa Landi, Adolphe Menjou, Gladys George, Mary Astor, Gene Raymond, Rochelle Hudson, Bruce Cabot, James Gleason, Gregor Piatigorsky, Anita Louise, Jose Iturbi, and Art Tatum, some of them appearing two or three times or more, plus those previously mentioned, as well as regulars (notably the Paul Taylor Choristers), sketch actors, and many others — all during 1936. As Barry Ulanov wrote, "The longhairs were shortened; the crew-cuts were lengthened."[17] The result was unprecedented cultural democratization.

The most important figure on the program, beyond Bing, was the writer who serendipitously became his collaborator in creating Bing's *KMH* self: the talented, elfin, and cheerfully sardonic Carroll Carroll. When Bing was hired, Thompson initially assigned him a writer in its West Coast office, Sam Moore. But two months after Bing took over, Moore left the agency. Rather than bring in an outsider, Reber asked Carroll to head west and take his place. Moore had spent the month before Bing's first *KMH* show trailing after him like a puppy, trying to learn the Crosby lingo, an effort that Carroll redoubled. He knew better than to create a character for Bing. Although radio was a medium of pioneering intimacy, its first dictum was to fake sincerity. But Crosby, Carroll acknowledged, had little capacity for fakery. He could not play a fictional character like Jack Benny's vain skinflint, nor could he assume the role of humanitarian or spokesman as Eddie Cantor had. Bing could only be himself — modest, playful, intelligent, and appealingly aloof. Carroll's challenge was to allow Bing to be Bing, only more so.

Though in later years he published an important memoir of his radio years, *None of Your Business,* Carroll was sparing with details about his background. He was born Carroll Weinschenk in New York in 1902 and dropped out of high school to write. He traveled for a while, working briefly as a farmhand, and when he returned to New

York, his stories and poems began to appear regularly in humor magazines as well as the *Saturday Evening Post, Life,* and *The New Yorker;* he wrote a radio column for the *New York Sunday World.* Sixty years later announcer Ken Roberts remembered his poems as "brilliant."[18] But they did not pay the rent, so Carroll began taking public-relations assignments, which led him to John Reber and his Chinese pajamas. Bespectacled and short and pleasantly owlish, he was soon recognized as one of the best comedy writers in radio. Actor Eddie Bracken described him as "a little unassuming guy who loved good comedy in a serious way, a pleasure to be with, just a regular old shoe, you know? You couldn't find anybody more natural or wonderful than Carroll Carroll."[19]

Bing was somewhat less enthralled and, to the writer's annoyance, kept Carroll at a distance. Their first meeting was a chance encounter outside Studio B, after a rehearsal. "Glad to know you," Bing said as Kuhl introduced them. But when he learned that Carroll was the new writer from New York, Bing said merely, "Ohhhhh? Lots of luck," and strode off.[20] Carroll had already sized up the man, observing him during the rehearsal: "Bing, wearing a porkpie hat, a dark blue outboard shirt, henna slacks, and black and white golf shoes, was smoking a pipe, doping a race, and running through a new tune, with Jimmy Dorsey reminding him of it on the saxophone. Nothing could have been more typical."[21]

Bing's clashing clothes, which reflected the fact that he was color-blind, became a running gag, as much a part of the Crosby persona as Jack Benny's cheapness — though, in this instance, grounded in reality. Bing could not tell red from green; he was able to drive because traffic lights were all the same to him — red on top, green on bottom. Carroll recalled once pointing out to Bing that he was wearing different socks, black and red. Bing looked down and replied, "That's funny. They both fit." Asked on another occasion if he knew the color of his socks, Bing answered, "Dark?"[22] Lines like that are found treasure for a comedy writer, but not necessarily usable. Color-blindness is no joke. The trick was to make fun of the Hawaiian shirts and array of hats (Bing never wore his rug on the air), the motley of plaids and stripes, without suggesting a disability.

As they began to work together, Carroll realized that he and Bing shared a fascination with language and a mutual love of show-business eccentrics. (Bracken recalled their hilariously trading stories about actor Charlie Butterworth.) Carroll played on those interests to flesh out Bing's radio character. For a while Bing resisted speaking more than was necessary; as late as 1946 he argued that listeners wanted to hear him sing, not talk, and he had a habit of severely pruning his dialogue. But as Joe Bigelow — formerly Bige of *Variety* and by 1946 the Thompson account executive in charge of *KMH* — noted, for all his protests Bing actually liked talking once he got going, especially trading lines with fast comics.[23] Carroll understood that. He began jotting down the odd words and bizarre slang that peppered Bing's conversation and put them into the scripts.

"That ain't English," Bob Burns observed, "that's a language called Crosby."[24] A 1938 issue of the sponsor's house magazine, *Cheesekraft*, published a Bing Crosby glossary: "the full treatment" (a good job), "prayer bones" (knees), "I pass" (I give up), "snozzy little ketch" (a yacht), "I seem to be playing infield" (I'm all confused), "let's have a recount" (I'm still confused), "go in there and pitch" (give them a good show), "a dinger" (a honey), "a whingdinger" (superlative), "frettin' cuticle" (worrying), "zingy" (quick), "in the groove" (down the alley), "shooting gallery" (movie theater),[25] and dozens more, some borrowed from vaudeville and jazz, others of unknown origin, like the one that tickled Miriam Hopkins about dropping a load of pumpkins, or Carroll's favorite among Bing's on-air quips, spoken to trumpeter Wingy Manone after a solo: "Man, that was dirtier than a Russian horse-doctor's valise."[26]

Carroll's routine was straightforward and full-time. He spent the weekend interviewing upcoming guests to get a feel for the way they spoke, looking for any quirks that could be written into the patter. He explained, "The policy was to talk to highbrows as if they were athletes and athletes as if they were highbrows."[27] On Monday and Tuesday he wrote the script, delivering complete copies to Bing and Burns, and applicable sections to the guests. The next day he collected okays and suggestions from the guests. Not until Thursday morning did he receive Bing's edits, which Carroll was free to incorporate or ignore. Thursday's rehearsal was conducted in segments, each timed, but usually not in order. There was never a complete run-through, so only Bing knew how the entire show would play. Carroll emphasized one reason the show seemed so informal: what other pro-

grams considered dress rehearsal, *KMH* presented as the actual program, aired live Thursday evening at seven.

For Bing, of course, *KMH* was anything but full-time. He was also
making three movies and recording, on average, forty records a year.
All of which he seemed, at times, to treat as necessary intrusions on
his primary interests, those of a gentleman sportsman. In that capacity, too, he made history. The year before he took charge of *KMH,*
Bing purchased his first racehorse, Zombie, who placed and showed
in two races at Santa Anita, representing Bing's colors of blue and
gold. At the same time, he hired as his trainer Albert Johnson, a
Spokane boy who left a few years before Bing to make his name as a
top jockey, winning the Kentucky Derby in 1922. Bing built stables
and an exercise track at Rancho Santa Fe, and before the year was out
he had fifteen horses, and soon after that twenty-one. He was betting
and losing heavily, and his compulsion would worsen before he had it
under control. But he earned respect for his serious love of the turf.
Trainer Noble Threewitt recalled him arriving at 4–4:30 A.M., an hour
before the track opened, to pad around the stables, schmooze with
the trainers, and read the papers.[28]

Thus, Bing was the obvious person to approach when William A.
Quigley, a former football star, successful stockbroker, and occasional
racing official, got the idea of establishing a track at Del Mar, not far
from Bing's Rancho Santa Fe getaway. Bing loved the idea, and the
Del Mar Thoroughbred Club was incorporated May 5, 1936. This
was to be largely a Hollywood project, financed and promoted by film
stars, whose regular presence at the track would heighten its appeal
for the general public. Bing, the primary stockholder, called for a
board meeting the day after incorporation, at Warner Bros.' studio.
Executives were elected: Bing president, actor Pat O'Brien (the
second-largest stockholder) vice president, Everett Crosby secretary-
treasurer, and Oliver Hardy and director Lloyd Bacon officers. The
other film people appointed to the executive committee were Gary
Cooper, Joe E. Brown, David Butler, William LeBaron, and Leo
McCarey, who soon dropped out, to be replaced by Clark Gable and
George Raft. Remaining directors, drawn from the business world,
included millionaire Charles Howard and his son Lindsay Howard.
Quigley was named general manager. When the stock offering failed

to take off, Bing and O'Brien borrowed on life-insurance policies to complete construction of the track. They filed an application with the California Horse Racing Board for a twenty-five-day meet, beginning July 3, 1937. On the day the world first learned of Amelia Earhart's disappearance, Bing, in a loose shirt and yachting cap, personally opened the gates and — as newsreel cameras turned — welcomed customers and collected their tickets. His horse, High Strike, won the first race.

At the same time, Bing pursued his primary love, golf. In 1936 he won the Lakeside Golf Championship, the first of several such victories. Though he didn't play on a professional level, he was widely conceded to be one of the best in Hollywood, his low handicap (two) occasionally contested by those who claimed he was a scratch player; twenty years after Bing's death, Bob Hope could be heard complaining that without the handicap they would have been more evenly matched.[29] On one occasion, Bing qualified for the national amateur golf championship. Golf expert Toney Penna noted, "If he could have hit the ball twenty to thirty yards farther, he could have been one of the country's top amateurs."[30]

Bing's main contribution to the game was as a popularizer and organizer. Penna (who scored fourth in the 1938 U.S. Open) put it into his head to create a pro-amateur invitational. Bing was intrigued by the idea of a competition in which Lakeside members and other low-handicap amateurs could team up with pros. The obvious place to hold it was the course near his home at Rancho Santa Fe. In February 1937, seven months before Del Mar opened, the Rancho Santa Fe Amateur-Pro — later known throughout the sporting world as the Bing Crosby National Pro-Am Tournament — made its debut. It was a triumph despite rains that washed out the first day's play as well as the bridge leading to a green; firemen and policemen in hip boots piggybacked the players across the water. Sam Snead won $500 carding a 68. Bing came in with an 87. The Crosby, the first and longest-running celebrity golf tournament, allocated all proceeds to charities.

All this was grist for Carroll Carroll's mill, albeit with alterations. Winning ponies, of which Bing had quite a few, were not as funny as losers, so Bing's limping nags became a running joke. His obsessive golfing, in Carroll's hand, was just another indication of Bing's laid-back, even lazy, approach to life. Obviously, Bing was never lazy, just relaxed. Fans, who confused the two, did not get many glimpses of the iron discipline that kept him on track and on time. His punctuality never wavered; the old days of sheepish arrivals were long past. Film, recording, and radio directors grew accustomed to arriving in the studio or on the set to find Bing already there. For Bing, a 5:30 A.M. call did not mean 5:40, and though he apparently never upbraided those who wandered in late, the sight of the leading man alone on an empty set, reading the newspaper or a racing form, humbled many of his coworkers into tightening their own schedules.

Conversely, Bing left promptly at the designated time, no matter what, even in the middle of a scene. "Tell him exactly when you wanted him and he'd be there," Carroll wrote, but the minute the session was over, he was "like a school kid who knew the bell ought to ring."[31] Bing considered punctuality a matter of courtesy. If he was on call to the studio from 6:00 to 4:00 and had another appointment at 4:30, he figured he ought to be prompt for both. The devil might tempt him with pleasures of the flesh, but never with idleness. That such exactitude could coexist with the insouciance and imperturbability for which he was renowned dumbfounded coworkers, especially those leading ladies who felt neglected because he was always pushing off to another appointment. Even fooling around had its place and time. By categorically following the clock, Bing was never rushed, never harried.

As Carroll fed Bing's own speech patterns back to him, Bing began to relish the tongue twisters that emerged from the dependable rhetorical device of mixing highfalutin words with slang. A few weeks into the job, Carroll wrote openings for Bing that even friends thought were impromptu. For example, the May 7 show:

> Good evening, ladies and gentlemen, Bing Crosby welcoming you to another of our regular Thursday-evening soirees in the *Kraft Music Hall*. And we hope you're all comfortably settled by your "soiradios" — the Bob Burns influence. At any rate, in addition to the insidious Burns, Jimmy Dorsey and his orchestra, and the Paul Taylor Choristers, we have with us in the Hall this evening my friend George Raft. We thought maybe the Raft wouldn't get back from location to be with us tonight, but I'm glad to report that the smooth and sinister yet romantic Georgie made it. Mr. Toscha Seidel, one of the greatest violinists in

the world, is also with us this evening, I'm proud to say. And Miss Una Merkel, MGM's very popular and extremely busy young commediene.[32]

This was followed by patter between Bing and Merkel, with exchanges like:

Bing: How long ago was that?
Una: Goodness, no southern gentleman asks a girl to name dates.
Bing: I'm from Spokane.
Una: That's far enough south of Alaska to make you a southern gentleman.

And:

Bing: Do you really think it's wise for a girl to give up school to go on the stage?
Una: What's the difference? It's an education. One way, you get smart by degrees. The other way, by stages.
Bing: I wonder what a southern gentleman would say to that?
Una: What do you say to it? Do you think a boy who wants to should go on the stage or stay in school?
Bing: What's the difference? It's an education. One way, you get smart by degrees. The other way, by stages.
Una: I just said that.
Bing: I know. I wanted you to hear how it sounded.

And for a closer to the five-minute "interview":

Una: By the way, now that you know all about me, how did you happen to get into show business?
Bing: Well, you see I was . . .
Una: Thank you. What was your first big dramatic part?
Bing: Miss Una Merkel, ladies and gentlemen . . .
Una: Do you think crooning is here to stay?
Bing: Miss Merkel will . . .
Una: Do the other two Rhythm Boys miss you much?
Bing: Jimmy, Una's on . . .

Bing was twenty-seven and Dixie was eighteen when they married, on September 29, 1930, at the Church of the Blessed Sacrament in Hollywood. She was far more famous than he was, and the wedding photo was widely published. *Susan Crosby Collection*

In 1934, shortly before the birth of the twins, Bing and Dixie bought a sixty-five-acre property in Rancho Santa Fe. Bing hired Lillian J. Rice to restore the nineteenth-century Spanish style, but added modern improvements, including a tennis court. *Susan Crosby Collection*

Bing, his mother, and James Cagney celebrate the christening of Bing's first son, Gary, on October 8, 1933.
Ron Bosley Collection

In 1936 Bing and Dixie built their beloved mansion on six acres at 10500 Camarillo Street in the Toluca Lake section of North Hollywood. It would be destroyed by fire in January 1943.
Architectural Digest

Dixie with her fourth son, Linnie, 1938. She was a dedicated tennis player until a kidney infection forced her to quit.
Rory Burke Collection

Bing was a voracious reader, even when he wasn't posing for publicity shots in his Camarillo Street home.
Architectural Digest

On the set of *Anything Goes*, Bing posed with his costar Ethel Merman and two Paramount players who dropped by, Fred MacMurray and Bing's old friend Gary Cooper.
Ron Bosley Collection

At a 1953 party Errol Flynn demonstrated his admiration for Bing's refusal to wear a toupee when he wasn't working. Linnie is seated on Bing's left.
Susan Crosby Collection

Bing named a horse Decca Joe, after Joe Perry, the prolific producer who recorded many celebrated hits in the thirties and forties.
Elsie Perry Collection

A frequent guest on Bing's *Kraft Music Hall* was Lucille Ball, shown here with Bing and an unidentified friend.
Gary Giddins Collection

ABOVE: The Crosbys' Westwood Marching and Chowder Club minstrel shows were major Hollywood social events in the late 1930s. Bing poses with (left to right) Bessie Burke, Midge and Herb Polesie, Dixie, and Johnny Burke. BELOW: Seated with an unidentified blackface actor, Pat O'Brien, and Jerry Colonna, Bing enjoys Bessie Burke's backless chaps. *Rory Burke Collection*

Bing takes the baton from bandleader and songwriter Harry Owens, after "Sweet Leilani" became the surprise hit of 1937 and helped turn Los Angeles into a Hawaiian theme park.
Len Weissman/Elsie Perry Collection

Jack Kapp, Joe Perry, and an engineer listen from the recording booth as Frances Langford, Bing, and Louis Armstrong record the *Pennies from Heaven* medley, August 17, 1936.
Elsie Perry Collection

The Boswell Sisters alternated with the Mills Brothers as regulars on Bing's Woodbury radio show. Bing later recorded famous duets with Connie Boswell, center.
Ron Bosley Collection

Bing looked forward to working with Louis in *Doctor Rhythm*, a picture plagued with mishaps; to Bing's chagrin, the Armstrong footage was cut and apparently lost, November 1937.
Gary Giddins Collection

Harry Crosby visited Bing on the set of *We're Not Dressing*, 1934.
Elsie Perry Collection

Bing and Dixie on the lawn of their home with, left to right, Phillip, Gary, Linnie, and Dennie, 1940.
Susan Crosby Collection

At which point the band struck up a loud and hasty introduction for her song.

Bing kept clear of the commercials, segueing with a line like "And here is Ken Carpenter to say a word on behalf of the management." Then he sang his first song, backed by Dorsey's "swanky swingsters." No matter what the song, Bing sang with his accustomed rhythmic lilt when Jimmy or his sub, Joe Venuti, led the band. Then he would trade a few lines with Bob Burns, whom Bing usually called by his given name, Robin. Burns would do seven or eight minutes about his relatives — the drunk uncle, the shrewish sister-in-law — and close with a bazooka solo. Frequently the patter with Burns or another guest would produce an uncommon word, like *bauxite,* that recurred as a comic motif throughout the show. One Crosby segment created a tradition, imitated on radio and TV: he would offer a few clues to a bygone day and give the audience the space of a station break to guess the correct year. Then he sang a representative song. On this show the year was 1928, and the song "June Night."

Time now for the second guest, George Raft, who spoke of his big break in *Scarface,* plugged the picture he was currently filming, and talked baseball — all very informal, very scripted, with a few inside curves:

Raft: Who's taking care of the store now?

Bing: You mean the studio? Paramount?

Raft: Yes. Any changes made since I've been away?

Bing: Oh, A. Zukor's back in charge.

Raft: You mean that racehorse, Azucar?

Bing: No, no — Adolph Zukor, the little giant. He's running things now.

Raft: Oh, I see. Say, what's this gag about bauxite? All I've heard since I've been here this evening is bauxite. What is the stuff?

Bing: I'll tell you, George. I'm going on location Saturday and you're going tonight. When I come back and you come back, there may be some report from the research committee. I'll tell you then.

Then Bing sang, sometimes a medley and sometimes one of his current records, but often not. The few surviving recordings of the 1930s Kraft shows are treasured not least because he never formally recorded more than half the songs featured on the air, including dozens of good ones, like Berlin's "I'm Putting All My Eggs in One Basket" and Ellington's "I Let a Song Go Out of My Heart."

Next came the longhair spot. Bing introduced Seidel with straightforward biographical remarks, noting his Oslo debut, his first American visit, and his 1,100 recitals, winding up with a peculiarly Crosbyan verbal turn, starting high and landing low: "Mr. Seidel favors us this evening with the scherzando movement from Lalo's violin concerto *Symphonie Espagnole,* and when you hear Mr. Seidel play it, if you don't think it's swell music, then you can't pick tunes for me." After the number, they talked a minute. Seidel was eager to get back East for the fights:

> Seidel: But before I leave for New York, I'd like to know what bauxite is.
> Bing: I'd be glad to tell you, but later. I don't want Burns to hear.
> Seidel: Well, I'll wait around then.
> Bing: And while he's waiting around, ladies and gentlemen, Toscha Seidel plays as an encore a composition by one of his colleagues, Fritz Kreisler's very lovely "Schön Rosmarin."

That number was followed by a combo from the Dorsey outfit playing an original jazz riff, "Coolin' Off." The show was winding down. After the third and final commercial, Burns explained to Bing that bauxite is "a ferruginous aluminum hydroxide," spelling the chemical equation. Bing, in what was often the hour's high point, settled into a ballad — tonight, "The Touch of Your Lips." He then named the guests for the next week's show as "Where the Blue of the Night" swelled behind him.

The show's most caustic critic was invariably the director. Kuhl described the May 7 program as "O.K.," before laying on his comments. Bing was on top of the mike again: "An elephant never forgets and a Crosby never remembers," he wrote in his report. The show suffered from "spring fever" and lacked "the usual pep, pace, and vivacity." Merkel was good, but she "should learn to play comedy." Raft had no material. Kuhl worried that Bing came across as "disrespectful of Seidel, a la Jolson" and thought he had trouble with the key on one number. He considered only Burns to be "very good." Even a cheese promo left a bad taste: "Kraft couples carry on the silliest conversations."[33] Kuhl's reservations were shared by few listeners.

*   *   *

Friends noticed that real Bing and radio Bing were sounding more and more alike, the former catching up with the latter. It was as if the object of Carroll's study had been liberated by the resulting caricature. Predilections stressed in his scripts were embraced by Bing, and he became indistinguishable from Carroll's takeoff. Put another way, Bing got a better sense of who he was from the role he played. In publicist Gary Stevens's analysis, "Carroll gave Bing the suavity, savoirfaire, the throwaway personality that Bing never had, and Bing lived that part for the rest of his life."[34] To Eddie Bracken, "Carroll's wonderful fey way of writing just fit Bing beautifully and literally made Bing a better actor. Carroll gave him a type of characterization different than anything else on radio and also different for Bing."[35] To Bing, Carroll's influence was comparable to that of Jack Kapp: "He'd send a script around to my home and I'd try to rewrite the speeches he'd written for me so as to make them sound even more like me. And I'd try to put in little jokes if I could think of any. Most of them were clumsy and pointless, but once in a while I hit something mildly amusing and Carroll wouldn't delete it if he thought it had a chance of getting a laugh. The way we worked together resulted in the next best thing to ad-libbing."[36]

But the next best thing was not good enough. To keep things lively, Carroll encouraged Bing to ad-lib a little, even if just an impromptu laugh — an infectious burbling that audiences loved. Observing how verbally dexterous Bing could be with his friends, Carroll was confident of Bing's ability to stand his ground and quip with the best. At first, with Kuhl's support, Carroll encouraged safe ad-libbing, the kind that takes place in rehearsal; if Bing (or a guest) came up with a zinger, it was written into the script. Carroll soon devised the subterfuge of handing Bing a slightly different script than that of his guests. The first time he tried it, he simply had a guest inquire about Bing's latest golf score. The studio went dead for a moment as Bing paled before finally responding, "Why, about eighty-two." When the guest asked another surprise question, Bing said, "Let's get back to the script here."[37] He had a fit when the show ended, threatening to quit when Kuhl told him to expect more of the same. He got used to it, however; his nervousness abated, and he began to sound more like himself. When Mischa Levitski made his third *KMH* appearance, the repartee began with Levitski remarking that he played better in the Music Hall than anywhere else because he could dress informally.

Bing: I'm delighted to hear it, and may I say that all day long I've been admiring your splendid red suspenders.

Mischa: A great many pianists wear suspenders exactly like these.

Bing: Any reason?

Mischa: Yes. To hold up their pants.[38]

The joke was older than vaudeville, a cousin to minstrelsy's road-crossing chicken, yet it generated an enormous response, in part because Levitski was delivering it, but chiefly because Bing did not see it coming and cracked up. His script read, "Because the flannel is soft and doesn't cut into the shoulders the way elastic suspenders do." Radio laughter galvanized audiences with its titillating suggestion of an indiscretion, especially Bing's, for he was almost always unflappable.

Kuhl marveled at Bing's ability to pilot the show no matter what the obstacles, sometimes sacrificing his own numbers. "Drastic cutting, late in the game, hurt show," Kuhl noted of one program, "but not as much as if Bing with typical, Quixotic gallantry, hadn't insisted Avalon Boys do two numbers at expense of his own medley, which we cut."[39] When Bette Davis's segment was shortened for time, Kuhl wrote, "an ad-lib of Bing's" (unpreserved) saved John Reber "the price of orchids."[40] At times, Bing's ad-libbing proved "the only way out when the free speech of the show gets beyond control — and it's the free speech that makes the show."[41]

After *KMH* had been rolling for a few months, the *New York Post* radio columnist observed that what began as "a slightly casual touch" quickly "crystallized into an attitude of catch-as-catch-can good humor," adding that no other show could so ingratiatingly offer artists of the caliber of Harold Bauer and Lotte Lehmann: "Mr. Crosby presents them not as something that the audience ought to like but as something that the audience will like."[42] Bing's presumption flattered his listeners. Their presumption that he was one of them, despite his much publicized prosperity in times of economic woe, flattered Bing. Movie-star wealth was an ancient story by the mid-1930s — the fantastic estates and servants and blocklong cars, the yachts and exotic playgrounds. But on Bing, who so obviously enjoyed his good fortune, it looked good, providing vicarious pleasure for his fans, as well as a measure of proof that the system — America itself — was not in irreversible decline.

*   *   *

The *KMH* Bing was almost instantly reflected on the silver screen. Paramount bought a Damon Runyon story, "Money from Home," that Ernst Lubitsch wanted to direct him in; the idea, in part, was to show off Bing's riding abilities. The story was rejected, however, in favor of *Rhythm on the Range,* a contemporary western designed to capitalize on Bing's success with cowboy songs. The plot, a wire hanger on which to drape the music and comedy, recycled one of the Depression's favorite fairy tales, apotheosized in Frank Capra's *It Happened One Night*: a wealthy and beautiful heiress runs out on her effete fiancé and finds happiness with a penniless, average Joe — average like Clark Gable or Bing Crosby. Bing himself had snared an heiress in *We're Not Dressing,* and he would get two more in *Double or Nothing* and *Doctor Rhythm.* In the early drafts, the heiress was a mere showgirl fleeing the bright lights, and Jack Oakie and singer Frances Langford were set to costar. Those plans were scuttled with many others. Paramount kept Bing on salary for three months before a story was finally approved.

After producer Benjamin Glazer hired director Norman Taurog, and a roomful of writers cobbled together the script, production was delayed by the search for a leading lady. The contenders included Jean Arthur and Olivia de Havilland, but the choice narrowed to two talented but little-known Paramount starlets: sweet-faced nineteen-year-old former model Marsha Hunt and stunning twenty-two-year-old University of Washington graduate Frances Farmer. "I lost out, and it broke my heart," Hunt recalled. "For once, instead of just being a pretty young thing, like most leading-lady roles, here was something where Bing sang to you. He would win her, lose her, and win her back, and then fade out. Frances, who was not a comedienne, got the role, and it broke my heart."[43] Hunt's booby prize was a publicity stunt: she escorted two frogs representing Bing and Burns to the annual jumping frog contest at Angel's Camp, a ghost town in northern California. Neither frog won.

By the time the film began to shoot, in late April, *KMH* had been on the air for three months, and Burns was tapped to reprise his role of Bing's pal on the big screen. He had already played small roles in a few Saturday-matinee westerns, but *Rhythm on the Range* established him as a briefly dependable if minor movie star in his own right. Playing opposite Burns was another newcomer, a veteran vaudevillian of nineteen, who some thought walked away with the picture. Martha

Raye was an original, and if her knockabout antics quickly dated, they overwhelmed audiences in the 1930s. Sharing a stage with her parents since the age of three, Maggie, as she was known to friends, climbed the lower rungs of show business, desperate to make herself known and liked. She perfected an aggressive and lusty attack, shorn of vanity. She was also a stunning singer, and her powerful rhythmic sense and brassy projection might have earned her a reputation as a Swing Era warbler. Yet she trusted only her comedic ability, a talent recognized by Charlie Chaplin, who cast her as his unsinkable victim in the 1947 *Monsieur Verdoux* and allowed her to steal their every scene. Maggie's wacky humor was bolstered by a rubbery face centered on a square maw of a mouth and a curvaceous figure that gave a shivery edge to her manhungry bellow, "Ooooh boy!"

While singing at a club outside Los Angeles, she signed up for a Sunday-night turn at the more glamorous Trocadero, where performers on the make entertained performers who could afford places like the Trocadero. In the audience were Jimmy Durante and Joe E. Lewis, who assisted her with friendly heckling, and an astonished Norman Taurog, who offered her a screen test. At Benjamin Glazer's request, Sam Coslow went down to the joint where she was working and volunteered to write a specialty number for her test. The result, "Mister Toscanini," was perfect — part fake ballad and part raucous swinger. The test delighted Glazer and Taurog, who resolved to add the song as well as Maggie to the picture. In order to avoid offending a living maestro, however, a change in title was mandated. Reborn as "Mr. Paganini," it became her trademark number. Coslow recalled that at a sneak preview of the picture, Raye's delivery of the song literally stopped the show — the audience cheered until the projectionist reran the scene.

That response was appropriate enough for a movie that was, in effect, filmed radio — specifically, filmed *Kraft Music Hall*. It is not a succession of radio numbers strewn around a plot, like *The Big Broadcast*, but rather a variety show in which plot is routinely interrupted to accommodate specialty numbers. The action revolves around Bing, but his character has little history or depth beyond his on-air personality. In this kind of picture, it does not matter whether he is decked out in a Stetson or a yachting cap; he is basically the same guy — winning, then losing, then winning the girl while singing like nobody's business. Ever the cordial host, he took it upon himself to soothe the nerves of movie newcomers Raye and Frances Farmer, calming them down and boosting their confidence.

It's a shame *Rhythm on the Range* didn't have a script worthy of the potential chemistry between Bing and Farmer, whose brief, stormy career virtually began here. (Howard Hawks saw the rushes and chose her for *Come and Get It,* her best film; the next year she joined New York's Group Theater to star in Clifford Odets's *Golden Boy.*) An opalescent blond beauty, she was obliged to dye her hair bright red, as was Raye, the better to accommodate Karl Struss's cinematography. Farmer was slim, secure, and observant, an expert listener with the manner of a patrician coed, cocking her head and looking at her costar with bemused innocence. She described the filming as "a long sweet nightmare,"[44] claiming that she never really knew what the film was about. But as the only cast member who wasn't called upon to be musical or funny, she brought depth to a shallow role. The fetching contrast between Crosby's chaste shyness and her glimmering frankness defined a new motif in Bing's movies: the *KMH*-era Bing, unlike the Sennett Bing, is always pursued, never in pursuit. Bing and Dixie invited Frances and her husband, actor Leif Erickson, to Rancho Santa Fe. Bing was enchanted by her. After the wrap he gave her a diamond necklace she treasured all her life.

Bing enjoyed making *Rhythm on the Range* and more than a decade later said the part of Jeff Larabee, the singing cattleman turned rodeo performer, was his favorite. Much of the filming was done on location in the High Sierras, where, as he wrote, "every prospect pleases and only work is vile."[45] He took full advantage of the opportunities to fish and ride and claimed that the experience of working on the picture inspired him to purchase, in 1943, his own working ranch in Elko, Nevada. Bing avowed that he wore no makeup beyond a suntan and dropped twelve pounds before shooting commenced, though he looks chunky in his flannel shirts and jeans. His most exhaustive preparation entailed two weeks' perfecting a technique for hand rolling cigarettes. In the film he hands the results to Frances; Mother Crosby's boy refrained from puffing onscreen.

With its quartet of stars and an octet of contributing songwriters, the picture is so free with in-jokes and non sequiturs that it doesn't even bother to deliver on the promised confrontation with the bad guys who vainly contrive to kidnap the heiress. Bing's Jeff Larabee was named after an offscreen character in *Two for Tonight*. His boss, the mannish Aunt Penny (Lucille Webster Gleason), suggests, as she stomps around Madison Square Garden, Bing's ancestor Cornelia Thurza Crosby, the trout expert who scandalized that very venue by wearing a green skirt seven inches above the floor. Since Martha Raye was known for a drunk routine, one was pointlessly thrown in, allowing her to murder "Love in Bloom." Bing, who routinely used his movies to employ friends, found a slot for Louis Prima, whose jazz was pulling them in at the Famous Door, and Bob Nolan's Sons of the Pioneers, including Leonard Slye, who later changed his name to Roy Rogers. His most important hand up was to a new acquaintance who had been working New York and Hollywood for years with infrequent success, Johnny Mercer.

Born in Savannah in 1909, Mercer got his break as Bing had, with Whiteman. Although he sang with southern-fried gusto and occasionally played juveniles (Leo McCarey thought he had potential as a film actor), Mercer was first and last a lyricist of genius, known for his peerless ear for the vernacular. Except for two or three revues, however, he enjoyed little attention on Broadway, and in two years out West he placed songs in only three pictures, notably *To Beat the Band* ("If You Were Mine"). But none were hits, and offers were drying up. While driving home to Savannah through Texas, he came up with an idea — words and music — for a song about ersatz westerners. He showed "I'm an Old Cowhand" to Bing, who put it in the film and later made a jolly and tremedously popular record with Jimmy Dorsey. "I really think he saved my Hollywood career," Mercer said.[46]

It marked the beginning of a long personal and professional relationship. "It was my good fortune to know him when he was married to Dixie and his boys were small," Mercer wrote a friend long afterward. "They often rode on my back and I enjoyed the happy days around the track and poolside with this most attractive couple. She was very kind to me, as I was in such awe of him and she knew it. Also, I was a Southerner, and she made me feel at home. I shall never forget their kindness to a very young writer and performer."[47] The film rendition of Mercer's song lacks the swinging élan of the record, but it's the picture's hot spot, a jam session in which Bing, Raye, Burns, Prima, and the Sons of the Pioneers trade choruses, each leading to a satirical break, for example:

I know all the songs that the cowboys know,
'Bout the big corral where the doagies go,
'Cause I learned them all on the radio.
Yippy I O Ki Ay.

Bing displays many facets of his vocal and comedic charms. When he sings "Empty Saddles" mounted on a horse in Madison Square Garden, his pianissimo head tones are uniquely affecting, a style derived from John McCormack and beyond the ken of most popular singers; Sinatra, for example, never attempted it, though Presley did. Bing's love of silent comedians comes through when least expected; while serenading Farmer in a boxcar headed west (and hanging a modesty curtain in the process), he does a funny Stan Laurel nod. When they finally reach the ranch and embark on "I'm an Old Cowhand," he demonstrates all his patented vaudeville shtick — jerky short-arm movements, tap dancing, torso wiggling — and, backed by guitar only, swings the tail of his solo chorus.

Rhythm on the Range easily returned its million-dollar investment as one of the top-grossing pictures of the year, number one on Paramount's roster. It was, as usual, a smash in towns and cities all over the country, breaking several house records, including one in Tucumcari, New Mexico, where the marquee promised, "Bessie Patterson in *Rhythm on the Range.*" Bessie, whose walk-on was so fast that even her mother had to forbear blinking to see it, was the girl who had won the Miss College Humor contest in 1933, for which she was promised a bit part. Now that she was eighteen, Paramount gave it to her, quietly. She was not necessary for the publicity campaign, which began with Bing, in cowboy regalia, whistling a few measures of "Where the Blue of the Night" while preserving his hands and feet in cement at Grauman's Chinese Theatre. Kraft delivery trucks were billboarded with the film for weeks. A thousand Kraft dealers in New York alone were provided window displays. Jukeboxes were prepped with Crosby records. The reviewers went along, although *Variety* was at a loss for a pigeonhole: not really a western, it advised, not really a musical — the cowboy stuff takes place in New York, the jazzy stuff takes place at the ranch, and most of it takes place on the road. Nevertheless, the paper concluded, Crosby "will satisfy most everybody."[48]

*   *   *

Bing had planned to spend the summer — the racing season — in New York with Dixie and made plans to travel there with Everett and his wife. But with *KMH* finding its footing, John Reber persuaded him to postpone the ten-week vacation stipulated in his contract until September, to continue broadcasting. Bing probably didn't need a lot of persuading. On June 1 the Crosbys took possession of their new home at 10500 Camarillo Street.[49] The custom-tailored southern colonial could accommodate three boys and more, should any arrive, as well as servants. It was a picture-postcard house, and the Crosbys loved it. Bing's dad regarded it with awe as a "mansion or palace." "It sure is some place," he remarked.[50]

A driveway curved through a ranging front lawn and up to the front door, while out back nearly half a block of trees made way for a tennis court, pool, bathhouse, and chicken coop. The roof, flat but for two modest gables, shaded a porch the length of the house with the help of six slim pillars. Inside, the spacious and pillared foyer faced a magnificent winding staircase that led to the bedrooms on a balconied second floor. Downstairs were Bing's den and bar, a playroom, and the living room — with fireplace and imposing chandelier — where Christmas and other parties were held. The design and furnishings mixed Georgian, Regency, Chippendale, Dresden, Victorian, and more; the walls were a panorama of linen, damask, and mirrors, the colors dark oak and a sedate blue-gray. The twenty rooms were, on balance, snug and lived-in. An official of the American Institute of Decorators remarked that no more than two rooms, the living room and dining room, could be described as formal.[51] The new house motivated Bing to renegotiate contracts; his price soared to $150,000 per picture, $3,500 per broadcast.

He decided to maximize his summer schedule by shooting the independent film he had wrangled from Paramount. Although the studio had fired Manny Cohen, he continued to hold contracts with Bing (and Mae West and Gary Cooper). If Paramount expected distribution rights, it was badly mistaken. Cohen formed Major Pictures Corporation with Bing, Everett, and John O'Melveny and sought bids for distribution of its first project, which as yet had neither story nor score, only Bing. Columbia's Harry Cohn won, and an agreement was drawn up. They would film a musical in which Columbia, Bing Crosby, Inc., and Cohen each owned a third. Paramount claimed not to care, shrugging off the deal as no different than a loan-out, which was true to a degree, except that loaning Bing was tantamount to making a cash donation to a rival studio, and an independent production relieved the recipient of any obligation to return the favor.

They decided to move ahead with a story called *The Peacock's Feather,* by Katherine Leslie Moore, as elaborated by screenwriter Jo Swerling *(The Whole Town's Talking, It's a Wonderful Life)* and retitled *Pennies from Heaven.* Within weeks of wrapping *Rhythm on the Range,* Bing was on a soundstage again, this time as an ex-con who dreams of singing and playing lute on a gondola in Venice. *Pennies from Heaven* was neither the best nor the most successful picture Bing made, but it was surely the most emblematic of those that preceded the *Road* series and *Going My Way,* presenting him literally in the role with which many people already associated him, that of an American troubadour. The film's immense impact on his career was manifest in its recruitment of Johnny Burke and John Scott Trotter, who became, respectively, his principal songwriter and musical director.

And, as it was Bing's project, he had the clout to repay an old debt. He wanted Louis Armstrong in the film. Cohen balked, seeing no reason to entail the expense of flying him in and having no desire to negotiate with Armstrong's crude, mob-linked but devoted manager, Joe Glaser. Bing refused to discuss the matter. The Reverend Satchelmouth was about to make his Hollywood debut. What's more, though his part was small (one musical number, two comic exchanges), Louis would be top-billed as part of a quartet of stars.[52] No black performer had ever been billed as a lead in a white picture. The combination of Louis's delightful performance and billing that presumed his magnitude as an artist greatly enhanced his career. Louis had previously appeared in two shorts and a (long-lost) independent feature; after *Pennies from Heaven* he became a Hollywood regular, instantly signed by Paramount for Martha Raye and Mae West vehicles and subsequently asked to provide cameos in pictures made for Warners, MGM, Columbia, Goldwyn, and others.

Sadly, Bing and Louis do not get to perform a vocal duet, though it would have been easy to schedule one in the nightclub scene that features Armstrong's band. Evidently, this was a bow to the color line, which was harder to breach in movies than on radio or records. The two do share a vaudeville sketch, however, in which Louis shows off his distinct yet never fully exercised acting skills for the first time. Their camaraderie is unmistakable. Bing, as usual, is the straight man and Louis the clown — a chicken-stealing, mathematically challenged yard worker who is also, conveniently, a genius entertainer. *Variety* found Armstrong the picture's strongest asset, not only "as an eccentric musician but as a Negro comedian."[53] Armstrong himself enthusiastically recounted his role thirty years later:

> Those scenes I had with Bing in that picture were Classics. Especially the scene where he wanted to open this Big Time Haunted House Night Club. But he didn't have enough loot to open this joint. And he liked our little seven piece band. So . . . He said Henry (that was my name in the film), I would like to hire your band and I will give you and your boys 'TEN' percent of the business, so you go and talk it over with your Musicians. Come back tomorrow and let me know as to what conclusion your boys came to. The next day I was right on time. And — Mr Poole (Bing's name) met me halfway in the back yard, saying Henry, have your boys decided yet? And I said, Mr Poole, I talked it over with my boys and told them you are willing to give them ten percent of the business. And my boys said that they cannot figure out ten percent as we're only seven men. So if you will be so kind as to give us seven percent, We'll — Just then Mr Poole said, OK Henry, it's a deal. And I smiled as I walked away saying Mr Poole, *thank* you *very* much. — I told those guys that you would do the right thing. — 'GAS-SUH' personified.
>
> Oh, I could run my mouth about my Man Crosby — those Broadcasts moments, and Stuff — why you'd be reading for years. But I must say this. Here's paying tribute to one of the finest Guys in this musical and wonderful world. With a heart as big. (As the world) Carry on Papa Bing, Ol Boy!! You will *still* be giving young singers food for thoughts (Musically) for Generations to come.[54]

Bing's other costars were less enchanting: Madge Evans, an attractive but wooden former child star who left Hollywood two years later, and Edith Fellows, a talented scampy thirteen-year-old who soon suffered her own problems making the transition to grown-up roles. As Patsy, the beleaguered orphan whom Bing befriends, Fellows was the first of several screen children he aided over the years. In his movie roles Bing more often rescued lost children than bore his own. He seemed genuinely fond of Fellows. Nanette Fabray, a child performer herself and Fellows's roomate, recalled Bing's visiting her when she was in bed with the flu and later arranging a fancy dinner for both girls.

The cursory plot has Bing feuding with Madge Evans for eight reels and marrying her in the ninth. Yet the picture opens with a startling scene: Bing behind bars on a smuggling charge, absurdly awaiting his impending release in the same cell block as a killer on his way to the electric chair. In a strangely upbeat mood, the killer asks Bing to deliver a letter to the family of his victim (Patsy and her grandfather, played by Donald Meek), leaving them an old abandoned house in New Jersey.

Pennies from Heaven, despite its fantastical script, is one of the few Depression musicals to acknowledge the Depression, albeit without actually using the D-word. In the pre-Code years Busby Berkeley invoked hard times and suicidal bitterness in his Warners musicals, but by 1935 Fred and Ginger and Eleanor Powell and even Berkeley himself were setting their work in the rarefied chambers of penthouse ballrooms and battleships. *Pennies from Heaven,* probably the only Hollywood musical set in a part of New Jersey other than Atlantic City, presents a vision of contented socialism in which everyone is pleasant except people with jobs: the latter are carnival tricksters, social workers, municipal officials, and landlords. The only direct political shot is taken at the Townsend Plan, a shady pyramid-pension scheme conceived by a retired doctor in California, subscribed to by millions in the period before Social Security. Larry Poole's view of privation is the familiar refrain of live and let live, formulated as only a Crosby character can: "I'm the last of the troubadours," he says, "the friend of man. I envy nobody and I'm sure nobody envies me."

Bing is most effective in early scenes. He kept his weight down this time, and he looks seasoned and even slightly angular. While singing for coins, he encounters Patsy at a fair and performs "So Do I" in an effectively sentimental episode, the song reinforced by plush strings and woodwinds, his audience a montage of working-class neighbors, the treacle cut by close-ups of Bing. His line readings are sharp, and his composure and canny physical movements contribute to the impression that he has the makings of a deeper actor than previously suspected. The *KMH* spirit is asserted in an improvised group-sing ("Old MacDonald") and in his dialogue with Armstrong and others. He mines laughs from lines that do not necessarily contain them.

The film is pushed amiably forward by director Norman Z. McLeod, an underrated comedy specialist, who presided when the Marx Brothers, W. C. Fields, Danny Kaye, and Bob Hope did some of their finest movie work; he later directed Bing and Bob in *Road to Rio*. But *Pennies from Heaven* derives its staying power largely from a remarkable score. Composer Arthur Johnston had, with Sam Coslow, written one of Bing's breakthrough songs, "Just One More Chance," along with the scores for *College Humor* and *Too Much Harmony*. He now surpassed himself in the company of a lyricist ten years his junior, Johnny Burke, who, like Carmichael and Mercer, achieved his place in Hollywood through Bing.

"One of the best things that's happened to me is a one hundred and forty-five pound Irish leprechaun named Johnny Burke," Bing wrote.[55] Born in northern California in 1908 and educated at the University of Wisconsin, Burke was a small, round-faced, hammy wag who endeared himself to Bing instantly. He had been knocking around music publishing houses for years, writing songs, mostly novelties, with Harold Spina. "Annie Doesn't Live Here Anymore" was their one substantial hit, thanks to Fred Waring and Guy Lombardo, though Fats Waller and the Dorseys had fun with their "My Very Good Friend, the Milkman." Burke did anonymous work-for-hire at Fox but never managed to get a song into the movies, so Bing was taking a chance on him for his first independent production. He was to become one of Bing's closest friends, until his drinking put a wedge in their relationship. For seventeen years Burke, whom Bing called the Poet, was his personal songwriter, the man behind a string of evergreens introduced by Bing through movies or records or both, among them "This Is My Night to Dream," "I've Got a Pocketful of Dreams," "Moonlight Becomes You," "An Apple for the Teacher," "What's New?," "Swinging on a Star," "Sunday, Monday or Always," "But Beautiful," "Like Someone in Love," and "It Could Happen to You." In all, he wrote twenty-three film scores for Bing, more than 120 expressly tailored songs.

Johnny got off to a rousing start with *Pennies from Heaven*, especially the title song, for which he wrote a singular, much imitated and parodied verse:

> *A long time ago, a million years B.C.*
> *The best things in life were absolutely free.*

But no one appreciated a sky that was always blue;
And no one congratulated a sun that was always new.
So it was planned that they would vanish now and then
And you must pay before you get them back again;
That's what storms were made for
And you shouldn't be afraid for . . .

And into the famous chorus, a winning variation on the Depression tenet that life is as often as not a bowl of cherries. The song was so cogent, Bing and McLeod elected to shoot it live, with the orchestra on the soundstage, forgoing the economy-minded practice of pre-recording. The even-keel swing of Johnston's *abac* melody, with its recurring rhythmic motif of four quarter notes ("Ev-ry-time-it rains it rains pen-nies-from-heav en") and an expansive double-triplet measure toward the close, make it memorably accessible and helped ensure its acceptance.

The whole score was popular and widely covered: Count Basie swung "Pennies from Heaven," and Billie Holiday and Artie Shaw each recorded three selections. Of the score's five songs, four yielded Decca hits for Bing ("Pennies from Heaven," "Let's Call a Heart a Heart," "So Do I," and the charged "One, Two, Button Your Shoe," with a counting game setting off the stanzas) and one for Armstrong, the exhilarating "Skeleton in the Closet." That tune — performed by a masked studio group with drummer Lionel Hampton in the film but recorded with Jimmy Dorsey's band — was singled out by many critics as the film's pinnacle.

Bing's "Pennies from Heaven" dominated sales of records and sheet music for more than three months. His record established a "new high in gross sales all over the country," according to *Down Beat,* which credited Bing's continuing popularity to his ability to "sing a sweet ballad with the same finesse he displays in warbling a 'get-off' tune."[56] Kapp was so certain of the record's success that before releasing it, he recorded a second version, with Bing, Louis, and Frances Langford. The song was nominated for an Academy Award (it lost, reasonably enough, to the Jerome Kern and Dorothy Fields ballad "The Way You Look Tonight"). In England it was said to be the most recorded movie melody since the start of talking pictures.

*　　*　　*

Writing songs is one thing, orchestrating them another. Because *Pennies from Heaven* was independent, the production did not have access to the Paramount music department. Columbia was not known for musicals, and Arthur Johnston was not sufficiently trained to arrange his melodies for a score. Burke suggested to Bing that he farm out the assignment to his friend, John Scott Trotter.[57] Knowing of Trotter's long association with the Hal Kemp band and admiring his arrangements for the band's singer, Skinnay Ennis ("Got a Date with an Angel"), Bing readily agreed. Trotter had been with Kemp from the beginning, when they organized a student band at the University of North Carolina that declined to play stock arrangements and, as a result, developed an original style. Kemp led a sweet band that occasionally played hot jazz; Bunny Berigan was the main soloist, and Trotter the pianist and chief arranger. He had met Bing once in 1930, on a night when Kemp was rehearsing late, long after the ballrooms had closed. Bing and Hoagy Carmichael walked in, the latter so excited about a new song he had written that, with Bing cheering him on, he took a running dive and slid the length of the dance floor on his belly, holding aloft the new manuscript: "Star Dust."

After Trotter left Kemp in 1936, he visited the West Coast for the first time, as a tourist. He had taken an apartment for a few months when Burke arrived with his wife to work on the film. Like Burke, he was twenty-eight, and for a while all three lived together. When Burke told him about the picture, Trotter protested that he was on vacation and turned it down — until he saw the songs. He arranged all but the Armstrong number. On the day the recording of the score was completed, Trotter packed his car and headed for New York, where a job awaited him with ARC, supervising recordings by the Andrews Sisters, Duke Ellington, Raymond Scott, and others, including a few historic sessions by Billie Holiday and Teddy Wilson. (John Hammond, the initiator of the Holiday series, dismissed Trotter as an intrusive executive, but the presence of Bunny Berigan and *Pennies from Heaven* songs would seem to support Trotter's claim to having produced those sides.) In June 1937 he received a wire from Larry Crosby: CAN YOU BE HERE 21ST. DORSEY LEAVING. YOURE TO TAKE OVER MUSIC ON KRAFT SHOW.

The Swing Era was in full flower, and Jimmy Dorsey felt he was missing out. Tommy and many musicians he came up with were now leading popular bands, and their record sales not only were unprecedented for jazz but were stimulating the whole recording industry. And here was Jimmy, nationally prominent because of his role on *KMH* yet reigned in by it all the same. He was encouraged to leave by Kapp, for whom he had already scored one hit, and his agent, Cork O'Keefe. With Fud Livingston writing his arrangements ("Too hot for you, Uncle Fud?" Bing ad-libs on their tub-thumping version of "I'm an Old Cowhand") and an appealing Crosby-style baritone in Bob Eberle (who attended each *KMH* broadcast as a band member but never sang on the show), Jimmy was ready for the road. Carroll Carroll later implied that had Jimmy not quit, he would have been removed by Kraft in favor of a more versatile musical director. In any event, Jimmy left after the July 1 broadcast and prospered with the Swing Era.

Trotter could hardly have been more different. Of his July 8 debut, Cal Kuhl's only comment was that the featured instrumental was "not effective."[58] But that was the season's final show. By the time it returned in October, John Scott and Bing had become working chums. Writing for Hal Kemp, Trotter had developed a vibratoless staccato style that he characterized as a refined Schottische rhythm; Johnny Mercer, a fan, more colorfully described it as a "typewriter" attack, clipped and orderly.[59] Trotter had also become accustomed to doubling the melody for singers who needed all the help they could get, while Bing preferred an arranger who let the singer alone. He surprised Trotter by emphasizing that opera orchestrations do not double the singer's line and asked him to write "just that way."[60] Bing chose the songs he sang on the air, in contradistinction to those he waxed for Jack Kapp. After each show, Trotter recalled, "Bing would go into the booth and select his numbers for the following week."[61] He listed them on the left-hand page of a loose-leaf binder; a secretary typed them on the right-hand page. Trotter took the selections and went to work arranging them, his job for the next seventeen years.

He was a huge but nimble and amiable man, as obsessed with cooking and antiques as he was with music. Though immensely well liked, Trotter was something of a loner, traveling the country to sample fabled restaurants or to London to visit Georg Solti, his lifelong friend. His solitary, self-sufficient manner appealed to Bing.

John Scott, a popular weekend and dinner guest, maintained a friendship with the Crosbys long past the *KMH* and Decca years, encouraged by Bing's second wife, Kathryn. Trotter never married, never lived with a lover; if he was gay, no one knew for certain. Alan Fisher, the Crosby butler during his second marriage, said, "He was totally asexual. Wasn't interested in women, wasn't interested in men, wasn't a closet anything. He was very close to the first Mrs. Crosby and, if anything, closer to the second Mrs. Crosby, who adored him. He formally helped decorate their homes. Extremely good taste, beautifully mannered, witty and funny, the children loved him. John Scott Trotter coming to stay was always a joy. Bing Crosby loved him, I'd have to say that. And if he was going to confide in anyone, I'd almost say it would have been him. They always sat in the library to talk."[62]

"He was fun," Johnny Burke's daughter, Rory, remembered. "He was at our pool all the time, a very large man in his swimming trunks, a little flamboyant with a big face, lots of curly brown hair, burly, strong, light on his feet — I can still see him jumping off the diving board."[63] Stories of his devotion to food are legion. "When we had the private house he used to come often," Frieda Kapp recalled. "A lovely fellow. Big. Once he came to the house after one of our holidays and we had a lot of gefilte fish left. And Jack says, 'Give some of this gefilte fish to John.' I said, Are you crazy? John, a southern gentile, what's he going to do with it? He ate the entire platter."[64] Carroll Carroll told of a weekend morning when John called Carroll's wife to say he was making vichyssoise and wanted to bring them some. They arranged to have dinner that night, but John never showed. He apologized in the morning, explaining that the soup was so good that he ate it all himself, then went to sleep.

In selecting musicians for the band, a new experience for Trotter, he drew on Hollywood studio players and added a small string section (it grew over the years) to the conventional big-band instrumentation. To sustain the swing and spontaneity Bing demanded, he peppered the ensemble with jazz musicians, including two former Whiteman trumpeters, Andy Secrest, whose solos carried a hint of Beiderbecke's bright lyricism, and (when he could get him) Manny Klein, whose lustier attack was in demand all over town. Trotter also recruited trombonist Abe Lincoln, who became a Dixieland regular; drummer Spike Jones, who achieved much fame as a musical parodist; and, most important, guitarist Perry Botkin, who had worked as a New York session man with Victor Young, Red Nichols, and Crosby himself, on the later Brunswicks. Like Trotter, Perry was a large man and a Crosby loyalist; he occupied Eddie Lang's chair for the next two decades. He was also a studio politician, and Trotter appointed him contractor, in charge of hirings. As the band grew, with violas and cellos, Trotter took to farming out many if not most of the arrangements. Among the young writers he apprenticed were Nelson Riddle and Billy May.

"Really, I can think of so many times when he has rescued me from glaring gaffes and melodic clichés," Bing wrote of Trotter, "when his choice of material, his arrangements, his use of voices and instruments meant the success of an album or a record." He continued with the usual excessive modesty: "If I am able to distinguish the good from the bad, if I know anything about music at all, what little I know rubbed off Trotter onto me."[65] What surely rubbed off on him was John Scott's musical conservatism. For if he helped make *KMH* homier than ever, the cost was the accelerated weaning of Bing from jazz and his corresponding conversion to a more decorous and conventional style. Trotter was Bing's man, not Decca's, but as a versatile musician who preferred the middle of the road, he was a dream come true for Jack Kapp. Trotter conducted the majority of Bing's records, but Jack knew better than to allow him full reign.

As the impoverished thirties caromed into the murderous forties, the middle of the road — alongside Bing — was for many the only place to be. Crosby embodied stability, his life an apparently open book, his voice a healing balm. "The other man puts a nickel in the phonograph," John Steinbeck writes in *The Grapes of Wrath*, "watches the disk slip free and the turntable rise up under it. Bing Crosby's voice — golden."[66] Bing was everywhere. *KMH* filled out the world's mental picture of the man it knew from records, pictures, and fan magazines. If those close to him found him remote, ultimately unknowable, those at a distance thought they knew him about as well as you could know a man. Everyone thought he could sum up the public and private Bing, including a calypso legend named Roaring Lion. In 1938, when Portuguese businessmen paid his way from Trinidad to New York to popularize the music of the islands, the Lion played for President Roosevelt and appeared on Rudy Vallée's show. After Bing dropped by for one of his recording sessions, the Lion commemorated his idol with a song released by Decca in 1939. It was called, simply, "Bing Crosby."

> *Of all the world's famous singers*
> *That I have ever seen*
> *On the movie screen,*
> *Of all the world's famous singers*
> *That I have ever seen*
> *On the movie screen,*
> *Lawrence Tibbett and Nelson Eddy,*
> *Donald Novis and Morton Downey,*
> *Kenny Baker and Rudy Vallée,*
> *But the crooning prodigy is Bing Crosby.*
>
> *Bing has a way of singing*
> *With his very heart and soul,*
> *Which captivates the world.*
> *His millions of listeners never fail to rejoice*
> *At his golden voice.*
> *They love to hear his la-da-de-da [whistles]*
> *So sweetly and with such harmony*
> *Thrilling the world with his melody.*
>
> *Mention must be made of Bing's romantic life,*
> *Centered on his wife.*
> *As lovely as the soft sylphs of poetic dreams*
> *Her smile is like the moonbeams.*
> *A former star, we know she can sing.*
> *But now her voice she has reserved*
> *for her sons and Bing.*
> *So, so happy must be Bing Crosby*
> *That he married a beauty like Dixie Lee.*
>
> *I wonder if you heard him singing that song*
> *"May I (be the only one to say I)?"*
> *And yet I'm wondering if you heard again,*

"(Every time it rains, it rains) Pennies from Heaven"?
But "Love Thy Neighbor" was the most thrilling song,
And "Git Along, Little Dogies, Git Along."
So sweetly and with such harmony
Thrilling the world with his melody.

Bing has a most interesting personality
Beloved universally.
He has two private horses, Double Trouble and Ligaroti,
Pipe smoking is his hobby.
He has a queer eccentricity —
Takes off his hat very infrequently.
So one and all, let's unanimously
Shout three cheers for this golden voice prodigy.[67]

21

PUBLIC
RELATIONS

*Where most of the Hollywood stars look upon personal
publicity as the lifeblood of their business, stooping to
inane invention and trickery to get it, Bing thumbs his
nose at it. . . . [He] is unco-operative because he just
doesn't give a damn.*
— H. Allen Smith, *Life in a Putty Knife Factory* (1943)[1]

Bing's role as the Technological Man reflected his introduction to the
world of music and entertainment; much as Louis Armstrong's career
reflected his reverse initiation in New Orleans's honky-tonks. For
Bing, the passkey had been the Edison gramophone his father
brought home when he was three. It introduced him to a procession
of performers — concurrently and without prejudice — that included
Irish tenors, Jewish vaudevillians, Sousa marching bands, barbershop
quartets, jazz bands, and dance bands. Canned music was unknown
to the young Louis, who encountered no less varied a musical banquet — from blues, rags, and minstrelsy to opera, quadrilles, and
marches — in the flesh, at picnics and funerals and on the street.
When Louis was able to purchase his first wind-up phonograph, as a
teenager, his favorites included Caruso and John McCormack, whom
he valued for his "beautiful phrasing."[2]

As Bing's interest in music matured, he continued to find inspiration in the recordings he and Al Rinker memorized and copied. The

Musicaladers were, in effect, a garage band — school kids emulating the popular music of the day. But Louis served a true apprenticeship with the very giants he venerated, learning their music and customs firsthand, working alongside experienced men who encouraged his every step. Louis established records as the definitive texts for a new art (his glorious bands, the Hot Five and Hot Seven, existed only to record), yet music remained for him a social experience that required an audience to complete the circle. Bing established all-time statistics with his extended stay at the Paramount Theater, yet music remained for him a skill best realized through mechanical reproduction. After the war, when he made several appearances on Bing's radio show, Louis played to the audience while Bing played to Louis.

Cocooning himself in technology at the same time he gamboled at sporting events and other public occasions, Bing was magically everywhere and nowhere, a perfect candidate for the ministrations of publicists charged with the assignment of riffing at length on what everybody already knew. The Bing that Paramount's publicity office spoon-fed the media was, overall, close enough to the truth to give all involved a clean conscience. The releases were written in a simple, mirthful, self-satisfied style that reinvented this most willfully independent of men as a blend of Tom Sawyer, Ragged Dick, Abe Lincoln, and Will Rogers — untouchably appealing, not unlike the folkloric hero of Roaring Lion's calypso.[3]

It has been written that the old studio demagogues spied on their screenwriters, listening for the sound of typing to make certain no one was dawdling. If they didn't bother checking the cubicles where their public-relations men worked, it was because a cluster of busier writers never lived. Day after day, studio publicists hammered out reams of copy about the company's principal assets, its stars, much of it laughably untrue. Who had time to check facts? And what star wanted to be pestered by facts? Actors with made-up names and made-up biographies were content to let the studio's press office reinvent them as it pleased.

The fictionalizing was often essential. The faintest whiff of moral turpitude could be ruinous, grounds to break a contract, although exceptions were made for stars who shone brightly at the box office. In the event of a problem too big for the publicists to hide, a patsy might have to take a fall. Hirelings could always be found to accept the blame for reckless accidents or acquiesce to sham marriages. Most stars, however, required no cover beyond the blizzard of press releases that found their way, virtually unchanged, into newspapers and magazines.

The power and arrogance of publicists was no secret. Hollywood lampooned them mercilessly, invariably portraying them as unscrupulous, ruthless, alcoholic, and utterly indifferent to the desires of the lost souls consigned to their unctuous hands. Onscreen, Lee Tracy (once cited by Bing as a favorite film actor) incarnated the role in *Bombshell*; Lionel Stander made it nastier in *A Star Is Born*. In Bing's *She Loves Me Not* the press flack is sleazier than the murderers. But the contempt of their associates by no means diminished the press agents' hold on the public's credulity. They were abetted by entertainment editors who cheerfully accommodated them, sometimes appending a reporter's byline to a standard press release. Since Bing's providential life made for a most seductive serial, Paramount flacks were obliged constantly to rehash it — spinning their own variations. Bing was of little help to them. He shunned invasions of his personal life.

He faced a Jesuitical conundrum: how to remain one of the sheep when everyone persists in treating you like the shepherd; how to keep that unruly mistress fame in her place. Success was a beautiful stranger who compromises a perfect evening by demanding unqualified love. Bing recognized that fans who loved him and expected the same in return were best handled from a distance. Yet even as he resisted public appearances, he assiduously responded to admirers, one at a time. As early as Cremo he made a point of answering his mail, dictating brief and businesslike responses. Several of his fan correspondences went on for years, leading to encounters and friendships. He was godfather to the child of at least one longtime letter writer.[4]

He blew hot and cold in the same way with colleagues. "Out here, all people want to do is to party and socialize," he told Cork O'Keefe in the late 1930s. "It got so I'd meet someone on the set for the first time, and next thing they'd be standing on my doorstep with a bunch of friends, expecting to be invited in and entertained. So my home's off-limits to everyone."[5] Yet his loyalties were absolute. "If you were his friend, he was a friend till the end," insisted Gary Stevens. "Look at all the song publishers he practically supported, like Rocco Vocco."[6] Vocco had befriended Bing in the Whiteman era, on occasion putting him to bed after a night's carousing; he could always call on Bing and ask him to debut a song on *KMH*. Bing was accessible; he answered his own phone. What he did not do very often was entertain guests — especially after 1939.

It was different in the mid-thirties, when Dixie occasionally instigated parties, though she, too, had second thoughts. After the night Joe Venuti came to dinner, she encouraged Bing to entertain his more colorful friends away from home. She had just purchased dining-room chairs with wood-framed wicker backs. Several drinks into the evening, Joe bet Bing he could butt his head through the wicker. Bing anted up, double or nothing, until Joe destroyed every chair, convulsing Bing and enraging Dixie, who banished them to the veranda till morning.

A more serious reason for keeping the world at bay was the fear of kidnappers, magnified by the police, who first warned the Crosbys of a plot before Gary was a year old. Three days after he had been cautioned, Bing obtained a permit to carry a gun, as did Ev; they were sworn in as deputy sheriffs. The publicity turned sour two years later when Bing was stopped for speeding, and the traffic cop noticed his revolver. Bing had forgotten the permit and had to explain himself at the Hollywood police station before he was allowed to continue on to Paramount. He began to realize that some threats were nothing more than unfounded rumors generated by publicity-seekers among the police or at the FBI. Yet if his sons were never endangered, they were nonetheless victimized. Obsessed with their safety, Bing hired bodyguards and imposed strict curfews. His attempt to raise them as regular kids was undermined by his constraining protectiveness.

Every few months, before a new Crosby film premiered, the newspapers and fan magazines published interviews, stories, even articles by Bing himself. Almost all were drawn from publicity releases. The result was fairly astonishing: the illusion that Bing was ubiquitous and approachable, when in fact he was harder to pin down for an interview than perhaps any other star of his stature. He was so pervasive on records and radio that his fans seemed not to notice his long absence from the stage. Bing liked to explain his aversion to live performance by insisting he was not a great entertainer, like Jolson or Fields. All his life, no matter how high his star rose, a part of him remained a fan with his nose pressed against the glass of the very business he ruled. The surest way to get his cold shoulder was to approach him with starry eyes.

The publicity assault had begun early. *College Humor* had just opened and *Too Much Harmony* was before the cameras when the studio issued its five-page opus, "The Life Story of Bing Crosby Written by Himself."[7] The best that can be said of the effort is that it reverses the venerable literary tradition in which fictional characters — from Robinson Crusoe to Huckleberry Finn — are made to seem real; here, without any morsal of literary distinction, a real person is made to seem fictional. "I love to sing," it commences, "and I can thank my lucky stars that other people like to hear me!" It gets worse, hitting notes that resonated for many years: "I'm one of those old-time bathroom baritones (since dignified by the title 'Crooner') and, in or out of the bathtub, Brother, I sing!"

Bing's days as a scalawag were recent enough to require acknowledgment: "I don't think a crazier guy ever lived than the Bing Crosby who sang at the Cocoanut Grove. Irresponsible? Say, I was so busy having a good time that I didn't know what responsibility was." Nor could the growth on his vocal cords be ignored, although he claims not to understand ("Honestly!") the "husky quaver" it yields. He calls Russ Columbo "a grand entertainer" and says they used to imitate each other (that one must have nettled Bing when he read it). In the "gay dog" days, he says, he broke contracts "without realizing what I was doing and without meaning to harm anyone intentionally."[8] Excerpted or whole, this stuff was widely published.

The mock Bing concedes he can't tell some things, so he asks Dixie Lee — "the wife, who has been putting up with me for a long time" — to continue. She also sighs a few enduring ditties, adding to a portrait of likable incorrigibility. His clothes: he "always looks as though he's been pulled out of the scrap bag." His innocence: "Bing is the most naive person in the world except Dick Arlen." His shyness: "When he was courting me, he was tongue-tied most of the time — like an awestruck little boy." His modesty: "He claims to be the laziest man in the world — and yet he works his head off." His willfulness: "We were having a party one night. At ten, Bing got up from his chair, said, 'Good night, have a good time.' With an admonition to me to carry on, he went to bed." His genuineness: "Today he's quite the same sort of person that he appears in the films — perhaps that's why he's so popular!"[9]

Rarely did Bing take the trouble to correct errors Paramount promulgated, as he did with the 1934 press release that insisted his son was "not named after Gary Cooper. Bing and Dixie just liked the name" or the canard that found him "shouting 'bing' louder than any kid in the neighborhood while playing cowboy in Washington."[10] It was usually too late. If one cycle of newspapers circulated a tale, the next repeated it. NBC distributed a biographical three-pager in the summer of 1939, in which nearly every line conveys misinformation.[11] Paramount releases made the malarkey more credible with touches of veracity — the weird clothing, whistling, fishing, self-deprecation, golf, pipe smoking. Some handouts were deemed so effective that the studio recycled them. The one that began "I love to sing" was updated with the title, "Some Sad Words Set to Gay Music," adding a paragraph about his recent pictures while omitting the passages about Russ Columbo, the husky quaver, and Dixie's observations. It ends: "I seem to be headed for success and I'm glad that it has come to me at this time, when I am no longer a gay dog, but a business man with a frog in his throat."[12]

By 1935 Crosby press releases had grown more subtle, less exclamatory. The gurus most responsible for the fabricated Bing were publicity men Ralph Huston and Dave Keene, who worked under Huston and often adopted Bing's byline. "Say It with Music: Bing Crosby's Life Story as Told to Dave Keene"[13] was initially written in the third person ("If Bing Crosby hadn't once tried to earn himself a few dollars by working as a lumberman . . ."),[14] then adapted as a memoir ("If I hadn't once tried to earn a few bucks for myself by being a lumberman . . ."). In yet another draft Keene took a completely new tack, beginning, "The most important thing in any man's life is a woman. I've been favored above most men. . . ."[15] It continues with hymns in praise of Bing's mother, Mildred Bailey, Dixie, and Broadway comedienne Elsie Janis, who, the release claims, was the most important woman in Bing's life after mother and wife because she prodded him to leave the Rhythm Boys — although "Barris was really the outstanding singer of the bunch. Al and I just made up the harmony."[16] (Bing may have known Janis, but he never publicly spoke of her.)[17] Keene's chronicle, a dozen pages parsed into five chapters, even revamped Bing's ancestors, making them Indian fighters as well as sea captains. Bing's dad was handsomely promoted: "Old Harry had a pickle factory."

By 1936 most of the elements in the Crosby legend were locked into place and references to his life as a gay dog disappeared. It is impossible not to love the character stitched together in Paramount's press office — generous, naive, humorous, happy, modest, unpretentious, pleasingly eccentric, devoted to family, bemused by good fortune. "Screen success hasn't altered his care-free good nature, his carelessness, nor his innate laziness," Ralph Huston enthused. "The only thing Bing resents is invasion of the privacy of his home. In public, he is perfectly willing to be a public figure. At home, like Garbo, he 'wants to be alone.'"[18]

By 1938 the releases were filled with tales of golf and the track and of his investments. For a few years he took a strong interest in prizefighting, buying the contract of heavyweight Georgie Turner and, more successfully, a half interest in Tacoma's Freddie Steele, who fought his way to middleweight champion. Turning his attention to another kind of boxer, he paid $1,500 for Gunda of Barmere (Bing renamed her Venus), whose stock inspired him to dabble in a commercial breeding kennel and enter his dogs in shows. His other investments included real estate and oil wells; an all-girl baseball team, the Croonerettes; Canadian gold mines; a majority share of Select Music Publishing Co.; and an actor's agency with a chancy roster: actresses Mary Carlisle and Genevieve Tobin, soprano Josephine Tuminia, songwriters John Burke and Arthur Johnston, and Dixie. His diverse interests were managed by Bing Crosby, Inc., the "very legal and secure" (as a finicky Paramount flack put it)[19] familyrun business created as an umbrella for his ever growing assets. Bing was president, Everett and Larry chief officers, and old Harry the bookkeeper of record.

Much was made of Bing's refusal to accept star billing, his insistence on crediting his success to luck and "swell friends"[20] ("as for acting, Bing doesn't know the meaning of the word"),[21] his imperturbable "naturalness and nonchalance."[22] He was often coupled with Eddie Cantor as one of Hollywood's proudest fathers. Not all

Paramount flacks read each other's copy, though; as late as 1938 a newcomer wrote, "There's no romance how he happened to become 'Bing.' He just shouted 'Bing! Bing!' louder and oftener than the other kids who played cops and robbers."[23]

One bulletin saluted talented women — namely, Dixie and the wives of Gary Cooper, Bill Boyd, Errol Flynn, among others — who gave up promising careers to marry Hollywood's leading men and "retire to plain, old fashioned housewifery."[24] In another Bing was described, incredibly, as a prophet without honor in his own country, because while he "serenely goes his placid way," few realize he "ranks high among the top 10 stars of Hollywood."[25] The most preposterous of them, however, cried poverty on behalf of stars who had to survive on strict allowances to protect them from cadgers and unsavory businessmen. It said Bing was obliged — along with Gary Cooper, Carole Lombard, Bette Davis, Fred MacMurray, and other magnanimous but impractical souls — to make do with a stipend, in his case administered through his company. "It may sound ridiculous that any person making as high as $5,000 a week actually has only $25 a week for pocket money. But as a matter of fact, some of the stars are allowed even less than that."[26] Actually, he was earning $10,000 a week, and as we will see, his "stipend" was $3,000.

Not infrequently, Paramount flacks celebrated the hand that fed them, in Bing's alleged voice: "Next to love, horse racing, golf, fishing, political speeches, and maybe a couple of other things, the greatest form of entertainment in the world is, to my mind, the motion picture" begins one redundant two-pager.[27] His name was regularly appropriated to tell amusing tales about the filming of his most recent pictures. A story put out in advance of *The Star Maker* was repeated months later in a release for *Road to Singapore*, with only the title and director altered; anecdotes were unchanged for both films. In a 1939 release Bing claims he will consider himself a success when he achieves "all the things I've always wanted to do."[28] His list begins with his desire to own a yacht ("Who doesn't, say you!") and fish for tarpon in Florida, which may have seemed eerily familiar to anyone who recalled the hero of *Here Is My Heart*.

But then, the idea was to blur the real Bing and the screen Bing. You need a scorecard to distinguish between facts, near facts, and fibs in many of the passages attributed to him, though the ghostwriter's motives are usually easy to catch. In 1934, for example, the obliging "Bing" writes:

> I don't smoke much, and I prefer a pipe [true]. Not that smoking might injure my voice [no need to rile potential sponsors], but I just don't care about it [not true]. I never rehearse a song, whether it's for a radio, picture or record, more than once [partly true; he rehearsed at home], and I always try to learn it by listening to somebody else sing the lyrics [true]. I always wear a hat or cap while broadcasting [true], for no reason except that it's comfortable [not true]. I'm not superstitious about anything [apparently true; religion, obviously, does not count]. I don't bother with a diet of any kind, except when the doctor orders me to [not true].[29]

And so on. A couple of months after that release, Bing signed an article about himself called "Me!" for *Picture-Play,* which published a specimen of his handwriting to prove his authorship.[30] Included with the usual attributes that show him to be quite human (goes to bed early, even at his own parties; is stubborn and unable to forget slights; can be thoughtless in putting golf ahead of everything else; credits his success to mother's prayers and blind luck) is the claim that he quit the Cocoanut Grove because management refused to give him his own orchestra! As to the diets he never bothered with: "I am forever bordering on the abyss of obesity. I have attempted many diets to overcome this dangerous inclination, but nothing helps."[31] He playfully takes issue with statements in a previous article by Dixie that was likely written by the same employee who wrote "Me!"

Still, in the realm of public relations, the Paramount pros might have learned a few things from Larry Crosby, who handled that mission for Bing Crosby, Inc. Basil Grillo, who straightened out Bing's business affairs after the war, once remarked of Larry that his job "consisted mostly of trying to keep Bing's name out of the paper. I say that facetiously, because with anybody in the public eye, from time to time somebody'll take a crack at him."[32] Larry did his share of spin doctoring. For example, there was the night of November 28, 1936, when Bing and his racing friend Lin Howard visited the College Inn in San Diego, after a day spent hunting quail. In the small hours Bing got into a fracas with a group of sailors. The big question: were Bing and the mariners allies or antagonists? Initially, Bing explained that a civilian insulted him and he invited him to step outside, where a fight took place involving sailors who "were on our side."[33] Larry was called in after a witness described the incident less patriotically: the sailors recognized Bing as he left the bar and heckled him until he offered to take them on one at a time, but police intervened after a couple of blows. "There wasn't much to it," Larry said, "a poke or two — but it was all settled to everybody's satisfaction. Let's forget it."[34] It was forgotten.

A few days later, in December, Bing instigated a suit that would not be forgotten for some time. He took action against Ben McGlashan, the owner and operator of station KOPJ in Los Angeles, for having played his records on two daily programs over the past ten months, presenting them in such a way as to suggest that Bing was in the studio. As filed by his attorney, John O'Melveny, Bing argued that he was known for "personal, original, and individual interpretations"[35] distinct from those of other performers; that the records were clearly labeled "Not Licensed for Radio Broadcast";[36] and that the defendant unfairly competed with his ability to earn royalties — estimated at two and a half to four and a half cents per record — and advertising revenue.

Ruling in Bing's favor, Judge Ruben S. Schmidt enjoined McGlashan from broadcasting the Crosby voice or otherwise profiting from it without written permission from Crosby.[37] He was probably irked by McGlashan's arrogant defense, which denied Bing's distinctiveness (then why play his records?), claimed every show ended with the announcement that the audience had been listening to phonograph records, and avowed that not-licensed stickers were without meaning — that once consumers bought a record, they could do with it as they pleased.[38] The judge's decision was no surprise. Fred Waring had won a parallel judgment a year before in Philadelphia. In 1939 both decisions were affirmed in federal court by Judge Vincent L. Leibell, in the case of *Paul Whiteman* v. *WNEW*.

A bargain would have to be struck, allowing radio access to records, and artists access to the profits. Beyond the lawsuits, the issue was forced by a congenial spieler named Martin Block, whose *Make-Believe Ballroom* in New York broadcast records he bought at the nearby Liberty Music Shop. In his chronicle of the music industry, David Sanjek writes that Block "made the profession of disc jockey a respectable one."[39] One of his early beneficiaries was Decca Records, which earned attention from Block at a time when merchants were intimidated by the established labels out to torpedo Jack Kapp. A few weeks before Judge Leibell's foregone ruling, Victor, Decca, and Columbia began offering broadcasters records for monthly licensing fees. Radio stations howled, to little avail. At long last the recording industry had its pound of flesh from the medium that a decade earlier almost destroyed it. Many stations continued to resist the record labels by signing contracts with transcription services, which produced discs by major performers exclusively for broadcast. But they soon capitulated. Bing's role in the battle prefigured his momentous struggle in 1946, when he took a different stand and single-handedly toppled network radio's policy of live entertainment in favor of prerecorded programs.

In terms of publicity, this was a neutral issue, as were most of the controversies surrounding Bing.[40] The press generally gave him a free ride for twenty years. The Treasury did not. Bing was assessed $128,524 in back taxes from 1933 and 1934. No sooner did he request that the Board of Tax Appeals redetermine the debt than the Treasury launched a publicity campaign of its own, pursuing such Hollywood notables as Chaplin, De Mille, Laughton, Dietrich, and the Will Rogers estate. Bing was charged with nonpayment of $159,810. Two years later he was dunned for another $178,000 for the same years. Most of his fans could not have cared less about governmental claims of overdue taxes, but many were dismayed when Bing and other players crossed a picket line in the studio strike of 1937, fueling later rumors of his rank-and-file conservatism. He had much to conserve. His 1936 income was gauged at $508,000: $375,000 for three pictures, $108,000 for thirty-nine *KMH* shows, $30,000 for a dozen recording sessions plus royalties.[41]

Yet that year and for several to come, Bing faced genuine financial jeopardy, a fact known only to his accountant, Todd W. Johnson; his attorney, John O'Melveny; and himself. Johnson attempted to explain the situation to Bing in a four-page letter in March 1937.[42] Working with the figure of $500,000 as Bing's probable 1937 income, he began by subtracting $100,000 for business expenses, including

Everett's 10 percent. Bing and Dixie's federal and state tax bills, on the remaining $400,000, would come to $236,900. Their taxes would be larger than in preceding years, he explained, because Bing's past salaries, excepting $3,000 a week, had been paid to Bing Crosby, Inc., not to Bing as an individual, which was now the case. The tax bite left Bing with $163,100.

After subtracting $13,100 for disallowed expenses, Johnson told Bing he would have $150,000, or $12,500 per month, for "personal use or investment." Yet in the preceding two months, Bing and Dixie had spent that much ($25,000) as follows: $9,575.03 to Dixie for household and other uses, $13,431.95 lost by Bing at the racetrack, and $1,868.98 for Bing's miscellaneous personal expenses. In addition, "large sums were spent for care of racehorses, wardrobe, entertainment, etc.," which the government would not allow. Even if Bing spent only his expected income, the accountant warned, he would be unable to repay an $85,000 bank note he had taken for investments, a racehorse, and other "capital expenditures." The bottom line, he emphasized, was that for every dollar Bing earned, only thirty cents was available for his discretionary use.

Johnson worried that he might be "taking a chance of incurring [Bing's] ill-will" in commenting on his "personal expenditures" but maintained that as his friend, he wanted to make sure "that your untiring efforts and long days and hours of work will result in your accumulating a considerable fortune, instead of having nothing left when your career is ended." Then he gave up the niceties and typed in panicky capital letters:

ALL OF YOUR PERSONAL EXPENDITURES COME OUT OF YOUR PART OF YOUR EARNINGS AND DO NOT COME OUT OF THE GOVERNMENT'S PART.

Such storm warnings would have seemed simply unbelievable to the public. Bing's fortune was part of his élan. In the mid-1940s, when his income from records was higher than that from films, his income as an entertainer would approach and finally settle in the area of seven figures — figures that did not take into account his diverse business interests. But even then the combination of confiscatory taxes and large expenditures gave his accountant palpitations.

Given those amounts and the frequent stories in which Bing was listed among the ten highest paid Americans (he was ranked eighth in 1936, in a list topped by William Randolph Hearst and including only two other entertainers, Mae West and Marlene Dietrich),[43] Larry's task was not merely to keep his name out of the papers but to underscore his most attractive qualities, not least his indifference to protocol. The public was so enamored of Bing's eccentricities that what might have been bad publicity for others redounded in his favor, as in 1937, when he attended the British film colony's Armistice Day celebration in an ordinary suit while the other men wore white tie and tails. When a few months later, in February 1938, he barred photographers from *KMH* broadcasts because they broke his concentration, the "bulb pressers," as he called them, knew they were licked and relented.

He even benefited from one of the era's strangest scandals. Four years earlier, in 1933, John Montague had arrived in Hollywood and quickly earned a reputation as an exceptional but mysterious golfer. With his 220-pound impeccably attired frame and a fedora or cap shading his ingratiating smile, he evidently charmed all he met and became the valued crony of several Hollywood notables, most prominently Bing. Actors appreciated his demand for privacy and his secrecy regarding the source of his wealth (his long disappearances into the desert led some to speculate gold mines). Mysterious Montague, as the press called him, refused to play in tournaments and shunned photographers; he broke the cameras of several who attempted to take his picture. His abilities were hyperbolized after he challenged Bing to a match using only a rake, shovel, and baseball bat, and won. Westbrook Pegler called him a modern Paul Bunyan, and Grantland Rice reported the rumor that he whacked a bird off a telegraph wire with a 170-yard drive. Former U.S. Amateur champion George Von Elm called him "the greatest golfer in the world."[44] *Time* glowingly profiled him twice, attesting to his sheer brawn with tales of his lifting Oliver Hardy, briefly Montague's roommate, with one hand, and ending an altercation at the Lakeside Club by "standing husky Cinemactor George Bancroft on his head in his locker and closing the door."[45]

The novelty match with Bing was his undoing. The publicity could not be contained. A photographer stalked them on the links and shot Montague with a telephoto lens, selling the pictures to newspapers and *Life*. An ex-con in upstate New York saw them and notified the police, who for seven years had been searching for the con's former partner. Montague was arrested in Beverly Hills in July and gave Bing as his reference. After fighting extradition for a month, he was returned to the Adirondacks, jailed for two days without bail, and denounced by the Essex County district attorney as a "vicious criminal."[46] His story, as it unraveled that summer, was too far-fetched for a movie.

In 1930 a man named La Verne Moore — known in his hometown of Syracuse as a prodigious athlete, pool-hall hustler, ladies' man, and well-mannered thug — and three others broke into a roadhouse, beat the owner's elderly father-in-law senseless, stole $750, and drove off in two cars, one of which overturned, killing the driver. Two of the thieves were arrested and served two years in jail, leaving the fourth, who vanished until he turned up in movieland, celebrated for his "phenomenal drives and deadly chip shots."[47] Montague denied the accusation, but Mr. and Mrs. Moore — and his fingerprints — confirmed that he was their son, La Verne. The witness against him was the putative accomplice who saw his picture in the papers. Testifying to his character were affidavits from Bing, Oliver Hardy, Guy Kibbee, Otto Kruger, and George Von Elm, among others. The only witness called to testify on his behalf in court was Montague's ailing mother, who insisted her boy was home in bed the night of the robbery. Immediately after his acquittal, Montague and the prosecutor who had called him a "vicious criminal" made a date to play golf. The press was amused.

When it was over, the only person to get a lift out of the episode was Bing. Cal Tinney of the *New York Post* declared him Man of the Week, because, as the headline read, he WENT TO BAT FOR GOLFER MONTAGUE AND SAVED HIM FROM JAIL.[48] The jury was probably more persuaded by the uncanny memory of Montague's mother, but Bing's affidavit received more attention. In the five years they had been friends, he wrote, he had "never known him to behave other than as a gentleman. . . . The circle that he moved in accepted him as an upright man."[49] Bing's loyalty was greatly admired: he offered, in vain, any amount of bond to get him out of jail in Los Angeles and posted

$25,000 to free him from jail in Essex County while he awaited trial. Everett signed him to a contract with Bing Crosby, Inc., which Montague boasted would earn him a million bucks.

That was too much for Larry. "Million dollars!" he yelped. "He's going to make a couple of shorts showing how he plays golf, but they won't bring in more than twenty thousand." Some magazine pieces were in the works, Larry said, and maybe a guest spot on *KMH* — "he'll probably get a thousand or so for that."[50] Now Kraft-Phenix was riled and declared flatly that he would never appear. Bing was, as usual, blithe if mischievous: "I don't know what Monty's plans are, but he ought to make a lot of money. I suppose he'll go into pictures. . . . I imagine he'll play roles such as George Bancroft plays."[51] At which point the story came to a full stop. Montague never worked in films, never capitalized on his immense fame in golf, never made any kind of news at all. Absent from the extended golfing section in *Call Me Lucky,* he had by the time of its publication seemingly vanished from the earth and all its memories.[52]

During the very months Montague was the tabloids' darling, Larry had his hands full with two remarkable publicity ventures. The second of them, a homecoming event, was a flawless coup that secured forever Bing's standing as Spokane's hometown boy. The first, however, was a fiasco. At the heart of the matter was the longest press release ever written about a film star: a 207-page biography, *Bing,* published in the spring of 1937, written by Ted and Larry Crosby, with an unattributed assist from Bing.

Poor Ted: life had not emulated the moral logic of his undergraduate stories. He married Hazel Nieman at twenty-four, and they had three daughters, including twins; it may or may not speak to the piety of his home that one of the latter entered the Holy Names order at eighteen, as Sister M. Catherine Joan.[53] Ted was a likable, hardworking family man, the only sibling to remain in Spokane, where he continued to harbor his long-standing ambition to write. He put his abilities to use as publicist for Washington Water Power but longed for a place in show business; to that end, he wrote songs and stories and kept on the lookout for talent he could promote. All his efforts in those areas came to nothing, while his brother seemed to fall upward from peak to peak, a charmed soul, living the life Ted had fantasized about in his college tales.

The book project began surprisingly early in Bing's career, in late 1934 or early 1935. For Ted it held the promise of additional income and the chance to publish — to mine the one commercial subject available to him. For a while he worked on the book alone, without input from Bing's office, though he kept Larry and Bing informed of his progress. At the same time, he was trying to interest Bing in various business ventures, soliciting him for seed money. Bing demurred, on one occasion telling him he could not afford the risk, as he was between contracts and had no guarantee of his standing in the coming year. Then a proposal fell into Bing's lap that he extended to Ted. *Collier's* had approached Grover Jones, a contributor to the magazine and one of the most resourceful of Paramount's screenwriters (*The Virginian, Trouble in Paradise, The Lives of a Bengal Lancer, The Milky Way*), about writing a three-part life of Bing.[54] Paramount, perhaps influenced by the labors of its publicity staff, was thinking along similar lines. In a letter that speaks to Hollywood's — and his — cavalier approach to biographical accuracy, Bing wrote Ted:

> Inasmuch as the studio has expressed a desire to make a picture covering my career, I see how we can mutually profit in the following manner. Before the articles in *Collier's* are released, Jones proposes to get a title okayed by the company. After the story appears there is no reason why it can't be sold to Paramount for $15,000 or even $20,000, as a starring vehicle for me, and I can urge its purchase. . . . I figure if [Grover] could take this material you are writing and revise and rewrite to suit his purposes, release it to *Collier's*, withholding, of course, picture and book rights, we would be in a much better position to collect on the latter two. Of course, any money coming to me I would assign to you. But for the business angle of the whole thing, I should appear. This deal with *Collier's* is already set, so your chance is on picture and book rights, where I have every reasonable belief you would be successful.
>
> I have no clear recollection of the interesting events prior to my going into show business and naturally rely on your material to supply these. What has happened in the meantime he and I can concoct. He plans the whole thing in story form, not an article, and in real down-to-earth fashion, not the stilted biographical things that have appeared in the various film and radio magazines.
>
> I would like to try and arrange the thing so some of the professional credit redounds to you, in addition to the financial gain for yourself if everything works out as planned.

What he is interested in chiefly are the minor incidents that happened around Spokane, and in school, that are real and interesting. These to be fictionized and colored a bit, and woven into a good tight story that avoids the cut and dried and makes good reading. The only parts of the yarn that need to be factual are the high points, such as marriage, the children, places of employment etc.[55]

The film and the article fell through — *Collier's* instead published "The Kid from Spokane" by Quentin Reynolds[56] — but the book took on a life of its own, as Ted composed first drafts and mailed them to Larry, who submitted them to Bing and returned the revised pages to Ted.[57] "I am mailing you 7 chapters of the book as we have finally completed them," Larry wrote Ted in April 1935, the month the Quentin Reynolds story ran.[58] "Bing has just finished one more — so I am having to keep after him to get them out."[59] Bing had recently wrapped *Misissipp* and, Larry confided, "he is tired of everything but horses & golf."[60] Yet somehow he found the energy to add the book to his regimen of obligations.

While the book progressed, Ted continued to pitch various enterprises, involving mining, medicine, and other projects for which he requested capital. Larry wrote him that Bing would be unable to underwrite them, as "his surplus money" was invested in *Pennies from Heaven*.[61] When Ted asked Bing to do a broadcast endorsing one venture, Larry explained that even if Bing donated his time, the cost of the orchestra and the station made it impractical. Ted put most of his energy into songwriting and a singer named Marion Boyle. He mailed a slew of songs to Larry, along with a stream of advice: "The enclosed 'Don't Look Behind You' is, I think, a natural, for a picture. . . . Of the *Pennies from Heaven* numbers I liked, 'So Do I' and 'Have a Heart' . . . Saw *Sailor Beware* the other night — very punk. Good thing Bing didn't get stuck to do that. . . . If a Mrs. Brosius calls to see you about some tunes she has, use your judgment."[62]

Larry submitted Ted's songs to Bing's publishing company, Select; when they were returned, Ted suggested other publishers and asked Larry whether Bing would sing one on the air. Their father told Ted that Bing had tried to fit one into a broadcast but was stopped by the sponsor. Ted persevered: "Any chance of my writing a story for a picture for him? Advise and will go to work."[63] Larry explained that his ideas were not powerful enough to "supplant what the writers on salary can turn out."[64] Months later Ted made demos of his own songs, and Larry sent them to Select's president, George Joy, who wrote back, "I went over those records of your brother Ted's songs, and there are a couple among them that sound pretty fair, but . . . we've got to get outstanding material; we cannot take just ordinary songs because of the opposition we are up against." He mentioned Berlin, Gershwin, and Porter and concluded, "Pass this along to Ted and tell him that I do hope one of these days we can get together with him on a song of his."[65]

Larry made a deal to syndicate the book in London, payment to be made when the finished manuscript was delivered, and had a rough draft printed for Bing's approval. While Ted eagerly waited for the English check, Bing lingered over two chapters. Larry assured him, "Bing is now going over the book — & has made some good changes. I have plenty offers — & hope to have good news soon."[66] With *Collier's* out of the picture, Larry tried the *Saturday Evening Post*, the weekly that sixteen years later enjoyed the best sales figures in its history serializing Bing's *Call Me Lucky*. For now, it preferred to commission an original Bing story, by humorist H. Allen Smith. In January 1937 Harry wrote Ted, "Flash: *Believe it or not,* Bing finished the last chapter of the story the other day and it's been mailed . . . ."[67] Proofs were rushed to Ted.

By March copies of *Bing* were available in two editions. Larry and Ted had misguidedly decided to publish and distribute it themselves, through the Bolton Printing Company. They produced a paperback version that Larry sold virtually at cost, for a dollar, through direct mail; the profit margin was too small to permit anything else. A two-dollar edition was bound in blue felt, with just the title, *Bing,* embossed in gold on the cover. They soon learned the vagaries of vanity publishing. "Response to cloth slow, but expect more when publicity breaks," Larry wrote Ted.[68] A department store in Spokane bought a hundred copies for a window display. By April they knew the book had flopped. "Even in my most conservative moments," Larry confessed, "I would have gambled the 100 copies wouldn't last there over a week."[69] They sold no more than a hundred copies at the Los Angeles theater showing Bing's latest film, *Waikiki Wedding.* "There isn't enough margin to place it in bookstores until the cost is cut in half on the second run," concluded Larry. "Besides they want a three-month consignment which is tough to carry."[70] He cautioned Ted not to buy a ranch.

They sold a total of 400 copies in the first weeks, mostly through fan mail, yet Larry put on a show for a reporter from England's *Gramophone,* who visited Crosby, Inc.'s three-story office building at 9028–30 Sunset Boulevard. He asked Larry if he thought fans would buy the book. "Larry led me to another part of the office to see the organization which deals with Bing's fan mail. I questioned the success of this project no longer. Bing's fan mail arrives in sacks from every part of the world."[71] An article in *Look* that year reported the number of letters as 10,000 per month.[72] Yet the books did not move. Larry could not distribute them to stores or afford the advertising that would have alerted fans who bought every magazine with Bing's picture on the cover. In the end, he asked Kraft and Paramount to accept the books as premiums: "It should make as good a theater give-away as crockery and the other junk they put out on grocery nights."[73] Paramount enclosed the book in *Double or Nothing* press packages in September, with the suggestion that theaters use it as an inducement. Decca mailed inserts, offering the book to dealers at a 25 percent discount.

Reviewers, not surprisingly, ignored it. The Crosbys had produced a bewildering puree of fact and fancy, crammed with conversation, much of it ludicrous. Written in the style of a novel for adolescents (Tom Swift in Hollywood), *Bing* is boy's life adventure, tracking the hero with the idiom's requisite luck-and-pluck sentimentality, bolstered with a decent selection of family pictures. H. Allen Smith wrote, "Bing must love [his brothers] deeply to have ever permitted its publication."[74] In his preface of four sentences, Bing appears to concur. He says he can't imagine why anyone would be interested in his biography, "but my brothers have long importuned me for permission to write it." He refers to their efforts as "sophomoric" yet claims that "all incidents are true."[75] Larry and Ted more cautiously added to the dedication page ("with fond recollections to Mother and Bing") a disclaimer: "For obvious reasons, some of the names and places are fictitious."[76] A truth rings through nonetheless, echoed by Smith: "Bing's career remains to me an American epic because it is the reverse of the traditional success story" — he violates the dicta of every schoolmarm, "and look at him!"[77]

"I was just beginning to dust off a few daydreams concerning a new house and one or two other things; so I will just put them back on the shelf," Ted wrote Larry.[78] Bing, realizing how little the project netted his brother, enabled Ted to finance a house that summer. But even after Ted received a promotion at Washington Water Power, he continued to dispatch songs, ideas, and candidates for stardom to Los Angeles. At Bing's second annual golf tournament in January 1938, Bing asked Roy Moe, the professional at Spokane's leading country club, if he could purchase a membership for his brother. Moe promised to raise the subject with the board. A board member wrote Bing that Ted would be welcome — "he is very well thought of"[79] — and that dues were $221. Bing wrote on the bottom of the letter, "Send check for $221.00. Advise Ted — send me bill for monthly dues — direct from club if necessary."[80]

Ted had not been the only family member circling the golden trough in 1937. Bing's childhood hero, Uncle George Harrigan, had come back into the picture, writing to the office with hard-luck tales. Bing sent him $500, to the consternation of his father. Kate's sister, Annie, had died, and the widower, Ed Walsh, married the nurse who had cared for her. During their honeymoon the Walshes visited Uncle George and were charmed by George's daughter, Marion, whom they brought to Los Angeles. The sudden appearance of all these relatives incensed the usually easy Harry. "[Marion] is about the biggest fool I ever saw," he griped to Ted. "Then old Walsh gets Mr. Wyatt [Dixie's dad] to take her out to Bing's house, and she moved in on them for about two weeks, till they left, this was without an invitation. Oh was Mother and I mad."[81] Bing and Dixie, however, enjoyed Marion's company.

The familial jockeying for favor peaked at Christmastime 1936. "Bing did not send checks to anyone this year, only presents, but *that old woman* (your uncle George Harrigan) wrote one of his sob letters to Bing," Harry wrote Ted. George had wanted to attend a football game, Harry howled, "and dam if Bing didn't send him a check for $100 — and 4 tickets to the game. I tried every way to stop it but to no avail. Bing and Dixie think George and Marion are tops. That dam liar and double crosser, I hate her. When she was here, she did not go see anyone, but stayed at Bing's all the time drinking with Dixie."[82]

Harry was pleased, however, that Kate had taken to calling him Caliban, "because I like to run around with young folks — ain't that mean though?"[83] Harry and Kate were spending increasing hours at the races. One day they took home $150. "Now Mother is having lots of Masses said for you all," Harry reported.[84]

Bing's favorite sister, Mary Rose, was having a harder time of it, raising her infant daughter while suffering from a thyroid condition ("I expect before long people will be mistaking me for Mae West").[85] Her marriage was crumbling, and she studied shorthand to compensate for her husband's unemployment ("the louse") while living on a stipend from Bing's office — barely enough, she complained, "to pay my board and schooling and keep the kid and I in Pants." She closed the same letter, "Dear me, if I'm not just like Dixie — always having to figure out how to save a nickel here and there."[86] Harry and Kate and all the siblings, except for the independent and happily married Catherine (Kay), seemed to have their eyes on the till. "Bing has put so much money into the Del Mar Race track, and gambling on horses," Harry fretted, "that we are having a time holding him down, in order that he will have enough left to pay the Income Tax."[87]

There were no real familial fissures, however, until 1944, when Bing invited Ted to join him in Los Angeles as a publicist for Del Mar, and Ted prepared a revised edition of his and Larry's long-forgotten book. The ensuing feud, which involved stock certificates, theft, Bing's divestment of his interests in Del Mar, and the book itself, would last nearly twenty years and rupture forever the relationship between Ted and his unforgiving parents. Yet no one could have imagined such a storm in the fall of 1937, when the Crosbys reunited in Ted's backyard for a gala homecoming befitting Spokane's prodigal son.

22

HOMECOMING

The interesting part of Bing to me is that he likes to be with jockeys, with millionaires, with beach boys and with caddies. He likes colorful people; he likes people who are amusing and aren't phonies. He's an unphony man. He's so distant, but he's a very genuine man.
— Johnny Mercer (1974)[1]

As trying as the book experience must have been throughout 1937, Larry looked beyond it to help craft one of the most pleasing publicity events of Bing's career, his official return to his hometown — twelve years to the month after he and Rinker drove off in their Tin Lizzy. Spokane had made overtures as far back as 1932, when hundreds of people signed a valentine, placed on display at a theater showing one of his Sennett shorts and then mailed to Bing in care of the New York Paramount. By 1937 he contemplated taking *Kraft Music Hall* on the road. When his old friend Mike Pecarovitch, Gonzaga's football coach, visited him in Hollywood, Bing pressed him with questions about summer training and said he might attend the September game between Gonzaga and Washington State, might even stay a week and do the show up there.

Pecarovitch reported the conversation, and Gonzaga responded with alacrity, offering Bing an honorary doctorate, the only one he would ever accept. The timing was perfect, as his visit would coincide with the university's fiftieth anniversary, its jubilee. Cal Kuhl and Kraft were delighted with the idea. Bing was committed to raising money for Gonzaga, a project that occupied much of his attention over the next forty years. He took the matter in hand and dictated a letter, which Larry amended with a few details before mailing to Bing's revered disciplinarian, the Reverend Curtis J. Sharp. Bing told Sharp that the event would have to be in October and that he would bring a well-known actor who had graduated from a Jesuit school, perhaps Pat O'Brien, Edmund Lowe, Andy Devine, or Walter Connolly, plus a band and other performers. Kuhl wanted to reserve the last five minutes of the broadcast for the presentation of the degree, Bing noted, so he needed to know the precise particulars and timing of the ceremony.

Paramount also got into the act. Bing wrote: "We are going to run a contest open to residents of the Pacific Northwest to select a boy and girl, both amateurs and both under twenty-one, to come to Hollywood for a screen test and possibly a part in a Paramount picture."[2] Bing, Kuhl, and others would choose the winners after entrants had been narrowed to a group of finalists. He added: "For the Kraft show, it is not considered a good thing to charge admission, so we will probably have to broadcast from a point where only a couple of hundred people would be admitted. Later they propose to give a monster dance and entertainment at the Armory, using the Dorsey band for dancing, and with Burns and myself and other acts we should have enough to put on a pretty good show." Bing offered to give two performances ("if not too strenuous"), "one for $1.10 which would admit everybody to the Armory or Auditorium and another for $10.00 a couple, for the people on Cannon Hill or those who think they can afford such a stiff tariff. . . . I'll be pleased to hear from you with any suggestions you might have relative to the show itself as a medium of garnering some shekels for the school."[3]

Sharp mailed him the Latin diploma and a tribute he wrote (along with citations for phrases he borrowed from Tennyson and Horace), which was to be read by the Reverend Leo Robinson, the president of Gonzaga. He enclosed an English translation of the diploma "for the less enlightened brothers in your troupe."[4] Sharp assured Bing he was doing all he could to keep their plans from leaking to the press, per

Bing's request, adding in an aside that Pecarovitch, to whom Bing had given a small bit in *Waikiki Wedding*, "is all agog about his part in your new picture *Double or Nothing.* Spokane certainly has had him over the barrel, paddling him generously."[5] Larry wrote the school's president that "Bing would prefer to arrive quietly without any fanfare, as our first item is the Mass, and then a day of radio rehearsal and the program with which no festivities must interfere."[6]

Larry went public in early August with the news that Bing would broadcast from Spokane and receive an honorary degree in music, causing much consternation at Gonzaga when the faculty realized that, not having a graduate school in music, the school could not confer such a doctorate. They changed it to doctor of philosophy, reasoning that philosophy was a staple of a Jesuit education, but Gonzaga did not graduate philosophers, either. The astute Sharp intended to correctly present Bing with a doctor of letters, yet the mistake was allowed to stand, by which time the press was so confused that the *Spokesman-Review* reported he would receive "the degree of doctor of philosophy in music."[7]

The Bing Crosby Talent Contest commenced a few weeks later. One could not help but notice that many applicants signed on with names that would not have made it onto a Hollywood marquee, although a few may have been invented for just that purpose: Carrie Mae Halz, Lyle Dolge, Grant Noble, Mrs. Charles Rainbow, Evelyn Thrasp, Hollis E. Wood.

Anticipation for the big weekend was stimulated by numerous news stories. Bing gave advice on how to hear your own voice by talking to a door; Jimmy Monaco and Johnny Burke wrote a marching song for GU; semifinalists were chosen for the Paramount competition; "Johnny" Trotter and Perry Botkin posed with Bing as they planned the show (Trotter had replaced Dorsey in the months since the original proposal); Pecarovitch announced that Bing was to be his assistant coach when Gonzaga's Bulldogs met the San Francisco Dons. The papers endlessly retold stories of the flivver, Rinker, Mildred, Whiteman, and Barris, as though they were grizzled fables collected by Bulfinch. "SEE! — MEET! — HEAR! BING CROSBY," the advertisements bellowed: "DINE With the Stars" Thursday at Civic Auditorium (five dollars a plate); "LAUGH With the Stars" Friday at the Armory (one-, two-, three-dollar tickets); "DANCE With the Stars" Saturday at Natatorium Park (ladies one dollar, men a dollar fifty); "CHEER With the Stars" Sunday afternoon at GU Stadium ($1.15, $1.75, $2.30 tickets).[8]

At last the day arrived, October 21: Bing's train pulled in at 7:00 A.M., without fuss, and he went directly to the university for mass. His retinue included Joe Perry, who had produced his monumental hit of the year, "Sweet Leilani," the best selling disc since 1929; his old friend Connie Boswell (formerly of the Boswell Sisters), with whom he recorded his current chartbuster, "Bob White"; his *KMH* guests, Edmund Lowe and Mary Carlisle; Bob Burns, Trotter and the band, Ken Carpenter, and Johnny Burke. A week earlier Ted was under the impression that Louis Armstrong was coming; if that was the case (Louis is not mentioned in the other existing correspondence), he may have been pulled because of a question Ted, who helped to arrange lodgings, ingenuously posed: "One thing — how about accommodations for Louis Armstrong. How do you handle that?"[9] Larry had arrived earlier in the week, as advance man. Harry and Kate followed. In a photograph taken by the *Spokane Chronicle*, Bing, wearing a mortarboard and gown and holding his degree, stands with his parents, Larry, and Ted, all looking inappropriately dour. Everett drove up later in the day. Dixie did not make the trip, as she was seven months pregnant.

After mass, at a commencement (rather than on the air), Bing received his degree. The statement written by Sharp and read by Robinson took note of Bing's technological handmaidens: "two of the greatest scientific achievements of the age, the radio and the cinema," whereby "the voice and personality of Harry Lillis Crosby have brought pleasure and many a happy moment to millions of his fellow men." It went on to praise his "steadfast loyalty and unswerving fidelity to his Alma Mater and his firm adherence to the principles of uprightness and moral courage taught by the University he attended."[10] Bing later recalled, "I almost broke down."[11]

From Gonzaga they trouped to City Hall, where Bing was named honorary mayor and Burns honorary chief of police. The *KMH* show and banquet followed that night. Thousands attended the various events, including the talent contest at the Fox Theatre, where the queuing began at 2:00 for a 9:30 curtain. Bing and Burns left the banquet to make a brief appearance at the Fox and return with the winners, chosen by Ted Lesser and James Moore, the head of Paramount's talent department and the studio's chief test director, respectively. Preliminary events reduced the field of a thousand contestants to a group of ten. Lesser assigned parts to the actors, and Moore filmed them, in case, Lesser observed, "talent develops that we can use outside of the winners."[12] As it happened, he found talent outside the circle of finalists. An attractive blonde named Barbara Ruth Rogers caught his eye selling tickets at a theater. Surprised but pleased by her good luck, she told a reporter, "I never thought much about pictures, but probably had the thought in the back of my head."[13] Paramount signed her along with one contest winner, Janet Waldo, to two-year contracts; they appeared in numerous movies over the next twenty-four months, before the bubble burst, first as walk-ons, then in supporting roles, and finally as leads in Poverty Row westerns.

Perhaps Bing was contemplating the likely future of young contract players or recalling his own futile auditions, because he was said to appear nervous at the show, furiously smoking his pipe and relieved to pass the mike to Bob Burns, who passed it to Carpenter, the evening's emcee. He was radiant, however, the next night at the Armory, presiding at a two-and-a-half-hour show before an elated audience of 3,500 — and in a tuxedo! When Carpenter introduced him, he brought down the house addressing the crowd as "fellow citizens." He continued, "You shouldn't thank me for coming here. Rather, I should thank you most sincerely for what you have done for me and for the honor which Gonzaga University has bestowed upon me. We came here to do something for Gonzaga and Spokane."[14] The highlight of the show was his duet with Connie Boswell on "Basin Street Blues."

Bing could do no wrong that week. In addition to raising more than $10,000 for the Gonzaga Athletic Fund, he presented the team with a $1,000 water wagon to replace paper cups carried around at halftime on a tray. (They lost anyway.) He visited a "home for unfortunate girls,"[15] called the House of the Good Shepherd, where he dedicated tennis courts, signed autographs, crooned a cappella, and executed a buck and wing. At the Shrine Children's Hospital, he walked among the beds with ready wit, talking and singing to one child after another — "My Little Buckaroo" to the smallest boy in the group,

"Sweet Leilani" to a girl in a head-to-foot cast with only her eyes showing. He staged an impromptu performance for the student priests at Mount St. Michael. He visited Inland Products, the former brewery that had brought the Crosbys east from Tacoma, and other haunts of his youth. On October 25 Bing boarded the train for Los Angeles. At a stop in Klamath Falls, Oregon, he was greeted by a crowd of 2,000. Call him lucky: the next day he abandoned the train in Oakland to attend the races at San Mateo. His horse High Strike won the Home Bred Handicap.

The four days cost Bing the substantial sum of $5,000. The headliners came out of friendship, but Trotter's band left five network shows without their regular musicians, and substitutes had to be paid, as did extra wire charges for broadcasting from Spokane. From a public-relations angle, it was a bargain; the national publicity was so upbeat, it started a wave of great-guy stories that all but washed away the drunk sailors, taxes, picket line, Mysterious Montague, and familial rancor. Three years earlier the *Los Angeles Examiner* had deemed him a "guardian angel" for seeing Mack Sennett through a period of financial hardship.[16] That kind of news item now became commonplace. In fact, within days of his return to Paramount, Bing was declared a lifesaver by makeup man Wylann Fieltz, whom Bing came upon unconscious in his dressing room and rushed to a hospital for an emergency appendectomy.

Bing's good deeds often concerned friends in the jazz world. In May 1937 he organized a five-hour benefit for the tubercular pianist Joe Sullivan at Pan-Pacific Auditorium. The 6,000 who attended and the tens of thousands who listened on the radio heard one of the Swing Era's benchmark evenings. Bing instructed Everett and Larry to produce the best swing concert ever, and the performers included Bing, Connie Boswell, Red Norvo, Johnny Mercer, Ella Logan, the guitar duo of Dick McDonough and Carl Kress, and the orchestras of Woody Herman, Earl Hines, Ray Noble, Jimmy Dorsey, Louis Prima, Harry Owens, Jimmy Grier, Victor Young, and Ben Pollack. It broke the house record and raised $3,000 for Sullivan. The next February *Down Beat* printed a story — "Bing Crosby (Dr. of Square Shooting) Known as Squarest Guy in Hollywood" — that itemized instances when he came to the aid of friends, often by giving them work in films or on radio: "Whenever the stork is hovering over a Hollywood home, the prospective 'Pappy' usually finds himself on Bing's program as a guest star — such were the cases of Andy Devine and Harry Barris."[17] At Easter he donated a $1,600 organ to St. Charles Church in North Hollywood, dedicating it with a few hymns. For a man who resisted the press, he had the press in thrall.

The gusher of goodwill soared after January 5, 1938, when Dixie gave birth to her fourth son (Bing told *Variety* they outfitted the nursery for a girl, hoping that might reverse their track record). Lindsay Harry was named for Lindsay Howard, with whom Bing founded Binglin Stock Farm that very week, and Bing's father. Quieter than the colicky Gary or the competitive twins, Linny (as he was called) would be the most indulged of the boys, though his life, marked by severe depression, would be no easier. "Linny was the only one of us with brown eyes," Gary recalled. "He differed in other ways as well. He was a quiet, dreamy, unaggressive child who read a lot, got good marks in school and liked to draw and paint."[18] In the excitement surrounding his arrival, all seemed rosy in the Crosby household and in what was rapidly becoming the Crosbys' world. Weeks after Linny appeared, the *New York Journal-American* editorialized that Bing's "current eminence" was one of "the grand stories" of the past year and hailed him as "the typical American, still young yet the father of four boys, singing his way honestly through life and brightening the way of others with his affable, smiling, melodious voice which radiates friendliness in the loudspeaker."[19]

Bing was celebrated in one poll as Hollywood's most typical father, and there were no signs that anything was amiss. Dixie's drinking was under control, she entertained, she accompanied Bing to numerous social functions. But trouble was around the corner, in part an unexpected consequence of Bing's homecoming broadcast, which spurred him and Kraft to take the show on the road, requiring longer absences from home. A year or two later, Dixie and the marriage would be in trouble, but not yet. "The children were all lovely boys," Dixie's friend Pauline Weislow recalled, "and she was very involved when they were young. She meant to be a wonderful parent. What was so very interesting is that such public persons as Bing and Dixie were so private."[20]

Since the demise of her film career, Dixie had reluctantly agreed to a few professional appearances, among them a guest spot on Al Jolson's radio show and a 1936 recording session with Bing, at which they sang two superb songs by Jerome Kern and Dorothy Fields, introduced that year by Astaire and Rogers in *Swing Time*. Astaire, Billie Holiday, and Guy Lombardo enjoyed hits with the arch "A Fine Romance" and the incomparably wistful "The Way You Look Tonight"; Bing and Dixie did not. But their renditions have a unique, unforgettable pathos that sets them apart. Bing's expertise at duets, from his apprenticeship with Al Rinker to his give-and-take with the Mills Brothers, was already known, though his unrivaled finesse as a quick-witted, funny, supportive partner of other singers was truly confirmed a couple of years later in records with Connie Boswell and Johnny Mercer. With Dixie, he is relatively guarded, but his formality is protective, mandated by their inability to sing in the same key. Their musical seclusion underscores an emotional detachment, despite Victor Young's spare and affectionate arrangements, which were devised to accommodate their disparate ranges.

Young was abetted by the material itself. "The Way You Look Tonight," one of the incontestable triumphs of American popular song, has two enharmonic changes, signaled by a transitional instrumental figure built into the melody — leading in to and out of the release. Young shrewdly employs those transitions to facilitate and minimize the shift in keys that occurs every eight bars, as Bing and Dixie exchange passages of that length. With his wide range and finesse, Bing carries the burden of those shifts, which are brought off so well that the listener is barely aware of the elevator ride transporting each singer to a harmonically suitable floor. Yet the manipulation of keys distances Bing and Dixie, who harmonize only briefly, on the title phrase. They sound at times as isolated as if they had been wired in from different studios, she passive and wounded, he expert and strong. Dixie's melancholy nasality, though passé, emanates feeling. Their attempts at humor on "A Fine Romance" are tense, despite Bing's fleeting mimicry of W. C. Fields ("potatoes") and Martha Raye ("oh boy"), but "The Way You Look Tonight" is an affecting record, lacking an essential bond of communication and in that absence striking a forlorn, immensely touching chord.

Any pretense of continuing her career was long over for Dixie by the time Linny was born. Except for parties, she rarely sang in public. Once on a Sunday night at the Century Club, Bing coaxed her, and she sang "You Are My Lucky Star" to an audience that included Jimmy Dorsey, Joe Venuti, and Zeppo Marx. Mostly she sang in the house. Her son Phillip remembered her chirping along with Ella Fitzgerald's "A-Tisket, A-Tasket" all day long.[21] When the kids accidentally broke the record, she ran out to buy another. Within a few years her shyness would congeal into reclusivity, but now she was regularly seen on Bing's arm: watching the boxing matches at Wrigley Field or attending the racetrack, sipping cocktails to celebrate the engagement of Anne Shirley and John Payne or at a party at Barbara Stanwyck's (Bing sang). She threw buffets for friends like the Johnny Burkes, the Edmund Lowes, the Johnny Mercers, the Joe Venutis, and the Andy Devines; celebrated anniversaries with the Pat O'Briens and the Joe E. Browns. The Crosbys dined at Chasen's and the Cocoanut Grove and the House of Murphy; after the races they stopped for drinks at Cafe La Maze or Club 17. When Bing appeared as a guest on the debut of Paul Whiteman's new Chesterfield show, she improvised a soiree, and she was there to cheer the gala debut of Earl Carroll's theater and restaurant.

And as if their dance cards were not filled top to bottom, Bing and Dixie formed a mummers society, the Westwood Marching and Chowder Club (North Hollywood Branch). However much Bing was a product and innovator of technology, he remained a son of the nineteenth century and the show-business traditions that dominated his youth. Though he married one of its daughters, Bing continued to view the South as a musical-comical never-never land, a state of mind and a trove of irresistible material. "He did like southerners," Kentucky's Rosemary Clooney recalled. "He loved southern women — it was almost a prerequisite. He wouldn't ask anyone if they were southern, but he got along with southerners very well."[22]

The Marching and Chowder Club was spurred by the Crosbys' friendship with their neighbors in Toluca Lake, Herb Polesie, a radio producer, and his wife, Mildred, whom everyone called Midge. (As Mildred Lovell, she wrote a society column for the New York *Daily News*). Phillip Crosby remembered Midge as a member of the circle of six who surrounded Dixie, along with Pauline Weislow, Kitty Sexton, Sue Carol, Alice Ross, and Julie Taurog, whom Phillip said had problems with her husband, director Norman Taurog, and spent more time at the Crosby home than at her own. Herb, who would soon produce *Kraft Music Hall* and two of Bing's movies, was described by Phillip as "one of the nicest guys in the world."[23] A press release identified him as the Marching and Chowder Club's president; the program for its first presentation, *The Midgie Minstrels,* credits him as "Interlocutor and ticket taker."

The show was held in the Crosby home on April 16, 1938. John Mercer and Joe Venuti were the end men. Bing appeared, according to a program note, by permission of the Emanuel Cohen Minstrels. As most of the wives had show-business experience, they performed along with their husbands; the couples included the Pat O'Briens, Johnny Burkes, Johnny Mercers, Larry Crosbys, David Butlers, Joe Venutis, Edmund Lowes, and Perry Botkins. Kitty Sexton performed under her maiden (and *Ziegfeld Follies*) name, Rasch; her husband, the veterinarian, also did a number. Bing printed up the jocular playbill ("one performance only"):

Part the First

1. Opening Chorus, "Hello, Hello" . . . . .Ensemble
2. Those Girls . . . . .Six bits of femininity
                                        or 75¢ worth of "Swanee"
3. "Frivolous Sal" . . . . .sung by Elsie Butler
                        with Rita Lowe and her three mocking birds
                        Off-Rhythm Boys, "Sailing Down Chesapeake Bay"
4. James Monaco . . . . .The original Ragtime Jimmy
                                From Red lights to kleig lights
5. "That Ever-lovin' Ziegfeld Follies Baby"
                                sung by Kitty Rasch (class of 1908)
6. Larry Crosby . . . . .The "IT" Boy in "Oh My Garden"
                        accompanied by THE Elaine Couper
                        Off-Rhythm Boys, "Sweet Cider Time"
7. "I Did It for the Red, White and Blue"
                                The Merry Mercers, Ginger and John
8. Jerry Colonna . . . ."The Clean Shaven Fillip"
                        Encore, "Louisville Lou" if requested
9. Perry (Union) and Virginia Botkin
                                        Two folks and one guitar
10. First Act Finale, "When You Wore a Tulip," Ensemble

Crackerjack, large peanuts and exceptional popcorn between the acts by David Butler, concessionaire. Very good prizes too.

Part the Second

1. The Natchez Sunshine Four . . . . .in "Bits and Tidbits"
"Jungle Town"
2. Lee & Burke, or Burke & Lee . . . . .Dixie and Johnny
in a potpourri of Chatter, Patter and Ja-Da
3. Ray Mayer . . . . .The Masked Musical Marvel
Demonstrates his latest invention THE PIANOLA
4. Bessie Patterson . . . . .A Lass and a Lasso!
Off-Rhythm Boys singing "Dearie Please Don't Be Angry"
5. Joe Venuti . . . . .The jiving alligator, or a bit of burp
accompanied by Sally
6. Bing Crosby . . . . .Refreshments served gratis
in lobby during recital
7. A lull
8. Pat O'Brien . . . . A bit of very old Erin
9. The Yacht Club Boys . . . . .Why?
10. Dr. William Sexton . . . . .For Men Only
11. Edmund Lowe . . . . .And away we go!
12. Finale "Waiting for the Robert E. Lee"
Entire Company

The above program, subject to change with plenty of notice. No money refunded once the curtain goes up. If it goes up.[24]

Though blackface was confined chiefly to an end-men number by Venuti and Mercer, the costumes replicated the wry buffoonery of an old-time minstrel show, with satiny stripes, clashing plaids, and bowlers or top hats. Bing looked especially natty in a black frock coat, broad-plaid trousers, a close-plaid vest with a watch fob, polka-dot bow tie, and top hat. O'Brien wore a suit of silver satin. Bessie Burke wore a studded leather belt, a satin blouse, cowboy hat, and chaps of sheep's wool with cutouts to display her buttocks. Johnny Burke and Dixie wore matching suits with fitted trousers and waistcoats, bow ties, and bowlers. The women in the sextet number blended satin, gingham, lace, and outlandish hats. David Butler tied a leopard skin over rolled-up trousers and cowboy shirt for a number with an un-billed John Scott Trotter.

Within weeks telegrams hastily went out for the club's second meeting:

THE WESTWOOD HILLS MARCHING AND CHOWDER CLUB NORTH HOLLY-
WOOD BRANCH ASKS YOU TO ITS 2ND BREAKWAY MINSTREL SHOW TO
BE PERPETRATED AT 10500 CAMARILLO NORTHHOLLYWOOD AT 7 PM
JUNE 25TH. BRING YOUR OWN ACT AND COSTUME OR COME AND KNOCK
YOURSELF OUT. CALL MISS ROSS AT NH 5645 WITH ACCEPTANCE OR ALIBI.
SUPPER AT MIDNIGHT.
— DIXIE AND BING CROSBY[25]

This show rounded up most of the same cast, along with Ken Murray, Wesley Ruggles, Jimmy Monaco, Andy Devine, Bill Frawley,
Eddie Sutherland, Skeets Gallagher, and Fred MacMurray. Trotter
led a five-piece band that included Tommy Dorsey and Spike Jones.
Now titled *The Breakaway Minstrel Show*, the company performed in
a huge tent erected on the Crosby tennis court, with an elaborate
proscenium arch and a painted backdrop.[26] The showstopper came
early, after an ensemble chorus of "Hello, Hello" and "The Little
Ladies, God Bless 'Em, in good ole 'Swanee River.'" Lasses Mercer
and Chitlins Crosby offered an "erudite analyseration of swing,"[27]
based on the vaudeville classic "Mr. Gallagher and Mr. Shean." Mercer wrote the lyric, an off-the-wall parody of jazz history; but what
dazzled the audience was the smooth running wit of the neovaudevil-
lians delivering it.

> JM: *Oh, Mr. Crosby [BC hums], Dear Dr. Crosby [BC scats]*
> *Is it true that swing's another name for jazz? [BC scats]*
> *And the first place it was played*
> *Was a New Orleans Parade*
> *And the Southern Negro gave it all it has?*
> BC: *Oh, Mr. Mercer, Mr. Mercer, Mr. Mercer, Mr. Mercer,*
> *I believe that its foundation came from them*
> *[JM: Are you positive?]*
> *Yeesss. They just slowed the tempo down*
> *And then they really went to town.*
> JM: *Allegretto, Mr. Crosby?*
> BC: *Alligators, Mr. M.*
> . . . .
> BC: *Mr. Mercer, [JM: Yes?] Oh, Mr. Mercer, [JM: Hm-hmm?]*
> *Well, I trust that I have made the matter clear.*
> *[JM: It's really too clear.]*

> *So when someone plays a thing*
> *You're gonna understand it's swing*
> *And appreciate the rhythm that you hear.*
> JM: *Oh, Mr. Crosby,* [BC: *Oh, hear me talking to ya*]. *No, Mr. Crosby*
> [BC scats]
> *I'm afraid that type of rhythm's not for me.*
> *I prefer my music played*
> *A la Schubert serenade.*
> BC: *Sort of ritardo, Mr. Mercer?*
> JM: *Sort of Lombardo, Mr. C.*[28]

The number went over so well that Bing and Mercer recorded it six days later for Decca, producing a major hit (hailed by *Time* as "the summer's most amusing ditty"),[29] an unflappable duet that remains a standard for rhythmic joshing on the boundary between vaudeville and jazz. They also recorded Hoagy Carmichael's "Small Fry," a more conventional reverie with southern minstrel badinage, which they performed with Fred MacMurray ("Fred plays the old dame") in the tent show, re-creating a scene from the as-yet-unreleased *Sing You Sinners*. Other highlights found Bing, as Gene Krupa Krosby, joining with Kenny Goodman Murray and Lionel Hampton Burke on "Maggie Blues"; and as Cracklins Crosby, rendering the classic "Nobody" ("Lifted bodily from a Bert Williams record"), which he later sang successfully on radio; the broadcast performance was issued as a Decca recording.

Bing's "private" shows, including impromptu productions at his golf and track meets, entranced much of Hollywood, adding to an allure that impressed his colleagues. In a town plagued by fear, he was seemingly fearless. His persona reflected an independence as admirable as it was rare. James Cagney had appeared as a guest on *Kraft Music Hall* early in 1937, but it was a year later, while listening to the show at his farm on Martha's Vineyard, that he experienced something of an epiphany about Bing. "I knew at once that this was a most extraordinary fella. I actually started to write a piece about him, 'The Miracle Known as Crosby,' but after a page or two, I stopped. I realized he was just beginning, and would add up to even more than he was."[30] Cagney was one of many *KMH* guests who marveled at his enigmatic grace.

A few weeks after the June Breakaway Minstrel Show, a young journalist named Marie Manovill wrote to several of Bing's radio guests, asking them to discuss his good and bad points. Lotte Lehmann observed, "It is very difficult for me to say whether the charm of his personality or the charm of his songs is more appealing to me."[31] The only correspondent who ventured any criticism was Rose Bampton. She began by remarking on Bing's ability to work hard and yet "make everyone about him feel that he is taking life easily, which is quite unique. Especially, since his work is always done and done well."[32] She pointed to the improvement in his singing as evidence of his labor and credited his "sincerity and absolute honesty" as additional reasons for his success. She continued:

> If one were hunting for bad points, I think his only one would be that perhaps he is too self-effacing. I can recall the occasion of one broadcast which demanded that Bing learn an arrangement of the sextette of "Lucia." Bing insisted that he didn't read music, that he wasn't a good musician, yet in spite of all this, inside of fifteen minutes he was singing as nonchalantly as any opera singer a most difficult arrangement which had been allotted to him.
>
> By this little criticism I do not mean to say that one must be arrogant, but surely Bing should be cognizant a little more of his own quite unique ability and standing.
>
> But then, perhaps that is just one of the reasons why every artist who is on his program comes away with a feeling of having made a very sincere new friend, and is just another Crosby fan for ever after.[33]

Bampton had hit on something. Her "little criticism" was much echoed, privately and in the press, as Bing's movies became increasingly routine; observers wondered why he seemed more energetic in pursuing golf and the ponies than in broadening his range as a performer. The public, of course, was satisfied. Bing was treasured in and out of the business. Hollywood had adopted him as its favorite crooner back when the Rhythm Boys played the Montmartre Cafe. The Marching and Chowder Club affirmed his likableness with insiders and amused the public when it learned of the get-togethers, initially through a charity-raising performance on Tommy Dorsey's *Raleigh-Kool Show*. The MCC sponsored a quintet: violinist Jack Benny, clarinetist Ken Murray, cornetist Dick Powell, pianist Shirley Ross, and drummer Bing.

An eager Paramount publicist ran with the ball: the Marching and Chowder Club performed every month (no less) and "turned back the pages of time to the gay '90s" with "approximately 150 stars" (no less). Why stop there? The Floradora Sextette number alone, he marveled, would "cost $500,000 to put on the screen."[34] Bing may have considered the ballyhoo a mistake, because Paramount quickly retreated with a bulletin that began on a more ominous note: "The screen colony's 'open door' policy is a thing of the past."[35] This release grieved for the film stars who were harassed by "chiseling hangers-on, blackmailers, souvenir hunters, and gate-crashing celebrity hunters"; they had no choice but to pare down parties and guest lists. "The West Side [sic] Marching and Chowder Club," it noted, hired "special guards to keep out the uninvited."[36] The Westwood revelers retired until 1940.

The mummers shows demonstrate Bing's capacity for fun, penchant for masks, and love for the venerable traditions of show business. They also underscore a leadership capacity he exercised more readily in his private life than in his professional one. If Bing was an unbending force who went his own way in his own time, he did not consider himself or want to be considered the architect of his career.

Like the indifferent college student who was pushed to the brink of show business by high schoolers, like the singing star who adopted the vision of his record producer, and like the radio star who had to be cajoled into spontaneity, Bing continued to heed the advice of those he deemed savvier than himself. Disciplined, inscrutable, and innovative artist that he was, he pretended to leave the big decisions to others as long as they suited his purposes. For example, at the time of the MCC shows, he accepted a ten-year contract, without options, to continue as *Kraft Music Hall*'s host. It was the longest commitment offered to anyone in radio history and would ultimately haunt NBC, when Bing made one of the biggest decisions of his life, to break free in 1946, and a judge ruled that a covenant of that length amounted to indentured servitude.

Playtime was another story: he called the shots. As Phil Harris recalled, "I knew him well enough to wait for him to call me."[37] In the late 1930s most of the calls he made were focused on making the Del Mar racetrack a going concern. Toward that end, the money Bing put up — essential though it was — probably counted for less than his

investment in energy and commitment. He coasted through the filming of *Double or Nothing* as if it were merely a venture to fill spare
time. "When not actually working in a scene or learning a song," a
reporter noted, "he was on the telephone talking to functionaries at
the track or at his stable, or he was out on the Paramount campus
rounding up other stars to be Del Mar 'guest stewards.'"[38] On the set
he convinced costars to appear on opening day for the next meet. At
the track he collected tickets, signed autographs, entertained, and
announced races.

He was no less engaged in the stables. Charlie Whittingham, who
trained for him in later years, met him in the early days at Del Mar.
"He'd be out every morning, and I got to know him quite well. Very
nice to be around, a regular guy, you know. Liked the horses and got
to know them, because Binglin had quite a good stable. They kidded
him about his nags, but he had decent horses. A lot of times, from the
races we'd go over to Bing's and have a cocktail, sit around and talk.
They had a softball team at Rancho Sante Fe, and he played on it.
Pretty good athlete."[39]

Though he never trained horses for Bing, Noble Threewitt admired
the way he handled himself on the grounds: "Lots of owners hate to
waste their time talking to you. But Bing would visit with anybody. He
was just an all-around good guy. The opening day at Del Mar with
him and Pat O'Brien — that was a great, great opening day."[40]

Yet in the year that followed that fabled afternoon, Del Mar
stumbled badly, failing to attract capacity crowds or a serious following. John O'Melveny had argued against the whole plan, but Bing
had uncharacteristically ignored his attorney's advice and invested
$45,000 for 35 percent of the stock. For a year and a half, Del Mar
lost money. Everything changed with the legendary meet of August
1938, which was heralded by the most famous track ditty ever composed. Midge Polesie came up with the catchphrase "Where the Turf
Meets the Surf," inspiring a sixteen-bar anthem — and a longer but
rarely heard verse — by Monaco, Burke, and Bing, played over the
loudspeakers before and after every set of races for seven decades
and counting. Bing, Pat O'Brien, and Oliver Hardy plugged it on
three NBC shows the week before the 1938 meet.

No effort was spared to attract the Hollywood community on
August 5, which was declared Motion Picture Day. Each contest was

titled like the entrées on a Sunset Boulevard menu: The Actors, The Exhibitors, The Producers, The Directors, The Cameramen, The Screen Writers, and The Stars. A Motion Picture Handicap offered a $3,000 purse for three-year-olds owned by people in the business. The horses raced by Robert Riskin, Clark Gable, and Joe E. Brown won, placed, and showed; Bing's entry, Rocco, came in last. But nothing could dampen his spirits that day. He announced the race and then signed hundreds of autographs. After the last race a screen was erected on the track for the premiere of Bing's new picture, *Sing You Sinners,* a racetrack story in which his own horses participated. This in itself was an event, "Hollywood's most novel preview," a reporter called it.[41] Drive-ins were practically unheard-of (the first one, erected in New Jersey in 1933, had few imitators until the late 1940s). The audience at Del Mar marveled at the sight of planes overhead and the sound of train whistles in the distance as they watched the movie. Bing was not around for the alfresco screening, however; he was rehearsing the script for the radio broadcast to follow. It began with Del Mar's theme song and proceeded with several stars lavishing praise on the picture and players, except for Bing, who in mock desperation asked Pat O'Brien, "How did you like *my* work in the picture, Pat?" The predictable reply: "Oh, were you in the picture, too?"

The press, including 375 writers and photographers who were delivered to the gates on a special train, focused on Motion Picture Day (Friday) and failed to report on Saturday evening's entertainment, which proved more consequential. Bob Hope had relocated to Los Angeles the previous year to appear in Paramount's *The Big Broadcast of 1938.* Having renewed their friendship on the links and at the studio, Bing asked Hope to join him onstage to re-create the routines they improvised at the Capitol Theater six years earlier. The crowd loved them, as did William LeBaron, an officer on the Del Mar board and Paramount's chief of production. The buzz that evening was, why doesn't somebody put these guys into a picture?

The incident that ensured Del Mar's survival took place the following Friday. Bing and Lin Howard had purchased the 6,000-acre La Portena ranch in Argentina and shipped several horses back to the United States, a slow, arduous journey by sea and rail. When the horses finally arrived, the six-year-old Ligaroti was promising but unsteady, and for a while Bing and Lin considered selling him — he was offered to Louis B. Mayer for $75,000. They were glad Meyer declined when, in March 1938, Ligaroti won a $5,000 handicap at Bay Meadows, San Mateo, by three lengths, completing the mile course in 1:40. Another of their Argentine horses, Sabuesa, also won that day. In July Ligaroti won the $5,000 Aloma Handicap at Hollywood Park. Unbilled, he also got to win the big race at the climax of *Sing You Sinners*. Word got around that Bing and Howard were claiming Ligaroti might be the best distance runner in the country, a boast that Del Mar's general manager, William Quigley, duly conveyed to Lin's father, who owned the famous Seabiscuit.

Charles Howard had made a fortune in Buick dealerships. Seabiscuit added to it, winning more than a third of his starts over a four-year period; in 1937 he was voted the nation's number one handicap horse. Howard could not resist Quigley's challenge, and a match race was staged with a $25,000 purse, no public wagering, though spectators could bet among themselves. Bing and Lin placed side bets with Howard (who grandly offered three-to-one odds) and Seabiscuit's backers. The distance was set at a mile and an eighth, with George (The Iceman) Woolf riding Seabiscuit and Noel (Spec) Richardson riding Ligaroti. A crowd of 22,000 overflowed the stands — larger by a third than the previous record crowd. The match was broadcast by Bing and O'Brien from a microphone on the grandstand roof, beneath which a cheering section wore Ligaroti sweaters and waved Ligaroti pennants, chanting, "You can try and try and try, but you can't beat Ligaroti!"

The race, euphemized by one sportswriter as "torrid,"[42] was remembered by the man who announced it, Oscar Otis, as the most violent he had ever seen. Seabiscuit broke out first, but at no time did either horse lead by more than half a length. The crowd went crazy, and so did the jockeys, flailing each other and the horses with whips, grabbing at each other's saddles and reigns. Seabiscuit won by a nose in 1:49, setting a new track record by four seconds. Spec Richardson immediately filed a protest against Woolf, who in turn claimed Richardson began the melee by grabbing his whip hand. Track stewards launched an inquiry, observing that Seabiscuit had taken severe punishment, showing welts on his neck and flank and breathing heavily, while Ligaroti, as one might expect of a Crosby horse, "appeared cool and relatively little exerted."[43] Both jockeys were suspended for the meet, with a recommendation that the California Horse Racing Board suspend them for the year. But as there was no pari-mutuel betting, the punishments could not be enforced. Dixie presented the prize money to Howard in the winner's circle. Bing graciously remarked to reporters, "It's no disgrace to be beaten by the world champion." Nationwide coverage put Del Mar on the map.

Paramount provided a punch line for all the fuss in the form of a press release with Bing's byline, in which he complains that he was "on the set one day" and had to endure a barrage of jokes about his horses. "Oh well, let the clowns laugh," he muses, "[my horses] will be winning races some day."[44] No horses or races are mentioned in the release, but Paramount's newest contract player makes an appearance. Bing laments that while driving to Lakeside, Bob Hope pointed to a decrepit nag and said, "It looks like one of your horses. It's stopped."[45] If the flacks were bent on reducing Bing to a routine of frazzled jokes, the front office seemed equally fixed on a standard recipe for film scripts. Small wonder he found more enchantment in the stables and more excitement at a tee.

23

A POCKETFUL
OF DREAMS

*I remember somebody once said that Bing would have
made a great Hamlet. I don't know what Bing had to say
about that. Oh, my gosh, he would have been scared to
death taking on Hamlet. But there was a feeling from
people that there was something much deeper about
Bing.*

— Anthony Quinn (1989)[1]

The *New York Sun* polled several personalities in 1938 for lists of
their ten favorite films. Bing's roster is individual, knowing, and surprisingly impolitic given his own predictable roles in the most capital-
oriented ("After all," says Sammy Glick, "our pictures are shipped out
in cans. We're in the canning business") of the arts.[2]

1. *The Crowd*
2. *The Birth of a Nation*
3. *The Informer*
4. *Vivacious Lady*
5. Any silent Chaplin film
6. Ditto
7. Ditto
8. *A Farewell to Arms*

9. *The Big Parade*
10. Lloyd Hamilton comedy

The list is striking in that seven of his selections are silent: Griffith's landmark *The Birth of a Nation;* King Vidor's two dramatic pinnacles, *The Crowd* and *The Big Parade;* and four comedies, three by Chaplin. Bing's lifelong love of silent comedy is apparent throughout his work, and his devotion to Chaplin in particular comes through on numerous occasions when he strikes a bowlegged pose or executes a pigeon-toed walk or some sleight of hand with a prop. The three talkies include his only ballot for a Paramount picture, Frank Borzage's pre-Code *A Farewell to Arms,* with Gary Cooper; *The Informer,* John Ford's celebrated treatment of a besotted traitor during the Irish Rebellion; and a new film, *Vivacious Lady,* George Stevens's comedy of the classes in which nightclub singer Ginger Rogers marries botanist James Stewart.

Bing's new film at the time his list appeared was *Sing You Sinners,* a determined effort to move beyond the standard Crosby persona movies that had grown increasingly similar. When William LeBaron took over as Paramount's chief of production (replacing the ill-suited Ernst Lubitsch), Adolph Zukor warned him he would have difficulty finding stories for Bing. From the beginning the studio had a firm notion of what a Crosby story entailed. Joseph Mankiewicz recalled Emanuel Cohen halting production on *Too Much Harmony* in 1933, explaining to him, "You have made one terrible mistake. You have Crosby falling in love with the girl. The public will never accept that. You must make the girl fall in love with him!"[3] A year later Charles Samuels, hired to doctor a few scripts, was instructed, "Don't forget that Crosby's love scenes are not like those of any other male star. He never makes love to the girl. She has to make love to him. Love and romance always have to sneak up on Bing when he isn't looking."[4]

Though *Pennies from Heaven* fits the template to a T, Bing was nevertheless aiming for greater variety when he and Manny Cohen produced it.[5] "I felt I had to play a different type of character, a real person," he told a reporter. "All this singing for no reason at all couldn't go on. So I went into business for myself."[6] Thirty years later he looked back on his 1930s films as a blur: "So much of what I did seems to run together. . . . A lot of those pictures were, dare I say, very similar."[7] His list of favorites show how well aware he was of the gap between Cinema and the general run of Hollywood product, particularly his own.

Returning to Paramount after *Pennies from Heaven,* in 1936, he worked for the fourth time with Frank Tuttle and for the fifth with Karl Struss, producing the blockbuster *Waikiki Wedding* — the third-highest-grossing picture of 1937. The project was chosen after two others fell through: *It Happened in Paradise,* a summer-camp musical, would have reunited him with Ida Lupino;[8] the more intriguing *Follow the Sun* would have reunited him with Burns and Allen and Norman Taurog (Paramount announced it as "made to the measure of that Crosby smash, *We're Not Dressing"*) while drawing directly on his ancestry in telling the story of a sea captain who ships from the Pacific Northwest to the Orient to start a nightclub.[9] The switch to a Hawaiian setting may have been swayed by an important recording session that summer.

To Jack Kapp, Hawaiian songs meant a standard category of music, like cowboy or Christmas songs. They represented another string for the Crosby bow, and Kapp was eager to record them. The Crosbys were planning to vacation in Hawaii in August, and Jack told him it would be a nice gesture to telegraph their arrival with a couple of appropriate tunes, "Song of the Islands" and "Aloha Oe." He hired the perfect accompanist, Dick McIntyre and His Harmony Hawaiians, a quartet with steel and acoustic guitars, ukelele, and bass. Five days after the record date, Paramount announced *Waikiki Wedding* as Bing's next picture, though the decision had not yet been finalized;[10] weeks later the studio reversed itself with an announcement that *It Happened in Paradise* was back on schedule. Yet in the end, Paramount, like Decca, succumbed to the appeal of placing a lei around Bing's neck.

If the years 1936 to 1940 were bumpy ones in Bing's movie career, with equal rations of highs and lows, they represented an important crossroads for his music. Once again his voice and attack were evolving. His newly modulated style was, as Rose Bampton discerned, more accomplished. He sang with greater economy, a more reflective approach to lyrics; he employed longer notes and balanced his expressive middle tones with polished plums from the high and low reaches of his range. The 1933 Jimmy Grier records had captured

Bing climbing peaks; now, tempered yet emotionally resolute, he was willing to survey the valleys. The voice was still round and robust, but he did not push it as hard. The nodes and attendant hoarseness had miraculously vanished, and the hollow ring that crept into his voice in the mid-1940s was not yet evident. Whether romping with his brother's jazz band or sighing of trade-wind breezes, Bing in the mid-thirties was the most quietly assured male pop singer alive.

For Bing, Hawaiian songs occupied a middle ground between cowboy songs and pop ballads, and he pursued all three idioms with unusually moody expressiveness. On Ray Noble's lovely "The Touch of Your Lips," his musing eloquence is befitting and expected. On the two comically theatrical numbers from Gershwin's *Porgy and Bess* ("I Got Plenty o' Nuttin'" and "It Ain't Necessarily So"), his interpretations are unexpectedly rueful. The most impressive of his new cowboy songs (including "We'll Rest at the End of the Trail," "A Roundup Lullaby," "Empty Saddles") was "Twilight on the Trail," a lament introduced that year by Fuzzy Knight in *The Trail of the Lonesome Pine* and sung by Bing as though it were an old western hymn. That's how it may have sounded to President Roosevelt, who declared it his favorite song after "Home on the Range"; Mrs. Roosevelt requested Bing's record for the Roosevelt Library.

Hawaiian songs combined affecting melodies and the down-home spirituality Bing found in western ballads. The glissandi of the steel guitar (guitars were always magic for him) complemented his vocal glides; the dilatory tempos exercised his handsome stalwart timbre. Yet Bing's affinity for South Seas idylls seemed clouded at the first session. The larghissimo tempo triggered a vague trembling and self-conscious use of mordents. Kapp immediately scheduled a follow-up, this time recording "South Sea Island Magic" and "Hawaiian Paradise," and the improvement is unmistakable; the mordents are natural and the high notes weighted by a robustness and subtly swinging pulse. "South Sea Island Magic," the more accomplished performance, sold decently in the period before "Pennies from Heaven" took over, dominating sales for the rest of the year. With "Hawaiian Paradise," Bing waved across the Pacific to its composer, Harry Owens, the bandleader who had auditioned him and Al Rinker at Cafe Lafayette in 1926. A professional since the age of fourteen, Owens had seemed so much more experienced back then, but he was only a year older than Bing. Now he led the band at Honolulu's Royal

Hawaiian Hotel, where Bing and Dixie would spend their first evening on the island.

On Sunday, August 30, 1936, two weeks after he returned to the studio with Dixie to record their duets, they boarded the SS *Lurline* for a five-week vacation. When the ship docked at Oahu on September 3, photographers captured Bing at breakfast and, as one reporter wrote, "shuffl[ing] his way through a jam of shrill flappers who ogled at the nonchalant swing of his 178-lb. body, the fluttering of his pale blue eyes."[11] The Crosbys had arranged to stay at a private home at Kaalawai with Lindsay Howard and his wife and other friends.

Like everyone else on the island, Owens was excited about their arrival and wondered whether Bing would remember him. His doubts were allayed that evening, when Bing strode to the bandstand and said, "Hi, Harry, is this tryout night?"[12] He asked the name of the tune the band had just played.

A couple of years earlier, Owens had written a ballad to commemorate the birth of his daughter, Leilani. When he told Bing the song was called "Sweet Leilani," Bing made a joke about not being able to pronounce it, but during the course of the evening he requested the unpronounceable title another five or six times. The following morning Bing phoned Harry to tell him he wanted the song for his next picture and asked whether he could ride over on a motorbike he had just rented. Harry was overwhelmed but ambivalent. The song was so personal to him and his family that he was disinclined to commercialize it. He asked Bing to listen to his other songs, including "Dancing Under the Stars," "Palace in Paradise," and "To You, Sweetheart, Aloha," all of which Bing eventually recorded. Undeterred, Bing proposed a characteristic solution to Owens's quandary.

For all his straightforwardness, Bing was in two areas a master of indirection. When it came to the requisite love songs in his movies, he asked Johnny Burke to avoid the phrase *I love you* in favor of roundabout metaphors (e.g., "You Don't Have to Know the Language," "Moonlight Becomes You," "Sunday, Monday or Always"). When it came to money, he devised intricate ways to be charitable without the appearance of actually giving away money. These ranged from schemes to allow Gonzaga to participate in a TV show to arranging bit work to making secret bequests. Indeed, his brother Bob resented him for years for refusing to help his band out of a bind early in his career, only to learn years later that the man who did help him was operating under Bing's instructions. According to Owens, Bing said, "I won't permit you to commercialize on 'Sweet Leilani,'" then offered to set up a trust fund that would collect all royalties for the education of Leilani and any future children Harry might have.[13] They made a test recording the next afternoon. Bing asked Harry to hum the tune so he would not miss any notes. "How fast he learned," Owens noted. "Once through and he knew it perfectly."[14]

The next few weeks were idyllic. Though besieged by fans, he swam, golfed, motorbiked, and tried surfing and motor gliding. He attended a meeting of Kamaaina Beachcombers' Hui, a sportsmen's organization dedicated to promoting swimming in the islands, and took a sampan from Honolulu to Kaunakakai, where a crowd paraded him through town to the steps of Molokai market. Deeply moved by the warmth of his reception, he sang "Hawaiian Paradise" and attempted "Na Lei O Hawaii," though he didn't know all the words. He stayed overnight on Molokai and hunted deer the next day.

Meanwhile, in Los Angeles, the film was beginning to take shape as producer Arthur Hornblow Jr. hired Don Hartman and Frank But- ler to write a script, and Eddie Sutherland (Hornblow's man on *Mis- sissippi*) to direct. Paramount renewed Bing's contract for another two years, though he had nine months remaining on the old one. Only five days earlier Bing had played his part in the negotiations by wiring columnist Sheila Graham that he might retire from the screen with the fulfillment of his present contract;[15] LeBaron thought Bing wholly capable of doing just that. Whether or not Bing was actually in contact with Hornblow, he did not inform him of "Sweet Leilani" until his return to the mainland on October 8, at which time he also displayed an expanded waistline that forced him to accept a stringent liquid diet.

Hornblow, an intelligent and cultured man in private life, was notoriously megalomaniacal on the set. Eddie Sutherland remem- bered him issuing pointless edicts, like "Crosby's got to be here at nine." "Well, Crosby can get there when he feels like it, you know," Sutherland explained. "What are you going to do, keep him after school? Crosby's a most generous man. He'll give you three months to work on a script if you're not ready, but then he'll say, 'I'm not coming in on Saturday, I want to go to the races.' You say, 'Fine,' and you shoot around him. But this man would say, 'He's got to be here Saturday.'"[16] Hornblow's response to "Sweet Leilani" was an emphatic no. Bing tried to convince him that the song had proved itself in Hawaii, and showed him a fitting spot for it in the script, to no avail. He let the matter slide — until shooting began.

Robin and Rainger, who wrote the picture's score, had been very good to Bing in the past with "Please," "Love in Bloom," and "June in January," among others. They were in no position to take umbrage at the insertion of a new song, as Rodgers and Hart did when Bing interposed "Swanee River" in *Mississippi*. Hornblow, on the other hand, remembered that tiff all too well, though he may have forgotten the positive things that came from Bing's stubbornness. For Bing, more than a song was at stake; there was the promise to Harry, and his pride in being able to recognize a winning number. After all, his previous attempts to help struggling tunesmiths had been rewarded with Carmichael's "Moonburn," Mercer's "I'm an Old Cowhand," and the score to *Pennies from Heaven*.

By the time the picture went into production in December, Hornblow had replaced Sutherland with Frank Tuttle, who was particularly enthusiastic about the challenge of creating Waikiki Beach on the Paramount lot, a feat he credited to the "ingenuity of the set designers and constructors, who built an entire Hawaiian village on one of the sound stages with an amazingly realistic sky backing."[17] Only scenic shots and a chase scene, using doubles, were photographed in Hawaii. While Tuttle busied himself staging the musical numbers, Bing behaved with customary professionalism, pleased to be surrounded by a cast of amusing friends, including Bob Burns, Martha Raye, George Barbier, and Grady Sutton, and an appealing and musical leading lady, Shirley Ross.[18] The filming was almost complete in February, when they came to the sequence where Bing thought "Sweet Leilani" belonged. He brought it up, and Hornblow refused. Bing told him, "When you change your mind, I'll be back," and left to play golf.[19] He stayed away for two days, until Hornblow relented. After they shot the scene, Bing cabled Hawaii:

DEAR HARRY, I FILMED SWEET LEILANI SEQUENCE TODAY. COME SATURDAY AM RECORDING SONG FOR DECCA. TRUST FUND DOCUMENTS IN MAIL. THINGS LOOKING UP. BETTER PLAN ON HAVING A DOZEN MORE KEIKIS. ALOHA TO ALL. BING.[20]

*   *   *

Like *Rhythm on the Range*, *Waikiki Wedding* is an elaboration of *Kraft Music Hall,* though more stylish than the earlier film. Tuttle's imaginative staging and limber camera are evident from the opening scene, a long traveling shot magnificently handled by Struss, showing a wedding ceremony and dwelling on the prettiest girls. He directed the film's primary song, "Blue Hawaii," as a duet, in which Bing recites each line of the lyric before Ross blends her voice with his, to avert the cliché of characters who are "letter perfect in the words of a song when they've never had a chance to learn them."[21] Only in Hollywood would a director aim for realism in presenting a song, when not an ounce of realism pertains anywhere else in the picture.

The plot requires Bing, playing a press agent, to romance Ross, the winner of a Miss Pineapple Princess competition, in order to dissuade her from returning to her California home and fiancé before the publicity value of her victory can be fully exploited. While love sneaks up on him, he contrives to keep her busy with a fake adventure involving hostile islanders; in effect, he frames a big con, engaging numerous actors to fool his mark. The device is engaging because through much of the picture the audience is no wiser than Ross, as a preposterous story unfolds, concerning an iconic pearl and a vengeful volcano. We learn shortly before she does that we have been duped by a scheming publicist who has conjured up a script within the script. After the fraud is exposed, *Waikiki Wedding* turns shamelessly routine: the leading lady must choose between her society fiancé on the mainland and a recumbent Bing on his boat.

In one scene Bing is obliged to knock out a tribal chief, played by Anthony Quinn, who recalled, "We were supposed to fight and I didn't know much about fighting in pictures. I had fought in the ring, so, I mean, a man is gonna hit me, he hits me. But Bing hit pretty hard. So I went down. I should have ducked. Then he apologized and that made us wonderful friends."[22] Quinn had been working in pictures for less than a year, mostly as an extra or a hood. *Waikiki Wedding* was his first substantial part. Because he was half Mexican and sensitive to studio discrimination, Quinn was gratified by Bing's easy tolerance:

> Bing was one of the most amazing people in the world because he had
> worked with so many minorities, and minorities were having a lot of

trouble in those days, my gosh. And Bing understood, he understood what I must have been going through and he was most helpful to me, his whole attitude. I always loved him because of the way he treated [people]. There was a shoeshine man at the entrance to the Paramount gate named Oscar. And Bing was one of his favorites because Bing came in and, I mean, he could talk the talk and he was wonderful at it. And Oscar and he would laugh, but there was nothing about Bing that was patronizing. He had worked with Louis and all the great musicians of the time and was used to being with blacks and Mexicans and all kinds of minorities. So he was actually wonderful to work with and made you at ease, put me at my ease.[23]

For all its polish, *Waikiki Wedding* is a minor period piece, dated by low humor — instead of *Rhythm on the Range*'s bull, the characters have to contend with Burns's pet pig — and the change-ups between patter and music. Bing holds the fort as the nominal star, looking youthful and earnest, coming to the fore chiefly in song. The real stars are Struss's depth-of-field photography and the songs, primarily "Blue Hawaii," an ideal vehicle for Bing; the first two phrases are confined to a range of four notes near middle C, the third leaps upward an octave, where the song remains until it descends for the second eight bars, and the release is lovely. "In a Little Hula Heaven" (an affable jump tune that Bing recorded swingingly with Jimmy Dorsey) and "Sweet Is the Word for You" are also effective. The one ineptly staged song is "Sweet Leilani," obscured by the squealing of the pig, which at the initial showing in Honolulu so affronted the patrons and composer that the print was angrily shipped back to Hollywood.

But, as Bing soon wired Owens: HEAR YE, HEAR YE! WAIKIKI WEDDING, AFTER FLOPEROO IN HAWAII, IS SMASH HIT ALL OVER THE USA. ALSO MY DECCA RECORD OF SWEET LEILANI JUST TOPPED ONE MILLION PLATTERS. SO SMILE MAN.[24] The reviews were modestly positive and generally out of touch. *Variety* prophesied, "None of the songs here will hit the top performance brackets," though it thought them deserving of "a minor play on the air."[25] *Time* dismissed the "pseudo-Hawaiian" ditties but considered the picture a "mild pleasantry," singling out for praise the pig, who "steals the show by oinking at suitable moments."[26] The *New York Times* found it "friendly, inoffensive, reasonably diverting."[27] *Melody Maker*, in England, huffed, "If this is the best that Paramount can do with Crosby, then I seriously suggest that they loan him permanently to Columbia — the firm which made such a success of *Pennies from Heaven*."[28]

The public loved *Waikiki Wedding* — *Variety* declared it socko everywhere, including Europe. In a season when theaters scrambled for patrons, Bing once again filled the coffers, eliciting trade-paper headlines like CLEVELAND PEACEFUL EXCEPT FOR CROSBY'S WHAM $21,500.[29] In three weeks it broke the Los Angeles Paramount's all-time house record, and then went on to ring up bigger numbers at its New York adjunct (on a bill with the Eddy Duchin band). The picture's domestic gross exceeded $1.5 million, ranking it third in 1937, after two MGM releases, *Maytime* and *The Good Earth*.[30] The one other top-ten entry from Paramount was a Gary Cooper vehicle, *The Plainsman*. Beyond that, news at the studio was bleak. Two of its matchless legends departed, diminished by the lilliputians in the Hays Office: Paramount canceled Mae West; Marlene Dietrich left in dismay. Ordered to reduce his budget of $30 million by a sixth, William LeBaron informed Zukor and the powers in New York that he preferred to step down and produce independently (an action he postponed until 1941).

When it came to musicals, each film factory claimed a discrete turf and stuck to it. MGM, self-consciously tony in every regard, had its *Broadway Melody* series, milking the Great White Way for ambience and source material. Warner Bros. sent its mugs and broads frolicking in the *Gold Diggers* movies, each climaxing with an erotic kaleidoscope of bare limbs. RKO had it both ways with Fred and Ginger, working-class hoofers who looked rich and stayed in the nicest places. Paramount alone made a complete reversal. Hollywood's most sophisticated establishment in the pre-Code era found its salvation in *Big Broadcasts* and was now content to advertise itself as the "radio recruitment studio" while boasting of profits from rubbish like *Mountain Music*, a hee-haw farce with Bob Burns and Martha Raye. Paramount's one sure attraction, money in the bank, was Crosby. In the long view of Bing's career, however, the popularity of *Waikiki Wedding* proved less significant than his handling of its songs.

Bing had not sung for Decca in six months, not since the duets with Dixie shortly before their vacation. In February 1937, accompanied by Lani McIntyre (Dick's brother) and His Hawaiians, he recorded

"Blue Hawaii" and "Sweet Leilani." The former, beginning with an attention-jolting steel-guitar glissando and superbly executed throughout, was a hit. The song endured for decades as a minor standard, recorded by Frank Sinatra, Ray Charles, and Elvis Presley, who made a movie of that name. "Sweet Leilani" did not fare as well in the long run. But it was a phenomenon in its day, commercially one of the most significant, and musically one of the most unusual, releases in the history of American popular music.

What did listeners think, in the spring of 1937, hearing "Sweet Leilani" on the radio? A plush glissando sets the stage for a high Hawaiian tenor — Lani McIntyre — singing a chorus backed by a humming ensemble and a contralto's obbligato. If forewarned by an announcer that this was the new Crosby record, did people wonder if he had joined the castrati? And if not forewarned, how surprised must they have been when, seventy-seven seconds into a three-minute side, the exotic vocalist is suddenly supplanted by the reassuring virility of Bing's dulcet baritone? It was a nervy arrangement, to say the least. Yet the switch from McIntryre to Bing underscored the latter's homey familiarity in a new and categorical way. It was like wandering through a strange city and suddenly meeting an old friend. Bing's reading is felt and faultless, from the ascending glide of the title phrase to the comely embellishment on the repeat of "heavenly flower" to the drawn-out closing "dream."

"Sweet Leilani" dominated sales charts for an astonishing six months, more than a third of that period in the number one spot (it was pushed aside briefly by another Bing Crosby record, "Too Marvelous for Words"). As the best-selling American disc in eight years, since the stock market crash, it was acclaimed as a turning point for the recording industry and a good sign for the national economy. That the record also boosted movie queues gave Hollywood reason to cheer as well.

The song was nominated for an Academy Award, in competition with the evergreens "That Old Feeling" and "They Can't Take That Away from Me" (a Gershwin song favored to win) and the deciduous "Whispers in the Dark" and "Remember Me?" (by Harry Warren and Al Dubin). The last probably would not have been nominated had it not also generated an enormous and delightfully whimsical Crosby hit, as arranged by John Scott Trotter to combine musty polka rhythms and a Bixian trumpet solo (by Andy Secrest), which Bing echoes in his jazzy finish.

The overwhelming popularity of "Sweet Leilani" vindicated Bing's faith in it, not only proving once again his interpretive powers but also trumping Hornblow, who never produced another Crosby picture. But the song's epochal success cannot disguise its essential triteness. The first of Bing's twenty-one gold discs is a quintessential bauble of the 1930s, a seductively nostalgic record that helped define its era — it helped trigger a craze for anything Polynesian — and yet echoes eerily in ours. The gold record and Oscar nomination were small potatoes compared with this statistic: it sold 54 million units of sheet music.[31]

Hawaii had been promoting itself as paradise in the Pacific for half a century, landing squarely on America's pop-culture map in 1915 when San Francisco's Pan-Pacific Exhibition introduced hula girls, steel guitars, and ukeleles. That year the mainland was swaying to songs like "On the Beach at Waikiki," "Song of the Islands," and "Hello, Hawaii, How Are You?" Bing heard them on the family record player, and the following summer he watched Jolson light up Spokane's Auditorium with "Yaaka Hula Hickey Dula." A fancy for ukeleles swept the nation in the 1920s. Yet it was not until the mid-1930s, when Hawaii started its own recording industry and began broadcasting shortwave, that kindling was provided for an all-out Hawaiian vogue. Bing lit the match in the spring of 1937.

Within months Hollywood resembled a Hawaiian theme park, as restaurants and nightclubs replaced 1920s jungle decor with bamboo, parrots, and waterfalls; floor shows complete with hula and/or sword dancers; and generic Cantonese cuisine masquerading as luau fixings. If you could not follow the Hollywood big shots to the Hawaiian surf for deductible holidays (they claimed to be scouting locations), you could hobnob at Luana, King's Tropical Inn, Hula Hut, Club Hawaii, Zamboanga, Seven Seas, and Hawaiian Paradise, among others. It did not last long. With the advent of the conga line, the bamboo was scrapped for gaucho chic and the steadfast pu-pu platter modified to accommodate coconut shrimp. But Hawaii was now regarded less as a distant territory than as a tropical extension of the United States, and by the mid-1940s the issue of statehood (unrealized until 1959) was on the table.

Hawaiian songs, mostly ersatz, were now a staple of American popular music. They answered the need for pure escapism, conjuring a world without breadlines, dust bowls, or the rumble of war while melding with the simple melodicism of country-and-western music — a connection manifested in the frisson of gliding steel guitars. Legend attributes the birth of that instrument to Joseph Kekuku, who got the idea in or about 1909, when he accidentally dropped a comb that slid across the frets of his guitar. Steel guitars were occasionally heard in country-music records in the 1920s, a mellower version of the slide techniques already familiar in the work of such black guitar innovators as gospel singer Blind Willie Johnson and bluesman Charley Patton. After Bob Wills featured Leon McAuliffe on "Steel Guitar Rag" in 1936, they were everywhere in country music, virtually plaiting the two styles as one, as in Roy Acuff's 1937 "Steel Guitar Chimes," an adaptation of "Maui Chimes."

Bing recorded more than forty Hawaiian or Hawaiian-style songs and arrangements, and several of those performances are sublime, notably those from 1939 and 1940, including "My Isle of Golden Dreams," which he singled out as a personal favorite ("I think I sounded fairly tolerable in that record"),[32] "Aloha Kuu Ipo Aloha" (words by Dick McIntyre, his most frequent Hawaiian accompanist), and a definitive adaptation of "Where the Blue of the Night," backed by the Paradise Island Trio. One of his most evocative records of 1937 connects Hawaii, country, and jazz in the context of a ballad that might have been written in the days of Carrie Jacobs Bond. Lani McIntyre composed "The One Rose," but Bing recorded it with a Victor Young ensemble (violins and harp, no guitars), producing a sui generis lament that breaches the generic boundaries. However much he disliked singing the phrase *I love you,* he could make of it a powerful cri de couer; reprising the line "Each night through love land," he evinces his flair for embellishment with Armstrongian finesse. In "The One Rose," Bing achieved the universality Jack Kapp envisioned.

At the March 1938 Academy Awards ceremony at the Biltmore Hotel, which Bing typically declined to attend (Bob Burns emceed, and Bob Hope made his Oscar night debut), Jimmy Grier conducted the nominated songs and confidently predicted the Gershwins would triumph. The trophy, however, went to Harry Owens, who accepted it with a short speech giving full credit to Bing. No one at the time seemed to find it ironic or farcical that Owens was handed the statuette by a gracious Irving Berlin. The relatively unknown Owens was the first songwriter to win as composer and lyricist — a distinction he held until 1943, when the fifty-five-year-old Berlin was at long last honored for the ultimate Crosby megahit, "White Christmas."

In the months leading up to Oscar night, Bing instigated contracts for Owens at Paramount and Decca; made his dramatic radio debut (opposite Joan Blondell) in an adaptation of *She Loves Me Not* for CBS's *Lux Radio Theater*, receiving rave notices; and completed two new pictures, filmed in the summer and autumn of 1937.

Double or Nothing stuck to the formula, with a recurring Depression twist. This time the four principals are brought together by a millionaire's will. The deceased has instructed his lawyers to drop twenty-five billfolds around the city containing $100 and the law firm's address. Every honest soul who returns the money is given $5,000 and the chance to participate in a competition. The first to legitimately double the money within thirty days wins the estate. Naturally, contemptuous heirs are on hand to foil their attempts, and naturally the most insidious of the heirs has an attractive daughter. The people who return the billfolds are played by Bing, Martha Raye, Andy Devine, and William Frawley. The romantic interest is provided by Mary Carlisle, of *College Humor,* who wore a "pale ice blue dress, perfectly beautiful," she said, that complemented Bing's eyes — "blue blue blue blue, they were gorgeous eyes."[33] The conceit was lost to black-and-white cinematography.

The stars, abetted by several specialty acts, provide an improbable number of diverting scenes in a film woodenly directed by Theodore Reed. This was his second Paramount film in a brief and negligible career, floated for a couple of years by the Henry Aldrich series (Paramount's answer to Andy Hardy). Not that Reed got much help from the quartet of credited scenarists, who probably never sat in the same room together.[34] Yet the performers are engaging, as are the songs, including three by Burke and Johnston (the *Pennies from Heaven* team) and two by Ralph Freed (Harry Barris's partner on "Little Dutch Mill") and Burton Lane, who six years before had helped Bing choose his theme song. "Smarty," the upbeat opening number, was the first of several Lane songs Bing recorded.

Sam Coslow, who helped put Martha Raye on the map with "Mr. Paganini," wrote another showstopper for her this time around, "It's On, It's Off," her character's theme song from her days in burlesque. Every time she hears it, she begins to strip. Frank Tuttle once described Maggie as a "combination of Marie Dressler and Fannie Brice. She appeals to the down-to-the-earth fans and the sophisticates."[35] Even the Hays Office approved, relieved that there was no "undue exposure,"[36] though Australian censors deleted a shot of a padlock on Raye's dress. The strip number was treated with a uranium-tone azure, the first time since the silent era that Paramount had used tinting. MGM and Fox also experimented with tints in this period, but after *The Wizard of Oz* (1939) and the rise of Technicolor, the practice was discontinued for good.

In compliance with Bing's demand not to be advertised as the "sole star," the studio top-billed him and Raye, a departure from custom, as she was not his romantic interest.[37] The reviewers were generally content, and the picture was a nationwide hit, yielding three top Crosby records: "The Moon Got in My Eyes" (a chart-topper), in which he effortlessly finesses a profusion of awkward *oo* and long-*i* diphthongs; "It's the Natural Thing to Do," with its singspiel interlude typifying Bing's *KMH* personality; and "Smarty," an insolently buoyant yet amusingly nuanced swinger. All were recorded at his first session with Trotter.

Double or Nothing is studded with personal references and jokes. The marriage of high and low that came to define *KMH* is evident as Bing swings "Smarty" in a diner while a chef bawls opera. Bing's love of silent comedy is manifest in a scene in which he sets his straw hat on fire to attract Carlisle's attention, a scene played at a leisurely tempo. As Mary's mother, Fay Holden reads *Hobo Harry's Revenge* to learn the lingo of lowlifes. Martha Raye interjects "Muddy Water" while belting "Listen My Children, And You Shall Hear." Mike Pecarovitch has a walk-on (as in *Waikiki Wedding*). Exceedingly strange vaudeville acts are interpolated. Bing's character's ambition is to open a nightclub, for which he hires a Singband — an all-girl choir dressed in tight black-satin dresses, scatting melodies conducted by Harry Barris (the first of his many bit parts in Crosby films). When Bing and Raye do their own scat number, Harry joins in for a few measures, closing with a Rhythm Boys *hahh!*

Of the singers who prerecorded the Singband tracks — gypsies who worked at all the studios — only a few were chosen to actually appear on camera, among them Trudy Erwin: "We sang on risers in this nightclub set, and we were there for days and days — you know how those things go. I was taking a rest on a little cot that was beside the set, and all of a sudden something was hitting me and I looked up and it was Bing throwing spit wads at me. That's when I first met him."[38] Within two years Trudy became a fixture on *KMH*, first as a member of the Music Maids, then as a single. "He was always completely relaxed — you'd never know he was acting. He always seemed the same to me. Singing was the same way, so natural and a wonderful ear."[39]

A private joke between Bing and Carlisle surfaces in dialogue leading into "It's the Natural Thing to Do." She asks him, "How's for a rousing game of backgammon?" Bing ad-libs, "Well, jacks is really my racket, but I'll pitch in with you." On *College Humor* Mary grew accustomed to Bing doing his job and leaving the set to pursue other interests. During *Double or Nothing* he casually asked if she played backgammon. "He was all gung ho for playing and on the set all the time," she recalled. "There were several years in between the first picture and the next and he had grown up, shall we say. But he hadn't changed a bit. He was very nonchalant about everything. He always knew his lines, but it wasn't like he was playing a part or acting. He was just there and he did it. He was delightful, never upstaged anyone, though he must have known the tricks of the trade — like you step back a bit and get your face in and everyone has to look at you. Bing was not like that. He was very generous and never tried to hog anything. He knew the tricks, but it wasn't his style."[40]

If he didn't compete for the camera, he struggled mightily to hold his own against Mary in their backgammon tournament. "It was a rage then," she said of the game, "and he wanted to learn it. He asked if I had a board and I said yes and he said, 'Bring it tomorrow.' We started to play and he said, 'Let's see, what'll we play for?' I said, 'Bing, you don't even know how to play the game, now why would you play for money?' And he said, 'Well, it's more fun like that.' We played through the whole picture and I kept winning and winning and winning. He never went to his dressing room like he used to — it was always, 'Get the board, come on, let's play.' When we finished the picture, he owed me a good bit of money, a fair amount in those days."[41] Reluctant to pay up, he persuaded her to play double or nothing until he was in the hole for $1,200. He promised to send a check but did not. Instead, he arranged for Mary, who was under contract to the Bing Crosby, Inc., talent agency, to star in *Doctor Rhythm,* which went into production a few months after *Double or Nothing* wrapped.

> Bing called and he said, "We're gonna do it together again," and I said, "Oh, I'm so pleased." I said, "You know, I bet I know why you want me in the picture." He said, "Why?" I said, "I bet you're gonna try and get your money back." And I want to tell you, we played. And Frank Tuttle was the director and they have pictures of us on the set, you know, with the board between us and playing away, with Frank looking on. And I kept winning and winning, and finally it was about two weeks before the picture finished and he said, "Why don't we play a really good big game?" And I said, "What do you mean by big?" And he gave me a figure. I said, "Why, Bing you're out of your mind. I don't play for that kind of money." He said, "Whose money are you playing with?" I said, "Oh, yeah. All right." So we started with this figure and it was an automatic double game. We both threw doubles. Then he was doing well, so he doubled it again. And then I thought I could beat him, so I doubled it again. So it was lot of money. And do you know that he won that game? We never played again.[42]

Mary concluded, "He didn't want to lose. He finally got the money back, he didn't have to pay me, and he didn't want to play again." One consequence of the time Bing and Mary spent together on the set was the rumor of an affair. Carlisle adamantly denied a romance, conceding that "there was so much gossip, it was unbelievable." She thought it was fueled because she accompanied Bing to Del Mar and to Spokane as part of the *KMH* troupe when he received his degree, though her mother chaperoned her on those occasions. "I bought a mink coat on one picture and people said, 'Oh, Bing bought the mink coat,' which is why I don't believe anything I read anymore." Yet the gossip never made the papers. "You have to remember, Louella Parsons was a good friend because I was a good friend of the Hearsts, and I would be up at the beach house, the ranch, San Simeon. So Louella is not going to print anything that isn't nice about me. And if she heard something, she'd say, 'Mary, what is this about a coat?' And

I'd say, 'Don't you believe it, I'll show you the check I paid for it,' you know, and she'd say, 'Okay, honey,' and that was it. They controlled everything in the press."[43]

The Hearst Editors' Radio Poll voted *Kraft Music Hall* best musical program and Bing the best male vocalist for 1937. He also reappeared on the Quigley box-office poll for the second time, ranking after Shirley Temple, Clark Gable, and Robert Taylor.

Bing started 1938 by completing *Doctor Rhythm,* arguably the most peculiar picture he ever made. Though routine enough in plot and variety-show diversions, it was a more personal project than its immediate predecessors. What began as a hip, funny, and stylish filmmaking party for old friends was derailed by accidents, infighting, and a capitulation to the sensibilities of southern exhibitors at the expense of Louis Armstrong. The film survives in a blundered post-release print as a fragmentary curiosity. *Doctor Rhythm* was Bing's second independent venture with Manny Cohen's Major Pictures, only this time there was no bidding for distribution. Paramount would release it under the rubric "Adolph Zukor Presents an Emanuel Cohen Production."

The comity suggested by the joint billing was entirely cosmetic. Zukor had disdained Cohen for years, ever since he had run the studio and signed Bing, Mae West, and Gary Cooper to personal contracts. He now saw the opportunity for a showdown. That was Zukor's way. A smiling cobra who bided his time before striking, he had taken control of Paramount twenty years earlier by taking note of the weaknesses of its founder, W. W. Hodkinson, and then using them to turn the board against him. With *Doctor Rhythm,* he found a way to rid himself of Cohen, whose name would never appear on another feature film. Executive machinations were of no concern to Bing, however, as he embarked on the venture, surrounding himself with friends and trusted colleagues.

Frank Tuttle was back, working for the first time with cinematographer Charles Lang, who was shooting his fourth Crosby picture. Tuttle credited Lang with breaking him of his penchant for arty foreground compositions that obscured the background action. Herb Polesie hired on as associate producer. John Scott Trotter wrote arrangements for a score supervised by Georgie Stoll. A new team was configured to write songs, as Johnny Burke joined James Monaco, a veteran composer recently signed to the studio. In his glory years Monaco had written such enduring ditties as "Row, Row, Row" for *Ziegfeld Follies of 1912,* "You Made Me Love You" for Al Jolson, and "Crazy People" for the Boswell Sisters, but his career had been in eclipse for several years. Jo Swerling and Richard Connell wrote the script, freely adapted from O. Henry's uninspired story "The Badge of Policeman O'Roon."

As usual, Bing was billed as part of a starring quartet, along with his backgammon adversary Mary Carlisle, fellow horse breeder Andy Devine, and — in a particular coup and the primary motivation for the entire project — Beatrice Lillie.[44] Bing had admired the outlandish Canadian-born comedienne ever since he saw her in *Charlot's Revue* in 1926. In the intervening years she had become the darling of the English stage, playing Shaw and Coward, though best known for turns in comic revues that earned her the accolade "the funniest woman on earth."[45] Yet her humor was hardly heartland material, and after a dismal vehicle in the early days of sound, she had been ignored by the film studios.

Wearing her hair in a mannish bob and trilling double entendres while gesticulating with a long cigarette holder, Bea Lillie combined wordplay, gender confusion, upper-crust parody, and spry physicality for a result that convulsed some and confused others. For her first picture in eight years (and the only suitable opportunity she would ever have in Hollywood), she was promised a major production number in addition to one of her trademark numbers, Rodgers and Hart's "There's Rhythm in This Heart of Mine," and the chance to revive her famous sketch from *At Home Abroad,* in which she orders "a dozen double damask dinner napkins."[46] Lillie arrived in Los Angeles in late September, appeared on *Kraft Music Hall,* and posed for *Doctor Rhythm* publicity photos with a horse, after which she thanked the photographer and his assistant and then turned to the horse and said, "Thank you, too, you walleyed son of a bitch."[47]

Louis Armstrong was also signed. After *Pennies from Heaven* he had appeared for Paramount in the Jack Benny comedy *Artists & Models* and in Manny Cohen's unsuccessful Mae West film, *Every Day's a Holiday.* Now he was back with Bing, purportedly in a more ambitious role, with two musical numbers and dialogue scenes, generating much publicity. Joe Glaser, Armstrong's manager, told the *Chicago Defender* (a black paper) that Louis would have "an opportunity to work throughout the picture in many scenes with Bing Crosby,"[48] enabling him to "surpass all of his acting in previous films."[49] That was in September. By October, when the picture went into production, Louis's role had been greatly reduced; though he worked two weeks (a glossy still of him and Bing was widely published), he was now limited to one production number, the climactic performance at a benefit for the police department, described with appalling insensitivity in the Paramount press book:

> The number opens with what seems to be a symphony orchestra in silhouette. Symphonic music swells from the screen. The number ends, the leader turns, bows and leans wearily against a pillar. Then as the light comes up we see that the musicians aren't a symphony orchestra at all, but a hot negro dance band, and the leader no Toscanini in black full dress, but a chubby darkie in a dress suit of silver cloth. He stands there dreamily until someone toots an impatient note at him from the rear, then he bestirs himself to reality, sighs, raises his trumpet and goes into "The Trumpet Player's Lament," which begins,
>> "I wish that I could play like José Iturbi,
>>> Instead of tootin' notes into a derby . . ."
> The disconsolate one is Louis Armstrong.[50]

The prevalent treatment of black performers in Hollywood musicals involved isolating their numbers so they could be snipped out when the pictures were distributed in the South. Despite all the publicity attending Armstrong's participation and the prominence accorded him in billing and press materials, that option became the fallback remedy for *Doctor Rhythm* — especially after it was understood that Tuttle had shot Louis in front of a racially integrated ensemble. Although MGM presented the mixed Benny Goodman quartet in *Hollywood Hotel* the year *Doctor Rhythm* was filmed, Tuttle's decision may have been viewed by the brass as a provocation; the only promotional stills of the sequence show Louis surrounded by black musicians.

Certainly, Zukor had the southern market on his mind after the brouhaha caused by Louis's performance in *Artists & Models*. Atlanta's *The Georgian* protested, "Martha Raye, thinly burnt-corked, does a Harlem specialty with a fat Negro trumpeter and a hundred other Negroes. It is coarse to the point of vulgarity. I have no objection to Negroes on the screen. I like them from Bill Robinson down the line. Their stuff is usually good. But I don't like mixing white folk — and especially a white girl — in their acts."[51] The managing editor of the *Shreveport Journal* personally wrote Zukor to warn him that any attempt to depict Negroes and whites "in social equality" was offensive and might generate repercussions.[52]

But that issue could wait; there were more pressing backstage problems, ranging from the ludicrous to the lunatic. Bing offered a small part to his recently acquitted golf friend, John Montague, arguing, "I knew he'd win out, he comes back here with clean hands and can start over again."[53] The Hays Office convened a meeting and flaunted its power in barring him from the film. Bing backed off. Then a problem arose with the title. The working title was that of O. Henry's story, but as the cameras started to roll, something snappier was sought, like *Swing Along Ladies* or *Come Along Lady.* One executive proposed *Doctor Rhythm,* to exploit the "reams of publicity printed about Crosby's doctorate from Gonzaga University."[54] Knowing Gonzaga might take umbrage, Larry telegrammed Father Sharp to tell him of the suggestion. As Sharp was out of town, the president, Leo J. Robinson, opened the wire and misread the title as *Doctor of Rhythm.* He wrote Larry, thanking him for directing the matter to the school's attention, and asked that the degree "not be referred to in any light manner." He was primarily irked by a radio burlesque on Fred Allen's *Town Hall Tonight* in which an actor portraying Robinson — "a cheap and undesirable caricature" — asked Bing for a job in the movies.[55]

Larry advised Cohen that Bing would not precipitate a clash with Gonzaga, and the studio relented, not knowing that Bing had taken the matter in hand with authoritative diplomacy, writing Father Robinson, "Larry has just shown me your letter of recent date and I am sorry that the undignified reference to the presentation of the degree was made on the *Town Hall Tonight* radio program. This is the type of thing that they generally do on their show. . . . I don't think there will be anything more of this nature, however. At least I hope not, as the ceremony and the honor the degree stands for is much too important to me to be either caricatured or referred to in the spirit of levity on the radio or in the newspapers." Concerning the title, he pointed out that it was *Doctor Rhythm,* a "substantial difference" from *Doctor of Rhythm,* implying no "connection with the ceremony at Gonzaga as the character I play in the picture is a doctor, a general practitioner in New York." He noted that the title was not finalized and "if we can think of anything better we will make the change."[56] That would not be necessary.

Bing's finesse was of no use a couple of weeks later, when Tuttle was directing a scene set in the Central Park Zoo in which Andy Devine's inebriated character frees the animals, including a cage full of monkeys. A net had been draped over the soundstage, but as the actor opened the latch, a lot of monkeys — 150 according to a newspaper account, 300 according to a Paramount press release, 350 according to Bing's autobiography — broke out, ripping the net apart and escaping. Four hysterical hours later forty of the monkeys had been seized; the rest toured Los Angeles, many of them swarming through trees in the district of Belmont High School. Cohen offered students a one-dollar bounty per head for every monkey captured. Monkey sightings were reported for weeks.

The studio got better publicity when Bing challenged Bob Hope to a round of golf. Hope was about to film *The Big Broadcast of 1938,* the picture in which he and Shirley Ross sing "Thanks for the Memory," so the outing bolstered two pictures. On the first hole only, for the benefit of press photographers, Ross caddied for Bob and Mary Carlisle for Bing. The loser was supposed to work as a stand-in for a day on the winner's picture. Bing won handily, though no one knows if Bob spent a day baking under the lights on the *Doctor Rhythm* set.[57]

The fun and games turned treacherous by late January 1938, after principal shooting ended, when the film was assessed at $350,000 over its $800,000 budget. Various technical problems were blamed, as well as Cohen's desire to give greater prominence to Bea Lillie. Zukor charged in, demanding control. Cohen's only leverage was his possession of the script and cutting print, and he withheld them. Paramount seized the negative, created its own print, and tried unsuccessfully to get Tuttle to supervise the editing. Why Tuttle refused is not clear, as he omits the episode from his unpublished memoir, though he writes at length of what a delightful experience the film was for him and Bing: he describes working with Bea Lillie as "one of the biggest kicks of our careers."[58] The studio assigned Herb Polesie the impossible task of cutting the film with no more than, as *Variety* noted, "his own conception of what the playwright had in mind."[59]

Emanuel Cohen was a tiny (under five feet) tin-pot Napoleon who became head of production in Paramount's darkest days, 1932, making numerous enemies as he bullied artists and displaced such industry stalwarts as B. P. Schulberg and Jesse Lasky. After his own fall some thought he was a model for the eponymous double-crosser in *What Makes Sammy Run?* by B. P.'s son, Budd, who denied it. Herman Mankiewicz said Cohen's only virtue was his diminutive size: "You don't have to see the sonofabitch — unless you look under the desk."[60] Yet in the early 1930s, when Paramount's value plummeted and Zukor (unable to repurchase stock he borrowed to acquire a chain of theaters) declared bankruptcy, ham-handed Manny was credited with keeping the studio afloat. He encouraged adult features like *A Farewell to Arms* and the sex farces of Mae West and Carole Lombard and launched the unexpectedly nimble crooner, Crosby. Now it was over for him. In exchange for a settlement of $400,000, he turned over all materials relating to *Doctor Rhythm* and relinquished claims to the nine pictures he made for distribution by Paramount, as well as the lease to his studio property. He was said to be planning productions with Gary Cooper and Mae West, but they never materialized.

Tuttle credited Polesie as "a contributor to the success of *Doctor Rhythm . . .* as adviser on story construction and picture planning," but others also had input on the post-production edit.[61] Acting on Zukor's orders to revise the footage to evenly balance Bing and Bea, LeBaron hired producer George M. Arthur to supervise, committing $150,000 for new scenes pending the response to a sneak preview. How much work was done is not known; but when the completed film was officially previewed several weeks later at the Los Angeles Paramount, it ran eighty minutes and there was no sign of Louis Armstrong. None of the remarkably favorable reviews noted his disappearance — except in black newspapers and England's *Melody Maker,* which raised a ruckus, reporting that the cut was made "in spite of Bing Crosby's urgent request to leave Louis in the film."[62]

Bing told the *Pittsburgh Courier,* a black paper, that cuts were made to accommodate increased footage of Bea Lillie, affecting his and Andy Devine's scenes as well as Louis's. He continued to exert pressure on Paramount, which ultimately agreed to supply a complete print with the Armstrong sequence to theaters requesting it. Only theaters in black communities did so, including the Regal in Chicago, which billed Louis as the star, and the Regent in Brooklyn. Those prints are not believed to have survived, and except for a few stills, the sequence is presumed lost. Late that summer Larry Crosby offered *Melody Maker* an explanation, denying "racial or professional jealousy" and repeating the need to give more footage to Beatrice Lillie.[63]

In truth, the film is so dizzy with specialty numbers, mistaken-identity gambits, and chases that Louis's number might very well have slowed the proceedings. Besides, his featured number, "The Trumpet Player's Lament," which Armstrong recorded for Jack Kapp at the same session that produced two of his masterpieces ("Struttin' with Some Barbecue" and "Jubilee"), was unworthy of him. Trashing jazz and everything he stood for ("I wish that I could play like José Iturbi . . ."), it was perhaps better off buried. Yet in noting that "Louis appeared in front of a white [actually mixed] band in the film," Larry leaves the unmistakable impression that Zukor took to heart the warnings of southern exhibitors.[64] Larry concluded, "Bing, who is Louis' bosom pal, was dissatisfied with the results and has sworn to get Louis a big part in the next Crosby musical."[65]

Alas, that musical was far from "next." It was postponed eighteen years, until they made *High Society* at MGM (1956), though there were many collaborations on radio, a movie cameo, and a hit record ("Gone Fishin'") in the interim. Bing's feelings for Louis are captured in a story told by Joe Bushkin, the pianist who led the quartet that backed Bing on his tours in the mid-1970s.

> This will give you an insight about Bing. We went to the track to see an Australian horse called Turn Unstoned. So I always like to bet, not as a big gambler or anything, at least fifty dollars. . . . So I see the fifty-dollar window, there's three people there. I can go right there and get the goddamn ticket and tell Bing, I got you covered. But I thought, that was not a housebroken way to operate with Bing. I was very con-scious of Bing's style and I figured if he said, Put two dollars down, I was going to give him a two-dollar ticket. I had to do that. The god-damn line at the two-dollar window — this was before they had the automatic teller — was huge and I get to the thing, sweating it out,

because the horses are on the track. And I order twenty-six two-dollar tickets, fifty dollars for me, two for him. And the guy keeps punching two-dollar tickets on me and the bells rang and people in back of me are really pissed off because they can't make a bet. It was a scene. So I go back and I told Bing what I bet. He said, What? He really got uptight with me. He said, For chrissake, if you win is it going to change your style of living? I said, No, Bing. He said, But if you lose, think of all the Louis Armstrong albums you could have picked up for that money.[66]

Doctor Rhythm made money, but not the usual windfall, although the reviews were generous. *Newsweek* reported that at one preview, the laughter drowned out "substantial portions of the dialogue" while "members of press, profession and public were heard to proclaim it Bing Crosby's best picture and many took in much more territory."[67] Lillie received much of the attention for her parody of a coloratura and her routine involving dinner napkins. The movie's grosses were helped by the early release of Bing's recordings of the film's songs, which received extensive radio play, especially the cheerful "My Heart Is Taking Lessons" and the winsome "On the Sentimental Side."

A great deal was made of the opening sequence, one of the most surreal in any American film of the period. Screenwriters Swerling and Connell created it as a throwback to the René Clair and silent-movie conceits Tuttle employed in *The Big Broadcast*. A doctor (Bing), policeman (Devine), Good Humor man (Sterling Holloway), and zookeeper (Rufe Davis) meet at night at the zoo, unfurl a banner proclaiming their fifteenth annual reunion of a relay race they won at P.S. 43, gorge on food and beer, sing the school song, strip down to running suits, and re-create the race around the seal pool. In the morning Bing, boozily blissful, sings "My Heart Is Taking Lessons" to birds in the park and is overheard by Carlisle, who tosses him a coin, while Devine dives into the pool and is bitten on the seat of his pants by a seal. Except for songs and grunts, the opening eight minutes of the picture are completely silent. Paramount boasted that *Doctor Rhythm* had less dialogue "than any American film in years" and claimed to have "evolved a new method of unfolding a story."[68]

The film becomes all too conventional when the dialogue kicks in, though the plot offers a twist on the usual Crosby formula: Bing loves the girl, but the girl loves a scoundrel, until one of Bing's ballads, "This Is My Night to Dream," brings her to her senses. Despite the title, rhythm is kept to a minimum. Yet Bing holds his own with Lillie in the concert parody, "Only a Gypsy Knows," complete with a patty-cake bit and a mock ballet.[69] "Bing, who is a born athlete, leaped into the air and did a couple of entrechats," Tuttle wrote. "I believe he was prouder of this accomplishment than of winning an Academy Award for *Going My Way*."[70]

Sing You Sinners was Claude Binyon's baby. In the years since *College Humor,* he and director Wesley Ruggles had developed an enviable track record with a series of edgy screwball comedies that advanced the careers of Paramount players Claudette Colbert, Fred MacMurray, and Carole Lombard, notably *The Gilded Lily, The Bride Comes Home, I Met Him in Paris,* and *True Confessions.* As a result, Binyon worked as an equal with Ruggles, an A-list director. The younger brother of Charles Ruggles, Wesley entered the business as an actor, leaving high school to organize a minstrel troupe. Mack Sennett made him a Keystone Kop in 1914, and he soon graduated to editor and director, assisting Chaplin on his last six films for Essanay.

Ruggles and Binyon had been looking for an idea that would suit Bing, their neighbor in Toluca Lake. The writer suggested, "I'd like to do a story about Crosby as I see him at his home and as I've watched him at the racetrack."[71] The director agreed, and Binyon came up with a story about three brothers who hate to sing but have no other way to pay the bills. Like princes in a fairy tale, the eldest is solid, responsible, and hardworking, and the second is a ne'er-do-well dreamer striving for a pot of gold and unwilling to settle for anything less. (The third brother is a boy caught between the two.) Bing was slated for the role of the no-account, who earns desperately needed money and squanders it on a racehorse. William LeBaron, who hoped to find a racetrack story for him, was pleased, as was Bing, who after reading the script remarked, "I guess I can act myself."[72]

The brothers, who live with their mother in the reduced circumstances of a working-class home stomped by the Depression, are Joe, David, and Mike Beebe, and the script was initially called *The Unholy Beebes,* a title Bing admired, though Paramount figured people would not know how to pronounce it and demanded a change. For a time the brass favored *Harmony for Three.*

Bing's siblings were originally to be played by Don Ameche and Mickey Rooney, but Ameche fell out quickly and Fred MacMurray replaced him as David. Rooney remained with the project until shortly before shooting began in April 1938, when he was suddenly pulled by MGM. Ignoring Paramount's casting department, Ruggles told his assistant director, Arthur Jacobson, "Find me another Mickey Rooney and we'll start the picture."[73] It so happened that Jacobson was scheduled to attend a benefit for the Motion Picture Relief Fund at the Biltmore Hotel, emceed by Bob Hope; in addition to movie stars, a few vaudeville acts were recruited to fill out the bill, among them the O'Connor Family, with its sparkling twelve-year-old wunderkind, Donald.

Jacobson made an appointment with O'Connor. "I asked him if he could act. He said, 'If it's entertainment, I can do anything. I can sing, I can dance, I can act.'" Asked if he could ride a racehorse, Donald replied, "No, but I'll learn," and did.[74] Jacobson asked him to listen to prerecordings by Bing and Fred and harmonize with them. Within days Donald knew the script cold. On Monday morning Jacobson brought him to see Ruggles, who immediately advised Paramount to sign him. O'Connor had been on the stage since he was three days old. He had played every kind of theater and circus. When he met Bing, he felt as though he already knew him:

I would see him on the screen in between shows and, like everybody else, I always thought he was a friend of mine. So when I met Bing, he was extremely nice. Had a wonderful smile. And he never said too much to me on the movie. He was very, very patient with me. I was a very small child at twelve and I was riding this big goddamned racehorse and I was scared to death of this horse. There was one scene down at the track, an exposition scene, where I tell him I've been bribed, I've got the money and I feel awful, I'm letting the family down. It's a long scene and Bing is in front leading me on the horse and he's pumping me and at the same time reassuring me not to be worried. We get right down to the end and I blow my lines. So we turn the horse around, all the way back, and it was a cold day at Santa Anita, and we have to start again with all the crying and everything. I blow the line again. We must have done that forty times. And Bing never complained, not once. I told him, "I'm so sorry, my mind just can't get this." He said, "Don't worry about it, kid, you'll get it, we have no place to go." We had a lot of fun on that movie. He treated me like a pal.[75]

Bing later said of O'Connor, "He could sing, dance, do comedy, do anything, thoroughly accomplished, thoroughly grounded in every aspect of show business because of his many years in vaudeville."[76]

Sing You Sinners was Bing's sixteenth picture as a film star and broke the pattern of all he had previously done. Johnny Burke and Jimmy Monaco wrote three songs (a fourth was not used), of which "I've Got a Pocketful of Dreams" was hugely popular; the interpolated "Small Fry," by Hoagy Carmichael and Frank Loesser, as performed by the Beebe brothers in rustic drag, was also considered a highlight of the film. Yet strictly speaking, the picture is not really a musical, as Bing sings only one solo and all the songs emerge from the plot. For the first and only time (except when he played a priest or, late in life, character roles), Bing does not get the girl and for the first time since *The Big Broadcast,* he plays a lout, complete with a drunk scene in which he reaches his nadir by making a pass at his brother's fiancée. "Sometimes I turn into such a heel, I surprise myself," he broods as Fred MacMurray undresses him and puts him to bed. Bing tells him, "You're the kind of fella I wanna be."

For the part of Martha, MacMurray's sweetheart, Artie Jacobson recommended an inexperienced seventy-five-dollar-a-week starlet named Terry Ray. Ruggles liked her but warned that she would have to be approved by Bing, per his contract. Jacobson brought her to Stage One, where Bing was prerecording, and, as she waited outside, told him about her. Bing said if he and Ruggles selected her, that was good enough for him. "He didn't want to see her," Jacobson said.[77] Artie had known Bing for years, mostly from luncheon encounters in the commissary. "I fell in love with the guy," he said, although they had never worked together. "I can go on all afternoon and tell you about the virtues of Bing Crosby. He was a wonderful guy, but he had to like you. He wasn't the easiest guy in the world to get to know."[78] Jacobson told him, "Since you're being so nice about it, you deserve the pleasure of seeing what will happen in her eyes when you tell her that she's got the job." He brought her into the stage and said, "Bing, will you tell this little lady something? Just say these words, 'You have the job.'" Bing deadpanned, "You have the job."[79] She fainted.

After walk-ons or bits in a dozen pictures (including *Rhythm on the Range*), Terry Ray suddenly found herself a leading lady, as Ellen Drew. The studio changed her name a couple of times before settling.

Bing joked that he was so confused by the name changes, he called her Ellen Terry, after the legendary dame of the nineteenth-century English stage. In a press release issued under his name, he expresses pleasure at not having to labor for her hand: "The only break I get in the picture is that I don't get the girl — Fred gets her. And believe me that's a relief. I've made enough love scenes in the past five or six years. And I haven't got a one in *Sing You Sinners*. Whoopee! What a break!"[80]

Artie Jacobson received a break as well. The roving head of the talent department was fired for auditioning female talent in hotel rooms. When a Paramount executive learned from Ruggles how O'Connor and Drew came to be in *Sing You Sinners,* he gave Jacobson the job.

The shoot was fun for Bing, not least because his costars included some two dozen of his horses; track scenes were filmed on location at the Pomona Fairgrounds and Santa Anita. On May 2 production on the soundstage was halted as a cake was wheeled out to salute Crosby's thirty-fourth birthday. Ironically, the character he played, Joe Beebe, is identified as being Bing's real age, thirty-five. As was the case with many of his previous pictures, *Sing You Sinners* overflows with biographical allusions, the kindest of which poke fun at Bing's persona, the rest taking him to task with a severity befitting a singing sinner. In the first two shots, Ruggles and Karl Struss establish a neighborhood not unlike the one Bing knew as "the holy land." As the willful Mother Beebe and her sons march to church and sing "Shall We Gather at the River," Joe (Bing) irreverently chews gum. At dinner Mother makes it clear that Joe is her pet; since macaroni will make him fat, she cooks his favorite dish, pot roast, which his brothers detest.

Dave is engaged to Martha but uses Joe's laziness and the family's insolvency as an excuse to postpone marriage. He resents having to sing in a trio for ten dollars a night, echoing the view of the combative young men who heckled Bing long ago at Lareida's Dance Pavilion. "I'm a man, doggone it," MacMurray's Dave says, "and I want to stay one." Mike (O'Connor) similarly complains that he's being turned into a Buster Brown. Bing, more than ever, embodies a version of Harry Crosby, the optimistic dreamer who never quite measures up. Mother Beebe (Elizabeth Patterson) observes, "His father was the same way. He just drifted along without a worry in the world until you boys started coming along." Bing takes Martha to a roadside dance hall where the bandleader, Harry Barris, persuades him to get up and sing. Barris is as kinetic as ever. Bing is so cool that you can't believe no one has advised him to go to Hollywood and become a star. He works the room, singing "Don't Let That Moon Get Away," dancing with customers, playing drums with cutlery on the bar, executing a nifty before resuming his seat.

The personal references keep on coming. Chagrined after making a fool of himself over Martha, he tells his mother, "I don't fit in this town, so I'm going somewhere I can do the family some good" — Los Angeles with a hard *g*. Relocated, he bets two bucks on a horse named Toluca. In a beautifully executed routine with actor Tom Dugan as a tout, Bing captures the madness of gambling and winning as he trades one ticket for another, finally winning a substantial sum. He sends for the family and meets the train wearing plaids and stripes that outstrip even Bing Crosby's hallucinogenic taste. The family is appalled to learn that he has invested all his money in a horse, Uncle Gus (played by Ligaroti and others). "Whatever you do, don't worry," he tells his mother, who is obliged to pay the cab fare. "Yes," she says, "I'm afraid we all know each other too well."

The study of a wastrel soon deteriorates into the familiar racetrack picture, but with a strange moral: long shots pay off better than dull jobs. The old-time revivalism of the title is nowhere echoed in the movie, but the combination of feckless optimism and family ties, bound within a veneer of realism, won over press and public. The New York *Daily News* implored Claude Binyon to devise a sequel, because the Beebes "are the sort of family, like the Joneses and the Hardys, that could continue indefinitely on the screen under Wesley Ruggles's astute direction."[81] *Time* conceded the picture was "tolerable comedy, jigging playfully from farce to melodrama like a kite with no tail," while lamenting that it was "no preachment for the typically American virtues."[82]

Bing received splendid reviews — not just for his portrayal but for the character of Joe Beebe. *Life* ran a pictorial on the fight scene, noting, "Crooner Bing Crosby abandons the romantic roles for which his stocky figure makes him unsuited and takes a comfortable, happy-go-lucky part that fits him like a glove. . . . His Joe Beebe is a model of simple, unpretentious acting."[83] Calling the picture "the funniest comedy on Broadway, including all the side streets," *New York Times* critic Bosley Crowther was inspired to offer a groaningly awkward *KMH*-style Crosby joke: "The only noteworthy difference between reality and *Sing You Sinners,* at the Paramount, is that in the movies Crosby's horse wins — an unprecedented thing which may be explained by the fact that Bing must have undoubtedly had a hand in the script."[84] To which Jimmy Durante might have exasperated, "Everybody wants to get into da act!"

But then, everyone *was* in the act. The *Times* reviewer's inclination to refer to Bing as he might to Stan or Ollie (as opposed to Mr. Cagney, Mr. Astaire, Miss Davis, et al.) implied an uncommon assumption of intimacy with the private identity of a movie star. "But you've got to know the character of Bing to appreciate the family comedy of *Sing You Sinners,*" Crowther adumbrated with a surplus of pronouns: "Bing is the type that's lovable, but that lies around reading in hammocks, or goes out and drinks too much, and come homes pie-eyed, and that propagates a new scheme for getting rich quick every weekend or so."[85] *The New Republic's* Otis Ferguson agreed: "The main thing was the character of Bing Crosby, who can sing and also be a swell feller."[86] *Life* could not distinguish between Bing on- and offscreen, even when it purported to be trying:

> To see Harry Lillis (Bing) Crosby on the Paramount lot is to set him down as the most modest and easygoing of Hollywood stars. This appearance is deceptive. For though Bing is modest, he is also one of the most enterprising actors in the film city. When his acting chores are over, he loves to hop in his bright red Cadillac, skip down 118 miles to his 120-acre ranch where he breeds and trains a stable of racehorses. . . . Between times he broadcasts weekly over the radio, turns out popular Decca records, plays the drums for pleasure, acts as adviser to a third brother's orchestra and raises his family of four boys including Twins Philip [sic] and Denis [sic].[87]

In short, when critics said that Bing plumbed new depths as an actor, they meant he was playing himself more credibly than ever before. His screen persona was not as ingenuous as Cooper's, or as manly as Gable's, or spirited as Cagney's, or funny as Grant's, but it had a matchless, overriding aplomb, a self-reliance that bordered on impertinence. It had always been there when he sang. Now it was evident when he acted. Bing retained the righteous assurance of silent-era movie clowns, vulnerable and impervious. Like Chaplin, he seemed most alone in a crowd. Small wonder Leo McCarey recognized in him the ideal movie priest. "There was a feeling from people that there was something much deeper about Bing," Anthony Quinn remembered.[88] And Donald O'Connor mused, "I think you have a tendency to dismiss someone acting so very natural. With the Stanislavsky kind of school, you try to act natural but you're acting. Bing was one of the finest natural actors who ever lived. To do that is a hell of an acting job. He studied that. The other person who was very close to that was Spencer Tracy, but Spencer was more dramatic than Bing. Bing was softer. Much softer. Came at you through the back door."[89]

Bing's revocation of Horatio Alger's school of gumption in *Sing You Sinners* represented a new turn in his persona. The ethical switch — from Hard Work, Pluck, and Ambition Conquer Adversity to Daydreamer Picks Winning Horse and Saves Family — was a fantasy designed to salve more than Depression worries. Economic burdens were now rivaled by international chaos. In the weeks surrounding the August 1938 *Sing You Sinners* premiere at Del Mar, Germany and Japan conscripted millions of reserves; Italy expelled its Jews; President Roosevelt pledged that the United States would not support Europe against the Reich; Prime Minister Chamberlain threatened war over Hitler's attack on Czechoslovakia, only to recant weeks later at Munich. Those stories vied with tales of native anxiety: on September 10, 55,000 hungry people trampled a Republican Party banquet in Pittsburgh; on October 30 Orson Welles staged a radio adaptation of *The War of the Worlds,* and hundreds of people abandoned their homes to escape martians. A year later, as Hitler invaded Poland, Dorothy would refuse to surrender on the Yellow Brick Road.

So eager were people to dream a dream of good luck and better times, they seemed "inured to hardship," as Barbara Bauer observed of the reception to *Sing You Sinners* and its "dispiriting soup kitchen and bread line atmosphere." Money or the lack of it, she wrote, was at the center of every scene: "Life has music for the Beebes only because the three brothers must sing for their supper. And there's something irredeemably pathetic about seeing a 'small fry' so heavily burdened by his family's problems."[90] Yet public and press roared at the pratfalls of the Beebes, trusting in Bing, whose existence was proof enough that hard times would pass. For a souvenir, one could bring home his ebullient recording of "I've Got a Pocketful of Dreams," number one in sales for a month and second only to Ella Fitzgerald's more clamorous fantasy "A-Tisket, A-Tasket" (also on Decca), as the year's best-selling record.

More remarkably, Bing was acknowledged as the second-highest-paid actor at any of the Hollywood studios.[91] Paramount's Claudette Colbert ranked first, at $426,944, followed by Bing, at $410,000, and freelancer Irene Dunne, at $405,222. They were the only three to top $400,000, though none ranked among the top ten 1938 box-office draws, according to the 1938 Quigley poll. Their incomes implied keen business sense and an autonomy that, in Bing's case, was fortified by his predominance in all media. His stature differed from the others in another way. While Paramount took great care to find suitable properties for Colbert, a Crosby property was presold by virtue of his presence alone. He was unlikely to find himself in a film he himself would have regarded as a potential classic. He was equally unlikely to find himself in a flop.

24

CAPTAIN COURAGEOUS

He never came on like a star, at least to anybody I ever saw. I've seen great singers choke, 'cause they're with the best. And whenever you did something like that, if you blew it, he blew it right behind you and blamed it on himself — you know, "Let's do another take, I fucked that up." He always sang the harmony part when he worked with somebody, always made it as easy as possible. He was a pleasure to work with.

— Gary Crosby (1991)[1]

On September 17, 1938, as *Sing You Sinners* rang box-office bells and "I've Got a Pocketful of Dreams" and "Alexander's Ragtime Band" (a duet with Connie Boswell) took turns crowning the hit parade, Bing, Dixie, and five-year-old Gary, along with Larry and his wife, Elaine, and twenty-four pieces of luggage, ascended the ramp of the SS *Monarch* for a three-week vacation in Bermuda. Bing's next film, *Paris Honeymoon,* was already in the can, shot during the summer between the two Westwood Marching and Chowder Club shows. In December he would begin preliminary work on his self-produced *East Side of Heaven.* Clearly, Bing and Dixie needed some time together. If he spread himself any thinner, nothing would be left but the stuff of caricature: pipe, hat, and golf club.

The trip, which concluded with a pleasant detour to Chicago and a reunion with baby brother Bob and Bob's new bride, proved a memorable jaunt that raised the family's spirits. Bing spent his time golfing, fishing, shopping, and shooting home movies with a 16mm camera he had acquired a couple of years earlier. The Crosbys returned with healthy tans and thirteen additional pieces of luggage containing purchases made along the way, including British military-style khaki shorts for each member of the *Kraft* team. Trotter's shorts, however, were a shiny blue; an NBC press release quoted Bing kidding him, "There just wasn't enough of this kind of khaki in Bermuda to make a pair of shorts for you."[2] Bing also brought Trotter a song to orchestrate, "Bermuda Buggy Ride," though he never recorded it.

Out shopping alone, Bing had bought a bolt of green doeskin cloth to have a suit made for his friend Edmund Lowe. "How's that for a nice green?" he asked Larry back at the cottage. "That's swell, Bing," Larry told him, "but it isn't green. It's pink, and a bad pink at that."[3] Bing returned to the store to exchange it, ordering by name rather than by sight.

The home movies Bing shot in Bermuda suggest nothing in the way of familial strain. In addition to touristy scenic pans, his camera dotes on Gary, golfing and riding in a horse-drawn cart, and captures a beach party and a deep-sea fishing expedition. During the years that Bing made most of his home movies (1936–40), he captured much of the same footage as numberless other dads in the era before camcorders and digitization replaced small movie cameras, tripods, portable screens, splicing Moviolas, noisy projectors that burned holes in the film stock, and social gatherings to display the results. That summer, in 1938, Bing edited years of footage into reels, complete with title cards that usually invoked the South: "Bing Crosby Presents Four Sons of Dixie," "The Sun Shines Bright on the Old Toluca Home," "Home on the Range, Where the Dears and Elder Folk Play." Filmed in Toluca or at Rancho Santa Fe, they display a young happy family indistinguishable from the one the public imagined.

In one sequence (Walt Disney's *Snow White* was the rage that year), the three elder boys are elaborately costumed as dwarfs while Sue Carol's daughter plays Snow White. Elsewhere, Bing can scarcely take the camera off the recently christened Linny, who lies on his stomach or reposes in a swing (the caption: "Swing It!") while his three brothers hold hands and play, turning somersaults in a sandpit, romping with the white terrier, Cremo, and other Crosby dogs, among them a matronly Saint Bernard that might have modeled for Nana in *Peter Pan*. A shot of Gary embracing the three-year-old twins is captioned "Gary Holds a Pair of Threes." Everyone looks sunny and pleased, especially Gary, who accompanies Bing fishing and riding; at four, he handles himself smartly on a pony, trotting toward the camera with no adult in view. The caption reads: "Another Crosby Learns About Horses (we hope)." At five, Gary dives and swims, under the tutelage of a trainer. The boys are surrounded by animals, including a goat and chickens in the backyard, and are as comfortable with them as if they lived on a farm. Dixie is introduced with the card "Momie Has Her Moments of Popularity," but she does not show up often and when she does, she is seen in the company of servants, nurses, and friends. Her hair is dark now, her smile broad yet shy; she wears dark glasses and gloves and a suit. One reel is called "Dixie Lee Presents Stepping Out" and documents Linny as he walked for the first time, with the caption "First Steps to Freedom from Feminine Autocracy."

The most frequently photographed friend is Andy Devine, with and without his son, fishing, mugging, comparing his own stomach with the bulk of the huge fish they've landed. Richard Arlen and Pat O'Brien and their daughters show up, as well as Edmund Lowe and Henry Fonda, Dixie's friends (especially Kitty) and parents, and Bing's: Harry in cap, cardigan, and tie; Kate in sweater and skirt, lifting Gary horizontally off the ground with take-charge brass. But the truly remarkable aspect of these private idylls is the authority of Bing, who is in front of the camera more often than behind it.

Bing's physical exuberance and style were shortchanged by his Hollywood features. Everything he does in the private reels is carried off with poised expertise. He rides at Santa Anita and Del Mar, with cap and pipe; walks the Alaskan coast among dozens of walruses and sizes up the seals; swims like a seal himself and plays tennis with an energetic grace; looks up from a backgammon game or down at a croquet ball; fishes for marlin; golfs; runs in a relay and hops in a sack race; dances the hula with a dozen or so grass-skirted beauties from *Waikiki Wedding*. Whatever the activity, he is invariably in his element, and his presence of mind shines through each frame.

Wearing shorts and a rolled-up bandanna to keep the thinning locks from his eyes, he is barechested on the fishing barge and, with his paunchy midriff and fleshy hips, suggests nothing of the torso of Apollo. Yet he is obviously in great physical condition, in perpetual motion, though very cool, with a pipe or a cigar and a twinkle for the camera when it meets his eye. He is surrounded by a crew of professionals. They land dozens of fish — someone is always ready with a club to finish off the largest; the deck and hold are awash in blood. The other amateurs occasionally get help from the pros, but not Bing, who wears a harness and reels in one monster after another as if he had grown up an apprentice to Disko Troop in *Captains Courageous*. He measures one catch against himself — they are the same height — and kisses another square on the mouth. Waiting for a bite, he holds his rod in one hand and with the other elaborately conducts the crew, unknowing members of his imaginary orchestra. In Chaplin's *Limelight* the old comic Calvero says, "That's all any of us are — amateurs. We don't live long enough to be anything else." Only in that sense does Bing convey amateur status.

As hard as Bing worked in the late 1930s, he was not the absentee father he became during the war, when army shows, charity work, and guest appearances kept him traveling around the country. The movies he shot at home and in Bermuda were hardly the labors of an indifferent or dilettante parent; they capture a long, rosy interval before the dam broke. If all happy families are alike, his was an ostensible paradigm. Signs of marital discord were few and confined. Dixie's drinking was not yet oppressive. If Bing stepped out in this period, his philandering — evident during the war but little noted before — was too incidental and discreet to merit attention.[4] After eight years he and Dixie were evidently committed to each other. Two years later Bing would threaten divorce for the first (but not the last) time since Dixie had raised the issue six months after their wedding. In the interim the mortal sin came to roost among Bing's siblings; four out of six (all but Larry and Kay) risked the wrath of God and Mother Crosby to divorce and remarry.

Everett separated from Naomi in 1936, though not until April 1938 did he sue for divorce, citing her drinking. He won custody of their daughter, Mary Sue, and a year later married light-opera singer Florence George, who was twenty-three; Bing featured her a few times on *Kraft Music Hall*.[5] Much later Ted also divorced and remarried.[6] Bing's favorite sister, Mary Rose, divorced and remarried twice.[7] The first to mortgage his soul was the youngest, Bob, whose band was playing at Chicago's Congress Hotel in 1938 when he met June Kuhn, a Sarah Lawrence student on Easter vacation. His first marriage, to Marie Grounitz, had lasted nearly four years, producing a daughter; letters suggest they parted over her involvement with a woman and initially planned to separate, not divorce.[8] His marriage to June got off to a terrifying start when she climaxed an argument by stabbing him in the back. Yet to the family's astonishment, he chose not to revoke the marriage, which lasted fifty-four years, producing three boys and two girls.[9]

To a proud, resolute Catholic like Kate, these marital changes bore consequences. While Harry figured that Marie had "no one to blame but herself" and left it at that, Kate lamented Bob's fall from grace.[10] Indeed, she held that grievance against him and the rest of her apostate children all her life. In the eyes of the Catholic Church, divorce, unlike the "humanly reparable" sin of adultery, warrants damnation.[11] Kate gave her children a preview, taunting those who had fallen and threatening those who had not. Ted's son, Howard, who never knew his grandmother, recalled, "I talked to Uncle Bob, I talked to Aunt Mary Rose, I talked to Aunt Kay, and I certainly talked to my dad, and they all said they felt no love for their mother at all. They were scared of her. As children, they respected her because she commanded a lot of fear. Now I don't know how Uncle Bing or Uncle Everett or Uncle Larry felt because I never talked to them about it."[12]

Bing and Dixie were in Bermuda when Bob and June married in Spokane, on September 22. Before heading home, they stopped in Chicago to meet the bride and provide Jack Kapp with a chance to record the brothers for the first time. Bob had become a commercial entity in his own right, fronting one of the era's most distinctive bands, the sole orchestral exponent of a music close to Bing's heart, Dixieland. "I'm the only guy in the business who made it without talent," Bob once remarked.[13] The musicians in his band would not have disagreed with him. An indifferent baritone who at best sounded like Bing and at worst did not, he became a bandleader through personality, good looks, and a famous name.

*　　　*　　　*

Bob had been picking cucumbers in Washington at twenty-five cents an hour when Bing told Anson Weeks, facetiously perhaps, that he had a younger brother who could sing. Hungry for a touch of Crosby magic, Weeks wired Bob an offer of $100 a week to join his dance band (Weeks's girl singer was Dale Evans). Dad Crosby handed him the telegram, laughing, saying it had to be a joke, because Bob could not sing. "I know," Bob told him, "but anything is better than picking cucumbers."[14] He took the train to Los Angeles to borrow a tuxedo from Bing, who spent the next ten days preparing him with voice lessons. Bob crooned with Weeks and then with the Dorseys, making little professional headway.

Bob's big chance came about when established bandleader Ben Pollack began devoting more energy to romancing and building the career of his singer, Doris Robbins, than to his orchestra, which boasted some of the finest musicians in the business. When he announced a long layoff in Los Angeles, the musicians stacked Pollack's music library on his doorstep one night and drove east, eventually reorganizing in New York under the leadership of Pollack's erstwhile musical director, Gil Rodin. Rodin was a talented leader behind the scenes, which is where he wanted to stay. The musicians formed a cooperative in 1935 and took their idea for a band to Rockwell-O'Keefe. Benny Goodman had just ushered in a new era at the Palomar Ballroom in Los Angeles, and Cork O'Keefe was intrigued by the idea of a collective in which the musicians, the leader, and his office held shares. Who did they have in mind as a leader? Rodin's men wanted the great trombonist and singer Jack Teagarden, but Paul Whiteman had him bound under a five-year contract. O'Keefe asked them to consider three of his clients. They thought Bob Crosby — young, pleasant, connected — the most promising. The job called for him to stand out front, smile, sing, and make introductions.

He took the opportunity seriously, especially when the Roger & Gallet perfume company offered to sponsor the band on a New York radio show. "This, of course, can either be the makings of the younger brother, or perhaps complete anhilization [sic] of the younger crooner's career," Bob wrote Ted. "Am hitting the piano every day, and running scales up and down in an effort to strengthen my voice a little and hope to show some improvement before the big program."[15] The first night he appeared with the band, Bob bought a baton. Bassist-composer Bob Haggart recalled, "He knew nothing about leading a band, knew nothing about music. He would beat off all these terrible tempos, and we'd take the baton away from him. [Drummer Ray] Bauduc and I would have to start the tempo the way we knew it was supposed to be."[16]

But the idea worked like a charm. Fans came to gawk at the new Crosby and stayed to enjoy his cordial demeanor and swinging band, which downplayed his singing in favor of stellar arrangements (by Haggart, Matty Matlock, Deane Kincaide) and solos (by Eddie Miller, Irving Fazola, Yank Lawson, Billy Butterfield, Joe Sullivan). Critic and producer Helen Oakley convinced Rodin to start a band within the band, an octet called the Bob Cats; inevitably, the tag stuck to all of Bob's musicians. Their swinging variation on the New Orleans style was received as a tonic. Duke Ellington, no less, described Crosby's Bob Cats as "a truly gut-bucket band with a strong blues influence."[17]

The jitterbugs were elated, though Bob felt they never accepted him as his own man. "They wanted to see what Bing's kid brother looked like," Haggart said, "and that was his cross to bear. His whole life he's been crying about the girls who would come up and ask, How tall is Bing? A lot of guys didn't want to work for him, but I felt a debt of gratitude because he mentioned my name, gave me all these plugs. In fact, he mentioned everybody in the band, and no other band-leader did that in those days. He wasn't much of a singer and he knew it, so he did a lot of talking."[18] Haggart, who over the years worked extensively with Bing, believed Bing was as ambivalent about Bob as the men in his band. "You know, he was never really proud of his kid brother," he observed, tracing the problem to Bob's inveterate gambling. Shortly before Bing and Dixie left for Bermuda, the orchestra drew crowds at Chicago's Blackhawk Restaurant, which harbored a bookie joint on the top floor. Bob wagered himself heavily into debt (Haggart thought $8,000), and the hoods running it issued an ultimatum. "The next thing I know, Larry and Everett came out from California to straighten the thing out. And that kept happening. Bing wasn't too fond of that."[19]

The ambivalence ran both ways. Publicly Bob often recounted the many things Bing did for him; privately he was known to grumble they were not enough. From Bob's perspective, Bing had progressed from his baby-sitter to a well-traveled entertainer, with no stops between. Eleven years and thousands of miles separated them. Maybe Bob believed he could close the gap by following in his brother's footsteps. But in the end, he conceded like many others, "I don't think I ever really knew Bing. I think Bing got frightened when he made his successful appearance, after he left the Whiteman band, at the Paramount Theater. And when he saw his name on the marquee in great big letters, he really got very frightened. And I think — I fantasize about this — that he built a cellophane bag and sealed himself inside and didn't let anyone inside because they knew he was shy and that he couldn't say no. He was an easy touch."[20]

Late in life Bob described him as "a fine man, a fine brother" and recalled how much Bing had done to establish him.[21] When Bob hit the big time, Bing presented his orchestra on *Kraft Music Hall,* introduced it at the Palomar Ballroom, and appeared as a guest on Bob's radio show. He also helped him out of financial problems and made records with him. Yet more often than not, they kept their distance.

When Bob sought management and publicity advice in 1939, Larry set him up with Barney McDevitt at Rockwell-O'Keefe. But when asked why he and Bing had never sung together, Bob could only answer, "I don't know. He never asked me. You don't argue with the Bank of America."[22] Bob never overcame a sense of hopeless competition. He explained why he agreed to front the big band: "I got sick and tired of everybody telling me, well, you don't sound as well as your brother Bing does when you sing. I figured, I'm a bandleader now and I got a better band than Bing has, because he never had one. So I topped him there."[23] Bob's most impervious fan, despite his fall from grace, was his mother, who once confided to a startled Rosemary Clooney, "You know, Bob's the real talent in the family."[24] His disengagement from Bing and his family was made evident to Rosemary at Bing's funeral when he walked over to her son, Miguel, and said, "Hi, I'm your uncle Bob." He had mistaken him for Bing's fifth son, Harry.

No feeling of competition intrudes, however, on the records Bing and Bob made that fall. The music appears to reflect their overall satisfaction with the reunion. If the incident with the bookies came up, it failed to dispel the warm feelings. Dixie instantly hit it off with June, who at nineteen (Dixie's age when she married Bing) was bewildered by her new circumstances. Bob was grateful to Dixie, and his affection for her never faltered. "She was a wonderful woman," he said, describing her as Bing's salvation.[25]

With Dixie and Gary listening in the control room, Bing recorded three numbers with the band. Two were covers of current Victor hits by bandleader Larry Clinton, "My Reverie" and "Old Folks" (Mildred Bailey covered them for Vocalion). Matty Matlock arranged "Old Folks," a new song by Willard Robison, the master of pastoral ballads, whose folklike melodies and nostalgic images influenced Hoagy Carmichael and Johnny Mercer. After a deft four-bar intro by clarinet and brasses, Bing enters brightly, in utter control of the narrative lyric, as if the consonant-heavy words and tempo changes presented no difficulties whatsoever. He floats over the rhythm like a kite on a breeze. Bing's version helped establish the song as an unlikely yet durable jazz standard, with interpretations ranging from Jack Teagarden to Charlie Parker to Miles Davis.

Bob Haggart initially arranged "My Reverie," Larry Clinton's adaptation of the Debussy theme, with an eight-bar introduction. "Jack Kapp came in and says, 'Wait a minute, we're playing "My Reverie," not "Clair de lune."'" And Bing says, 'Leave it alone, he worked all night on this thing.' And it was true. So he left it in."[26] Haggart, though, realized that eight bars at a slow tempo might kill the record, so he cut the intro in half. Bing attacks the number with authority, enlivening the tempo to rid it of any dawdling. His articulation denatures the labored rhymes, even the dreadful couplet "My dreams are as worthless as tin to me / Without you, life will never begin to be." He sings the *h* in *whirlpool* and uses his entire range, plus head tones and mordents — his timing is as natural as a heartbeat. The record was a solid hit.

But the blockbuster of the session was a new song by Mercer and Harry Warren, written for a Dick Powell movie (*Hard to Get*). "You Must Have Been a Beautiful Baby" is quintessential Bing, a rejoinder to those who thought jazz was something he relegated to his past, the kind of performance that inspired pianist Ralph Sutton to marvel: "He's right there, right on the button, man. You know — a musician. And so loose. Jesus Christ, it's unbelievable."[27]

Here he is: swinging with such poise that he lifts the whole band, but with that choirboy voice that speaks right to you even as it suggests a sleepy-eyed nonchalance. This is not a singer to commune self-consciously with his muse or to emote for the hipster musicians. His approach is disarmingly, almost nakedly, artless, yet so artful that he never shows his hand, never shows off his phrasing or his easy way of rushing or retarding a phrase, never does any of the things singers do to show you how hard they are working. He is so smooth, you may not notice the flawless diction of the rhymes *startin'* and *kindergarten* in a phrase that ends with a model mordent on the last word *(wild)*; the impeccably timed cadences of the phrase "I can see the judges' eyes as they handed you the prize"; and the neat embellishment on the reprise of "judges' eyes." Haggart's excellent arrangement puts the verse in the middle for a change of pace and shows off the ensemble and tenor saxophonist Eddie Miller in an interlude that begins with a hint of "Muskrat Ramble." The sustained chords at Bing's return have the effect of suspending the rhythm. A number one hit, "You Must Have Been a Beautiful Baby" was reckoned as one of the top sellers in a year dominated by big bands. Bing won the *Down Beat* poll as best jazz singer of 1938.

Hits aside, Bing enjoyed a state of musical grace in the late 1930s. Having pared away the most avid of his youthful mannerisms, he now personified a style beyond style. He made singing seem so easy that amateurs imagined they could sound as good as he did, an illusion that flattered Bing. In his own way, he was as much a musical populist as the self-styled people's singers, like Woody Guthrie, who disparaged Crosby as the commercial tool of a soulless industry. Many of the same people who wanted to be Guthrie around a campfire became Crosby in the shower. Nineteen thirty-eight turned out to be Bing's busiest year as a recording artist since 1928, when he was at Paul Whiteman's beck and call. In fifteen sessions he recorded forty-seven songs (as opposed to an average of thirty during the preceding decade), of which twenty-three were important hits, scoring among the year's bestsellers. As most of his other records were issued on the flip sides of hits, virtually every number made money, an average he sustained in 1939 (again forty-seven songs) and 1940 (sixty songs). In terms of quantity, his most fruitful year was 1947 (seventy-nine songs), but that was a time of spoken-word albums and a rush to stockpile material before the recording ban of 1948. For a ratio of bull's-eyes to discards, the years 1937 to 1940 were nonpareil.

In addition to Hawaiian songs and tailor-made Johnny Burke lyrics, duets became a major element in Bing's recording regimen. Even more than *Kraft Music Hall,* they emphasize his spontaneity and good humor, partly because they concentrate so much interplay in such a brief span, but largely because the interplay is conducted over musical rhythms with people Bing admired and enjoyed. One might argue that of all the manifestations of his art, duets best exemplify the real Bing.

The pop vocal duet is a peculiar art. Though obviously assisted by compatible vocal ranges, it is absolutely dependent on personal empathy. Sinatra, attempting to replicate Bing's career in his early years, tried to blend with several colleagues and almost always proved too stiff to bring it off, until he and Bing chimed in *High Society* (1956). Bing, on the other hand, was never more honestly and affably himself than in duets. He employed the format more frequently than anyone else — on records, radio, and television. Near the end of his life, he cited the *High Society* duet with Sinatra ("Well, Did You Evah?") as his favorite scene from any of his movies. Among his many other partners were Connie Boswell, Johnny Mercer, Al Jolson, Louis Armstrong, Peggy Lee, Bob Hope, Judy Garland, Fred Astaire, Jack Teagarden, Louis Jordan, Frances Langford, Jimmy Durante, Ella Fitzgerald, Lee Wiley, Gary Crosby, Mary Martin, Mel Tormé, Burl Ives, Donald O'Connor, Mildred Bailey, Perry Como, Trudy Erwin, Danny Kaye, Mitzi Gaynor, Dean Martin, Maurice Chevalier, Patty Andrews (and her sisters), and Rosemary Clooney — a particular favorite, as their vocal ranges and esprit were a perfect match.

The duet gave him a challenge, like golf, with a modified degree of competition. He was as generous to other singers as to fellow actors, and his supreme confidence relaxed and inspired them. The laughter in a Crosby duet is never scripted, while the scripted material often sounds improvised; it is generally impossible to tell just how much was planned. An illuminating example of Bing's disregard for safety nets and his ability to get another performer to share his derring-do comes from late in his career, when he recorded with Fred Astaire, an inveterate rehearser. Ken Barnes, who produced their 1975 album, recalled that Fred "treated every vocal like a choreographic routine.

He would want to know what happened here, did he hear the brass there — he was really very precise. Whereas Bing would just say, 'Well, the tempo's good, the key's fine. I'll leave it to you fellows.'"28 The week prior to the recording date, Astaire fretted in London while Bing toured Scotland's golf courses.

Barnes tried to track him down at various courses but kept missing him until he returned to London, two days before the session. Reaching him at Claridge's, he explained that Fred required six or seven hours of rehearsal. Bing laughed and said that was impossible: "I've got nineteen appointments tomorrow" (Bingspeak for eighteen holes and a drink after the game). Bing asked, "What does he want to rehearse for? Fifteen minutes in front of the piano. How sweet it is. No problem." Bing finally offered to arrive half an hour early on the morning of the session. When Ken phoned Fred to tell him the plan, there was a long silence before he erupted: "Oh, my God. I should have known. He has always been like this. I'll tell you what he is, he's irresponsible!" Ken pointed out that Bing had never let him down and was always delightful in the studio. Fred remonstrated, "Well, we all know the great Crosby can just walk in and turn it on. I can't do that. I'm not his kind of performer. I've got to be prepared."29

Fred insisted he had to rehearse with somebody, so he and Barnes went to the home of musical director Pete Moore, where Ken sang Bing's parts. Fred began feeling more confident, but he was concerned about the confusing lead sheets and asked for one that had only his lines. "Can't I have a part of my own so I know exactly what I'm doing? Why must I know what Bing's doing?" Barnes said, "Well, I think you have to. It's a duet. You guys have to interact."30 Another eruption. In Barnes's recollection, their conversation went like this:

Fred: Interact? That's another thing. Crosby's a great ad-libber, I can't ad-lib at all. He's going to destroy me. I shouldn't have done this.
Ken: Fred, I'm sure it's gonna be fun, it's gonna be like a party. We've got the band there. You'll like the songs and you'll like Bing.
Fred: I *love* Bing, he's great. But he's gonna crucify me. He's a much better ad-libber than I am. And these parts, I don't know what I'm looking at.
Ken: Well, look, it says Bing, very clearly there, and then Fred, and then both.
Fred: I know how to fix that.31

Whereupon Fred took out two colored pencils and proceeded to underline his own lines in red and Bing's in blue.

On the morning of the session, Bing arrived to run down the material with Fred, accompanied by Pete Moore on piano. As they sang, Bing looked over Fred's shoulder at the red and blue lines, then down at his own part, and kept singing. "I could see he was up to something," Barnes recalled. When they finished, Bing said, "You know, I think it would be much better if I sang these lines and you sang those. It's better for your personality, Fred." "Oh my God. Are you sure?" Fred asked. Bing reassured him. So Fred took out the pencils and scratched out the blue and replaced it with red and vice versa. They sang it again. Bing said, "No, I think it was better the way it was before." Fred said, "I can't see anything now." Ken offered a clean copy, but Fred declined, asking, "Now, Bing, are we gonna stay with those lines?"[32]

They proceeded to the studio, where the forty-three-piece orchestra awaited them, and handled the material like the pros they were, completing most numbers in two takes. Fred was so loosened up by the morning's experience that he parried every Crosby thrust with aplomb, answering each in kind. "It was just beautiful," Barnes said, "and I can tell you Fred's ad-libbing on that record was genuine." Bing made him laugh several times, cracking him up at the finish of "Pick Yourself Up," with an improvised spiel about teaching him to sing; you can hear the musicians roaring as well. "Ken, what a lovely album," Fred enthused at the end of the day. Bing invited Fred to dinner and asked him to appear on his next Christmas special, telling him, "We got on so well."[33] As to billing on the jacket, *A Couple of Song & Dance Men,* Fred overruled Barnes's inclination and insisted that Bing's name come first.

Bing's penchant for duets resounded in 1937 and 1938, when he recorded the Gallagher and Shean parody with Johnny Mercer and several numbers with Connie Boswell. "He loved Johnny Mercer," Rosemary Clooney recalled, "got along with him brilliantly. He liked Johnny's patterns of speech." Clooney explained a technique Bing used for duets, adapted from his radio work: dummy lines at rehearsal to mask the real lines. "For example, we did 'You Came a Long Way from St. Louis,' and on the verse, I say, 'You breakfast with Bardot,' and he says, 'Oh, my, she's something,' so I know he has a line there.

But when we get down to the final take, he says, 'You know, somebody ought to knit that girl a hug-me-tight,' which is a little shrug old ladies used to wear in the South. Well, I started to laugh, you know, because it was just so out of left field — a hug-me-tight for Bardot. He would do a dummy line until you were close to the take and then hit you with the one he had worked out."[34]

One of Bing's most compatible partners was Connie Boswell, who embarked on a successful twenty-five-year career as a soloist in 1935, after her sisters Martha and Vet married and left show business. Struck by poliomyelitis at three, she performed in a wheelchair rendered invisible by lighting and the drapery of her gowns; she disdained sympathy. After her death in 1976, Bing remembered her as "a dear woman, a brave woman."[35] Connie (she changed her name to Connee during the war so she would not have to dot the *i* while signing countless autographs for servicemen) played cello, piano, and saxophone, and her instrumental skills enhanced her rhythmic poise, as did her admiration for Louis and Bing, whose slurs and syncopations suited her sultry timbre. She was a singer's singer and a favorite of musicians. Ella Fitzgerald acknowledged Connie as her idol, and Harry Belafonte once called her "the most widely imitated singer of all time."[36] Bob Crosby's band accompanied her at her first solo engagement and on many of her best Decca records, evading the radar of Kapp, who tried to tone down her jazziness.

Yet it took the compound of her molasses drawl and Bing's brisk virility to secure her a couple of chart-topping hits, the winningly imaginative "Bob White" and an offhanded sprint through "Alexander's Ragtime Band." The last, backed by a raucous, swinging Victor Young band, was released with an Eddie Cantor speech asking for help to fight infantile paralysis. The performers and Decca donated the disc's royalties to the cause.

The first Boswell-Crosby encounter, "Basin Street Blues," was a gift to Connie. She dominates the number while Bing plays straight man, harmonizing or humming obbligato, never singing more than eight consecutive solo bars but blending dreamily with her on the last unison chorus. When Bing sings a trombone-style counterpoint, his deep authority makes her shine. Their comportment suggests a family affair, as they call each other by name and refer to John Scott Trotter, practically extending an invitation to the listener to join them on "the street where all the light and dark folks meet." Andy Secrest's fine trumpet solo pays homage to Louis Armstrong, incorporating figures from Louis's two celebrated recordings of Spencer Williams's tune. Bing messed up a phrase, "where welcome's free," but let it ride, an instance of his credo (expressed to Les Paul at another session) to "let them see I'm human."[37] Bing and Connie are more equal and ebullient on Johnny Mercer's "Bob White," a tantalizing confection packed with puns about birds and singing.[38] This time Connie plays it straight, and Bing turns in one of his most playful performances, indulging the staccato and vibrato called for in the lyric.

Bing's solo sessions of this period also produced gems, but sometimes you had to pan through a lot of silt to find them. The biggest risk in taming Bing was the threat of a middlebrow blandness, imposed not through songs or arrangements but coming from within Bing himself. As the all-purpose troubadour, he could no longer play the jazzman who subverts corny material with the tact of his own musical impulses, who subordinates the "what you do" to the "how you do it." Kapp didn't want that from him, and the Decca schedule, with its relentlessly diverse range of material, made such knowing detachment almost impossible to sustain. Bing had a genius for popularity. His major achievement was to plait the many threads of American music into a central style of universal appeal. But the price was exorbitant. To achieve universality, he had to dilute individuality.

Drawing from the payload Bing had helped strike a few years back with "Swanee River," Kapp returned to the nineteenth century for two classics, the abolitionist threnody "Darling Nelly Gray," and the Negro spiritual "Swing Low, Sweet Chariot." They served Jack's strategy to establish Bing as the American bard and suited his purposes in other ways: those tunes were known to millions, spoke to a nostalgic longing for the past, and were in the public domain. The songs of Stephen Foster probably never enjoyed greater popularity than in the 1930s, when they were not widely perceived as underscoring racial stereotypes. Deeply ingrained in the American memory, like fairy tales handed down through generations, they, too, were sweet, sentimental, and unprotected by copyright. Kapp revived many of them for his roster, as did producers at other companies, and the songs were recycled in numerous movie scores. His initial selections for Bing were politically astute even by the standards of half a century later.

"Darling Nelly Gray," written by Benjamin Hanby, a twenty-two-year-old white minister, four years after *Uncle Tom's Cabin* was published, similarly dramatizes southern barbarism in the form of a slave's lament for his lover who had been sold off and sent to the Georgia cotton fields. Louis Armstrong and the Mills Brothers recorded it for Decca a year before Bing, creating a richly emotional performance, tender and defiant. In Trotter's arrangement, the combination of soloist and choir is replicated by Bing and Paul Taylor's Choristers, but the result is studied and detached. The Choristers restore the darkest passage of the lyric ("the white man bound her with his chain"), omitted from the Armstrong version, and Bing sings with much elegance, especially on the verse. But the throaty warmth associated with his nodes has been replaced by a thin echo in his upper midrange, and although he counters it with frequent low-note swoops, he is too remote from the material to engage it meaningfully. In the last section of "Swing Low, Sweet Chariot," his voice softens to as low and hushed a level as he ever achieved on records, but the effect is nonetheless dated.

Still, those songs were preferable to newer creations like the nondescript "Let Me Whisper I Love You," with a Trotter arrangement that combines classical borrowings and a habanera beat, or the stupefying "When Mother Nature Sings Her Lullaby," for which Bing was backed by pipe organ — a throwback to his days at the Paramount Theater and Jesse Crawford, and no more enchanting. Yet the same session that produced "Let Me Whisper I Love You" generated a memorable version of the Edgar Sampson swing anthem "Don't Be That Way," three months after Benny Goodman opened his fabled Carnegie Hall concert with it. In place of Benny's thumping four-four, Trotter's arrangement bounces not unpleasantly over a two-beat rhythm. Bing, slow and sinuous, glides through the melody, smoothly mining the lyric for nuance: the low *way,* the drawn-out *sky,* the mordent on *me,* the jazzily enhanced "don't break my heart." Trotter provides a bona fide swing interlude, with Spike Jones's splashing cymbals setting up Secrest's solo, until Bing ends the party with a decisive "Stop it!"

He proved no less masterly on "Summertime," recorded at his first reunion with Matty Malneck, who had played so prominent a role in establishing Bing with the Paul Whiteman band. Matty's medium-slow arrangement has enough bounce to animate Bing, who inflects the descriptive, cautionary lyric for meaning, employing those bass-baritone swoops that were influencing numerous young singers in the 1930s. After the ensemble plays a one-bar unison Bixian rip in the interlude, Bing closes with a surprise reprise of the phrase "don't you cry."

"A Blues Serenade" also summoned recollections of days gone by, though the song itself was only three years old. It was written by Frank Signorelli, whose Original Memphis Five kept Bing's circle jumping in Spokane, and Mitchell Parish, who wrote the lyric to "Star Dust." The first try ended in a Crosby fluff take, which begins with a nice muted trumpet solo by Manny Klein but is otherwise stilted. The botched take might have sufficed if Bing had not veered out of tune on the coda; holding fast to the wrong pitch, he drones, "What the hell happened to me, son of a bitch," and then tells Malneck, "Let them play the melody." The blunder snapped him to attention, and the second take is far more persuasive. He floats the dreamy melody, underscoring the consonants in the phrase "one that I could kiss and cling to," and employs a long rest to syncopate the reprise.

The quintessential Crosby ballad of 1938, however, emerged from the session that produced "I've Got a Pocketful of Dreams," as well as the less memorable *Sing You Sinners* songs and a mildly engaging Robin and Rainger cowboy song ("Silver on the Sage"). "Mexicali Rose" was written by bandleader — and later California state senator — Jack Tenny, while working a border town in 1923. The piece languished until the mid-thirties, when Gene Autry sang it on records and in a movie. It was brought to Bing's attention by Carroll Carroll's secretary at a *KMH* rehearsal, when Bing could not come up with a tune. "I heard my mother humming a pretty song," she told him.[39]

Bing sang "Mexicali Rose" for four months on the air before making a record that infused it with the vivid and wistful melancholy he had used to transform so many commonplace and even trite songs ("Home on the Range," "Black Moonlight"). He made the song resonate as a quasi-western hymn for the last days of the Depression. Autry reclaimed it a year later in a movie of the same name, but in his or anyone else's hands, it was merely a sentimental love song. Bing's interpretation produced a frisson, an eerily palpable suggestion of what the times sounded and felt like. We tend to recall 1938 with the images of swing — stomping feet and flying skirts. "Mexicali Rose" renders the flip side, far from the ballrooms, where the night is black, inert, and full of longing. The force of his reading transcends the lyric and its southwestern setting.

John Trotter's clever arrangement, with its staccato wind instruments marching against a small contingent of strings, is more polka than mariachi — a neat trick either way for a waltz. Aldous Huxley observed that the waltz was originally conceived, in 1770, as a "jovial, bouncing, hoppety little tune" fit for a child's nursery, "almost completely empty of emotional content," but that by a century later it had become the very rhythm of eros, "densely saturated with amorous sentiment, languor and voluptuousness."[40] In waltzes such as "The One Rose" and "Mexicali Rose," strong emotions are retained, but despite the romantic text, eros — now the province of swinging four-four — is supplanted by chilling loneliness, relieved only by the cathartic identification between the listener and singer. Bing admired Trotter's arrangement and navigates it with confidence, holding back the sentiment like a dam. Bing is in the details: the goldfish puckering on the *b*s in "big brown eyes"; the tender head tone on *hold* followed by the barrel-chested *me* in the phrase "kiss me once again and hold me"; the contrast between the distant hollow timbre on the first syllables of *crying* and *pining,* and the satisfying mordent on the suffixes.

Bing's sides with Bob Crosby followed "Mexicali Rose" onto the hit parade in the closing weeks of the year, but his last hit of 1938 was a return to solemnity that launched a new tradition for the record business and the country. In December Kapp issued Bing's "Silent Night": not a new version, but the one he had made in 1935. Before 1938 reissues of any kind were rare and usually came out on bargain-label subsidiaries so as not to compete for consumer dollars with new product; during the past decade Victor, Brunswick, and Columbia combined enjoyed no more than six or seven reissue hits. But with the vast increase in record sales in 1938, reissues became more profitable. RCA re-released old records by Tommy Dorsey and Kay Kyser; Brunswick did the same with early sides by Raymond Scott, Louis Armstrong, and most timely of all, the Boswell Sisters — their 1935 "Alexander's Ragtime Band" rode the coattails of the duet by Bing and Connie. Jack followed the trend when he reissued Decca's first big hit, "The Music Goes 'Round and Around," and its first Christmas song, "Silent Night."

But "Silent Night" was like no other reissue, thanks to its seasonal attachment. Kapp realized that it had the makings of a national observance. Bing's holiday classic could be brought to market year after year, with dependable results. Over the next few years, the annual release of Christmas songs would become a recording-industry staple and a holiday tradition as steadfast as Christmas trees, fruitcakes, and Dickens. Where once Americans had celebrated with carols, hymns, and the *Messiah*, they would now grow accustomed to hearing — and buying by the millions — pop-record perennials, first Bing's "Silent Night" and (as of 1942) "White Christmas," and then a spate of new songs conceived to exploit the demand, from Nat "King" Cole's "The Christmas Song" and Gene Autry's "Rudolph the Red-Nosed Reindeer" to Harry Simeone's "The Little Drummer Boy" and Bobby Helms's "Jingle Bell Rock," and on and on.

And what of his concurrent movies? *Paris Honeymoon* was remembered by its participants for a pun, alas not in the picture, delivered grandiloquently by Bing in reference to his costar, Franciska Gaal. The Budapest-born actress and cabaret star was brought to America by Cecil B. De Mille for *The Buccaneer,* the first of three Hollywood pictures she made in 1938, after which — her starlight diminished — she returned to Europe. A beautiful, wired Kewpie doll with beseeching Luise Rainer eyes and the pep of Miriam Hopkins on a diet of triple-espressos, she played basically the same role in *Paris Honeymoon* (which has no honeymoon and only a few minutes of Paris) and MGM's *The Girl Downstairs*: an unyielding peasant girl who lands a millionaire. When she wasn't chewing up scenery and actors, she raged off camera at cast and crew. After one violent tantrum, she stormed off the set. Bing broke the stunned silence: *"I'd like to divide Gaal into three parts."*[41]

The picture, rushed to fulfill Bing's three-picture quota that year, was not without promise. Paramount reassembled the *Waikiki Wedding* team. Frank Tuttle and Karl Struss shot a Frank Butler and Don Hartman script, and Leo Robin and Ralph Rainger supplied the songs. The studio certainly appeared confident. It issued a publicity release revealing that Bing might rethink the "freak"[42] clause in his contract prohibiting it from billing him above the title: "It may be 'Bing Crosby and Franciska Gaal in *Paris Honeymoon,*'" the release timorously announced.[43] The studio even attempted to have a print of the film interred, instead of a Crosby record, in a 6,177-year time capsule created by Thornwell Jacobs of Oglethorpe University.[44] Paramount assured Jacobs that its latest cellulose film stock would last 100 years but failed to explain what use that would be to a capsule under seal until 8114. (Jacobs chose 6,177 years because that's how far back from 1938, he said, the Egyptians developed calendars.)

Bing himself knew the picture was a runt, and far from accepting star billing had his name listed, after the title, on the same card as five other actors, of whom Akim Tamiroff, possibly inspired by Gaal, wins honors for over-the-top histrionics that broke up Tuttle and Bing. His big speeches, as the con-man mayor of a Ruritanian country, are filmed in single-camera setups over Bing's shoulders, with few reaction shots to break his timing. The plot reverses the male fantasy of a few years earlier in favor of a Cinderella variation; instead of an heiress forsaking her kind for a common Joe, the self-made millionaire abandons his wealthy fiancée to anoint a poor serving girl. The trouble is that Bing's heiress as played by Shirley Ross (his leading lady in *Waikiki Wedding*) is more appealing than the wacky laundress played by Gaal. By the time Gaal's Manya tells Bing's Lucky she loves him (really? he had no idea), Bing plays their scenes as though he were contemplating root canal.

Bing's Lucky is every bit as superstitious as Fred Astaire's Lucky in the 1936 classic *Swing Time*, which is also contrived around a postponed engagement. Strangely, no one remarked on the similarities. The movie begins with an inside joke. Lucky's butler, Edward Everett Horton (known for his pictures with Astaire, but an old acquaintance of Bing's from *Reaching for the Moon*), retrieves a shoe from a horse that trumpet player and memoirist Max Kaminsky would later describe as "a moth-eaten, sway-backed, ancient yellow nag."[45] The horse had been a birthday gift from Joe Venuti, so Bing put it in the picture. Returning with the horseshoe, Horton points out a joke that Bing's radio audience could appreciate: Lucky wears argyle socks with his dress suit.

Frank Capra rated Bing "in the top ten of all actors" and explained why: "He has a complete faculty of being able to work with props; you give many actors props and they can't do it, but he can juggle balls and have Bob Hope cracking ad-libs on the side and still say his stuff."[46] Bing's first song as Lucky, a rich cowboy, is a sterling example. He dons his Stetson and sings "The Funny Old Hills," casually performing a world of shtick: making and twirling a lariat, chewing, spitting, hopping up and down on a bed, stroking a nonexistent mustache (a favorite bit of mime he repeated in *East Side of Heaven, If I Had My Way,* and elsewhere). Bing amused the crew with one ad-lib that did stay in the picture. He is supposed to kiss Ross, who wears a veil. Instead of lifting the veil and taking her in his arms, as every other actor would have done, he tells her, "You better lift up that pup tent," before bestowing his peck.[47] Ross and Bing sing a bathtub duet that got past the censors because Bing telephones his part, crooning, "I have eyes to see with," long-distance, as she soaks.

The mediocre score yielded three substantial hits, arranged by Trotter: the loping "Funny Old Hills," the exceptionally well-sung "I Have Eyes," and the patronizing "You're a Sweet Little Headache." Bing's energetic warbling could not, however, salvage "Joobalai," a fatuous attempt at a peasant folk song that portends the kind of novelties Perry Como made his province in the 1950s. The records did not help the picture, Bing's least successful to date. When it debuted at the New York Paramount in January 1939, live music won the day. Bob Crosby's Bob Cats, wrote the New York *Daily News* reviewer, were "the answer to an alligator's prayer."[48]

East Side of Heaven was an altogether more pleasant experience for Bing and moviegoers. It developed a situation that had first been exploited in *Pennies from Heaven:* Bing as a surrogate father. After the back-to-back disappointments of *Doctor Rhythm* and *Paris Honeymoon,* he needed a pick-me-up movie quick and, having fulfilled his Paramount obligation for the year, was entitled to produce this one himself. His friend David Butler said, "Why don't you let me do your outside picture?"[49] Butler, riding high as the director responsible for the incredibly profitable stardom of six-year-old Shirley Temple, had left Fox and was negotiating a deal with Universal. Bing told him to go for it.

Butler surrounded himself with story men, chiefly the then ailing William Conselman (he died a year later) and James Kern, who had come to Hollywood as a member of the comedy-vocal group the Yacht Club Boys (sort of a musical Ritz Brothers). Out of respect for

Conselman, Butler gave him the screenwriting credit on *East Side of Heaven* but in interviews for the Directors Guild of America's oral-history program said that he and Kern devised the story. In any case, Universal pounced. To be sure, the studio was desperate and would likely have signed Bing had he wanted to play Ming the Merciless in a Flash Gordon serial. Deanna Durbin was its only moneymaker and, for that matter, only star. Early in the year two erstwhile RKO executives, Nate Blumberg and Cliff Work, were recruited to revive Universal's fortunes, and by the early 1940s the company would be in the chips with W. C. Fields, Abbott and Costello, Maria Montez, and a monster revival. *East Side of Heaven* was a transitional project, and in order to get Bing back on the lot for the first time since *King of Jazz*, Universal conceded him a 50 percent profit split in exchange for his services and personal investment of half the final budget.

It was a wise deal for all concerned. With Bing's money on the line, he was doubly inspired to make an entertaining picture while keeping an eagle eye on the budget. The latter function he delegated to Herb Polesie, who served as his associate producer (the movie credits do not acknowledge a producer, though Polesie shares a card with Butler for original story). A wonderful cast was assembled, with Joan Blondell, Mischa Auer, Irene Hervey, C. Aubrey Smith, Jerome Cowan, and a personality from Bing's first days in Los Angeles, Jane Jones, the big-boned singer and hostess of the speakeasy where Mildred Bailey worked. The production number with Jones, as the owner of the Frying Pan Cafe, introduced — as singing waitresses — the Music Maids, who simultaneously became regulars on the *Kraft Music Hall*. For good measure, Matty Malneck and his orchestra and pianist Joe Sullivan were also drafted.

For Universal, the most important member of the supporting cast turned out to be the infant daughter of a milkman, who upon hearing of the studio's need for a ten-month-old baby dropped four snapshots along with the morning milk on the doorstep of Charles Previn, Universal's musical director. The pictures were turned over to Butler, who told *Life* he hired the baby without asking its sex and did not know he had a girl in a boy's part for two days.[50] He later admitted he tested numerous babies and found the milkman's, Sandra Henville, to be the cutest. "I said, 'Nobody will know if this is a boy or girl. We'll call it a boy.' We put the kid in as Baby Sandy, and the kid was wonderful."[51] The studio made another picture with Baby Sandy, then disclosed that she was a girl and made a bunch more — eight in all, and all moneymakers. Only the studio of Maria Montez could have mined silver from a gurgling genderproof infant. When her three-year contract ended, Sandy did a cameo for Republic and retired at age four.

"East Side of Heaven was good fun under the expansive aegis of D. Wingate Butler," a buoyant Bing wrote Johnny Mercer after completion. "Never engaged in a more pleasant and, I hope, profitable enterprise. The budget was astonishingly low and, if John Public takes to the picture favorably, we're a cinch to make a meg or two."[52] Butler had known Bing since the Cocoanut Grove. He directed Dixie in *Fox Movietone Follies* and mistakenly believed that Dixie and Bing met at a party he and his wife gave for a visiting German opera company. "Bing was there, and he sang with all the opera fellows, and we were very friendly," he recalled.[53] The two men grew closer at Del Mar ("the happiest days of my life").[54] An early investor, Butler led the cheering squad for Ligaroti at the famous match race.

Born in San Francisco in 1894, Butler began in movies as an actor for Thomas Ince in 1913 and earned major parts in numerous pictures for D. W. Griffith, King Vidor, and John Ford before he turned to directing in 1927. An impersonal but prolific and reliable filmmaker, he made lucrative comedies and musicals for every major studio over a thirty-year period before turning to television in the late 1950s (all six seasons of *Leave It to Beaver*, among dozens of episodes for other programs). The year before his death in 1979, Butler was awarded an honorary lifetime membership in the Directors Guild of America — the fifth director so honored. A portly, funny, easygoing man with a passion for sports, he was a perfect match for Bing.

As Universal anticipated, the production was pragmatic and efficient. With a script completed early in the new year of 1939, the cameras began to roll on Friday, January 13. Polesie's first status report was optimistic; they scheduled the picture for thirty-six days, but figured forty more reasonable. A week later he presented a budget — "worked over and reduced in every possible way"[55] — of $686,000, noting they had fallen behind two days and would exceed that sum if they fell behind any more. The weekly status reports were written with an inflated sense of drama ("only fair progress during the past week," "a rather disastrous setback last night"),[56] as if to lowball expectations, but the model production averaged fifteen minutes of footage a week, and most of the delays concerned Sandy, who was not permitted to work more than four hours a day. Butler maximized the shoot by switching to a different set when Sandy was whisked away; if he did not have to shoot close-ups, he replaced her with a doll.

Bing sang all the songs, so the prerecordings were a snap, though they were made in a novel way. He was accompanied solely by a pianist playing softly. The orchestra dubbed its part onto his playback recordings, Butler recalled, "because Bing ad-libbed a lot. We had a piano playback that wasn't very loud, so that the other music would cover it."[57] Butler enjoyed his professionalism: "He was the fastest man that I ever saw in my life with learning a song. He'd get a song, and come over and say to Johnny Burke, 'Play it.' Johnny would play it a couple of times. He'd start humming it, and then the third time he'd sing it — he'd know it perfectly."[58] He was no less gratified by Bing's acting: "He did everything you wanted him to do. I never saw such an actor. He'd do it, and do it very well. The only thing — we always kidded him about wanting to leave his hat on. He never wanted to put that toupee on."[59]

Some exteriors were shot day-for-night between dinner and sunrise, to accommodate Bing's radio obligations, and one street scene with seventy-five extras was ruined by unexpected rainfall followed by winds that "blew all rain clouds away but made recording and photographing impossible."[60] To make up for lost time, they often worked Saturday nights until the small hours. Polesie estimated midway that they would need forty-two days (six more than scheduled), provided the big production number in the Frying Pan Cafe ("Hang Your Heart on a Hickory Limb") went smoothly,[61] but a week later two more days were lost when Joan Blondell fell ill during makeup and was hospitalized for "a severe cold and throat infection"[62] — not a total loss, because in her absence the rest of the company could rehearse the musical number. Filming finished March 7, after forty-four shooting days and an overrun of $10,000.[63]

During the next ten days, the 137½-minute rough cut was edited to eighty-six minutes in time for a successful preview. Even so, a battle with the censors had to be decided. Joseph Breen had warned against shooting certain bits: "This gag of the baby wetting its diapers must be omitted"; "This gag of Danny investigating the baby's sex must be omitted"; "The following line is suggestive and must be changed or omitted: 'This is just like spring practice, but wait till the season starts.'"[64] When studio chief Cliff Work informed Breen he would go to the New York board to persuade it — "in the friendliest possible manner"[65] — to allow the baby to wet its diaper, Breen harrumphed in a letter to Will Hays that Universal disregarded his script warnings and shot offensive scenes, urging him to block the trespass of "what we call, here, toilet gags."[66] In almost every instance Universal prevailed. The picture premiered April 7 in Miami and opened a month later at Radio City Music Hall — Bing's debut in New York's landmark movie theater. As Bing anticipated, it made a meg or two, but Paramount was probably more envious of the billing than the profits: "Bing Crosby and Joan Blondell in *East Side of Heaven.*"

Bing's usual routine was in no way hindered by the six days per week shooting schedule — a phenomenon no less remarkable for being absolutely typical. Each week he produced an hour program for *Kraft Music Hall,* requiring his presence at two-hour rehearsals on Wednesdays at 3:30 and seven-and-a-half-hour rehearsals on Thursdays at 11:00, followed at 7:00 by the broadcast, after which he ate at the Universal commissary and worked all night, reporting again on Friday morning. His *KMH* guests in that month and a half included the usual motley of Hollywood players and concert stars, among them Grete Stuckgold, Spring Byington, Colonel Snoopnagle, Humphrey Bogart, Nigel Bruce, Emanuel Feuermann, Elizabeth Patterson, Gregor Piatigorsky, Wayne Morris, Henry Fonda, Ellen Drew, Rose Bampton, Joan Bennett, Joseph Calleia, Lloyd Nolan, Frances Langford, and William Frawley. Some of his finest singing in the period was heard on radio, including fully realized interpretations of songs he never recorded, for example Hoagy Carmichael's "I Get Along Without You Very Well" (a new song he offered in two discrete arrangements) and DeSylva, Brown, and Henderson's old ditty "Together." One major change took place at *KMH,* when Paul Taylor's Choristers concluded their contract with the February 9 show. The program report for February 16 notes, "Didn't seem to miss the choir,"[67] but the next week a new choir of five debuted, the Music Maids, *KMH* fixtures for the next six years.

Two Music Maids had crossed Bing's path before. Alice Ludes, married to NBC audio engineer Ed Ludes, was one of the Williams Sisters, a trio that performed regularly on Bing's Woodbury show, and Trudy Erwin (who later married Bing's audio engineer, Murdo MacKenzie), freelanced in the *Double or Nothing* Singband. Each of the five members was between seventeen and twenty-three when the group was formed early in 1939 by Erwin and Dottie Mesmer; the others were Denny Wilson and Bobbie Canvin, who soon left to sing with Tommy Dorsey's band and was replaced by Trudy's high-school classmate, Pat Hyatt. They won instant acceptance. Though their popularity on the air did not translate into much of a recording career beyond a handful of discs with Bing, they appeared in a few movies and on the soundtracks of a few more. By the time *East Side of Heaven* circulated, they had been on *KMH* for several weeks, and many assumed they were put in the film to capitalize on their radio renown. Actually, they were hired for the film — their agent was Larry Crosby — before Bing approved them for the program.

"Larry called us one day and said, would we like to audition for some show on NBC," Trudy Erwin recalled. "So we did 'Hawaiian War Chant' in Studio B at NBC, no accompaniment, nobody onstage, just Larry, ourselves, and the mixer — my husband now, though we didn't know each other then, of course."[68] Bing listened to their transcriptions, and a week later Larry called and asked whether they would like to be on *Kraft Music Hall*. They had no idea they were auditioning for Bing. Some nights they were allowed to perform on their own, but mostly they backed Bing and provided half-chorus interludes for his songs. "It was a lot of fun. Once in a while, he would take us to the Brown Derby on Vine. He didn't eat very much, maybe a salad. In those days, he'd have a big breakfast and no dinner, that's how he finally took off weight. I never thought he was too heavy, but that's what he did. Very disciplined, except when he went wild — in his work, I mean. The most fun was the dress rehearsal that just preceded the show by maybe an hour. He would kid around and try to break us up and sing the wrong lyrics and just do all kinds of stuff."[69] Bing, who invented monikers for everyone (Murdo MacKenzie was Heathcliff, Johnny Mercer was Verseable), called the Music Maids the Mice. "I don't know why he did that," Trudy said, "maybe because we got in a little circle and talked at rehearsal."[70] Alice Ludes speculated, "Well, the sponsor made cheese."[71]

The combined radio and movie work failed to sate Bing's energy. On his first free Sunday, he took Dixie, the Edmund Lowes, and Lin Howard to the races and then to Club 17, where the great stuttering comedian Joe Frisco entertained. The picture's third weekend coincided with Bing's third annual pro-am tournament at Rancho Santa Fe. The first in which Bob Hope played, it is now chiefly remembered for the presence of Babe Didrikson Zaharias, the 1932 Olympic gold medalist who became a championship golfer in the 1940s. At the 1939 Crosby she was accepted as a competitor by mistake; she remains the only woman to have participated in the tournament. In 1974, when Bing futilely lobbied to permit women pros to play the Crosby on Monterey Peninsula, he recalled how much Babe had added to the event. The following Sunday he guest-starred on a new CBS series, *The Gulf Screen Guild Show*, a popular anthology to which Hollywood stars donated services because fees were given to the Motion Picture Relief Fund. A few weeks later Bing and Dixie attended a preview of David Butler's *Kentucky*, his last Fox picture and one close to the director's heart, as it concerned horse breeders. A photograph of the couple entering the theater shows Dixie in a sheath gown and fur jacket, smiling, while Bing, in a light overcoat and fedora, mugs, thumbs at chin and fingers spread to frame his exaggerated grin.

East Side of Heaven is little remembered today, a victim of MCA's disregard for most of the Universal catalog, which it acquired in 1962. To be sure, the film was a mild amusement in its day and seems no more profound today; the sentimental final shot of Bing and Baby Sandy will make you coo or wince. But it entertains throughout. Butler, who did not consider himself a thinker, knew how to avoid longueurs. The picture also represents a change in Bing's screen character, a transition that points ahead to the deadpan comedy he perfected in the *Road* pictures and the maturity that defined his 1940s persona. Photographed by George Robinson (a Universal veteran better known for his work on horror films), *East Side of Heaven* looks and feels like an early-forties film, with grayer shades and a relaxed tempo, not to mention Bing's shorter and wavier toupee.

One reason Crosby accepted billing above the title was the prominence of Joan Blondell; he allowed the same exception for *Sing You Sinners* because of Fred MacMurray's stature. Blondell was the first major Hollywood actress to play opposite Bing since Miriam Hopkins in 1934. Some of his leading ladies became stars after working with him (Carole Lombard, Joan Bennett, Ida Lupino, Frances Farmer), but the only Crosby cast members during the past five years with box-office clout were MacMurray and W. C. Fields. Joan Blondell had spent her entire childhood in vaudeville and emerged in the 1930s as one of the most popular and reliable performers on the Warners lot. She was equally at home in gangster pictures (usually opposite James Cagney or Warren William) and musicals (usually opposite her husband, Dick Powell). Now, however, she was freelancing. *East Side of Heaven* was an important role for her, secured by Bing, who had enjoyed working with Joan a year earlier on the *Lux Radio Theater*.

The movie opens with a private joke. Jimmy Monaco, who wrote the score with Johnny Burke, had gotten married in November and recently returned from his honeymoon. In the first scene Bing is at work at the Postal Union, singing greetings on the phone. One message — to Alice from Kitty — probably refers to Dixie's friends, but there is no doubt about the next one: to Mr. and Mrs. James Monaco, whom we see in the midst of a violent quarrel, until she slams the phone down. After work Bing walks into a hotel lobby and casually exchanges greetings (he poses à la Hermes and twirls his invisible mustache) with Matty Malneck, who is leading a band no one else pays any attention to.[72] Bing had gone to hear Malneck in a Los Angeles club and impulsively offered his band a part in the picture; as there was no nightclub sequence, Butler planted it in the crowded lobby. Bing then strolls to the receptionist, Blondell, and attempts to pick her up, but it's a game. They are, in fact, engaged; their marriage has been postponed, as so often occurs in Depression movies. Unlike in *Sing You Sinners,* she is the one who wants to delay until he gets a decent job. Their interplay throughout the film is appealing and funny.

The Production Code is tweaked in the next scene, in which we see Bing and his roommate, Mischa Auer, asleep in a double bed (one of the few scenes in which Bing does not wear a hat); under the Code, married couples were required to sleep in single beds, but single men could cozy up under the same sheets. Asked by Bing to be his best man, Auer responds: "If the best man is the best man, why does the bride marry the groom?" The censors were more concerned about the villain of the piece, a radio gossip named Claudius De Wolfe, played to unctuous perfection by Jerome Cowan. Butler based the character on real-life society wag Lucius Beebe, known for his tag line "Are you happy, honey?" Seeing the phrase in the script, Breen wrote Universal, "There must be of course no 'pansy' suggestion about the line, 'Are you happy, honey?'"

The convoluted plot involves an imperious old millionaire who is trying to take his infant grandson from the wife of his alcoholic son. Meanwhile, Bing takes a job as a singing driver for the Sunbeam Taxi Company, auditioning for the job with the peppiest song in the under-rated Monaco-Burke score, "Sing a Song of Sunbeams." "The cruising troubadour," as he is known, offers a free ride and song to customers to build up business. The Crosby hero has come a long way in one year from the hard-work-is-for-saps credo of *Sing You Sinners,* but he continues to exemplify the idea of the common-man singer.

The mother leaves the baby in his cab, allowing Bing a kind of "spring practice" to be the perfect dad. His apprenticeship is accompanied by two fine ballads, "That Sly Old Gentleman (from Feather-bed Lane)," which he delivers so convincingly that Blondell, listening in the hall, thinks he's got an older babe in there, and the title number, a lullaby composed with Bing-friendly low-note swoops (bars five to seven and twenty-one to twenty-three). Thanks to Bing and pals, the millionaire is reunited with his family. The malevolent Claudius DeWolfe, whose show the millionaire sponsored, is fired, giving Bing his program. And that's how crooners are born.

"In New York they're on their knees begging for business," *Variety* lamented, blaming the dearth of moviegoers on the World's Fair, a disabling heat wave, and sporting events.[73] Under the circumstances, *East Side of Heaven* would be lucky to take in $55,000 at Radio City, the paper warned. Yet a week later the tide came in and Bing's picture emerged as a sizable hit in the most fabled of movie seasons, 1939. Reviews helped. The New York *Daily News* gushed, "Bing Crosby's pictures are getting better and better. *East Side of Heaven* is the most delightfully amusing film he's ever done."[74] *Variety* called it a "grand package of entertainment," singling out its smart pace ("hitting a nice tempo at the start and rolling merrily to the finish"), and noted how unusual it was for a star to "toss his own coin into productions to get a shot at a cut of the profits."[75] Baby Sandy was declared by New York's *Herald Tribune* "our favorite actor of the month."[76]

In the year dominated by *Gone With the Wind,* the ten highest-grossing movies of record were dramas, with the exception of two nostalgic Judy Garland pictures: *Babes in Arms,* which re-creates minstrelsy and glorifies middle America, and *The Wizard of Oz,* which tells how Dorothy regains her middle-American home after bringing order to a foreign land. This was the year of *The Hunchback of Notre Dame, Jesse James, Mr. Smith Goes to Washington, Stagecoach,* and *Drums Along the Mohawk.* Pundits who divined a trend toward sobriety, however, had but a year to find out how wrong they were: *Road to Singapore* and Preston Sturges's films were just around the corner. Butler told a reporter in 1946 that *East Side of Heaven* earned between $3 million and $4 million and saved Universal from going under.[77] Had those numbers been accurate, his picture would surely have ranked in the top ten. On the other hand, everyone acknowledged that it did bail out Universal.

In tracking the fortunes of far more conventional folks than the unholy Beebes, *East Side of Heaven* marked a moderating turn in the selling of Bing Crosby. Ahead of him lay his wackiest comedies, powerful dramatic roles, and nostalgic detours, but Bing's days as an acquiescent romantic lead, forever wooed, reluctantly wooing, were over.

25

WHAT'S NEW

Al Jolson was like Mr. Great Singer of all time. Maurice
Chevalier was like Mr. Entertainer of all time. Frank
Sinatra is like Mr. Balladeer of all time. But Bing
Crosby is like Mr. Everything of all time.

— José Ferrer (1974)[1]

When Universal hired Cliff Work as its new production chief, it fired
Charles R. Rogers, who then attempted to stay afloat as an independent producer. One night at the Brown Derby, Rogers ran into the
legendary vaudevillian and songwriter Gus Edwards, who had recently announced his retirement and was rumored to be suffering
from paresis. They spoke of the old days, and Rogers told Gus that his
life might make a good picture. After Edwards sent him an old autobiographical article he had written for *Collier's*, Rogers made a preliminary production deal with United Artists. There was only one actor
for the lead, and Rogers went to Paramount to see whether he could
borrow Bing. Paramount had no intention of loaning him and did not
have to worry about Rogers's going to him directly, because *East*
Side of Heaven fulfilled Bing's outside option for the year. William
LeBaron recognized a good idea, however, and invited Rogers to make
the picture for him.

It was, in fact, a brilliant idea — on paper. Bing had just scored a
hit as a vicarious papa, waving good-bye at the close of *East Side of*

Heaven with Baby Sandy in his arms. Playing Gus Edwards, he would be surrounded by dozens of vicarious kids. The more you thought about the possibilities, the more compelling they became. Edwards was the king of kiddie acts back when Bing was first entering elementary school. He initially made his mark in 1896 as a member of the Newsboy Quintet, an act that consisted of teenage boys dressed in raggedy clothes, hawking papers and singing ballads. The German-born Edwards eventually proved a formidable Tin Pan Alley composer and publisher, with songs like "In Zanzibar," "In My Merry Oldsmobile," "Sunbonnet Sue," "By the Light of the Silvery Moon," and "Jimmy Valentine." In 1907 he wrote his biggest hit, "School Days," which sold 3 million records (sung by Byron G. Harlan) and encouraged him to create a Broadway show in which forty young players strutted their stuff, to the utter indifference of the Great White Way. Undaunted, Edwards distilled from the show a vaudeville act, "School Boys and Girls," that went on to enjoy phenomenal success for more than a quarter of a century. Imitators were legion.

By 1913 *Variety* reported sixty-two *School Days* acts touring the country, all of them sure-fire and very inexpensive, for as show-business chroniclers Abel Green and Joe Laurie Jr. observed, "The only props were a few desks and chairs [and] there were always stagestruck youngsters available to sing and dance."[2] In his many variations on the act ("Kid Kabaret," "Band Box Revue," "Blonde Typewriters"), Edwards introduced countless boys and girls, many later prominent, among them Eddie Cantor, George Jessel, Groucho Marx, Walter Winchell, Elsie Janis, Sally Rand, Eleanor Powell, Georgie Price, Lila Lee, Jack Pearl, Bert Wheeler, Mervyn LeRoy, Ina Ray Hutton, Ricardo Cortez, Charles King, Ann Dvorak, and Ray Bolger. In 1939, a world remade by the Depression and an inevitable war, the country was once again gripped by kiddiemania. Shirley Temple, pushing twelve, had only another year or two at the top, but the public responded to children of all ages, from infancy (Baby Sandy) to teens (Deanna Durbin, Judy Garland). Had Humbert Humbert spent more time at the movies, he might have been a happy, happy man.

One can imagine the humming of Paramount's wheels: perfect vehicle for Bing, perfect vehicle for child performers, perfect opportunity for shamelessly exploitative publicity (like importing sixteen orphans from as many orphanages for a press preview), perfect opportunity to discover and launch its very own Deanna Durbin. Her name was Linda Ware, a fourteen-year-old orphan from Detroit. The plenary possibilities of Gus Edwards's story and the wonderful talents he discovered were sacrificed to the studio's vain hope that her golden locks and faux-operatic voice would hit the kiddie jackpot. She was billed as "the new singing discovery of Charles R. Rogers, Discoverer of Deanna Durbin."[3] But Ware was no more a match for Durbin than Kitty Carlisle and Gladys Swarthout had been for Jeanette MacDonald.

Worse, the script somehow devolved from the story of Edwards to the story of Bing. By the time it was ready to shoot, *The Star Maker* so little resembled Edwards and his career that the name of the protagonist was changed to Larry Earl and history was mooted with the attribution "suggested by the career of Gus Edwards." That did not restrain Paramount from promoting "the heart-happy story of America's greatest showman, Gus Edwards."[4] The fictional plot concerned a conflict involving a children's welfare organization that bans the hero's shows and forces the hero to pioneer a newfangled invention. "It's what they call radio or something," one character remarks, allowing Bing/Larry/Gus to predict: "In a few years — remember this now — that little gimmick will have every star in show business singing and acting over it." Every star but Gus Edwards, whose sole connection to radio was a local amateur talent program in Los Angeles for a couple of seasons in the mid-thirties, shortly before his retirement.

That was not the only instance of Bing's story subsuming Edwards's. In the tradition of *Kraft Music Hall, The Star Maker* offered seventy-seven-year-old Walter Damrosch his cinema debut, playing himself, as well as accompanying and avowing the greatness of Linda Ware. What Damrosch, who had convinced Andrew Carnegie to build a concert hall on New York's Fifty-seventh Street and Tchaikovsky to conduct its opening night, thought of her number — Tchaikovsky's "Valse des Fleurs" with words by Frank Loesser — is anyone's guess, as no journalist is known to have asked him. Ware is less annoying as a trilling soprano than as a barrelhouse interpreter of "The Darktown Strutters' Ball," to which she brings the very mannerisms Bing parodied a few years later in *Going My Way.* The public did not encourage her career, but several reviewers kvelled:

"a brilliant coloratura, a winning personality and a pleasing countenance" (*Variety*).[5]

The drearily familiar Crosby character as personified by Larry Earl may be summed up by the titles of two of the songs he sings: Edwards's "If I Was a Millionaire" (1910) and Burke and Monaco's "A Man and His Dream." Once again, he is the stubborn dreamer who cannot abide conventional jobs and seizes the day. What makes the picture different is that Earl acquires a wife. The preeminent stars of the Hollywood musical, like those of horror films, were rarely depicted with spouses, except in biopics. "Can you pay the grocer off with dreams?" asks Larry's fiancée, Mary (a poorly written role played by a redheaded Mary Martin lookalike, Louise Campbell). "Sure, if you'll just say yes," Larry tells her, and in contrast to all his previous movies and most of those to follow, Bing marries.

The Star Maker is, in fact, the only picture Bing ever made playing a happily married man. He was on the brink of divorce in Mack Sennett's *One More Chance* and would marry and divorce in *Blue Skies*. He would be bitterly divorced in *Man on Fire*, philosophically divorced in *High Society*, widowed in *Just for You*, and in deep marital trouble in *The Country Girl*. He was on the prowl or celibate in everything else.

It is not far-fetched to surmise that, in part, Bing plays a composite of his younger self and his father: the irresponsible husband who will not allow his wife to work yet cannot hold down respectable jobs that interfere with his joie de vivre. When he proposes to Mary, Larry promises her furs, diamonds, servants; eighteen months later we see her ironing in a cold-water flat as Larry spends their savings on a piano — not unlike Harry Crosby bringing home the phonograph and theater tickets while Kate despaired of paying the grocery bill. Like Kate and Dixie, Mary takes steps to ensure Larry's success, sneaking into the car of impresario F. F. Proctor and charming him into seeing her tactless husband. Proctor installs Larry on the bottom of a bill that lists several of Bing's favorite vaudeville artists, notably Eddie Leonard, Julian Eltinge, Van and Schenck, and Blanche Ring, most of whom he and David Butler would soon contrive to present in *If I Had My Way*.

The first half of *The Star Maker* has many pleasantries, not least a re-creation of the Newsboys (Larry is too old to be in the act, so the

June Kuhn was a Sarah Lawrence student when she met Bob Crosby on her Easter break. Their marriage got off to a rocky start but lasted fifty-four years. This picture was taken in October 1938, about the time of the "You Must Have Been a Beautiful Baby" session.
Rory Burke Collection

Harry and Kate Crosby loved the Hollywood life. Bing claimed his father used to buttonhole strangers to show them his (Bing's) press clippings; his more forbidding mother became a habitué at the racetrack.
Courtesy of the Academy of Motion Picture Arts and Sciences

Bing volunteered for military service and was asked to entertain servicemen. During a break on the sixty-five-city Victory Caravan in 1942, he relaxed with Bert Lahr, Oliver Hardy, and James Cagney. *Gene Lester*

Several members of the Crosby circle were united when the twin daughters, Rory and Regan, of Bing's friend and lyricist Johnny Burke were baptized. Shown on the steps of Saint Ambrose Church on Fairfax Avenue, January 11, 1942, are (left to right) Sammy Cahn, Jack Mass, Barney Dean, John Scott Trotter, Phil Silvers, Bing (Rory's godfather), Dixie (holding Rory), Bob Hope, Delores Hope (holding Regan), Skitch Henderson, Pat O'Brien, Bessie Burke (in front), David Butler (Regan's godfather), Eloise O'Brien, Johnny Burke, Elsie Butler, Jean Stevens, and Dr. Arnold Stevens.
Quinn Burke Collection

Bing was almost as accomplished a fisherman as he was a golfer. He owned many dogs, and even showed some of them off at competitions.
Susan Crosby Collection

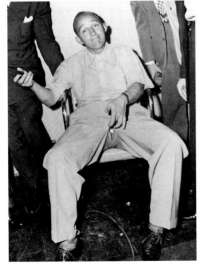

Bing showed up intoxicated to record "Ave Maria" on April 25, 1945, and Jack Kapp had to reschedule the session. When photographer Gene Lester asked Bing if he was aware of the hole in his pants, Bing put his finger in it and said, "Oh, Jesus, hey, but that makes it convenient, doesn't it?"
Gene Lester

Bing shakes hands with Frank Tuttle, his favorite director of the 1930s, who brought a touch of René Clair whimsy to *The Big Broadcast* and achieved a blockbuster with *Waikiki Wedding*.
Gary Giddins Collection

A lobby card for *Double or Nothing* (1937) shows Bing with Mary Carlisle, who taught him something about backgammon, and Martha Raye, who made her film debut with Bing. Each appeared in three of his movies.
Gary Giddins Collection

David Butler, who first directed Dixie and then Bing (*East Side of Heaven*) posed with Bing's music director on the *Kraft Music Hall*, John Scott Trotter, at a Westwood Marching and Chowder Club production.
Rory Burke Collection

Bing records at Decca with a full complement of strings.
Gene Lester/Elsie Perry Collection

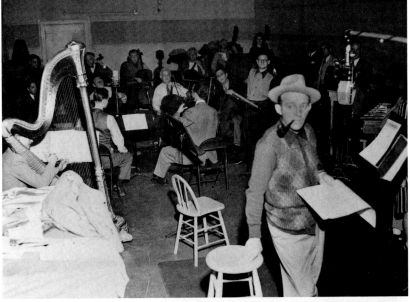

Bessie Burke, Barney Dean, Everett Crosby, and Bing's friend and neighbor Dave Shelly at a Crosby party, 1940.
Rory Burke Collection

In 1935 Dixie costarred with John Boles, who had aced Bing out of a big number in *King of Jazz*. Her career soon ended, however, and she became reclusive, though she often accompanied Bing to the track.

above: Gary Giddins Collection
below: Courtesy of the Academy of Motion Picture Arts and Sciences

Bing, the silent-comedy connoisseur, affects a Chaplinesque stance during one of his countless charity golf matches with Bob Hope, who almost always lost.
Bill Milkowski Collection

Bing and Bob wrestle during a break on *Road to Singapore*, 1939. Usually they wrestled over lines.
Bill Milkowski Collection

Dorothy Lamour had to fight for her every line once Bob and Bing got started. No one expected *Road to Singapore* to break attendance records and begin a twenty-year series.
Gary Giddins Collection

The fake feud between Bob and Bing continued for thirty-seven years. During a trip to Spain in 1953, Bing could not resist taking his best shot. *Susan Crosby Collection*

By 1940 Bing was on top, but all he had achieved would soon seem like a mere prelude to what was to come during the war and after. *Gary Giddins Collection* picture has him discovering them on a street corner, dancing to a hurdy-gurdy). Bing enjoyed the seven newsboys, among them Darryl Hickman, whom the Crosby talent agency signed and placed in *The Grapes of Wrath,* a prelude to his dozens of film roles in the forties and fifties; Danny Daniels, who did much of the solo tap dancing in the picture and went on to a long career as a choreographer on stage and screen; and Dante DiPaolo, who was a specialty dancer in movies, a dance director in Las Vegas, and an actor in Italian epics and *giallos.* "I auditioned five times," DiPaolo remembered. "Bing was only at the final audition. That's when Le Roy Prinz, our dance direc-tor, told me not to change a thing, because I was singing 'Star Dust,' and he told me, Do it exactly that way because Bing really likes 'Star Dust.' There must have been six, seven hundred kids from Hollywood auditioning, not just for the seven newsboys, but all the kids in 'School Days,' tons of auditions."[6]

Indeed, the producer claimed he auditioned 1,583 kids for the pic-ture. Several incidents from those tryouts were added to the script, including the child who turned out to be a midget and the girl who would not sing despite her mother's panicked pleas. Bing had fun on the set. The newsboys bought him a cake to celebrate his assumed thirty-sixth birthday. When Dante failed to hear the director call cut and kept dancing, Bing put his hat on him and it came down to his mouth. Nearly sixty years later, Dante married Rosemary Clooney, who remembered an incident in the 1970s, when they were in a pro shop: "Bing said to Dante, Try on this hat, and he took off the hat and threw it to him and the hat went down to the same place as when he was a kid. 'Cause Bing had a big head. So Dante said he felt just exactly the same way as he did back then. Oh God, it was funny, to see the admiration Dante had for Bing after all those years."[7] On sev-eral occasions Bing brought his own kids to the set to show off the three-part harmonies of Gary (almost six) and the twins (almost five).

That some uneasiness also existed is evident from Bing's under-stated remark when asked, in 1976, about his most difficult film. "I've done some pictures where you didn't quite know where they were going," he answered. "I remember a picture called *The Star Maker.* The director didn't like the picture but he had to do it — a guy named Roy Del Ruth, he was a good director — and the atmosphere on the set wasn't too congenial because of that. Roy always treated me very well but wasn't happy because he disliked things they had done with the script, but he had to go ahead with it. And that's the only picture I can think of where there was even a smidgen of unpleasantness."[8]

On one occasion, as Barry Ulanov reported, Bing exercised his power with unruffled dispatch. By this time the star was accustomed to disbursing bit parts to old friends on their uppers. He examined the cast lists for possibilities and asked assistant directors to call the people he had in mind, leaving Bing's name out of it. Bing had asked Del Ruth's man to contact a friend to play an elevator operator. Making up one morning, he noticed someone else in the role and asked Del Ruth, "What happened? Couldn't you get the guy I suggested?" Del Ruth told him, "We didn't try. We thought this fellow would be better." Bing nodded, "Well, maybe you're right."[9] He took off his toupee and observed what a lovely day it was, perfect for golf. Del Ruth quickly assured Bing that he would get hold of his choice right away and that both actors would get paid.

Bing was in superb voice. The old songs suited him as well as the new ones or better, especially the non-Edwards relic "I Wonder Who's Kissing Her Now," beautifully sung by Bing to encourage a shy little girl during an audition and prettily shot by Karl Struss, who elsewhere puts shadows on Bing's cheeks and focuses on his big, limpid eyes. In several scenes he is more aggressive than usual, reciting self-righteous speeches, but is splendidly disarming when teaching the kids confidence in a number that begins with a rhyming section reminiscent of Bert Williams and turns pure Bing as he sidles into Burke and Monaco's "Go Fly a Kite." As usual, he was billed after the title card, this time with five other cast members, undistinguished but for Ned Sparks, who was never funnier than as Larry's child-loathing publicist.

The Star Maker received respectable reviews and made lots of money, beating the competition in almost every city. Paramount took a full-page ad, headlined BING BUSINESS! — inexplicably crowing that it outgrossed its own competing blockbuster, Cecil B. De Mille's *Union Pacific*, in seven markets, from San Francisco to Boston. Louella Parsons praised Bing for daring to appear with those little "picture stealers," noting, quite rightly, "Never have the old songs been sung with more feeling. Yesterday's favorite tunes take on a new flavor when Bing croons them."[10] *Time* agreed that he sang them "as well as they have ever been sung" and praised the movie as "an engaging archaeological exploration into a vanished world of the U.S. amusement industry,"[11] which was certainly true of the elaborate "School Days" number, with Bing in mortarboard, goatee, and glasses on the tip of his nose.

Despite *The Star Maker*'s success, Linda Ware disappeared, and poor ailing Gus Edwards, who lived another six years, got little in the way of a professional boost. One of the studio's publicity stunts was an August 18 dinner in his honor at the Ambassador Hotel. It attracted freeloading newsmen in large numbers, but few luminaries. Bing was not present. The day before the premiere, he played in a California state golf championship at Del Monte, then went straight to Rancho Santa Fe, some said as an excuse to miss the opening. "One thing is certain," a *Time* correspondent memoed his editor, "after he is through with a picture Crosby treats his time as his own, won't go sailing around the country for studio publicity."[12]

The Star Maker, compromised though it is by the producer's ambition to create a star, added to Bing's prestige as an entertainer who covered the waterfront of American show business. It also helped usher in a new genre in musicals: sham biographies of popular entertainers who made their mark before or beyond movies. Many films were made in the 1930s about nineteenth-century composers — half a dozen about Johann Strauss alone. Many others exploited pop gossip. (Jolson decked Walter Winchell in 1933 for writing a Russ Columbo melodrama, *Broadway Through a Keyhole*, that everyone knew was about Ruby Keeler's involvement with a gangster before she married Jolson.) But the only major attempt at dramatizing the story of a great showman was MGM's lavish and immensely successful *The Great Ziegfeld*, in 1936.

Suddenly, in 1939, Paramount, Fox, and RKO turned out five musical biographies. Like *The Star Maker*, Fox's *Rose of Washington Square* used a pseudonym for its thinly disguised depiction of Fanny Brice, but that was made without Brice's consent — she sued and won a settlement. Real names were used in films purportedly telling the stories of Stephen Foster, Victor Herbert, and Vernon Castle, but they were dead, though Vernon's wife and dancing partner, Irene, allowed RKO to turn their marriage into a Fred and Ginger vehicle.

After Michael Curtiz directed James Cagney in the glimmering *Yankee Doodle Dandy* (George M. Cohan) in 1942, the floodgates opened: dozens of biopics, none as good, all of them fictitious, many ludicrous, especially in the casting: Victor Mature as Paul Dresser, Mickey Rooney as Larry Hart, Robert Walker as Jerome Kern (Jews were always played by conspicuously gentile Gentiles). Bing partook of the idiom, playing minstrel Dan Emmett in *Dixie* (1943) and testing as Will Rogers for a picture David Butler tried to launch.

Yet *The Star Maker* represented for Bing not an entry into a new decade but the closing of a door on the old. Where could he have gone from there? Screening Bing's last picture of the 1930s, how could studio bosses fail to recognize a sad portent, a future of conventional marital amusements, a dozen versions of the same script: misunderstanding at breakfast, song, compromising situation with a secretary, song, mistaken identities, song, denouement, song. Yes, Bing was a far more accomplished actor than ever before, but he was also considerably harder to cast. His comedy was mellow, not brazen; his personality likable, not fervent. He could no more essay Cary Grant screwballs than Errol Flynn swashbucklers. Bing created the quintessential light leading man with a stunning voice, and — though he had not enjoyed a genuine smash since *Waikiki Wedding* — his popularity continued to hold. In 1939 he was Paramount's top-ranked male draw (ahead of Ronald Colman, Gary Cooper, and Jack Benny) and Universal's second-ranked (after Charles Boyer).[13] But no one could predict how his persona might develop beyond the sort of decorous romances that sneaked up on him throughout the 1930s.

A transformation loomed ahead, triggered by the February 1940 release of *Road to Singapore*. In the brief interval before that picture began shooting, Bing concentrated on his recording career, continuing the prolific schedule of 1938. Usually, records had to be sacrificed when Bing was juggling a movie and his radio show, and not just because of time constraints. Each film required prerecording sessions; additional pressure on his voice was considered reckless. Yet between March and June — before and after *The Star Maker* — Kapp managed to squeeze in nearly a dozen sessions, eking out more than two dozen hits, though no megahits; it was the year (1939) when Glenn Miller's sugared swing and Kay Kyser's infantile gimmicks held sway.

Every change in Bing's vocal style precipitated an alteration in his stature, in the nature of his renown. This Kapp understood too well. Just as Bing's recent movies prefigured an increasingly housebroken maturity, so his new records would reflect his standing as a classicist, the troubadour laureate of American song. Considering Crosby's beginnings at Decca ("Just a-Wearyin' for You") and the wistful successes of 1938, Kapp's increasingly retro direction was surprising only in its tenacity. The good and the bad went hand in hand: Bing made many exceptional records in 1939 while hacking his way through sentimental fluff, patriotic airs, and songs from his own distant past. As always, his primary recording obligations were his movie songs, which occasioned few complaints — the Deccas were often vastly superior to the screen versions. For the rest, he was saddled with a profusion of mossy evergreens, and looking backward more often than ahead.

His first major hit of the New Year, recorded the previous December, four years after he turned it down as too high-class, was Victor Herbert's "Ah! Sweet Mystery of Life." It was a fitting beginning to the year of *The Star Maker,* a year largely consecrated to a revival of old styles of show business Bing had so decisively helped bury. Beyond movie and vaudeville songs, he recorded a few good standards; a couple of terrible songs, as favors; six remakes of youthful Crosby classics (plus two from the Whiteman period); and brief returns to Hawaii and the West. The patriotic songs added a new flavor to the mix. In all those sessions, he added only one number to the catalog of enduring pop standards, "What's New?"

Yet 1939 was a good year for new songs. Among those Bing did *not* record that might have suited him to a T were "Day In — Day Out," "All the Things You Are," "I Thought About You," "I Get Along Without You Very Well," "Some Other Spring," "If I Didn't Care," "I Didn't Know What Time It Was," "South of the Border," and "Over the Rainbow." Instead, he enriched Decca's coffers with the likes of "Little Sir Echo" (an adaptation of the Boy Scouts' anthem), "Whistling in the Wildwood," and the inscrutably maudlin "Poor Old Rover," which one would like to think was intended as a jape — after all, it was cowritten by Del Porter, an architect of Spike Jones's City Slickers, and recorded with Spike himself on drums.[14] Audible evidence fails to support that hope.

Beyond the dubious material was the issue of John Trotter's one-an-a-two-an-a arrangements and a clique of soloists who, outside the

Hollywood studio system, would have made no bandleader's A-list. Compared with Bob Crosby's band, for example, which enjoyed an outstanding year with its new trumpet star, Billy Butterfield, and clarinetist Irving Fazola, Trotter's regulars (trumpeter Andy Secrest, saxophonist Jack Mayhew) were also-rans, and while they served his arrangements proficiently, the question remains: in an era of phenomenal musicianship, why was its most prized vocalist (voted, in January 1939, number one crooner of the United States by song promoters and, more democratically, best male singer by the readers of *Down Beat*) so rarely challenged by his peers?

"What's New?," one of Bing's two mightiest hits that year, resulted from a distant collusion with his baby brother's band. While experimenting with a cycle of chord changes, Bob Haggart devised a melody and arranged it as a concerto for Billy Butterfield, whom he and Bob Crosby discovered playing in a Kentucky band shell. The record, "I'm Free," made Butterfield a jazz star and convinced many that, with a lyric, the song could be a smash. Johnny Mercer, who wrote the band's greatest success of the year, "Day In — Day Out," tried his hand and, for once, was stumped. "He worked on it for two months," Haggart remembered, "but he said, 'I keep coming up with the same thing — I'm free, free as the birds in the trees, da da da da.' And so he just never did it, and then along comes Johnny Burke, who changed the whole idea."[15]

Burke liked the tune and, as Haggart later learned, had a conversation at the time with Larry Crosby. Larry told him, "You know, I love your lyrics, but they're all very poetic. Couldn't you write something more conversational?" "Like what?" he asked. Larry said, "Like 'what's new?' 'how's things?' something like that, one-on-one."[16] Haggart, who never met Burke, did not know he had written a lyric until he heard Bing's record, arranged for Trotter by the gifted bandleader Claude Thornhill. As Bing's record took off, other bandleaders (Benny Goodman, Charlie Barnet, Hal Kemp) adapted the song as a feature for their vocalists, and it endured as a standard, cropping up decade after decade in versions by Louis Armstrong, Peggy Lee, Frank Sinatra, Linda Ronstadt, and many others. Bing's performance is piquant in its conversational tact: the coolly interrogative "what's new?" belying the difficulty of a phrase that changes key after the first bar, from C to A flat; the atypical dropped-*g* on *treatin'*; clipped consonants on *bit* and *admit;* all contrasted with polished mordents and mellifluous high notes.

"What's New?" typified the evolution in Bing's style from, as critic John McDonough wrote, the "husky baritone of the 1931 Brunswicks to the mellow pipe organ"[17] of the 1940s — an organ so seemingly unaffected that, to paraphrase Huey Long, it made every man a crooner, at least in his own mind. Even *Time,* in its give-and-take manner, was touched: "Once more Crooner Crosby illuminates a dull song by singing it as though it were the best song he had ever heard."[18]

But consider the other five sides recorded at that June 30 session. Bing did himself and Harry Barris no service by recording his former partner's laborious "Neighbors in the Sky," which Kapp buried on the B-side of a middling duet with Connie Boswell, "Start the Day Right." (A few months before, Bing had done Barris the real kindness of reprising three of his great songs from the Cocoanut Grove.) He was similarly at a loss trying to mine something from Walter Donaldson's "Cynthia," recorded at the behest of his song publisher friend Rocco Vocco. Donaldson had ruled the roost in the 1920s, turning out dozens of enduring hits, but by the mid-1930s his style was outmoded, and despite Hollywood assignments, he wrote only a few important songs, notably "Did I Remember?" With its wordy imagery and disharmonious repetition of the name Cynthia, his new opus had no chance. Bing's forgotten record is not without appeal, despite an error (he turns a verb into a gerund), but Kapp buried it until 1940, when Bing scored Donaldson's last two hits, written with Johnny Mercer, who joined Bing for buoyant duets on "Mister Meadowlark" and "On Behalf of the Visiting Firemen."

The rest of the session was devoted to Gus Edwards — two admirable collaborations with the Music Maids. The first is a medley set up by the Maids ("School Days") followed by savory Crosby snippets of "Sunbonnet Sue," "Jimmy Valentine," and the nimble "If I Was a Millionaire." The last two are so pleasing, he might easily have made entire records of them. In the case of "Jimmy Valentine," that may have been the initial intention, as a fluff take, from the movie prerecordings, survives with an ominous spoken introduction in the manner of "Skeleton in the Closet." Just as Bing was finishing the first chorus, he slipped up and, without breaking stride, sang it into oblivion:

Look out! Look out!
For when you see his lantern shine
That's the time to jump right up and shout
uh, Help!, Oh Jesus Christ, I blew the time
And I'm a dirty son of a bitch
When Jimmy Valentine . . .

Edwards had learned his trade in the early years of Tin Pan Alley vaudeville, when topicality meant everything. The year he wrote "Jimmy Valentine," O. Henry's good-hearted burglar had been revived as the hero of a popular play. In 1905 Edwards wrote "In My Merry Oldsmobile," in recognition of the two automobiles that traversed half the country, from Detroit to Portland, in forty-four days. Composing the first hit tune to glorify the horseless carriage did not get Gus the free Olds he tried to pry out of the company, but it made him enough money to buy several. In later years, though, radio stations refused to play the song because it was considered akin to an advertisement. The embargo hurt sales of Bing's superb version with the general public (the BBC banned it outright), but Decca scored all the same when Oldsmobile bought 100,000 discs as part of a pact with Paramount to cross-promote its 1940 model and *The Star Maker*.

Bing's recorded treatment is far superior to that in the movie. Trotter's brisk arrangement starts as a waltz, permitting one chorus each for Bing and the orchestra; then it switches to four-four for the Music Maids, followed by Bing, who enters swinging. Accompanied by the rhythm section and the Maids, he peaks with a suavely injected "automo-bub-bub-bubbel-in'," before finishing with a Barris-style *shhh!* Four choruses in less than two and a half minutes: imagine if Trotter had opened it up with soloists and given Bing another chorus. Bix Beiderbecke rescued a tedious version of the song back in 1927, but for sheer élan, his chorus had nothing on Bing's.

The movie songs produced other gems, often alchemized from chancy material. Three days after wrapping *East Side of Heaven*, he insightfully interpreted the songs for Decca. In the title number, his pearly vowels and nuances — he makes the word *same* ("it's the same old Manhattan") a worldly sigh of routine — make more of the song than it's worth. (The first orchestral interjection will be recognized by many as the four-note riff from *The Twilight Zone*.) Burke took the idea for "Hang Your Heart on a Hickory Limb" from a maxim his wife often repeated, and inserted a Jesuitical piece of advice he figured Crosby would appreciate: "For every bit of pleasure there'll be pain / If you feel that's no bargain, then abstain." Bing capers through the verse and into the chorus, employing his old technique of squeezing in extra syllables toward the end, leading Crosby expert and singer Arne Fogel to comment, "Only Bing can be so funky, swingy, and funny at the same time."[19] Jimmy Monaco used an unusual forty-eight-bar *aba* format for "Sing a Song of Sunbeams," a song that ushered in a spate of Crosbyan odes to sanguinity, most famously the 1944 "Swinging on a Star."

Burke once explained his method for writing Bing's lyrics, and it was no different than Carroll Carroll's for writing radio scripts. "The most successful device," he said, "was to listen to Bing's conversation and either take my phrases directly from him or pattern some after his way of putting phrases together."[20] An evident example among the four songs he and Monaco wrote for *The Star Maker* is "Go Fly a Kite" (he rhymes *wind* and *chagrined*), which in Trotter's staid arrangement makes for a less than impassioned record — until Bing's Armstrongian closing chorus. The flat sentimentality of "A Man and His Dream" and "Still the Bluebird Sings" are partly redeemed by "An Apple for the Teacher" — in the picture a Linda Ware nonentity, but on record a jaunty duet for Bing and Connie Boswell, whose pouty on-the-beat southern inflections show precisely why the youthful Ella Fitzgerald (whom Bing later named as the best singer alive) adored her. Propelled by Perry Botkin's guitar, it preceded "What's New?" as a top seller.

Jack Kapp's instincts aside, Bing's new style lent itself to old songs, an ironic circumstance for the man who not too long before embodied Jazz Age modernity. Bing plainly delighted in the simple diatonic melodies of the bygone era, and the songs brought out his most ingenuous charm. Frank Sinatra debuted on records in 1939, with Harry James's band, though it was little noted at the time. Yet four years later, to exploit his momentous triumph as a single, one of those selections with James, "All or Nothing at All," was re-released and rocketed up the charts to become his first million-seller. In retrospect, the irony was unmistakable: at the moment Sinatra had extended the interpretation of lyrics — patented by Bing on records like "What's New?" — into a darker and more personal realm, Bing had reserved much of his most poignant work for the easier mercies of nostalgia.

Despite the rearguard repertory, Bing did not succumb to musical apathy. He continued to find ways to enliven the old with nuance and power. "If I Had My Way" is exemplary, a Crosby waltz in which phrases resonate like gongs, thanks to perfect parallel mordents, over a slow but pulsing tempo; the voice is lovely, the high notes exquisite, and the emotions deeply persuasive and of a sort no one else could have mustered. The romantic vulnerability of a Sinatra is unsuited to these elemental melodies. They demand a bounteous voice and temperament to avoid bathos while cutting through the cobwebs. Despite its egregiously antiquated minstrel lyric, Bing's "The Missouri Waltz" is a neglected gem. It suggests that the king of technology and prince of jazz was also the last nineteenth-century man, an artist genuinely besotted by the past — that is, genuinely capable of extracting nuggets of beauty and sentiment where his contemporaries found only corn.

On a few sessions Bing's accompaniment combined John Scott Trotter's Frying Pan Five (a name that promised more steam than it delivered) and the Foursome, a vocal choir that doubled on a variety of instruments. Bing had casually met two of the singers, Ray Johnson and Del Porter, in Spokane, when he was a Musicalader and they were appearing with a band at the Davenport Hotel. They later teamed with two other singers, worked for Mack Sennett, and scored on Broadway in *Girl Crazy*. A few Hollywood films followed, but they were about to head East again when Bing invited them to appear on *KMH;* soon they became regulars on Bob Burns's summer replacement show. What Bing and Trotter liked about the Foursome, beyond their efficient harmonies, was their unison playing of the ocarina, a potato-shaped wind instrument with ten holes that produces pure tones (no partials or overtones). The combination of ocarinas and Del Porter's clarinet provided a catchy freshness to oldies ("Ida, Sweet as Apple Cider" and "Down by the Old Mill Stream") and western songs ("When the Bloom Is on the Sage" and the bestselling "Allá en el Rancho Grande," Bing's first time singing in flawless Spanish). The sound inspired Burke and Monaco to write a song about the ocarina for *Road to Singapore*.

*　　*　　*

Bing recorded every week in March, early April, and — after completing *The Star Maker* — every week in June. His radio show continued to wax in popularity with the usual guests, including Frances Langford, William Frawley, Bert Lahr, Joan Bennett, Matty Malneck, Pat O'Brien, Leo McCarey, Florence George (Everett's new wife), Freddie Bartholomew, Rudolph Ganz, Jackie Cooper, John Wayne, Gladys Swarthout, Walter Damrosch, Basil Rathbone, Walter Huston, Lucille Ball, and so forth. Bing filled his downtime with sporting events. He played tennis at the Palm Springs Racquet Club (along with Errol Flynn, Frank Morgan, and other film stars); participated in the broadcast of a two-minute Joe Louis fight; and traveled to Boston to watch Ligaroti come in next to last at Suffolk Downs, ending a meteoric career. Bing had bad luck of a different kind when his horse Midge raced at Hollywood Park and he sent a friend to bet a large sum on the nose; Midge won, but the friend did not get to the track on time. Bing found a few days to join Dixie in Palm Springs, where they threw a party at Cafe La Maze for the Eddie Lowes, the Dave Butlers, and the Herb Polesies. Then it was back to *The Star Maker* and Jack Kapp.

Part of Decca's invasion of the past focused on new versions of Crosby classics from before 1934, before Decca. Jack and Bing had several possible motives. For one, they were good songs and, as Bing's style had radically changed, warranted new interpretations. For another, many of the songs were by Bing's friends and associates, so he was doing them a favor. For a third, the idea of making a movie based on Bing's life had been in the air for a couple of years, since the deal Bing attempted to broker for Ted Crosby and Grover Jones, and was thought more likely now, given the vogue for pictures about contemporary entertainers. In that event, Decca would want to own versions of the essential records Bing had recorded for Brunswick. That was the nub of the matter. Brunswick had recently been acquired by CBS, guaranteeing an impending rivalry.

In 1938 William Paley, who had declined to invest in Decca when the recording business was moribund, bought ARC (the holding company for Brunswick and Columbia), with the intention of reviving Columbia as a prominent label. RCA Victor's executive, Edward Wallerstein, itching to leave the company, had convinced Paley to purchase ARC for $700,000. Paley did not need much convincing. As the economy revived, he looked with increasing jealousy at David

Sarnoff's NBC, which not only controlled two networks to his one but operated the profitable and prestigious RCA. The record business had rallied: Kapp's visionary pricing, Crosby's steady and increasing sales, and the tremendous commercial breakthrough of the swing craze brought the industry back to heights approaching the glory days of 1927. The turnabout would be complete by 1940. Yet Paley had more than business on his mind. He wanted revenge.

Paley and Sarnoff had competed bitterly for ten years, frequently over cultural programming. At a time when intellectuals disdained radio and Capitol Hill vetted its contributions to the national good, the networks strove for prestige; highbrow signings were essential, even if they could not attract sponsors. In 1930 Paley brought off a historic coup by hiring the New York Philhamonic, under the direction of Arturo Toscanini, for Sunday-afternoon broadcasts. Toscanini remained a CBS staple until 1936, when he declined to renew his contract with the orchestra. Paley and the Philharmonic hoped he would change his mind but in the interim reluctantly accepted his no. Sarnoff and his programming chief, John Royal, did not. Toscanini was a prize catch, and they came up with an offer he could not refuse: NBC would create for him his own symphony orchestra. It was a stunning, buccaneering gamble, the kind Paley prided himself on making. Paley went to war. With RCA's former chief, Wallerstein, in his camp and ARC in his pocket, he hoped to cut RCA off at the knees. His timing could not have been better.

By 1939 the synergy between records and radio had grown so significant, *Variety* initiated a new feature, "Network Plugs, 8 A.M. to 1 A.M." — a list of the records most played on the flagship stations of the NBC (WEAF and WJZ) and CBS (WABC) networks, computed over a week. Twenty to forty plays in a week was considered high and certain to increase the sales of sheet music and records. The need for accurately tracked sales and playlists was answered in July 1940, when *Billboard* aced *Variety* and published its first chart of bestselling records, a signal tribute to a flourishing industry. By then, as *Time* reported in a September 1939 survey of the "Phonograph Boom," it had "fattened into one of the fastest growing business in the U.S., with an annual gross of some $36,000,000."[21] *Time* assigned most of the credit to "the five-year-old Decca concern, with Crosby as its Caruso."[22] Decca sold 12 million records in 1939, second only to

RCA (with 13 million), for an estimated annual gross of 4 million dollars. Bing accounted for a sixth of Decca's sales — "a post-Caruso record record." *Fortune* reported that Decca ceased to advertise because the company could no longer keep up with orders. In 1940 Decca sold 18 million records, still a close second to RCA.

Paley soon killed the various smaller ARC logos as well as Brunswick, reserving Columbia for his status signings, which included several symphony orchestras, along with such conductors as Stokowski (Toscanini's rival), Mitropoulos, Rodzinski, and Stock, and just about any swing band with an open contract, including Goodman, Basie, Ellington, James, Krupa, Red Norvo and Mildred Bailey, and Kay Kyser. Then he borrowed a page from Decca's playbook. Kapp's reduced prices had revitalized the whole industry; Paley reduced the price of twelve-inch classical discs by half, to a buck apiece, driving a wedge into RCA's dominance in the field (the one area Kapp neglected). Meanwhile, there was now the issue of who owned the Brunswick catalog that Kapp had nursed before leaving the company to create Decca. A deal was made. All Brunswick records made before Warner Bros. leased the company to ARC, in December 1931, would go to Decca — in which Warner Bros. maintained a financial interest.[23] All Brunswicks made after Warner Bros. had given ARC a ten-year lease, including most of the Crosby sides, would remain part of CBS's ARC holdings.

With Columbia going toe-to-toe with RCA and the increased acceptance of reissues, it was only a matter of time before both companies would release old Crosby sides. At Kapp's suggestion, Bing recorded new versions of his benchmark recordings, including a couple that remained in the Decca trove. Kapp believed that the Bing of 1939 was far more acceptable to audiences than the Bing who originally recorded "Star Dust," "I Surrender, Dear," "It Must Be True," "Wrap Your Troubles in Dreams," "Home on the Range," and "Just One More Chance." Most of those songs had been hits in late 1930 and early 1931; however mannered or naive they may have sounded in 1939, they had been lanterns in the musical landscape of their day. Good songs ought to withstand many and diverse interpretations, as indeed these did. Yet Bing's remakes could only display, at best, a great singer singing great songs. They could not recapture the novelty of brand-new songs rendered in a brand-new style. The originals helped define the time in which they were created; the remakes helped define the ripening of Crosby.[24]

All the same, some were improvements over the originals. Bing was right to reclaim "Star Dust," which had become one of the most performed of all songs in the eight years since he introduced the lyric. Unfortunately, he dropped the verse, but his entrance — after a spacey introduction with a long harp arpeggio (the kind Spike Jones later parodied in "Holiday for Strings") — is alluring and his follow-through is flawlessly composed, if a bit stentorian. After *East Side of Heaven*, Bing invited Matty Malneck to record with him on this session, and passages in Malneck's swirling arrangement would later be referenced by Gordon Jenkins in the setting he devised for a definitive 1956 Nat "King" Cole version. Malneck's ensemble included Manny Klein and accordionist Milton DeLugg, both of whom are scored high so that Bing's voice is the low instrument, an anchor for the others, especially on another strong tune from the session, "Deep Purple," notable for Bing's range and expansive low notes.

He was unable to replicate the magic of the 1933 "Home on the Range," but he did bring a renewed authority to the Harry Barris remakes, ensuring their survival as standards. The new "I Surrender, Dear" is more deeply felt and conversational than the original. The long instrumental prelude and jazzy tempo changes of the Jimmy Grier arrangement are gone, but a comparison of the vocals reveals the greater finesse and weightiness he now brought to the song that had hastened his journey to network radio.

"Wrap Your Troubles in Dreams" is more remarkable, supernally relaxed, especially in the effortlessly dramatized bridge. The song lends itself to Bing's legato phrasing with a two-bar rhythmic pattern that occurs eleven times — that is, for twenty-two of its thirty-two bars: quarter note (*wrap*) quarter note (*your*) eighth note eighth note (*trou-bles*) quarter note (*in*) dotted half (*dreams*) quarter note (*and*). On every occasion, Bing expands the dotted half note, pushing the following quarter note into the next bar, producing a subtle syncopation and a canny example of his musical pulse at work. In a second take, sung at a brighter tempo, his embellishments are more overt, and it might have been chosen for release, except that an apparent change in the arrangement confused Bing as he headed into the final bridge, resulting in the most famous of Crosby fluffs, played out to the bitter end:

> *Castles may tumble, that's fate after all*
> *Life's really funny that way*
> *Sang the wrong melody, we'll play it back*
> *See what it sounds like, hey hey*
> *They cut out eight bars, the dirty bastards*
> *And I didn't know which eight bars he was gonna cut*
> *Why don't somebody tell me these things around here*
> *Holy Christ, I'm going off my nut.*

The fluff take was instantly bootlegged, and fifty or so copies were released on a label stamped Triple-X. Soon numerous bootlegs of the bootleg were pirated — an underground hit.

Other kinds of nostalgia permeated Bing's 1939 recordings. Accompanied by Victor Young, he turned to Gershwin for the first time in three years to essay exceedingly slow and reflective versions of "Somebody Loves Me" and "Maybe." He also returned, after three years, to Dick McIntyre for two of his best Hawaiian songs, "To You, Sweetheart, Aloha" and "My Isle of Golden Dreams," displaying the candor that enriched his readings of songs from the Gus Edwards era. His affection for the melodies is unmistakable, as is his evident enjoyment in the sound of his voice. On two occasions, in 1955 and 1960,[25] Bing cited "My Isle of Golden Dreams" as his favorite record, an intriguing selection because Decca declined to reissue it during the entire LP era. Say this much: it represents the purity of his voice and his agile control at a glorious peak. The phrasing is unerring, the high notes full and fair, and the mordents — varied in stress and duration — are never merely ornamental; they *do* something, advancing meaning and feeling.

Those qualities were no less apparent when, with Johnny Mercer's lyric, he transformed "And the Angels Sing," Benny Goodman's jazzed-up *fraylich* — a Yiddish dance tune drawn from klezmer music — into a ballad. Goodman's record propelled the jitterbugs with its heady two-beat interlude by trumpet player Ziggy Elman, who devised the piece. In turning it into a love song, Bing understates everything yet brings his own undulations into play: on the superb release, his mordents roll out like ripples in a stream.

For sentiment of another kind, in March Kapp recorded Bing singing Irving Berlin's "God Bless America," written in 1917 but suppressed by the composer because he thought it a shameless flag-waver, until Kate Smith asked him for a patriotic song on the eve of the Second World War. He also recorded Francis Scott Key's "The Star Spangled Banner," written in 1814 and decreed by an act of Congress as the national anthem in 1931. They were not chosen for musical or commercial value, though the convincingly sung Berlin song sold remarkably well — almost as well as Kate Smith's. Bing's take on the national anthem is unsurprising; he sings it straight and sober, as though he were standing in a ballpark. These records convey little significance today. They are musical heirlooms. But in their day they imparted a political meaning beyond rote patriotism.

In March 1939, when the Berlin and Key songs were recorded, patriotism was a sorely contested idea. In one of the strangest consequences of political opportunism, the far left (communists) and far right (American Firsters) snuggled together under the covers of isolationism. Hitler was not the problem, they agreed; it was either J. P. Morgan and Jewish bankers or commies and Jewish radicals, or the imminent invasion of an Asian horde (the Yellow Peril) sweeping westward to wipe out civilization, Christianity, and white people. Personalities as anomalous as Father Charles E. Coughlin and Charles Lindbergh were heard by millions on radio, arguing that Hitler was the last bulwark against greater evils. The country refused to consider war, and Roosevelt despaired of mobilizing aid for Europe. Even as he pushed through the Lend-Lease Act in 1941, providing credit for opponents of the Axis, the Almanac Singers sang, "Franklin D., listen to me / You Ain't a-gonna send me 'cross the sea."[26]

"The Star Spangled Banner" is not an isolationist song. Before Bing, the last singer to make a popular record of it was John McCormack, in the spring of 1917, as General Pershing's American Expeditionary Forces headed for France. In the immediate weeks before Bing made his version, Franco marched on Madrid, and Hitler — after conscripting all German youth and refusing to meet with Roosevelt — invaded Prague and Memel. A couple of weeks before that, in the United States, 22,000 Nazis congregated in Madison Square Garden; anti-Nazi protests of equal size followed. Music was invariably caught in the crosshairs: the Daughters of the American Revolution declared Marian Anderson unfit to perform in Constitution Hall because of her color; Germany banned jazz and swing; Russia purged the leadership of the Komsomol for permitting music that encouraged the rumba, tango, and jitterbug; Italy allowed swing but barred Jewish music and musicians as well as most American movies. In 1940 the recently resigned ambassador to Great Britain, Joseph P. Kennedy, addressed fifty top Hollywood executives at a luncheon and told them to "stop making anti-Nazi pictures or using the film medium to promote or show sympathy to the cause of the democracies versus the dictators." He warned them to "get those Jewish names off the screen."[27]

In that context, the act of recording patriotic songs was neither pro forma, sentimental, nor innocent. Any doubts that Bing's recordings endorsed a particular vision of America were swept aside the following summer when Decca released his four-sided *Ballad for Americans*. Earl Robinson, who wrote the music for John Latouche's libretto, was not a rote liberal preaching tolerance; he was a loyal communist who supported the Hitler-Stalin pact, though his personal politics ran largely to issues of racial equality. A prolific composer, he was best known at the time for the classic union protest song "Joe Hill." In 1938 he and Latouche created a forerunner to *Ballad for Americans*, "Ballad of Uncle Sam," for the Federal Theater Project, which was roundly vilified by Texas congressman Martin Dies's committee investigating "un-American" activities — like racially integrated theater. He slandered their work as "an American version of the 'Internationale.'"[28] "It died early," Louis Untermeyer wrote in his notes to Bing's LP release of *Ballad for Americans*, "with a noose of red tape around its neck."[29]

After Hitler invaded Poland on September 1, 1939, the public grew resistant to native demagogues. *Ballad for Americans* debuted on CBS in November, introduced by Burgess Meredith and sung by the princely African American baritone Paul Robeson, and was a sensation. *Variety* described it as "a masterpiece of authentic American love of country."[30] *Reader's Digest* concurred: "the finest piece of American propaganda."[31] Robeson recorded it in February. Numerous singers (hundreds according to Earl Robinson), including Lawrence Tibbett and James Melton, performed it over the next few years. But Bing was the only popular singer to record it, in four parts, accompanied by Victor Young conducting the Decca Concert Orchestra and the Ken Darby Singers. Robinson thought Tibbett's version too operatic, but "Bing Crosby recorded the piece beautifully on Decca, and his version sold another twenty thousand copies. I remember gently exaggerating the Crosby style when I described his crooning to friends." Robinson added, "By the way, he sang it in the lower Robeson key."[32]

Bing did not approach the project lightly. He studied the work before the session, and his concentration in the studio was painstaking; everything had to be right. In contrast to his usual speed (five tunes in two hours, rarely more than two takes), he devoted an hour to each of the four segments. If the reviews were not overtly political, political righteousness fueled the cheers of latecomers to the world of popular music. "Bing Crosby came of age, musically speaking, in his last week's album, *Ballad for Americans*," wrote *New York Post* critic Michael Levin. "This is the finest recorded performance Bing had done to date and shows that in the last few years he has gone far beyond binging and has really learned how to sing." When he finished patronizing Bing, Levin chanced a risky comparison with Paul Robeson's Victor set that undoubtedly gladdened the hearts of Kapp's team: "For all of Robeson's magnificent voice, we prefer the Crosby version. The recording is better, the orchestration is better, and the chorus is better trained."

Ballad for Americans is now antiquated: a rabble-rousing, melting-pot, bleacher-cheer oratorio, narrated and sung by a bard who identifies himself, at the very end, as the personification of America. It begins:

In '76 the sky was red,
Thunder rumbling overhead,
Bad King George couldn't sleep in his bed,
And on that stormy morn,
Old Uncle Sam was born. (Some birthday!)
Old Sam put on a three-cornered hat,
And in a Richmond church he sat,
And Patrick Henry told him that,

While America drew breath,
It was liberty or death.
(Did they all believe in liberty in those days?)
Nobody who was anybody believed it.
And everybody who was anybody, they doubted it.
Nobody had faith, nobody — nobody but, uh, Washington, Tom Paine,
    Benjamin Franklin, Haym Salomon, Crispus Attucks, Lafayette.
    Nobodies.

One imagines Kapp leaping at the opportunity to record it with the man he had helped establish as the personification of American song. Surely no great political courage was required, because suddenly every political group wanted to claim the work as its private anthem. The Republicans hired Ray Middleton (after Robeson declined) to sing it at the convention that nominated Wendell Willkie as its 1940 presidential candidate. One week earlier it was sung at the Communist Party convention. The political significance of Bing's version lay in his personal standing, specifically the ethnicity he was now intent on making a crucial component of his public persona. Bing's radio audience was estimated as high as 50 million. But when most people thought of an Irish Catholic on the air, the figure brought to mind was the increasingly repudiated Father Coughlin, whose pro-Hitler tirades had grown so bellicose that they provoked Irish American gangs to descend on Jewish neighborhoods to start fights.

Coughlin's family had come to America in the same pre-Famine era as the Harrigans and, like them, had settled in Canada, where he was born in 1891. He and Bing started their radio careers on CBS and were considered among the idiom's first masters. (Wallace Stegner has described Coughlin's delivery as "such mellow richness, such heartwarming, confidential intimacy.")[33] William Paley refused to renew Coughlin's contract after he accused CBS of censorship, but the relationship could not have survived the priest's rabid anti-semitism. NBC also refused to broadcast him, so Coughlin organized his own network of twenty-six independent stations and reached more people than ever before. By 1940 he was so far over the edge that Catholics turned from him in embarrassment (two years later Archbishop Edward Mooney, with the support of the Vatican, ordered him to cease publication of *Social Justice,* his noxious magazine). That same year Bing recorded the work in which the founding of America is traced to a family of patriots that includes a Jewish financier (Haym Salomon) and a runaway slave (Crispus Attucks). *Ballad for Americans* was American history as refracted by New Deal liberalism and served with a spoon. But it worked, and through it Bing spoke his piece and balanced the scales.

Bing had never made much of his ethnicity. Every aspect of big-time entertainment discouraged him, and in any case, it would have been a stretch; his paternal Anglican side settled in America well before the Revolution, and his maternal Irish side arrived in New Brunswick in the 1830s. Unlike minstrelsy and vaudeville, which were steeped in ethnic stereotypes, Hollywood and radio insisted upon common denominators. The thinking was that a picture about Jews would attract only Jews, and a picture about Catholics would attract only Catholics, and so forth. No all-Negro picture had ever earned much money. Leo McCarey's affecting *Make Way for Tomorrow* (1937) flopped, it was argued, because it was about old people, and they never turned out in sufficient numbers. The picture business was tough enough without deliberately limiting the number of ticket buyers. Since the end of the early-thirties gangster cycle, Hollywood's product had steadily slouched toward the ethnically rinsed paradise of Louis B. Mayer's beloved Carvel, MGM's city on a hill, home to the confessor/jurist Judge Hardy and his son, Andy. Only character players could keep their accents, receding hairlines, noses, and names. In all the feature films he had made to date, Bing had never played a character with a name — Crosby, Danvers, Bronson, Williams, Jones (twice), Lawton, Grayson, Gordon, Crocker, Larabee, Poole, Marvin, Boland, Remsen, Beebe, Lawton, Martin, Earl — that could be construed as remotely Irish.

He now commenced a conversion, from all-American crooner to hyphenated-American nationalist, an ethnic in a land of ethnics, publicly and privately. At his behest, Larry and Ted began to investigate the family's genealogy; in later years Bing would wear the emblem of his Irish forebears on his blazers. Yet long before that, as Coughlin's name faded from public discourse and memory, Bing's name became inextricably linked to the community of Irish American Catholics. American popular song derived from a motley of ethnicities; the one address where the efficacy of the melting pot could not be denied was Tin Pan Alley. It succeeded because the Jews, blacks, Italians, Anglos, southerners, westerners, midwesterners, and others refused to melt, all priding themselves on the particular heritages that fed their art. Bing, the prodigy of the Inland Empire raised on the diversity of recordings, found his cultural corner in rediscovering the Irish in his pedigree.

The transformation was apparently triggered by *Ballad for Americans* and was undoubtedly hastened by the war. Four months after recording the Robinson-Latouche cantata, Bing took the only outright political stand of his career, which seemed to undermine all he stood for by aligning him with the movie colony's most conservative element. On the eve of the election, he gave a radio address in support of Wendell Willkie and lent his name to an advertisement in the *New York Times,* signed by 165 Hollywood figures determined to refute the notion that the "Mighty Motion Picture Industry" was united in supporting FDR's third-term candidacy.[34] Willkie, a moderate businessman who came to the public's attention when he denounced special interests on the radio show *Information, Please,* could have passed for a liberal Democrat in any other season. But not in 1940, and not in opposition to FDR. Bing's reputation as a reactionary was sealed through his affiliation with such right-wing signatories as Walt Disney, Gary Cooper, Hedda Hopper, Adolph Menjou, George Murphy, Mary Pickford, and Lew Ayres, who, having taken his role in *All Quiet on the Western Front* to heart, created his own tempest by declaring himself a conscientious objector. Inevitably, Bing was singled out. The *Philadelphia Record* published a vicious editorial, accusing Crosby alone of ingratitude and corruption; the first because he was "a two-bit crooner" when Roosevelt came to office and now boasted an income equal to "the titans of industry," the second because Del Mar, referred to as "one of his racetracks," used WPA money slated for a park.[35]

Bing was taken aback by the brouhaha. His politics, such as they were, had never been monolithic. He was no Roosevelt hater. In 1935 he had participated in fund-raising celebrations for the president's birthday on the Warner Bros. lot. Moreover, when he returned to *Kraft Music Hall* after the election, on November 14, he made a plea for the nation to unite behind the president now that the contest was over. The editorial attack may have prompted that statement, but it was not the only way in which he distanced himself from the other signatories. When Roosevelt died in 1945, Bing sang "Faith of Our Fathers" and Brahms's "Lullaby" on NBC's two-hour memorial broadcast. Nor did he join the belligerents a few years later as a "friendly witness" during the HUAC's reign of terror. Nor did he allow politics to influence his professional relationships. He sat out politics for good.

A month after the election, Bing surprised Kapp with a request to do a record. He rarely bothered to suggest numbers; he had always been content to leave repertory to Jack, except when he was doing a favor for someone. Now he wanted an arrangement prepared and studio time set aside to record "Did Your Mother Come from Ireland?" It was his first Irish song, opening up a new area that even Jack had failed to consider. Victor Young was selected to write the arrangements and conduct the December 10 session, which produced four sides. Two of them reflected Bing's authentic if neglected heritage (the other Irish song was "Where the River Shannon Flows"), and two reflected the southern Negro heritage he so often borrowed as his own, albeit as construed by Stephen Foster ("My Old Kentucky Home" and "De Camptown Races"). During the next few years he extended both lineages, playing minstrel Dan Emmett in *Dixie* and Irish American priest Father O'Malley in *Going My Way* and *The Bells of St. Mary's,* his way of tipping the scales in favor of liberal benovolence.

26

EASY RIDERS

You know, when we were doing a Road *picture, he'd get out of his car at Paramount with his shoelaces untied. I'd say, "Don't you have time to tie your shoelaces before you leave the house?" He'd say, "Oh, I stopped at Wilshire to hit a bucket of balls." This was before we went to work in the morning.*

— Bob Hope (1992)[1]

Bob Hope arrived in Los Angeles in September 1937 with his wife, Dolores, and, he would later admit, a "log-size chip on my shoulder."[2] He had been lured by a Paramount producer who thought he showed potential. But as an established Broadway star, he was defensive, suspicious, and truculent. Hollywood was not going to get the better of him. He had money saved, he told his agent, and if he did not like his part in *The Big Broadcast of 1938,* he was ready to return to New York. Dolores, dismayed when she realized her husband's name meant nothing in Hollywood, was not too keen on moving anyway. Hope was nearing thirty-five, an advanced age to start out in pictures — not for a character actor, certainly, but for the leading man he meant to be. Between 1934 and 1936 he had made eight shorts in New York. After the first opened, Walter Winchell reported, "When Bob Hope saw his picture at the Rialto, he said, 'When they catch John Dillinger . . .

they're going to make him sit through it twice.'"[3] Bob was more sanguine about his stage and radio work.

Leslie Townes Hope was born on May 29, 1903, the fifth of seven sons, in Eltham, England, a suburb of London. His father was a stonemason, his mother a singer who accompanied herself on harp and piano. The family moved to Cleveland, Ohio, in 1907, and at ten Leslie demonstrated his inclination toward show business by impersonating Chaplin, the sensation of 1914. He dropped out of high school to study dancing with a hoofer, taking whatever jobs he could get — soda jerking, boxing, hustling pool. Soon Hope was giving dancing lessons, and he drafted his girlfriend for an act that played midwestern vaudeville houses. Later, teamed with dancer George Byrne, he traveled the Keith circuit all the way to New York, by which time he had changed his name. Hope and Byrne found work around, but rarely in, Manhattan before splitting up.

Bob's first substantial stage role, as a butler (Screeves) in the 1928 flop *Ups-a-Daisy,* came to nothing. Yet while emceeing in small out-of-the-way joints, he discovered his ability to get laughs. He had no material and little experience telling jokes, but his fearlessly snappy style and determination to win approval pleased customers. He charmed them. Realizing that charm could take him only so far, he scrambled for jokes, collecting them from magazines, books, and other performers. His break came not as a comedian but as the second lead in Jerome Kern's *Roberta.* His easy ability to get laughs earned him rave notices, which led to other Broadway shows and offers to appear on radio and in film shorts.

Mitchell Leisen and Harlan Thompson, the director and producer of a forthcoming movie in *The Big Broadcast* series, caught Hope in the *Ziegfeld Follies of 1936,* in which he and Eve Arden sang "I Can't Get Started." Paramount had a similar love duet lined up for its picture but was hesitant to cast an unknown. After Jack Benny turned down the role, however, they went back to Hope, who was now wowing audiences with Jimmy Durante and Ethel Merman in Cole Porter's *Red, Hot and Blue!* He had one prior commitment — Bob had signed a twenty-six-week contract to deliver monologues on *The Rippling Rhythm Revue,* a Woodbury soap program with bandleader Shep Fields. Paramount guaranteed him a transcontinental hookup enabling him to fulfill the contract.

*   *   *

While Dolores unpacked at the Beverly Wilshire Hotel, Bob impatiently left for the studio, where he knew nobody but Leisen and Thompson. When they showed him his song, Robin and Rainger's "Thanks for the Memory," he was disappointed to learn that it was a duet, with Shirley Ross, not a solo. He changed his mind when a rehearsal pianist played it; he knew the song was a sure-fire hit. Before filming began, Bob called Bing. Theirs was the sort of friendship that thrives on competition, as became evident in the key interests that seemed to bind them at the hip — golf and a brinkmanship approach to comedy. They had little else in common. As Dolores noted, "Bing loved to hunt and fish, and Bob wouldn't be caught hunting or fishing anything but a golf ball. Bob had no interest in horses. They lived entirely different lives, but they respected each other and loved working together. And eventually they found they loved each other very much."[4]

Their millions of fans in the 1940s and 1950s, when Bing and Bob emerged as one of the most adored teams in show-business history, would have been astonished to learn that the love Dolores spoke of did not blossom fully until 1961, when the two families shared a castle in England during the filming of *The Road to Hong Kong,* the least successful entry in the *Road* series but the most important to their relationship. Prior to 1961 their friendship, although genuine, was largely professional. Grievances, petty or serious, were not acknowledged or discussed, and socializing was sporadic, in part because Bob remained slightly in awe of Bing and because Bing believed that actors' chemistry ought to be saved for the set. Yet they worked together so often, they saw more of each other than many avowed buddies: seven *Road* pictures, the Victory Caravan, charity events, radio and television broadcasts, Bing's cameos in Bob's movies, endless rounds of publicly covered golf. Bing died just as Melville Shavelson completed the script for what would have been their eighth road trip, *Road to the Fountain of Youth.*

Dolores had known Bing before she met Bob, in Philadelphia in 1927, when she and Ginger Meehan worked in *Honeymoon Lane.* She next saw him in 1932, when she sang at New York's Richmond Club and a columnist referred to her as the female Crosby. Bing and Dixie came by the club, and she told them that the comparison unnerved her. That was the year Bing and Bob first met near the Friars Club and shared the stage at the Capitol Theater. Bob and

Dolores were married in 1933. In the summer of 1935, while Bing and Dixie vacationed in Saratoga, Bing ran into Bob at Paul Whiteman's opening at the Riviera Club — their only encounter in the interim between the Capitol and the Hopes' arrival in Hollywood.

Yet within a few weeks, Bob's name was appearing in the columns as a Crosby crony. A Paramount publicist orchestrated the November golf match in which the loser was purportedly obliged to work a day as an unpaid stand-in for the winner. The newspapers went along. "Crosby, champion of the Lakeside Club, is the favorite. Hope, a former Broadway stage actor, is new to the movies. Little is known here of his golfing prowess," wrote a stringer for the *New York Herald Tribune,* as if the match were a serious sporting event.[5] Hope carded an 84 to Bing's three-over-par 73.

The studio was less successful in its attempts to remodel Bob's face. Unlike Bing, who refused to consider ear surgery, Hope was actually willing to have his nose unsloped if required. Dolores talked him out of it. The nose issue vanished, along with his anonymity west of the Mississippi, when *The Big Broadcast of 1938* opened. "Thanks for the Memory" was greatly admired (though it did little for Shirley Ross); and Paramount's advertising campaign, depicting the all-star cast in caricatured profiles, made Hope's nose almost iconic. It remained only for Bing to call him Ski-nose — and Spoonface and Trout Snout and Ratchedhead and the Pepsodent Pinnochio, et al. — for a defect to be reassessed as a major asset.

Three months after the Woodbury series ended, Bob was added to the cast of *Your Hollywood Parade,* a Warner Bros. promotional program with emcee Dick Powell, sponsored by Lucky Strike and its intrusive despot, George Washington Hill, whom Hope remembered as constantly demanding more and more violins. It lasted only a few months, through March 1938. But that was time enough to draw national attention to Hope's topical and leering one-liners and his fast, wisecracking delivery. Bob debuted as Bing's guest on *Kraft Music Hall* in July, to promote his picture. Frank Woodruff, a J. Walter Thompson program director, called it "a very good show" but thought "Hope not quite at home in this set up."[6] That remarkable evaluation may not have been completely off base; the show was little noticed, unlike Hope's pas de deux with Bing two weeks later at Del Mar.

Bing invited Bob and Dolores to the track for the weekend. Dolores recalled of the August 6 clambake, "Bing was, naturally, master of ceremonies and he called Bob up and they started fooling, doing these same funny little things that they did at the Capitol when they were there. And somebody from Paramount said, They're like cream and sugar. They were just marvelous together, really, a natural."[7] The executives at ringside included Paramount producers William LeBaron and Harlan Thompson. "So they went back to the studio," Bob recalled, "and everybody said, 'How can they work that good together? My God.' They didn't know that we had done it for two weeks at the Capitol. And they said, 'We gotta put these guys in a picture.'"[8]

Yet back in Hollywood, second-guessing tempered the initial enthusiasm. Bing was Paramount's bread and butter; Bob was, the studio hoped, up-and-coming. When the front office saw prints of *The Big Broadcast of 1938,* it picked up his option and rushed him into a tepid Burns and Allen vehicle, *College Swing.* He fared no better in *Give Me a Sailor* or the desperately titled *Thanks for the Memory,* all rolled out that year. Confidence in the idea of teaming him with Bing waned. How much interest could be generated by a crooner and a comedian, or for that matter, any two men who were not united by stormy drama? Buddy pictures had not yet found a niche in Hollywood beyond Laurel and Hardy and Saturday-matinee cowboys and their sidekicks. In his memoir Bob credits Bing with getting the project rolling: "Not everyone knows how shrewd he is when it comes to the entertainment business. He instantly recognized the value of the *Road* pictures as a way of getting a spontaneous ad-libby type of humor. There were doubters in the studio who shook their heads and said, 'Well . . . I don't know.' But Bing was an important star. They listened to him. He was right."[9]

Captains of industry, like politicians, often trust the opinions of others more than their own, most especially in show business, where the sine qua non of survival is someone else to blame. Lord and Thomas, the advertising agency that placed Hope in *The Rippling Rhythm Revue* and *Your Hollywood Parade,* was unable to secure him his own program until his success on the Lucky Strike show and reviews of his first picture convinced Pepsodent toothpaste, which was looking to replace the ratings-damaged — how times had changed! —

Amos 'n' Andy. The thirty-minute *Pepsodent Show Starring Bob Hope* triumphed from the start, ruling its Tuesday-night time slot (and lasting defiantly through 1950). With guest stars and regulars — at first, Judy Garland, bandleader Skinnay Ennis, and comedian Jerry Colonna, who sang like a police siren and hailed Hope with a trademark phrase, "Greetings, Gate!" — the show was brisk and surprising, chiefly because of Hope's timely one-liners, which were often aimed at Hollywood. The popularity of *The Pepsodent Show,* in turn, convinced Paramount that it was on the right track and propelled the search for a script to team Hope and Crosby.

Screenwriters Frank Butler and Don Hartman — the duo behind *Waikiki Wedding, Paris Honeymoon,* and *The Star Maker* — were given the task of finding a suitable property. They did not have far to look. After briefly considering a spurned Burns and Allen project called *Havana,* they turned to their own rusting script based on a story by Harry Hervey, a veteran of exotic intrigue (he plotted von Sternberg's *Shanghai Express*). Initially adapted as a project for Bing in 1936, titled *Follow the Sun,* it was revised in 1938 by Butler and Ken Englund, to tell the story of Josh Mallon, heir to the Mallon Mercantile fortune, and his pal Ace Winthrop, the son of a horse thief, who board a ship and find themselves bound for Indochina. With Hartman on board, the script was retooled, retitled *(Road to Mandalay),* and offered as a knockabout escapade for Jack Oakie and Fred MacMurray, who had clicked in a couple of 1936 films.[10] They or their agents turned it down. Now Hartman and Butler re-revised it for Bing and Bob, tricking it up with gags and places to insert songs.

To underscore a rivalry, it was decided to situate one woman between them. The studio chose Dorothy Lamour, formerly Mary Leta Dorothy Slaton of New Orleans, where she was born in 1914. When her parents divorced, her devoted mother married Clarence Lambour just long enough for Dorothy (as she was known) to take his name. At sixteen Dorothy won a beauty contest, and she and her mother relocated to Chicago, where she operated a hotel elevator and looked for a place to sing. A hotel acquaintance set her up with Everett Crosby, who took her to hear his brother Bing and introduced her to bandleader Herbie Kay, who hired and married her. On a tour in Texas, she showed Herbie a poster that providentially dropped the *b* from Lambour. Dorothy decided to keep it that way. She was soon hired to sing at New York's Stork Club and the Greenwich Village boîte, One Fifth Avenue, where her repeat customers included Bob Hope. Paramount gave her a screen test, and she made a splash in 1936, as *The Jungle Princess*, draped in a strip of cloth called a sarong. She appeared that year on *Kraft Music Hall*. After a few more tropical epics — famously, John Ford's *The Hurricane* — Lamour and sarong were all but synonymous.

Lamour liked to tell a story about leaving the Paramount commissary, laughing to herself, and running into two writers who asked her what was so funny. She told them she had just seen Bing and Bob hamming it up at a table, and said she would love to make a picture with them. Whether or not the incident had anything to do with her recruitment, the studio could not have dreamed up anyone more appropriate. Her beauty suggested a sultry innocence, nothing too serious; she could handle a melody, so there was no need to overdub her vocals; and she was a genuine mainstay of the very type of adventure movie they were about to burlesque.

In April 1939, while Bing was shooting *The Star Maker*, the studio announced that as soon as that film wrapped, he, Hope, and Lamour would begin work on Harlan Thompson's production of *Road to Mandalay*. Filming was delayed until late in the year, by which time the title had evolved into *Road to Singapore*, ostensibly because that locale was considered more treacherous-sounding.[11] Perhaps the studio also wanted to deflect an association with Kipling, one of whose *Barrack-Room Ballads*, "On the Road to Mandalay," had been adapted (by Oley Speaks) as a popular song in 1907. The Burmese city had been appropriated for subsequent songs — Bing recorded "Rose of Mandalay" — which diluted any menace associated with the place. Kipling created the genre mocked by the *Road* movies, with his imperialist adventures set in United Kingdom protectorates, notably his short story "The Man Who Would Be King." A measure of the *Road* series' extended influence is John Huston's enthralling 1975 film of Kipling's tale, ripe with comical "ad-libby" colloquies between Sean Connery and Michael Caine that were inspired by Bing and Bob, not Kipling. The scene in which their laughter causes a lifesaving avalanche might have worked in *Road to Utopia*.

The magic of the *Road* movies has little to do with parody, romance, or music, though all three are essential to the blend. Rather, it stems from the interaction between the protagonists and what they bring out in each other. Bing was never more comically broad and inventive than with Bob; Bob was never more human and credible than with Bing. They are opposites who attract. Hope is brash and vain, yet cowardly and insecure. Crosby is romantic and self-possessed, yet manipulative and callous. Hope is hyperbole, Crosby understatement; Hope is the dupe, Crosby the duper. No one had the faintest notion of a series as *Road to Singapore* went before the cameras in early October, but everyone could see that it was not going to be an ordinary production.

Paramount assigned Victor Schertzinger to direct, an odd but salutary decision. He began as a concert violinist and entered Hollywood in 1916, writing the score for Thomas Ince's *Civilization*. Within a year he had a duel career as a prolific director and songwriter; his *One Night of Love*, a hit picture and an even bigger hit song, in 1934, provided Grace Moore with her greatest success. By then he had directed dozens of films, and many more followed — not least a handsome adaptation of *The Mikado*. Schertzinger got the job because of his association with musicals, not farce. (His friendship with the Crosbys — he served as best man at Everett's wedding to Florence George — could not have hurt.) Today, however, he is remembered almost entirely for his work during the two years preceding his death, in 1941: four pictures with Bing, including the first two *Road* ventures, and one with Lamour, *The Fleet's In*, for which he wrote his most durable songs, "I Remember You" and "Tangerine." Johnny Burke was retained to write the lyrics, but this time he wrote three songs with Jimmy Monaco and two with the director.

In the weeks before he was to begin the picture and resume duties at *KMH*, Bing took a break. He traveled by train to New York, chiefly to play golf at Meadowbrook with his friend Harvey Shaeffer. This was the trip when he bet Shaeffer $100 he could — anonymously — dive from the fifty-foot board at Billy Rose's *Aquacade Revue*, collecting sixty-five dollars because he aborted the dive midair and landed feet first.

Dixie was relieved to have Bing out of town. The twins required tonsillectomies, and not wishing to distress him with recollections of Eddie Lang, she admitted them secretly to the Good Samaritan

Hospital after his departure. The procedures went off without a hitch. Bing's one professional obligation in New York was to record two songs — at Jack Kapp's request — with the Andrews Sisters, a relatively new act Jack's brother Dave had signed to the label. A year earlier the Andrews Sisters had recorded one of Decca's all-time megahits, the English-language version of the Yiddish song "Bei Mir Bist du Schön."

Although Bing's collaboration with the Andrews Sisters would stall for the next four years, it ultimately meant as much to his recording career as the Hope connection meant to his screen and radio careers in the same period. Call him lucky? The nuns of the order of the Poor Clares must have been working overtime. To him, it was just another session, one of Jack's ideas, which he agreed to with some reluctance. Incredibly, he did not see the material until he arrived at the Fifty-seventh Street studio — early, as usual, for the 8:00 A.M. session. He was perched on the piano when the sisters, shivering with doubt, walked through the door.

They had become singers because of Bing Crosby and the Boswell Sisters, whose Woodbury broadcasts they listened to with the rapt attention Bing brought to the jazz records he and Al Rinker copied at Bailey's. Maxene Andrews recalled: "My sister LaVerne had a fantastic musical memory. Her great love, outside of loving Bing, was the Boswell Sisters. LaVerne would very patiently teach Patty and me the intricate parts of their arrangements. But in our minds, Bing and the Boswell Sisters came together. You didn't think of one without thinking of the other. So when Mr. Jack Kapp called us into his office and said, How would you like to record with Bing Crosby? — well, do you know what that felt like?"[12] Kapp told them they could choose one tune, but the other would have to be "Ciribiribin," an English-language version of a turn-of-the-century Neapolitan folk song — introduced, coincidentally, by Grace Moore in Victor Schertzinger's *One Night of Love*.

After meeting with Kapp, they and arranger Vic Schoen repaired to the small apartment of Lou Levy, a music publisher and, subsequently, their manager and Maxene's husband. "So we started to talk about it, all the nervous talk," Maxene remembered: "How can we record with him? What's he going to sing? How is he to sing with? What are we going to do? We don't read music. It went back and forth."[13] Vic wrote vocal and small-band arrangements for "Ciribiri-bin" and a novelty number, "Yodelin' Jive," and Dave Kapp hired Joe Venuti to lead a swinging little band with Bobby Hackett on trumpet.

"We walked into the studio and Bing never said a word. So we didn't know whether we should say hello to him. We didn't know any-thing." Maxene did observe that his hat was slightly back on his head, but she did not yet know what that meant. Years later it was the first thing she looked for: "He could be very moody, but we could always tell what mood he was in because I never saw him without his hat in all the years I knew him. When he'd walk in, if his hat was square on his head, you didn't kid around with him. But if it was back a little bit, sort of jaunty-like, then you could have a ball."[14]

Bing called Vic over and asked him to play the melodies, which he did with a one-finger demonstration at the piano. "My sister Pat sang along with him. From that point on, Bing always said, when we went in to a recording date, 'Hey, Patty, come over here and show me what we're going to sing.' But at that time, we walked in and we had a sheet of paper, just one sheet, with all the lyrics of the songs typed out, and that's all he got."[15] The four singers shared the same mike — the sis-ters looking straight at him, mesmerized, and Bing singing away from them, in profile.

The date was over in a flash, and the women ran. "We flew out of that studio," Maxene said. "I don't think we said good-bye to any-body. We had been so uncomfortable and we were so nervous that maybe the record wouldn't be good, and maybe we felt we weren't good enough. We talked about it and we thought, you know, that would be the one record we'd make with Bing, but at least in our career we could say we recorded with Bing Crosby."[16] The 78 was a two-sided hit.

While they fretted, Bing said to Jack, or so Jack reported to the sis-ters, "I will record with them anytime they want. They can pick the material. I want nothing to do with it. I just want to sing with them."[17] In truth, he did go on to record nearly four dozen numbers with the sisters, as well as duets with Patty when she went out on her own; and Schoen did select and arrange most of the material. A third of their recordings reached *Billboard*'s top ten, and four — "Pistol Packin' Mama" and "Jingle Bells," 1943; "Don't Fence Me In," 1944; "South America, Take It Away," 1946 — were certified with gold discs as million sellers.

Ranging in age from nineteen to twenty-four, the Andrews Sisters grew up in Minneapolis and apprenticed in vaudeville. They had little of the southern sass, improvisational bravado, or casual swing of the Boswells. But they had pizzazz, a unison pep that drove and inspired Bing. No personal connection ever developed. Although he presented them on the radio and used them in one film (the 1948 *Road to Rio*), the partnership existed almost exclusively on records, the most copious and commercially productive vocal alliance of his recording career. Their work is overall less compelling than entertaining, but the best of it is highly entertaining. The first two collaborations betray no nervousness or lack of preparation — though, to be sure, the charts did not require much in the way of interplay. Bing bends "Ciribiribin" to his rhythmic will, chimes with the girls, and sings the reprise in Italian. For good measure, Joe Venuti wails a sixteen-bar solo. Nothing could be done with the banal "Yodelin' Jive" except soldier through it. Patty noted a physical facet of Bing's time: "He had a thing with his foot. He would move it right to left, right to left, and so on — just like a metronome."[18]

Schertzinger was blindsided his first day on the set. He called for action, and the actors came to life, but much of the dialogue was strangely alien. "Victor was a nice fellow and he'd directed some fine pictures, but he'd had little experience with low comedy," Bing states in his memoir. "For a couple of days when Hope and I tore freewheeling into a scene, ad-libbing and violating all of the accepted rules of movie-making, Schertzinger stole bewildered looks at his script, then leafed rapidly through it searching for the lines we were saying."[19] He complained in the beginning but conceded that he had something special after he noticed the usually indifferent crew beaming. To the astonishment of his cameraman, William Mellor, Schertzinger relied more and more on master shots, often first takes. "After a couple of days," Hope recalled, "he went to the commissary, to the table where we ate, and said, 'You know, I know how to say start with these guys, but I don't know when to say stop, because they ad-lib all the time.' We did so much ad-libbing and kidding around, it was so different for the *Road* pictures, that everybody got a big kick out of it."[20]

Bing was in particularly good humor after the first week of shooting and traveled to San Francisco for the weekend. On Sunday afternoon he sang two free sets at the Golden Gate International Exposition on Treasure Island, backed by George Olsen's band. The announcement of his participation drew a record crowd of 187,730, causing such widespread congestion on the island that the roads were blocked and Bing had to be brought in by yacht.

Back on the set, Schertzinger received another wake-up call while they filmed a scene in which Bing and Bob crawl into bed. Bing would not remove his cap. The director became indignant as Bing coolly explained that he was not going to get up and retrieve the toupee; it was the last scene of the day and the golf course beckoned. He advised him to shoot the scene. Schertzinger decided on a show-down and sent a messenger to the front office, demanding arbitration. He learned where the power at Paramount rested when two executives rushed over to the recumbent Bing and asked, "Is everything all right, Bing? Do you need anything?"[21] Not a thing, Bing told them, everything was just fine. The executives left without a word to Schertzinger, who resumed filming, though the scene was later reshot.

Hope, bowled over by Bing's savoir faire, to say nothing of his muscle, was certain that the hat stayed in the picture — much as Bing believed that Carole Lombard's kicking-and-punching tantrum remained in *We're Not Dressing*. But the scene in question finds him wearing his hairpiece. David Butler recalled a similar incident during the filming of *Road to Morocco* (the third journey), but without an executive summons. "Hell, Bing, you can't wear a hat to bed," he said of a turban. Bing said, "Sure I can, they wear 'em all the time out there."[22] That scene was also cut or reshot. Bing wears a copious assortment of hats throughout the series; in *Road to Utopia* he wears one in all but five or six scenes, perhaps a record. They served a purpose beyond relieving him of the toupee; they also made it easier to disguise the use of stunt doubles.

The writers were less amused by the antics. Hartman visited the set when the boys were in full throttle. He was visibly upset, and Hope baited him. "If you recognize anything of yours, yell 'Bingo!'" he shouted.[23] Hartman shot back, "Shut up, or I'll put you back in the trunk" — meaning the script, on which the actors, however cocky, were ultimately dependent. "That was the truth," said Melville Shavelson, who later collaborated with Hartman on many of Hope's and Danny Kaye's films, while contributing — "incognito, no credit, not very much money" — lines to the *Road* pictures. "Basically, [Bing and Bob] did not change characters or anything else. That was the invention of Don Hartman and Frank Butler and continued through the other pictures."[24] Hartman complained about line changes to the producer. Bing claimed that he and Bob sneaked up to the projection room where rushes were viewed that evening, and when they heard the top brass laughing, they knew they were safe.

Lamour contributed to the ad-libbing legend, describing herself as stymied by their banter, struggling to "find the openings."[25] Hope recalled her pleading, "Why don't you give me something to say?" and his retort, "Just twirl your sarong, you'll be all right."[26] Told that Bing's secretary on *Road to Utopia* said they gave Dottie a hard time, he laughed: "No, we never gave her a hard time. We gave her a good time. She was in every picture."[27] Lamour developed a sense of humor about it, though one can imagine the ratio of humor to anger at work when, after a scene in which they splashed soapsuds on her, she followed them into the commissary and dumped an entire canister of suds on their heads. The diners were amused, she wrote in her autobiography, "but the director wasn't too thrilled. It meant that our hair, along with all our clothes, had to be dried again."[28]

Her anger prevailed when it came to Anthony Quinn, playing her unsavory dance partner, Caesar. "Bing got me out of some embarrassing spots," he conceded. "He always defended me."[29] The main incident concerned a routine with Dorothy that required him to snap a whip around her waist and reel her in for a snug dance. The great character actor Akim Tamiroff, though not in the cast, was accomplished with a bullwhip and instructed him. For safety's sake, however, Quinn cracked the whip a foot away from her; then it was wrapped in place and he pulled her close. When they played the scene, she shoved him away and shouted, "I can't dance with him. The son of a bitch has a hard-on!"[30] Everyone on the set froze. Quinn did not feel he could respond: "I was just a small player then. I didn't dare."[31] The tension dissolved into laughter after Bing piped up: "You should be happy you can give someone a hard-on, Dottie."[32]

Lamour once insisted, "After the first *Road* film, I never studied dialogue. Never. I'd wait to get on the set to see what they were planning. I was the happiest and highest-paid straight woman in the business."[33] Yet she cannot have been pleased by her abrupt demotion — second-billed in *Road to Singapore,* third-billed in *Road to Zanzibar* and ever after. Her roles were increasingly designed to support the boys. Even in *Singapore* she does not arrive until twenty minutes into the story. By the fifth trek, *Road to Rio,* Bing and Bob were able to force Paramount into a three-way split, and she never forgave them for not cutting her in. But by then her career had fallen apart. The *Road* movies were all she had, though she remained a mandatory ingredient. When Bing and Bob made the mistake of reducing her participation in *The Road to Hong Kong* to a glorified cameo, audiences bristled, especially as she was replaced by the dreary Joan Collins. Lamour's predicament is implied in a publicity photograph taken during the shooting of *Road to Singapore.* All three are dressed in striped caftans, laughing. Dottie, in the center and holding a sitar, is doubled over with hilarity. On each side, looking no less merry, Bing and Bob lock eyes over her head, as if she weren't there.

What each of them had that she lacked was a team of kibitzing writers. In truth, little of the ad-libbing was genuinely ad-libbed. For decades the scriptwriters privately seethed less at sabotage than at the notion that their work was improvised by actors. In later years Bing and Bob explained their peculiar ideas of ad-libbing. "You see, I just started my radio show," Bob said, "and I had the greatest staff of writers, all young people like [Norman] Panama and [Melvin] Frank, who had just gotten out of college in Chicago; [Melville] Shavelson and [Milt] Josefsberg, two more young guys, brilliant. I had about six or seven, and I used to give them the *Road* scripts, and they'd make notes on the margins, so and so and so and so, and I'd go into Bing's dressing room in the morning and say, 'What do you think of this?' and he would say, 'Oh, that's funny, that's funny.' And so we'd ad-lib these things into the pictures and people would fall down laughing."[34]

The biggest laughs came when Hope neglected to visit Bing's dressing room, which was the case most of the time. The onscreen battle between Bing's Josh Mallon and Bob's Ace Lannigan (changed from Winthrop) over Lamour's Mima was a Lindy hop compared to the offscreen competition for last laughs, which included *Road*-like double crosses. For example, Bob would have a writer provide Bing with a comic line on the QT, which Bing would happily deliver, expecting to stump Bob, not knowing that the writer had already given Hope a better rejoinder. Dolores Hope recalled, "There was a natural rivalry, which was a very healthy one, and what you see in the *Road* pictures is Bob and Bing as they really were. Typical of their personalities and everything about them — Bob low man on the totem pole most of the time. I think the *Road* pictures capture a great deal of their personalities."[35]

Josh and Ace were a canny amalgam of Bing and Bob, as their friends knew them, and the manipulating partner and naive stooge invented by Butler and Hartman. The two men raced on and off the set to the writers — never those who received screen credit — for punch-ups and reassurances, attempting to outdo each other, much like the characters they played. To each of them, a writer would counsel, When Bob says this, you say that, or, When Bing does that, you do this. The rivalry invigorated them. "I heard they didn't pal around so much outside their work, and yet they seemed like the greatest friends on the set," Quinn recalled. "I must say Bob Hope was very challenging to him, because Bing was very fast on his feet and Bob had to keep him off balance constantly with his ad-libs. But Bing's great asset was the facility of his mind, really quite remarkable."[36] Shavelson noted, "Bob obviously wanted to be as sharp as he could, so he and Bing and the writers would go off the set and then come back and start off with a line that nobody knew where in the world it came from, and build from there."[37]

"We thought it would lend spirit, you know, to the piece if we wouldn't tell one another exactly what we were going to say," Bing said in 1976. "You had to stick to the script in a general way, just keep the story line intact, but I would always prepare a few snappers, and of course he would have a sheath of snappers ready for me, and [Lamour] would be standing there in the middle, trying to get in something, crawl in somewhere. I think it helped the pictures and gave them an ad-libbed flavor . . . like a couple of hall-room boys clowning around. The writers didn't like this too much. They were good-natured about it, I guess, but once in a while they put in an objection that we were tinkering with the story too much."[38] In another 1976 conversation, he said most of the carrying-on took place during the first two films. Told by a fan that "each movie, as a whole, seemed like an ad-lib," Bing responded: "That was the brilliance of the entire enterprise. By the second or definitely the third *Road,* our styles had become so finely — I don't want to say chiseled, but it does seem to apply — that the extremely superlative writers were able to create dialogue that appeared to be improvised off the cuff, but it wasn't. Most of that material was completely scripted. . . . Of course, every now and then, we'd tear off a leaf of our own."[39]

Bing protested too much. According to Paramount files, *Road to Morocco* was filled with bad ad-libbing, which Buddy DeSylva, who had become chief of production, ordered cut. Generally, the films are so seamless, it is difficult to believe that any genuine ad-libs survive beyond under-the-breath comments, like one in *Road to Zanzibar,* when Bing, counting a parcel of bonds, drops a reference to treasury secretary Henry Morgenthau. For one of his most memorable authentic ad-libs, in *Morocco,* he played straight man to a camel that spat across the set directly into Bob's eye. Bob staggered into camera view, but before he could howl or David Butler could stop action, Bing merrily patted the camel's flank and said, "Good girl, good girl." Butler kept the whole incident in the film.

A comparison of *Road to Morocco* scripts, the margins offering alternative lines and jokes, reveals the kinds of written "ad-libs" that survived. Epigrammatic they are not. Several punch-ups are accomplished with a few added words. Bob's character was intended to say, "You mean you're thinkin' of eatin' me?"; instead, he says, "You mean you'd eat me? Without vegetables?"[40] Bing's character says of Bob's departed aunt Lucy, "When you're dead, you're dead," to which Bob was supposed to say, "Not Aunt Lucy"; instead he says, "Not Aunt Lucy. She was a Republican." Sometimes each gets a zinger to replace dull dialogue, as when they are lost in the desert: "Any idea where we are?" "Unh-huh" was changed to (Bob:) "This must be the place where they empty all the old hourglasses"; (Bing) "I think this is what's left after I clean my spinach." One can imagine a writer secretly, as if touting a hot tip at the track, passing to Bing an improvement on (to Bob) "Why, you slimy, double-crossin' eel" and (to Lamour) "We've been together since we were kids." Instead, Bing calls Hope a "dirty, underhanded, sickle-snoot" and tells Lamour, "We were kids together, in the same class for years — till I got promoted."

At other times Bing simply translates phrases into Bingese, as he often did ("Who's that cute little nipper?" becomes "Who is that headstrong, impetuous boy?"). Butler admired Bing's feeling for language, describing him as a "conversational" actor.[41] He told a reporter that Bing never read a script verbatim, that he added, deleted, and changed words to find a better fit. Butler gave him free reign, arguing, "You get some damn good stuff that way. You can always cut afterwards."[42] Reviewing *Road to Zanzibar* in *The New Republic*, Otis Ferguson enlarged on that aspect of his ability. Noting Bing's facile lingo, he wrote, "I believe him to be the first artist in popular expression today — not just slang for its own newness or to be different, but the kind of speech that is a kind of folk poetry, with its words of concision, edge, and cocky elegance fitted to speech rhythms, so that they may run free to the point, musical and easy."[43]

Mort Lachman, a longtime Hope writer, began contributing to the series with the fourth outing, *Road to Utopia,* and traced the illusory ad-libbing to the way Bob and Bing interacted on radio. "Let me explain how it was done," he said:

> We did the same thing in movies as in radio. We would do a basic script and we would play it to the audience, on Monday night, a half-hour rehearsal. Then we would meet afterwards, and rewrite all night, and then on Tuesday, we would do it again, live, on the air. Bob liked a little extra, so we would give him a few asides, a few changes, a few things that belonged to him that Bing did not see. Bing would come with his writers — Bill Morrow, for one — who gave him things. Now on the movie set the same thing would happen. They would go through rehearsal and Hope would say, "You know I could use something here, I could use something there," and we'd all write some jokes to go there. Then he'd pick the ones he wanted. . . . You have to understand they were playing to the guys on the set. What stayed in and didn't stay in depended on what got a laugh from the crew. The cameramen broke up, the lighting men broke up, the carpenters broke up, set people broke up, sound people broke up. So the attitudes in the *Road* pictures were different than in most movies. And that led to the breaking of the fourth wall, because they started working directly to the audience.[44]

The writer — if one could call him that, since he never actually wrote anything — most often found in the crossfire of the Crosby-Hope food fight for nearly fifteen years was Barney Dean, the most fabled member of Bing's extended family, beloved by all, as perhaps only a jester can be. He was the least likely figure in the inner circle: a short, round, shiny-headed, Jewish gnome with bright blue eyes. "A pixie in human form,"[45] wrote Bing, comparing him to the seven dwarfs — "not Grumpy," he stipulated, though his facial expression was so intense that he was sometimes called Cement Head. Reporters did not know what to make of him, because out of fierce loyalty to his benefactors, he had one answer to any question about Bing or Bob. He would put his right forefinger to his forehead, ponder deeply, and say, as if imparting privileged information, "Gee, I can't remember now."[46]

Barney Fradkin was born in Russia, in 1904, and came through Ellis Island to Brooklyn, at twelve. In 1920, after learning a time step, he got a job in vaudeville with Eddie Leonard's minstrels; "I was the guy that got the sand from the shuffle dance because I had the least talent," he told Barry Ulanov.[47] He told Shavelson he was the "world's youngest whirlwind dancer," whatever that meant.[48] Bing remembered he shuffled poorly and could not tap at all. Yet he toured in vaudeville for a decade before teaming up with dancer Sid Tarradasch. Barney convinced his partner that Fradkin and Tarradasch would never fit on a marquee, so — eyeing silent film actress Priscilla Dean's name on a billboard — they renamed themselves the Dean Brothers. They fared no better. Barney went into a short-lived comedy act and found stand-in work in Hollywood. By early winter 1939 he was peddling Christmas cards. Paramount allowed him to push his wares on the lot. When he went over to the stage where *Road to Singapore* was filming, Bing and Bob were delighted to see him.

Barney had shared vaudeville bills with Bob and was present, in 1931, when the Friars saluted Bing. While reminiscing, Dean took out of his pocket a card from a penny weight machine promising he would never lose his fortune. He said, "If I go back to my hotel and find they locked me out of my room, I'm going to sue the weighing machine people."[49] They returned to the set to shoot the "Sweet Potato Piper" number, involving dance breaks. Barney suggested a step, and they incorporated it into the routine. Bob recalled: "I said to Bing, 'This guy's too funny. He could help us with a lot of lines. Why don't we get him on the set?' So Bing called the assistant director and said, 'Tell them I want to put Barney Dean on for writing here.' About five people came out from the front office to check, you know. They were so thrilled to be talking to Bing, they never even mentioned Barney Dean, and Barney went on working with us until he died. Every scene, we'd discuss it, and he would come up with a couple lines."[50]

Barney demurred, for the most part. They devised the gags by themselves, he said, then gave him the credit. But he was always around, trading off between Bob's pictures and Bing's and aiding both when they collaborated. For a number of years, they arranged for Barney's salary to be figured into the budget of each movie. In the *Road to Morocco* financial report, his contribution is described as twenty-nine bits and gags; a few are detailed, the rest summed up as "And several pieces of business which are very difficult to explain."[51] After the war, concerned about his future, Bing and Bob asked Paramount to install Barney permanently on the writing staff. Paramount did not decline outright but dragged its heels.

Basil Grillo, who had just been hired to supervise Bing's business interests, was inadvertently caught up in the dispute over Barney's job. At that time he hardly knew Bing and needed him to sign some checks. Bing told him to meet him in his dressing room the next morning at nine but never showed. Instead, Leo Lynn came and told Basil to meet Bing in his dressing area on the set. It was early 1946, and they were filming *Welcome Stranger*. "I go out there and they're shooting this big production number, 'Country Style,' with maybe a hundred dancers. And all of a sudden Bing comes off the set, and I think he's coming to the dressing room. But he never shows. Now I'm really hurt. I'm taking all of this very personally, because I am sure he doesn't like me."[52] Bing disappeared for more than an hour, then returned to the set as Basil silently composed his resignation speech. "He saunters in and they get ready to shoot when he says, 'Wait a minute, one of my men is here, I have to see him.' A hundred extras are waiting and Bing comes over to the dressing room. He greets me like I was his long-lost son, puts on that damn Irish charm — could charm you right out of your socks. And he sat down, signed the checks, chitchatted, and so on, wasting time. None of this makes sense to me at all."[53]

Leo Lynn eventually explained it to him. "This particular day," Grillo learned, "Bing and Bob went into the front office as soon as they got in the studio, and said, 'Look, we want Barney Dean to have a contract, and we want it now. And we feel very bad, we feel very ill about this whole thing and we're not going to be able to do much work until Barney gets a contract.'" Bing had been stalling everyone all day — his idea of a work stoppage. Bob, also filming on the lot, did the same thing. "At two o'clock that afternoon," Basil said, "Barney had his contract signed, sealed, and delivered. That's the kind of power they had, though they never really used it except as a last resort."[54]

Shortly afterward, Bing put Grillo in charge of Bing Crosby Enterprises dictating a letter to that effect to his staff; no deals of any kind could be consummated without Basil's personal approval. But Grillo continued to feel like an interloper until he went to see Bing one day in his dressing room. "I'm sitting there, waiting for Bing, and Barney comes in. He was a real nice little guy, but he didn't know that anybody in the world existed other than Bing and Bob. Everybody else he called Major. He says, 'Hi Bas, how are you today?' Well, geez, I nearly fell off my chair. From Barney, this was real recognition. It meant I was accepted."[55]

Songwriter Johnny Lange recalled a number he wrote for Walt Disney's *Song of the South* ("Uncle Remus Said"): "Bing sang it several weeks in a row on his show, because I put the name Barney in the song. I drove Barney once to see the Ritz Brothers so he could sell postcards. Not long after that Bing and Bob Hope made a job for him at Paramount and he was making five hundred dollars a week."[56] Gary Crosby recalled Barney sitting off to the side of the set as the scenes were blocked. "After you block, you step out to get your makeup fixed while the lighting men light the thing and there's about a twenty- or thirty-minute period there, and the old man and Hope would go over to Barney and say, 'Give us something to make this thing better.' So Barney threw lines to them. Then they come back and the director would say, 'Roll 'em,' and the dialogue would be different from what they had just rehearsed. Barney was a sweet guy. Dad loved Barney Dean to death. He was at our house all the time."[57]

Bing's aversion to hospitals and funerals, evident after Eddie Lang's death and more pronounced after the media circus attending Dixie's, was absolute. His friends accepted his detachment as characteristic. He was consistent, demanding that his own funeral be held privately and secretively, before the cock crowed. So while some people groused, few were surprised that he did not visit Barney in the hospital, where he died of cancer in 1954. Barney's death, two years after

Dixie's, was hard on Bing, but his way of acknowledging it was typical, a fitting gesture that — mutual friends agreed — Barney would have relished. Within weeks of the burial, Bing was interviewed by Edward R. Murrow on *Person to Person,* a popular television program that specialized in fake candor, with Murrow sitting in the studio, asking prearranged questions of famous people who were filmed in their homes.

As Bing's segment concluded, Murrow said, "Bing, thanks for letting us come visit you tonight. . . ." Bing interrupted him. "Wait a minute, you're not gonna get away. I have something else I want to show you. Don't take off. This is really my pride and joy." He strode into the hallway, as another camera picked him up, and, standing before a huge painting, said, breathlessly and without garbling a word:

> Everyone has something in their home that they really like to go into rhapsodies about. This is a canvas by Sir Alfred Munnings, who was the head of the British Royal Academy for years. He's considered the finest painter of the English country life and country scene. It represents the hunting scene and it recalls a very amusing story to me. Barney Dean, the late Barney Dean, the beloved gag writer who worked for us for so many years. We were having a party here. It was getting late-ish, four-ish or so. Just a few stragglers out in the hall, two or three people, you know how they like to dawdle at a party, hate to say good night. And Barney was looking up at the picture sort of ruminatively and I said, 'Barney, what's on your mind?' Barney was from New York, Brooklyn, never left the pavement, never been off the bricks in his life, and he looked at the picture and said, 'How come we never do this no more?' Ed, I know you're in a hurry. You've got a time factor back there in television that you're fighting all the time, so I want to say good night to you.[58]

Another remembrance was inserted two years later into *High Society,* when Trummy Young, the trombonist in Louis Armstrong's band, mutters, as they approach C. K. Dexter-Haven's mansion, "I forgot my library card." Barney made the crack when Bing brought him to a New Year's Eve party at Winthrop Rockefeller's estate in Tarrytown, as he recounts in his autobiography (Barney makes an early appearance, page two). Later at that same affair, as they stood unrecognized — Bing wasn't wearing his hairpiece — on a gallery watching an indoor tennis game, a reveler asked them, "Has anyone seen Millicent?" Barney offered, "Maybe she's upstairs playing polo."[59]

Barney Dean stories, like those told of comedians Groucho Marx, Joe Frisco, W. C. Fields, or Phil Harris, became part of the currency of Hollywood wit. Skitch Henderson, the pianist whose career Bing launched when he made him a regular on his 1946 radio show, was present for one of Barney's most frequently cited one-liners. "There was a coffee shop across Hollywood Boulevard and all of us would go — Bing, the writers, Barney, of course. And the Hollywood cops suddenly decided they didn't want any jaywalking on Hollywood Boulevard. So we all cross the street, about five of us, and a cop strides up to us and puts his shoulder over Barney Dean, and before the cop can say a word, Barney asks, 'How fast was I going officer?'"[60]

"I loved that man," Eddie Bracken said. "He was great. We were doing a picture and a horse stepped on his toe. The first thing a normal person would say is 'Ow!' or scream. Barney turned around, looked at the horse, and said, 'Jew hater.'"[61] The picture was Paramount's wartime flag-waver, *Star Spangled Rhythm,* in which Bing and Bob also appear. Barney showed up in *Variety Girl, Duffy's Tavern,* and *Thanks for the Memory* — in all, two pictures with Bing and Bob, one with Bing, one with Bob. He is himself the subject of a punch line in *Road to Zanzibar:* Bob complains that he wants to return to the United States, and Bing says, "Yeah, you'll wind up in Barney Dean's Beanery, blowing up bloodwurst," which doubled as a joke about Bing's bu-bu-bu *b*s.

"There were nine million writers on the set, and all Bing or Bob wanted to talk to was Barney," Mort Lachman recalled. "You know what they were jealous of? They were jealous of Barney's affection."[62] "He was their lucky charm," Shavelson said. "They had to have Barney around, and he was such a nice guy. Bing was going to New York once, so he said to Barney, 'Can I do anything for you?' Barney says, 'Yeah, go up to One hundred and twenty-first Street and so-and-so, the big building on the corner; you go to the thirteenth floor, ring the bell for Mrs. Rosenzweig. She'll come to the door, she's a nice lady. Give her five thousand dollars.' Bing asks why. Barney says, 'She's my mother.' Barney was the kind of guy who gave the head of the studio, Buddy DeSylva, a gold watch, and he had engraved on it, 'This is a lot of shit, but when you don't have any talent, you have to do these things.'"[63]

"Barney didn't have a lot of confidence with women," Rory Burke, Johnny's daughter, recalled.[64] After Jimmy Van Heusen joined the inner circle as Burke's partner, he took it upon himself to fix up Barney. A bachelor of legendary appetites and connections, Van Heusen, a licensed pilot, was once presented with an airplane by one of Hollywood's top madams. "They would go whoring," Rory recalled. "I really should not have been hearing these things, but we had big ears and we'd kind of listen around the corners. But they couldn't talk about it when Bing was around; he wouldn't have liked that. Not at all. Bing was something of a gentleman in that respect. He might have gone along with them, but he wouldn't be talking about it. Everybody had their part in looking out for Barney."[65] Barney called his protectors the hoodlum gentlemen, and with Bing and Bob occupying different social circles, he became a tether between them.

But there was a dark side to the friendship. Antisemitism was rife, and Bing occasionally received hate mail, calling him a "Jew lover." Rory Burke remembered Bing reading aloud one letter after the war, which said all the Jews should be gassed. Barney said, "Well, that's one way to handle us."[66] Intolerance was a bond between them, because anti-Catholic hatred was also rampant. Rory recalled that before she and her siblings were sent to parochial schools, their father cautioned them not to tell anyone they were Catholic.

Barry Ulanov grew smitten with Barney while writing his book about Bing in 1948, invoking Etienne Gilson and Saint Augustine in his attempt to describe "the 'cry' and the 'clamor' of Barney's heart." He concluded, "It is no mere coincidence that this little Russian Jewish dancer with four steps should be such a close associate of the American Catholic singer."[67] Fifty years later he continued to ruminate about the relationship. "He was the jester, but there was a sour note, a pathos — if not tragic, then at least pathetic — that reinforces my understanding of Bing's irony. Bing never freed himself from the fear that the source of his gift would dry up. There was always some small element of anxiety that fed into his sense of irony, which I have persuaded myself is his great talent — not just an amiable standing aside, but something better than that, more thoughtful than that. You'd never think of Barney Dean and Bing Crosby as a natural connection — so different in their backgrounds, in their attitudes. But I think Bing saw in him his shadow. Things Bing could not quite acknowledge, he could accept in Barney, some of whose stories had a very somber aspect. Of course, he was a very lovable man, too."[68]

It is nonetheless obvious that many of Barney's lines don't travel well; the cautionary adage "you had to be there" is inescapable. The same is true of many *Road* wisecracks, at least on paper — not much to daunt the Marx Brothers, let alone Oscar Wilde or Billy Wilder.[69] Yet the pictures abide as classic comedies, able to sustain grateful smiles even when they fail to elicit outright yucks. Along with the films of Preston Sturges and the last works of Lubitsch, they are among the few Hollywood comedies to survive the war years, successfully recycled for every subsequent generation. The film historian David Shipman expresses a prevalent tone when he writes, "They have turned out — surprisingly, I think — to be ageless."[70] Gilbert Seldes called them the "second great series of comedies with a group of stars made after sound came in," the first being those of the Marx Brothers.[71] Their enchantment derives not from the jokes — whether copyrighted, kibitzed, or ad-libbed — but from the infinitely appealing and enigmatic rapport between the two principals.

Barney Dean aside, Bob was the shadow figure who transformed the cinematic Bing, alleviating the intrusive blandness and whetting Bing's wit to a fine nub. As a foil, Bob deepened Bing's ironic stance, his detachment, encouraging the sadistic touch present in almost all movie comedy, from Sennett and Chaplin to Fields and the Marxes, though inhibited in Bing's post-Sennett work. Bing's anxiety occasionally drove his characters to a stubborn solitude, a desire to escape to the ranch or the boat, to be left alone, to wallow in a lack of ambition. Even when the plot did not demand it, the actor's nerveless independence suggested a willingness on the part of his characters to retreat from the world, a disposition his friends recognized in Bing. But love always sneaked up and roped him back. The absurdity of the *Road* movies gave him a lot more rope.

Like the torpid *Paris Honeymoon*, *Road to Singapore* is superficially concerned with a rich man who abandons his rich fiancée for a peasant girl. This time, he is not self-made but rather the heir to a shipping fortune who renounces responsibility, money, sex, and luxury in favor of a mock marital relationship with a buddy on whom he wreaks havoc. Bing's Josh sets out for Singapore but (as usual for the series) never gets there. He does, however, get away. In the made-up province of Kaigoon, he is liberated, remade with an uncanny compound of independence, intelligence, cruelty, warmth, and indifference — no longer the romantic crooner of the 1930s, but more like the complicated man his associates recognized as Bing. As one Spokane classmate remarked to a reporter in the 1940s, the *Road* pictures unleashed the Bing he knew as a kid.

Road to Singapore begins a cycle in which Bing's characters are obsessed with getting away for the sake of getting away. They rebel against inclusion. In *Rhythm on the River, Holiday Inn,* and *Blue Skies,* he is hell-bent on escaping the city, celebrity, fortune, and accountability; specifically, he spurns his too easily won — virtually unavoidable — success. When in *Holiday Inn* a Hollywood producer besieges him with offers other entertainers would die for, he gazes around at his isolated homestead and complains: the idea that he could be left alone to hibernate with his talent was too good to be true. In *Road to Zanzibar* and *Road to Utopia,* he and Bob are on the lam, fleeing evildoers or the repercussions of their own schemes. The furthest Bing could go to duck the mammon and romance eternally dropped in his unwilling lap was Father O'Malley's cloister; in his last films the earth itself can no longer hold him — he flies in and out of the frame at the close of *High Time* (1960) and lands on the moon in the road trip that was supposed to end in Hong Kong.

Many of Bing's roles lacked history beyond the conventions of *Kraft Music Hall* and light comedy. As Josh Mallon, he has a pedigree: his first movie father and a heritage of seafarers not unlike that of the Crosbys. Josh is agreeable, cocky, and attractive, but somehow not whole. He dismisses family tradition out of hand as stodgy and pompous: "That's not for me, Dad, I want to be one of the boys, a regular guy." His father (Charles Coburn) is reasonable and his fiancée (Judith Barrett) is pretty and pleasant, though he is so indifferent to her that one wonders how the engagement came about. The obligations of the business are hardly onerous. Yet Josh prefers to rough it with Ace, broke.

Audiences in 1940 understood the gist, even if they could articulate it no better than Josh or Ace. With recovery imminent and the war in Europe threatening to snare the United States, the Huck

Finn reverie of a retreat from civilization and its feminizing ways had renewed appeal. Men in particular responded to the camaraderie of two resourceful and comical friends at a time when they were about to be plunged into the homosocial environment of combat. As Huck learned, you can escape only when the wolf (in this case, his father) is no longer at the door. Josh finds that feminization is everywhere he goes — and so is America.

The latter revelation was comforting. You could leave the United States without leaving it behind. Wherever Bing and Bob travel, they bring American outlooks, American morals, and most of all, American show business, primarily vaudeville. Even in Kaigoon, they hawk their wares with song and dance, like two old troupers on a small-time circuit. From *Road to Zanzibar* on, the vaudeville connection is explicit — they play cheapjack performers of one sort or another, auguring the entrenchment of American pop culture around the world. They adapt and burlesque local customs and rituals, ultimately changing them into exotic reflections of home. The natives are their straight men, the villains their stooges, the women their props, the clothing their costumes. Yet the mayhem is quelled by decency and light. They are anarchists with sweet souls.

A month before the Los Angeles preview of *Road to Singapore*, in February 1940, *Variety* published its annual analysis of film stars and their box-office clout during the preceding year. Bing still ranked as the top male player at Paramount, while Bob straggled in at number ten. *Variety* expressed a guarded optimism about Bob's future: his "questionable star quantity last year, progressed with *Cat and Canary* [a haunted-house comedy with Paulette Goddard], and properly tailored with material [he] can become a standard box office figure for the company."[72] After *Singapore* Bob ascended to box-office heaven. In 1941 he was the first clown in five years, since Joe E. Brown, to make the Quigley top-ten poll. For a couple of seasons, his numbers eclipsed Bing's. Yet rarely did one of Bob's solo efforts make as much money as the *Road* films, while Bing's solo vehicles often surpassed them.

The chemistry between Crosby and Hope was "like magic," Mort Lachman said of *Singapore*. "It didn't compare with *Morocco* or any of those later ones, but compared to the pictures it was playing against, it was a miracle to see those two guys come to life on the screen. They were wild. It was *Wayne's World* in 1940."[73] In the first scene, a ship bearing Josh and Ace docks in Hawaii and they watch from the bow as fellow sailors are berated by their waiting wives.

> Josh: You know, if the world was run right, only women would get married.
> Ace: Hey, can they do that?
> [Josh gives him a look.]

The lines are idiotic — the kind of thing you expect from Abbott and Costello. But something in their contrasting attitudes, in the ingenuousness of Bob's delivery and the wry forbearance of Bing's look, lets the audience know instantly that it has been introduced to a bona fide team — not just two actors but a rare and skillful duet, "cream and sugar," in Dolores Hope's phrase. Their timing is as reflexive and infallible as that of two jazz musicians trading fours. Bob insisted that Bing was the greatest straight man he ever saw, but as Lachman pointed out, "Hope was also the greatest straight man for Bing that there ever was. Hope was such a good target, and the audience loved when Bing put him down."[74]

As in the next scene: a couple of menacing bruisers demand to know which of them dallied with their relation, Cherry, and Josh unhesitatingly points to Ace. When they order Ace to come with them, however, the unlikely heroes go into a practiced patty-cake routine, an infantile diversion that stymies their adversaries, until the last pat turns into two fists, aimed at their jaws. Here, in embryo, is the enigma of the friendship. They are at once true blue and murderously competitive. The relationship was not terribly puzzling to contemporaries, who lived in a world saturated with Crosby and Hope insult gags. They were ultimately as omnipresent as talk of DiMaggio's streak or the war.

The gibes never did let up. They ricocheted back and forth from radio to movies to live appearances, eventually to television. Hope counted on them. Bing's cameos in his films often got the last and best laughs, as in the closing shot of *The Princess and the Pirate*, when Virginia Mayo walks past Bob's open arms and into Bing's. Earlier in the picture Bob tells her about a show he did on the road to Morocco, ruined by "some overaged crooner with laryngitis [who] kept cramping my act." But by then the jokes were no longer confined to his films. In *Best Foot Forward* (1943), Lucille Ball remarks, "We've covered more road than Bing Crosby and Bob Hope." Until Bing's death, thirty-seven years after *Road to Singapore*, neither performer could appear anywhere without making an obligatory crack about the other. The audience deciphered them as proof of an exemplary friendship.

Bing's comic disdain may have been influenced by his friend Oliver Hardy, who originated the quiet, long-suffering gaze. But where Hardy's impatience is a response to the fine mess he blames on Stan Laurel, Bing as often as not precipitates the mishaps that jeopardize him and Bob. His passive hostility is consistent with his male relationships in two previous films; he talked Stu Erwin into a suicide pact and betrayed his generosity in *The Big Broadcast* and tried to seduce his brother's girl in *Sing You Sinners*. "I like most Bing Crosby films," Martin Scorsese once remarked. "I was fascinated by his character. He's charming, he sings all the time — and meanwhile, he's swindling everybody. In the *Road* pictures, he takes advantage of Bob Hope from beginning to end — and still winds up with the girl. He uses Hope so badly, but with such integrity, such confidence. I used a variation of that in the *Mean Streets* relationship between Robert De Niro and Harvey Keitel."[75]

As usual, autobiographical touches abound in *Road to Singapore*. In the homecoming scene in his father's office, Bing references both sides of his own parentage. The writers drew on the Crosby sea captains to flesh out Josh's background. And when his fiancée, Gloria, walks in, Bing reflexively removes his gum and hides it under the desk, as though she were his mother about to catch him with a cigarette or a drink. A newspaper headline reporting on the brawl also suggests the Crosby touch (or that of writers who, like Carroll Carroll and Johnny Burke, drew on his lingo): AGAIN IN DURANCE VILE. In the next episode Josh reels in a swordfish with overheated comical clumsiness, in stunning contrast to home movies in which Bing catches far larger fish with the aplomb of a Hemingway hero — an instance of his lack of actorly vanity.

Schertzinger delivered on his promise to spruce up the major musical numbers. The first, set in the stateroom of Josh's prospective in-

laws, serves as a template for the off-kilter union between him and
Ace. Surprisingly, Hope is the picture's first singer, in a Burke and
Schertzinger lampoon, "Captain Custard," about a uniformed movie
usher who fancies himself a military figure, replete with references to
Bank Night, double features, and free dishes. When Gloria's smug
and insulting brother, Gordon — the sort of wealthy snob Josh does
not want to become — sneers at Ace, Josh chivalrously announces
that they are a team. He puts a fezlike box on his head and leaps into
the number with a phrase about "pitching for Paramount," which virtually erases the line between Josh and Bing and lets the audience
know that it is in on a marvelous joke: this is a movie that *knows* it's a
movie.

This subtle assault on the fourth wall, which became less subtle in
later *Road* films when a camel or a bear spoke directly to the audience, surprised people not because the device was untried but
because of the context in which it appeared. It built on a tradition of
character breaking employed by the zaniest of comedians, from
Oliver Hardy looking straight at the audience in *Two Tars,* as if to say,
"Look what I have to contend with," to Groucho Marx in *Animal
Crackers* cautioning the audience not to expect every joke to be good.
Groucho revived the gambit in 1939, in *At the Circus,* but it was
rarely used except in cartoons. In *Singapore* the actors never address
the audience, but they make cracks to let us know that they know
that we know that it is all artifice. They are goofing on their celebrity
and the social contract celebrity implied in that era. From the first,
when he played a crooner named Bing, Bing's pictures often toyed
with the audience's involvement in his life. Now he conjured the illusion of letting down his guard entirely, and the audience felt it was
seeing a new and brighter Bing.

With Bing/Josh involved in "Captain Custard," it becomes a full-
fledged vaudeville number, firmly establishing Bing and Bob as a
couple. Indeed, Bob emerges for all practical purposes in a femme
role; real women are employed tangentially in the piece and discarded on Bing's entry. Bob wraps himself in a dresslike cape, shakes
his hips, and bestows upon Bing a military kiss. In later films, the
gender-bending was sometimes reversed. (In *Zanzibar* as they drink
champagne in a nightclub, Bing squeaks in a little-girl voice, "Daddy,
the bubbles make my nose tickle." Bob looks around and asks, "Was

that at this table?") But either way, Bob was the schlemiel, a condition telegraphed by the names of his characters, which, except for Ace, were never monosyllabic. Bing played Chuck, Jeff, and Duke; Bob played Hubert, Orville, and Chester, except when he answered to nicknames like Turkey and Junior.

The "Captain Custard" number ends with the second patty-cake brawl in eighteen minutes. Clearly, they need to get away. Josh and Ace sail for Singapore and get as far as Kaigoon, with $1.28 between them. They make a curious pact to swear off women and go out to a saloon where the floor show is Mima and Caesar and his whip. ("I think he wants her to give up cigarettes," Bing says after he lashes one from her mouth.) Yet another brawl ends as they spirit Mima to their hut, where she takes over, buying food, cleaning, and forcing Bing and Bob to sleep together under the same net. As they slumber, she sings "The Moon and the Willow Tree." Ace begins to get up, but Josh grabs him: "The night air's bad for you, Junior, back in the net." Instead of driving them apart, Lamour's Mima brings them closer. Bound by jealousy, each is afraid to let the other out of his sight.

Desperate for money, Ace remembers an old con called Spotto, a phony cleaning fluid (one of the writers probably remembered it from Bing's Sennett short, *One More Chance*). To lure a crowd, they become vaudevillians, dressed alike in dark yachting caps, dark shirts, light pants. Mima, wearing an ankle-length skirt (no sarong in this ménage), joins them for a few whimsical bars of "An Apple for the Teacher." Josh stops them and goes straight into the ocarina number "Sweet Potato Piper," which includes diverting interplay as Bob exhibits his dancing skills and Bing fakes it, game as ever. Bing's prerecording of the song for the film is far more jubilant and inventive than the Decca record he made a few weeks later. All three are supposed to be playing ocarinas, and at one point he acknowledges the prerecording by taking his fingers off the instrument as Bob's eyes bug.

Having gathered the marks, they hawk Spotto, pulling the effortlessly funny Jerry Colonna from the crowd and sacrificing his white suit to its degenerative powers. While the trio dodges the police, Colonna is the subject of the best directorial conceit in the picture. Josh's father, in search of his son, has cabled his branch in Kaigoon. As a clerk reads the message, he hears a high-pitched siren. Exasperated, he gets up and leaves his office to locate the source. The siren continues as he makes his way to a nearby building. Inside, seated at an upright organ, is his associate, Colonna, the siren. The camera cuts to him just as he finishes bleating what turns out to be the first note of "Carry Me Back to Old Virginny."

Meanwhile, Josh and Ace decide they cannot tolerate their sudden domesticity and argue about which of them will send Mima packing. This is perhaps the scene that best exemplifies what is most appealing about Crosby and Hope. The smooth and credible badinage is effective not because of the writing, which is mundane, but because its locker-room naturalness does not feel written or even acted. Bob was the most persuasively charismatic actor Bing had ever played against, his equal in most respects short of singing, and his better at physical comedy. Bing's unmistakable pleasure in playing with a genuine accomplice is contagious.

They dispatch Mima only long enough to rescue her again from Caesar. Her return signals an abrupt change in mood. Josh and Ace have surrendered their bachelor mode; they are now on the road to domesticity, as each sells out the other in the contest for Mima. Any doubts about who will win are put to rest when Josh finally, nearly an hour into the movie, delivers the one indispensable ingredient in a Crosby film, a ballad. If Burke and Monaco's "Too Romantic" is less memorable than songs Burke and Van Heusen composed for later *Roads*, it marked a turning point for Burke; it's the best love song he had written for a Crosby film to date. (Significantly, the far superior "Imagination" and "Polka Dots and Moonbeams" appeared a few months later, written with Van Heusen for Sinatra. For *Zanzibar* Van Heusen was on the Crosby team.)

Bing's edict to Burke to avoid *I love you*s was not strictly enforced; Johnny slid one in at the end of "What's New?" tied to a cadence that obliges the singer to dispense with it quickly. But the challenge compelled him to be extra-inventive in getting the message across, sometimes with evasive results, as in "On the Sentimental Side" or "East Side of Heaven." "Too Romantic," however, is astutely tailored to emphasize Bing's passive allure. It has him conceding a fear of intimacy because he is too romantic, too vulnerable: "moonlight and stars can make such a fool of me"; "wouldn't I look a sight on bended knee." He wants a sure thing: "Don't let me fall unless it could all come true." Bing's rendition in the picture is more robust than his hit record but not nearly as aggressive as Lamour's. She knows what she wants but has to put up with an obbligato of wisecracks. The song ends as Hope comes from behind and dunks Bing in the lagoon.

The feminization proceeds apace. Starving for food, they use another of Ace's concoctions, an intended roach killer called Scramo, to darken their skins (Kaigoon requires more of a tanning than a blackening) so they can masquerade as natives at a feast. Josh and Ace wear womanly caftans that cover their breasts, and Bing plays even more broadly than Bob. After an obligatory bring-on-the-girls native dance, they flee from a ceremonial marriage requirement, at which point Gloria and Josh's father arrive. Josh refuses to leave, but Mima, meaning to protect him from losing his fortune, pretends to love Ace. That sends him packing, after he delivers a maudlin tribute to good old Ace, the first and last time the series would forget itself so egregiously and descend to rank depths of stoic poignancy. Josh learns the truth and returns to Mima, as Ace happily presides like a child who has reconciled his divorced parents (a Hollywood convention of the period, popularized by Deanna Durbin). Still, the audience knows who the real couple is; a Spotto victim comes running in with a policeman, and the movie fades as Bing and Bob go into their patty-cake crouch.

The reviews were so tepid, Paramount excluded even the good ones from trade-paper ads, preferring to display the numbers as *Singapore* broke records at one theater after another. *Time*'s man plainly dozed: "Crooner Crosby, the lyric son of a businessman, has an irrepressible urge to be a beachcomber. He and Bob Hope take Miss Lamour beachcombing with them. Bing Crosby sings one song ('Kaigoon') in Esperanto."[76] He does not. Many thought that though the film was slight, Bing and Bob deserved a reunion. The *New York Times* was less encouraging: "We would not go so far as to call the road closed, merely to say one proceeds at his own risk, with heavy going after Lamour." The *Times* bestowed "an E for effort . . . and an SEC for an investigation of the possibilities it has squandered."[77]

The movie opened, grandly enough, at the New York Paramount on a bill with the eagerly awaited revamped edition of Tommy

Dorsey's band. Under a huge display for the film and its stars, the marquee promised: "In person — Tommy Dorsey and His Orchestra; Bunny Berigan, Buddy Rich, Frank Sinatra, Pied Piper Quartette, [tap dancers] Winfield and Ford; Extra Added Attraction — Red Skelton."[78] Sinatra had recently cut his first discs with Dorsey, two songs, the second a boyishly anemic cover of "Too Romantic." The movie and the stage show made for an unbeatable combination, one *Variety* said gave the lie to the myth that Holy Week was bad for business.[79] An elated New York *Daily News* headline blared: PARAMOUNT GOES GAY IN A LARGE WAY. But *Singapore* did not need live music to lure crowds. By March it had broken two-year records in New York, Los Angeles, Miami, and Chicago.[80] By April Paramount's ads listed thirty cities where it was held over two, three, and four weeks.[81]

Kate Cameron of the *Daily News* caught the spirit that ignited audiences. After expressing astonishment that Bing and Bob had not been teamed before — "Separately, they're good, but together they're a riot!" — she noted: *"Road to Singapore* is something I can't explain. It is as goofy a bit of make-believe as I have seen upon a screen. . . . After the long list of heavy and so-called 'significant' films that hit the screen lately, *Road to Singapore* is a blessed relief. It's naughty — but nifty."[82] Cameron knew her readers. Hollywood flaunted its talent and diversity in 1940, producing a trove of films that made money and endured as classics or semi-classics: *The Shop Around the Corner, Rebecca, His Girl Friday, The Great Dictator, Christmas in July, The Letter, The Bank Dick, The Sea Hawk, Brother Orchid, Dr. Ehrlich's Magic Bullet, Pinocchio, The Great McGinty, The Grapes of Wrath, The Mortal Storm, Foreign Correspondent, My Favorite Wife, Rhythm on the River, The Mark of Zorro, The Philadelphia Story, Pride and Prejudice,* and several others. Yet as splendid as those pictures were, *Road to Singapore,* with receipts of $1.6 million, was the top-grossing picture of the year.[83]

This was hardly a tribute to the public's discernment. Most of the year's top-ten moneymakers, excepting *Rebecca* and *Road to Singapore,* are forgotten today — *The Fighting 69th, Arizona, Buck Benny Rides Again, North West Mounted Police, Kitty Foyle.* While they disappeared, however, *Singapore* inaugurated a franchise that echoed through the culture during and after the war, persistently for more than twenty years. Until James Bond, the *Road* series was the most lucrative ever produced. For Bing, it indicated redefinition. His contemporaries had followed him for a decade; now a much younger audience was drawn to him as well. Neither Crosby nor Paramount nor, for that matter, Jack Kapp and Kraft could have imagined in 1940 that everything he had already achieved would be remembered, within a few short years, as merely a prelude to what followed — a bagatelle compared with the symphony of adulation he roused in the 1940s, when Bing Crosby was remade in the crucible of war.

Bing Crosby Discography: The Early Years

This section includes all studio recordings in which Crosby participated between 1926 and July 6, 1940. With the exception of two "fluffs" and dramatically different versions of "St. Louis Blues," alternate or rejected takes are omitted.

The parenthetical information denotes Bing's instrumental and vocal accompaniment. Bandleaders appear to the left of the slash and vocalists to the right. When Bing shared billing with other artists, beginning in 1931, the costarring performer's name is preceded by a dash.

Vocal group refers to singers in the Whiteman band other than the Rhythm Boys, though on occasion (as on "Changes") the Rhythm Boys were part of the vocal group; S denotes a Bing Crosby solo. In those instances when no musical director was credited, the ensemble is identified by the name of the label, e.g., Brunswick (Brunswick Studio Orchestra).

All sessions before May 1931 were released under the names of various bandleaders or Paul Whiteman's Rhythm Boys, except for a handful by Bing. Beginning with the May 4, 1931, session ("Were You Sincere?"), all recordings were released under Bing's name.

1926
Oct. 18: I've Got the Girl!   (Don Clark/Al Rinker)
Dec. 22: Wistful and Blue   (Paul Whiteman/Al Rinker)

1927
Feb. 10: Shanghai Dream Man   (Paul Whiteman/vocal group)
Feb. 25: That Saxophone Waltz   (Paul Whiteman/vocal group)
Feb. 28: Pretty Lips   (Paul Whiteman/Al Rinker)
Mar. 7: Muddy Water   (Paul Whiteman)
Apr. 29: I'm Coming, Virginia   (Paul Whiteman/S–Al Rinker)
         Side by Side   (Paul Whiteman/Rhythm Boys)
May 9: I'm in Love Again   (Paul Whiteman/S–vocal group)
May 24: Magnolia   (Paul Whiteman/Rhythm Boys)
June 20: Mississippi Mud/I Left My Sugar Standing in the Rain
                                          (Rhythm Boys)

Sweet Li'l/Ain't She Sweet   (Rhythm Boys)
July 6: My Blue Heaven   (Paul Whiteman/vocal group)
Aug. 12: The Five Step   (Paul Whiteman/Rhythm Boys)
Aug. 19: The Calinda   (Paul Whiteman/S–vocal group)
Aug. 20: It Won't Be Long Now   (Paul Whiteman/Rhythm Boys)
Sept. 21: Missouri Waltz   (Paul Whiteman/vocal group)
Nov. 11: That's Grandma   (Rhythm Boys)
Nov. 17: Miss Annabelle Lee   (Rhythm Boys)
Nov. 23: Changes   (Paul Whiteman/S–vocal group)
Nov. 25: Mary   (Paul Whiteman)

1928

Jan. 11: Ol' Man River   (Paul Whiteman)
Jan. 12: From Monday On   (Rhythm Boys)
Jan. 20: Mississippi Mud   (Frank Trumbauer)
Jan. 27: Make Believe   (Paul Whiteman)
Feb. 7: Poor Butterfly   (Paul Whiteman/vocal group)
Feb. 8: There Ain't No Sweet Man That's Worth the Salt of My Tears
    (Paul Whiteman/S–vocal group)
Feb. 13: Sunshine   (Paul Whiteman/S–vocal group)
    From Monday On   (Paul Whiteman/S–vocal group)
Feb. 18: Mississippi Mud   (Paul Whiteman/S–vocal group,
    Irene Taylor)
Feb. 28: From Monday On   (Paul Whiteman/S–vocal group)
    High Water   (Paul Whiteman)
Mar. 1: What Price Lyrics?   (Rhythm Boys)
Mar. 12: I'm Wingin' Home   (Paul Whiteman/S–vocal group)
Mar. 14: Metropolis (Part 3)   (Paul Whiteman/vocal group)
Mar. 15: Lovable   (Paul Whiteman)
Mar. 16: March of the Musketeers   (Paul Whiteman/S–vocal group)
Apr. 21: I'm Afraid of You   (Paul Whiteman)
Apr. 22: My Pet   (Paul Whiteman/S–vocal group)
    It Was the Dawn of Love   (Paul Whiteman/S–vocal group)
    Dancing Shadows   (Paul Whiteman/vocal group)
Apr. 23: Louisiana   (Paul Whiteman/S–vocal group)
Apr. 24: Grieving   (Paul Whiteman/vocal group)
    Do I Hear You Saying?   (Paul Whiteman/vocal group)
Apr. 25: You Took Advantage of Me   (Paul Whiteman/S–vocal group)
May 21: Evening Star   (Paul Whiteman/vocal group)
May 22: Get Out and Get Under the Moon
    (Paul Whiteman/S–vocal group)
June 10: 'Taint So, Honey, 'Taint So   (Paul Whiteman)

I'd Rather Cry Over You	(Paul Whiteman/S–vocal group)
June 17: I'm on the Crest of a Wave	(Paul Whiteman/S–vocal group)
That's My Weakness Now	(Paul Whiteman/Rhythm Boys)
June 18: Because My Baby Don't Mean "Maybe" Now	
	(Paul Whiteman/S–vocal group)
Out-o-Town Gal	(Paul Whiteman/Rhythm Boys)
June 19: Wa Da Da	(Rhythm Boys)
That's Grandma	(Rhythm Boys)
Nov. 10: My Suppressed Desire	(Rhythm Boys)
Rhythm King	(Rhythm Boys)
Dec. 22: Makin' Whoopee	(Paul Whiteman/S–vocal group)
Dec. 28: I'll Get By (As Long as I Have You)	
	(Ipana Troubadours)
Rose of Mandalay	(Ipana Troubadours)

1929

Jan. 25: I'm Crazy Over You	(Sam Lanin)
Susianna	(Sam Lanin)
If I Had You	(Sam Lanin)
Jan. 26: The Spell of the Blues	(Dorsey Brothers)
Let's Do It	(Dorsey Brothers)
My Kinda Love	(Dorsey Brothers)
Feb. 28: Coquette	(Paul Whiteman)
Mar. 7: My Angeline	(Paul Whiteman)
Mar. 14: My Kinda Love	(Bing Crosby/Matty Malneck)
Till We Meet	(Bing Crosby/Matty Malneck)
Mar. 15: Louise	(Paul Whiteman)
Apr. 5: I'm in Seventh Heaven	(Paul Whiteman/Rhythm Boys)
Apr. 10: So the Bluebirds and the Blackbirds Got Together	
	(Rhythm Boys)
Louise	(Rhythm Boys)
Apr. 25: Little Pal	(Paul Whiteman)
May. 3: Reaching for Someone	(Paul Whiteman)
May. 4: Oh, Miss Hannah	(Paul Whiteman)
Orange Blossom Time	(Paul Whiteman)
May 16: Your Mother and Mine	(Paul Whiteman/S–vocal group)
S'posin'	(Paul Whiteman)
May 24: I Kiss Your Hand, Madame	(Bing Crosby/Matty Malneck)
Baby, Oh Where Can You Be?	(Bing Crosby/Matty Malneck)
Sept. 6: At Twilight	(Paul Whiteman/S–vocal group)
Sept. 13: Waiting at the End of the Road	
	(Paul Whiteman)

When You're Counting the Stars Alone

(Paul Whiteman/S–vocal group)

Sept. 27: Can't We Be Friends?   (Bing Crosby/Matty Malneck)

    Gay Love   (Bing Crosby/Matty Malneck)

Oct. 9: Great Day   (Paul Whiteman/S–vocal group)

    Without a Song   (Paul Whiteman)

Oct. 16: I'm a Dreamer, Aren't We All   (Paul Whiteman/S–vocal group)

    If I Had a Talking Picture of You

(Paul Whiteman)

Oct. 18: Southern Medley   (Paul Whiteman)

    A Bundle of Old Love Letters   (Paul Whiteman)

    After You've Gone   (Paul Whiteman)

1930

Feb. 10: Happy Feet   (Paul Whiteman/Rhythm Boys)

Mar. 21: Song of the Dawn   (Paul Whiteman/S–vocal group)

Mar. 22: Livin' in the Sunlight, Lovin' in the Moonlight

(Paul Whiteman)

Mar. 23: A Bench in the Park   (Paul Whiteman/Rhythm Boys,

Brox Sisters)

    I Like to Do Things for You   (Paul Whiteman/Rhythm Boys)

    You Brought a New Kind of Love to Me

(Paul Whiteman)

May 23: A Bench in the Park   (Rhythm Boys)

    Everything's Agreed Upon   (Rhythm Boys)

Aug. 26: Three Little Words   (Duke Ellington/Rhythm Boys)

Oct. 29: Fool Me Some More   (Gus Arnheim)

    It Must Be True   (Gus Arnheim)

Nov. 20: Them There Eyes   (Gus Arnheim/Rhythm Boys)

Nov. 25: The Little Things in Life   (Gus Arnheim)

1931

Jan. 19: I Surrender, Dear   (Gus Arnheim)

Mar. 2: Thanks to You   (Gus Arnheim)

    One More Time   (Gus Arnheim)

    Wrap Your Troubles in Dreams

(Gus Arnheim)

    Just a Gigolo   (Gus Arnheim)

Mar. 30: Out of Nowhere   (Bing Crosby/Brunswick)

    If You Should Ever Need Me   (Bing Crosby/Brunswick)

May 1: Ho Hum!   (Gus Arnheim/Loyce Whiteman)

    I'm Gonna Get You   (Gus Arnheim)

May 4: Were You Sincere?	(Brunswick)
Just One More Chance	(Brunswick)
June 12: I'm Through with Love	(Brunswick)
Many Happy Returns of the Day	
	(Brunswick)
I Found a Million Dollar Baby (in a Five and Ten Cent Store)	
	(Brunswick)
June 24: At Your Command	(Harry Barris, piano)
Aug. 19: I Apologize	(Victor Young)
Dancing in the Dark	(Victor Young)
Star Dust	(Victor Young)
Sept. 14: Sweet and Lovely	(Victor Young)
Oct. 6: Now That You're Gone	(Victor Young)
A Faded Summer Love	(Victor Young)
Oct. 8: Too Late	(Victor Young)
Goodnight Sweetheart	(Victor Young)
Oct. 25: Gems from George White's Scandals, Part 1 ("The Thrill Is Gone")	
	(— Victor Young)
Gems from George White's Scandals, Part 2 ("Life Is Just a Bowl of Cherries")	
	(— Victor Young, Mills Brothers, Boswell Sisters)
Nov. 23: Where the Blue of the Night (Meets the Gold of the Day)	
	(Brunswick)
Dec. 3: I'm Sorry Dear	(Brunswick)
Dec. 16: Dinah	(— Mills Brothers/ Bennie Kreuger)
Dec. 21: Can't We Talk it Over	(Helen Crawford, organ)
I Found You	(Helen Crawford, organ)

1932

Jan. 21: Snuggled on Your Shoulder	(Bennie Kreuger)
Feb. 11: St. Louis Blues (take A)	(— Duke Ellington)
St. Louis Blues (take B)	(— Duke Ellington)
Feb. 16: Starlight	(Brunswick)
How Long Will It Last?	(Brunswick)
Feb. 23: Love, You Funny Thing	(Brunswick)
My Woman	(Brunswick)
Feb. 29: Shine	(— Mills Brothers/Brunswick)
Mar. 8: Face the Music Medley, Part 1 ("Soft Lights and Sweet Music")	
	(— Victor Young)
Shadows on the Window	(Victor Young)

Mar. 15: Paradise   (Victor Young)
   You're Still in My Heart   (Victor Young)
Apr. 13: Lawd, You Made the Night Too Long
            (— Don Redman/Boswell Sisters)
Apr. 23: Sweet Georgia Brown   (Isham Jones)
   Waltzing in a Dream   (Isham Jones)
   Happy-Go-Lucky You   (Isham Jones)
Apr. 24: Lazy Dream   (Isham Jones)
   Let's Try Again   (Isham Jones)
May 25: Cabin in the Cotton   (Lennie Hayton)
   With Summer Coming On   (Lennie Hayton)
May 26: Love Me Tonight   (Lennie Hayton)
   Some of These Days   (Lennie Hayton)
Sept. 16: Please   (Anson Weeks)
Oct. 14: How Deep Is the Ocean?   (Brunswick)
   Here Lies Love   (Brunswick)
   I Don't Stand a Ghost of a Chance with You
            (Brunswick)
Oct. 25: Linger a Little Longer in the Twilight
            (Lennie Hayton)
   We're a Couple of Soldiers   (Lennie Hayton)
   We're a Couple of Soldiers   (fluff take)
            (Lennie Hayton)
   Brother, Can You Spare a Dime?
            (Lennie Hayton)
   Sweet Sue — Just You   (Lennie Hayton, piano)
Oct. 28: Let's Put Out the Lights and Go to Sleep
            (Brunswick)
   I'll Follow You   (Brunswick)
Nov. 4: Just an Echo in the Valley   (Brunswick)
   Someday We'll Meet Again   (Brunswick)
Dec. 9: Street of Dreams   (Brunswick)
   It's Within Your Power   (Brunswick)

1933
Jan. 9: I'm Playing With Fire   (Brunswick)
   Try a Little Tenderness   (Brunswick)
Jan. 12: You're Getting to Be a Habit with Me
            (— Guy Lombardo)
   Young and Healthy   (— Guy Lombardo)
   You're Beautiful Tonight, My Dear
            (— Guy Lombardo)

Jan. 26: I've Got the World on a String (— Dorsey Brothers)
      My Honey's Lovin' Arms   (— Mills Brothers/
                                       Dorsey Brothers)

Feb. 9: What Do I Care, It's Home   (Brunswick)
      You've Got Me Crying Again   (Brunswick)

Mar. 14: Someone Stole Gabriel's Horn (— Dorsey Brothers)
      Stay on the Right Side of the Road
                           (— Dorsey Brothers)
      Here Is My Heart   (— Dorsey Brothers)

June 9: Learn to Croon   (Jimmy Grier)
      Moonstruck   (Jimmy Grier)
      My Love   (Jimmy Grier)
      I've Got to Pass Your House to Get to My House
                           (Jimmy Grier)

June 13: Blue Prelude   (Jimmy Grier)
      I Would If I Could but I Can't
                           (Jimmy Grier)
      Learn to Croon   (Jimmy Grier)
      Shadow Waltz   (Jimmy Grier)

June 16: I've Got to Sing a Torch Song (Jimmy Grier)
      There's a Cabin in the Pines   (Jimmy Grier)
      Down the Old Ox Road   (Jimmy Grier)

Aug. 27: I Guess It Had to Be That Way
                           (Jimmy Grier)
      Thanks   (Jimmy Grier)
      The Day You Came Along   (Jimmy Grier)
      Black Moonlight   (Jimmy Grier)

Sept. 27: Beautiful Girl   (Lennie Hayton)
      The Last Round-Up   (Lennie Hayton)
      After Sundown   (Lennie Hayton)
      Home on the Range   (Lennie Hayton)

Oct. 22: We'll Make Hay While the Sun Shines
                           (Lennie Hayton)
      Temptation   (Lennie Hayton)
      Our Big Love Scene   (Lennie Hayton)

Dec. 11: Did You Ever See a Dream Walking?
                           (Lennie Hayton)
      Let's Spend an Evening at Home
                           (Lennie Hayton)

1934
Feb. 25: Love Thy Neighbor   (Nat W. Finston)

Once in a Blue Moon	(Nat W. Finston)
Good Night Lovely Little Lady	
	(Nat W. Finston)
May I?	(Nat W. Finston)
Mar. 10: Little Dutch Mill	(Jimmy Grier)
Shadows of Love	(Jimmy Grier)
Mar. 13: She Reminds Me of You	(Jimmy Grier)
Ridin' Around in the Rain	(Jimmy Grier)
July 5: I'm Hummin', I'm Whistlin', I'm Singin'	
	(Irving Aaronson)
Love in Bloom	(Irving Aaronson)
Straight from the Shoulder	(Irving Aaronson)
Give Me a Heart to Sing To	(Irving Aaronson)
Aug. 8: I Love You Truly	(Georgie Stoll)
Just a-Wearyin' for You	(Georgie Stoll)
Let Me Call You Sweetheart	(Georgie Stoll)
Someday Sweetheart	(Georgie Stoll)
Oct. 5: The Moon Was Yellow	(Georgie Stoll)
The Very Thought of You	(Georgie Stoll)
Two Cigarettes in the Dark	(Georgie Stoll)
The Sweetheart Waltz	(Georgie Stoll)
Nov. 9: With Every Breath I Take	(Georgie Stoll)
June in January	(Georgie Stoll)
Love Is Just Around the Corner	
	(Georgie Stoll)
Maybe I'm Wrong Again	(Georgie Stoll)

1935

Feb. 21: Soon	(Georgie Stoll)
Down by the River	(Georgie Stoll)
It's Easy to Remember	(Georgie Stoll/Rhythmettes, Three Shades of Blue)
Swanee River	(Georgie Stoll/Crinoline Choir)
Silent Night	(Georgie Stoll/Crinoline Choir)
Feb. ??: Adeste Fideles/Lift Up Your Hearts/Stabat Mater	
	(unknown organ)
Aug. 14: From the Top of Your Head to the Tip of Your Toes	
	(Dorsey Brothers)
I Wish I Were Aladdin	(Dorsey Brothers)
Takes Two to Make a Bargain	
	(Dorsey Brothers)
Two for Tonight	(Dorsey Brothers)

Without a Word of Warning	(Dorsey Brothers)
I Wished on the Moon	(Dorsey Brothers)
Nov. 12: Red Sails in the Sunset	(Victor Young)
Take Me Back to My Boots and Saddle	
	(Victor Young)
On Treasure Island	(Victor Young)
Adeste Fideles	(Victor Young/Guardsmen Quartet)
Nov. 13: Sailor Beware	(Georgie Stoll)
My Heart and I	(Georgie Stoll)
Silent Night	(Victor Young/Guardsmen Quartet)
Moonburn	(Georgie Stoll Trio)

1936

Mar. 24: We'll Rest at the End of the Trail	
	(Victor Young)
Twilight on the Trail	(Victor Young)
The Touch of Your Lips	(Victor Young)
Lovely Lady	(Victor Young)
Corrine, Corrina (parody)	(Victor Young)
Mar. 29: Would You	(Victor Young)
Robins and Roses	(Victor Young)
I Got Plenty o' Nuttin'	(Victor Young)
It Ain't Necessarily So	(Victor Young)
Robins and Roses (parody)	(Victor Young)
July 14: Empty Saddles	(Victor Young/Guardsmen Quartet)
A Roundup Lullaby	(Victor Young)
July 17: I Can't Escape from You	(Jimmy Dorsey)
The House Jack Built for Jill	(Jimmy Dorsey)
I'm an Old Cowhand	(Jimmy Dorsey)
July 23: Song of the Islands	(Dick McIntyre)
Aloha Oe	(Dick McIntyre)
July 24: So Do I	(Georgie Stoll)
Pennies from Heaven	(Georgie Stoll)
July 29: Let's Call a Heart a Heart	(Georgie Stoll)
One, Two, Button Your Shoe	
	(Georgie Stoll)
Aug. 4: Shoe Shine Boy	(Jimmy Dorsey)
South Sea Island Magic	(Dick McIntyre)
Hawaiian Paradise	(Dick McIntyre)
Aug. 10: For Love Alone	(Victor Young)
I Never Realized	(Victor Young)
Beyond Compare	(Victor Young)

Aug. 12: Dear Old Girl   (Ivan Ditmars/The Three Cheers)
       Just One Word of Consolation

                                         (Ivan Ditmars/The Three Cheers)

Aug. 17: Pennies from Heaven Medley ("So Do I")

                                     (— Jimmy Dorsey/
                                     Frances Langford)

       Pennies from Heaven   (— Jimmy Dorsey/Louis

                                     Armstrong, Frances Langford)

Aug. 19: The Way You Look Tonight   (— Dixie Lee/Victor Young)
       A Fine Romance   (— Dixie Lee/Victor Young)
       Me and the Moon   (Victor Young)

1937

Feb. 23: Sweet Leilani   (Lani McIntyre)
       Blue Hawaii   (Lani McIntyre)
Feb. 28: In a Little Hula Heaven   (Jimmy Dorsey)
       Never in a Million Years   (Jimmy Dorsey)
Mar. 3: What Will I Tell My Heart   (Jimmy Dorsey)
       Too Marvelous for Words   (Jimmy Dorsey)
       Peckin'   (Jimmy Dorsey)
Mar. 5: The One Rose (That's Left in My Heart)

                                     (Victor Young)

       Sweet Is the Word for You   (Victor Young)
       Moonlight and Shadows   (Victor Young)
Mar. 8: Sentimental and Melancholy   (Victor Young)
       My Little Buckaroo   (Victor Young)
       What Is Love?   (Victor Young)
July 12: It's the Natural Thing to Do   (John Scott Trotter)
       All You Want to Do Is Dance   (John Scott Trotter)
       The Moon Got in My Eyes   (John Scott Trotter)
       Smarty   (John Scott Trotter)
Sept. 11: Dancing Under the Stars   (Lani McIntyre)
       Palace in Paradise   (Lani McIntyre)
       When You Dream About Hawaii

                                     (Lani McIntyre)

       Sail Along, Silv'ry Moon   (Lani McIntyre)
Sept. 20: Can I Forget You   (John Scott Trotter)
       The Folks Who Live on the Hill

                                     (John Scott Trotter)

       I Still Love to Kiss You Goodnight

                                     (John Scott Trotter)

       Remember Me?   (John Scott Trotter)

Sept. 25: Basin Street Blues   (— Connie Boswell/
             John Scott Trotter)
    Bob White (Whatcha Gonna Swing Tonight?)
             (— Connie Boswell/
             John Scott Trotter)
Nov. 12: There's a Gold Mine in the Sky
             (Eddie Dunstedter, organ)
    When the Organ Played "O Promise Me"
             (Eddie Dunstedter, organ)
Nov. 15: Let's Waltz for Old Times' Sake
             (Eddie Dunstedter, organ)
    In the Mission by the Sea   (Eddie Dunstedter, organ)

1938

Jan. 21: My Heart Is Taking Lessons   (John Scott Trotter)
    This Is My Night to Dream   (John Scott Trotter)
    On the Sentimental Side   (John Scott Trotter)
    The Moon of Manakoora   (John Scott Trotter)
Jan. 26: Alexander's Ragtime Band   (— Connie Boswell/
             John Scott Trotter)

    Home on the Range   (Victor Young)
Apr. 13: Sweet Hawaiian Chimes   (Harry Owens)
    Little Angel   (Harry Owens)
Apr. 22: Let Me Whisper I Love You   (John Scott Trotter)
    Don't Be That Way   (John Scott Trotter)
Apr. 25: Little Lady Make-Believe   (Eddie Dunstedter, organ)
    When Mother Nature Sings Her Lullaby
             (Eddie Dunstedter, organ)

    Darling Nelly Gray   (Paul Taylor Choristers)
    Swing Low, Sweet Chariot   (Paul Taylor Choristers)
May 23: Now It Can Be Told   (John Scott Trotter)
    It's the Dreamer in Me   (John Scott Trotter)
July 1: Small Fry   (— Johnny Mercer/Victor Young)
    Mr. Gallagher and Mr. Shean   (— Johnny Mercer/Victor Young)
July 8: Summertime   (Matty Malneck)
    A Blues Serenade   (Matty Malneck)
July 11: I've Got a Pocketful of Dreams (John Scott Trotter)
    Don't Let That Moon Get Away
             (John Scott Trotter)
    Silver on the Sage   (John Scott Trotter)
    Laugh and Call It Love   (John Scott Trotter)
    Mexicali Rose   (John Scott Trotter)

Oct. 14: You Must Have Been a Beautiful Baby
                                              (— Bob Crosby)

      Old Folks   (— Bob Crosby)

      My Reverie   (— Bob Crosby)

Nov. 4: You're a Sweet Little Headache (John Scott Trotter)

      I Have Eyes   (John Scott Trotter)

      The Funny Old Hills   (John Scott Trotter)

      Joobalai   (John Scott Trotter)

Dec. 2: When You're Away   (Victor Young)

      Ah! Sweet Mystery of Life   (Victor Young)

      Sweethearts   (Victor Young)

      Thine Alone   (Victor Young)

Dec. 9: Gypsy Love Song   (— Frances Langford/
                                         Victor Young)

      I'm Falling in Love with Someone
                                    (— Frances Langford/
                                         Victor Young)

Dec. 12: My Melancholy Baby   (John Scott Trotter)

      I Cried for You   (John Scott Trotter)

      The Lonesome Road   (John Scott Trotter)

      When the Bloom Is on the Sage
                                    (John Scott Trotter)

Dec. 19: Between a Kiss and a Sigh (John Scott Trotter)

      Just a Kid Named Joe   (John Scott Trotter)

      It's a Lonely Trail   (John Scott Trotter)

      Let's Tie the Old Forget-Me-Not
                                    (John Scott Trotter)

1939

Mar. 10: East Side of Heaven   (John Scott Trotter)

      Hang Your Heart on a Hickory Limb
                                    (John Scott Trotter)

      That Sly Old Gentleman (from Featherbed Lane)
                                    (John Scott Trotter)

      Sing a Song of Sunbeams (John Scott Trotter)

Mar. 15: Ida, Sweet as Apple Cider (John Scott Trotter/The Foursome)

      Poor Old Rover   (John Scott Trotter/The Foursome)

      Down by the Old Mill Stream (John Scott Trotter/The Foursome)

Mar. 22: Deep Purple   (Matty Malneck)

      Star Dust   (Matty Malneck)

      God Bless America   (Max Terr Chorus/
                                     John Scott Trotter)

The Star Spangled Banner	(Max Terr Chorus/ John Scott Trotter)
Mar. 31: If I Had My Way	(John Scott Trotter)
Little Sir Echo	(John Scott Trotter/Music Maids)
I Surrender, Dear	(John Scott Trotter)
I'm Building a Sailboat of Dreams	
	(John Scott Trotter)
Apr. 3: Allá en el Rancho Grande	(John Scott Trotter/The Foursome)
It Must Be True	(John Scott Trotter/Music Maids)
S'posin'	(John Scott Trotter/Music Maids)
Apr. 5: Whistling in the Wildwood	(John Scott Trotter)
And the Angels Sing	(John Scott Trotter)
June 9: Wrap Your Troubles in Dreams	(John Scott Trotter)
Wrap Your Troubles in Dreams	(fluff take) (John Scott Trotter)
Girl of My Dreams	(John Scott Trotter)
The Missouri Waltz	(John Scott Trotter)
Still the Bluebird Sings	(John Scott Trotter)
Go Fly a Kite	(John Scott Trotter)
A Man and His Dream	(John Scott Trotter)
Just One More Chance	(John Scott Trotter)
June 13: To You, Sweetheart, Aloha	(Dick McIntyre)
My Isle of Golden Dreams	(Dick McIntyre)
Maybe	(Victor Young)
Somebody Loves Me	(Victor Young)
Home on the Range	(Victor Young)
June 22: Start the Day Right	(— Connie Boswell/ John Scott Trotter)
An Apple for the Teacher	(— Connie Boswell/ John Scott Trotter)
June 30: Neighbors in the Sky	(John Scott Trotter)
What's New?	(John Scott Trotter)
Cynthia	(John Scott Trotter)
Medley of Gus Edwards Song Hits ("Sunbonnet Sue," "Jimmy Valentine," "If I Was a Millionaire")	
	(John Scott Trotter)
In My Merry Oldsmobile	(John Scott Trotter/Music Maids)
Sept. 20: Ciribiribin	(— Andrews Sisters/Joe Venuti)
Yodelin' Jive	(— Andrews Sisters/Joe Venuti)
Dec. 15: Too Romantic	(John Scott Trotter)
The Moon and the Willow Tree	
	(John Scott Trotter)

Sweet Potato Piper   (John Scott Trotter/The Foursome)
Between 18th and 19th on Chestnut Street
      (— Connie Boswell/
      John Scott Trotter)

1940

Feb. 9: Marcheta   (John Scott Trotter)
      Tumbling Tumbleweeds   (John Scott Trotter)
      If I Knew Then (What I Know Now)
            (John Scott Trotter)
      The Girl with the Pigtails in Her Hair
            (John Scott Trotter)
Feb. 25: Devil May Care   (John Scott Trotter)
      The Singing Hills   (John Scott Trotter)
      I'm Waiting for Ships That Never Come In
            (John Scott Trotter)
Mar. 22: Beautiful Dreamer   (John Scott Trotter)
      Jeanie with the Light Brown Hair
            (John Scott Trotter)
      Yours Is My Heart Alone   (John Scott Trotter)
      Sierra Sue   (John Scott Trotter)
Apr. 12: Meet the Sun Half-Way   (John Scott Trotter)
      April Played the Fiddle   (John Scott Trotter)
      I Haven't Time to Be a Millionaire
            (John Scott Trotter)
      The Pessimistic Character (with the Crab Apple Face)
            (John Scott Trotter)
Apr. 15: Mister Meadowlark   (— Johnny Mercer/Victor Young)
      On Behalf of the Visiting Firemen
            (— Johnny Mercer/Victor Young)
July 1: Trade Winds   (Dick McIntyre)
      A Song of Old Hawaii   (Dick McIntyre)
      Aloha Kuu Ipo Aloha   (Dick McIntyre)
July 3: When the Moon Comes Over Madison Square
            (John Scott Trotter)
      Only Forever   (John Scott Trotter)
July 6: Ballad for Americans: (Victor Young/Ken Darby Singers)
      Part One
      Part Two
      Part Three
      Part Four

Bing Crosby Filmography: Complete

This section lists all major feature films and short subjects made for theatrical release, plus five television dramas (*High Tor, Dr. Cook's Garden,* and three inspirational two-reelers produced by the Christophers). It does not include pictures made by Bing Crosby Productions in which Bing does not appear. Credits are given only for those in which he has a substantial role. Unless otherwise noted, all pictures were released by Paramount.

S = short subject
V = voiceover (musical or narrative)
C = cameo or supporting appearance
HC = Bob Hope movie with Crosby bit-part cameo

1930

King of Jazz (Universal) (C,V) Directed by John Murray Anderson. Produced by Carl Laemmle Jr. Written by Edward T. Lowe, Harry Ruskin, and Charles MacArthur. Photographed by Hal Mohr, Ray Rennahan, and Jerome Ash. Songs by Milton Ager–Jack Yellin; Mabel Wayne–Billy Rose; Harry Barris–James Cavanaugh; others. Cast: Paul Whiteman and His Orchestra with the Rhythm Boys, the Brox Sisters, John Boles, Laura La Plante, Jeanette Loff, Merna Kennedy, Walter Brennan, Stanley Smith, William Kent, Glenn Tryon, Russell Markert Girls.

Two Plus Fours (Pathe) (S,C) Directed by Ray McCarey. Written by McCarey and Charles Callahan. Cast: Nat Carr, Thelma Hill, Bing Crosby, Harry Barris, Al Rinker, Ed Deering, Spec O'Donnell.

Check and Double Check (RKO) (V) "Three Little Words" performed by Duke Ellington and His Orchestra with the Rhythm Boys.

Reaching for the Moon (United Artists) (C) "When the Folks High Up Do the Mean Low Down" sung by Bing Crosby, Bebe Daniels, and June MacCloy.

1931

Confessions of a Co-ed (C) "Out of Nowhere" sung by Bing Crosby; "Ya Got Love" sung by the Rhythm Boys.

I Surrender Dear (Educational-Sennett) (S) Directed by Mack Sennett. Written by John A. Waldron, Earle Rodney, and Harry McCoy. Songs by Harry Barris–Gordon Clifford; Barris–Bing Crosby–Harry Tobias; John Green–Edward Hayman; Ernest Ball–J. Keirn Brennan. Cast: Bing Crosby, Arthur Stone, Marion Sayers, Luis Alberni, Julia Griffith. The Sennett-Crosby shorts were later reissued as parts of compilation films, notably *Road to Hollywood* (1947) and *Down Memory Lane* (1949).

One More Chance (Educational-Sennett) (S) Directed by Mack Sennett. Written by John A. Waldron, Earle Rodney, Harry McCoy, and Lew Foster. Songs by Arthur Johnston–Sam Coslow; Harry Barris–Billy Moll–Ted Koehler; Barris–Gordon Clifford; Lew Brown–Sidney Clare. Cast: Bing Crosby, Arthur Stone, Patsy O'Leary, Matty Kemp.

1932

Dream House (Educational-Sennett) (S) Directed by Del Lord. Written by John A. Waldron, Earle Rodney, Harry McCoy, and Lew Foster. Songs by Harry Barris–Gus Arnheim–Gordon Clifford; Irving Kahal–Pierre Norman–Sammy Fain. Cast: Bing Crosby, Ann Christy, Katherine Ward, William Davidson, Eddie Phillips, Vernon Dent. Reissued in edited version as *Crooner's Holiday* (1935).

Billboard Girl (Educational-Sennett) (S) Directed by Leslie Pearce. Written by John A. Waldron, Earle Rodney, Harry McCoy, and Lew Foster. Songs by Jack Meskill–Vincent Rose; Al Dubin–Joseph Burke. Cast: Bing Crosby, Margie Babe Kane, Dick Stewart, Jimmy Eagles, Lincoln Stedman, George Pearce. Reissued in edited version as *Bring On Bing* (1935).

Hollywood on Parade Z2: No.2 (S,C) "Auf Wiedersehen" sung by Bing Crosby.

The Big Broadcast Directed by Frank Tuttle. Written by George Marion Jr., from a play, *Wild Waves,* by William Ford Manley. Photographed by George Folsey. Songs by Leo Robin–Ralph Rainger; Sam Lewis–Joe Young–Harry Akst; Harry Barris–Gordon Clifford; others. Cast: Bing Crosby, Stuart Erwin, Leila Hyams, Sharon Lynne, George Burns, Gracie Allen, Spec O'Donnell, George Barbier, Major Sharp and Minor, Arthur Tracy, Mills Brothers, Boswell Sisters, Kate Smith, Donald Novis, Cab Calloway, Vincent Lopez, Eddie Lang.

1933

Sing Bing Sing (Educational-Sennett) (S) Directed by Babe Stafford. Written by John A. Waldron, Earle Rodney, Harry McCoy, and Lew Foster. Songs by Harold Arlen–Ted Koehler; Joe Young–Carmen Lombardo; Gus Kahn–Harry Woods. Cast: Bing Crosby, Florine McKinney, Franklin Pangborn, Irving Bacon, Arthur Stone.

Blue of the Night (Educational–Sennett) (S) Directed by Leslie Pearce. Written by John A. Waldron, Earle Rodney, Harry McCoy, and Lew Foster. Songs by Roy Turk–Fred Ahlert–Bing Crosby; Milton Ager–Ed Nelson–Al Hoffman–Al Goodhart; Gerald Marks–Benny Davis; Edward Heyman–Dana Suesse. Cast: Bing Crosby, Margie Babe Kane, Franklin Pangborn, Toby Wing, Bud Jamison.

Hollywood on Parade Z3: No.1 (S,C) "The Old Ox Road" sung by Bing Crosby.

Hollywood on Parade Z3: No.4 (S,C) "Boo Boo Boo" sung by Bing Crosby and Jack Oakie; "Buckin' the Wind" sung by Crosby.

Hollywood on Parade Z3: No.7 (S,C) Bing appears in a skit with John Barrymore, Harry Langdon, others.

Please (S) Produced and directed by Arvid E. Gillstrom. Written by Dean Ward and Vernon Dent. Songs by Leo Robin–Ralph Rainger; Al Dubin–Harry Warren; Victor Young–Ned Washington–Bing Crosby; others. Cast: Bing Crosby, Mary Kornman, Vernon Dent.

College Humor Directed by Wesley Ruggles. Written by Claude Binyon and Frank Butler, from a story by Dean Fales. Photographed by Leo Tover. Songs by Arthur Johnston–Sam Coslow; others. Cast: Bing Crosby, Jack Oakie, Mary Carlisle, Richard Arlen, Mary Kornman, George Burns, Gracie Allen, Lona Andre, Joseph Sauers (Sawyer), Grady Sutton.

Too Much Harmony Directed by A. Edward Sutherland. Produced by William LeBaron. Written by Joseph L. Mankiewicz and Harry Ruskin. Photographed by Theodor Sparkuhl. Songs by Arthur Johnston–Sam Coslow. Cast: Bing Crosby, Jack Oakie, Judith Allen, Skeets Gallagher, Harry Green, Lilyan Tashman, Ned Sparks, Kitty Kelly, Grace Bradley, Mrs. Evelyn Offield Oakie, Henry Armetta.

Going Hollywood (MGM) Directed by Raoul Walsh. Produced by Walter Wanger. Written by Donald Ogden Stewart, from a story by Frances Marion. Photographed by George Folsey. Songs by Nacio Herb Brown–Arthur Freed. Cast: Marion Davies, Bing Crosby, Fifi D'Orsay, Ned Sparks, Stuart Erwin, Patsy Kelly, Sterling Holloway, Bobby Watson, Radio Rogues, Lennie Hayton.

1934

Just an Echo (S) Produced and directed by Arvid E. Gillstrom. Written by Dean Ward, Vernon Dent. Songs by Harry Woods–Jimmy Campbell–Reg Connelly; Joe Young–Carmen Lombardo; others. Cast: Bing Crosby, Mary Kornman, Vernon Dent.

We're Not Dressing Directed by Norman Taurog. Produced by Benjamin Glazer. Written by Horace Jackson, Francis Martin, and George Marion Jr., from a play, *The Admirable Crichton*, by Sir J. M. Barrie. Photographed by

Charles Lang. Songs by Mack Gordon–Harry Revel. Cast: Bing Crosby, Carole Lombard, Ethel Merman, Leon Errol, George Burns, Gracie Allen, Ray Milland, Jay Henry.

She Loves Me Not Directed by Elliott Nugent. Produced and written by Benjamin Glazer, from a play by Howard Lindsay and a novel by Edward Hope. Photographed by Charles Lang. Songs by Leo Robin–Ralph Rainger; Mack Gordon–Harry Revel. Cast: Bing Crosby, Miriam Hopkins, Kitty Carlisle, Eddie Nugent, Henry Stephenson, Lynne Overman, George Barbier, Warren Hymer, Judith Allen.

Here Is My Heart Directed by Frank Tuttle. Produced by Louis D. Lighton. Written by Edwin Justus Mayer and Harlan Thompson, from a play, *The Grand Dutchess and the Waiter,* by Alfred Savoir. Photographed by Karl Struss. Songs by Leo Robin–Ralph Rainger; Robin–Lewis Gensler. Cast: Bing Crosby, Kitty Carlisle, Roland Young, Alison Skipworth, Reginald Owen, Akim Tamiroff, William Frawley, Cecilia Parker, Marian Mansfield.

1935

Mississippi Directed by A. Edward Sutherland. Produced by Arthur Hornblow Jr. Written by Francis Martin and Jack Cunningham, adapted by Herbert Fields and Claude Binyon, from a play, *Magnolia,* by Booth Tarkington. Photographed by Charles Lang. Songs by Richard Rodgers–Lorenz Hart; Stephen Foster. Cast: Bing Crosby, W. C. Fields, Joan Bennett, Gail Patrick, Queenie Smith, Claude Gillingwater, John Miljan, Five Cabin Kids.

Two for Tonight Directed by Frank Tuttle. Produced by Douglas MacLean. Written by George Marion Jr. and Jane Storm, from a play by Max and J. O. Lief. Photographed by Karl Struss. Songs by Mack Gordon–Harry Revel. Cast: Bing Crosby, Joan Bennett, Mary Boland, Lynne Overman, Thelma Todd, James Blakely, Douglas Fowley, Ernest Cossart.

The Big Broadcast of 1936 (C) "I Wished on the Moon" sung by Bing Crosby.

1936

Star Night at the Cocoanut Grove (MGM) (S,C) "With Every Breath I Take" sung by Bing Crosby.

Anything Goes Directed by Lewis Milestone. Produced by Benjamin Glazer. Written by Howard Lindsay and Russel Crouse, from their play. Photographed by Karl Struss. Songs by Cole Porter; Hoagy Carmichael–Edward Heyman; Leo Robin–Frederick Hollander; Robin–Richard Whiting. Cast: Bing Crosby, Ethel Merman, Charles Ruggles, Ida Lupino, Arthur Treacher, Grace Bradley, Robert McWade, Margaret Dumont.

Rhythm on the Range Directed by Norman Taurog. Produced by Benjamin Glazer. Written by Walter DeLeon, Francis Martin, Sidney Salkow, and John C. Moffitt, from a story by Melvin J. Houser. Photographed by Karl Struss. Songs by Billy Hill; Johnny Mercer; Sam Coslow; Leo Robin–Richard Whiting; Robin–Frederick Hollander; Gertrude Ross–Badger Clark. Cast: Bing Crosby, Frances Farmer, Bob Burns, Martha Raye, Lucille Webster Gleason, Samuel S. Hinds, George E. Stone, Warren Hymer, Leonid Kinsky, Martha Sleeper, Louis Prima, Sons of the Pioneers.

Pennies from Heaven (Columbia) Directed by Norman Z. McLeod. Produced by Emmanuel Cohen. Written by Jo Swerling, from a story, "The Peacock Feather," by Katherine Leslie Moore. Photographed by Robert Pittack. Songs by Johnny Burke–Arthur Johnston. Cast: Bing Crosby, Madge Evans, Edith Fellows, Louis Armstrong, Donald Meek, John Gallaudet, Tom Dugan.

1937

Waikiki Wedding Directed by Frank Tuttle. Produced by Arthur Hornblow Jr. Written by Frank Butler, Don Hartman, Walter DeLeon, and Francis Martin. Photographed by Karl Struss. Songs by Leo Robin–Ralph Rainger; Harry Owens; others. Cast: Bing Crosby, Shirley Ross, Bob Burns, Martha Raye, George Barbier, Anthony Quinn, Leif Erikson, Grady Sutton.

Double or Nothing Directed by Theodore Reed. Produced by Benjamin Glazer. Written by Charles Lederer, Erwin Gelsey, John C. Moffitt, and Duke Atteberry, from a story by M. Coates Webster. Photographed by Karl Struss. Songs by Johnny Burke–Arthur Johnston; Burton Lane–Ralph Freed; Sam Coslow–Al Siegel. Cast: Bing Crosby, Mary Carlisle, Martha Raye, Andy Devine, William Frawley, Fay Holden, Samuel S. Hinds, John Gallaudet, Frances Faye, Harry Barris.

1938

Doctor Rhythm Directed by Frank Tuttle. Produced by Emanuel Cohen. Written by Jo Swerling and Richard Connell, from a story, "The Badge of Policeman O'Roon," by O. Henry. Photographed by Charles Lang. Songs by Johnny Burke–James Monaco; Lorenz Hart–Richard Rodgers. Cast: Bing Crosby, Beatrice Lillie, Mary Carlisle, Andy Devine, Laura Hope Crews, Rufe Davis, Sterling Holloway, Franklin Pangborn, William Austin, Harold Minjir, Louis Armstrong (original cut only).

Sing You Sinners Directed and produced by Wesley Ruggles. Written by Claude Binyon. Photographed by Karl Struss. Songs by Johnny Burke–James Monaco; Hoagy Carmichael–Frank Loesser. Cast: Bing Crosby, Fred MacMurray, Donald O'Connor, Ellen Drew, Elizabeth Patterson, Tom Dugan, John Gallaudet, Irving Bacon, Harry Barris.

1939

Paris Honeymoon Directed by Frank Tuttle. Produced by Harlan Thompson. Written by Frank Butler and Don Hartman, from a story by Angela Sherwood. Photographed by Karl Struss. Songs by Leo Robin–Ralph Rainger. Cast: Bing Crosby, Franciska Gaal, Akim Tamiroff, Shirley Ross, Edward Everett Horton, Ben Blue, Rafaela Ottiano, Gregory Gaye.

East Side of Heaven (Universal) Directed by David Butler. Produced by Herbert Polesie. Written by William Conselman, from a story by Butler and Polesie. Photographed by George Robinson. Songs by Johnny Burke–James Monaco. Cast: Bing Crosby, Joan Blondell, Baby Sandy, Mischa Auer, C. Aubrey Smith, Irene Hervey, Jerome Cowan, Robert Kent, Jane Jones, Music Maids, Matty Malneck.

The Star Maker Directed by Roy Del Ruth. Produced by Charles R. Rogers. Written by Frank Butler, Don Hartman, and Arthur Caesar, from a story by Caesar and William Pierce. Photographed by Karl Struss. Songs by Johnny Burke–James Monaco, Gus Edwards–Will D. Cobb; Edwards–Vincent Bryan; Shelton Brooks; others. Cast: Bing Crosby, Louise Campbell, Linda Ware, Ned Sparks, Janet Waldo, Laura Hope Crews, Thurston Hall, Billy Gilbert, Walter Damrosch.

1940

Road to Singapore Directed by Victor Schertzinger. Produced by Harlan Thompson. Written by Frank Butler and Don Hartman, from a story by Harry Hervey. Photographed by William Mellor. Songs by Johnny Burke–James Monaco; Burke–Victor Schertzinger. Cast: Bing Crosby, Bob Hope, Dorothy Lamour, Charles Coburn, Anthony Quinn, Jerry Colonna, Judith Barrett, Gaylord Pendleton, Miles Mander.

Swing with Bing (Universal) (S) Directed and produced by Herbert Polesie. Written by Grant Garret. Photographed by Al Wetzel. Music by Johnny Burke–James Monaco. Cast: Bing Crosby, Richard Keene, Bud Ward, Toney Penna, Jimmy Thompson, Arthur W. Bryan, Ty Cobb, Richard Arlen.

If I Had My Way (Universal) Directed and produced by David Butler. Written by William Conselman and James V. Kern, from a story by Butler, Conselman, and Kern. Photographed by George Robinson. Songs by Johnny Burke–James Monaco. Cast: Bing Crosby, Gloria Jean, Charles Winninger, El Brendel, Allyn Joslyn, Eddie Leonard, Blanche Ring, Grace La Rue, Julian Eltinge, Trixie Friganza, Paul Gordon, Six Hits and a Miss.

Rhythm on the River Directed by Victor Schertzinger. Produced by William LeBaron. Written by Dwight Taylor, from a story by Billy Wilder and Jacques Théry. Photographed by Ted Tetzlaff. Songs by Johnny Burke–James

Monaco. Cast: Bing Crosby, Mary Martin, Basil Rathbone, Oscar Levant, Charley Grapewin, William Frawley, John Scott Trotter, Ken Carpenter, Wingy Manone, Harry Barris.

1941

Road to Zanzibar Directed by Victor Schertzinger. Produced by Paul Jones. Written by Frank Butler and Don Hartman, from a story by Hartman and Sy Bartlett. Photographed by Ted Tetzlaff. Songs by Johnny Burke–James Van Heusen. Cast: Bing Crosby, Bob Hope, Dorothy Lamour, Una Merkel, Eric Blore, Douglass Dumbrille, Iris Adrian, Leo Gorcey, Ernest Whitman, Ken Carpenter.

Birth of the Blues Directed by Victor Schertzinger. Produced by B. G. De Sylva. Written by Harry Tugend and Walter DeLeon, from a story by Tugend. Photographed by William C. Mellor. Songs by B. G. DeSylva–Lew Brown–Ray Henderson; W. C. Handy; Johnny Mercer; Gus Edwards–Edward Madden; others. Cast: Bing Crosby, Mary Martin, Brian Donlevy, Carolyn Lee, Jack Teagarden, Eddie "Rochester" Anderson, J. Carrol Naish, Warren Hymer, Harry Barris, Perry Botkin, Ronnie Cosbey, Hall–Johnson Negro Choir.

Angels of Mercy (Red Cross newsreel, Metrotone News, released by Paramount, MGM, and 20th Century-Fox) (S,V) "Angels of Mercy" sung by Bing Crosby.

1942

Don't Hook Now (S) Produced by Herbert Polesie and Everett Crosby. Music by Johnny Burke–James Van Heusen. Cast: Bing Crosby, Bob Hope, Ben Hogan, Sam Snead, Jimmy Demaret.

My Favorite Blonde (HC)

Holiday Inn Directed and produced by Mark Sandrich. Written by Claude Binyon, from an idea by Irving Berlin adapted by Elmer Rice. Photographed by David Abel. Songs by Irving Berlin. Cast: Bing Crosby, Fred Astaire, Marjorie Reynolds, Virginia Dale, Walter Abel, Louise Beavers, John Gallaudet, Irving Bacon, Harry Barris.

Road to Morocco Directed by David Butler. Produced by Paul Jones. Written by Frank Butler and Don Hartman. Photographed by William C. Mellor. Songs by Johnny Burke–James Van Heusen. Cast: Bing Crosby, Bob Hope, Dorothy Lamour, Anthony Quinn, Dona Drake, Vladimir Sokoloff, Mikhail Rasumny, George Givot, Andrew Tombes, Leon Belasco, Dan Seymour, Yvonne De Carlo.

Star Spangled Rhythm (C) Directed by George Marshall. Produced by Joseph Sistrom. Written by Harry Tugend, others. Photographed by Leo

Tover. Songs by Harold Arlen–Johnny Mercer. Cast: Bing Crosby, Eddie Bracken, Betty Hutton, Walter Abel, Victor Moore, Bob Hope, Fred Mac-Murray, Mary Martin, Alan Ladd, Dorothy Lamour, Veronica Lake, Ray Milland, Eddie "Rochester" Anderson, William Bendix, Jerry Colonna, Cecil B. De Mille, Gary Crosby, the Golden Gate Quartet, Paulette Goddard, Dick Powell, Franchot Tone, Vera Zorina, Katherine Dunham.

1943

Dixie Directed by A. Edward Sutherland. Produced by Paul Jones. Written by Karl Tunberg and Darrell Ware, from a story by William Rankin adapted by Claude Binyon. Photographed by William C. Mellor. Songs by Johnny Burke–James Van Heusen; Dan Emmett. Cast: Bing Crosby, Dorothy Lamour, Marjorie Reynolds, Billy De Wolfe, Raymond Walburn, Grant Mitchell, Lynne Overman, Eddie Foy Jr., Fortunio Bonanova, Carl Switzer, Harry Barris.

1944

Going My Way Directed and produced by Leo McCarey. Written by Frank Butler and Frank Cavett, from a story by McCarey. Photographed by Lionel Lindon. Songs by Johnny Burke–James Van Heusen; Franz Schubert; Georges Bizet; James Royce Shannon. Cast: Bing Crosby, Barry Fitzgerald, Frank McHugh, Risë Stevens, Stanley Clements, Jean Heather, Gene Lockhart, James Brown, William Frawley, Porter Hall, Fortunio Bonanova, Carl Switzer, Robert Mitchell Boys Choir.

The Shining Future (Warner Bros.) (S,C) Directed by LeRoy Prinz. Produced by Gordon Hollinshead and Arnold Albert. Written by James Bloodworth. Songs by Frank Loesser and Joe Bushkin–John DeVries. Cast: Bing Crosby, Frank Sinatra, Jack Carson, Cary Grant, Benny Goodman, Harry James, Irene Manning, Dennis Morgan, Charles Ruggles. Made for Canada's Sixth War Loan and reissued in edited version as *The Road to Victory* (1944).

Swingtime with the Stars (US Coast Guard) (S) Songs by Harold Arlen–Johnny Mercer; Cole Porter. Cast: Bing Crosby, Leo "Ukie" Sherrin, Lt. Jimmy Grier and the Eleventh Naval District Coast Guard Band.

Here Come the Waves Directed and produced by Mark Sandrich. Written by Allan Scott, Ken Englund, and Zion Myers. Photographed by Charles Lang. Songs by Harold Arlen–Johnny Mercer. Cast: Bing Crosby, Betty Hutton, Sonny Tufts, Ann Doran, Gwen Crawford, Noel Neill, Catherine Craig, Marjorie Henshaw, Mae Clarke, Minor Watson, Harry Barris, Yvonne De Carlo, Mona Freeman.

The Princess and the Pirate (Goldwyn/RKO) (HC)

1945

Duffy's Tavern (C) Numerous Paramount players make guest appearances in an adaptation of a popular radio show. Bing Crosby sings a parody of "Swinging on a Star"; Gary, Phillip, Dennis, and Lindsay briefly appear.

Out of This World (V) Eddie Bracken comedy with songs dubbed by Bing Crosby. Gary, Phillip, Dennis, and Lindsay briefly appear.

All-Star Bond Rally (20th Century–Fox, made for the War Activities Committee and U.S. Treasury Department for Seventh War Bond Drive) (S, C) Directed by Michael Audley. Cast: Bing Crosby, Frank Sinatra, Bob Hope, Harpo Marx, Betty Grable, Harry James, Linda Darnell, Jeanne Crain.

Hollywood Victory Caravan (S,C) (Made for the War Activities Committee and U.S. Treasury Department). Directed by William Russell. Written by Mel Shavelson. Song by Jimmy McHugh–Harold Adamson. Cast: Bing Crosby, Bob Hope, Betty Hutton, Humphrey Bogart, Alan Ladd, Barbara Stanwyck, Franklin Pangborn, Robert Benchley.

The Bells of St. Mary's (Rainbow/RKO) Directed and produced by Leo McCarey. Written by Dudley Nichols, from a story by McCarey. Photographed by George Barnes. Songs by Johnny Burke–James Van Heusen; Grant Clark–George W. Meyer; Douglas Furber–A. Emmett Adams. Cast: Bing Crosby, Ingrid Bergman, Henry Travers, Ruth Donnelly, Joan Carroll, Dickie Tyler, Una O'Connor, Rhys Williams, Martha Sleeper, William Gargan, Jimmy Dundee.

1946

Road to Utopia Directed by Hal Walker. Produced by Paul Jones. Written by Norman Panama and Melvin Frank. Photographed by Lionel Lindon. Songs by Johnny Burke–James Van Heusen. Cast: Bing Crosby, Bob Hope, Dorothy Lamour, Douglas Dumbrille, Jack LaRue, Robert Barrat, Robert Benchley, Nestor Paiva, Hillary Brooke, Will Wright, Jimmy Dundee.

Blue Skies Directed by Stuart Heisler. Produced by Sol C. Siegel. Written by Arthur Sheekman, from an idea by Irving Berlin adapted by Allan Scott. Photographed by Charles Lang. Songs by Irving Berlin. Cast: Bing Crosby, Fred Astaire, Joan Caulfield, Billy De Wolfe, Olga San Juan, Frank Faylen, Victoria Horne.

1947

Welcome Stranger Directed by Elliott Nugent. Produced by Sol C. Siegel. Written by Arthur Sheekman, from a story by Frank Butler adapted by Sheekman and N. Richard Nash. Photographed by Lionel Linden. Songs by Johnny Burke–James Van Heusen. Cast: Bing Crosby, Barry Fitzgerald, Joan Caulfield, Wanda Hendrix, Frank Faylen, Elizabeth Patterson, Robert

Shayne, Larry Young, Percy Kilbride, Thurston Hall, Don Beddoe, Clarence Muse.

Variety Girl (C) Practically everyone on the Paramount lot made a cameo appearance in this backlot variety show. Bing Crosby sings "Harmony" with Bob Hope and others.

My Favorite Brunette (HC)

Road to Rio Directed by Norman Z. McLeod. Produced by Daniel Dare. Written by Edmund Beloin and Jack Rose. Photographed by Ernest Laszlo. Songs by Johnny Burke–James Van Heusen. Cast: Bing Crosby, Bob Hope, Dorothy Lamour, Gale Sondergaard, Frank Faylen, Joseph Vitale, George Meeker, Frank Puglia, Nestor Paiva, Robert Barrat, Tor Johnson, the Andrews Sisters, the Wiere Brothers, the Stone–Barton Puppeteers, the Carioca Boys, Jerry Colonna.

1948

The Emperor Waltz Directed by Billy Wilder. Produced by Charles Brackett. Written by Brackett and Wilder. Photographed by George Barnes. Songs by Johnny Burke–Joseph J. Lilly; Burke–Richard Heuberger; Burke–Johann Strauss; Sam Lewis–Joe Young–Ralph Erwin–Fritz Rotter. Cast: Bing Crosby, Joan Fontaine, Roland Culver, Richard Haydn, Lucile Watson, Harold Vermilyea, Sig Ruman.

1949

A Connecticut Yankee in King Arthur's Court Directed by Tay Garnett. Produced by Robert Fellows. Written by Edmund Beloin, from a novel by Mark Twain. Photographed by Ray Rennahan. Songs by Johnny Burke–James Van Heusen. Cast: Bing Crosby, Rhonda Fleming, William Bendix, Sir Cedric Hardwicke, Murvyn Vye, Virginia Field, Henry Wilcoxon, Joseph Vitale, Julia Faye, Alan Napier.

Top o' the Morning Directed by David Miller. Produced by Robert L. Welch. Written by Edmund Beloin and Richard Breen. Photographed by Lionel Lindon. Songs by Johnny Burke–James Van Heusen; others. Cast: Bing Crosby, Barry Fitzgerald, Ann Blyth, Hume Cronyn, Eileen Crowe, John McIntire, Tudor Owen, Jimmy Hunt.

The Adventures of Ichabod and Mr. Toad (Disney/RKO) (V) Directed by Jack Kinney, Clyde Geronimi, and James Algar. Production supervised by Ben Sharpsteen. Written by Geronimi, Bill Peet, and others, from a novel, *The Wind in the Willows,* by Kenneth Grahame, and story, "The Legend of Sleepy Hollow," by Washington Irving. Songs by Don Raye–Gene de Paul. Bing Crosby narrates "Ichabod" (Basil Rathbone narrates "Mr. Toad") and sings three songs.

1950

Riding High Directed and produced by Frank Capra. Written by Robert Riskin, Melville Shavelson, and Jack Rose, from a story by Mark Hellinger. Photographed by George Barnes and Ernest Laszlo. Songs by Johnny Burke–James Van Heusen; Stephen Foster; others. Cast: Bing Crosby, Coleen Gray, Raymond Walburn, Frances Gifford, Clarence Muse, William Demarest, Charles Bickford, Frankie Darro, Harry Davenport, Douglass Dumbrille, Ward Bond, Gene Lockhart, James Gleason, Percy Kilbride, Margaret Hamilton, Oliver Hardy, Joe Frisco.

Mr. Music Directed by Richard Haydn. Produced by Robert L. Welch. Written by Arthur Sheekman, from a play, *Accent on Youth,* by Samson Raphaelson. Photographed by George Barnes. Songs by Johnny Burke–James Van Heusen. Cast: Bing Crosby, Nancy Olson, Charles Coburn, Ruth Hussey, Robert Stack, Tom Ewell, Ida Moore, Charles Kemper, Donald Woods, the Merry Macs, Peggy Lee, Groucho Marx, Dorothy Kirsten, Marge and Gower Champion.

1951

Here Comes the Groom Directed and produced by Frank Capra. Written by Virginia Van Upp, Liam O'Brian, and Myles Connolly, from a story by Robert Risken and O'Brien. Photographed by George Barnes. Songs by Johnny Mercer–Hoagy Carmichael; Jay Livingston–Ray Evans; Giuseppe Verdi. Cast: Bing Crosby, Franchot Tone, Jane Wyman, Alexis Smith, James Barton, Anna Maria Alberghetti, Connie Gilchrist, Robert Keith, H. B. Warner, Minna Gombell, Walter Catlett, Carl Switzer, Louis Armstrong, Phil Harris, Dorothy Lamour, Frank Fontaine, Cass Daley.

The Fifth Freedom (Chesterfield Cigarettes) (S,C) Korean War propaganda. Bing Crosby sings "You're a Grand Old Flag."

Angels in the Outfield (MGM) (C) A fantasy about baseball; Bing Crosby appears as part-owner of the Pittsburgh Pirates.

You Can Change the World (The Christophers) (S) Directed by Leo McCarey. Produced by William Perlberg. Song by Johnny Burke–James Van Heusen. Cast: Bing Crosby, Bob Hope, Jack Benny, Irene Dunne, Eddie "Rochester" Anderson, William Holden, Paul Douglas, Loretta Young, Ann Blythe, Fr. James Keller.

1952

The Greatest Show on Earth (C) Circus melodrama; Bing Crosby and Bob Hope are glimpsed in the bleachers.

Son of Paleface (HC)

Just for You Directed by Elliott Nugent. Produced by Pat Duggan. Written by Robert Carson, from a story, "Famous," by Stephen Vincent Benét. Photographed by George Barnes. Songs by Harry Warren–Leo Robin. Cast: Bing Crosby, Jane Wyman, Ethel Barrymore, Bob Arthur, Natalie Wood, Leon Tyler, Cora Witherspoon, Ben Lessy, Regis Toomey, the Mexican Ballet.

Road to Bali Directed by Hal Walker. Produced by Harry Tugend. Written by Frank Butler, Hal Kanter, and Bill Morrow, from a story by Butler and Tugend. Photographed by George Barnes. Songs by Johnny Burke–James Van Heusen. Cast: Bing Crosby, Bob Hope, Dorothy Lamour, Murvyn Vye, Ralph Moody, Leon Askin, Peter Coe, Michael Ansara, Carolyn Jones, Bob Crosby, Jane Russell, Humphrey Bogart, Dean Martin and Jerry Lewis.

1953

Little Boy Lost Directed and written by George Seaton, from a story by Marghanita Laski. Produced by William Perlberg and Seaton. Photographed by George Barnes. Songs by Johnny Burke–James Van Heusen; others. Cast: Bing Crosby, Nicole Maurey, Christian Fourcade, Claude Dauphin, Gabrielle Dorziat, Colette Deréal, Georgette Anys, Peter Baldwin.

Scared Stiff (C) Comedy starring Dean Martin and Jerry Lewis; Bing Crosby and Bob Hope show up in the last scene.

Faith, Hope and Hogan (Christopher Thoughts) (S,C) Produced and directed by Jack Denove. Cast: Bing Crosby, Bob Hope, Ben Hogan, Ralph Kiner, Phil Harris, Fr. James Keller.

1954

White Christmas Directed by Michael Curtiz. Produced by Robert Emmett Dolan. Written by Norman Krasna, Melvin Frank, and Norman Panama. Photographed by Loyal Griggs. Songs by Irving Berlin. Cast: Bing Crosby, Danny Kaye, Rosemary Clooney, Vera-Ellen, Dean Jagger, Mary Wickes, Sig Ruman, John Brascia, Richard Shannon, Ann Whitfield, Grady Sutton, Herb Vigran, Johnny Grant, Percy Helton, Barrie Chase, George Chakiris.

The Country Girl Directed and written by George Seaton, from a play by Clifford Odets. Produced by William Perlberg and Seaton. Photographed by John F. Warren. Songs by Ira Gershwin–Harold Arlen. Cast: Bing Crosby, Grace Kelly, William Holden, Anthony Ross, Gene Reynolds, Eddie Ryder, Ida Moore, Jacqueline Fontaine.

1955

Bing Presents Oreste (S,C) Bing introduces opera singer Oreste Kirkop; a one-reel trailer for *The Vagabond King* (1956).

1956

High Tor (Ford Star Jubilee, CBS–TV) Directed by James Neilson. Produced by Arthur Schwartz. Written by Maxwell Anderson and John Monks Jr., from a play by Anderson. Photographed by Lester Shorr. Songs by Schwartz and Anderson. Cast: Bing Crosby, Nancy Olson, Julie Andrews, Everett Sloane, Hans Conreid, Lloyd Corrigan.

Anything Goes Directed by Robert Lewis. Produced by Robert Emmett Dolan. Written by Sidney Sheldon, from a play by Guy Bolton and P. G. Wodehouse as revised by Howard Lindsay and Russell Crouse. Photographed by John F. Warren. Songs by Cole Porter; Sammy Cahn–James Van Heusen. Cast: Bing Crosby, Donald O'Connor, Jeanmaire, Mitzi Gaynor, Phil Harris, Kurt Kaszner, Walter Sande, Richard Erdman, Argentina Brunetti, Ruta Lee, Marcel Dalio.

High Society (MGM) Directed by Charles Walters. Produced by Sol C. Siegel. Written by John Patrick, from a play, *The Philadelphia Story,* by Philip Barry. Photographed by Paul C. Vogel. Songs by Cole Porter. Cast: Bing Crosby, Grace Kelly, Frank Sinatra, Louis Armstrong, Celeste Holm, Louis Calhern, John Lund, Sidney Blackmer, Margalo Gillmore, Lydia Reed, Richard Garrick, Trummy Young, Edmond Hall, Billy Kyle, Arvell Shaw, Barrett Deems.

1957

Man on Fire (MGM) Directed and written by Ranald MacDougall, from a story by Malvin Wald and Jack Jacobs. Produced by Sol C. Siegel. Photographed by Joseph Ruttenberg. Song by Paul Francis Webster–Sammy Fain. Cast: Bing Crosby, Inger Stevens, Mary Fickett, E. G. Marshall, Malcolm Brodrick, Richard Eastham, Anne Seymour, Dan Riss.

The Heart of Show Business (Columbia) (V) Documentary on Variety Clubs International. Directed by Ralph Staub. Narrated by Bing Crosby, Edward G. Robinson, James Stewart, Burt Lancaster, Cecil B. De Mille.

1958

Showdown at Ulcer Gulch (Saturday Evening Post) (S,C) A one-reel magazine promotion with Bing Crosby, Bob Hope, Ernie Kovacs, Edie Adams, Groucho Marx, Chico Marx.

1959

Alias Jesse James (United Artists) (HC)

Say One for Me (20th Century-Fox) Directed and produced by Frank Tashlin. Written by Robert O'Brien. Photographed by Leo Tover. Songs by Sammy Cahn–James Van Heusen. Cast: Bing Crosby, Debbie Reynolds,

Robert Wagner, Ray Walston, Les Tremayne, Connie Gilchrist, Frank McHugh, Joe Besser, Stella Stevens.

1960

Let's Make Love (20th Century–Fox) (C) Romantic comedy with Marilyn Monroe and Yves Montand; Bing Crosby sings "Incurably Romantic" and gives Montand a lesson in crooning.

High Time (20th Century-Fox) Directed by Blake Edwards. Produced by Charles Brackett. Written by Tom and Frank Waldman, from a story by Garson Kanin. Photographed by Ellsworth Fredericks. Songs by Sammy Cahn–James Van Heusen; others. Cast: Bing Crosby, Nicole Maurey, Fabian, Tuesday Weld, Richard Beymer, Patrick Adiarte, Yvonne Craig, Gavin MacLeod.

Pepe (Columbia) (C) Cameo–studded vehicle for Cantinflas; Bing croons a medley and autographs a tortilla.

1962

The Road to Hong Kong (United Artists) Directed by Norman Panama. Produced by Melvin Frank. Written by Panama and Frank. Photographed by Jack Hildyard. Songs by Sammy Cahn–James Van Heusen. Cast: Bing Crosby, Bob Hope, Joan Collins, Robert Morley, Dorothy Lamour, Walter Gotell, Felix Aylmer, Roger Delgado, Mei Ling, Peter Madden, Peter Sellers, Jerry Colonna, David Niven, Frank Sinatra, Dean Martin.

1964

Robin and the 7 Hoods (Warner Bros.) Directed by Gordon Douglas. Produced by Frank Sinatra. Written by David R. Schwartz. Photographed by William H. Daniels. Songs by Sammy Cahn–James Van Heusen. Cast: Frank Sinatra, Dean Martin, Sammy Davis Jr., Bing Crosby, Peter Falk, Barbara Rush, Victor Buono, Allen Jenkins, Jack La Rue, Phillip Crosby, Sig Ruman, Edward G. Robinson.

1966

Stagecoach (20th Century-Fox) Directed by Gordon Douglas. Produced by Martin Rackin. Written by Joseph Landon, from a screenplay by Dudley Nichols from a story by Ernest Haycox, "Stage to Lordsburg." Photographed by William H. Clothier. Cast: Bing Crosby, Ann-Margret, Michael Connors, Alex Cord, Red Buttons, Robert Cummings, Van Heflin, Slim Pickens, Stephanie Powers, Keenan Wynn.

Cinerama's Russian Adventure (United Roadshow Presentations-Sovexportfilm) (V,C) Narrated and introduced by Bing Crosby.

1968

Bing Crosby's Washington State (Cinecrest) (S,V) Directed by Dave Gardner. Written and photographed by Robert Brown and Ruth Davis. Narrated by Bing Crosby.

1971

Dr. Cook's Garden (Paramount Pictures Television/ABC–TV) Directed by Ted Post. Produced by Bob Markell. Written by Art Wallace, from a play by Ira Levin. Photographed by Urs Ferrer. Cast: Bing Crosby, Frank Converse, Blythe Danner, Bethel Leslie, Abby Lewis, Barnard Hughes, Staats Cotsworth, Jordan Reed.

You Can Still Change the World (The Christophers) (S,C) Produced and written by Jeanne Glynn. Directed by Beatrice Conetta. Narrated and introduced by Bing Crosby. Compilation of film clips from television programs produced by The Christophers on the occasion of their twentieth anniversary.

1972

Cancel My Reservation (MGM–EMI) (HC)

1974

That's Entertainment! (MGM) (V,C) Directed, produced, and written by Jack Haley Jr. Complilation of film clips introduced by Bing Crosby, Elizabeth Taylor, Peter Lawford, Frank Sinatra, James Stewart, Mickey Rooney, Gene Kelly, Donald O'Connor, Debbie Reynolds, Fred Astaire, and Liza Minnelli.

Notes and Sources

AI   author interview
AMPAS   Academy of Motion Picture Arts and Sciences — Margaret Herrick Library
Rinker   Unpublished memoir, *The Bing Crosby I Knew,* by Al Rinker, completed in 1978
BCCGU   Bing Crosby Collection, Foley Center Library, Gonzaga University
HCC   Howard Crosby Collection
JWTPR   J. Walter Thompson program reports for *Kraft Music Hall*
KGM   Unpublished memoir by Kitty (Lang) Good, recorded and transcribed during the 1980s and 1990s. Courtesy of Kitty Good and her son, Tim Good
Lucky   *Call Me Lucky,* by Bing Crosby and Pete Martin
RBT   *Remembering Bing*: interview transcripts for a 1987 Chicago WTTW television documentary, produced and written by Jim Arntz and Katherine MacMillin, executive producer: Glenn DuBose.
TIA   Time Inc. Archive

Introduction

1. Seldes, *The Public Arts,* p. 126.

2. Thompson, *The Complete Crosby,* p. 252.

3. Death certificate filed with the American embassy in Madrid, Oct. 21, 1977.

4. Edmund Wilson, *The Wound and the Bow* (1941; reprint, New York: Oxford University Press, 1965), p. 3.

5. *Newsweek,* June 28, 1999.

6. Shepherd and Slatzer, *Bing Crosby: The Hollow Man,* and Crosby and Firestone, *Going My Own Way.*

7. Among the most egregious were a memoir by Joan Rivers that called him a drunken wifebeater (for which there is no evidence); the pilot for a syndicated TV show, *Hollywood Babylon,* with Tony Curtis, that recycled demonstrative untruths concerning his will; and a December 22, 1999, story in the *New York Post* that distorted Crosby's readily available FBI file (see note 40 to Chapter 21).

8. Smith, *Life in a Putty Knife Factory,* p. 258.

9. An article in the *New York Times,* "Watched by Millions," Aug. 25, 2000, reported that the only programs to attract more than 50 million viewers in the preceding eight months were two special events, the Super Bowl (88.5 million) and the final episode of *Survivor* (51.7 million).

10. Cited in the *Philadelphia Courier,* Nov. 22, 1947.

11. 1960 radio interview by Tony Thomas, for Canadian Broadcasting Company, released on LP, *Conversations in Hollywood,* vol. 2 (Citadel).

12. Emerson, *Representative Men* (1850).

13. Rourke, *American Humor.*

14. According to Whitburn, *Pop Memories 1880–1954* and *Top Pop Singles 1955–1986.* Much of Whitburn's figuring is based on speculation, so it would be folly to place too much emphasis on his pop-chart rankings, but the general picture he offers has proved reliable.

15. According to the annual Quigley Publications poll; Steinberg, *Reel Facts.*

16. There are many others. Crosby made twenty-three gold and two platinum singles, including the only double-sided gold record ("Play a Simple Melody"/"Sam's Song"); he was the leading record seller through two decades, the 1930s and 1940s; more than half his feature films were among the ten highest grossing pictures of the years in which they were released; in 1946 three of the five top-grossing pictures of the year (*The Bells of St. Mary's, Blue Skies, Road to Utopia*) were Crosby vehicles, each a sequel to one of his earlier successes; he introduced more Academy Award–nominated songs (fourteen) and more winners (four) than any other film star.

PART ONE
1. The Harrigans

1. *Kraft Music Hall* radio broadcast, Mar. 15, 1945.

2. This section is based largely on genealogical research by King and Fitzgerald. See their *The Uncounted Irish* and King's *The Irish Lumberman-Farmer,* as well as King's "Bing Crosby's Irish Roots: The Harrigan Family of County Cork, New Brunswick Can., Minnesota, and Washington" in *Minnesota Genealogist*, vol. 14, no. 4 (1983); a letter from Joseph A. King to Sheelah Carter of Spokane Public Library, dated Jan. 27, 1979, in library files; and a 1994 AI with King. Much information was also culled from the Crosby family's *Crosby Genealogy,* commissioned by Larry Crosby and published privately.

3. Her full name was Catherine Driscoll Harrigan. In several essays and books, King inadvertently gives her birth date as 1782 (which would make her fifty at the time of Dennis Jr.'s birth), yet it was King who discovered, in the 1851 census for Williamstown, New Brunswick, that she was actually born in 1791. (See *Lumberman-Farmer,* Appendix A, p. 172.)

4. King speculates that Dennis sold his leases in the townlands at Driane and Derryleary, which bordered Schull, in order to purchase the fares. In Parliamentary Report of 1835 and 1836, two parish priests, Father James Barry and Reverend Robert Trail, estimated that no more than ninety people of the parish emigrated in 1831 — "they were, with very few exceptions, Protestants, and in comfortable circumstances."

5. Swift, "A Modest Proposal," 1829.

6. Edmund Burke, in a letter in 1792, described the code as "a machine as well fitted for the oppression, impoverishment and degradation of a people, and the debasement in them of human nature itself, as ever proceeded from the perverted ingenuity of man."

7. Wellington, cited in Woodham-Smith, *The Great Hunger,* p. 20.

8. Gustave de Beaumont, *Ireland: Social, Political and Religious,* 1839), cited in ibid., p. 19.

9. The story of John of Skibbereen is based on an undated letter from Bing Crosby's first cousin, Margaret Harrigan Kendell, of Redmond, Washington, accessed by King, who says Kendell's information was given her by William Harrigan, a

first cousin of Bing's mother. Larry Crosby was under the impression that John used two surnames, Harrigan and O'Brien, and was known as Organ O'Brien because he played the organ in church at Skibbereen, a part of West Cork where (King writes) "the population lived so exclusively on the potato that no trade in any other description of food existed."

10. Cited in Woodham-Smith, *The Great Hunger*, p. 24.

11. Ibid., p. 26.

12. See Van Der Merwe, *Origins of the Popular Style*, pp. 10–14, for a fuller treatment of how the Oriental influence was sustained in Europe's northwestern countries.

13. *Chambers's Encyclopaedia*, cited in the 1972 supplement to the *Oxford English Dicitonary*, under *croon*.

14. AI, Ronan Tynan.

15. It might perhaps be more accurate to say that Crosby "allowed to be written in his memoir," *Call Me Lucky*, as he did not so much write as speak it to his collaborator, Pete Martin. But he did scrutinize the manuscript, and though he permitted many inaccuracies (not nearly as many as he blithely approved in his brothers' book), the volume reflects his wishes. Indeed, it is not impossible that he took an active hand in sections of *Lucky*.

16. King interviewed Father John Deasy of Schull, who said, "[Bing] mistakenly thought his grandfather was born in Ireland." *The Uncounted Irish*, p. 290. Several early books on Crosby trace the Harrigans to County Mayo and describe Dennis Jr. as a plumber, misinformation that Bing unaccountably declined to correct when he vetted Thompson's 1976 biography.

17. King, *The Uncounted Irish*, p. 101.

18. Others include Louis B. Mayer, production chief at MGM, and Robert C. Gillis, who in 1904 helped purchase and design much of the Hollywood community.

19. According to the 1900 census, Dennis Jr. initially entered the United States in 1859, as a carpenter and contractor. He returned to Canada, however, and married Catherine (Katie), bringing her to the United States in 1867. She was born in March 1836 or 1837 in New Brunswick, the daughter of John Ahearn and Ann Meghan of Ireland and Miramichi, and died on October 25, 1918, in Tacoma. Also "Dennis Harrigan Dies[;] Prominent Contractor, Resident of Tacoma Since 1888 Passes," *Tacoma Daily Ledger*, Sept. 19, 1915, and "Crosby's Mother, State Native, Dies," *St. Paul Pioneer Press*, Jan. 8, 1964.

20. The Harrigan children were William John Harrigan (1867), Alexander Ambrose (1869), Edward (1870), Catherine (1873), Anne (1875), Francis Albert (1876), and George Leo (1879).

21. This was her accepted family name, but there is no *Helen* on her Stillwater birth certificate.

22. *Lucky*, p. 52.

23. The dry-goods store run by Albert H. Sanford and George H. Stone sold fabrics, clothing, and hardware. It was across the street from the library at 1115–17 Tacoma Avenue and is listed as Kate's place of employment in the 1893–94 city directory. AI, Judith Kipp.

2. The Crosbys

1. Blankenship, *Early History of Thurston County*, p. 267.

2. Ibid.

3. *Crosby Genealogy.* Larry Crosby's privately printed chronicle was completed in 1960. Although he kept complete files on the genealogy in the Crosby offices, they were not available for research and may have disappeared. The *Genealogy* is not an infallible source: it has obvious mistakes (the date of Harry Lowe Crosby's death is given as 1949, instead of 1950) and contradictions.

4. Ibid. Larry also claimed earlier English Crosbys: a Yorkshire constable in 1204; a property owner named Golfrides de Crosseby; and John de Crosseby, a procurator appointed by the abbot of St. John's in Colchester early in the fourteenth century.

5. Bing refers to him as Edmund in *Lucky,* and other biographers name him Thomas, but William is the name in *White's Biographical Bulletin* on Bing, 1946; in Larry's genealogy; and in the rolls of the General Society of Mayflower Descendants.

6. Institute of American Archives, certified by director Mendell Peterson.

7. *Correspondence of James Fenimore-Cooper,* edited by his grandson James Fenimore Cooper (New Haven: Yale University Press, 1922), p. 284.

8. Mary E. Phillips, *James Fenimore Cooper* (New York: John Lane Company, 1913), p. 86. For more on Enoch, see *The Spy Unmasked, or Memoirs of Enoch Crosby, alias Harvey Birch, The Hero of Mr. Cooper's Tale of the Neutral Ground,* edited by H. L. Barnum in 1831. Also James Grossman, *James Fenimore Cooper* (New York: William Sloane Associates, 1949).

9. Susan Feninore Cooper, "Small Family memories" (1883), in *Correspondence of James Fenimore-Cooper,* p. 42.

10. The name Nathaniel became a Crosby good-luck piece. Nathaniel Sr. begat Nathaniel Jr., who begat Desire Crosby (born 1772), Bethiah, and David from his first marriage, and from his second, Tabitha, Mary, and Captain Nathaniel Crosby I, who was born in 1782. Nat I married Ruby Foster, begetting in 1810 Captain Nathaniel Crosby II, and later married (in 1831) Mary Lincoln in Wiscasset, Maine, begetting another Nathaniel in 1835, as well as Mary Lincoln and Martha Ruby.

11. The passenger list for the *Grecian* included Captain Clanrick Crosby, his wife, Phebe F. Crosby, and their three children, Clanrick, Phebe Luisa, and Cecilia; First Officer Washington Hurd and his wife (Clanrick's sister) and their two-year-old daughter, Ella; Second Officer Albert Crosby (Clanrick's younger brother) and his wife; Mrs. Mary Crosby, wife of Captain Nathaniel Jr. and three children, Nathaniel, Mary, and Martha; Mrs. Holmes, companion-housekeeper; Captain Nathaniel Crosby Sr., the father of the captain and second officer; and one passenger, Mr. Converse Lilly of New York — all in the cabin. Forward, there were seven more, including the three brothers of Mrs. Nathaniel Crosby Jr: Joseph Taylor, Foster Lincoln, and Nathaniel Lincoln.

12. Martha married a ship chandler and remained in China until 1864, when she brought her son to San Francisco to escape a cholera epidemic. She resettled in Olympia, where her mother and siblings were. Her husband died of cholera in China, and she lived in Tumwater for the next two years, then married Andrew Burr, Capital City's postmaster and a loquacious politician, and had three children.

13. Goldie Robertson Funk, "The Old Crosby Home at Tumwater," *Seattle Times,* Mar. 20, 1949.

14. AI, Ken Twiss.

15. Catherine Crosby, "A Mother's Day," unidentified magazine clip (c. 1947). BCCGU.

3. Tacoma

1. Burt McMurtrie, "It Seems to Me," *Tacoma Daily News*, Sept. 29, 1948.

2. Most of the material on the treasurer's office and Harry's early employment is from an analysis of county records by Judith Kipp of the Tacoma Public Library, Northwest Room. Election results from Bonney's *History of Pierce County*.

3. *Tacoma Daily Ledger*, Dec. 14, 1902. The deed was turned over by Alexander T. Hosmer to Catherine H. Crosby for $850 on January 6, 1903.

4. *Tacoma Daily Ledger*, May 4, 1903. "Summer arrived full blown in Tacoma yesterday," the story began, "and the whole city was out taking the open air. The day was perfect, with twelve hours of warm, mellow sunshine and a gently stirring breeze, ideal weather for outdoor recreation."

5. *Tacoma Daily Ledger*, May 5, 1903: "The home of Mr. and Mrs. H. L. Crosby was gladdened yesterday by the arrival of a son."

6. *Tacoma Daily News*, May 6, 1903.

7. *Tacoma Daily Ledger*, May 7, 1903: "A little son arrived May 3 in the home of Mr. and Mrs. H. L. Crosby."

8. Reverend Anthony LeBlanconce was parish priest and signed the register, which reads "Henrieum Lillis."

9. Paul Vandervoort II, "Uncle Sam Sans Whiskers," *Band Leaders Magazine*, Jan. 1946.

10. Intrepid researchers in the 1940s had little difficulty finding the truth — indeed, until the mid-eighties, the only book to get it right was Mize's *Bing Crosby and the Bing Crosby Style*. The Associated Press Biographical Service had the correct year (wrong day) in a 1946 Crosby sketch but altered it to 1904 as of 1949, presumably acceding to pressure from the Crosby organization. In 1949 Bing's business manager, Basil Grillo, noticed discrepancies regarding his age on several life-insurance policies: "Everyone of them had a different age, all the way from 1901 to 1904. When an insurance policy doesn't state the right age, they adjust the payments accordingly when it comes time to pay off. So not understanding the actor's mind, I innocently went to Bing and I said, 'Bing, we've got a lot of policies here and they all have a different birth date for you, which really changes the amount of insurance we carry.' I asked, 'When were you actually born?' He says, 'Nineteen hundred and four.' Even for business reasons, he was born in 1904. Everything related back to his success as a movie actor. He tried to protect it, and I think the age thing was an outgrowth of that. He once told me, 'In this business, youth is everything.' Maybe he convinced himself that he was born in 1904. Who knows?" Grillo believed that Crosby was born in 1901, because Larry said so. Yet by 1957 no one in the family could have been in doubt. That year, in advance of his second marriage, Bing himself obtained a baptismal certificate with the correct date; shortly thereafter, Larry prepared the genealogy he distributed to the family, correctly identifying his brother's year of birth. Yet 1901 and 1904 continue to crop up in reference works. AI, Basil Grillo.

11. Catherine Cordelia was the first of the Crosby children whose birth was recorded by Tacoma's Department of Public Health.

12. AI, Ken Twiss, who spoke with Mary Rose and said she reluctantly conceded her role in the May 2/3 controversy.

13. Reed was replaced by his former cashier, Edgar M. Lakin, who succeeded Reed as treasurer in the election of 1904. At first, the change boded well for Crosby, who was soon advanced to the position of deputy. Yet for unknown reasons, he was

fired before the end of 1905, possibly to reward an elusive clerk named William Turner, who with far less experience was given Harry's job. His dismissal was followed by that of all the men promoted by Lakin. Only Turner returned to a demoted post in 1910.

14. For many years Tacoma's port was larger than Seattle's because it was thirty miles farther west and saved a day in transporting goods to the Pacific — a system known as "rail to sail." Tacoma was shaped by a series of booms and busts that began in 1852, when the first sawmill was opened by a Swede who then bought a large tract of land, hoping the Northern Pacific Railroad would come through. The NPRR was given land to do just that, and the lumber companies followed.

15. Ted Crosby, *The Story of Bing Crosby*, p. 20. This is the 1946 edition of a book originally published in 1937 and credited to Ted and Larry Crosby. (See Chapter 21.) In addition to being updated, the second version is revised in numerous small ways. Both are essentially fictions, however, and are referenced here with much caution.

16. *Lucky*, p. 56.

17. Ibid., p. 55.

18. Deed #230077, received Jan. 5, 1907.

19. *Spokesman-Review*, Sept. 13, 1908. BCCGU.

4. Spokane

1. Ralph Ellison, "On Bird, Bird-Watching, and Jazz," *The Collected Essays*. Also Melville writes in *Moby Dick* (Chapter XLV) of the "rights, privileges, and distinctions of a name" bestowed by an admiring community.

2. Stratton, *Spokane & the Inland Empire*, p. xiv; Spokane city directory of 1914.

3. For some twenty years the NPRR treated the city as little more than a dependent, hindering its growth with monopolistic pricing so that Spokane's businessmen lost out to rivals in Seattle, where competing railroads charged half as much to transport products from the East.

4. Motto engraved on a Northern Pacific Railway arch in Sept. 1883. See Stratton, *Spokane & the Inland Empire*, pp. 109–21 for a concise history of the NPRR's impact on Spokane.

5. Ted and Larry, *Bing*, p. 6. This passage was deleted from the 1946 edition.

6. *Lucky*, p. 56.

7. NET-TV interview, *Close-Up on Bing Crosby*, 1967.

8. "Heiber Incorporates Brewery," *Spokesman-Review*, Apr. 12, 1892; "Hieber Brewery Changes Hands," Oct. 1, 1905; "Plan Beer Agency," Apr. 15, 1906; "Erect New Ice Plant," Nov. 16, 1906; and "Pays $35,000 for Lease," Sept. 29, 1908. Also, Spokane city directories, 1906–34.

9. Ad, 1911 city directory.

10. "A Mother's Day," op. cit.

11. Harry L. Crosby Sr. as told to Jack Holland, "My Boy Bing," *Movies* (undated, probably spring 1940). BCCGU.

12. "The Kid from Spokane," *Collier's*, Apr. 27, 1935.

13. The "Bingville Bugle" references are from the *Spokesman-Review* for March 13, 1910; August 7, 1910; September 13, 1910; January 29, 1911; April 2, 1911.

14. Despite references to a floppy-eared Bingo in *Lucky*, a 1949 Associated Press sketch, and elsewhere, a search of the "Bingville Bugle" for 1910 turned up no such character, though there was a drawing of an unnamed fellow with outsize ears.

15. "Uncle Sam Sans Whiskers," op. cit.

16. Gertrude Kroetch, 1946 interview memo. TIA.

17. "A Mother's Day," op. cit.

18. They were Ted, Bob, Mary Rose, and Kay. AI, Howard Crosby.

19. Bing Crosby, "My Second Family," from the early 1960s, reprinted in *The Crosby Voice,* Sept. 1984, Australia.

20. NET interview, op. cit.

21. "My Boy Bing" op. cit.

22. *Lucky,* p. 56.

23. Helen Finnegan, 1946 interview memo. TIA.

24. *Lucky,* p. 57.

25. In his book, Ted Crosby says Kate proudly refused the offer, but he told his son Howard that Kate was all for it and Harry stopped her. AI, Howard Crosby.

26. Radio interview with Jack O'Brien, New York, Dec. 10, 1976.

27. Wilbur W. Hindley, "In Clemmer and Liberty New Record Is Made by Spokane," *Spokesman-Review,* Feb. 28, 1915.

28. Corporation deed between Pioneer Educational Society and Catherine H. Crosby, filed June 1, 1911; warranty deed between Catherine H. Crosby and Inland Brewery & Malting Company, filed July 2, 1911; quitclaim between Inland Brewery and Catherine H. Crosby, filed Jan. 15, 1913.

29. Born ten years after Bing and seven years after Mary Rose, Bob was born at 508 East Sharp Street and baptized on September 7, 1913, at St. Aloysius, birth certificate from Bureau of Vital Statistics. Harry Lowe was forty-three, Kate was forty.

30. Bob Crosby, RBT.

31. *Lucky,* p. 56.

32. Ted Crosby, *The Story of Bing Crosby,* p. 30.

33. Alice Watts, "Bing Was Her Favorite," *The Daily Olympian,* Aug. 14, 1981.

34. Ibid.

35. Gregg Hammond, "Mary Rose Crosby Poole," *The Crooner,* no. 50, Nov. 1990. Also AI, Ken Twiss.

36. *Tacoma Daily Ledger,* Sept. 19, 1915: He died September 18, at eighty-three, and was buried in Calvary Cemetary, Tacoma. In 1909 Dennis had been struck on the head by falling timber while inspecting construction of the governor's mansion; his condition worsened in 1911. The death certificate gives the primary cause of death as myocarditis and a contributing cause as nephritis. In addition to his widow and seven children, he was survived by a brother, Patrick Harrigan, in Oregon, and fourteen grandchildren — seven of them Kate's and Harry's.

37. Bing told the same story on Radio Erin in 1961: "I remember my mother telling me that when her mother was on her deathbed . . ."

38. Cottrell in "Belly Flops at Little Vatican" (unsigned), *The Inside Passage,* Oct. 28, 1977.

39. *Lucky,* p. 66. Also William Stimson, "Bing We Hardly Knew Ye," *Pacific Northwest,* Dec. 1987.

40. "My Boy Bing," op. cit.

41. NET interview, op. cit.

42. Ibid. A fin is slang for five dollars.

43. *Spokesman-Review,* Jan. 7, 1916.

44. The poem by Thomas Dunn English was set to music by Nelson Kneass; Ben is implored to remember the long dead "sweet Alice."

45. Also known as "A Dog Named Rover" and "What D'Ye Mean You Lost Yer Dog

(Where's That Dog-gone Dog-gone Dog of Mine)," and not to be confused with "Poor Old Rover," which Bing did record. One night at a hunting lodge, in the 1960s, oilman George Coleman taped him singing it.

Bing: I've got a dog named Rover.

> Hey Rover, come over.
> He roams around all over.
> He's only home three times a day.
> [whistles] I'm looking for a dog called Rover.
> I'm looking for him now all over.
> But he's a hunter dog all right
> 'Cause he keeps me hunting day and night.
> This is what I worry over.
> Say, who put the rove in Rover?
> [whistles, says, "My whistle's getting dry"].
> Sometimes I wish I were a tree.
> Then Rover'd have to look for me.
> Oh where's that goddamn goddamn dog of mine?
> [ends song, laughter]

Bing: My mom's got a picture, took a picture . . .

Coleman: How old were you then?

Bing: Twelve. And I had that — you know, the knee pants?

46. Few people recorded that song or "A Perfect Day." One who recorded both was contralto Elsie Baker, a Victor recording star during the mid-teens. Bing might have been surprised to learn that one of the most prolific composers of the kind of song marking his debut was a relative, albeit one so distant not even his parents knew of her. Larry uncovered the connection when he compiled his genealogy. Blind poet Fanny Jane Crosby was the protégée of George Frederick Root and the lyricist for his Civil War hit, "Rosalie the Prairie Flower." She later published 8,000 hymns and songs, most under her married name, Mrs. Alexander Van Alstyne.

47. NET interview, op. cit.

5. Gonzaga

1. O'Brien interview, op. cit.

2. The classroom story was related by Corkery to a background reporter for *Time*. TIA. Francis Prange, who presided over the physics lab, later became known for his work in prison rehabilitation as chaplain at McNeil Island.

3. AI, Ray Flaherty.

4. Much of this section was drawn from Schoenberg, *Gonzaga University*, and Edward J. Crosby (Bing's brother), "Gonzaga Past, Present and Future,"*Gonzaga* 11:1 (Oct. 1919).

5. Many contemporary education practices were established in such sixteenth-century texts as Saint Ignatius of Loyola's *Spiritual Exercises* and the *Ratio Studiorum* (Plan of Studies). Material here is based on John W. Donahue, S.J., "Notes on Jesuit Education," *America*, Oct. 26, 1983, and AI with Father Donahue.

6. Ibid.

7. "But wait. These worldly things too are sweet; the pleasures they give is not inconsiderable; we must not be too hasty about rejecting them, because it would be a shame to go back to them again." *Confessions,* bk. 6, chap. 12.

8. Flannery O'Connor, "A Memoir of Mary Ann," in *Mystery and Manners*.

9. Radio interview with Father Caffrey, issued on LP, *Sunday in Hollywood with Ann Blythe and Bing Crosby*, by the Maryknoll Fathers in the 1950s.

10. *Lucky*, p. 72.

11. Ibid., p. 70.

12. Schoenberg, *Gonzaga University*, p. 267.

13. Crosby, *The Story of Bing Crosby*, p. 47.

14. Thompson, *Bing*, p. 6.

15. Caffrey interview, op. cit.

16. Bob Crosby, RBT.

17. O'Brien interview, op. cit.

18. *Crosby Genealogy.*

19. Ibid.

20. Schoenberg, *Gonzaga University*, p. 249.

21. Bing especially enjoyed the team of Willie and Eugene Howard, who did Jewish dialect humor and impressions of top vaudeville stars.

22. The team was Sam Lewis and Joe Young.

23. Interview by George O'Reilly at Shepperton Studios, London, 1961.

24. "Brewing Concern to Make Vinegar," *Spokesman-Review*, Jan. 17, 1917.

25. Theis as president, Lang as vice president, William Huntley as treasurer, and H. L. Crosby as secretary.

26. AI, Robert Kipp.

27. Bob Crosby, RBT.

28. AI, Peggy Lee.

29. Interview taped in Bing's Paramount Pictures dressing room by Bill Tusher, 1951.

30. "A Mother's Day," op. cit.

31. "Belly Flops at Little Vatican," op. cit.

32. Hal Prey, "Readers Knew the Famous When They Weren't So Famous," *Reminisce*, Sept. 1994. Mrs. Stickney's granddaughter recovered.

33. Dyar, *News for an Empire.*

34. Ibid.

35. "A Mother's Day," op. cit.

36. Ibid.

37. AI, Alan Fisher.

38. "Uncle Sam Sans Whiskers," op. cit.

39. *Gonzaga* 9:2. (Dec. 1917). The school magazine, *Gonzaga*, a key source for much of the material in this section, appeared between 1910 and 1922 and was considered an exemplary student publication by educators. Each issue ran between forty-two and forty-eight pages and sold for twenty cents, averaging a $500 annual profit, most of which was sent to Pope Benedict XV's relief program.

40. AI, Ray Flaherty.

41. *Gonzaga* 11:3 (Dec. 1919).

42. AI, Ray Flaherty.

43. *Gonzaga* 11:1 (Oct. 1919). Bing was mistakenly listed as class of '21, which would have been correct had Kate not started him early.

44. *Lucky*, p. 68.

45. The debate: "Resolved: A national referendum should he held to determine support for Wilson's League of Nations."

46. *Confessions,* bk. 2, chap. 2. A tradition at Gonzaga encouraged instructors to "turn out men who not only absorbed a great amount of knowledge, but who could use it, express it and get up and make a talk in a creditable manner," William DePuis, "School Dramatics," *The Gonzaga Year-Book,* 1924.

47. *Lucky,* p. 71.

48. Ibid., pp. 71–72.

49. "School Dramatics," op. cit.

50. Transcribed from his dedication speech at Gonzaga, 1957.

51. *Gonzaga* 11:4 (Jan. 1920).

52. The student was Doug Dyckman, *Gonzaga* 11:6 (Mar. 1920).

53. Father Art Dussault, a friend and classmate of Bing's and later his primary liaison at Gonzaga, told columnist Earl Wilson (*New York Post,* Aug. 4, 1952) that Bing owed a lot to "having been jugged," suggesting that it had helped train his phenomenal memory for songs and scripts.

54. *Gonzaga* 11:7 (Apr. 1920). Ted was one of the most prolific and ambitious writers at the school. His numerous works include the poem "Gonzaga" ("And all in their breasts the teachings of their Alma Mater hold / Nor barter their birthright precious for passion or fame or gold!"), 11:1 (Oct. 1919); verse tributes to the Crosby seafearers and Lincoln; such short stories as "The Girl on the Job" (a woman who takes a wartime job then gives it up to a man), 11:2 (Nov. 1919), and "Trying Days" (set in a logging camp), 11:4 (Jan. 1920); and a long journalistic tribute, "Major Gerhard L Luhn, USA," about a recently departed German-born (yet "every inch an American . . . no lurking loyalty for the old land"). Luhn had been a hero of the Mexican and Civil Wars, a cavalryman and Indian fighter, the veteran of forty army posts, and "a Christian above all"; he organized the first cadet corps at Gonzaga in 1900. *Gonzaga* 11:6 (Mar. 1920).

55. *Gonzaga* 11:9 (June 1920). This long-forgotten juvenilia, clunky but vivid, seems to anticipate many aspects of his career, from his dusky caricature in the Mack Sennett two-reeler *Dream House,* through parodied caravans in the *Road* pictures. The central image recurs unconsciously in his exalted description (*Lucky,* p. 43) of meeting Paul Whiteman, the first potentate Bing ever knew. No less prescient is the cymbal, the instrument he brought with him into the big time, or the pagan setting he came to know in the sodden arms of Prohibition. The young Bing's vision of a white-robed ruler served by vassals while an audience sings his praises and music flows suggests how far Bing's dreams had begun to distance him from Spokane.

6. Mr. Interlocutor

1. Rourke, *American Humor,* p. 103.

2. AI, Ray Flaherty.

3. The cost breakdown for college day students was as follows: $50 tuition per semester for College of Arts and Sciences, $5 breakage deposit, $3 bulletin and library fee, $10 student activities (including season tickets to all ordinary games, as well as debating and dramatic societies, orchestra, band, and other events) $10 laboratory fee, $2.50 partly refundable deposit for chemicals.

4. *Gonzaga Register,* 1920–21.

5. Ibid.

6. Gonzaga hired Charles E. "Gus" Dorais in May 1920, after Jim Thorpe was obliged to decline because of a prior contract.

7. "Dorais Gives Recruits Tryout," *Spokane Daily Chronicle,* Mar. 31, 1922.

8. *Lucky,* p. 303. Bing's mother worked with Father Sharp in her role as treasurer of the Mother's Club, which raised money for scholarships and school functions. He served on its executive board as faculty representative. Mrs. T. J. Corkery, mother of Frank, served as secretary and later as president. The April 26, 1921, *Spokane Daily Chronicle* lists Mrs. H. L. Crosby as one of two dozen patronesses of a play, *Gonzaga's Chief.* See also, Schoenberg, *Gonzaga University,* p. 302; *Gonzaga* 12:5 (Mar. 1921); *Gonzaga* 14:1 (Autumn 1922).

9. *Lucky,* p. 39.

10. Ibid.

11. Ad, *Gonzaga Bulletin,* Oct. 7, 1921.

12. "Work of Michael Pecarovitch Lauded by Southern Critics," *Spokane Daily Chronicle,* May 5, 1922. Pecarovitch lived in San Pedro, California, and participated in theatricals at Santa Clara, Seattle College, and Gonzaga.

13. *Gonzaga* 12:2 (Nov. 1920).

14. Ibid. 12:3 (Dec. 1920).

15. Another member was George Twohy, Bing's high-school debating partner.

16. Rourke, *American Humor,* p. 103.

17. Donald O'Connor, for example, has spoken of the sincerity with which an actor was expected to approach a black role. AI.

18. Ellison, "An Extravagance of Laughter," in *The Collected Essays.*

19. AI, Bob Hope.

20. Rourke, *American Humor,* p. 103.

21. For example, whites played Charlie Chan and Fu Manchu decades after they were no longer allowed to play blacks, except in classical theater; consider *The Road to Hong Kong* or *Dr. No* in the 1960s.

22. Rourke, *American Humor,* pp. 103–04.

23. In "Vintage Glimpses of a Lost Theatrical World," Margo Jefferson writes of a silent film of black pantomimist and dancer Johnny Hudgins: "His charm so palpable that the burned-cork makeup, which we have come to read as intrinsically degrading, seems as incidental as the white makeup circus clowns have worn for centuries," *New York Times,* Oct. 20, 1996.

24. AI, Gerald Marks. Coincidentally, Marks and Sy Oliver were both New Yorkers born in Michigan.

25. Letter from Father Arthur L. Dussault, S.J. Jesuit Oregon Province Archives.

26. AI, Father Patrick J. Ford. S.J., academic vice president of Gonzaga.

27. Ibid.

28. Letter from Dussault to "Cathy and Hobie," Apr. 9, 1990. Jesuit Oregon Province Archives.

29. Letter from Dussault to Mr. Marion Simms, Sept. 14, 1950. Jesuit Oregon Province Archives.

30. Tony Thomas interview, op. cit.

31. George O'Reilly interview, op. cit.

32. NET interview, op. cit.

33. Goldman, *Jolson,* p. 36.

34. Ibid., p. 4.

35. Waters, *His Eye Is on the Sparrow,* p. 218.

36. *Gonzaga* 13:2 (Apr. 1922).

37. "Gonzaga Pupils Rehearse Play," *Spokane Daily Chronicle,* Feb. 8, 1923. Also *Gonzaga* 14:2 (Winter 1923).

38. Strangely, Bing tells a story in *Lucky* about a fan who insisted upon calling him Bim Crosland, which is how he signed the fan's autograph book.

39. "Gonzaga Actors Delight Crowd," *Spokane Daily Chronicle,* Nov. 8, 1923.

40. Anne Shaw Faulkner, "Does Jazz Put the Sin in Syncopation?" *Ladies' Home Journal,* Aug. 1921.

7. Musicaladers

1. *Confessions,* bk. 4, chap. 1.

2. Rinker. *The Bing Crosby I Knew* is a 110-page draft for a proposed book, finished in 1978 (a year after Crosby's death) when Al was seventy-one; he died three years later. At one point, his suggested title was *It's a Treat to Beat Your Feet on the Mississippi Mud.* Courtesy of Julia Rinker.

3. Ibid.

4. Rinker interview from *The Old Guy on the Orange Juice Commercial: A Biography for Radio of Bing Crosby,* written and narrated by Ron Connibear, c. 1977.

5. Rinker.

6. The Cotton Pickers, which made its key recordings in 1922 and 1923, should not be confused with McKinney's Cotton Pickers, a black band that began recording in 1928.

7. Rinker.

8. Ibid.

9. Ibid.

10. Ibid.

11. Rinker interview by John McDonough, 1976.

12. *Lucky,* p. 75.

13. H. Allen Smith, "Mildred Bailey Plans to Sing Her Life Story from the Stage of Town Hall Next Fall," *New York World Telegram,* Apr. 12, 1941.

14. Rinker.

15. Connibear interview, op. cit.

16. Ibid.

17. *Lucky,* p. 75.

18. Sidney Copeland, office memorandum, Aug. 3, 1946. TIA.

19. Ibid.

20. Ibid.

21. TV interview, *The Pat Collins Show,* WCBS, New York, 1976.

22. Crosby interview, radio documentary by John Salisbury, KXL, Portland, Oregon, 1976.

23. Connibear interview, op. cit.

24. Copeland memo, op. cit.

25. William Stimson, "Bing Crosby: The Road to Hollywood," *Spokane Magazine,* Dec. 1977.

26. Bing Crosby, "Requiem for Rock 'n' Roll," *Music Journal,* Jan. 1962. "A music company in my native Spokane was our jazz classroom. We met there to listen to the latest and practice playing by ear. With my pal Al Rinker, I practically lived in the place. I'm sure that our parents were as worried about our 'crazy' music as today's parents have been about Rock 'n' Roll."

27. Joseph Mitchell, "In Which Bing Crosby Debunks Himself; Broken Hearts? No, Just Broken Bottles," *New York World Telegram,* Dec. 16, 1931.

28. AI, Don Eagle, a Spokane musician, a generation younger than Bing, who worked with him in *A Connecticut Yankee in King Arthur's Court* and interviewed Rinker and others for a series of sketches published in *Bingang.*

29. Bing's June 24, 1937, letter to Stubeck and Stubeck's comments from Copeland memo, op. cit. The store was at Sprague and Wall.

30. Lincoln Barnett, "Bing, Inc.," *Life,* June 18, 1945.

31. Jack Sheehan, "A Brush with Celebrity," *Showbiz,* 1995, reprinted in *Bing,* no. 114 (Dec. 1996). In November 1975 Bing read an article by Sheehan about Bud Ward, the Spokane-born amateur golfer, and sent him a flattering letter with his own recollections of Ward. Sheehan wrote Bing and told him of his aunt Dorothy's death. Bing wrote him to say he remembered meeting him at Hayden Lake.

32. Rinker.

33. Ibid.

34. Copeland memo, op. cit.

35. Ibid.

36. "Bing We Hardly Knew Ye," op. cit.

37. Ibid. Material on Lareida's also drawn from AI with of Nancy Gale Compau of the Northwest Collection, Spokane Public Library, who, in addition to research aid, related information from her father, who frequented Lareida's. Also Stimson, *A View of the Falls,* unidentified clip. BCCGU.

38. Letter from H. Neal East to Bing Crosby, Feb. 19, 1935. HCC.

39. "Bing Crosby: The Road to Hollywood," op. cit.

40. Ibid.

41. Bill Salquist, "Hometown Remembers Because Bing Did," *Spokane Daily Chronicle,* Oct. 15, 1977.

42. Rinker.

43. Ibid.

44. McDonough interview, op. cit.

45. Rinker.

46. *Spokane Chronicle,* May 19, 1918. After the resolution was passed by the County Council of Defense banning *The Birth of a Nation* from "Spokane county," it was made public in an announcement by Clemmer on behalf of the league of motion picture men of the Spokane district.

47. "Now the Klemerklink for Doc Clemmer's Young Friends," *Spokane Chronicle,* Apr. 28, 1916.

48. "New Firm Takes Over Clemmer," *Spokesman-Review,* May 2, 1925. It was the 149th theater that Carl Laemmle's Universal Pictures had taken over in a period of sixty days. Universal operated the theater until 1929, when Ray Grombacher leased it and renamed it the Audian. It later became the State Theater and is now the Met, a concert theater.

49. *Lucky,* p. 74.

50. Rinker.

51. Ibid.

52. Author visit, also AI, Michael Smith, manager of the Met, and *Spokane Chronicle,* May 30, 1986. After the State (Clemmer) and Garland (which opened in 1945) closed, the only single-auditorium theater in Spokane was the Dishman, which

showed pornography. In 1988 the Metropolitan Mortgage & Securities Co. restored the Clemmer/State as the Met, magnificently re-creating the original design by E. W. Houghton and structure by August Paulsen.

53. Dussault attended Bing's tryout at the Clemmer and later recalled, "Many of the boys from school used to go down and cheer Bing and Al on." Letter to Stanley Antepenko, Sept. 22, 1976. Jesuit Oregon Province Archives.

54. Dyar, *News for an Empire*.

55. *Lucky*, p. 74.

56. See Chapter 8 for Crosby's use of the term in his letter to Dirk Crabbe.

57. Thompson, *Bing*, p. 16.

58. Rinker.

59. "My Boy Bing," op. cit.

60. Rinker.

61. *Lucky*, p. 78.

62. Madeleine Carroll, a twenty-two-year-old neighbor was interviewed by a *Time* reporter; Copeland memo, op. cit.

8. Vaudeville

1. Billing reproduced in numerous ads in the trades and on stage bills, 1926.

2. Nevertheless, the word *phonograph* obtained prominence in the United States, while *gramophone* became standard in the United Kingdom.

3. Gelatt, *The Fabulous Phonograph*, p. 146.

4. In a 1980s radio interview with Bill Osborne in Seattle, Bob Crosby recalled the Meyers campaign. "It was done tongue in cheek. They were going to have a lot of fun. They dressed Vic up and put a white sheet on him like Mahatma Gandhi had and gave him a goat to lead around town. They had a lot of fun. Their only campaign issue was that Vic was going to put hostesses on all the streetcars and serve coffee and tea at the end of the line, and cookies. That was his campaign promise. What happened was, it just astounded everybody, including brother Larry, that Vic Meyers got elected lieutenant governor. He studied parliamentary law, and they tell me, at least my uncle did, Judge Harrigan, who's in the House over in Olympia, he said he became one of the finest Speakers of the House, knew parlimentary law. So Vic stayed lieutenant governor for over twenty years, I believe."

5. At least that's what Bing recalled; Al thought they sang with Meyers himself. In most instances where disputed accounts between Crosby and Rinker can be verified, the former's recollections, written thirty years closer to the events, have proved to be the more reliable. In instances that could not be verified, Bing's account is often more colorful than Al's. It should be noted that when the Crosby memoir was a 1953 bestseller, Whiteman, Rinker, Barris, Malneck, and other principals were alive, and none found reason to correct the record as he created it — not even in private interviews from that era.

6. Rinker.

7. Ibid.

8. *Lucky*, p. 79.

9. Rinker.

10. Ibid.

11. Ibid.

12. Jones was seen briefly twelve years later as a member of a trio singing

"The Ragtime Violin," in the 1938 20th Century-Fox musical *Alexander's Ragtime Band*. Bing gave her a prominent spot in *East Side of Heaven* that same year. See Chapter 24.

13. AI, Red Norvo.

14. "Mildred Bailey Plans to Sing . . . ," op. cit.

15. Crosby liner notes, *Mildred Bailey: Her Greatest Performances 1929–1946*, Columbia Records, 1962.

16. Rinker.

17. Ibid.

18. AI, Milt Bernhart, Red Norvo.

19. Rinker.

20. Crosby liner notes, op. cit.

21. Mildred later auditioned for talent scout and record producer John Hammond with Smith blues.

22. Rinker.

23. AI, Barry Ulanov.

24. Pete Martin may have jumbled some facts in the Lyman passage in *Lucky,* or Bing, who liked to mention the names of people he admired or thought were neglected, may simply have added him to the historical record. Lyman is not mentioned in Ulanov or other early accounts. Yet the older Bing got, the more insistent he became about the Lyman gig, sometimes extending it to a few weeks. He would also extend his yearlong pre-Whiteman vaudeville experience to eighteen months or two years.

25. Owens, *Sweet Leilani*, p. 21.

26. Ibid., p. 22. Owens misremembered the songs they auditioned and named "Mississippi Mud," which lay two years in the future.

27. Ibid., p. 23.

28. Rinker.

29. Collins interview, op. cit.

30. *Variety,* Oct. 20, 1926.

31. Cited in Slide, *The Vaudevillians*, p. 159.

32. *Spokane Daily Chronicle,* Jan. 1, 1926.

33. Doreen Taylor, who danced as Doreen Wilde, was interviewed at length in 1981–82, shortly before her death, by her granddaughter, Alison McMahan, who later transcribed and collated the tapes.

34. Ibid.

35. Ibid.

36. Bing Crosby, *Live at the London Palladium* (K-Tel, United Artists), 1976.

37. Wilde interview, op. cit.

38. *Confessions*, bk. 2, chap. 1.

39. This four-page handwritten letter, written to Dirk Crabbe on January 24, 1926, was sent by the recipient's widow, Lillian Crabbe Hanson, to the Minneapolis radio personality Arne Fogel and first published in *Bingang* in July 1988. Some of the addenda appeared as "Don Eagle Provides Further Insight into Early Bing Letter," *Bingang*, July 1990.

40. Wilde interview, op. cit.

41. Ibid.

42. Norman, *The Film Greats*, p. 197.

43. *Lucky,* p. 80.

44. That same week *Variety* ran an ad taken out by a young vaudevillian named Harry Barris, who toured the Midwest with his Blu Blowing Baby Grand; in little more than a year, he would change all their lives. Also that week, on May 4, Bing's brother Larry, an editor at the *Wallace-Press Times* in Wallace, Idaho, married Elaine Couper of Spokane.

45. Thompson, *Bing,* p. 18.

46. Rinker.

47. Ibid.

48. AI, Phil Harris.

49. The humor of Ole Olsen and Chic Johnson, largely forgotten today, was brought to a fevered pitch in the 1938 stage hit *Hellzapoppin'*, which ran three years and has been called "the greatest vaudeville revue of all time." Slide, *The Vaudevillians,* p. 111.

50. Harris later said, "The first ballad I really remember him singing was 'I Kiss Your Hand, Madame,' at the Montmartre, in 1929." AI.

51. Cited as "a San Diego newspaper" in Shephard and Slatzer, *Bing Crosby: The Hollow Man,* p. 58.

52. *Lucky,* p. 81.

53. One grace note during their run was the marriage of Bing's sister Catherine to Edward Mullin at San Francisco's St. Ignatius Catholic Church, in a ceremony read by Gonzaga's dean of faculty, Father Carroll.

54. Rinker.

55. Ibid.

56. *Lucky,* pp. 42–43.

57. *Variety,* Oct. 6, 1926; the review (signed Land.) appeared under "New Acts." The version used here is the one that ran in *Variety*'s second edition; the first had a few different words and altered punctuaton.

58. AI, Red Norvo.

59. Thompson, *Bing,* p. 18.

60. *Lucky,* p. 80.

61. Rinker.

9. Whiteman

1. *Variety,* Feb. 16, 1927, signed by Gus Kahn, Jean Goldkette, Roger Wolfe Kahn, Joe Rea, Eddie Edwards, Paul Ash, Phil Napoleon, Art Kahn, and five others. Cited in DeLong, *Pops,* p. 58.

2. Hugh C. Ernst, original program notes. He characterized the piece as follows: "The shrieking clarinet, thumping piano and the clattering traps describe vividly a husky hostler dragging his wife by the hair around their squalid hut behind the stable. The 'G-r-r-r!' of the cornet and the moan of the trombone are Fido and Towser barking, yapping and howling outside the door, eager to get into the fray."

3. DeLong, *Pops,* p. 104.

4. Thompson, *Bing,* p. 21.

5. *Lucky,* p. 43.

6. Thompson, *Bing,* p. 21.

7. Ibid.

8. Rinker.

9. Ibid.

10. Ibid.

11. *Lucky,* p. 83.

12. Rinker.

13. For Columbia's U.K. release, even Clark's name vanished, though not entirely. His band was billed as the Charleston Serenaders and Betty Patrick became Tillie Clarke.

14. *Variety,* Oct. 20, 1926.

15. *Spokane Chronicle,* Nov. 17, 1926.

16. Letter from Larry Crosby to Ed Mello, Feb. 2, 1951.

17. *Spokane Chronicle,* Nov. 17, 1926.

18. Interviews with M. L. Higgins and Madeleine Carroll, Copeland memo, op. cit.

19. *Spokane Chronicle,* Nov. 24, 1926.

20. Rinker.

21. *Spokane Chronicle,* Nov. 17, 1926.

22. *Spokane Chronicle,* Nov. 25, 1926.

23. *Spokesman-Review,* Nov. 1926, cited in Dyar, *News for an Empire.*

24. "Crosby, Rinker Win Home Town and Boys Go Big at Liberty," *Spokane Chronicle,* Nov. 1926, undated clip. BCCGU.

25. Ibid. The reporter went on to write that the "remarkable reception they received last night before a 'hardboiled' home town audience left little doubt that they would succeed in the east."

26. *Lucky,* p. 83.

27. Rinker.

28. Ibid.

29. Ibid.

30. DeLong, *Pops,* p. 105.

31. Jack Fulton was still angry about the incident sixty-five years later, conceding Crosby's talent yet protesting that Bing's way had to be the only way. AI, Fulton.

32. *Lucky,* p. 92. He goes on to say, "As there had been nothing like it, it was very popular."

33. Mezzrow and Wolfe, *Really the Blues,* p. 120.

34. Ken Murray, "Louis, Bix Had Most Influence on Der Bingle," *Down Beat,* July 14, 1950. He also said, "You know, Ken, I got a lot out of Bix Beiderbecke when we were both beating around the country with the Whiteman band. And just as Bix himself found inspiration in Louis Armstrong out on the South Side in the late '20s, so did I."

35. Whiteman's marquee billing.

36. *Variety,* Feb. 16, 1927.

37. Ibid.

38. DeLong, *Pops,* p. 108.

39. O'Brien interview, op. cit.

40. *Lucky,* p. 84.

41. McDonough interview, op. cit.

42. Rinker.

43. Ibid.

44. Mize, *Bing,* p. 27.

45. *Lucky,* p. 84.

46. Thompson, *Bing,* p. 27.

47. The top five vocal records of 1927. Whitburn, *Pop Memories.*

48. Slide, *The Vaudevillians,* p. 51.

10. Rhythm Boys

1. Interview memo for *Time,* on Francis Cork O'Keefe, M. Gleason, August 1946. TIA.

2. AI, Marti Barris and Joe Porter.

3. *Variety,* May 5, 1926.

4. O'Brien interview, op. cit.

5. Rinker.

6. Ibid.

7. *Variety,* June 8, 1927.

8. *Variety,* June 22, 1927.

9. *Lucky,* p. 96.

10. AI, Donald Mills.

11. *Spokane Daily Chronicle,* Aug. 23, 1927.

12. AI, Bill Challis.

13. Ibid.

14. Ibid.

15. Carmichael, *The Stardust Road,* p. 121.

16. AI, Bill Challis.

17. Mezzrow and Wolfe, *Really the Blues,* p. 148.

18. AI, Bill Challis.

19. Ibid.

20. Fred Romary liner notes, Bing Crosby, *Wrap Your Troubles in Dreams* (RCA Vintage), 1972.

21. Alistair Cooke, *Letter from America,* BBC, October 1977, reprinted in *Bing,* Summer 1999.

22. Promotional interview disc for Decca Records, 1955.

23. *Confessions,* bk. 4, chap. 6. The song lyric is "I'm tired of living and scared of dying."

24. Kart, *Chicago Tribune* Oct. 15, 1977.

25. Crosby interview; Evans and Kiner, *Tram,* p. 92.

26. AI, Bill Challis.

27. Sudhalter and Evans, *Bix: Man and Legend,* p. 240.

28. *Lucky,* p. 94.

29. Rinker.

30. AI, Dolores Hope.

31. *Time* memo on O'Keefe, op. cit.

32. Ibid.

33. Western Union telegram from Bing Crosby to Ginger Meehan, New York, January 4, 1928, 12:49 A.M. Georgia State University, Special Collections.

34. Ibid., Chicago, July 4, 1928, 5:07 P.M.

35. Ibid., Chicago, July 10, 1928, 8:07 P.M.

36. Bogue, *Ish Kabibble.*

37. Ibid.

38. Thomas interview, op. cit.

39. *Variety*, Apr. 18, 1928.

40. AI, Marti Barris and Joe Porter.

41. *Lucky*, p. 94.

42. Rinker.

43. O'Brien interview, op. cit.

44. Rinker.

45. *Variety*, Aug. 15, 1928.

46. Ibid.

47. Letter from Louis Armstrong to unknown recipient, c. 1967. Louis Armstrong House and Archives at Queens College/CUNY.

48. Dance, *The World of Earl Hines*, p. 146.

49. AI, Gary Crosby.

50. Osborne interview, op. cit.

51. The full inscription reads, "Am I too suave or sveldt [sic]. To Ted, Hazel and the little one. Bing. Brush by Fuller."

52. Rinker.

53. Ted Crosby, *The Story of Bing Crosby*, p. 143; also *Lucky*, p. 95.

54. Challis interview by Ira Gitler, Oral History Program, Institute of Jazz Studies, Rutgers University, N.J.

55. "Popular Records," *The New Yorker*, Dec. 29, 1928.

56. *Variety*, December 26, 1928.

11. Of Cabbages and Kings

1. Universal ad for *King of Jazz*, in *Variety*, Dec. 11, 1929.

2. The writer was Paul Schofield, known for the 1926 *Beau Geste*.

3. For what it's worth, rumors at the time blamed the rancor on Olsen's concern that Shutta was carrying on with Cantor.

4. Evans and Kiner, *Tram*, p. 105.

5. Vallée, *Let the Chips Fall*, p. 15. "If further proof were needed that there is little or no vanity in Rudy Vallée, I need only point out that throughout the course of four marriages over a period of forty-seven years, there has never been a single progeny to bear my name!" (p. 16).

6. DeLong, *Pops*, p. 122.

7. Abel Green, "Whiteman–Old Gold Social Bunch Ride De Luxe — 50 Aboard and Happy," *Variety*, May 29, 1929.

8. Evans and Kiner, *Tram*, pp. 114–15.

9. KGM.

10. Ibid.

11. Ted and Larry Crosby, *Bing*, p. 149.

12. Ibid., p. 157.

13. Evans and Kiner, *Tram*, p. 115.

14. AI, Kurt Dieterle.

15. Thompson, *Bing*, p. 34.

16. Ted and Larry Crosby, *Bing*, p. 156.

17. TV interview, *The David Frost Show*, Feb. 10, 1971.

18. *Lucky*, p. 121.

19. AI, Dorothea Ponce.

20. Vallée, *Let the Chips Fall*, pp. 91–92.

21. Shepherd and Slatzer, *Bing Crosby: The Hollow Man*, p. 124.

22. Various ads, *Los Angeles Evening Express*, July 1929.

23. Ibid.

24. Ibid.

25. AI, Phil Harris.

26. Various ads, op. cit.

27. Earl Wilson, "It Happened Last Night," *New York Post* (undated clip), 1946.

28. Evans and Kiner, *Tram*, p. 118.

29. Rinker.

30. Ibid.

31. *Lucky*, p. 98.

32. Cardinal O'Connell made his remarks before a thousand members of Boston's Holy Names Society in January 1932, cited in Eberly, *Music in the Air*, p. 103.

33. Ibid.

34. *Lucky*, p. 88.

35. Ibid., p. 89.

36. In *Variety*, Nov. 29, 1929, Bob Landry wrote of the "Gay Love"/"Can't We Be Friends" disc, "looks like a possible favorite, properly piloted."

37. Cited in Daniel, *Chronicle of the 20th Century*, p. 375.

38. *Variety*, Dec. 11, 1929.

39. DeLong, *Pops*, p. 143.

40. AI, Bobbe Van Heusen.

41. AI, Kurt Dieterle.

42. Ted and Larry Crosby, *Bing*, p. 170.

43. *Lucky*, p. 100.

44. Ibid., p. 102.

45. AI, Bobbe Van Heusen.

46. Ibid. The wire would have been dated 1969. Bobbe married Perlberg before a justice of the peace in Pasadena in February 1928, though she insisted that it was a couple of years later. The sisters' career began when Irving Berlin's producer, Hassard Short, heard them in Edmonton and asked them to sing for Berlin over the phone. Short then changed their name from Brock to Brox. They appeared on stage in *The Cocoanuts* and the *Ziegfeld Follies of 1927* and then signed with MGM. Bobbe, whose real name was Josephine, was also known as Dagmar (after silent film actress Dagmar Godowsky). Her sisters were Lorayne, who married trumpet player Henry Busse in 1935, and Pat.

47. *Variety*, Feb. 26, 1930.

48. *Variety*, May 7, 1930.

49. Regina Crewe, *New York American*, May 3, 1930.

50. The picture opened with a running time of ninety-eight minutes, according to *Variety*, May 7, 1930, suggesting a last-minute cut (restored prints play 105 minutes). The live show opened at forty-two minutes and was soon cut to thirty-seven. Gershwin was paid $5,000 and Whiteman $12,500. Tickets sold for two dollars.

51. *New York Times*, May 3, 1930.

52. The new sequences for the German edition and one made for Spain were directed by a twenty-four-year-old German immigrant, Kurt Neumann, yet another newcomer launched by *King of Jazz*; he went on to make many low-budget genre

films, e.g., *The Unknown Guest, Cattle Drive, Rocketship X-M, Tarzan and the She-Devil,* and most famously, *The Fly.*

53. *Variety,* Apr. 9, 1930.

54. *Lucky,* p. 102.

55. Ibid.

56. AI, Rosemary Clooney, to whom Kathryn Crosby told the story in spring 2000.

57. Rinker.

58. Coslow, *Cocktails for Two,* p. 105.

59. These include the 1935 feature *Broadway to Hollywood* and such shorts as *Roast Beef and Movies* and *Nertsery Rhytmes* (with Ted Healy's Three Stooges). Most of the surviving footage was marketed in Germany in 1930, including the remarkable "Lockstep" prison number, which debuted in the United States in *That's Entertainment III* (1994). For Bing the experience marked the beginning of his lifelong friendship with actor William "Buster" Collier Jr. (the son of matinee idol William Collier Sr., who was also in *The March of Time*), a fishing buddy and neighbor.

60. *Lucky,* p. 102.

61. Challis's swing arrangements include "Clarinet Marmelade" and "Singing the Blues" for Henderson and "Stardust" for Ellington.

12. Dixie

1. "Bing Crosby Debunks Himself," op. cit.

2. AI, Frank Lieberman.

3. AI, Rory Burke.

4. Pulliam, *Harriman.*

5. The movie was *Happy Days,* and the number with the Boswells was cut from the final print.

6. Letter from Dixie Lee to Edward J. Meeman, 1930, on the occasion of the first of her movies, *Cheer Up and Smile* (her sixth film), to open in Harriman. Meeman was editor of the *Knoxville News-Sentinel.* Cited in Pulliam.

7. AI, Pauline Weislow.

8. Meeman letter, op. cit.

9. "It Happened Last Night," op. cit.

10. Vocco also came to Bing's aid in Chicago ("My goodness, in the old days, I used to put Bing Crosby to bed — he was drunk all the time, you know — but we became really good friends," he recalled after Bing's death); the aid he provided Dixie cemented a lifelong friendship. Vocco interview, Columbia University Oral History Research Office.

11. "It Happened Last Night," op. cit.

12. The pictures were *Let's Go Places, Harmony at Home, Happy Days, Cheer Up and Smile,* and *The Big Party.*

13. "One of the most elaborate song and dance numbers probably ever screened is 'Crazy Feet' with Dixie Lee singing and 32 girls doing tap and jazz routines." *Variety,* Feb. 19, 1930.

14. Atkins, *David Butler;* AI, Robert O'Brien; Ulanov, *The Incredible Crosby.* For Richard Keene (aka Raymond Keene, said by Bing [*Lucky,* p. 121] to have arranged Bing's unsuccessful screen test at Fox), Shepherd and Slatzer, *Bing Crosby: The Hollow Man.* For White, *Los Angeles Times,* Sept. 30, 1930. Movies White appeared in with Dixie are *Happy Days* and *Fox Movietone Follies.*

15. Charles Samuels, "Bing Crosby the Groaner," unidentified magazine clip, 1946. BCCGU.

16. Anne Edwards, "Bing Crosby the Going My Way Star in Rancho Santa Fe," *Architectural Digest,* April 1996.

17. "It Happened Last Night," op. cit.

18. AI, Pauline Weislow.

19. AI, Flo Haley.

20. AI, Dr. George J. (Jed) Hummer.

21. AI, Marsha Hunt.

22. Larry and Ted Crosby, *Bing,* p. 184; also, "Bing Crosby the Groaner," op. cit.

23. Cooper, *Please Don't Shoot My Dog,* p. 23.

24. This was directly before he left with Whiteman on the aborted trip to Vancouver, which led to his breaking his association with the bandleader.

25. Larry and Ted Crosby, *Bing,* p. 178.

26. "It Happened Last Night," op. cit.

27. Rinker.

28. Al Hine, "Million Dollar Kettle Drummer," *Esquire,* May 1953.

29. Leroy, *Mervyn Leroy: Take One,* p. 88.

30. Anthony Quinn, RBT.

31. Rinker.

32. Waters, *His Eye Is on the Sparrow.*

33. "The Survival of African Music in America," *Popular Science Monthly,* Sept. 1899. Cited in Van Der Merwe, *Origins of the Popular Style,* pp. 134–36.

34. AI, Joe Bushkin.

35. AI, Jake Hanna.

36. AI, Milt Hinton.

37. Letter from Walter Huston to Marie Manovill, Dec. 31, 1938. Courtesy of Marie Manovill and Gloria Burleson.

38. AI, Bud Brubaker.

39. AI, June MacCloy.

40. Ibid.

41. Armstrong letter, c. 1967, op. cit.

42. Crosby and Firestone, *Going My Own Way,* p. 112.

43. *Spokesman-Review,* Sept. 30, 1930.

44. *Spokane Daily Chronicle,* Sept. 30, 1930.

45. *New York Times,* Sept. 30, 1930. This was an AP dispatch. Bing was twenty-seven and had not yet clipped a year from his age; the incorrect age given Murray Crosey is simply one of many errors, including Dixie's real name and birthplace.

46. AI, Basil Grillo.

47. "Dixie Lee Weds Bing Crosby," *Los Angeles Times,* Sept. 30, 1930.

48. AI, Flo Haley.

49. Armstrong letter, c. 1967, op. cit.

50. Rinker.

51. Armstrong, *Swing That Music,* p. viii.

52. *Los Angeles Examiner,* Mar. 5, 1931.

53. This occurred only two weeks before the death of Knute Rockne, the beloved Notre Dame football coach, in a plane crash (March 30), an event that so disturbed Bing that he did not fly again until 1944, occasionally losing work as a result.

54. Bob Crosby, RBT.

55. This line appears in an unproduced teleplay, *Bing and Dixie,* by Mel Frank, based largely on interviews gathered by Frank and producer Meta Rosenberg; in this instance, the line was related to Meta by George Rosenberg, her husband and Bing's longtime agent. AI, Meta Rosenberg, Elizabeth Frank.

56. *Confessions,* bk. 2, chap. 4.

13. Prosperity Is Just Around the Crooner

1. Sennett, *King of Comedy,* p. 258.

2. Coslow, *Cocktails for Two,* p. 111.

3. The show also included an interview with Marlene Dietrich, possibly the first time they met.

4. Coslow, *Cocktails for Two,* p. 112

5. Sennett, *King of Comedy,* p. 257.

6. Ibid.

7. AI, Jack Hupp.

8. Mack Sennett Collection, Folder 1450, AMPAS. The letter was written by Bea Englander, representing Sennett. Bing's ambivalence about leaving the trio is also suggested by an agreement he made with songwriter Walter Donaldson involving an endorsement and photograph ("Featured by The Rhythm Boys") on the sheet music for the 1931 song "Hello Beautiful." Neither the Rhythm Boys nor Bing recorded it (Wayne King had the hit; Maurice Chevalier made it a signature theme), but a cover depicting the boys was published and soon withdrawn.

9. The Boswells had had their first hit in April; the Mills Brothers would have one in the fall.

10. Rinker.

11. *Lucky,* p. 105.

12. Ibid.

13. Kenneth Frogley, "IDN Radio," *Los Angeles Illustrated Daily News,* May 28, 1931.

14. Ibid., June 2, 1931.

15. *Lucky,* p. 107.

16. Rinker.

17. "In those days, every place had a trio, and these guys were heroes to us high-school kids. So when Crosby left, the Cocoanut Grove was without a trio and they had a contest to see who would succeed him." AI, Jack Hupp. The winners were Jack Smith, Milton Spersal, and Al Teeter, who would get together in school and imitate "So the Bluebirds and the Blackbirds Got Together." Smith took Bing's role and remained at the Grove for a few years with Arnheim and, later, Phil Harris, then appeared on the *Hit Parade* and other shows and with Doris Day in *On Moonlight Bay.* AI, Phil Harris.

18. Rinker.

19. "[Rinker] was salaried to Bing Crosby Ltd which is owned by Crosby, Barris and Roger Marchetti, local lawyer." *Variety,* July 28, 1931.

20. AI, Marti Barris.

21. AI, Marguerite Toth.

22. AI, Basil Grillo.

23. AI, Joe Porter.

24. AI, Basil Grillo.

25. AI, Julia Rinker.

26. Shepherd and Slatzer, *Bing Crosby: The Hollow Man.*

27. Rinker.

28. Ibid.

29. AI, Skitch Henderson.

30. AI, Don Eagle.

31. AI, Kurt Dieterle.

32. *Photoplay*, Sept. 1931.

33. *Motion Picture Herald*, Oct. 10, 1931.

34. *Variety*, Nov. 10, 1931.

35. Eberle, *Music in the Air*, p. 13.

36. Another excellent number is "I'd Climb the Highest Mountain," a fine song he never otherwise recorded.

37. According to the original cast notes, Ginger Rogers was proposed for the role of Bing's beloved, which went instead to Ann Christy.

38. "Bing Crosby Signs with Columbia," Columbia Broadcasting System press release, Aug. 22, 1931.

39. "CBS Gets Crosby; Musicians' Ban in L.A. Only," *Variety*, Aug. 25, 1931.

40. Ibid.

Part Two
14. Big Broadcast

1. Louis Armstrong, *Time* (1955).

2. AI, Artie Shaw.

3. Young would go on to conduct more Crosby recordings that anyone except John Scott Trotter.

4. AI, Burton Lane. Arthur Jarret, "a fairly popular singer in those days," chose Lane's song as his theme after Bing turned it down, "but my song never made it."

5. AI, Marti Barris.

6. Circumstantial evidence of his involvement in "Where the Blue of the Night"'s pretty if rarely heard verse was provided by rival Russ Columbo, who, upon hearing Bing sing the chorus on the air, rushed to record it. Columbo's version, made five days before Bing's, lacks the verse, probably because he had no way of knowing that one had been added.

7. Crosby's authorship has been challenged on only one song, by Harry Tobias, the lyricist who submitted "At Your Command" to Harry Barris. Yet Tobais, in an interview conducted sixty years after the fact, also insisted that he wrote the music, which, if true, would make it the only melody he wrote during a long career as a lyric writer. Lane said Bing did not request participation in "Love Came Into My Heart," though he performed it on the air before introducing "Where the Blue of the Night." Bing minimized his work as a songwriter in a 1976 radio interview with John Salisbury: "I wrote a couple of things with Harry Barris, nothing serious. I wrote a lot of material, parodies, verses, special material on television, radio, and in the films, gag songs, nothing popular, nothing that made a hit."

8. Thomas, *Harry Warren and the Hollywood Musical*, p. 2.

9. *New York Times*, Aug. 30, 1931.

10. Transcription of Sept. 2, 1931, CBS broadcast, *The Chronological Bing Crosby, Vol. 11* (Jonzo).

11. Salisbury interview, op. cit.

12. Smith, *In All His Glory*, p. 92.

13. Shepherd and Slatzer, *Bing Crosby: The Hollow Man*, p. 161.

14. *Time* memo on O'Keefe, op. cit.

15. Memo of background interview with Simon Ruskin, M. Gleason, Aug. 14, 1949. TIA.

16. "Bing Crosby Debunks Himself," op. cit.

17. *Lucky*, p. 111.

18. Letter from Agnes Law to Philip K. Eberle, cited in Eberle, *Music in the Air*, p. 102.

19. Memo of background interview with Edgar Sisson, May 16, 1949. TIA.

20. AI, Gary Stevens.

21. AI, Artie Shaw.

22. AI, Gary Stevens.

23. *Variety*, Sept. 8, 1931; the same article listed the selections performed on that first show.

24. AI, Gary Stevens.

25. AI, Artie Shaw.

26. AI, Gary Stevens.

27. *Variety*, Sept. 8, 1931.

28. Columbo's 1928 recording (with Gus Arnheim) of "Back in Your Own Backyard," made shortly after Bing's "Ol' Man River," shows how stiffly rearguard his original attack was. The more winning Columbo sides ("Prisoner of Love," "All of Me") followed in 1931, by which time he had assimilated the Crosby style, though he avoided mordents along with rhythm.

29. AI, Ken Roberts. "I think Freddy conducted Monday and Tuesday nights, when Bing wasn't there. Victor Young was hired specifically for Bing — that's all he did."

30. Ibid.

31. Ibid. Roberts worked with Bing again during the war, when Bing specifically requested him, and at charity events: "And then many many years later — I guess at about 1976 — I was still working at CBS doing a soap opera every day, and I was walking through the corridors and a friend of mine brought Bing in to be on an interview show with Pat Collins and he saw me and said 'Kenneth, are you still here?' He was still such a nice, sweet, simple fellow."

32. *Variety*, Oct. 27, 1931.

33. *Variety*, 1931, cited by Wilbur W. Hindley in the *Spokesman-Review*, Dec. 27, 1931.

34. Mildred Bailey, Jack Oakie, and Bob Hope also claimed to have coined the name "the Groaner." Hope and Oakie are out of the question — they did not know Crosby until 1932. Dorsey may have picked up the phrase from Bailey, known for her verbal swiftness (Tommy was not), but he was apparently more aggressive about using it.

35. Duke Ellington, Carter Harmon Interview Collection, Smithsonian Institution, cited in Nicholson, *Reminiscing in Tempo*, p. 119.

36. Kiner, *Directory & Log of the Bing Crosby Cremo Singer Radio Series*.

37. Ruskin memo, op. cit. Dr. W. James Gould, Ruskin's successor as throat specialist to stars and politicians, pointed out in the 1990s that performing surgery on Bing's node would have been irresponsible.

38. *Lucky,* p. 113.

39. Ibid.

40. Ibid.

41. *Billboard,* Nov. 13, 1931.

42. *Variety,* Nov. 10, 1931. The reporter, Bige, was Joe Bigelow, who later became an account executive in charge of *Kraft Music Hall.*

43. Memo of background interview with McInerny and others, 1940s (undated). TIA.

44. Sisson memo, op. cit.

45. AI, Donald Mills.

46. AI, Frieda Kapp.

47. AI, Burton Lane.

48. AI, Artie Shaw.

49. AI, Red Norvo.

50. AI, Ken Roberts.

51. AI, Gary Stevens.

52. AI, Ken Roberts.

53. They were Paul Bracco and Phil Taylor, interviewed by *Time.* McInerny memo, op. cit.

54. AI, Artie Shaw.

55. Mack Sennett Collection, Folder 1450, AMPAS.

56. In the 1976 John Salisbury interview, Bing was asked to comment on Ellington: "I recorded a couple of times with Duke and used to see him all the time. We were friendly, but I never worked a great deal with Duke. I had great admiration for him as a composer and a bandleader — one of the greatest, one of the all-time greats in both fields, conducting, arranging. A giant, a real giant. And a nice man, a real reasonable type, good taste. Classy guy."

57. Mize, *Bing Crosby and the Bing Crosby Style,* p. 125.

58. *Gramophone,* Dec. 1932, cited in *Bing,* Apr. 1996.

59. Bing collaborated on the lyrics of this with two obscure songwriters, Irving Wallman and Max Wartell.

60. Ulanov, *The Incredible Crosby,* p. 88.

61. Thompson, *Bing,* p. 52.

62. Adams, *Here's to the Friars,* p. 155.

63. *New York Daily News,* Feb. 25, 1932.

64. "Crooner Crosby Faces Suit for Earnings Share," *Los Angeles Times,* June 3, 1932.

65. Letter from Eleanor Hard, Editorial Department, *Time,* to Mr. E. J. Crosby, Dec. 12, 1931. HCC.

66. Letter from E. J. Crosby to Eleanor Hard, undated. HCC.

15. The Crosby Clause

1. Paramount ad, *The Big Broadcast* (1932), reprinted in *Bingtalks,* May–Aug. 1995.

2. KGM.

3. *Variety,* Apr. 26, 1932.

4. KGM.

5. This refers to the second take (B) of "Sweet Georgia Brown."

6. *Los Angeles Times,* June 13, 1932.

7. Evans and Kiner, *Tram,* p. 154.

8. KGM.

9. The working title was *The Girl in the Transom.*

10. "Stereophonic Sound," from the film *Silk Stockings* (1955).

11. At one point Paramount planned to call Crosby's character Bing Hornsby, and a cast list went out with that name; numerous reviews, including those in *Variety* and the *Spokesman-Review,* stated that Bing played Hornsby despite numerous references to Crosby throughout the film.

12. The Tuttle material was drawn from an unpublished memoir, *They Started Talking,* which despite the ironic title ignores the HUAC hearings; plus "Frank Tuttle Discusses Why He Is 'Informer'," *New York Herald Tribune,* May 25, 1951; "Tuttle Confesses Paying 10G Into Red Coffers — Brands 39 as Commies," *Variety,* May 25, 1951; "Film Old Timer Frank Tuttle 10 Yrs. a Red, Names 36 More," *New York Daily News,* May 25, 1951; "Film Maker Rues 10 Years a Red," *New York Times,* May 25, 1951; "Tuttle Admits to 10 Years as Red; Names 30 Other Commies," *Hollywood Reporter,* May 25, 1951; "Tuttle, Ex-Film Director, Ex-Red, Broke," *Los Angeles Examiner,* July 3, 1954; "Frank Tuttle, Veteran Movie Director, Dies," *Los Angeles Times,* Jan. 7, 1963; and press releases issued by Paramount in 1934 and by Warner Bros. in 1956. The witness who named Tuttle was screenwriter and superinformer Richard J. Collins.

13. McGilligan and Buhle, *Tender Comrades,* p. 148.

14. Ibid.

15. AI, Nancy Briggs.

16. AI, Basil Grillo.

17. AI, Helen Votachenko. Tuttle was also diabetic. Bing wrote of an incident when producer Herb Polesie and Tuttle visited him to go over a new script: "About half way through, Frank began getting slower and slower in his reading. Finally, with bowed head, he was able to gasp out, 'orange juice.' He was going into a coma or some kind of blackout." Bing and Herb dashed into the kitchen and found oranges, but not a knife to cut them. Bing frantically tore open oranges with his hands until he had a glassful. The moral, he concluded: "Know thine own kitchen." Bing Crosby, unpublished papers.

18. Clair, who pioneered the creative use of sound, initially declared talking movies "a redoubtable monster." Many years later, in a 1959 TV interview (*Le Million,* DVD), he pointed out the decline of the great physical comedians of the silent era and observed that the best comedians of the sound era came from radio.

19. Westmore and Davidson, *The Westmores of Hollywood,* p. 94.

20. Frost interview, op. cit.

21. Tuttle memoir.

22. "Crosby-Lombardo billing keeps Guy out of Par picture!" *Variety,* July 5, 1932.

23. *Hattie,* by Carlton Jackson (Madison), cited in *Bing,* Dec. 1991.

24. *Variety,* Oct. 18, 1932.

25. *Spokesman-Review,* Oct. 28, 1932.

26. *New York Daily Mirror,* cited in Alvin H. Marill, "Bing Crosby," *Films in Review,* June–July 1968.

27. *New York American,* in ibid.

28. In a letter from Jason S. Joy of the MPAA to Harold Hurley at Paramount, Sept. 30, 1932: "The exception referred to is the sequence in the bathroom, into

which are injected a couple of undress shots which we cannot help but consider unfortunate in that they do not seem to be called for by the action, and in fact appear almost offensively out of place in a story as free as this is from sex implications. While we have not yet got to the point of making scenes like these a Code matter, nevertheless they are being so generally injected into pictures that we are becoming more than a little concerned. Censors in a number of places inevitably cut them out; and so, if you are thinking of trimming the picture at all, we would urge you very earnestly to consider eliminating at least one of these shots, in the interest of censorship and, we believe, good taste and sound policy." MPAA files, AMPAS.

29. Tuttle memoir.

30. *Variety,* Dec. 13, 1932.

16. Brother, Can You Spare a Dime?

1. AI, Rosemary Clooney.

2. Whitney Balliett, *Saturday Review,* June 27, 1953.

3. AI, Gary Crosby.

4. AI, Barry Ulanov.

5. CBS signed blackface singer and future character actor Jay C. Flippen to fill out its programming in Bing's absence.

6. *Variety,* Aug. 8, 1932.

7. John A. Myer, M.D., "Cigarette Century," *American Heritage,* Dec. 1992.

8. Strangely, Bing's version is ponderous and orotund. It survived as a classic tenor saxophone solo by Chu Berry until Sinatra found the right gait for it, though the definitive version was recorded in 1958 by Billy Eckstine (*Imagination,* EmArcy), who often revived Crosby ballads.

9. Informed in 1994 of Bing's true birth date, Hope paused, then howled with pleasure, "That Bing! That Bing!"

10. AI, Bob Hope.

11. Ibid.

12. *Variety,* Dec. 6, 1932.

13. *New York Herald Tribune,* Dec. 3, 1932.

14. *Variety,* July 26, 1932.

15. A 1944 ad, C. Liggett & Myers Tobacco Co., unidentified magazine. Collection of Eric Anderson.

16. *Variety,* Jan. 31, 1933: "Bing Crosby pays the Shuberts $50 for the rights to do 'Brother Can You Spare a Dime at the Palace.'"

17. Vallée begins his October 27, 1932, Columbia recording as follows: "This is Rudy Vallée again, stepping perhaps a bit out of character."

18. Studs Terkel liner notes, *Songs of the Depression,* a record anthology issued by Book of the Month Club, 1980.

19. Crosby and the nation would have been astonished to learn that twenty years on, "the Depression's theme would become prosperity's forbidden melody," as Murray Kempton wrote (*Part of Our Time,* 1955), after Jay Gorney was probed by the House Un-American Activities Committee as a communist.

20. On that record, Lennie had accompanied Jack Fulton's vocal on celesta. Another connection with the song is that Sue Carol helped introduce it.

21. Writing about "Brother, Can You Spare a Dime?" in the 1970s, musicologist Charles Hamm concluded, "It was difficult to lose faith in a country that had produced

a Bing Crosby." Liner notes, *Brother Can You Spare a Dime?: American Song During the Great Depression* (New World), 1977.

22. *Variety*, Jan. 10, 1933.

23. *Variety* ranked the top twelve shows as follows: Jack Pearl, Eddie Cantor, Ed Wynn, Amos 'n' Andy, Rudy Vallée, Burns and Allen, Myrt and Marge, Al Jolson, Bing Crosby, Ben Bernie, Fred Allen, Kate Smith. Feb. 28, 1933.

24. Milton Berle and Haskell Frankel, *Milton Berle* (New York: Dell, 1975), p. 144.

25. AI, Tony Martin.

26. Friedwald, *Jazz Singing*, p. 103.

27. Ibid.

28. Earl Coleman, a self-described Black Bing who recorded with Charlie Parker in 1947 and revived his career as a ballad singer thirty years later, insisted that the first Black Bing was LeRoy Felton, who sang with Benny Carter's band (e.g., Carter's recording of "More than You Know"). Carter himself took a flier at singing in the Crosby style ("Synthetic Love," 1933). As early as 1932, Harlan Lattimore, the vocalist with Don Redman's orchestra, was billed as "the Negro Bing Crosby." After the enormous success of Billy Eckstine, other Black Bings included Herb Jeffries, Al Hibbler, Arthur Prysock, and Johnny Hartman. AI, Earl Coleman, Benny Carter.

29. This was Bing's second consecutive hit with a Victor Young tune, after "I Don't Stand a Ghost of a Chance."

30. Thompson, *Bing*, p. 58.

31. AI, Barry Ulanov.

32. KGM.

33. Ibid.

34. Bing Crosby, "Mutual Liking for Spaghetti Made Eddie and Bing Pals," *Down Beat*, May 1939.

35. AI, Barry Ulanov.

36. Ibid.

37. Oakie, *Jack Oakie's Double Takes*, p. 118.

38. Ed Sullivan, "Little Old New York," *New York Daily News*, Apr. 10, 1944.

39. Smith, op. cit., p. 264.

40. Coslow, *Cocktails for Two*, p. 134.

41. Oakie, *Jack Oakie's Double Takes*, p. 63.

42. Ibid.

43. Coslow, *Cocktails for Two*, p. 135.

44. AI, Mary Carlisle.

45. Ibid.

46. AI, Nancy Briggs.

47. Dietrich, *Dietrich*, p. 104.

48. Harrison Carroll, *Los Angeles Evening Herald Express*, Sept. 25, 1934.

49. AI, Max Wilk.

50. Frank Steiner of Paramount to Frank Murphy, *Bing*, Oct. 25, 1967.

51. Andre Sennwald, *New York Times*, June 23, 1933.

52. *Los Angeles Times*, June 14, 1933.

53. *Variety*, July 25, 1933.

54. "Musicomedies of the Week," *Time*, July 1933.

55. MPAA files, AMPAS.

56. AI, Alan Fisher.

57. AI, Rosemary Clooney.

58. AI, Sheila Lynn.

17. Under Western Skies

1. "Bing Crosby Debunks Himself," op. cit., cited in *Time*, Jan. 1, 1934.

2. Long thought to be lost, *Please* was discovered and marketed in the 1990s by film preservationist Bob DeFlores. Only one reel of *Just an Echo* is believed to exist; as of 2000, the collector who found that reel has refused to let anyone else see it. In 1976 DeFlores asked Bing about *Just an Echo*: "And he says, 'Well, I'm just not happy with it.' I said, 'What's the matter?' He says the editing was real poor. He said, 'I'd be in a Mountie uniform on a horse and the camera angle would be from the left and then all of a sudden a sharp cut and I'd be somewhere else.' He remembered this after forty-five years."

3. Letter from Bing to Ted Crosby, Tuesday (undated) 1934. HCC.

4. Collins interview, op. cit.

5. W. E. Oliver, "Bing Calm Despite Stress," *Los Angeles Evening Herald Express*, June 14, 1933.

6. KGM.

7. Ibid.

8. Ibid.

9. Paramount press release by Dave Keene, Oct. 27, 1933.

10. Ibid.

11. Oakie, *Jack Oakie's Double Takes*, p. 129.

12. *Lucky*, pp. 117–18.

13. Mordaunt Hall, *New York Times*, Sept. 23, 1933.

14. *Variety*, Sept. 26, 1933.

15. Louella O. Parsons, Hearst syndicate, Sept. 29, 1933.

16. *Variety*, Oct. 1933.

17. *Variety*, Nov. 14, 1933.

18. *Time*, Jan. 1, 1934.

19. Walsh, *Each Man in His Time*, p. 257.

20. Davies, *The Times We Had*, p. 119.

21. *Lucky*, pp. 119–20.

22. Davies, *The Times We Had*, p. 120.

23. Ibid.

24. *Lucky*, p. 121.

25. Transcribed from *Both Sides of Bing Crosby* (Curtain Calls).

26. Walsh, *Each Man in His Time*, p. 271.

27. Barrios, *A Song in the Dark*, p. 398.

28. MPAA files, AMPAS.

29. *Lucky*, p. 120.

30. Louella O. Parsons, Hearst Syndicate, Jan. 26, 1934.

31. Andre Sennwald, *New York Times*, Dec. 23, 1933.

32. *Time*, Jan. 1, 1934.

33. *Time*, Jan. 22, 1934.

34. *Variety*, Sept. 19, 1933.

35. AI, Roy Rogers.

36. Salisbury interview, op. cit.

37. Ibid.

18. More Than a Crooner

1. Robert Trout, transcribed script for *Wilkins Coffee Time,* Oct. 6, 1933. Collection of John McDonough.

2. *Billboard,* undated clip, 1934.

3. Between Arnheim and Grier, the band was conducted for three shows by Carol Lofner.

4. Alton Cook, "Bing Crosby Record Stayer," *New York World Telegram,* July 12, 1934.

5. *Fortune* (Aug. 1935) described FDR as "the best voice in radio. Until Mr. Roosevelt taught the world how that titanic trombone of tubes and antennae could be played no one had any idea of the possible range of its virtuosity."

6. Manchester, *The Glory and the Dream,* p. 81.

7. Leuchtenburg, *Franklin D. Roosevelt and the New Deal,* p. 330.

8. Gross, *I Looked and I Listened,* p. 172.

9. It's too late to order it, but the kit contained "a trial-size cake of Woodbury's facial soap, generous tubes of Woodbury's germ free, cold, and facial creams, and six baby packets of Woodbury's facial powder, a sample of each of the six shades."

10. Bob Crosby, RBT.

11. After shooting wrapped on Catalina, the crew moved to the Paramount lot, where Bing entertained a few visiting Gonzagans, including Mike Pecarovitch (then Gonzaga's coach) and Ray Flaherty, who arrived with members of his team, the New York Giants, winners of the 1934 National Football League championship. "Bing had one of the greatest memories I have ever seen," Ray recalled. "As those football players came in, he would stand at the door and greet them, 'Hello, George,' 'Hello, Max,' 'Hello, Bill.' I think maybe he used to get a program and rehearse it a little bit." AI, Flaherty.

12. *Lucky,* p. 125.

13. Ibid., p. 126.

14. Ibid., pp. 127–28.

15. Ibid., p. 128.

16. Several comic lines were punched into Horace Jackson's script by writers George Marion Jr. (*The Big Broadcast*) and Francis Martin (*Mississippi*).

17. Especially after Bette Davis throttled her on camera in *Old Acquaintance* with a vengeance unstipulated in the script.

18. Kobal, *People Will Talk,* p. 361.

19. Hart, *Kitty,* p. 65.

20. AI, Kitty Carlisle Hart.

21. Letter from Bing Crosby to Ted Crosby, Tuesday (undated) 1934. HCC.

22. This passage obviously augurs the famous "a little sex" scene in Preston Sturges's *Sullivan's Travels.*

23. AI, Kitty Carlisle Hart.

24. Ibid.

25. Salisbury interview, op. cit. On another occasion, he told Ireland's George O'Reilly that he "fought like the dickens" against having to sing it and that when it became the hit of the picture, he realized he had no ability to predict hits.

26. Benny and Marks, *Jack Benny,* p. 71.

27. Salisbury interview, op. cit.

28. AI, Kitty Carlisle Hart.

29. Westmore and Davidson, *The Westmores of Hollywood,* p. 94.

30. Frost interview, op. cit.

31. Ferguson, *The Film Criticism of Otis Ferguson,* p. 49.

32. *Time,* Sept. 17, 1934.

33. *New York Herald Tribune,* May 6, 1934, writer unknown.

34. KGM.

35. Ibid.

36. AI, Howard Crosby.

37. KGM.

38. *Variety,* Sept. 4, 1934.

39. KGM.

40. *Variety,* May 1, 1935.

41. Letter from Larry Crosby to Ted Crosby, Saturday (undated) 1935. HCC.

42. Ibid.

43. Swindell, *Screwball,* p. 154.

44. Letter from Larry Crosby, op. cit.

45. AI, Kitty Carlisle Hart.

46. Tuttle memoir.

47. AI, Kitty Carlisle Hart.

48. *New York Daily News,* Dec. 22, 1934.

49. *Variety,* Dec. 25, 1934.

50. *Time,* Dec. 31, 1934.

51. Marquis Busby, *Los Angeles Examiner,* Jan. 7, 1934.

19. Decca

1. Lester Velie, "Vocal Boy Makes Good," *Collier's,* Dec. 13, 1947.

2. Interview, Australian radio, April 1977.

3. *Bing Crosby Album,* Dell 1949, reprinted in *Bingang,* Dec. 1988.

4. AI, Frieda Kapp.

5. Ibid.

6. Ibid.

7. *Lucky,* p. 142.

8. Principle sources for Kapp's background and Decca's early history are John McDonough's comprehensive unpublished account, "Decca: 60th Anniversary History," commissioned and withheld by MCA in 1994; an interoffice memo by Sir E. R. Lewis; AI, Geoffrey Milne; Ronnie Pugh liner notes, *Decca Country Classics 1934–1973;* and Herman Paikoff, "The American Record Corporation (A Corporate Overview)," *The New Amberola Graphic,* Autumn 1992, excerpted in *Bingang,* Dec. 1992.

9. Lewis memo, op. cit.

10. Ibid.

11. Ibid.

12. *Variety,* Aug. 7, 1934.

13. AI, Elsie Perry.

14. Garland was one of several performers (including the Boswells and Deanna Durbin) Joe Perry is said to have introduced to making records.

15. Dave Kapp interview by John Krimsky, July 27, 1971. BCCGU.

16. This exchange was facilitated by Herman Starr, another of Jack's longtime loyal friends. Starr was the chief of Warner Bros.' film music, but he had been president of Brunswick when Jack was hired. In 1941, when the ten-year Brunswick lease lapsed and returned the company to Warners, Starr sold the company to Decca. Because the original contract between Warners and ARC was signed December 3, 1931, all records made before that date as well as the name Brunswick belonged to Decca, and all records made after that date belonged to Columbia, which is why Brunswick recordings by Bing and others are, to this day, split between the two companies.

17. AI, Frieda Kapp.

18. Mezzrow and Wolfe, *Really the Blues*, p. 211.

19. Gelatt, *The Fabulous Phonograph*, p. 268.

20. Letter from Jack Kapp to *Time*, Jan. 17, 1936.

21. *Variety*, Feb. 26, 1936.

22. Unpublished interview with Jack Kapp by Lea Nicholson, for *Time*, Mar. 22, 1941. TIA.

23. Letter from Jack Kapp to Bing Crosby, Aug. 30, 1934.

24. Nicholson interview, op. cit.

25. Although this was a unique gambit for Bing, codas of this sort became a trademark of Billy Eckstine's ballads in the 1940s.

26. *Lucky*, p. 141.

27. Ibid. Contrary to all his earlier protestations of not being a crooner, he wrote in this context that he was unworthy precisely because he was a crooner.

28. Seldes, *The Public Arts*, p. 131.

29. "Bing Crosby a Choir Boy in 'Silent Night' Record," unsigned review in unidentifiable New York newspaper, Dec. 3, 1936. TIA.

30. Eyman, *Ernst Lubitsch*, p. 234.

31. Another reason Hart may have been incensed was his apprehension of a comparison with the most famous of all Broadway interpolations — Jerome Kern's use of "After the Ball" in *Show Boat*. No one today would think of comparing Kern's masterwork with *Mississippi*, but similarities were all too evident in 1935, when the use of Foster's song might have been interpreted as an overt imitation of Kern.

32. AI, Peggy Lee.

33. In 1924, as *The Fighting Coward*, and in 1929, as *River of Romance*.

34. Edward Sutherland, Columbia University Oral History Research Project.

35. Taylor, *W. C. Fields*, p. 236.

36. AI, Bob DeFlores.

37. Quentin Reynolds, "The Kid from Spokane," *Collier's*, Apr. 27, 1935.

38. In widely circulated newstories, Bing was reported to have received between $75,000 and $110,000 per film. The higher figure, which seems most likely in the context of top film salaries for the period and in regard to Bing's previous contracts, was confirmed by reporting done by *Fortune* in 1946, for "The Great Throat" (*Fortune*, Jan. 1947).

39. Another amusing moment occurs early when a music publisher fails to hear a plane crash directly over his head — "deaf as a post, but picks the biggest song hits."

40. *The Spectator*, Sept. 27, 1935, collected in Greene, *On Film*, p. 24.

41. This took place two days before the death of Will Rogers and may have contributed to the drinking that resulted in his near debacle with "Home on the Range."

42. Simon, *The Big Bands,* p. 144.

43. Transcribed from session tape.

44. Letter from Joseph Breen to B. B. Kahane, RKO, Jan. 10, 1935. MPAA Files, AMPAS.

45. Typed note from K.L. of Breen office, Aug. 8, 1935. Ibid.

46. Letter from Joseph Breen to Paramount executive John Hammell, Sept. 9, 1935. Ibid.

47. Ibid.

48. *Variety,* Feb. 12, 1936.

49. *Time,* Feb. 3, 1936.

50. Letter from Joseph Breen to John Hammell, Jan. 28, 1936. MPAA Files, AMPAS.

20. *Kraft Music Hall*

1. JWTPR, Oct. 29, 1936, by H. C. Kuhl.

2. Oakie, *Jack Oakie's Double Takes,* pp. 9–11.

3. Ibid.

4. Ibid.

5. JWTPR, Mar. 5, 1936, by H. C. Kuhl.

6. Niven, *The Moon's a Balloon,* p. 210.

7. Carroll, *None of Your Business,* p. 3.

8. Final revisions of script for *Kraft Music Hall,* Dec. 5, 1935.

9. JWTPR, Dec. 5, 1935, by H. C. Kuhl.

10. George McCabe, "Watching the Kraft Music Hall in 1936," *Bing,* Spring 1999.

11. Ibid.

12. JWTPR, Jan. 2, 1936, by H. C. Kuhl.

13. Ibid. Jan. 9, 1936, by H. C. Kuhl.

14. In November 1936 Bing wired Venuti: "THE THOMPSON AGENCY ASKED ME LAST WEEK IF YOU WOULD BE ACCEPTABLE TO ME FOR THE EIGHT-WEEK PERIOD [when Dorsey took a break] AND I ASSURED THEM THAT YOU CERTAINLY WOULD BE IN FACT I STIPULATED THAT I WOULD HAVE NO ONE ELSE SO I IMAGINE IF ROCKWELL IS ABLE TO WORK OUT ARRANGEMENT WHEREBY JIMMY'S ABSENCE FROM THE PROGRAM FOR EIGHT WEEKS WILL DEFEAT STANDBY CHARGES YOU SHOULD BE COMING ON FOR THAT PERIOD STOP THINK YOUD BETTER LEAVE THOSE TEXAS MUSTANGS ALONE IF YOU COME HERE ILL PUT YOU ON SOME REAL WINNERS BEST REGARDS TO SALLY. BING CROSBY"

15. JWTPR, Feb. 6, 1936, by H. C. Kuhl.

16. John Salibury interview for radio series *The Crosby Years,* 1973, cited in Vernon Wesley Taylor, "Hail KMH!," *The Crosby Voice,* no. 29, Sept. 1984.

17. Ulanov, *The Incredible Crosby,* p. 122.

18. AI, Ken Roberts.

19. AI, Eddie Bracken.

20. Carroll, *None of Your Business,* p. 123.

21. Ibid., p. 122.

22. AI, Gary Crosby.

23. Interviewed by M. Gleason as background for *Fortune,* Aug. 4, 1946.

24. "'Crosby-isms' Win Praise as Smart Airwave Patter," *Cheesekraft,* May 1938.

25. Ibid.

26. "Hail KMH!," op cit.

27. Ibid.

28. AI, Noble Threewitt. Also AI, Charlie Whittingham and Dan Smith, and Eddie Read, "The Del Mar Story," file copy, Del Mar Publicity Office, courtesy of Dan Smith, director of publicity.

29. AI, Bob Hope.

30. Penna, *My Wonderful World of Golf.*

31. Carroll, *None of Your Business,* p. 125.

32. This and all subsequent excerpts are from Carroll Carroll's final-version script for the *Kraft Music Hall* of May 7, 1936. No recording of the actual show is known to exist.

33. JWTPR, May 7, 1936, by Cal Kuhl. Around this time Kuhl began signing the reports with his nickname rather than his initials.

34. AI, Gary Stevens.

35. AI, Eddie Bracken.

36. *Lucky,* p. 150.

37. Alton Cook, "Bing Crosby Trick Revealed," *New York World-Telegram,* Feb. 29, 1938.

38. Carroll, *None of Your Business,* p. 159.

39. JWTPR, May 21, 1936, by Cal Kuhl.

40. Ibid., May 28, 1936, by Cal Kuhl.

41. Ibid., July 1, 1936, by Cal Kuhl.

42. Aaron Stein, "Radio Today," *New York Post,* Nov. 20, 1936.

43. AI, Marsha Hunt.

44. Arnold, *Shadowland.*

45. Bing Crosby, "The Role I Liked Best," reprinted in *Bingang,* Oct. 1983.

46. Bach and Mercer, *Our Huckleberry Friend,* p. 56.

47. Letter from Johnny Mercer to Leslie Gaylor, undated, early 1970s.

48. *Variety,* Aug. 5, 1936.

49. During the interim, they had rented Marion Davies's house in Benedict Canyon.

50. Letter from Harry Crosby to Ted Crosby, Mar. 20, 1936.

51. Harold Grieve, president of the California division.

52. In *Anything Goes, Rhythm on the Range,* and many films to come, Bing billed himself at the head of a foursome, following the title card.

53. *Variety,* Dec. 16, 1936.

54. Armstrong letter, c. 1967, op. cit.

55. *Lucky,* p. 162.

56. *Down Beat,* Mar. 1937.

57. Much of the material on Trotter is based on a radio interview he did with his friend Eddie Rice on behalf of the British Crosby Society, late 1960s; and a personal (unpublished) interview he gave James T. Maher, Apr. 5, 1959.

58. JWTPR, July 8, 1937, by Cal Kuhl.

59. Cited in Will Friedwald liner notes, *Hal Kemp* (Columbia).

60. Maher interview, op. cit.

61. Rice interview, op. cit.

62. AI, Alan Fisher.

63. AI, Rory Burke.

64. AI, Frieda Kapp.

65. Bing Crosby liner notes, John Scott Trotter, *A Thousand and One Notes,* reprinted in *Bingang,* Mar. 1996.

66. Steinbeck, *The Grapes of Wrath* (New York: Viking, 1939). Ironically, Steinbeck described Bing singing "Thanks for the Memory," which became Bob Hope's theme song and was not recorded by Bing until 1956; he did perform it on *KMH,* however, and like many people, Steinbeck failed to distinguish between Crosby records and Crosby radio.

67. Roaring Lion, who headlined at the Village Vanguard in 1945, during the height of his career, wrote *Calypso from France to Trinidad — 800 Years of History* in 1987 and was still performing as of 2000. In another song, "Four Mills Brothers," he muted his praise for Bing, describing him as "interesting" in *We're Not Dressing* ("Love Thy Neighbor" clearly made an impression on him) and acknowledging his unparalleled "voice control" yet concluding, "But I still prefer to hear the Four Mills Brothers sing, 'I Ain't Got Nobody (and nobody cares for me)'." Asked if he recalled the Lion's record thirty-seven years after it was recorded, Bing said, "Cute song. 'Takes off his hat infrequently' — isn't that in there?"

21. Public Relations

1. Smith, op. cit., p. 258.

2. Ward, *Jazz,* p. 64.

3. Too old to play Dick or Tom, he briefly tried the mantles of Abe and Will during the Second World War, costumed as the former for a song in *Holiday Inn* and as the latter in a screen test for a proposed Rogers biography.

4. AI, Pamela Crosby Brown, his goddaughter.

5. Cited in Michael Brooks liner notes, *Bing Crosby: The Columbia Years, 1928–34,* 1988.

6. AI, Gary Stevens. See note 10 in Chapter 12 on Vocco.

7. The Paramount press releases alluded to in this section are identified by the obscure system in use at the time. This one, for example, is marked, "Paramount fp September 1933." The significance of the initials is unclear, and dates are not always provided. Many releases without dates were later inventoried and dated with a *ca.* They are found in the Paramount files, AMPAS.

8. Ibid.

9. Ibid.

10. Paramount de lapp fp ca. 1934.

11. Part of a series called *NBC Personalities,* issued by the National Broadcasting System, June 8, 1939. Sample: "All the other kids shouted 'Bang' as they shot their make-believe revolvers, but little Harry Lillis was an individualist." He is also described as playing the title role in *Julius Caesar,* narrowly averting the falling curtain and taking several bows, and attending college with Al Rinker.

12. Paramount kc ca. 1934.

13. Bing: Paramount huston ca. 1934.

14. Untitled draft, ca. 1934.

15. A completely different release, identically titled "Say It with Music: Bing Crosby's Life Story as Told to Dave Keene." Paramount huston ca. 1934.

16. Ibid.

17. That didn't stop *Look* from repeating the story that Janis helped give him his start, in a five-page pictorial almost entirely drawn from Paramount press releases, including the cowboys-and-Indians story and his refusal to diet.

18. Paramount huston hb ca. 1935.

19. "Crosby, Inc." Paramount Lyle Rooks nhf Feb 1938.

20. Paramount huston eb ca. 1935.

21. Paramount Huston kc ca. 1935.

22. Ibid.

23. "Crosby, Inc.," op. cit.

24. Paramount Bonnet jp-f Aug. 11, 1939.

25. Paramount Bradfield jaf Nov. 11, 1938.

26. Paramount Bradfield vwf Jun. 13, 1938.

27. "By Bing Crosby," Paramount Bonnet jp Dec. 28, 1938.

28. "By Bing Crosby," Paramount edwards jp Jan. 8, 1939.

29. Paramount 1934, identifying page missing.

30. A subhead reads, "The crooner king looks himself over and after listing his good points tears down the perfect picture by admitting some really scandalous shortcomings." *Picture-Play,* Nov. 1934.

31. Ibid.

32. AI, Basil Grillo.

33. *New York Sun,* Nov. 30, 1936.

34. Ibid.

35. Complaint for Injunction, no. 410003, filed in California Superior Court Dec. 17, 1936, by O'Melveny, Tuller & Myers on behalf of Harry L. Crosby Jr., also known as Bing Crosby, Plaintiff.

36. Ibid.

37. Judgment by Judge Rubin S. Schmidt, filed in California Superior Court, Jan. 4, 1937, in case of *Harry L. Crosby Jr. v. Ben S. McGlashan.*

38. Answer to Injunction, filed in California Superior Court, Dec. 25, 1936, by Rollin L. McNitt on behalf of Ben S. McGlashan.

39. Sanjek and Sanjek, *American Popular Music Business in the 20th Century,* p. 51.

40. One controversy that did not arise until more than two decades after Crosby's death derived from an FBI memo, written June 21, 1937, by Clyde Tolson to J. Edgar Hoover, concerning racketeers and con men preying upon the Hollywood community. The sole reference to Crosby is as follows: "An instance was cited in this connection of an individual who preyed upon the sympathies of a number of motion picture actors and actresses on the plea that he was afflicted with a disease, and was unable to support himself. It seems that as a result of his contacts with a number of persons in the industry he received considerable sums of money. He is reported in one instance to have received $10,000 from Bing Crosby, and $1,600 from the mother of Ginger Rogers, and it is stated that in all he probably secured between $40,000 and $50,000. One of the persons involved took it upon herself to make certain inquiries concerning the individual and found that he was hiring expensive automobiles with some of the money which he secured from persons in the motion picture colony." In December 1999, three days before Christmas, the *New York Post* ran an inexplicably vicious attack on Crosby in which virtually every statement was misreported. It summed up the foregoing account: "Tolson revealed that Crosby had once coughed up $10,000 because of a threat hanging over his head." It claimed that Tolson's memo and Crosby's other FBI files had just been released; in fact, they had become public knowledge in 1992 and had been widely posted on the Internet for

more than five years. Bill Hoffmann and Murray Weiss, "Bing Crosby's Single Life," *New York Post,* Dec. 22, 1999.

41. His financial records for the years 1933 through 1946 were assembled by *Fortune* and set out in a memo by M. Gleason, Aug. 13, 1946. TIA.

42. Letter from Todd W. Williams to Bing Crosby, Mar. 18, 1937. Courtesy Mark Scrimger.

43. The list, published in the *New York Sunday News,* Jan. 6, 1936: 1. William Randolph Hearst, 2. Mae West, 3. steel executive C. W. Guttseit, 4. General Motors president Alfred Sloane Jr., 5. Marlene Dietrich, 6. 20th Century-Fox president Winfield Sheehan, 7. General Motors executive William F. Knudsen, 8. Bing Crosby, 9. Woolworth president B. D. Miller, 10. IBM president Thomas J. Watson.

44. "Mysterious Montague," *Time,* July 19, 1937.

45. Ibid.

46. Dick Lee, "Golf Wizard 'Vicious Thug,' Refused Bail," *New York Daily News,* Aug. 25, 1937.

47. Ibid.

48. Cal Tinney, "Went to Bat for Golfer Montague," *New York Post,* Oct. 30, 1937.

49. Lamoyne A. Jones, "Film Friends Say Montague Led Good Life," *New York Herald Tribune,* Oct. 24, 1937.

50. "Montague's 'Million' in Films Drops to Shorts at $20,000," AP story in *New York Herald Tribune,* Oct. 28, 1937.

51. Ibid.

52. An exhaustive attempt to locate an obituary for Montague proved unsuccessful.

53. The same month she took her vows (July 1952) a son, Howard, was born to Ted, who had divorced and was remarried to Margaret Mae Mattes.

54. Bing wrote of Jones, "Grover is an excellent writer and commands considerable respect both in the picture business and in the magazine field. As far as picture scripts are concerned, I don't imagine he has [a] superior." Letter from Bing Crosby to Ted Crosby, dated Wednesday (probably early 1935). HCC.

55. Ibid.

56. *Collier's* ran the article on April 27, 1935.

57. The story of Ted and the book and subsequent repercussions (which will be detailed in volume two) was pieced together through correspondence between the principals as well as AIs with Basil Grillo, Gary Crosby, Phillip Crosby, Howard Crosby, Mary Francis Crosby, Ray Flaherty, Nancy Briggs, Mozelle Seeger, Lillian Murphy, and Gloria Haley. Also Kathryn Crosby, *My Life with Bing.*

58. Letter from Larry Crosby to Ted Crosby, Apr. 12, 1935. HCC.

59. Bing's participation in a book he claimed reluctantly to condone makes it a more stimulating work. Passages that suggest Bing's touch ("Everett was cognizant of the more than moderate popularity of Bing") may indeed be his; snippets of dialogue may relate more truth than the synthetic context indicates — the bitterness Bing displays at having been aced out of "Song of the Dawn," for example, waxes in piquancy if one imagines Bing vetting the manuscript.

60. Letter from Larry to Ted, Apr. 12, 1935, op. cit.

61. Letter from Larry Crosby to Ted Crosby, July 22, 1935. HCC.

62. Letter from Ted Crosby to Larry Crosby, Oct. 6, 1936. HCC.

63. Letter from Ted Crosby to Larry Crosby, Dec. 1, 1936. HCC.

64. Letter from Larry Crosby to Ted Crosby, Mar. 9, 1937. HCC.

65. Letter from George Joy to Larry Crosby, May 7, 1937. Dad Crosby told Ted that Bing tried to fit one of his songs into a broadcast but was stopped "at the last moment" by the sponsor. Letter from Harry Crosby to Ted Crosby, Mar. 20, 1937. HCC.

66. Letter from Larry Crosby to Ted Crosby, Saturday, undated. HCC.

67. Letter from Harry Crosby to Ted Crosby, Jan. 20, 1937. HCC.

68. Letter from Larry to Ted, Mar. 9, 1937, op. cit.

69. Letter from Larry Crosby to Ted Crosby, Apr. 27, 1939. HCC.

70. Ibid.

71. E. Nils Holstius, *Gramophone,*Oct. October 1937, reprinted in *Bing,* Feb. 1971.

72. *Look,* July 6, 1937. The article reported that all the stamps were removed and given to a missionary society, which sold them to collectors.

73. Letter from Larry to Ted, Apr. 27, 1939, op. cit.

74. Smith, op. cit., p. 255.

75. Ted and Larry Crosby, *Bing,* Preface.

76. Ibid., unnumbered dedication page.

77. Smith, op. cit, p. 258.

78. Letter from Ted Crosby to Larry Crosby, Apr. 30, 1937. HCC.

79. Letter from Francis J. McKevitt to Bing Crosby, Mar. 21, 1938.

80. Ibid.

81. Letter from Harry Crosby to Ted Crosby, Sept. 29, 1936. HCC.

82. Letter from Harry Crosby to Ted Crosby, Dec. 29, 1936. HCC.

83. Letter from Harry Crosby to Ted Crosby, Oct. 13, 1936. HCC.

84. Letter from Harry Crosby to Ted, Jan. 20, 1937, op. cit.

85. Letter from Mary Rose Peterson to Ted Crosby, Dec. 17, 1934.

86. Ibid.

87. Letter from Harry to Ted, Jan. 20, 1937, op. cit.

22. Homecoming

1. Recorded for a fourteen-part BBC radio series, cited in Thompson, *Bing,* p. 242.

2. Letter from Bing Crosby to the Reverend Francis [sic] Curtis Sharp, May 4, 1937. BCCGU.

3. Ibid.

4. Letter from the Reverend Curtis J. Sharp, S.J., to Bing Crosby, May 14, 1937. BCCGU.

5. Ibid.

6. Letter from Larry Crosby to the Reverend Leo Robinson, S.J., June 12, 1937. BCCGU.

7. "Zippy Air of His Old Home Is Delight to Bing Crosby," *Spokesman-Review,* Oct. 22, 1937.

8. Ad, *Spokesman-Review,* Oct. 20, 1937.

9. Letter from Ted Crosby to Larry Crosby, Oct. 13, 1937. HCC.

10. "Gonzaga University Golden Jubilee, Harry Lillis Crosby Doctor of Letters," submitted by Reverend Sharp, July 1937. BCCGU.

11. *Spokesman-Review,* Oct. 22, 1937.

12. "Crosby Talent Quest Winners Will Be Chosen at Fox Theatre Tonight," *Spokesman-Review,* Oct. 21, 1937.

13. "Hollywood Bid Surprised Her," *Spokesman-Review,* Oct. 23, 1937.

14. "3500 'Pals' Give Ovation to Bing," *Spokesman-Review,* Oct. 23, 1937.

15. *Spokesman-Review,* Oct. 24, 1937.

16. Lloyd Pentages, "I Cover Hollywood," *Los Angeles Examiner,* Aug. 10, 1934.

17. Sharon A. Pease, "Bing Crosby (Dr. of Square Shooting) Known as Squarest Guy in Hollywood," *Down Beat,* Feb. 1938.

18. Crosby and Firestone, *Going My Own Way,* p. 39.

19. *New York Journal-American,* Jan. 23, 1938.

20. AI, Pauline Weislow.

21. AI, Phillip Crosby.

22. AI, Rosemary Clooney.

23. AI, Phillip Crosby.

24. A few spelling errors, almost certainly made by the printer, have been corrected: the mistakes included *feminity* for *femininity, Cooper* for *Couper, Bodkin* for *Botkin, Colona* for *Colonna, Chesapeak* for *Chesapeake, Swanee* for *Swannee.*

25. Telegram as sent to John and Ginger Mercer four days before the second presentation, with misspellings *(Breakway, Northhollywood)* intact. From DIXIE AND BING CROSBY, Western Union, June 21, 1938.

26. All references from the second playbill, "The Westwood Marching and Chowder Club North Hollywood Branch Presents its 2nd Breakaway Minstrel Show Saturday, June 25, 1938."

27. Ibid.

28. Transcribed from the Decca record "Mr. Crosby and Mr. Mercer," recorded July 1, 1938, also known as "Mr. Gallagher and Mr. Shean."

29. *Time,* 1938 (undated clip). TIA.

30. Cagney, *Cagney by Cagney,* p. 109.

31. Letter from Lotte Lehmann to Marie Manovill, Apr. 1, 1938.

32. Letter from Rose Bampton to Marie Manovill, Apr. 4, 1938.

33. Ibid.

34. Paramount Bradfield vwf, July 6, 1938.

35. Paramount Bonney jaf, August 5, 1938.

36. Ibid.

37. AI, Phil Harris.

38. "Picture Making Second to Crosby's Track Winners," *New York Daily Mirror,* Aug. 20, 1938.

39. AI, Charles Whittingham.

40. AI, Noble Threewitt.

41. Harrison Carroll, *Los Angeles Evening Herald-Express,* Aug. 8, 1938.

42. *New York Times,* Aug. 14, 1938.

43. Ibid.

44. "By Bing Crosby," 5 Paramount Bradfield SW, July 26, 1938. This release was published verbatim in the *New York Journal-American,* Sept. 4, 1937, with the headline, CROSBY'S HAY-BURNERS BEAR BRUNT OF HOLLYWOOD JIBES.

45. Ibid.

23. A Pocketful of Dreams

1. Anthony Quinn, RBT.

2. Budd Schulberg, *What Makes Sammy Run?* (New York: Random House, 1941).

3. Geist, *Pictures Will Talk,* p. 58.

4. "Bing Crosby the Groaner," op. cit.

5. The rapscallion Bing of the Sennett shorts was not entirely displaced; he often ended up competing with a suitor (*Waikiki Wedding*) or a parent (*Double or Nothing*). Yet the plots of all but a few of his 1930s films are shaped from the same mold.

6. "Bing Crosby Works for Bing Crosby Now," *New York World-Telegram*, Aug. 6, 1936.

7. Mel Neuhaus, "Interview: Bing Crosby," 1976, published in *Laser Marquee*, Nov. 1994.

8. *Variety*, June 17, 1936.

9. *Variety*, July 15, 1936.

10. *Variety*, July 29, 1936.

11. *Hawaii Star-Bulletin*, cited in "The Musical Tantrum," *Honolulu Magazine*, June 1988, reprinted in *Bingang*, Dec. 1988.

12. Owens, *Sweet Leilani*, p. 70.

13. Ibid., p. 72.

14. Ibid., p. 72.

15. Sheila Graham, "Crosby Plans to Quit Film," syndicated column, Sept. 4, 1936.

16. Interview with Edward A. Sutherland, Columbia University Oral History Research Project.

17. Tuttle memoir.

18. A talented performer, Ross deserved a better career than she had. Born in Omaha in 1909, she introduced "Blue Moon" in a small role in the picture *Manhattan Melodrama* in 1934. *Waikiki Wedding* was her big break, leading to her celebrated duet with Bob Hope in *The Big Broadcast of 1938*. She made two more films with Hope and reunited with Bing, albeit in a secondary role, for *Paris Honeymoon*, then went to Broadway, where her career ended in the 1940s, after she turned down the lead in *Guys and Dolls* because her husband was dying. Ross died in 1975.

19. Thompson, *Bing*, p. 113.

20. Owens, *Sweet Leilani*, p. 77.

21. Tuttle memoir.

22. Anthony Quinn, RBT.

23. Ibid.

24. Owens, *Sweet Leilani*, p. 80.

25. *Variety*, Mar. 31, 1937.

26. *Time*, undated clip. TIA.

27. *New York Times*, Mar. 25, 1937.

28. *Melody Maker*, Apr. 17, 1937.

29. *Variety*, Mar. 31, 1937.

30. *Variety*, Jan. 5, 1938.

31. "Timeline: Hawaiian Entertainment Milestones," *Billboard*, Apr. 30, 1994.

32. Promotional interview disc for Decca Records, 1955.

33. AI, Mary Carlisle.

34. The picture is replete with howlers. Frawley turns in the money, yet he is supposed to be a small-time crook; Bing provides the accompaniment for a song by flicking on a car radio, without turning on the ignition; Bing outwits the heirs with an architectural trick that would have cost more than the fortune he hoped to snag; etc.

35. Irene Thirer, "Frank Tuttle Specialty Is Holiday Movie Wares," *New York Post*, Mar. 25, 1937.

36. Letter from Joseph Breen to John Hammell, Apr. 16, 1937. Also letter from F. S. Harmon of MPAA to Breen, Sept. 16, 1937, on Will Hays's response to the scene in question. MPAA files, AMPAS.

37. The clause forbidding Paramount to bill him as the "sole star" is in his contract for *Double or Nothing*. AMPAS. In the film's onscreen credits, Crosby and Raye are listed in larger type, followed by Devine and Carlisle in smaller type, thus continuing what had become a Crosby tradition of billing him as part of a quartet.

38. AI, Trudy Erwin.

39. Ibid.

40. AI, Mary Carlisle.

41. Ibid.

42. Ibid.

43. Ibid.

44. Ironically, Devine plays the character O. Henry describes as "a well-set-up, affable, cool young man." *Pocket Book of O. Henry Stories* (New York: Washington Square Press, 1948).

45. Phyllis Hartnoll and Peter Found, *The Concise Oxford Companion to the Theater* (New York: Oxford University Press, 1992).

46. The famous sketch was written for her by Dion Titheradge, and in the film is played by Lillie and three Hollywood specialists in flustered, effete servility: William Austin, Harold Minjir, and the matchless Franklin Pangborn.

47. AI, Mary Carlisle.

48. *Chicago Defender,* Aug. 7, 1937, cited in Stratemann, *Louis Armstrong on Screen.*

49. *Chicago Defender,* Sept. 25, 1937. Cited in Stratemann, p. 73.

50. Paramount's *Doctor Rhythm* press book, which credits Armstrong with "Specialty Numbers."

51. Dudley Glass, *The Georgian,* cited in *Variety,* Sept. 15, 1932.

52. Dolph Franz to Adolph Zukor, Aug. 25, 1937. AMPAS.

53. *Hollywood Citizen News,* Oct. 28, 1937.

54. Music Files, Paramount Pictures, cited in Bloom, *Hollywood Song.*

55. Letter from Father Leo J. Robinson, S.J., to Larry Crosby, Oct. 31, 1937. BCCGU.

56. Letter from Bing Crosby (on Major Pictures Corporation letterhead) to Father Leo J. Robinson, Nov. 3, 1937. BCCGU.

57. Crosby scored 37 36 73 to Hope's 40 44 84.

58. Tuttle memoir.

59. *Variety,* Jan. 26, 1938.

60. Cited in Bach, *Marlene Dietrich,* p. 189.

61. Tuttle memoir.

62. *Melody Maker,* May 28, 1938.

63. Ibid., Aug. 6, 1938.

64. Ibid.

65. On the *David Frost Show,* Feb. 10, 1971, Bing and Louis exchanged the following comments (note: Louis was not in *Rhythm on the River*):

DF: How many different things have you done together? *High Society* . . .

BC: *Pennies from Heaven. Rhythm on the River.*

LA: There were some other pictures, too, you know.

BC: *Doctor Rhythm.* We did a lot of radio together.

LA: We had some nice hustles together.

66. AI, Joe Bushkin.

67. *Newsweek,* May 9, 1938.

68. Paramount's *Doctor Rhythm* pressbook.

69. Indeed, Bing plays his comic scenes with aplomb, underscoring his *KMH* persona by prescribing "continuous pedular agitation" to a patient who needs to walk more and fighting a pack of sailors as a way of winking at those who read in the papers of his navy encounter. He affects a number of silent-comedy stances.

70. Tuttle memoir.

71. Sidney Skolsky, "Tintypes," *New York Daily Mirror,* Aug. 18, 1938.

72. Ibid.

73. Atkins, *Arthur Jacobson,* p. 107.

74. Ibid., p. 108.

75. AI, Donald O'Connor.

76. Salisbury interview, op. cit.

77. Atkins, *Arthur Jacobson,* p. 110.

78. Ibid., p. 199.

79. Ibid., p. 110.

80. "By Bing Crosby," Paramount herbert vpf, Jan. 24, 1938.

81. Kate Cameron, "Crosby, MacMurray in Paramount Hit," *New York Daily News,* Aug. 18, 1938.

82. *Time,* Aug. 20, 1938.

83. *Life,* Aug. 1938.

84. *New York Times,* Aug. 29, 1938.

85. Ibid.

86. *The Film Criticism of Otis Ferguson,* p. 231.

87. *Life,* op. cit. The upper case *T* in *twins* is *Life*'s, as are the misspellings of the boys' names.

88. Anthony Quinn, RBT.

89. AI, Donald O'Connor.

90. Bauer, *Bing Crosby,* p. 119.

91. Rosten, *Hollywood,* p. 342.

24. Captain Courageous

1. AI, Gary Crosby.

2. "Crosby Returns from Bermuda Trip with Many Stories but No Shirts," NBC press release, Oct. 27, 1938.

3. Ibid.

4. Since the early 1980s Crosby has often been portrayed as a virtuoso philanderer, sometimes with a snide zealotry that would have made the Puritans roll their eyes. That Crosby disported himself in his early years we have seen. That he cheated on Dixie during the 1940s and after, embarking on a love affair for which he almost cashiered their marriage, we shall see, in volume two. But rumors aside, instances of such behavior in the period under discussion are not substantiated.

5. Since more than one research archive includes in its files for Florence George and/or Everett Crosby an arrest record concerning a woman of the same name and one Ira Sturman, charged at his apartment, on February 9, 1929, with possession of

narcotics and ten gallons of liquor, it may be prudent to note here that *that* Florence was a dancer and no relation to Everett's wife, who was twelve years old at the time of her namesake's misadventure. Everett was forty-two when he married Florence in New York, on May 9, 1939 (director Victor Schertzinger was best man); they had no children.

6. Ted married Hazel Nieman (children, Patricia Antonia, Catherine Anne, and Helen Delores, who entered the Holy Names order as Sister M. Catherine Joan). His second marriage was to Margaret Mae Mattes (children, Howard Mattes and Edward Nathaniel).

7. Mary Rose married Albert Peterson (a daughter, Carolyn), William Miller (a son, William), and James Pool.

8. Letters from Harry Crosby to Ted Crosby, Sept. 7 and Sept. 29, 1936. From the latter: "[Dell] was the cause of it all, after Mother got Bob to send for her, for that woman Dell to go along, we knew would spoil it all, so Marie writes us that Dell is through with her, and we take it that Dell has departed." HCC.

9. The marriage to Marie Grounitz produced a daughter, Elizabeth Ann. The children of Bob's second marriage are Cathleen Denyse, Christopher Douglas, George Robert Jr., Stephen Ross, and Junie Malia. The remaining siblings, Kay and Larry, married, respectively, Edward Mullin (a daughter, Marilyn) and Elaine Couper (a son, John, and a daughter, Molly).

10. Letter from Harry Crosby to Ted Crosby, Sept. 7, 1936. HCC.

11. *Catechism of the Catholic Church.*

12. AI, Howard Crosby.

13. Simon, *The Best of the Music Makers,* p. 147.

14. Bob Crosby, RBT.

15. Letter from Bob Crosby to Ted Crosby, Sept. 21, 1935. HCC.

16. AI, Bob Haggart.

17. Chilton, *Stomp Off, Let's Go,* p. 72.

18. AI, Bob Haggart.

19. Ibid.

20. Bob Crosby, RBT.

21. Osborne interview, op. cit.

22. Ibid.

23. Ibid.

24. AI, Rosemary Clooney.

25. Bob Crosby, RBT.

26. AI, Bob Haggart.

27. AI, Ralph Sutton.

28. AI, Ken Barnes.

29. Ibid.

30. Ibid.

31. Ibid.

32. Ibid.

33. Ibid.

34. AI, Rosemary Clooney.

35. *Joe Franklin Show,* WOR-TV, Dec. 3, 1976.

36. Lamparski, *Whatever Became Of . . . ?* (8th series), p. 37.

37. AI, Les Paul.

38. Mercer recorded his own version in the 1960s with Bobby Darin.

39. Alton Cook, "Taking Rest Cure in Gay Night Life," *New York World Telegram*, Sept. 7, 1940.

40. Aldous Huxley, "Popular Music," in *Along the Road*.

41. AI, Helen Votachenko.

42. Paramount Bradfield hf Aug. 4, 1938.

43. Ibid.

44. Paramount Bradfield jhf Aug. 11, 1938.

45. Kaminsky, *My Life in Jazz*, p. 68.

46. Thompson, *Bing*, p. 243.

47. Erskine Johnson, "Behind the Makeup," *Los Angeles Examiner*, June 23, 1938.

48. Kate Cameron, "Bing and Bob Crosby Star at Paramount," New York *Daily News*, Jan. 26, 1939.

49. Atkins, *David Butler*, p. 183.

50. *Life*, Aug. 14, 1939.

51. Ibid., p. 184.

52. Letter from Bing Crosby to John Mercer, Apr. 13, 1939. Georgia State University, Special Collections.

53. Atkins, *David Butler*, p. 181.

54. Ibid., p. 181.

55. University of Southern California Archive, Universal Collection, Weekly Status Reports on *East Side of Heaven*, Jan. 20, 1939.

56. Ibid., Jan. 27, 1939.

57. Atkins, *David Butler*, p. 186.

58. Ibid., p. 186.

59. Interviewed by Atkins for Directors Guild of America Oral History project, Jan. 14–June 22, 1977.

60. Weekly Status Reports, op. cit, Feb. 3, 1939.

61. Ibid., Feb. 17, 1939.

62. Ibid., Feb. 24, 1939.

63. Ibid., Mar. 10, 1939. The forty-four days do not count the delay caused by Blondell's illness. At first, estimates of the overrun were $13,000, but that figure was reduced to $10,000 after five weeks of polishing the budget. The lower figure was approved April 14.

64. Letter from Joseph Breen to Maurice Pivar at Universal, Jan. 9, 1939. MPAA files, AMPAS.

65. Letter from Joseph Breen to Will H. Hays, Mar. 25, 1939. MPAA files, AMPAS.

66. Ibid.

67. JWTPR, Feb. 16, 1939, by R. J. Brewsrer. Many radio references have the Music Maids appearing with Bing in January and earlier; they made their debut on February 23.

68. AI, Trudy Erwin.

69. Ibid.

70. Ibid.

71. AI, Alice Ludes.

72. The more prominent members of the band were Manny Klein, Bobby Van Eps, and Milton DeLugg.

73. *Variety,* May 10, 1939.

74. Kate Cameron, "Bing Crosby Bows in the Music Hall," *New York Daily News,* May 5, 1939.

75. *Variety,* Apr. 12, 1939.

76. Ad pull-quote, *Variety,* May 10, 1939.

77. Background interview by M. Gleason, Aug. 4, 1946. TIA.

25. What's New

1. Recorded for a fourteen-part BBC radio series, cited in Thompson, *Bing,* p. 243.

2. Green and Laurie, *Show Biz from Vaude to Video,* p. 45.

3. Ad, *Spokesman-Review,* Aug. 31, 1939.

4. Ibid.

5. *Variety,* Aug. 23, 1939.

6. AI, Dante DiPaolo.

7. AI, Rosemary Clooney.

8. Salisbury interview, op. cit.

9. Ulanov, *The Incredible Crosby,* p. 149.

10. Louella Parsons, "Children Vie with Bing in 'Star Maker,'" Hearst syndicate, Aug. 22, 1939.

11. *Time,* Sept. 4, 1939.

12. Memo from Alfred Wright Jr. to David W. Hulburd Jr., "Subject: The Star Maker," Aug. 23, 1939. TIA.

13. *Variety,* Jan. 3, 1940.

14. Not to be confused with "My Dog Rover," sung at his mother's sodality with leash in hand. See note 45 to Chapter 4.

15. AI, Bob Haggart.

16. Ibid.

17. John McDonough, *Down Beat,* Mar. 1994.

18. *Time,* Nov. 6, 1939.

19. Letter from Arne Fogel to author, 1995.

20. William Ruhlmann, "The Road to Bing Crosby," *Goldmine,* Dec. 24, 1993.

21. *Time,* Sept. 4, 1939.

22. Ibid. An article in *Fortune* weeks before *Time*'s (both came out in September 1939) said that Crosby's "records compose no less than 9 percent of [Decca's] output." *Time*'s far larger figure would appear to be the accurate one, however, as *Time* acknowledged *Fortune* as its main source and changed the number according to its own subsequent fact-checking.

23. See note 16 for Chapter 19.

24. Although the rule indicated here holds generally for pop records, exceptions abound. Al Jolson's 1940s remakes, for example, are the ones for which he is remembered, in part because the technology had improved and Jolson had become a better singer — the comforting baritone (rather than nattering tenor) popularized by the movie based on his life, *The Jolson Story* (1946). Similarly, any late-career Judy Garland version of "Over the Rainbow" has greater iconic power than the original for reflecting all the intervening personal drama. With Crosby, the iconic power generally resides with the earlier versions, though the later ones are often musically superior.

25. The 1955 Decca promotional disc (op. cit) and a 1960 interview with Wilfred Thomas, Oct. 15, 1960, cited in Reynolds, *Part Two*, p. 139.

26. "Washington Breakdown," recorded by the Alamanac Singers, March 1941.

27. A. Scott Berg, *Goldwyn* (New York: Knopf, 1989), p. 346.

28. Robinson and Gordon, *Ballad of an American*, p. 77.

29. Louis Untermeyer liner notes, Bing Crosby, *The Man Without a Country* and *What So Proudly We Hail* (featuring *Ballad for Americans*), Decca DL 8020.

30. Robinson and Gordon, *Ballad of an American*, p. 96.

31. Ibid., p. 95.

32. Ibid., p. 100.

33. Wallace Stegner, "The Radio Priest and His Flock," by Wallace Stegner, cited by Albert Fried, *FDR and His Enemies*, p. 224. Fried himself writes of Coughlin's "superb delivery, his beautifully modulated baritone voice, his rolling cadences, his delicate trills, his endless alliteration. He was an artist of the airwaves."

34. Peters, *The House of Barrymore*, p. 441.

35. *Philadelphia Record*, Nov. 11, 1940, cited in unidentified clip, "Philly Record Attacks Crosby for F.D.R. Blast," Nov. 12, 1940. BCCGU. Also "Race Track by WPA," *New York Daily News*, May 16, 1940.

26. Easy Riders

1. AI, Bob Hope.

2. Bob Hope, *Have Tux, Will Travel*, p. 131.

3. Ibid., p. 129.

4. AI, Dolores Hope.

5. *New York Herald Tribune*, Nov. 7, 1937.

6. JWTPR, July 14, 1938, by Frank Woodruff.

7. AI, Dolores Hope.

8. AI, Bob Hope.

9. Hope, *Have Tux, Will Travel*, p. 140.

10. *Champagne Waltz* and *The Texas Rangers*.

11. The new title required arbitration when Columbia Pictures complained that it was planning an epic called *Singapore*. The Columbia entry was never made.

12. Maxene Andrews, interviewed by Mark Scrimger and Bob Pasch, 1992, as transcribed by the author; an edited version was published in *Bingang*, Dec. 1992.

13. Ibid.

14. Ibid.

15. Ibid.

16. Ibid.

17. Ibid. According to Vic Schoen, Dave Kapp produced the session and Jack was not present in the studio, though, of course, Bing may have said as much to him after the fact.

18. Joseph F. Laredo liner notes, *Bing Crosby and the Andrews Sisters* (Decca).

19. *Lucky*, p. 157.

20. AI, Bob Hope.

21. Ibid.

22. *Time* memo regarding interview with David Butler from M. Gleason to S. Olson, Aug. 4, 1946. TIA.

23. *Lucky*, p. 157.

24. AI, Melville Shavelson.

25. Lamour, *My Side of the Road,* p. 88.

26. AI, Bob Hope.

27. Ibid.

28. Lamour, *My Side of the Road,* p. 89.

29. Anthony Quinn, RBT.

30. Marx, *The Secret Life of Bob Hope,* p. 140.

31. Anthony Quinn, RBT.

32. Marx, *The Secret Life of Bob Hope,* p. 140.

33. Parish, *The Paramount Pretties,* p. 340.

34. AI, Bob Hope.

35. AI, Dolores Hope.

36. Anthony Quinn, RBT.

37. AI, Melville Shavelson.

38. Salisbury interview, op. cit.

39. Neuhaus interview, op. cit.

40. This line and those that follow taken from Crosby's copy of the script for *Road to Morocco.* AMPAS.

41. *Time* Butler memo, op. cit.

42. Ibid.

43. *The Film Criticism of Otis Ferguson,* p. 356.

44. AI, Mort Lachman.

45. *Lucky,* p. 158.

46. *Time* memo, "Cottrell and Company," 1946. TIA.

47. Ulanov, *The Incredible Crosby,* p. 165.

48. AI, Melville Shavelson.

49. *Lucky,* p. 159.

50. AI, Bob Hope.

51. A few of the itemized gags are "What are you, yellow?"; "It's only a kangaroo"; "No thanks, we ate four days ago"; "[Lamour] disappears during song and Bob and Bing kiss each other"; "I could have won the Academy Award." Legal papers, *Road to Morocco.* AMPAS.

52. AI, Basil Grillo.

53. Ibid.

54. Ibid.

55. Ibid.

56. AI, Johnny Lange.

57. AI, Gary Crosby.

58. *Person to Person,* CBS-TV, 1954. Bing tells the same story in *Lucky,* pp. 161–62.

59. *Lucky,* p. 35.

60. AI, Skitch Henderson.

61. AI, Eddie Bracken.

62. AI, Mort Lachman.

63. AI, Melville Shavelson.

64. AI, Rory Burke.

65. Ibid.

66. Ibid.

67. Ulanov, *The Incredible Crosby,* p. 169.

68. AI, Barry Ulanov.

69. Gerald Mast describes Crosby, Hope, and Lamour as "the Marx Brothers with heart," *Can't Help Singin',* pp. 223–26.

70. Shipman, *The Story of Cinema,* p. 597.

71. Seldes, *The Public Arts,* p. 131.

72. *Variety,* Jan. 3, 1940.

73. AI, Mort Lachman.

74. Ibid.

75. Martin Scorsese, "Guilty Pleasures," undated article, *American Film,* 1994.

76. *Time,* Mar. 25, 1940.

77. Frank S. Nugent, "Posting a Proceed-With-Caution Sign on Paramount's 'Road to Singapore,'" *New York Times,* Mar. 14, 1940.

78. Photograph, *New York Times,* Mar. 13, 1940, cited in Dupuis, *Bunny Berigan,* p. 223.

79. *Variety,* Mar. 20, 1940.

80. Ibid.

81. Ibid., Apr. 10, 1940.

82. Kate Cameron, "Paramount Goes Gay in a Large Way," *New York Daily News,* Mar. 14, 1940.

83. Kay, *Box Office Champs,* p. 16.

Interviews and Bibliography

The primary interviews on which this work is based were conducted by the author or research associates. Vital interviews were also made available by John McDonough (Frank Capra, Matty Malneck, and Al Rinker), James T. Maher (John Scott Trotter), and Mark Scrimger and Bob Pasch (Maxene Andrews). Numerous interviews with Bing Crosby and others, taken from radio and TV broadcasts and diverse publications, are identified in the source notes. The author interviews are as follows:

Scott Ables, Anna Maria Alberghetti, Steve Allen, Mike Alpert, Bill Angelos, Army Archerd, Bob Bakewell, Danny Bank, Ken Barnes, Marti Barris, Rose Baylis, Tom Bell, Milt Bernhardt, Ann Blythe, Victor Borge, Jimmy Bowen, Eddie Bracken, Buddy Bregman, Nancy Briggs, Earl Brown, Les Brown, Pamela Crosby Brown, Violet Brown, Bud Brubaker, Pat Stanley Burke (Matthews), Rory Burke, Fran Bushkin, Joe Bushkin, Red Buttons, Billy Byers, John Cahill, Sammy Cahn, Frank Capp, Mary Carlisle (Blakely), Bill Challis, Saul Chaplin, Doc Cheatham, Rosemary Clooney, Alan Cohen, Dawn Coleman, George Coleman, Perry Como, Frank Converse, Alex Cord, Gary Crosby, Gregory Crosby, Harry Crosby, Howard Crosby, Janet Crosby, Mary Francis Crosby, Nathaniel Crosby, Phillip Crosby, Susan Crosby, Blythe Danner, Fred DeCordova, Bob DeFlores, Alan Dell, Norman Dewes, Dante DiPaolo, Kurt Dieterle, Ivan Ditmars, Ray Dolby, Father John W. Donahue, S.J., Robert Dornan, Gordon Douglas, Richard Drewitt, Ted Durein, Don Eagle, Harry "Sweets" Edison, Blake Edwards, Trudy Erwin, Nanette Fabray (MacDougall), Robert Farnum, José Feliciano, Bob Finkel, Alan Fisher, Ray Flaherty, Rhonda Fleming, Father Patrick J. Ford, S.J., Sister Mary Francis, John Frigo, Jack Fulton, Milt Gabler, Beverly Garland, Leslie Gaylor, Mitzi Gaynor, Dick Gibson, Johnny Grant, Hy Grill, Basil Grillo, Bob Haggart, Florence Haley, Gloria Haley, Jack Haley Jr., Jake Hanna, Bill Harbach, Phil Harris, Kitty Carlisle Hart, Edmund Hartman, Skitch Henderson, Sid Herman, Ray Herzog, Jim Hillbun, Milt Hinton, Celeste Holm, Bob Hope, Dolores Hope, Dr. George J. Hummer, Marsha Hunt, Jack Hupp, Carl Jefferson, Herb Jeffries, Hank Jones, Hal Kantor,

Frieda Kapp, Mickey Kapp, Joseph H. King, Robert Kipp, Buz Kohan, Miles Krueger, Mort Lachman, Duncan Lamont, Burton Lane, Johnny Lange, Peggy Lee, Gene Lester, Howard Levine, Lou Levy, Frank Liberman, Rich Little, Jay Livingston, Alice Ludes, A. C. Lyles, Shiela Lynn, June MacCloy (Butler), Murdo MacKenzie, James T. Maher, John Mandel, Carolyn Manovill, Gerald Marks, Tony Martin, Billy May, Ginger Mercer, Don Mike, Henry Miller, Donald Mills, Geoff Milne, Lyle Moore, Pete Moore, Tom Moore, John Mullin, Lillian Murphy, Farlin Myers, David Nelson, Sheri North, Red Norvo, Robert O'Brien, Donald O'Connor, Jerry O'Connor, Lillian Oliver, Nancy Olson, Bill Osborn, Norman Panama, Marty Passetta, John Patrick, Les Paul, Elsie Perry, William Perlberg Jr., Jerry Pickman, Terry Polesie, Dorothea Ponce, Joey Porter, Mike Post, Leslie Raddatz, Fred Reynolds, Carole Richards, Julia Rinker, Max Roach, Bob Roberts, Kenneth Roberts, Buddy Rogers, Roy Rogers, Lina Romay (O'Brien), Bob Roose, Meta Rosenberg, Kevin Ross, Cal Rossi, Jimmy Rowles, Iris Flores Schirmer, Vic Schoen, Mozelle Seeger, Nick Sevano, Hazel Sharp (Diane Notestine), Melville Shavelson, Artie Shaw, Virgil H. Sherrill, Bob Sidney, Kevin Silva, Frank Sinatra Jr., Nancy Sinatra, Ann Slater, Daniel G. Smith, Francis X. Smith, Johnny Smith, Michael Smith, Paul Smith, Kay Starr, Gary Stevens, Rise Stevens, Gloria Stuart, Ralph Sutton, Jim Tainsley, Norma Teagarden (Friedlander), Todd Thomas, Noble Threewitt, Mel Tormé, Marguerite (McGhee) Toth, Arthur Tracy, Barry Ulanov, Mickey Van Gerbig, Bobbe Van Heusen, Felisa Vanoff, Betty Caulfield Vietor, Helen (Tuttle) Votachenko, Robert Wagner, Ray Walston, Pauline Weislow, Sandy Wernick, Paul Weston, Charlie Whittingham, Spiegel Wilcox, Max Wilk, Joe Williams, Jane Wyman.

Books and Selected Articles about Bing Crosby

Arnold, Maxine. "Man at the Top." *Photoplay,* March 1947.

Barnes, Ken. *The Crosby Years.* New York: St. Martin's Press, 1980.

Bauer, Barbara. *Bing Crosby.* New York: Pyramid Publications, 1977.

Bishop, Bert and John Bassett. *Bing: Just for the Record.* Gateshead, England: International Crosby Circle, 1980.

Bookbinder, Robert. *The Films of Bing Crosby.* Secaucus, N.J.: Citadel Press, 1977.

Carpozi, George Jr. *The Fabulous Life of Bing Crosby.* New York: Manor Books, 1977.

Crosby, Bing with Pete Martin. *Call Me Lucky.* New York: Simon & Schuster, 1953.

Crosby, Gary with Ross Firestone. *Going My Own Way.* Garden City, N.Y.: Doubleday, 1983.

Crosby, Kathryn. *Bing and Other Things.* New York: Meredith Press, 1967.

———. *My Life with Bing.* Wheeling, Ill.: Collage, 1983.

Crosby, Ted. *The Story of Bing Crosby.* Cleveland: World, 1946.

Crosby, Ted and Larry. *Bing.* Los Angeles: Bolton Printing Co., 1937.

Edwards, Anne. "Bing Crosby The Going My Way Star in Rancho Santa Fe." *Architectural Digest.* April 1996.

Feather, Leonard, "Bing: The Father of Pop." *Melody Maker.* June 19, 1976.

Hamann, G. D., editor. *Bing Crosby in the 30's.* Hollywood: Filming Today, 1996.

———. *Bing Crosby in the 40's.* Hollywood: Filming Today, 1997.

———. *Bing Crosby in the 50's.* Hollywood: Filming Today, 1998.

———. *Bing Crosby in the 60's.* Hollywood: Filming Today, 1999.

———. *Bing Crosby in the 70's.* Hollywood: Filming Today, 1999.

Hentoff, Nat. "Bing Crosby Is Coming to Town." *New York News Magazine.* December 5, 1976.

Kiner, Larry. *Directory & Log of the Bing Crosby Cremo Singer Radio Series.* Self-published, 1973.

King, Joseph A. "Bing Crosby's Irish Roots: The Harrigan Family of Co. Cork, New Brunswick (Can.), Minnesota, and Washington." *Minnesota Genealogist* 14, no. 4 (1983).

Marill, Alvin H. "Bing Crosby Photographed as Pleasingly as He Sang." *Films in Review.* June–July 1968.

Macfarlane, Malcolm. *Bing: A Diary of a Lifetime.* Gateshead, England: International Crosby Circle, 1997.

Mielke, Randall G. *Road to Box Office: The Seven Film Comedies of Bing Crosby, Bob Hope and Dorothy Lamour.* Jefferson, N.C.: McFarland, 1997.

Mello, Edward J. and Tom McBride. *Crosby on Record.* San Francisco: Mello's Music, 1950.

Mize, Dr. J. T. H. *Bing.* Chicago: Who Is Who in Music, 1946.

Morgereth, Timothy A. *Bing Crosby: A Discography, Radio Program List and Filmography.* Jefferson, N.C.: McFarland, 1987.

Murray, Ken. "Louis, Bix Had Most Influence on Der Bingle." *Down Beat.* July 14, 1950.

Neuhaus, Mel. "Interview: Bing Crosby." *Laser Marquee,* November 1994.

O'Connell, Sheldon with Gord Atkinson. *Bing: A Voice for All Seasons.* Tralee, Ireland: Kerryman Ltd., 1984.

Osterholm, J. Roger. *Bing Crosby: A Bio-Bibliography.* Westport, Conn.: Greenwood Press, 1994.

Pairpoint, Lionel. *". . . And Here's Bing!" Bing Crosby: The Radio Directories.* Gateshead, England: International Crosby Circle, 2000.

Pugh, Colin. *Alternate Bing Crosby.* Bristol, England: John Joyce, 1988.

Reilly, Jim. *The Songs of Bing Crosby on Compact Disc.* Self-published, 1996.

Reynolds, Fred. *The Road to Hollywood.* Rev. ed. Bristol, England: John Joyce, 1986.

———. *The Crosby Collection, Part One: 1926–1934.* Self-published, 1991–97.

———. *The Crosby Collection, Part Two: 1935–1941.* Self-published, 1991–97.

———. *The Crosby Collection, Part Three: 1942–1950.* Self-published, 1991–97.

———. *The Crosby Collection, Part Four: 1951–1960.* Self-published, 1991–97.

———. *The Crosby Collection, Part Five: 1961–1977.* Self-published, 1991–97.

Reynolds, Quentin. "The Kid from Spokane." *Collier's.* April 27, 1935.

Ruhlmann, William. "Swinging (On a) Star: The Road to Bing Crosby." *Goldmine,* December 24, 1993.

Scrimger, Mark. "An Intimate Tour of Bing's Hometown, Spokane." *Bingang,* April 1984.

Shepherd, Donald and Robert F. Slatzer. *Bing Crosby: The Hollow Man.* New York: St. Martin's Press, 1981.

Staff. "Bing Crosby: He Is Still Falling Uphill." *Time,* April 7, 1941.

———. "Going His Way Is a Nation's Habit After Twenty Years of Crosby Song." *Newsweek,* January 28, 1946.

———. "The Crosby Story." *Billboard,* October 26, 1946.

———. "The Great Throat: Bing Crosby, First in Films, First on the Air, and First on the Phonographs of His Countrymen." *Fortune,* January 1947.

———. *Bing Crosby Album* (magazine). New York: Dell, 1949.

———. *The Bing Crosby Story* (magazine). New York: Lopez, 1977.

Stimson, William. "Bing Crosby: The Road to Hollywood." *Spokane,* 1977.

———. "Bing We Hardly Knew Ye." *Pacific Northwest,* December 1987.

Taylor, Vernon Wesley. "Hail KMH!" (six parts). *The Crosby Voice,* Bing Crosby Victorian Society, September 1984, February 1985, May 1985, September 1985, November 1985, February 1986.

Thomas, Bob. *The One and Only Bing.* New York: Grosset & Dunlap, 1977.

Thompson, Charles. *Bing.* New York: David McKay, 1976.

———. *The Complete Crosby.* London: W. H. Allen, 1978.

Ulanov, Barry. *The Incredible Crosby.* New York: Whittlesey House, 1948.

Vandervoort, Paul II. "Uncle Sam Sans Whiskers." *Band Leaders,* January 1, 1946.

Venables, Ralph. "Cross-Section on Crosby." *Vocal Jazz,* London, 1945.

Zwisohn, Laurence J. *Bing Crosby: A Lifetime in Music.* Los Angeles: Palm Tree Library, 1978.

Selected Bibliography

Adams, Joey. *Here's to the Friars.* New York: Crown, 1976.

Adams, William Forbes. *Ireland and Irish Emigration to the New World.* Baltimore: Genealogical Publishing Co. (reprint), 1980.

Agee, James. *Agee on Film.* New York: McDowell, Obolensky, 1958.

Andre, Marcella, editor. *Columbia: Portrait of a Label.* New York: Sony Music Entertainment Inc., 1991.

Andrews, Maxene and Bill Gilbert. *Over Here, Over There; The Andrews Sisters and the USO Stars in World War II.* New York: Zebra Books, 1993.

Arce, Hector. *Gary Cooper.* New York: William Morrow, 1979.

———. *Groucho.* New York: G. P. Putnam's Sons, 1979.

Armstrong, Louis. *Swing That Music.* London: Longmans, Green and Co., 1936.

———. *Satchmo: My Life in New Orleans.* New York: Prentice-Hall, 1954.

Arnold, William. *Shadowland.* New York: McGraw-Hill, 1978.

Astaire, Fred. *Steps in Time.* New York: Harper & Row, 1959.

Atkins, Irene Kahn, editor. *Arthur Jacobson.* Metuchen, N.J.: Directors Guild of America and Scarecrow Press, 1991.

———. *David Butler.* Metuchen, N.J.: Directors Guild of America and Scarecrow Press, 1993.

Bach, Bob and Ginger Mercer. *Our Huckleberry Friend: The Life, Times, and Lyrics of Johnny Mercer.* Secaucus, N.J.: Lyle Stuart, 1982.

Balio, Tino. *Grand Design: Hollywood as a Modern Business Enterprise, 1930–1939.* Berkeley, Calif.: University of California Press, 1995.

Barnouw, Erik. *A Tower in Babel*. New York: Oxford University Press, 1966.

———. *The Golden Web*. New York: Oxford University Press, 1968.

Barrett, Mary Ellin. *Irving Berlin: A Daughter's Memoir*. New York: Simon & Schuster, 1994.

Barrios, Richard. *A Song in the Dark: The Birth of the Musical Film*. New York: Oxford University Press, 1995.

Basie, Count with Albert Murray. *Good Morning Blues*. New York: Random House, 1985.

Beck, Jerry and Will Friedwald. *Looney Tunes and Merrie Melodies*. New York: Henry Holt, 1989.

Behr, Edward. *Prohibition*. New York: Arcade, 1996.

Bell-Metereau, Rebecca. *Hollywood Androgyny*. New York: Columbia University Press, 1993.

Beloff, Jim. *The Ukukeke: A Visual History*. San Francisco: Miller Freeman Books, 1997.

Bennett, Tony with Will Friedwald. *The Good Life*. New York: Pocket Books, 1998.

Benny, Jack and Joan. *Sunday Nights at Seven: The Jack Benny Story*. New York: Warner Books, 1990.

Benny, Mary Livingstone and Hilliard Marks with Marcia Borie. *Jack Benny*. New York: Doubleday, 1978.

Berger, Edward, editor. *Bassically Speaking: An Oral History of George Duvivier*. Metuchen, N.J.: Institute of Jazz Studies and Scarecrow Press, 1993.

Bergman, Ingrid and Alan Burgess. *My Story*. New York: Delacorte Press, 1980.

Bergreen, Laurence. *As Thousands Cheer: The Life of Irving Berlin*. New York: Viking, 1990.

———. *Louis Armstrong: An Extravagant Life*. New York: Broadway Books, 1997.

Blankenship, Mrs. George E. *Early History of Thurston County, Washington Together with Biographies and Reminiscences of Those Identified with Pioneer Days*. Self-published, 1914.

Bloom, Ken. *Hollywood Song*. 3 vols. New York: Facts on File, 1995.

Blumenthal, Ralph. *Stork Club*. Boston: Little, Brown, 2000.

Bogdanovitch, Peter. *Who the Devil Made It*. New York: Alfred A. Knopf, 1997.

Bogue, Merwyn. *Ish Kabibble*. Baton Rouge, La.: Louisiana State University Press, 1989.

Bordman, Gerald. *American Musical Theatre*. New York: Oxford University Press, 1986.

Bowen, Jimmy and Jim Jerome. *Rough Mix*. New York: Simon & Schuster, 1997.

Buxton, Frank and Bill Owen. *The Big Broadcast 1920–1950*. Rev. ed. New York: Viking, 1966.

Cagney, James. *Cagney by Cagney*. Garden City, N.Y.: Doubleday, 1976.

Cahn, Sammy. *I Should Care*. New York: Arbor House, 1974.

Cantor, Eddie and David Freedman. *Ziegfeld: The Great Glorifier*. New York: Alfred H. King, 1934.

Capra, Frank. *The Name Above the Title*. New York: Macmillan, 1971.

Carmichael, Hoagy. *The Stardust Road*. Bloomington, Ind.: Indiana University Press (reprint), 1983.

Carroll, Carroll. *None of Your Business or My Life with J. Walter Thompson*. Toronto: Cowles, 1970.

Catechism of the Catholic Church. Liguori, Mo.: Libreria Editrice Vaticana/ Liguori Publications, 1994.

Chaplin, Saul. *The Golden Age of Movie Musicals and Me.* Norman, Okla.: University of Oklahoma Press, 1994.

Chilton, John. *Who's Who of Jazz.* Rev. ed. New York: Da Capo, 1972.

————. *Stomp Off, Let's Go! The Story of Bob Crosby's Bob Cats & Big Band.* London: Jazz Book Service, 1983.

————. *Let the Good Times Roll: The Story of Louis Jordan and His Music.* London: Quartet, 1992.

Citron, Stephen. *Noel & Cole.* New York: Oxford University Press, 1993.

Clooney, Rosemary with Raymond Strait. *This for Remembrance.* Chicago: Playboy Press, 1977.

Clooney, Rosemary with Joan Barthel. *Girl Singer.* New York: Doubleday, 1999.

Cohan, Steve and Ina Rae Hark, editors. *The Road Movie Book.* London: Routledge, 1997.

Condon, Eddie. *We Called It Music.* Rev. ed. New York: Da Capo, 1988.

Conrad, Barnaby. *Name Dropping: Tales from My Barbary Coast Saloon.* New York: HarperCollins, 1994.

Cooper, Jackie with Dick Kleiner. *Please Don't Shoot My Dog.* New York: William Morrow, 1981.

Coslow, Sam. *Cocktails for Two.* New Rochelle, N.Y.: Arlington House, 1977.

Cronkite, Kathy. *On the Edge of Darkness.* New York: Doubleday, 1994.

Crowe, Cameron. *Conversations with Wilder.* New York: Alfred A. Knopf, 1999.

Crowther, Bruce and Mike Pinfold. *The Jazz Singers.* Poole, England: Blanford Press, 1986.

Curtis, Jenny. *Bob Hope.* New York: Metro Books, 1999.

Dance, Stanley. *The World of Swing.* New York: Scribners, 1974.

————. *The World of Earl Hines.* New York: Scribners, 1977.

Daniel, Clifton, editor. *Chronicle of the 20th Century.* Mount Kisco, N.Y.: Chronicle, 1987.

Davies, Marion. *The Times We Had.* Indianapolis: Bobbs-Merrill, 1975.

Davis, Ronald L. *The Glamour Factory.* Dallas: Southern Methodist University Press, 1993.

Deffaa, Chip. *In the Mainstream.* Metuchen, N.J.: Institute of Jazz Studies and Scarecrow Press, 1992.

————. *Blue Rhythms.* Urbana, Ill.: University of Illinois Press, 1996.

Delaunay, Charles. *Django Reinhardt.* New York: Da Capo (reprint), 1981.

DeLong, Thomas A. *Pops: Paul Whiteman, King of Jazz.* Piscataway, N.J.: New Century, 1983.

Dexter, Dave Jr. *Playback.* New York: Billboard Publications, 1976.

Dietrich, Marlene. *Marlene.* New York: Avon (reprint), 1990.

Donaldson, Ellen, editor. *The Walter Donaldson Songbook.* Winona, Minn.: Hal Leonard, 1988.

Douglas, Mike with Thomas Kelly and Michael Heaton. *I'll Be Right Back.* New York: Simon & Schuster, 2000.

Dunning, John. *On the Air: The Encyclopedia of Old-Time Radio.* New York: Oxford University Press, 1998.

Dupuis, Robert. *Bunny Berigan: Elusive Legend of Jazz.* Baton Rouge, La.: Louisiana State University Press, 1993.

Dyar, Ralph E. *News for an Empire: The Story of the Spokesman-Review.* Caldwell, Idaho: Caxton Printers, 1952.

Eames, John Douglas. *The Paramount Story.* New York: Crown Publishers, 1985.

Eberly, Phillip K. *Music in the Air.* New York: Hastings House, 1982.

Edmonds, I. G. *Paramount Pictures and the People Who Made Them.* San Diego: A. S. Barnes, 1980.

Eisenberg, Evan. *The Recording Angel.* New York: McGraw-Hill, 1987.

Ellington, Duke. *Music Is My Mistress.* Garden City, N.Y.: Doubleday, 1973.

Ellison, Ralph. *The Collected Essays of Ralph Ellison.* New York: Modern Library, 1995.

Emerson, Ken. *Doo-Dah! Stephen Foster and the Rise of American Popular Culture.* New York: Simon & Schuster, 1997.

Epstein, Daniel Mark. *Nat King Cole.* New York: Farrar, Straus and Giroux, 1999.

Evans, Philip R. and Larry F. Kiner. *Tram — The Frank Trumbauer Story.* Metuchen, N.J.: Institute of Jazz Studies and Scarecrow Press, 1994.

Ewen, David. *Great Men of American Popular Song.* Rev. ed. Englewood Cliffs, N.J.: Prentice-Hall, 1972.

Eyman, Scott. *Ernst Lubitsch: Laughter in Paradise.* New York: Simon & Schuster, 1993.

———. *The Speed of Sound: Hollywood and the Talkie Revolution 1926–1930.* New York: Simon & Schuster, 1997.

Fein, Irving A. *Jack Benny: An Intimate Biography.* New York: G. P. Putnam's Sons, 1976.

Ferguson, Otis, edited by Robert Wilson. *The Film Criticism of Otis Ferguson.* Philadelphia: Temple University Press, 1971.

Ferguson, Otis, edited by Dorothy Chamberlain and Robert Wilson. *In the Spirit of Jazz: The Otis Ferguson Reader.* New York: Da Capo, 1997.

Feuer, Jane. *The Hollywood Musical.* Bloomington, Ind.: Indiana University Press, 1993.

Fidelman, Geoffrey Mark. *First Lady of Song: Ella Fitzgerald for the Record.* New York: Carol Publishing Group, 1994.

Fields, Armond and L. Marc. *From the Bowery to Broadway: Lew Fields and the Roots of American Popular Theater.* New York: Oxford University Press, 1993.

Finler, Joel W. *The Hollywood Story.* New York: Crown, 1988.

Fisher, Eddie. *Eddie: My Life, My Loves.* New York: Harper & Row, 1981.

Fitzgerald, Margaret E. and Joseph A. King. *The Uncounted Irish.* Toronto: P. D. Meany, 1990.

Fontaine, Joan. *No Bed of Roses.* New York: William Morrow, 1978.

Fowles, Jib. *Starstruck.* Washington, D.C.: Smithsonian Institution Press, 1992.

Foy, Eddie and Alvin Harlow. *Clowning Through Life.* New York: Dutton, 1928.

Frank, Gerold. *Judy.* New York: Da Capo (reprint), 1999.

Frank, Rusty E. *Tap!* Rev. ed. New York: Da Capo, 1994.

Franklin, Joe. *Joe Franklin's Encyclopedia of Comedians.* New York: Bell, 1985.

Franklin, Joe with R. J. Marx. *Up Late with Joe Franklin.* New York: Scribners, 1995.

Freeman, Bud. *You Don't Look Like a Musician.* Detroit: Balamp, 1974.

Freidel, Frank. *Franklin D. Roosevelt: A Rendezvous with Destiny.* Boston: Little, Brown, 1990.

Fried, Albert. *FDR and His Enemies.* New York: St. Martin's Press, 1999.

Friedwald, Will. *Jazz Singing*. New York: Scribners, 1990.

———. *Sinatra! The Song Is You*. New York: Scribners, 1995.

Furia, Philip. *Ira Gershwin*. New York: Oxford University Press, 1996.

Gabbard, Krin. *Jammin' at the Margins*. Chicago: University of Chicago Press, 1996.

Gabler, Neal. *An Empire of Their Own*. New York: Doubleday, 1989.

Garnett, Tay with Fredda Dudley Balling. *Light Your Torches and Pull Up Your Tights*. New Rochelle, N.Y.: Arlington House, 1973.

Gehring, Wes D. *Leo McCarey and the Comic Anti-Hero in American Film*. New York: Arno Press, 1980.

Geist, Kenneth L. *Pictures Will Talk*. New York: Scribners, 1978.

Gelatt, Roland. *The Fabulous Phonograph*. Philadelphia: Lippincott, 1955.

Giddins, Gary. *Riding on a Blue Note*. New York: Oxford University Press, 1981.

———. *Satchmo*. New York: Doubleday, 1988.

Gioia, Ted. *The History of Jazz*. New York: Oxford University Press, 1997.

Goldberg, Isaac. *Tin Pan Alley*. New York: John Day, 1930.

Goldenson, Leonard H. with Marvin J. Wolf. *Beating the Odds*. New York: Scribners, 1991.

Goldman, Herbert G. *Jolson: The Legend Comes to Life*. New York: Oxford University Press, 1988.

———. *Banjo Eyes: Eddie Cantor and the Birth of Modern Stardom*. New York: Oxford University Press, 1997.

Goodman, Ezra. *The Fifty-Year Decline and Fall of Hollywood*. New York: Simon & Schuster, 1961.

Gottfried, Martin. *Nobody's Fool: The Lives of Danny Kaye*. New York: Simon & Schuster, 1994.

Gourse, Leslie. *Louis' Children*. New York: William Morrow, 1984.

Green, Abel and Joe Laurie Jr. *Show Biz: From Vaude to Video*. New York: Henry Holt, 1951.

Green, Stanley. *Encyclopaedia of the Musical Film*. New York: Oxford University Press, 1981.

———. *Hollywood Musicals: Year By Year*. Milwaukee: Hal Leonard, 1990.

Greene, Graham. *Graham Greene on Film*. New York: Simon & Schuster, 1972.

Gross, Ben. *I Looked and I Listened*. New York: Random House, 1954.

Grudens, Richard. *The Best Damn Trumpet Player*. Stony Brook, N.Y.: Celebrity Profiles, 1996.

Guiles, Fred Laurence. *Marion Davies*. New York: McGraw-Hill, 1972.

Hadlock, Richard. *Jazz Masters of the 20's*. New York: Macmillan, 1965.

Hale, Lee with Richard D. Neely. *Backstage at the Dean Martin Show*. Arcadia, Calif.: Dean Martin Fan Center, 1999.

Halliwell, Leslie. *Mountain of Dreams*. New York: Stonehill Publishing, 1976.

Hamann, G. D., editor. *Clarence Muse in the 30's*. Hollywood: Filming Today, 1996.

———. *Hollywood Scandals in the 30's*. Hollywood: Filming Today, 1996.

Hamill, Pete. *Why Sinatra Matters*. Boston: Little, Brown, 1998.

Hamm, Charles. *Yesterdays*. New York: W. W. Norton, 1979.

Hammond, John with Irving Townsend. *John Hammond on Record*. New York: Summit Books, 1977.

Handy, W. C. *Father of the Blues*. New York: Macmillan, 1941.

Harmon, Jim. *The Great Radio Comedians*. Garden City, N.Y.: Doubleday, 1970.

Hart, Kitty Carlisle. *Kitty*. Garden City, N.Y.: Doubleday, 1988.

Harvey, James. *Romantic Comedy in Hollywood from Lubitsch to Sturges*. New York: Alfred A. Knopf, 1987.

Hemming, Roy and David Hajdu. *Discovering Great Singers of Classic Pop*. New York: Newmarket Press, 1991.

Hinton, Milt and David G. Berger. *Bass Line*. Philadelphia: Temple University Press, 1988.

Hirschhorn, Clive. *The Hollywood Musical*. New York: Crown, 1981.

Hoopes, Ray. *When the Stars Went to War*. New York: Random House, 1994.

Hope, Bob. *They Got Me Covered*. Self-published, 1941.

Hope, Bob with Pete Martin. *Have Tux, Will Travel*. New York: Simon & Schuster, 1954.

Hope, Bob with Melville Shavelson. *Don't Shoot, It's Only Me*. New York: G. P. Putnam's Sons, 1990.

Horowitz, Joseph. *Understanding Toscanini*. New York: Alfred A. Knopf, 1987.

Howard, John Tasker. *Stephen Foster*. New York: Crowell, 1934.

Hunt, Marsha. *The Way We Wore*. Fallbrook, Calif.: Fallbrook Publishing Group, 1993.

Huxley, Aldous. *Along the Road*. London: Chatto and Windus, 1925.

Hyland, William G. *The Song Is Ended*. New York: Oxford University Press, 1995.

Inman, David. *The TV Encyclopedia*. New York: Perigee Books, 1991.

Jablonski, Edward. *Harold Arlen*. Boston: Northeastern University Press, 1996.

———. *Irving Berlin: American Troubadour*. New York: Henry Holt, 1999.

Jacobs, Dick. *Who Wrote That Song?* White Hall, Va.: Betterway Publications, 1988.

Jasen, David A. *Tin Pan Alley*. New York: Donald I. Fine, 1988.

Jasen, David A. and Gene Jones. *Spreadin' Rhythm Around*. New York: Schirmer Books, 1998.

Johnson, Dorris and Ellen Leventhal, editors. *The Letters of Nunnally Johnson*. New York: Alfred A. Knopf, 1981.

Jones, Max. *Talking Jazz*. New York: Norton, 1988.

Jones, Max and John Chilton. *Louis: The Louis Armstrong Story*. Boston: Little, Brown, 1971.

Kaminsky, Max with V. E. Hughes. *My Life in Jazz*. New York; Harper & Row, 1963.

Kanter, Hal. *So Far, So Funny*. Jefferson, N.C.: McFarland, 1999.

Karney, Robin, editor. *Chronicle of the Cinema*. New York: DK Publishing, 1995.

Kashner, Sam and Nancy Schoenberger. *A Talent for Genius: The Life and Times of Oscar Levant*. New York: Villard Books, 1994.

Katz, Ephraim. *The Film Encyclopedia*. 2d ed. New York: HarperPerennial, 1994.

Kay, Eddie Dorman. *Box Office Champs*. New York: Portland House, 1990.

Kempton, Murray. *Part of Our Time*. New York: Simon & Schuster, 1955.

King, Joseph A. *The Irish Lumberman-Farmer*. 2d ed. Self-published, 1987.

Kinkle, Roger D. *The Complete Encyclopedia of Popular Music and Jazz: 1900–1950*. 4 vols. New Rochelle, N.Y.: Arlington House, 1974.

Klamkin, Marian. *Old Sheet Music*. New York: Hawthorn Books, 1975.

Kobal, John. *People Will Talk*. New York: Alfred A. Knopf, 1985.

Kreuger, Miles, editor. *The Movie Musical: From Vitaphone to 42nd Street.* New York: Dover, 1975.

Lally, Kevin. *Wilder Times.* New York: Henry Holt, 1996.

Lamour, Dorothy with Dick McInnes. *My Side of the Road.* Englewood Cliffs, N.J.: Prentice-Hall, 1980.

Lamparski, Richard. *Whatever Became Of . . . ?* 8th series. New York: Crown, 1982

Laurie, Joe, Jr. *Vaudeville.* New York: Henry Holt, 1953.

Lax, Roger and Frederick Smith. *The Great Song Thesaurus.* 2d ed. New York: Oxford University Press, 1989.

Lee, Peggy. *Miss Peggy Lee.* New York: Donald I. Fine, 1989.

Lejeune, C. A., edited by Anthony Lejeune. *The C. A. Lejeune Film Reader.* Manchester, England: Carcanet, 1991.

LeRoy, Mervyn with Dick Kleiner. *Mervyn LeRoy: Take One.* New York: Hawthorn Books, 1974.

Lester, Gene with Peter Laufer. *When Hollywood Was Fun!* New York: Birch Lane Press, 1993.

Leuchtenburg, William E. *Franklin D. Roosevelt and the New Deal, 1932–1940.* New York: Harper & Row, 1963.

Levant, Oscar. *Memoirs of an Amnesiac.* G. P. Putnam's Sons, 1965.

Levine, Lawrence W. *Black Culture and Black Consciousness.* New York: Oxford University Press, 1977.

———. *Highbrow/Lowbrow.* Cambridge: Harvard University Press, 1988.

Levinson, Peter J. *Trumpet Blues: The Life of Harry James.* New York: Oxford University Press, 1999.

Levy, Shawn. *King of Comedy: The Life and Art of Jerry Lewis.* New York: St. Martin's Press, 1996.

Lewis, Judy. *Uncommon Knowledge.* New York: Pocket Books, 1994.

Linet, Beverly. *Ladd.* New York: Arbor House, 1979.

Lipsitz, George. *Rainbow at Midnight.* Urbana, Ill.: University of Illinois Press, 1994.

Louvish, Simon. *Man on the Flying Trapeze.* New York: W. W. Norton, 1997.

Lowry, Ed with Charlie Foy, edited by Paul M. Levitt. *Joe Frisco.* Carbondale, Ill.: Southern Illinois University Press, 1999.

Loza, Steven. *Barrio Rhythm.* Urbana, Ill.: University of Illinois Press, 1993.

MacDonald, J. Fred. *Don't Touch That Dial!* Chicago: Nelson-Hall, 1979.

Maltin, Leonard. *Selected Short Subjects.* New York: Da Capo, 1972.

———. *The Great American Broadcast.* New York: E. P. Dutton, 1997.

Manchester, William. *The Glory and the Dream.* Boston: Little, Brown, 1974.

Manone, Wingy with Paul Vandervoort II. *Trumpet on the Wing.* Garden City, N.Y.: Doubleday, 1948.

Marek, George R. *Toscanini.* New York: Atheneum, 1975.

Marmorstein, Gary. *Hollywood Rhapsody.* New York: Schirmer Books, 1997.

Martin, Mary. *My Heart Belongs.* New York: Quill, 1984.

Martin, Pete. *Pete Martin Calls On. . . .* New York: Simon & Schuster, 1962.

Marx, Arthur. *The Secret Life of Bob Hope.* New York: Barricade Books, 1993.

Mast, Gerald. *Can't Help Singin'.* Woodstock, N.Y.: Overlook Press, 1987.

Mattfield, Julius, editor. *Variety Music Cavalcade.* New York: Prentice-Hall, 1952.

McBride, Joseph. *Frank Capra.* New York: Simon & Schuster, 1992.

McCabe, John. *Mr. Laurel & Mr. Hardy.* New York: Doubleday, 1961.

McCarthy, Albert. *Big Band Jazz.* New York: G. P. Putnam's Sons, 1974.

McGilligan, Patrick. *Backstory.* Berkeley. Calif.: University of California Press, 1986.

McGilligan, Patrick and Paul Buhle. *Tender Comrades: A Backstory of the Hollywood Blacklist.* New York: St. Martin's Press, 1997.

Mezzrow, Mezz and Bernard Wolfe. *Really the Blues.* New York: Random House, 1946.

Mize, Dr. J. T. H., editor. *International Who's Who In Music.* 5th ed. Chicago: Who Is Who in Music, 1951.

Monti, Carlotta with Cy Rice. *W. C. Fields & Me.* Englewood Cliffs, N.J.: Prentice-Hall, 1971.

Mordden, Ethan. *The Hollywood Musical.* New York: St. Martin's Press, 1981.

———. *The Hollywood Studios.* New York: Simon & Schuster, 1989.

Morgenstern, Dan and Ole Brask. *Jazz People.* New York: Harry D. Abrams, 1976.

Mueller, John. *Astaire Dancing.* New York: Wings Books, 1991.

Murray, Ken. *Life on a Pogo Stick.* New York; Holt, Rinehart and Winston, 1960.

Murray, William. *Del Mar: Its Life & Good Times.* Del Mar, Calif.: Del Mar Thoroughbred Club, 1988.

Murrells, Joseph. *Daily Mail Book of Golden Discs.* London: McWhirter Twins Ltd., 1966.

Nachman, Gerald. *Raised on Radio.* New York: Pantheon Books, 1998.

Nasaw, David. *The Chief: The Life of William Randolph Hearst.* Boston: Houghton Mifflin, 2000.

Netland, Dwayne. *The Crosby: Greatest Show in Golf.* Garden City, N.Y.: Doubleday, 1975.

New York Times Directory of the Film, The. New York: Arno Press/Random House, 1971.

Nicholson, Stuart. *Ella Fitzgerald.* New York: Scribners, 1994.

———. *Reminiscing in Tempo: A Portrait of Duke Ellington.* Boston: Northeastern University Press, 1999.

Niven David. *The Moon's a Balloon.* London: Hamish Hamilton, Ltd., 1971.

Nolan, Frederick. *Lorenz Hart: A Poet on Broadway.* New York: Oxford University Press, 1994.

Norman, Barry. *The Film Greats.* London: Hodder and Stoughton, 1985.

Nugent, Elliott. *Events Leading up to the Comedy.* New York: Trident Press, 1965.

Oakie, Jack. *Jack Oakie's Double Takes.* San Francisco: Strawberry Hill Press, 1980.

O'Neill, Eileen, editor. *The Thalians: Stars and Stripes.* San Bernadino, Calif.: Franklin, 1976.

O'Toole, Andrew. *Branch Rickey in Pittsburgh.* Jefferson, N.C.: McFarland, 2000.

Owens, Harry. *Sweet Leilani.* Pacific Palisades, Calif.: Hula House, 1970.

Parish, James Robert. *The Paramount Pretties.* New Rochelle, N.Y.: Arlington House, 1972.

Peary, Danny, editor. *Close-Ups.* New York: Simon & Schuster, 1978.

Penna, Toney with Oscar Fraley. *My Wonderful World of Golf.* New York: Centaur House, 1965.

Perry, Jeb H., editor. *Variety Obits.* Metuchen, N.J.: Scarecrow Press, 1980.

Peters, Margot. *The House of Barrymore.* New York: Touchstone, 1991.

Pitrone, Jean Maddern. *Take It from the Big Mouth.* Lexington, Ky.: University Press of Kentucky, 1999.

Pleasants, Henry. *Serious Music and All That Jazz.* New York: Simon & Schuster, 1969.

———. *The Great American Popular Singers.* New York: Simon & Schuster, 1974.

Poague, Leland A. *The Hollywood Professionals.* vol. 7. San Diego: A. S. Barnes, 1980.

Pulliam, Walter. *Harriman: The Town That Temperance Built.* Maryville, Tenn.: Brazos, 1978.

Pye, Michael. *Moguls.* New York: Holt, Rinehart and Winston, 1980.

Quirk, Lawrence J. *Jane Wyman.* New York: Dembner Books, 1986.

———. *Bob Hope: The Road Well-Traveled.* New York: Applause Books, 1998.

Raymond, Jack. *Show Music on Record.* Washington, D.C.: Smithsonian Institution Press, 1992.

Roberts, John Storm. *The Latin Tinge.* New York: Oxford University Press, 1979.

Roberts, Mary Beth, editor. *The Famous Music Publishing Companies Professional Song Guide.* New York: Famous Music, 1993.

Robinson, Earl with Eric A. Gordon. *Ballad of an American.* Lanham, Md.: Scarecrow Press, 1998.

Rogin, Michael. *Blackface, White Noise.* Berkeley, Calif.: University of California Press, 1998.

Rosten, Leo C. *Hollywood.* New York: Harcourt, Brace, 1941.

Rourke, Constance. *American Humor.* New York: Harcourt Brace Javonovich, 1931.

———. *The Roots of American Culture.* New York: Harcourt, Brace and World, 1942.

Rust, Brian. *Jazz Records 1897–1942.* Rev. ed. New Rochelle, N.Y.: Arlington House, 1978.

———. *The American Record Label Book.* New York: Da Capo, 1984.

———. *The Dance Bands.* New Rochelle, N.Y.: Arlington House, 1974.

Sackett, Susan. *Hollywood Sings!* New York: Billboard Books, 1995.

Sanders, Coyne Steven and Tom Gilbert. *Desilu.* New York: William Morrow, 1993.

Sanford, Herb. *Tommy and Jimmy: The Dorsey Years.* New Rochelle, N.Y.: Arlington House, 1972.

Sanjek, Russell. *American Popular Music and Its Business.* Vol. 3 (1900–1984). New York: Oxford University Press, 1988.

Sanjek, Russell and David. *American Popular Music Business in the 20th Century.* New York: Oxford University Press, 1991.

Santoro, Gene. *Stir It Up.* New York: Oxford University Press, 1997.

Satchell, Tim. *Astaire.* London: Century Hutchinson, 1987.

Schatz, Thomas. *The Genius of the System.* New York: Pantheon, 1988.

Schickel, Richard. *His Picture in the Papers.* New York: Charterhouse, 1973.

Schmeltzer, Michael. *Spokane: The City and the People.* Helena, Mont.: American Geographic Publishing, 1988.

Schoenberg, Wilfred P., S.J. *Gonzaga University Seventy-five Years 1887–1962.* Spokane, Wash.: Gonzaga University, 1963.

Schuller, Gunther. *Early Jazz*. New York: Oxford University Press, 1968.

———. *The Swing Era*. New York: Oxford University Press, 1989.

Seldes, Gilbert. *The Seven Lively Arts*. New York: Harper, 1924.

———. *The Public Arts*. New York: Simon & Schuster, 1956.

Sennett, Mack with Cameron Shipp. *King of Comedy*. Garden City, N.Y.: Doubleday, 1954.

Sennett, Ted. *Hollywood Musicals*. New York: Harry N. Abrams, 1981.

Shacter, James D. *Piano Man: The Story of Ralph Sutton*. Chicago: Jaynar Press, 1975.

Shapiro, Nat and Nat Hentoff. *Hear Me Talkin' to Ya*. New York: Dover (reprint), 1966.

———. *The Jazz Makers*. New York: Rinehart and Company, 1957.

Shaughnessy, Mary Alice. *Les Paul*. New York: William Morrow, 1993.

Shaw, Arnold. *The Street That Never Slept*. New York: Coward, McCann and Geoghegan, 1971.

———. *The Rockin' '50's*. New York: Hawthorn Books, 1974.

———. *The Jazz Age*. New York: Oxford University Press, 1987.

Shindler, Colin. *Hollywood Goes to War*. London: Rutledge & Kegan Paul, 1979.

Shipman, David. *The Great Movie Stars: The Golden Years*. New York: Da Capo, 1982.

———. *The Story of Cinema*. New York: St. Martin's Press, 1982.

———. *Judy Garland: The Secret Life of an American Legend*. New York: Hyperion, 1992.

Shorris, Sylvia and Marion Abbott Bundy. *Talking Pictures*. New York: New Press, 1994.

Sikov, Ed. *On Sunset Boulevard: The Life and Times of Billy Wilder*. New York: Hyperion, 1998.

Simon, George T. *Glenn Miller*. New York: Thomas Y. Crowell, 1974.

———. *The Best of the Music Makers*. Garden City, N.Y.: Doubleday, 1979.

———. *The Big Bands*. 4th ed. New York: Schirmer Books, 1981.

Sinatra, Nancy. *Frank Sinatra: An American Legend*. Santa Monica, Calif.: General Publishing Group, 1995.

Skretvedt, Randy. *Laurel and Hardy: The Magic Behind the Movies*. Beverly Hills: Past Times Publishing, 1994.

Slide, Anthony. *The Vaudevillians*. Westport, Conn.: Arlington House, 1981.

Smith, H. Allen. *Life in a Putty Knife Factory*. New York: Doubleday, Doran, 1943.

Smith, Jay D. and Len Guttridge. *Jack Teagarden*. New York: Macmillan, 1960.

Smith, Joe. *Off the Record*. New York: Warner Books, 1988.

Smith, Sally Bedell. *In All His Glory*. New York: Simon & Schuster, 1990.

Snowden, Clinton A. *History of Washington: The Rise and Progress of an American State*. Vol. 2. New York: Century History Company, 1909.

Sobol, Louis. *The Longest Street*. New York: Crown, 1968.

Sommers, Robert T. *Golf Anecdotes*. New York: Oxford University Press, 1995.

Spada, James. *Grace: The Secret Lives of a Princess*. Garden City, N.Y.: Doubleday, 1987.

Springer, John. *All Talking! All Singing! All Dancing!* New York: Cadillac Publishing Co., 1966.

Steinberg, Cobbett. *Reel Facts*. New York: Vintage Books, 1982.

Stenn, David. *Clara Bow: Runnin' Wild*. New York: Doubleday, 1988.

Stimson, William. *A View of the Falls: An Illustrated History of Spokane*. Northridge, Calif.: Windsor Publications, 1985.

Stowe, David W. *Swing Changes*. Cambridge: Harvard University Press, 1994.

Stratemann, Dr. Klaus. *Louis Armstrong on Screen*. Copenhagen: JazzMedia ApS, 1996.

Stratton, David H., editor. *Spokane & The Inland Empire*. Pullman. Wash.: Washington State University Press, 1991.

Stroff, Stephen. *Red Head: A Chronological Survey of Red Nichols and His Five Pennies*. Lanham, Md.: Institute of Jazz Studies and Scarecrow Press, 1996.

Stuart, Gloria with Sylvia Thompson. *I Just Kept Hoping*. Boston: Little, Brown, 1999.

Sudhalter, Richard M. *Lost Chords*. New York: Oxford University Press, 1999.

Sudhalter, Richard M. and Philip R. Evans with William Dean-Myatt. *Bix: Man and Legend*. New Rochelle, N.Y.: Arlington House, 1974.

Swindell, Larry. *Screwball: The Life of Carole Lombard*. New York: William Morrow, 1975.

————. *The Last Hero: A Biography of Gary Cooper*. Garden City, N.Y.: Doubleday, 1980.

Taylor, Robert Lewis. *W. C. Fields: His Follies and Fortunes*. Garden City, N.Y.: Doubleday, 1949.

Taylor, Theodore. *Jule: The Story of Composer Jule Styne*. New York: Random House, 1979.

Thomas, Tony. *Harry Warren and the Hollywood Musical*. Secaucus, N.J.: Citadel Press, 1975.

Toll, Robert C. *Blacking Up: The Minstrel Show in Nineteenth-Century America*. New York: Oxford University Press, 1974.

————. *The Entertainment Machine*. New York: Oxford University Press, 1982.

Tormé, Mel. *My Singing Teachers*. New York: Oxford University Press, 1994.

Tosches, Nick. *Dino: Living High in the Dirty Business of Dreams*. New York: Doubleday, 1992.

Tucker, Mark, editor. *The Duke Ellington Reader*. New York: Oxford University Press, 1993.

Vallée, Eleanor with Jill Amadio. *My Vagabond Lover*. Dallas: Taylor Publishing, 1996.

Vallée, Rudy. *Vagabond Dreams Come True*. New York: E. P. Dutton, 1930.

————. *Let The Chips Fall. . . .* Harrisburg, Pa.: Stackpole Books, 1975.

Vallée, Rudy and Gil McKean. *My Time Is Your Time*. New York: Obolensky, 1962.

Van der Merwe, Peter. *Origins of the Popular Style*. New York: Oxford University Press, 1989.

Viera, Mark. *Sin in Soft Focus*. New York: Harry N. Abrams, 1999.

Walker, Leo. *The Big Band Almanac*. Rev. ed. New York: Da Capo, 1989.

————. *The Wonderful Era of the Great Dance Bands*. New York: Da Capo (reprint), 1990.

Walsh, Raoul. *Each Man in His Time*. New York: Farrar, Straus and Giroux, 1974.

Ward, Geoffrey C. *A First-Class Temperament: The Emergence of Franklin Roosevelt*. New York, Harper & Row, 1989.

————. *Jazz*. New York: Alfred A. Knopf, 2000.

Waring, Virginia. *Fred Waring and the Pennsylvanians*. Urbana, Ill.: University of Illinois Press, 1997.

Waters, Ethel with Charles Samuels. *His Eye Is on the Sparrow*. Garden City, N.Y.: Doubleday, 1951.

Watkins, T. H. *The Great Depression*. Boston: Little, Brown, 1993.

Welles, Orson and Peter Bogdanovich. *This Is Orson Welles*. New York: HarperCollins, 1992.

Wertheim, Arthur Frank. *Radio Comedy*. New York: Oxford University Press, 1979.

Westmore, Frank and Muriel Davidson. *The Westmores of Hollywood*. Philadelphia: Lippincott, 1976.

Wexler, Jerry and David Ritz. *Rhythm and the Blues*. New York: Alfred A. Knopf, 1993.

Whitcomb, Ian. *After the Ball*. New York: Simon & Schuster, 1972.

White, John I. *Git Along, Little Dogies*. Urbana, Ill.: University of Illinois Press, 1989.

Whitburn, Joel. *Pop Memories 1890–1954*. Menomonee Falls, Wis.: Record Research, 1986.

———. *Top Pop Singles 1955–1986*. Menomonee Falls, Wis.: Record Research, 1987.

Whiteman, Paul. *Records for the Millions*. New York: Hermitage Press, 1948.

Wilder, Alec with James T. Maher. *American Popular Song*. New York: Oxford University Press, 1972.

Wiley, Mason with Damien Bona. *Inside Oscar*. New York: Ballantine Books, 1986.

Wilk, Max. *The Wit and Wisdom of Hollywood*. New York: Atheneum, 1971.

———. *They're Playing Our Song*. New York: Atheneum, 1973.

Williams, Martin. *Jazz Masters in Transition 1957–69*. New York: Macmillan, 1970.

Woodham-Smith, Cecil. *The Great Hunger*. New York: Harper & Row, 1962.

Young, Jordan R. *Spike Jones Off the Record*. Beverly Hills: Past Times Publishing, 1984.

———. *Let Me Entertain You*. Beverly Hills: Moonstone Press, 1988.

Ziegfeld, Richard and Paulette. *The Ziegfeld Touch: The Life and Times of Florenz Ziegfeld, Jr.* New York: Harry N. Abrams, 1993.

Zierold, Norman. *The Moguls*. New York: Coward-McCann, 1969.

Zolotow, Maurice. *Billy Wilder in Hollywood*. New York: G. P. Putnam's Sons, 1977.

Zukor, Adolph with Dale Kramer. *The Public Is Never Wrong*. New York: G. P. Putnam's Sons, 1953.

Unpublished Manuscripts

Frank, Melvin. *The Crosbys: Bing and Dixie*. Teleplay. Courtesy of his daughter, Elizabeth Frank.

Good, Kitty. Untitled memoir by the widow of Eddie Lang, taped by her son, Tim Good. Courtesy of Kitty and Tim Good.

Gordon, Julia M. *What a Life: The Eddie Bracken Story*. Life of the actor by his granddaughter, written on a Senior Fellowship from Dartmouth. Courtesy of Eddie Bracken and Julia M. Gordon.

McDonough, John. *Decca: 60th Anniversary History.* Commissioned by MCA. Courtesy of John McDonough.

Porter, Joey. *Never Been So Lost.* Screenplay by the son-in-law of Harry Barris. Courtesy of Joey Porter and Marti Barris.

Rinker, Al. *The Bing Crosby I Knew.* Written memoir. Courtesy of his daughter, Julia Rinker, and widow, Elizabeth Rinker.

Taylor, Doreen. Untitled memoir of dancer Doreen Wilde, taped by her granddaughter, Alison McMahan. Courtesy of Alison McMahan.

Tuttle, Frank. *They Started Talking.* Written memoir. Courtesy of his daughter, Helen Votachenko.

Selected Fan Magazines

Bingang. Since 1936, published twice a year by Club Crosby. President, Mark Scrimger. Membership inquiries: vice president and editor Wayne L. Martin, 435 So. Holmes Ave., Kirkwood, MO 63122-6311, USA. European representative: Ken W. Crossland, 9 Arden Drive, Dorridge, Solihull, W. Midlands B93 8LP, UK. Club Crosby@aol.com

Bing. Since 1950, published three times a year by the International Crosby Circle. Edited by Malcolm Macfarlane. Membership inquiries: Hon. Secretary and Treasurer Michael Crampton, 19 Carrholm Crescent, Chapel Allerton, Leeds LS7 2NL, UK. American representative: F. B. Wiggins, 5608 North 34th Street, Arlington, VA 22207, USA. icc@iccircle.globalnet.co.uk

The Crosby Voice. Published by the Bing Crosby Victorian Society. Inquiries to Bob Neate, 22 Pakenham Street, Blackburn, Victoria, 3130 Australia.

Bingtalks. Published by the Bingthings Society, founded and edited by Bob Lundberg, 1989 to 1995.

Bing Crosby Home Page. On-line only, created by Steven Lewis. www.kcmetro.cc.mo.us/crosby

Acknowledgments

My primary debt is to the people — friends, relations, colleagues, and acquaintances of Bing Crosby — listed in Interviews and Bibliography. I spoke to some for just minutes and others for many hours, but *Bing Crosby: A Pocketful of Dreams* would be poorer without any one of them, and I thank them all. Many graciously made available letters, photographs, and other mementos.

I cannot overstate my gratitude to curators and librarians at public and private archives. For two weeks at Gonzaga University, I was aided with charity and skill by the chair of the Special Collections, Stephanie Edwards Plowman, and her assistant, Sharon Prendergast, who led me through the maze of hundreds if not thousands of documents in the Bing Crosby Collection at Foley Center Library. My thanks to Robert Burr, Gonzaga's library dean, Marty Pujolar, director of the alumni association at the Crosby Alumni House; Brother Edward Jennings S.J., Jesuit archivist assistant; and Father William Yam, S.J., Jesuit archivist.

I benefited greatly from the aid of Judith Kipp, the conservator of the Tacoma Public Library's Northwest Room and Special Collections, whose zest for research inspired my own as she found the answers to my every query; I am grateful to her associates, Brian Kamens and Gary Fuller Reese. Nancy Gale Compau, head of the Northwest Room of the Spokane Public Library, was unstintingly helpful.

At the Academy of Motion Picture Arts and Sciences, I was assisted by Samuel A. Gill, Margaret Herrick Library Archivist at the Center for Motion Picture Study; chief librarian Dr. Linda Mehr; and Russell Good, Sondra Archer, and Michael Friend. At the University of Southern California Film Archive, I relied on the expertise of director Ned Comstock and Leith Adams. My friend Dan Morgenstern, director of the Institute of Jazz Studies at Rutgers University, assembled Crosby clippings and sent other materials. Michael Cogswell, director of the Louis Armstrong House and Archives, found major documents; I am grateful to the always loyal Phoebe Jacobs and Dave Gold of the Louis Armstrong Educational Foundation for allowing me to use them. Marion Hirsch, archivist at the Center for Sales, Advertising, and Marketing History of Kraft General Foods at Duke University, provided complete *Kraft Music Hall* program reports; my thanks to Elizabeth W. Adkins, archives manager for Kraft General Foods.

One of the luckiest calls I received was from Alan Farnum, then at *Fortune,* who introduced me to two other *Fortune* writers, Sean Tully and Terence Pare. The three Crosby enthusiasts enabled me to explore the Time Inc. archive with its memoranda on background interviews done for, but usually not used in, stories that ran in *Fortune, Time,* and *Life.* The files allowed me to hear the voices of people who were part of Bing's early years — elementary-school teachers, boyhood friends, physician, agents, stage hands, engineers, and so forth. I am grateful to my old friend Elizabeth Pochoda, for access to the morgue at the New York *Daily News,* and Ken Chandler for clippings from the *New York Post.* Everyone writing about movies ought to know the work of G. D. Hamann, a one-man clipping factory; in addition to publishing five volumes on Bing, he located and sent me many unexpected gems.

Daniel G. Smith, chief of publicity for Del Mar Thoroughbred Club, provided me with various papers on the origin of the track and a comprehensive tour — filled with many anecdote-rich people — so intoxicating that I considered becoming a tout. I am grateful to Mary Shepardson of Del Mar Special Projects and Marketing and everyone I encountered there. I thank Jack Disney, the historian of Santa Anita Race Track, and Michael Smith, manager of Spokane's The Met, a restoration of the old Clemmer Theater. Cossette Gutierrez was most helpful at the County Clerk's Office in Redwood City. My thanks to Mary Beth Roberts at Famous Music, Jim Hillbun of the defunct Ampex Museum of Magnetic Recording, John Mulderig of The Christophers, Andy McKaie at MCA, and Christopher Ann Paton, archivist of the Popular Music Collection at Georgia State University.

I am grateful to Herb Scheer of the Lincoln Center Library of Performing Arts, along with the New York Public Library staff; Sylvia Kennick Brown, special collections librarian and college archivist at Williams College; John Farris, the curator at Hyde Park; Rosemary Hanes, Joseph Balian, and the AFI film collection of the Library of Congress; Ronald C. Simon, curator of New York's Museum of Broadcasting; Howard W. Hays of the UCLA Film and Television Archive; UCLA Theater Arts Library; the University of Southern California's Cinema and Television Library; Laura Arksey of the Eastern Washington State Historical Society; Valerie Sivinski of the Tacoma Historical Preservation Office; Columbia University's Oral History Research Office; and the AFI's Louis B. Mayer Library and Leo McCarey Collection.

*　　*　　*

My thanks to Bryan Johnson and his staff at Film Syndicate (*Bing: His Legendary Years 1931–1957*) for sharing research, including reels of rare footage, and to Derek Bailey and Landseer Productions (*Bing Crosby — the Voice of the Century*), for also sharing research. I am indebted to the crew that made the PBS documentary *Remembering Bing,* and to its producers and director, Glenn DuBose, Jim Arntz, and Katherine MacMillin, who allowed me access to their interviews.

Many people provided me with letters: I am especially grateful to William H. David, son of producer Henry Ginsberg; Carolyn Manovill and Gloria Burleson, who came upon Ms. Manovill's letters in an old suitcase; and Violet Brown and her daughter Pamela Crosby Brown. I am humbled by the generosity of Howard Crosby, who sent me a decade's worth of correspondence between Bing, his siblings, and father, enabling me to straighten out a hopelessly tangled narrative; and Susan Crosby, who taught me about bipolar illness and loaned me the remarkable journal and scrapbook of her former husband, Lindsay Crosby.

The memoirs of the former Kitty Lang were a revelation to me that I hope will be edited and published in their own right. I am deeply indebted to her son, Tim Good, for entrusting me with them. I am equally in debt to Julia Rinker, for her insights as well as the irreplaceable memoirs of her father, Al Rinker. Alison McMahan phoned when she heard about my project to offer transcript, tape, and photos of her grandmother, Doreen Wilde, an incredible boon. My thanks to Helen Votachenko for the memoir of her father, Frank Tuttle; Julie Gordon, for her study of her grandfather, Eddie Bracken; and James T. Maher, for preparing and annotating his extensive notes from his interviews with John Scott Trotter.

Rory Burke is a constant source of encouragement and good cheer. She flew to Spokane when I was researching there and gave me many hours of candid recollections, then sent a carton of correspondence, photos, scrapbooks, and other materials. I thank her daughter, Quinn Burke, for the baptismal photograph used in this volume. Elizabeth Frank offered good advice and packed a shopping bag with the relevant scripts and papers of her father, writer-producer Mel Frank. I thank Sonny Rollins for being who he is and for playing "Prisoner of Love" and "Sweet Leilani" when I most needed to hear them — coincidences, of course, but evidence that jazz is God's gift.

I miss Jimmy (Dr. W. James) Gould, who with his wife, Maureen, offered encouragement, friendship, and a quiet place to work when I began, in 1991. I am indebted to Richard W. Weiss for helping me to see that the examined life is worth living. No one has been more encouraging over the years than Michael Anderson, a masterly editor who always knows just when to call, and Mary Cleere Haran, singer, chanter, humorist, and my main source on Irish Catholic angst. I owe more than I can ever repay to Geoffrey C. Ward, though none of his many kindnesses has meant as much as his and Diane Ward's friendship.

The enthusiasm and generosity of Bing Crosby's fans have been a tonic. Mark Scrimger, the president of Club Crosby, one of two international fan clubs that publish outstanding fanzines, sent me a freezer-size carton of *Bingang*, books, magazines, and other materials — so many that it took a year to work my way down to the bottom. He subsequently provided invaluable photographs and letters. The late Bob Lundberg, who founded and edited *Bingtalks*, and the late James S. Johnson introduced me to Bing fandom, including that most congenial and magnanimous of fans, Bill Hunt, who sent me numberless audiotapes, videotapes, articles, and suggestions. Some collectors build fortresses around their acquisitions; Bill wants everyone to enjoy his.

Malcolm Macfarlane, editor of the other exceptional fanzine, the International Crosby Circle's *Bing*, has provided endless aid and comfort, not least through his invaluable *Bing: A Diary of a Lifetime*, but also through swift e-mail responses to my relentless barrage of queries. Always ready to help, Malcolm forwarded useful materials and hooked me up with Ron Bosley, who provided several of this book's photographs. I am grateful to the ICC's American representative, F. W. Wiggins, for many kindnesses, and to John Marshall and his intelligently acerbic early-1990s Crosby newsletter, *The Grapevine*.

Arne Fogel, the Minnesotan singer and radio personality who has given as much thought to the Crosby style as anyone, has generously shared his expertise while sending me dozens of audio- and videotapes, including most of the existing Crosby interviews. My old friend Will Friedwald, whose passion for Cros runs just as deep (see *Jazz Singing*), was the first to come by bearing a truckload of Crosbyana. Where would we be without the ministrations of Uncle Wilski? Records Will and Arne did not have were put on tape for me by BMI's singer maven, Dan Singer. Peter Levinson offered me contacts, phone numbers, clippings, Los Angeles hospitality, and worthy advice. My thanks to Saint Clair Pugh of Liz Smith's office, for phone numbers and advice, and to Ms. Smith for publishing an item about the book that brought numerous responses.

John McDonough provided me with the manuscript of his comprehensive history of Decca Records, commissioned for the company's sixtieth anniversary, in 1994, by MCA, which then chose not to celebrate it. John also made available interviews he conducted for his newspaper stories, as well as the Robert Trout epigram. Chip Deffaa recorded and annotated audiotapes of materials so rare that I would not have known enough to go looking for them. James Gavin revealed a gift for locating impossible-to-find films and sent other items he happened upon. Bill Milkowski's Crosby anecdotes, writings, and photographs proved treasurable.

Film preservationist Bob DeFlores enabled me to see several rare films (including the splendid *Here Is My Heart*); my thanks to him and Brenda for their hospitality. Until the day he died, Leslie Gaylor was a relentless Crosby propagandist whose name was known to every broadcaster in England; they had all received his letters demanding more Bing. (Bing felt guilty about the postage Leslie paid and sent him small checks, which he refused to cash.) Leslie sent me his correspondence from Crosby, Johnny Mercer, and others — many times. Peter Cakanic Jr., always an encouraging correspondent, sent tapes and clips. John Newton shared several remarkable finds from his collection of showbiz memorabilia. I had hardly met Eric Anderson when he loaned me his collection of Bing ads. The late Bill Osborn transferred to tape a complete collection of Crosby radio broadcasts. The late Ken Twiss, who created the Bing Crosby Historical Society, shared print materials and time when he had precious little of it left.

Ernest H. Sutkowski, who has long sponsored a thrice-weekly Crosby show on WRTN-FM in New Jersey, took an early interest in this book and offered his considerable assistance in acquiring recordings and meeting people. I am grateful to him and his assistant Mary Beth Del Balzo for many things, not least for introducing me to Francis X. Smith, former city councilman and justice of the New York Supreme Court. When Frank was named "Judge of the Year" in 1984, Congressman Gary Ackerman took note in the *Congressional Record* of his collection of Crosbyana, assembled with "boundless zest, wide-eyed rapture, and an unquentable thirst to expand his knowledge." After dinner with Ernie and Frank, the judge opened his car trunk and entrusted me with two huge volumes of memorabilia.

With apologies to those inadvertently omitted, I thank Alice Fay, Alan Nahigan, Allen Sviridoff, Andrew O'Toole, Ann McKee, Arnold J. Smith, Barnaby Conrad, Ben Sonnenberg, Bill Christine, Bill Daugherty, Bob Ellis, Bob Gottlieb, Bob Larsson, Bob Mohr, Campbell Burnap, Charles D. Baillie, Charles Graham, Chica Boswell Minnerly, Chris Bozeman, Curtis F. Brown, Dan Levinson, Daniel Okrent, David Lobosco, David Lotz, David McCain, David Nasaw, David Stenn, Deborah Grace Winer, Derek Parkes, Dorothy Rivers, Dr. Jock Jocoy, Duncan Lamont, Dwayne Netland, Eddie Brandt's Saturday Matinee, Edward Cramer, Eileen Van Buren, Evan Challis, Gene Santoro, Gord Atkinson, Greg Van Beek, George Scorpy Doyle, Hank O'Neal, Hobie Wilson, Jack Bean, Jack Ellsworth, James Spada, Jane

Kovner, Jay Diamond, Jean Bach, Jean Strouse, Jean-Louis Brindamour, Jeff Abraham, Jeff Atterton, Jeanine Bassinger, Jewell Baxter, Jim Reilly, Joe Sinnott, John R. T. Davies, John Joyce, John McNicholas, Father John Russo, S.J., Joyce Jamison, Joyce Jansen, Joyce Lundberg, June Waller, Ken Bloom, Keith Parkinson, Kent Jones, Leith G. Johnson, Leonard Maltin, Lyn Erikson, Marian McPartland, Michael Bloom, Michael Avallone, Michael Feinstein, Michael Modero, Miguel Ferrer, Nancy Franklin, Nancy Gordon, Nat Hentoff, Pam Sharp, Patricia O'Hare, Perry Robinson, Peter O'Brien, S.J., Peter Minton, Peter and Susan Straub, Philip Yampolsky, Raphael Ferrer, Richard Lamparski, Richard M. Sudhalter, Richard Stone, Ridge Walker, Romy Kaufman, Ron Hutchinson, Ronan Tynan, Ross Firestone, Sherwin Dunner, Stan White, Stanley Dance, Steve Dolley, Steve Futterman, Steven LaVere, Stuart Oderman, Susan Terry, Sy Johnson, Terry Carter, Thomas M. Hampson, Tom Dardis, Walter Surovy, Ward Grant, Wayne L. Martin, Wilfrid Sheed, William Bastone, William E. Redpath, and William Ruhlmann.

My chief researcher was Libby Pace, an extraordinary investigator who efficiently rounded up people, legal papers, and archival material; expertly helped with interviews; and enabled me to navigate Los Angeles. Nancy Snyder, who took over midway, is a canny researcher to whom I confidently delegated interviews. A few early interviews were conducted by Arlene Hellerman; others were set up by Joe Gilford.

I remain grateful for the efficiency and kindness of Mary Beth Hughes, who ran my office and planned my research trips when she should have been writing. She introduced me to Charles Bock, who examined countless issues of *Variety* and fanzines when he, too, should have been working on his novel. Connie Julian found research material and transcribed tapes until she was called away by political uprisings. Deborah Wenzel and Joan Hirsch did many transcriptions. Lee Rothchild, now bringing order to Australia, brought order to hundreds of bulging Crosby files. Thanks also to Christopher Luongo, Gloria James, Jenny Rothchild, Lea Jacobson, and Peter Lubell. Special thanks to my assistant Elora Charles, whose beguiling voice and Alexandrian zeal have brought refreshing charm and efficiency to an office in need of both.

The one person without whom this book would not exist is its original editor, Paul Bresnick, who persisted for years in convincing me to tackle it, then watched the manuscript grow larger and larger until it finally burst into two volumes. The original publisher was swallowed by one that wanted nothing to do with it. I am grateful to Paul for his loyalty and friendship, and hope he takes pride in the finished work.

Bing Crosby: A Pocketful of Dreams was an orphan for no more than the blink of an eye thanks to my radiant editor and publisher, Sarah Crichton, who said yes in thunder. She also conned me into thinking the manuscript was as clean as I needed to believe until it was finished, and then covered page after page with her "suggestions." I cannot enumerate all the ways in which Sarah has helped me to focus, pare, and open the narrative. Have I said, "Thank you?" Thank you! And thank you to Steve Lamont, who copyedited the final manuscript with ingenious fastidiousness and empathy and did yeoman fact-checking that saved me all kinds of humiliation and grief. My thanks to editor Chip Rossetti for piloting the entire project; managing editor Mary Tondorf-Dick; John Fulbrook III, who designed the cover (with a photograph made available by Mickey Kapp); publicists Beth Davey and Heather Rizzo; publisher's assistant Rita Omark; Jon Protas; and everyone at Little, Brown. Also to Don Forst, Robert Christgau, Doug Simmons, and everyone at the *Village Voice,* my second home.

I owe a lot more than 10 percent to my canny agent, Georges Borchardt — not that I want to plant a seed. But he did restore my sanity more than once during an often tumultuous decade. Thanks also to Anne Borchardt and DeAnna Heindell.

Bing Crosby never had a better friend than Rosemary Clooney, and neither have I. She's become a member of the family, or have I become a member of hers? Hers is certainly larger, and I love them all. Rosemary's encouragement, beyond her substantive help and extraordinary generosity to me and Debbie and especially Lea, has meant more than she can imagine. At the same time, she is the critic about whom I am most nervous — 'cause she *knows,* and thanks to her I know more than would otherwise have been possible.

My thanks to Alice Giddins and Helen and Norman Halper are boundless. I am grateful to Aaron Donner, and his mom, Ronnie Halper, for the loan of his computer-wizard dad, Marc Donner, and to Donna and Paul Rothchild for their computer savvy and the loan of their children — listed above, earning their keep. Many thanks to Norma Salfarlie.

My wife, Deborah Halper, and daughter, Lea, lived through every sentence of this book. My only regret is the weekends and evenings it kept me from them. On the other hand, I don't expect ever to forget the look on Lea's face the night she met Bob Hope; you would have thought he was Derek Jeter. No writer ever had a more loving and supportive family — all of my books are for them, but this one is truly theirs.

Index